ORGANIZATIONAL BEHAVIOR:
Theory and Practice

RICHARD M. HODGETTS
Florida International University

Merrill, an imprint of
Macmillan Publishing Company
New York

Collier Macmillan Canada, Inc.
Toronto

Maxwell Macmillan International Publishing Group
New York   Oxford   Singapore   Sydney

Cover Art: Marko Spalatin
Editor: Charles E. Stewart, Jr.
Production Editors: Victoria M. Althoff and Sheryl Glicker Langner
Art Coordinator: Vincent A. Smith
Text Designer: Debra A. Fargo
Cover Designer: Russ Maselli
Production Buyer: Pamela D. Bennett

This book was set in Century Old Style.

Macmillan Publishing Company
866 Third Avenue, New York, NY 10022

Collier Macmillan Canada, Inc.

Hodgetts, Richard M.
    Organizational behavior : theory and practice / Richard M.
  Hodgetts.
      p.   cm.
    Rev. ed. of: Organizational behavior / Steven Altman, Enzo
  Valenzi, Richard M. Hodgetts. c1985.
    Includes bibliographical references and index.
    ISBN 0-675-21275-8
    1. Organizational behavior.   I. Altman, Steven. Organizational
  behavior.   II. Title.
  HD58.7.H62 1991
  658.4—dc20   90-13433
                                                                    CIP

Printing: 1 2 3 4 5 6 7 8 9   Year: 1 2 3 4

PREFACE

Modern organizations face many challenges, from increasing internal efficiency to more effectively interacting with their external environments. In all of these endeavors people play a key role, and for this reason more and more attention is now being directed toward understanding behavior in organizations. We know that intuition and common sense can help us to understand, predict, and control human behavior, but they are no substitute for a systematic, analytical approach to the field. It is this need that has given rise to the academic discipline of organizational behavior.

The purpose of this book is to familiarize the reader with the field of organizational behavior by first introducing its major elements and then explaining each in detail. We begin with a consideration of the individual and the organization and then move on to groups, structure, processes, and finally future horizons. It is assumed that the reader is either a newcomer or a practitioner with little formal training in organizational behavior. Hence, this book can be used effectively for the first behavioral course in management. It can also be employed in professional training courses and should prove useful to practicing executives who want to update their knowledge of the field.

DISTINGUISHING FEATURES

In this book, the concepts of organizational behavior have been presented in an interesting, easy-to-read style through the use of these special features: organization, stop-action cases, organizational behavior in action stories, exhibits and margin comments, self-feedback exercises, chapter goals and review and study questions, cases, and a glossary.

Organization

This book is organized into six major parts. Part I introduces the foundations of modern organizational behavior. You will learn what the term *organizational behavior* means, become acquainted with the three major fields of study that constitute organizational behavior, and be introduced to the ways in which behavioral scientists go about studying behavior in organizations. Part II is devoted to an examination of individual behavior in organizations. Topics such as personality, perception, attitudes, job satisfaction, learning, and motivation will be the major focus of attention as we attempt to shed light on the question "Why do people act as they do?" Part III investigates this question further through an analysis of groups in organizations. In this part of the book you will be examining group norms, roles, status, and composition. You will also learn about group decision making and communication, as well as some of the most recent findings on effective group leadership, power, organizational politics, and conflict. In Part IV the focus of attention switches to organizational structure and the ways in which individuals, groups, and the structure all come together in an organizational setting. The major consideration is given to basic and contingency factors in organizational design, job design, and stress in the work place. Part V examines the organizational processes used in bringing together the individual, the group, and the structure. Our attention in these chapters will be on decision making, communication, organizational climate and structure, and organizational change and development. Finally, in Part VI the focus will be on future areas of concern, including international organizational behavior and career planning and development.

Stop-Action Cases

Each chapter begins with a stop-action case that presents a situation and a series of accompanying questions. After making a preliminary analysis of the case, you are given the opportunity to revise your answers based on in-chapter information. As the case questions are revisited in the chapter, recommended answers to each question are offered as a way of providing feedback and reinforcing learning.

Organizational Behavior in Action Stories

Each chapter contains a boxed story of an organizational behavior concept applied in a practical way. The purpose of these stories is to illustrate the linkage between organizational behavior theory and practice.

Exhibits and Margin Comments

A large number of tables and illustrations are employed in this text, both to highlight important concepts and to present them in an easy-to-understand manner. Also, comments are located in the margin throughout the book to aid in both understanding and reviewing the material.

Self-Feedback Exercises

A self-feedback exercise has been placed at the end of each chapter. The purpose of this exercise is to provide insights into your own behavior, attitude, and philosophy regarding the concepts you have studied in the chapter. These exercises should help make the chapter material more relevant to you.

Chapter Goals and Review and Study Questions

Behavioral goals are set forth at the beginning of each chapter. These goals relate what you will be learning in the chapter. At the end of the chapter review and study questions are tied directly to these goals. These questions enable you to measure your own progress and go back and read any parts of the text you feel you did not sufficiently understand.

Cases

All too often students learn theories without understanding their practical application. For this reason, two cases have been included at the end of each chapter. These cases provide an opportunity to apply the behavioral concepts presented in the chapter and thus reinforce these major ideas.

Glossary

At the end of the text is a glossary of terms. This glossary is comprehensive and provides a definition or explanation of the most important topics contained in the book.

INSTRUCTIONAL SUPPORT

An Instructor's Manual/Test Bank has been specially developed for use with this book. This manual contains a synopsis of the goals and materials in each chapter, as well as suggestions for teaching the chapter. In addition, there are answers to the Cases' questions and to the review and study questions at the end of each chapter. The Test Bank contains a large pool of true-false and multiple-choice questions for testing purposes. There are also comprehensive cases that can be used in tying together the materials for Parts II through V. Transparencies are also available to adopters.

ACKNOWLEDGMENTS

Many people were instrumental in helping me write this book. My family, from whom I took so much time, deserves my deepest thanks. I also would like to express my appreciation to the staff at Merrill, an imprint of Macmillan Publishing, who worked so closely with me on this project: Sally MacGregor, Vicki Althoff, and Sheryl Langner.

The reviewers who read the manuscript and offered substantive suggestions were instrumental in helping create the final product. These include: David B. Greenberger, The Ohio State University; Robert A. Figler, University of Akron; Linda L. Neider, University of Miami; Karin Fulton, University of Tennessee; Paula B. Alexander, Seton Hall University; Norbert Elbert, Bellarmine College; Arthur L. Darrow, Bowling Green State University; Paula C. Morrow, Iowa State University; John E. Mack, Salem State College; Paul Lyons, Frostberg State University; Foad Derakhshan, California State University–San Bernadino; James K. Swenson, Moorhead State University; A. Thomas Hollingsworth, St. John's University; George C. Witteried, University of Missouri–

St. Louis; Elmer Burack, University of Illinois–Chicago; Gene Murkison, Georgia Southern College; Roger Dean, Washington and Lee University; Bruce D. Wonder, Western Washington University; Alan Cabelly, Portland State University; William J. Traynor, California State University–Long Beach; and Paul Greenlaw, Pennsylvania State University.

Finally, for their input and advice, I would like to thank: Fred Luthans, University of Nebraska; Ronald Greenwood, General Motors Institute; Jane Gibson, Nova University; Dana Farrow, Len Chusmir, and Galen Kroeck, my colleagues at Florida International University; and Minnie Dunbar, my doctoral student. Thanks also goes to Ruth Chapman for her typing of the manuscript.

Richard M. Hodgetts

CONTENTS

CHAPTER 9
The Leadership Process

CHAPTER 10
Power, Organizational Politics, and Conflict

PART V
ORGANIZATIONAL PROCESSES

CHAPTER 14
The Decision-Making Process

CHAPTER 15
The Communication Process

CHAPTER 19
Career Planning and Development   503

GLOSSARY   531

NAME INDEX   543

SUBJECT INDEX   551

ORGANIZATIONAL BEHAVIOR

PART I
FOUNDATIONS OF MODERN ORGANIZATIONAL BEHAVIOR

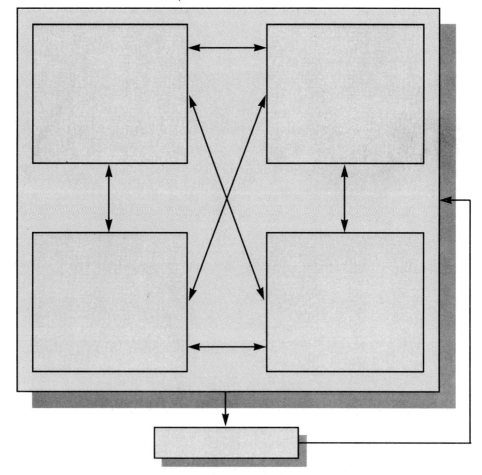

Conceptual Model for this Book

O rganizational behavior is a topic of major concern to every practicing manager, regardless of organization or hierarchical level. Many questions confront and perplex most modern managers: How do you motivate people? Which leadership style is most effective in which situation? What are the main causes of communication breakdown?

The major goal of the first part of the book is to study the foundations of modern organizational behavior, thereby setting the stage for a systematic analysis of the field. When you are finished reading this part, you will not be able to answer the three questions posed in the preceding paragraph, but you will have a sound understanding of what organizational behavior is and how modern psychologists, sociologists, and anthropologists study such behavior.

Chapter 1 provides a historical perspective on modern organizational behavior. The objectives in this chapter are to define the term organizational behavior, to provide some illustrations of this behavior in action, and then to trace the development of the store of knowledge about human social behavior from the early classical contributors to today's modernists. You will learn in this chapter that we have come a long way from the factory manager who was convinced that people work for money and that everything else is secondary to them. You will also learn that despite some great strides in behavioral research, there is a long way to go in truly understanding why people act the way they do.

Chapter 2 examines the field of behavioral science, noting who behavioral scientists are and how they go about investigating behavior in the workplace. You will learn that many of your assumptions about behavior are probably based on limited experience. For example, if you have ever worked in a large office you may have noted that many of the personnel are working far below their real potential. This observation may have led you to think that the organization could fire half of its staff with no consequent loss in efficiency. However, modern behavioral scientists would be unwilling to draw such a conclusion until the effects of worker layoff had been studied and the investigators were certain that if half the workers were fired, the others would indeed be able (and willing) to do all the work. Were these scientists to find that the remaining workers became panicky and that most of them started looking for other jobs (a not unlikely result of a mass firing), then your idea about dismissing half the workers would be perceived as detrimental rather than helpful. In short, we all have ideas about how and why people act as they do, but modern behavioral scientists put their biases aside and try to study each situation on its own merits. In Chapter 2 we will examine some of the research designs used by these scientists in gathering data and formulating behavioral hypotheses.

When you are finished with this part of the book you should have a sound understanding of where the field of organizational behavior is and where it seems to be heading. You should also know what the term organizational behavior means and how the individuals who work in the field go about conducting their research and formulating their theories. ◆

CHAPTER 1
Organizational Behavior: A Historical Perspective

GOALS OF THE CHAPTER

Organizational behavior is a subject that has long intrigued and perplexed managers. Perhaps the major reason is that employees do not always act in a predictable way, and this leads managers to view subordinate behavior as unpredictable or unorthodox. Why do managers believe that their own concept of appropriate behavior is right and the employee's is wrong? Perhaps the best answer is that the managers cannot see themselves acting as the employees do, and "correct" behavior is regarded as what the managers themselves would do.

In the initial chapter of this book, we examine what organizational behavior is all about. We will also take a historical look at the emergence of modern organizational behavior and examine the status of modern theory. When you have finished reading this chapter, you will be able to:

1. define the term *organizational behavior*;
2. describe the philosophy of the classical theorists of organizational behavior and give its shortcomings;
3. describe how the human relationists adopted and extended classical theory;
4. explain some of the shortcomings of the human relationists' theory;
5. describe the human resource philosophy of organizational behavior;
6. note how the modernists have formulated a flexible, empirically based approach to understanding behavior at work.

OPENING CASE: JAKE'S PHILOSOPHY

At Kirsten, Inc., new employee orientation is important. New managers are taught the philosophy and culture of the firm, and they are given a series of lectures by top managers. At the recent orientation, Jake McGullen talked to the group about his experiences.

When I started with the firm, I was strictly work-oriented. My focus was on getting my people to do as much as possible. I once designed a special incentive program that resulted in my group achieving more sales during the month of December than any other group—and we had one of the smallest sales territories in the country!

However, over the years my philosophy of management has changed. I don't think I've become less work-oriented, but I have become more people-oriented. For example, I've gotten a lot wiser about the importance of group norms and the need to listen to people and treat them with respect.

Most importantly, I've learned that people are important assets and need to be treated as such. They want work that allows them to use creativity and that offers them job autonomy and feedback. I suppose you could say that I've gone through an extended learning period—and I'm still learning. But I'd like to think

that I'm better at managing people today than when I started here 27 years ago.

1. When Jake began his management career was he a classical manager?
2. Does Jake believe in any of the ideas espoused by human relations theory?
3. How would you describe Jake's thinking today? Put it in your own words.

Write down your answers to these questions and put them aside. We will return to them later.

ORGANIZATIONAL BEHAVIOR IN ACTION

Organization behavior is concerned with understanding and controlling human behavior.

Organizational behavior is an academic discipline concerned with describing, understanding, predicting, and controlling human behavior in an organizational environment. When applied to individuals and groups, organizational behavior includes norms, values, perceptions, attitudes, and a series of other behavioral determinations, all of which we will be studying. For the moment, however, we would like you to think of organizational behavior in *action terms* by examining five specific cases.

Case 1: What's the Score?

Having earned his doctoral degree in marketing, Louis King accepted a two-year contract, with renewal dependent upon satisfactory performance, at a nationally-known university. The department chairperson was in Europe during the interview process, so the dean of the College of Business had filled in by meeting Louis at the plane, taking him to dinner, arranging for him to meet the marketing faculty, and then seeing him off at the airport. In the course of this visit the dean had told Louis that although publications were important, most of the students came from very wealthy families and were accustomed to high-quality teaching and counseling. As a result, Louis devoted most of the year to preparing his lectures, designing two new courses for the curriculum, and serving on one university and two college committees.

Toward the end of his first year, Louis was called in by the newly elected chairperson of the department for a progress talk. At this meeting it was revealed that Louis had the highest student evaluations in the department for the preceding semester and the second highest in the entire college.

Nevertheless, the chairperson noted, there was a problem: Louis had not submitted one article for publication that year and had not appeared on one panel at either a national or a regional meeting. Louis explained that when he was hired the dean had made it clear that publication was of secondary importance. Unfortunately for

Louis, the chairperson disagreed, noting that the dean had spoken out of turn and had no direct control over who was hired and fired in the department, a matter that was decided solely by the departmental faculty. Upon checking with the dean, Louis learned that the chairperson was right. He also found out that while he was busy with other matters, the chairperson and top members of the department had been bringing in people to fill new openings in the department and that many of these candidates were research-oriented.

Before the end of the second semester the chairperson informed Louis that the college would stand behind its two-year commitment, but that his contract would not be renewed for a third year. This advance notice would enable him to find a new job before the second year was out.

Louis went to the dean but did not receive a very favorable hearing. In fact, when asked if teaching were not the most important role of a professor, the dean replied that although it was, "We are still in an era of publish or perish." Louis spent the first semester of his second year interviewing for a job. He eventually accepted a position at a large university in the midwest where he was told that they expected him to publish one article a year if he hoped to get tenure. Although Louis was sorry to leave his old job, he was optimistic about his new one. "At least," he said, "I know the score at this new school." ◆

This case illustrates a typical behavioral problem that confronts individuals in organized environments. The person's expectations are not in accord with those of the organization. We can put the blame (if we want to assign one) on any number of people. The dean inadvertently misled the young professor. The people in the department in general, and the chairperson in particular, failed to provide guidance and support to the individual. Finally, the professor himself failed to react appropriately to cues in the environment that indicated he was not pursuing all the right activities. When he saw everyone else working on research and writing, he should have realized that these activities were high on the organization's priority list. For the moment, we won't examine why the problem occurred or how it could have been avoided. Rather, we simply note that there are many organizational behavior problems with which individuals must deal. Individual behavior will be the topic of discussion in Chapters 3–6.

Case 2: The Work-Oriented Supervisor

Barbara Gilbert was a new supervisor at the Lake Point plant. The first two weeks of Barbara's tenure had been taken up with orientation and training. The firm spent a good deal of time stressing the importance of work output. At the end of the training session, Barbara felt she understood the company's operating philosophy quite well.

During the next six months Barbara practiced what she had been taught. Specifically, she noted that of the fourteen workers under her direct control, four were very productive, eight were average, and the other two were generally very poor. In an effort to encourage the top four, she continually reminded them that the company rewarded high productivity, and at the first semiannual review she recommended the four for the highest salary increases allowed under the contract. This, she felt, would show them how much management appreciated what they were doing.

However, the salary adjustment brought about a problem. The four high producers were now making more money than anyone else in the group, and the others retaliated by interacting less and less with them. In fact, within three weeks of the salary increases the four workers were totally ostracized by the others.

Barbara encouraged the high producers to ignore these pressures, and she was initially successful. Unfortunately, within a month of the second review period, all four indicated that they would be quitting. One of them put it this way: "I want to work in a friendlier, more relaxed atmosphere." The others echoed these sentiments. Their terminations took place over a two-week period and resulted in a large decline in work output. The departures and reduced productivity led Barbara's boss to tell her, "You've lost your best four workers. What type of manager are you? If you don't straighten out that mess down there and get us back the lost productivity, you'll be the next to go."

On her way out of the manager's office Barbara reflected on the problem. "Maybe," she thought, "if I hadn't pushed so hard for high productivity, the four wouldn't have done so well at raise time and they'd still be working here. On the other hand, the company said I was supposed to get high output and I did. I don't understand. I thought I was doing the right thing." ◆

In contrast to the first case, this is an illustration of group behavior. The norms, values, and attitudes of a work group can directly affect the output of individual members. Although Barbara's intentions were commendable, she singled out the high producers and split the work group into two camps. If she had had more supervisory experience, she might have exercised more effective leadership and gotten the lower producers to do more work, or reduced the negative effect that these employees had on the high producers, or both. Group behavior and effective leadership, primary topics in the study of organizational behavior, will be the subject of our attention in Chapters 7–10.

Case 3: One Heck of a Job

Roberta Anderson was hired by Woodling Memorial Hospital to develop a management development department that would provide training for the supervisors and other managerial personnel in the organization. Although Roberta had a bachelor's degree in English and a master's degree in psychology, she was very interested in management training and spent the first six months reading a great deal of management literature and attending professional training courses. This was fine with her boss, Paula Castle, the hospital administrator, who wanted her to become as well-rounded as possible in all fields of management training and development.

Once this initial training period was over, Roberta started contacting all of the departments in the hospital and asking each the type of training it would like over the next year. The lists that were submitted included: (a) improved communication; (b) time management; and (c) effective leadership styles. Roberta developed training programs in all these areas. By the end of the year she felt that her work had been very successful and, from a personal standpoint, highly rewarding. Much of the feedback she received from department heads in the hospital reinforced these feelings.

At the beginning of the new year, however, she received some bad news. Paula Castle announced that she was taking early retirement. Her replacement, Phil Winthrop, told Roberta that he would like to see her temporarily continue in her current job, but that he wanted to decentralize control over training and development to the departmental level by increasing these departments' budgets and letting them send people outside for much of this training. As Roberta's job was phased out, Phil wanted her to move into the public relations department of the hospital.

After giving the matter serious thought, Roberta announced she was leaving to take a job with another hospital, helping them start up a management development department of their own. "This is one heck of a job," she told Phil, "and I just can't see myself doing any other type of work." ◆

In this case a person who loves her job refuses to be phased into some other activity that is less personally rewarding. Situations like this can arise any time an organization restructures its departments or activities. Sometimes these changes involve specific individuals, as in this instance; other times they affect entire groups. The latter situation occurs when people who have been working together for long periods of time and have established warm personal relationships suddenly find themselves transferred to different parts of the organization. Yet, whether individuals or groups are affected, the behavioral problems involved relate to organization design, job design, and stress, topics that will be discussed in Chapters 11–13.

Case 4: Getting Out Ahead

When Harry White started working for the Rutherford Investment Company, he took a training program designed to teach him how the firm analyzed and evaluated its investment proposals. Harry learned that the company was basically conservative, although from time to time it did take big risks. Six months after Harry began, his boss, Fred Audrey, was scheduled to go on vacation. Fred called Harry in and told him, "Next week a personal friend of mine is going to apply for a loan on a real estate deal he is putting together in South Florida. I'd appreciate it if you'd look at the proposal very closely and do what you can for him." Harry promised to do so.

When the proposal came in Harry looked it over carefully. The investment was a bold one and promised both high risk and high reward. As a result, Harry gave the proposal a marginal acceptance, calling it "pretty much of a gamble when compared to other safer investments we can make." The committee, acting on Harry's evaluation, turned down the application.

Harry's boss returned the Monday after the proposal was rejected. He was very upset. "I thought I told you to take care of this man's proposal. Sure it's something of a gamble, but I know the individual personally and he would never get into anything he could not get out of profitably. Now he's going to go somewhere else and we're going to lose the loan. What's wrong with your judgment?"

The next week, Harry received his first six-month evaluation. He was rated as low average. His boss said that Harry "does not have a sufficient understanding of investment analysis. His work is not on a par with that of many other trainees in the firm." Harry was shocked. All of the other trainees he knew had received good evaluations. Two weeks later, having secured employment with another financial institution, Harry tendered his resignation. When his fiancee asked him why he had decided to leave Rutherford, Harry said, "I like to think that I'm getting out while I'm still ahead." ◆

In this case we see a person who misinterpreted a communication he received. As a result, he made a decision that was wrong and elicited a negative personal evaluation. Situations like this are not uncommon. Although the firm has a basic set of rules, management expects its people to know when to bend those rules. Harry did not. As a result he terminated his relationship with the organization. The functions at work in this case, decision making and communication, constitute major organizational processes that take place in every enterprise. These are functions that individuals and groups use when they interact in an organizational environment. They will be the focus of Chapters 14 and 15.

Case 5: Straightening Out a Mess

When Anthony Rodriguez became head of Production Plant 6, he knew that output had been slipping for almost eight months. He was determined to find out why and correct the situation as quickly as possible.

It took Tony less than two weeks to pinpoint the major problems. The production groups and the quality control sector in the plant were at each other's throats. The reason was that all production output moved quickly down a conveyor-like assembly line. There was time to perform only the particular assembly function; if any mistakes were made, the unit had to continue to the end, at which point the quality control people took over and determined whether the unit was acceptable or not. Those units that were not acceptable were sent to a rework department where they were fixed.

The production groups hated this process because the quality control people were responsible for identifying and listing all errors that they found. These lists were then posted in the production area. The production people felt as if the quality control people were holding them up to ridicule. The quality control people, in turn, felt that the production people ought to have done their work correctly the first time.

In order to deal with the problem, Tony brought in an outside consultant known as a change agent. For the next two weeks, this individual examined the problem and worked to find a solution to the intergroup conflict that existed. When his boss called him yesterday, Tony gave him a status report on the problem. The boss told him, "I don't care what you do, Tony, just as long as you straighten out the mess. The last guy we had in there was unable to do that, and we had to get rid of him. I'd hate to see that happen to you." Tony promised to have the matter at least partially resolved by the end of the month. "If you can do that," the boss told him, "you should start to see an increase in productivity by the beginning of the fiscal quarter and results by the end of it. Good luck!"

When Tony put down the phone, he wondered how successful the consultant would be in helping to resolve the group conflict problem. "The toughest thing about this job," he thought to himself, "is that problems like this never end. When I solve this one, there will be another waiting for me. No wonder so many people in this plant take early retirement." ◆

In this case, we see a manager who is facing a problem of intergroup conflict that is affecting organizational effectiveness. These types of problems are often resolved with the help of an outside consultant known as a change agent. These individuals work with the organization to help create an environment more conducive to increased output. This entire area of conflict, change, and the resolution of such problems in order to achieve organizational effectiveness is a major one in modern enterprise. Sometimes the issue requires cooperation from the personnel as well as support from top management. It also calls for the use of many of the tools and techniques you will be studying in this book. That is why we have reserved the topics of climate, culture, change, and conflict resolution for Chapters 16 and 17.

From the five cases we have just examined, it is evident that organizational behavior is a very broad field. In examining it, we will be studying individuals, groups, organization design, organizational processes, and organizational effectiveness. Before beginning our study, however, it is helpful first to obtain a historical perspective on the field. Where has it been and where is it going? This question can be answered by a brief review of classical management theory and human relations theory followed by modern theory.

CLASSICAL MANAGEMENT THEORY

Managers have always been concerned with organizational behavior problems. With the advent of industrialization, these problems increased. In particular, management discovered that attaining high productivity required a systematically designed organization that adhered to basic rules of order and logic. Three major groups helped formulate these ideas: (a) scientific managers; (b) administrative theorists; and (c) bureaucracy advocates. The thinking of the three constitutes **classical management theory**. In the following pages we examine each, together with its implications for organizational behavior.

Scientific Management Movement

The **scientific management** movement in the United States began in the post–Civil War era. The scientific managers, in many cases, were mechanical engineers who attempted to apply time-and-motion study concepts in the workplace. Through the use of such scientific procedures they were often able to significantly increase productivity. At the heart of their work was the **task concept,** described by Frederick Taylor, the most famous member of their group, in this way:

The task concept was central to scientific management.

> The most prominent single element in modern scientific management is the task idea. The work of every workman is fully planned out by the management at least one day in advance, and each man receives in most cases complete written instructions, describing in detail the task which he is to accomplish, as well as the means to be used in doing the work. And the work planned in advance in this way constitutes a task which is to be solved. . . . This task specifies not only what is to be done but how it is to be done and the exact time allowed for doing it.[1]

Philosophy and Behavioral Implications.   From an organizational behavior standpoint, why would workers be willing to do more work simply because a mechanical engineer had discovered some time-saving shortcuts? There were two reasons. First, if an employee failed to do the required work, there was a good chance of being fired. Second, in most cases the company offered a financial incentive for high output. Taylor, for example, designed a *differential piece-rate system* based on two different rates of pay. For those who did less than the expected output (standard), there was a low rate. For those who did standard or above, there was a higher rate.

The workers were viewed as adjuncts to the machine.

Four behavioral conclusions about the scientific managers can be drawn from this discussion. First, they believed that by carefully designing each job, high efficiency and profit could be obtained. Unfortunately, in the process they tended to lose sight of the worker as a person. Most scientific managers viewed the worker as a mere adjunct to the machine.

Money was considered a prime motivator.

Second, by offering financial incentives for high productivity they illustrated a belief in the maxim "money motivates." On the negative side, however, they made no allowances for people who did not want to maximize their financial gain.

There was a lack of understanding about group behavior.

Third, because these incentive plans were typically geared to individuals rather than to groups, it indicates that the scientific managers lacked a solid understanding of group behavior. Note that we did *not* say that these managers understood nothing about group behavior. They knew from their research that ten people working independently would typically have greater total output than ten people working as a group. What they did not know was *why*.

The worker was viewed as a totally rational person.

Fourth, these managers tended to see the worker as a totally rational person, who would perform the work in the most efficient manner and maximize his or her income in the process. Actually, people do not function this way; they are too complex to be reduced to such a simple description.

The scientific managers raised more behavioral questions than they answered. They did, however, make organizations more aware of these behavioral challenges. Certainly if businesses were to continue along the road of industrialization, they would have to pay more attention to the area of human behavior in organizations.

Administrative Theory and Bureaucracy

Principles of administration were formulated and developed.

The success of the scientific management movement resulted in a shift of attention farther up the organizational hierarchy. This focus on management led to the eventual formulation by administrative theorists of management rules and principles.[2] Some of the more commonly cited were the following:

1. Authority and responsibility ought to be equal; you cannot have one without the other.
2. The goals of the organization should take precedence over those of individuals or groups of employees.
3. The remuneration of personnel must be fair and should be tied to successful effort.
4. Everyone should have one and only one boss.

5. In order to preserve the integrity of the hierarchy, communication should follow formal channels, unless employees have permission from their superior to cut across organizational lines.

These principles were much more general than the engineering-oriented rules employed by the scientific managers, which is to be expected, given that they were designed for managing people.

Bureaucracy is based on rules, standards, and impersonality.

Some people tried to blend the thinking of scientific management and administrative theory by recommending organization structures based on strict, logical laws of order. The result was a **bureaucracy** in which the personnel all held specialized jobs, operated in accordance with specific rules and standards, and carried out their duties in a spirit of formalistic impersonality.[3]

Philosophy and Behavioral Implications. The philosophies of the administrative theorists and bureaucracy advocates were similar in that both wanted to formulate ideas related to managing people. The major differences between the two were that: (a) the administrative theorists were concerned with all phases of management activity, whereas the bureaucracy advocates were primarily interested in organization structure; and (b) the administrative theorists had more flexible views related to their primary interest areas. From a behavioral point of view, however, both groups are important.

Administrative theory guidelines were often too general or overly rigid.

The administrative theorists tried to develop principles to help individuals manage more effectively. The biggest problem with these guidelines was that some were so general that they provided no substantive recommendations, whereas others were so rigid that they could not be satisfactorily implemented. For example, although their rules required authority and responsibility to be equal, the administrative theorists never explained how to ensure this equality. Conversely, while pointing out that everyone should have one and only one boss, they failed to consider the value of multiple bosses (as used in some modern organization structures). In retrospect, it is clear that the administrative theorists recognized the importance of managing people effectively but failed to incorporate any behavioral awareness into their philosophy.

The bureaucracy advocates were still farther off the mark. Although modified bureaucracies can be appropriate in certain situations, these advocates believed that personnel should be forced to conform to organizational requirements. Of course, they realized that people would occasionally be unpredictable or irrational, or both. However, they believed that such problems could be minimized through the use of structured job environments, job tools and instructions, and job content. One of the primary problems with this thinking was its view of the worker as a totally rational individual who would gladly conform to organizational objectives in the name of efficiency. However, as Blau has observed, "To administer a social organization according to purely technical criteria of rationality is irrational, because it ignores the nonrational aspects of social conduct."[4]

The administrative theorists and bureaucracy advocates were aware of the human element in the organization, but they were not able to deal with it effectively.[5]

STOP

Review your answers to Question 1 and make any changes you would like before continuing.

1. When Jake began his management career was he a classical manager?

When he began Jake was a classical manager. He was work-oriented and even developed an incentive program designed to dramatically increase sales. He believed in many of the concepts espoused by classical management theory.

HUMAN RELATIONS THEORY

Classical management theory was eventually supplemented by **human relations theory**. We say "supplemented" rather than "replaced" because, to a great degree, the human relations model actually *incorporated* and *extended* classical theory.

By the early 1920s businessmen had begun to note some of the dysfunctional effects associated with trying to standardize workers and jobs. It was becoming clear that the individual could no longer be thought of as a mere appendage to the machine.

On the other hand, the human relationists did *not* challenge the basic tenets of task specialization, orderliness, stability, and control that were central to classical management theory. They merely sought to add a slightly human dimension to management's orientation. In this regard some of them argued that although money was an important motivator, most people were willing to take part of their reward in the form of humane treatment, personal attention, and the chance to feel important. Major support for many of the human relations ideas were provided by social science studies in industry. The most famous of these was the Hawthorne studies, which illustrate the type of research inquiries with which the human relationists were concerned.

> Human relationists sought to add a human dimension to classical theory.

The Hawthorne Studies

> No relationship between illumination and output was found.

The **Hawthorne studies** began in 1924 at the Hawthorne Works of the Western Electric Company near Cicero, Illinois. The initial objective was to examine the effect of illumination on output. However, after two and a half years and numerous experiments, the researchers were unable to determine the effects of lighting on productivity. Despite repeated experiments, output in both the test and control groups increased. Even though the researchers were confused, further studies were proposed. At this point, Elton Mayo and his Harvard colleagues were invited to study the situation.

> Small-group research was undertaken.

In order to make a systematic analysis of the factors affecting work performance, the researchers decided to isolate a small group of female workers from the regular work force and put them under close observation. Although an observer was placed in the room with the women to record everything that happened and to maintain a friendly atmosphere, the women were told that the experiment was not designed to boost production. They were to work at their regular pace and not be distracted by the change in the environment. Then the researchers began introducing changes such as hot lunches, rest periods, days off, and Saturday morning work. As the study continued, the output of the women rose and stayed high. Similar results were obtained from a second experiment with another group of workers. These results led the researchers to conclude that there was simply no easy-to-identify, direct relationship between changes in the work environment and productivity. Nor did individual wage incentives or relief from fatigue and monotony seem to be the underlying causes of the observed increases in output. The answer seemed to rest more with *social factors* than with anything else. As a result, the study moved into its third phase, the massive interviewing program.

A massive interviewing program was carried out.

The initial purpose of the interviewing program was to obtain information that would be helpful in improving supervisory training. During this phase of the studies, over 20,000 interviews were conducted. One discovery the interviewers made was that people tend to give standard, stereotyped answers to direct questions. Therefore, a nondirect approach was substituted. The outcome of the switch to a nondirect approach was very favorable. The employees began talking about all sorts of things that interested them, or bothered them, on the job. The result was a wealth of information about employee attitudes and group dynamics. One of the researchers' findings was that the individual's work performance, position, and status in the organization were determined not only by the person himself but also by the group members. Peers had an effect on individual performance. In order to study this area of informal norms more closely, the research entered its fourth and final phase, that of the bank wiring room.

In this room there were three types of workers: wiremen, soldermen, and inspectors. After the equipment was wired and soldered, the inspector would check to see that it was acceptable. The researchers decided to study these workers and learn as much about their behavior as possible.

One of the researchers' discoveries was that the workers deliberately restricted their output. Another finding was that the men treated the managers differently; the supervisors lower down the hierarchy were shown less respect than managers further up the line. A third discovery was that the group divided itself into two subgroups or cliques, and, based on their respective cliques, the workers either did or refrained from doing certain things such as engaging in games or trading jobs. A fourth was that there were certain codes of conduct that individuals had to follow if they wanted to be accepted as a member of a clique. Roethlisberger and Dickson[6] identified these as follows:

A number of group norms were uncovered.

1. You should not turn out too much work. If you do, you are a "rate buster."

2. You should not turn out too little work. If you do, you are a chiseler.

3. You should not tell a superior anything that will redound to the detriment of an associate. If you do, you are a squealer.

4. You should not attempt to maintain social distance or act officious. If you are an inspector, for example, you should not act like one.

Philosophy and Behavioral Implications. The philosophy of the human relationists extended classical management theory to encompass some consideration of the individual. Through their research the human relationists made some important behavioral contributions. First, they recognized and identified some of the major determinants of informal group development. Second, they studied the characteristics of these informal groups so that they could better understand behavior within them. Third, they realized that although division of labor enhanced productivity, the fatigue and monotony brought about by job specialization had to be dealt with from a *psychological* as well as a physical standpoint. They were also aware that organization plans are often disrupted by internal friction. As a remedy, they prescribed means for eliminating organizational conflict, including participative management, improved communication, and recognizing human dignity.

It was found that happy workers are not necessarily productive workers.

In retrospect, however, human relations theory had a number of serious shortcomings in regard to organizational behavior. First, its proponents believed that employee participation would lead to job satisfaction, which would in turn bring about increased productivity. Supporters of this viewpoint are often referred to as members of the "happiness school." Empirical research has not validated the "satisfaction leads to performance" thesis.

Second, many human relationists regarded the formal and informal organizations as separate and distinct entities. Moreover, these theorists believed that the goals of both organizational groups were often irreconcilable.

Third, the Hawthorne findings, which helped form the foundation for human relations thinking, were criticized for not being sufficiently scientific.[7]

Fourth, after Hawthorne the human relationists seemed content to conduct empirical research that had little meaning outside of its own context and to engage in descriptive generalizations.[8] This led critics to call the movement's findings nothing more than a trivial mass of empirical and descriptive information. By the mid-1950s it was obvious that the human relationists were running out of steam and had nothing more substantive to contribute to management and organization theory. This led to the emergence of modern theory, which makes heavy use of the scientific method and rigorous research designs.

Modern theory, based more on scientific methods and rigorous research designs, began to emerge.

STOP

Review your answers to Question 2 and make any changes you would like before continuing.

2. Does Jake believe in any of the ideas espoused by human relations theory?

He certainly does. His comments about the importance of group norms and the need to listen to people and treat them with respect indicate that he accepts some of the thinking of human relations theory.

MODERN ORGANIZATIONAL BEHAVIOR THEORY

Modern behavioral theorists have extended the thinking of the human relationists, viewing the employee as a highly capable entity with untapped resources. According to this theory, the manager's role should not be to control subordinates, as the classicists and to some degree the human relationists perceived it, but to facilitate employee performance. This attitude has resulted in the emergence of **human resources theory**, which is presented in Table 1–1 and contrasted with the classical and human

TABLE 1–1

Behavioral Theories of Management

Classical Management Theory	Human Relations Theory	Human Resources Theory
People work in order to be assured of food, clothing, shelter, and survival. Money motivates!	People work in order to be assured of food, clothing, shelter, and survival, but they are also interested in the chance for social interaction with their fellow workers.	People work in order to fullfill needs, such as to contribute to organizational objectives, attain a feeling of accomplishment, and use their creativity in a job-related setting, as well as to earn a living and enjoy social interaction.
If the pay is good enough, people will put up with just about anything.	If the pay and social interaction are good enough, people will put up with just about anything.	People are most highly motivated by work that allows them to use creativity and offers them job autonomy and feedback.
Objectives should be set for people, not by them.	When useful, suggestions and recommendations should be considered in setting objectives for employees.	Mutual goal-setting processes are important in creating employee commitment to organizational objectives.
The manager's job is to tell people what to do and see that these orders are followed.	The manager's job is to tell people what to do and be willing to listen to both their work suggestions and their complaints.	In getting things done, the manager should use mutual goal-setting and problem-solving approaches with personnel.
Managers should communicate downward, giving orders and advice in the process.	Managers should communicate orders downward and receive upward input from subordinates regarding work progress and performance.	Managers should encourage communication (upward, downward, horizontal, vertical) in whatever way is necessary to promote organizational effectiveness.
Most people cannot handle work that calls for self-direction, self-control, or creativity. The scientific management task concept is very important.	People do not want self-direction or self-control. They enjoy social interaction with other employees and this should be addressed in the task concept.	People do welcome self-direction and self-control and will perform well under these conditions.
When people do things wrong, the manager should use technical retraining programs so as to prevent these mistakes in the future.	When people do things wrong, the manager should listen to their problems and use tactful disciplining in getting them into line.	When people do things wrong, the manager should make use of whatever training (technical, human, conceptual) is necessary to ensure continued short- and long-range performance.
The manager's primary emphasis should be on using personnel efficiently.	The manager's primary emphasis should be on treating personnel well.	The manager's primary emphasis should be on using personnel as if they are important human assets.
Managers should say, "You'd better do it!" The worker is to be treated as a child.	Managers should say, "You ought to do it." The worker is to be treated as an adolescent.	Managers should say, "You can do it." The worker is to be treated as an adult.

Adapted from Raymond E. Miles, *Theories of Management* (New York: McGraw-Hill Book Co.,1975).

relations thinking. Notice that the latter two models are similar in nature and differ dramatically from the human resources model. Modern behaviorists offer an approach to managing human resources that differs markedly from that of Taylor and his associates.

There are three significant ways in which modern theory extends human relations theory. First, it is based on more rigorous *empirical research*. Propositions about human behavior must be formulated on the basis of formal scientific investigation and not according to a personal philosophy of how and why people act as they do. Second, modern theory is concerned with bringing together all of this information into an overall framework that can be examined by those interested in learning about management and organizational behavior. Those wishing to do research in the area can use the framework as a point of departure. Third, modern theory accepts the premise that the only meaningful way to study organizations is through a *systems approach*. In so doing, modern theorists pick up where the Hawthorne researchers left off.

Modern theory is empirical, broadly based, and systems oriented.

STOP

Review your answers to Question 3 and make any changes you would like before continuing.

3. How would you describe Jake's thinking today? Put it in your own words.

Jake subscribes much more heavily to modern behavioral theory than to classical or human relations theory. His comments about creativity, job autonomy, and feedback clearly illustrate this. In fact, a review of Table 1–1 shows that Jake has been progressing from classical thinking to human resources thinking. This is undoubtedly what he meant when he said he has gone through an extended learning period.

A Systems Approach to Organizations

A system is an organized unit that consists of two or more interdependent parts.

A **system** is an organized unit that consists of two or more interdependent parts, or subsystems, and can be distinguished from the environment in which it exists by some identifiable boundary. As applied to the study of organizations, there are five interdependent parts that are of interest to modern theorists.

First, there is the *individual*. This person comes to the organization with a particular personality structure. There are certain things he or she is prepared to give to the organization and certain things he or she wishes to receive in return.

Second, there is the *formal organization*. Within this structure there are divisions, departments, and units, and within each of these are individual positions that carry authority and responsibility.

Third, there is the *informal organization,* which has already been discussed in some depth. Only two notations need to be made here: (a) The informal organization, like the formal, makes demands on the individual, and in order to remain a member, the person must behave appropriately; and (b) the formal and informal organizations are not always in conflict; sometimes there is harmony between them.

FIGURE 1–1

The Organizational System (Note: The double-headed arrows represent the fusion process.)

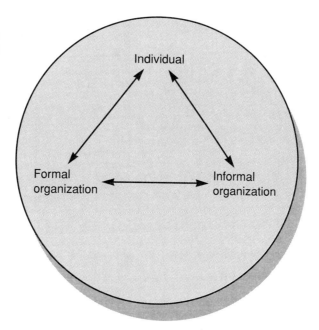

External environment

Fourth, a *fusion process* takes place among the foregoing three elements, in the course of which each modifies and shapes the other. This give-and-take results, ultimately, in preserving organizational integrity.[9]

Fifth, the work is performed in the *physical environment*. Interaction of individuals and machine systems takes place in this setting.

These five parts constitute what is known as the organizational system (Figure 1–1). Implied within the conceptual scheme is the fact that the system operates in, and is in constant interaction with, the external environment. A further elaboration of this relationship is presented in Figure 1–2. It is thus evident that behavioral theorists have extended the classical and human relations approaches to include the external environment (economy, competitors, government regulation, customers, and so on), as well as the internal environment. In so doing, modern theorists see the organization as an ecosystem that must continually adapt to its surroundings by receiving inputs from the external environment and modifying its relationship with this environment accordingly. The organization is viewed as a basically open system.

Other Characteristics

In addition to the open-system viewpoint, modern theorists incorporate five other important organizational characteristics into their conceptual framework.

First, organizational systems are seen as being probabilistic rather than deterministic. **Deterministic systems** do as they are told, and for all practical purposes their outcomes are predictable. If an adding machine is in proper running order and the

FIGURE 1–2
Organization's Dynamic Interaction
with Its Environment

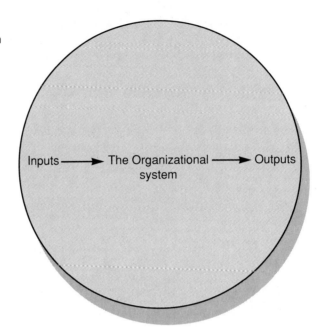

External environment

operator enters the number 182, presses the "add" button, enters the number 118, and then presses the "equals" button, the answer 300 will print out. The machine will not give any other answer. However, in **probabilistic systems** outcomes are not uniquely determined. It is possible to make predictions about the outcome when a probabilistic system is involved, but we can never be sure. For example, if a coin is flipped into the air and allowed to fall to the ground, there is a 50 percent chance of a head and a 50 percent chance of a tail. Statistical probabilities can be assigned to the flip, but the outcome cannot be determined with certainty before the coin's toss. Human beings also fall into this probabilistic system category, although at a much more sophisticated level.

Second, modern theorists see a need for certain *processes* to continue in operation if the organization is to survive. These processes help the enterprise interact with both its internal and external environments. These processes entail decision making, communication, and performance evaluation.

Third, individuals in organizations are seen as being *multimotivated*. There may be many things driving a person toward a particular objective, and there may be more than one way of satisfying the individual's desires. In contrast to the classical view of the worker as an economic being, modernists see the individual as a complex entity who can be motivated in a multitude of ways.

Fourth, modern theory tends to be *descriptive* (here is how people behave) rather than normative or prescriptive (here is how managers ought to deal with their people). Modern theorists seek to describe characteristics of organizations and management and provide alternative courses of action while leaving the specific choice of the needs to pursue and the means to obtain them up to the individual manager.

Fifth, and finally, modern theory is *multidisciplinary*. Concepts from many different disciplines are relied upon in the study of organization and management. These include psychology, sociology, and anthropology, to name but three.

Behavior is multifaceted and should be studied from an empirical and open-system focus.

Philosophy and Behavioral Implications. The philosophy of the modernists states that behavior in organizations is multifaceted and must be studied from both empirical and open-system viewpoints. Heavy reliance is placed on scientific proof as contrasted with intuitive feelings, and the organizational setting is given as much consideration as the individual or the group. For example, modernists are interested in studying human resource management trends. What developments will impact on the way organizations will function during the 1990s?[10] At the same time, these researchers would be unwilling to assume that management values will be changing dramatically between now and 2001. "Organizational Behavior in Action: Business as Usual" (pp. 20–21) explains why.

It is still too early to put modern theory in perspective. On the positive side, we can applaud the attention being given to empirical research. Additionally, the great amount of behavioral research currently under way should provide further important insights into individuals in organizations.

On the negative side, modern theorists seem to be running into the same problem that confronted the human relations theorists. Although a great deal of research is being done, little attempt is being made to fit everything together into a general model or theory of organizational behavior.

CONCEPTUAL MODEL FOR THIS BOOK

Now that you are familiar with the behavioral sciences and modern organizational behavior theory, you are ready to begin your study of organizational behavior. Before doing so, however, we want to introduce you to the conceptual model that will be used in this book. This model comprises a series of interrelated parts. In each of the next four sections of the text we will examine one of these parts, beginning with individual behavior and then going on to group behavior, organization structure, and organizational processes. Figure 1–3 on page 22 illustrates this conceptual model.

Individual Behavior

The primary component of organizational behavior is the individual, a very complex being whose needs, drives, and motives merit close analysis. In our examination of individual behavior we will be studying personality, perception, attitudes, learning, job satisfaction, reinforcement, and a host of other factors that help determine how and why people act the way they do. We will also be looking at the motivation process, which helps explain why people do (or fail to do) certain things. This discussion will review the role of such key motivational factors as money, working conditions, security, challenge, and work responsibility.

Organizational Behavior In Action

BUSINESS AS USUAL

Are managerial values going to change dramatically during the 1990s? In contrast to what many people believe, recent research shows that they are not. One longitudinal study, for example, gathered data on fifteen different characteristics of ideal managerial behavior over a twenty-one-year period from a number of different organizations. Opposite are rankings from Sperry Rand's Aeronautical Equipment Division for 1965-1986 inclusive, one of the firms in the study.

Commenting on the conclusions and implications of these data, James Lee notes:

> In the twenty-one years covered by the study of Sperry managers, very little change took place in values measured by rankings of fifteen characteristics of the ideal manager. This very slow change rate better matches other studies of the American cultural change rate. In their 1978 updated study of Muncie, Indiana (first studied in 1929 and 1937 as a typical American community by sociologists Robert and Helen Lynd), Theodore Caplow and his team of sociologists concluded that not much has changed: "We have not been able to find any trace of the disintegration of traditional social values described by observers who rely on their own intuitions. . . . Almost all the social forces shaping life in modern-day Muncie were already present in 1924. It amounts to a startling message about the nation: that American life has not changed very much in 50 years."

There will be many major organizational behavior changes taking place during the 1990s. However, management values will not be one of them. As behavior

---

Group Behavior

Just about everyone in an organization is a member of at least one group, the one to which they have been assigned by the management. In addition to this formal group, however, most are also members of one or more informal groups. The behavior of individuals in groups is a function of many factors, including the values and norms of the members and the composition of the groups. People in groups influence each other in such a way that group behavior is more than just the sum of the individual behaviors. For this reason we will be studying and comparing the differences between individual and group behavior. We will also be considering leadership and how the effective leader induces the group to attain organizational objectives. Power and organizational politics will also be considered.

Organizational Structure

Individuals and groups interact within the confines of the organizational structure. This structure derives from four basic factors: job definitions, departmentalization, span of control, and the decentralization and delegation of authority. The basic structure is also

research indicates, when it comes to managerial values, it is going to be business as usual.

Median Ranks on Ideal Manager Characteristics of Sperry Managers for 1965, 1972, 1978, and 1986

Ideal Manager Characteristic	1965 (N = 69)	1972 (N = 59)	1978 (N =67)	1986 (N = 114)
Future Planning	4.1	3.3	3.4	3.6
Respect for Authority	7.4*	9.5	9.5	9.2**
Quantifiable Variables	6.1	5.8	5.9	7.3
Sensitivity to Feelings	6.0	5.6	5.9	4.9
Personal Friendships	13.1	13.6	13.5	13.4
Decision Making	3.4	2.4	2.7	3.7
Religious or Ethical Values	10.1	8.9	9.8	8.7
Develop New Methods	3.7	4.0	4.2	4.3
Support of Government	12.5	13.1	13.5	12.8
Hard Work	7.7	8.7	9.4	9.7**
Family Obligations	11.1	10.2	11.1*	9.0**
Maint. of Status Differences ...	12.4	13.7	13.8	13.5
Willingness to Take Risks	11.0*	7.8*	9.4	9.6
Capacity for Loyalty	6.0	7.1	7.8	6.4
Belief in Subordinates	5.0	5.4	6.5	5.0

*Indicates significant differences between median ranks of samples on each side of the symbol.
**Indicates significant differences of at least 1.7 ranks between 1965 and 1986.

Source: James A. Lee, "Changes In Managerial Values, 1965–1986," Business Horizons, July–August 1988, pp. 29–37.

modified by contingency factors, such as organizational size, the characteristics of the employees, perceived complexity of the environment, dependence on the external environment, turbulence of the external environment, and technology. Within this structure, individuals and groups carry on organizational activities. Sometimes, however, people find the structure too confining or restrictive. They want more flexible or rewarding work. This is where job design comes in. Today many organizations are redesigning jobs so that workers gain autonomy, challenge, and opportunity for personal satisfaction from their jobs. In this part of the book we will study basic design factors and a job design. Stress and work will also be examined.

Organizational Processes

If individuals and groups are to achieve the objectives of the organization, three organizational processes must be carried out. First, decisions have to be made. Second, information about these decisions must be communicated to the personnel. Third, some

Conceptual Model for this Book

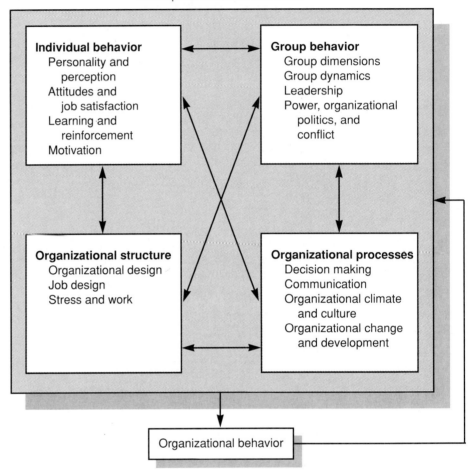

FIGURE 1–3
Conceptual Model for This Book

form of evaluation and corrective action must be taken in the form of evaluating climate and culture and adapting to change through the use of effective organizational development. These three processes of decision making, communication, and organizational development allow the people in an enterprise to interface with one another.

Our formal discussion of organizational behavior begins with the study of individuals and groups, and we will finish by examining the organizational processes which help ensure overall effectiveness. Such effectiveness is important because it serves as a gauge to evaluate organizational behavior and, where necessary, take corrective action.

SUMMARY

1. Organizational behavior is an academic discipline concerned with describing, understanding, predicting, and controlling human behavior in an organizational setting. Much of what we know about organizational behavior has been gathered over a long period of time.

2. Classical theorists had fixed views of human behavior in organizations. For example, the scientific managers applied time-and-motion study concepts to the workplace and then tried to motivate workers toward higher productivity by using incentive wage schemes. They also believed that money was the primary motivator.

3. The administrative theorists and bureaucracy advocates tried to develop scientific, rational principles for use at the management level. Both groups, however, lacked a solid understanding of organizational behavior. The theorists provided principles that were either too general or too rigid; the bureaucracy advocates failed to realize that a social organization cannot be administered according to purely technical criteria of rationality.

4. The human relationists adopted and extended classical thinking by adding a human dimension. In particu-lar, they argued that management had to deal with the worker as a whole person having needs and wants that demanded satisfaction. Many of the bases for such conclusions were found in the studies they conducted in industry. The best known were the Hawthorne studies.

5. The greatest problems with the human relationists were that they generalized their findings, and they tended to believe that happy workers were productive workers. In overall terms, their work was heavily descriptive, and they were eventually replaced by the modernists, who are much more empirical in their approach.

6. The modernists view individuals as highly capable, untapped human resources. They also place great reliance on empirical research data, an overall framework, and a systems approach. Some of the other important character-istics of modern theory are the belief that individuals are multimotivated and that the best way to study people in organizations is by a multidisciplinary approach.

KEY TERMS

organizational behavior	bureaucracy	system
classical management theory	human relations theory	deterministic systems
scientific management	Hawthorne studies	probabilistic systems
task concept	human resources theory	

REVIEW AND STUDY QUESTIONS

1. What is meant by the term *organizational behavior?* Define it in your own words.

2. Did the scientific managers understand organizational behavior? Defend your answer.

3. Did the administrative theorists understand organizational behavior? Explain.

4. What did the bureaucracy advocates overlook when it came to organizational behavior? Give your reasoning.

5. How did the human relationists extend the thinking of the classical management theorists? Be complete in your answer.

6. What did the Hawthorne researchers learn about organizational behavior as a result of this massive research study?

7. In your own words, what was the basic philosophy of the human relationists?

8. What contributions did the human relationists make to organizational behavior theory?

9. In recent years the human relations philosophy has come under attack. What are some of the criticisms leveled against it?

10. How does the human resources model differ from the

human relations model? How does the human resources model differ from the classical model? Compare
and contrast the three models.

11. In what way does modern organizational behavior theory extend human relationist thinking?

12. Modern theorists see the social structure as consisting
of five basic parts. What are they? Describe them.

13. Modern theory tends to be descriptive rather than
normative or prescriptive. What does this statement
mean?

CASES

You Just Can't Get Good Help Anymore

The Greenley Corporation's profit over the last five years
had increased at an annual rate of 13.5 percent. Most of this
increase was a direct result of subcontracts the firm had
secured from other companies.

    Six months ago, to deal with its ninety-day backlog of
orders, Greenley introduced an incentive plan to increase
output. There were several versions of the plan, each tailored to specific jobs. The one for assemblers and packers
offered a bonus of 25 percent for all work over standard.
The average assembler-packer was making $7.50 an hour
and was expected to assemble and pack ten units within this
time period. With time allowed for lunch and rest breaks,
people put in seven hours of work and were expected to
produce seventy units, resulting in a base of $.70 per unit.

    If the assembler-packer chose to work on Saturday,
the rate was time and a half, and management also promised
to pay the 25 percent bonus for output over standard. One
of the assembler-packers who turned out eighty-two units a
day received a weekly gross pay of $409.50. The calcula-
tions were as follows:

Average weekly pay
(7 hours × $7.50 per hour × 5 days)   = $262.50

Bonus for 12 extra units per day
($.70 per unit × 1.25 percent
bonus × 12 extra units × 5 days)   =   52.50

Saturday overtime
(7 hours × $11.25 [$7.50 per
hour × 1.5 for overtime])   =   78.75

Saturday bonus for 12 extra units
($.70 per unit × 1.5 for overtime ×
1.25 percent for incentive × 12 units)   =   15.75

                                              $409.50

    Last week the production department reported that
there was a one hundred-day backlog of orders. The vice-
president in charge of production told the president that he
would like to start finding subcontractors for some of these
orders. The president gave his consent but urged the manager to try to get as much of the work as possible done in
house. "If necessary," he said, "raise the incentive to 35
percent of base pay." The vice-president agreed to do so,
but pointed out to the president that only 6 percent of the
total plant work force was willing to work on Saturday. "I
don't think we're having much success with our incentive
program. If you ask me, you just can't get good help any-
more."

1. Does the Greenley management think that money motivates people? Explain.

2. Why is the incentive plan not proving effective?

3. Based on the vice-president's last comment, to which
theory of management does he subscribe: classical, human relations, or human resources? Explain.

The Pampered Workers

Gloria Anderson, a department head in a large midwestern
bank, has seven people reporting to her. In contrast to most
of the other departments in the bank, Gloria's people admit
that they feel little pressure on a day-to-day basis. The
major reason is because Gloria takes care of most matters
herself, delegating very little work to her subordinates. She
believes that managers should only ask their people to do
work that they themselves cannot do. In addition, Gloria
thinks that most workers want to feel important and useful,
but above all they want to be recognized as individuals. By

keeping them as happy as possible, she believes she can get the greatest quality and quantity of work from her people.

Gloria's boss, however, disagrees with this basic philosophy. He thinks she spends too much time worrying about whether the workers are happy or not. "With that philosophy," he has told her, "you are treating your people like little children. Workers don't want to be kept happy; they want challenging, meaningful work that allows them to contribute to objectives. You've got to think of your people as untapped human resources. Instead of sheltering them from work, get them involved. Delegate more and quit worrying about whether it disturbs them. People want to be used well, not pampered. You mean well, but you really underrate your people terribly."

Gloria has promised to think over what her boss has said. She was particularly disturbed by his remarks about pampering the people and underestimating their abilities. She knows that three department heads got higher performance appraisals than she did, and they tend to delegate quite a bit of work to their staff. Nevertheless, she is not sure how accurate her boss' statements are.

1. Does Gloria's philosophy of management place her in the classical, human relations, or human resources model? Explain.
2. Do you agree or disagree with Gloria's boss? Give your reasoning.
3. What would you recommend that Gloria do? Why?

SELF-FEEDBACK EXERCISE

Identify Your Philosophy of Management

Carefully read each of the following statements and indicate your attitude toward each by using this scale:

5	Strongly agree
4	Agree
3	Indifferent
2	Disagree
1	Strongly disagree

Put the number corresponding to your answer on the line at the right.

1. Few employees can handle work that requires self-control. _____
2. Most employees want to feel important. _____
3. Managers should continually allow subordinates to exercise more self-direction and self-control. _____
4. Work is not inherently distasteful. _____
5. Money is the most important motivator of all. _____
6. Employees have a great desire to belong. _____
7. If the pay is good, employees will tolerate just about any job. _____
8. Most people are capable of more self-direction than their jobs demand. _____
9. People want to be recognized as individuals. _____
10. The manager must create an environment in which all employees can contribute to the limits of their ability. _____

11. Most employees can exercise more self-control than their jobs demand. _____
12. The manager's basic job is to closely supervise subordinates. _____
13. Workers want to be kept informed about what is going on in the organization. _____
14. The manager's basic task is to make use of his or her untapped human resources. _____
15. Managers must establish detailed work procedures and routines. _____
16. Managers should listen to the objections of employees to their plans. _____
17. Most employees are lazy. _____
18. Subordinates should be allowed to exercise some self-direction and self-control. _____
19. Expanding subordinate influence will lead to direct improvements in operating efficiency. _____
20. On routine matters, managers should allow subordinates to exercise some self-direction and self-control. _____
21. The use of threats is important in keeping workers productive. _____
22. Managers should encourage full employee participation in important matters. _____
23. Most people dislike work. _____

24. People work best under benevolent autocratic leadership. _____

25. Few employees can handle work that requires self-direction. _____

26. The manager's basic responsibility is to make each employee feel important. _____

27. Most employees are more creative than their jobs require. _____

28. Social needs are more important than money in motivating employees. _____

29. People want to contribute to meaningful goals that they have helped establish. _____

30. It is extremely important for managers to closely control subordinate performance. _____

Go back and make sure that you have indicated your attitude toward each statement. Then transfer your answers to the scoring key below and total each column.

I	II	III
1. _____	2. _____	3. _____
5. _____	6. _____	4. _____
7. _____	9. _____	8. _____

12. _____	13. _____	10. _____
15. _____	16. _____	11. _____
17. _____	18. _____	14. _____
21. _____	20. _____	19. _____
23. _____	24. _____	22. _____
25. _____	26. _____	27. _____
30. _____	28. _____	29. _____
Total _____	_____	_____

Column I indicates your preference for or belief in classical management concepts and philosophies. Column II reflects your preference for or belief in human relations concepts and philosophies. Column III indicates your preference for or belief in human resources concepts and beliefs.

On the chart opposite construct a bar graph for each of your scores. This figure will help you see your initial philosophy of organizational behavior. By the time you have finished reading this book, we hope your human resources score will be much higher than the other two. For the moment, however, use these scores as feedback on where you are now.

NOTES

1. Frederick W. Taylor, *Principles of Scientific Management* (New York: Harper Brothers, 1911), p. 39.

2. For an excellent discussion of administrative theory principles see L. Urwick, *The Elements of Administration* (New York: Harper Brothers, 1943).

3. Robert M. Blau, *Bureaucracy in Modern Society* (New York: Random House, 1956), pp. 28–33.

4. *Ibid.*, p. 58.

5. For more on bureaucracies during this period see Peter Miller and Ted O'Leary, "Hierarchies and American Ideals," *Academy of Management Review*, April 1989, pp. 250–265.

6. F. J. Roethlisberger and William J. Dickson, *Management and the Worker* (Cambridge, MA: Harvard Univ. Press, 1939), p. 522.

7. Alex Carey, "The Hawthorne Studies: A Radical Criticism," *American Sociological Review*, June 1967, pp. 403–416.

8. For more on the Hawthorne studies see Henry A. Landsberger, *Hawthorne Revisited* (Cornell: Cornell Univ. Press, 1958); "Hawthorne Revisited: The Legend and the Legacy," *Organizational Dynamics*, Winter 1975, pp. 66–80; Richard Franke and James Kaul, "The Hawthorne Experiments: First Statistical Interpretations," *American Sociological Review*, October 1978, pp. 623–643; Berkeley Rice, "The Hawthorne Defect: Persistence of a Flawed Theory," *Psychology Today*, February 1982, pp. 70–74; and Richard H. Franke, "The Hawthorne Experiments: Empirical Findings and Implications for Management," paper presented at the National Academy of Management Meetings, New Orleans, August 1987.

9. E. Wight Bakke, *The Fusion Process* (New Haven: Labor and Management Center, Yale Univ., 1953).

10. L. James Harvey, "Nine Major Trends in HRM," *Personnel Administrator*, November 1986, pp. 102–109.

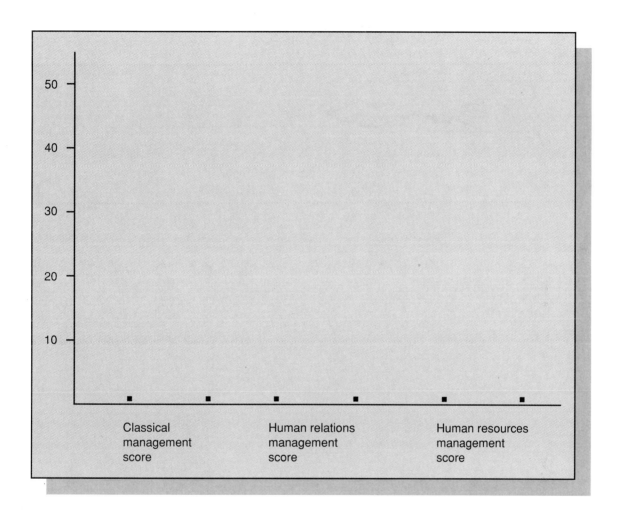

Classical management score	Human relations management score	Human resources management score

CHAPTER 2
Behavioral Science and Organizational Behavior

GOALS OF THE CHAPTER

Organizational behavior involves the scientific study of individuals and groups in an organizational setting. The people who are most active in this scientific inquiry are known as behavioral scientists. The primary goal of this chapter is to examine the basic disciplines that make up the behavioral sciences and to study the ways in which behavioral scientists conduct their organizational behavior inquiries. The secondary goal of the chapter is to present a conceptual model for the book, illustrating how we are going to go about studying organizational behavior. When you are finished reading this chapter you should be able to:

1. identify and describe the three basic disciplines that constitute modern behavioral science;
2. describe the basic components of a research design;
3. explain some of the basic research design fundamentals, including hypothesis formulation and the formation of experimental and control groups;
4. list some of the hallmarks of a scientific approach;
5. compare and contrast such common research designs as the field study, the laboratory experiment, and the field experiment;
6. relate the advantages and limitations of such data collection methods as observation, secondary sources, interviews, and questionnaires;
7. discuss the ethical responsibilities of modern behavioral scientists to those who participate in their research studies.

OPENING CASE: FITTING IN FROM DAY ONE

For over a year Paul Trimble, chief executive officer for a large conglomerate, has been negotiating a joint venture with a Korean manufacturing firm. The latter would like Paul's company to give them a license to manufacture and sell certain high tech products in the Far East market. Last week the two parties finalized the agreement. One of the provisions of the contract calls for Paul's firm to directly supervise some of the manufacturing operations.

Paul knows that many American firms have had problems in supervising Far East operations because they do not understand the norms, values, and behaviors of the local people. He intends to prevent this from happening to his firm. There are three outstanding behavioral scientists on his staff—a psychologist, a sociologist, and a cultural anthropologist—and he is going to send one of them to Korea to study Korean management practices. His overseas partners have promised him full cooperation. Then, drawing on this information, Paul intends to have a training program developed that will prepare the managers for their overseas assignment.

"I want our people to fit in from day one," Paul told his senior vice-president. "We stand to make a lot of money on this deal if everything works out right. And I'm determined that it will."

1. Which behavioral scientist should Paul send? Why?
2. What type of research design should the behavioral scientist use? Explain.
3. What form(s) of data collection should the individual use? Why?

Write down your answers to these questions and put them aside. We will return to them later.

THE BEHAVIORAL SCIENCES

The behavioral sciences consist of three basic disciplines: psychology, sociology, and anthropology. Each has made important contributions to the field of organizational behavior. In fact, much of what we know about behavior is a result of interdisciplinary findings from these three areas.

Psychology

Psychology is the study of individual behavior.

Psychology is the study of human behavior, and over the last one hundred years this field has undergone a great transition. Early psychologists were basically interested in mental processes such as memory and perception of sensation. Modern psychologists, however, have broader concerns.[1] One of their current interests is the biological-physiological aspects of behavior, such as the effect of heredity and environment on intelligence. Which is the major determinant? Additionally, what is the brain's role in behavior? Of even greater interest to most psychologists are the processes of learning, perception, motivation, and self-efficacy,[2] and an awareness of these processes is essential to understand organizational behavior. Another major area of interest is personality.

In recent years the number of professional psychologists has been growing. Today they hold important positions in many different fields. Some are academicians with specialties in experimental, social, or clinical psychology. Others can be found in business, industrial, and governmental organizations. For example, there are educational psychologists and counselors who work with schoolchildren. Some industrial psychologists function chiefly in industry, where they are involved in screening and training employees.

Sociology

Sociology is the study of social behavior.

Sociology is the study of social behavior within societies, institutions, and groups. Modern sociologists are particularly concerned with investigating interdependent social behavior. In a societal context, for example, they are interested in: (a) the internal problems of the society; (b) the components common to most societies; and (c) the way societies allocate responsibility for various tasks. On an institutional level, they are concerned with the various organizations that make up a society, including political, legal, business, industrial, governmental, and religious institutions.

We will be most concerned with the work of sociologists who study group behavior, because the group is the unit of analysis most closely associated with modern society. Group analysis encompasses two areas of concern: primary groups and small-group research. **Primary groups** are characterized by "intimate, face-to-face association and cooperation."[3] The most common examples of primary groups are the family and the peer group. Both have a major impact on behavior and constitute one of the basic building blocks of American society.

The objective of small-group research (which is not limited to primary groups) is to study the forms of behavior that evolve in the course of social interaction. Sociologists conducting small-group research are more interested in "*how* the small group interacts than in *what* it interacts about."[4]

Anthropology

Anthropology is often defined as the science of man. In the study of organizational behavior, the most important subfield is **cultural anthropology,** which is concerned with the impact of culture on behavior. **Culture** consists of ideas, values, and behavioral patterns that have been learned as a result of living in a particular society. Culture commonly dictates both *what* people learn and *how* they behave.

For purposes of organizational behavior, many anthropologists are interested in comparing behavior between cultures. For example, the way businesses in the United States manage their personnel is quite different from the way firms in other countries do so. Many of these differences can be accounted for by the managerial attitudes that prevail in the specific culture. For example, the Japanese are more collective in their approach and employ slower decision-making processes, and the role of the company in personal affairs is much greater in Japan than in the United States.[5] Cultural values foster a style of management so markedly different from American managerial practice that a U.S. firm can encounter difficulty when it tries to put its management methods into effect in another country. Consider some of the following examples.

> An American firm in Japan introduced individual incentive payment plans. The workers asked management to do away with them because to single out one person as more productive than others is personally humiliating. The company complied.
>
> In another American firm the company promised to reward individuals who came up with productivity-related ideas. There were no suggestions. The company then changed the approach to a group suggestion system. Productivity improvement ideas rained down on the firm.[6]

In other areas of the world, organizational behavior is influenced less by a desire to make correct decisions and more by the belief that everything will work itself out. This is particularly true in Arab countries.

> Arab behavior is greatly influenced by the belief that destiny is more dependent on the will of a Supreme Being than on individual behavior. A higher power dictates the outcome of important events, so individual action is of little consequence. This thinking affects not only individuals' aspirations but also their motivation. Additionally, the status of the individual Arab is determined primarily by one's family position and social contacts, not necessarily by one's own accomplishments. This helps explain why many Middle Easterners take great satisfaction in appearing to be helpless. In fact, helplessness can be used as a source of power for in this area of the world the strong are resented and the weak are compensated.[7] Examples such as these illustrate how cultural attitudes affect the way people in different societies behave.[8]

Cultural anthropologists are interested in the impact of culture on behavior.

Culture can affect managerial behavior.

STOP Review your answer to Question 1 and make any changes you would like before continuing.

1. Which behavioral scientist should Paul send? Why?

Paul should send the anthropologist. This assignment requires someone to study the impact of culture on behavior. The individual will need to find out what people learn and how they behave. This assignment is more in line with the anthropologist's training than with that of the other two behavioral scientists.

BEHAVIORAL SCIENCE RESEARCH

Most modern behavioral scientists—psychologists, sociologists, and anthropologists—apply an empirical approach to the study of organizational behavior. As a result, they take pains not to confuse common sense and scientific findings, for when dealing with organizational behavior, the two can easily overlap. Consider some maxims that we often hear: Spare the rod, and spoil the child; never trust a used-car dealer. In some cases these sayings may be accurate, but not always. Modern behavioral scientists put aside their personal beliefs, values, attitudes, and emotions and concentrate on gathering and analyzing information in an *objective, systematic* way.

> A research design is a plan, a structure, and a strategy of investigation.

The first step in conducting any scientific inquiry is formulating the research design. A **research design** comprises the plan, structure, and strategy of investigation to be used in obtaining answers to the researcher's questions.[9] The **research design plan** "is the overall scheme or program of the research."[10] It includes everything the investigator is going to do, from writing the hypothesis to collecting and analyzing the data to submitting the final report.

The **research design structure** is more specific than the plan. In it the researcher specifies the variables that are to be measured and the relationships that exist between these variables. For example, an individual might want to measure the influence of a management training program on leadership effectiveness. Hypothesizing that effective leaders supervise higher-producing units than less effective leaders, the behavioral scientist will form two groups—an experimental group and a control group—that are equal in productivity. The experimental group will be given management training; the control group will not. After the training is complete, production from the two units will be measured in order to determine the effect of the program. The structure is diagrammed in Table 2–1.

The **research design strategy** is also more specific than the plan. In the strategy the investigator decides on specific methods for gathering and analyzing data. (Some of these methods will be examined later.)

Finally, the behavioral scientist decides how the research objectives will be met and how problems encountered along the way will be resolved. With regard to this point, for example, if a questionnaire is mailed to a random sample of two hundred people and one hundred responses are needed, the investigator will have decided

TABLE 2–1
Research Design Structure

	Experimental Group	Control Group
Premeasurement of unit output	X	X
Training program	X	O
Postmeasurement of unit output	X	X

Note: X = yes; O = no.

beforehand what to do if the first mailing elicits only eighty-seven usable responses. There may be a second mailing, and if this proves insufficient, then the questionnaire may be sent out to another twenty-five people selected at random. All of this, however, is worked out in the research design strategy.

Some Design Fundamentals

A research design has two basic objectives. First, it must provide answers to specific questions. Second, it has to help the researcher control any nonrelevant factors that can affect the results. In pursuing these two objectives, the behavioral scientist will rely on some design fundamentals, such as hypothesis formulation, constructing experimental and control groups, and assigning people to these groups.

  One of the most common design fundamentals is the formulation of a hypothesis. A *hypothesis* is a statement about the relationship between two or more variables. This relationship is usually stated in terms of an independent, or causal, variable(s) and a dependent, or effect, variable(s). For example, the introducing of a sales incentive plan (independent variable) will bring about a 30 percent increase in sales (dependent variable); memorizing key terms in the text (independent variable) will lead to higher grades on multiple-choice exams (dependent variable); approving a 10 percent salary increase for all hospital personnel (independent variable) will bring about reduced job turnover (dependent variable).

A hypothesis is a statement about the relationship between two or more variables.

  A second design fundamental involves the use of *randomly* chosen members of the experimental and control groups. The experimental group is the one that receives some treatment, whereas the control group is untreated. By comparing the two groups both before and after the treatment, the behavioral scientist can determine the effect of the treatment.

  It is essential when forming experimental and control groups to ensure that the two are as similar as possible in makeup. Only then will the behavioral scientists be able to measure the effects of the treatment and establish a basis for inferring that any difference in results between the two groups is attributable to the treatment. For example, if a behavioral scientist believes that incoming freshman students who take a two-day course entitled "How to Study" will have higher grades during their first two semesters than those who do not, an experimental and control group can be formed and the hypothesis tested. However, the researcher must be sure that the groups are equivalent in composition. This means that all "A" students cannot be assigned to one group and all "C" students to the other. There should be some of each type in both groups, and this mix can be secured by the use of random assignment.

With random assignment, everyone has an equal opportunity to be in either the experimental or the control group.

When random assignment is used, everyone has an *equal* chance of being in either the experimental or the control group. One way of making a random assignment is to list each person's name on a piece of paper, put all the names into a basket, shake up the basket to mix the papers, and then draw them out one at a time. The first person is assigned to the experimental group, the second to the control group, etc., until all names are drawn and assigned.

Hallmarks of a Scientific Approach

There are six characteristics of a scientific approach.

There are many ways in which a researcher can collect and analyze data, but all research efforts should manifest the six characteristics of a scientific approach (often referred to as the *hallmarks of an ideal science*[11]):

1. *The procedures are public.* A complete description of the study is provided so that other researchers in the field are able to follow each step of the investigation.
2. *The definitions are precise.* The procedures that were used, the variables that were measured, and the methods that were employed for measuring must all be clearly stated.
3. *The data collecting is objective.* There must not be any bias in either the collection or interpretation of the data.
4. *The findings are replicable.* If other researchers were to conduct the same study, they would arrive at the same basic findings.
5. *The approach is systematic and cumulative.* The study should contribute to a united body of knowledge by helping to build a theory.
6. *The purposes are explanation, understanding, and prediction.* The basic objective of the scientific approach is to determine how and why things happen. If these questions can be answered, then predictions can be made about what will happen in particular situations. For example, having determined how and why money motivates individuals, a behavioral scientist would then be able to predict which individuals would be most motivated by financial incentives and which would be least motivated.

Common Research Designs

A number of research designs are commonly used to study organizational behavior. The following examines three of the most popular: the field study, the laboratory experiment, and the field experiment.

The basic purpose of a field study is to gather information.

Field Study. The basic purpose of a **field study** is to gather information from the respondents, as opposed to trying to change or influence them in any way (see "Organizational Behavior in Action: How Real Managers Really Work"). There are two types of field studies: *naturalistic observation,* in which the experimenter simply observes what goes on; and the *survey method,* in which researchers may use either interviews or questionnaires to obtain their data. Also, in order to reduce time and cost, a random sample of the total population is usually selected.

Organizational Behavior In Action

HOW REAL MANAGERS REALLY WORK

What do managers do with their time? A recent field study conducted among 457 managers revealed some extremely interesting and new findings. The researchers found that the "real managers" (RMs for short) they studied performed four different types of tasks:

1. networking—politicking, socializing, interacting with outsiders;
2. communications—exchanging information, handling paperwork;
3. human resource management—motivating, training, developing, disciplining;
4. traditional management activities—planning, decision making, controlling.

Even more interesting, an analysis of the data from this field study found that there are three types of RMs: successful, effective, and average. Successful RMs have a very rapid rate of promotion. Effective RMs are well liked by their people and have high work output. Average RMs tend to devote an almost equal amount of time to all four management activities. Here was the percentage breakdown for all three groups:

	Successful RMs	Effective RMs	Average RMs
Networking	48%	11%	19%
Communications	28	44	29
Human Resource Management	11	26	20
Traditional Management Activities	13	19	32

What do these data illustrate? A number of important conclusions have been drawn, including: (a) some managers achieve rapid promotion by politicking rather than by working hard and achieving objectives; (b) communication is more important, on average, than any of the other management activities; and (c) organizational success is greatly influenced by one's ability to interact with others.

Source: Fred Luthans, Richard M. Hodgetts, and Stuart A. Rosenkrantz, *Real Managers* (New York: Ballinger, 1988).

Each of the respondents in the survey is asked the same questions. These questions are usually related to people's behaviors or attitudes. For example, an organization might want to gather data on how people feel about working there. In this case, the following questions might be among those asked: Are the working conditions good? Does your boss treat you well? Is the pay adequate? Overall, how well do you like your job?

If the questionnaire is reliable and valid (topics we will study in Chapter 15), the results can tell the organization a great deal about worker satisfaction. They can also provide insight into potential problems of which the organization should be aware. Such early warnings can prevent minor problems from becoming major ones.

The field study is limited, however, in that some kinds of data cannot be validly obtained. For example, the survey can only collect information of which the respondent is consciously aware. Subconscious motives cannot be determined. Additionally, if the researchers use a questionnaire and mail it to prospective respondents, the number who properly complete and return it can be quite small. (National mailings, for example, often achieve but a 1 to 2 percent return.) If the original sample is small or the response rate is very low, the return may not constitute a representative sample.

Laboratory Experiment. The *laboratory experiment* requires a research design more rigorous than that for a field survey. The basic purpose of such an experiment is to observe the effects that an independent variable(s) has on a dependent variable(s). If the behavioral scientist can control the conditions under which the experiment is conducted, it is possible to draw conclusions regarding the relationships between the independent and dependent variables.

The basic purpose of a lab experiment is to observe the effects of an independent variable on a dependent variable.

One of the most interesting, significant, and controversial laboratory experiments ever conducted on human behavior was done by Stanley Milgram, who sought to determine the conditions under which people would follow or disobey orders (causal variable) to administer electric shocks (result variable) to a person giving an incorrect response.[12] The subject was told that his task was to teach the learner a list of paired associates, to test him on the list, and to administer punishment whenever the learner erred. The punishment was an electric shock delivered from a shock generator that the subject controlled. As the experiment progressed, the learner, according to plan, gave many wrong answers, and the naive subject began administering what he thought were increasingly severe shocks. Actually, the learner was not being shocked at all.

As the shock level increased, some people refused to administer any further voltage. However, the subjects were far more obedient than forty psychiatrists affiliated with leading medical schools expected they would be. Some of the conclusions Milgram drew from his work on obedience and authority are the following:

1. Obedience decreases when the victim is in the same room as the teacher, and decreases further when the teacher must touch the victim directly to administer the shock.
2. Obedience drops sharply when the experimenter is absent.
3. Obedience drops when the subject is in a group of rebellious peers.
4. Obedience increases when the subject is merely an accessory and does not have to pull the shock lever himself.[13]

Laboratory experiments such as this are very useful in studying behavior. There are, however, some drawbacks that should be noted. First, the laboratory experiment participants must be carefully chosen. College students, for example, are often a poor choice if the behavioral scientist wants to study managerial behavior, since few students have had experience in this capacity. Second, it has to be possible to isolate and systematically study the causal variables. Third, the results have to be applicable to the real world. If the situation created in the lab is too artificial, the findings are of no real value.

The basic purpose of a field experiment is to apply the laboratory method to a real-life situation.

Field Experiment. A **field experiment** can be thought of as an "applied" laboratory experiment. It is designed to apply the laboratory method to a real-life situation. An example was provided in Chapter 1 in the case of the Hawthorne studies (although they were far less scientific than the work done by modern behavioral scientists). Today we see many other examples of the field experiment. A typical case is the managerial training example in which the test group is given training and the control group is not. This illustration appeared earlier in our discussion of design structure. The behavioral scientist would measure the effect of the training program by calculating as follows:

$$\text{Effect of training} = (E_A - C_A) - (E_B - C_B)$$

where E_A is the performance of an experimental group after the training program

C_A is the performance of the control group after the training session

E_B is the performance of the experimental group prior to the training session

C_B is the performance of the control group prior to the training session

Note that the field experiment is like the laboratory experiment because it allows for measurement both before and after the independent variable is introduced or changed.

Despite its wide use by behavioral scientists, however, the field experiment does present some problems. First, the subjects usually know they are under investigation, so procedures are necessary to decrease the likelihood of people changing their behavior during the observation period. A second problem centers around how the organization will handle the results. In our illustration, the workers supervised by the managers who attended the training program might perform better than the staff of those who did not. At performance appraisal time, however, how will the managers evaluate their people? If ratings are given strictly on the basis of performance, does this not discriminate against those not chosen for the program? Issues such as these should be resolved well in advance of the appraisal period.

Review your answers to Question 2 and make any changes you would like before continuing.

2. What type of research design should the behavioral scientist use? Explain.

The behavioral scientist should use a field study. Remember, the individual's objective is to gather information from the respondents as opposed to trying to change or influence them in any way. In doing so the scientist would undoubtedly rely on both naturalistic observation and the survey method.

Choosing a Research Design

Which research design is best? This depends on what the behavioral scientist wants to measure or study. Each of the designs we have discussed has strong and weak points.

By selecting one, the researcher often has to give up some of the advantages associated with the others. The five factors most often considered when choosing a research design are realism, precision, control, scope, and cost.

Realism refers to how close the research design is to the real world. A field experiment offers a great deal of realism. However, there may be things going on in the environment that the researcher either is unaware of or cannot control. A laboratory experiment, on the other hand, enables the investigator to control most variables, but the setting is not very realistic. Often there has to be a trade-off between realism and control of the variables.[14]

Precision refers to how accurately the variables under consideration can be measured. For example, the researcher might want to determine the effect of a change in leadership on the performance of subordinates. In a laboratory experiment the participants could be videotaped to permit close analysis of the way everyone responds when the new leader takes over. Here again the laboratory setting often provides a better opportunity to measure precisely what happens. However, does the increased precision offset the loss in realism?

Control refers to how well the researchers can manage the experimental situation so that they can establish cause-and-effect relationships, such as investigating the correlation between salary raises and work output. Control also allows the researchers to reproduce a situation over and over again, so that they do not have to rely on a single observation in drawing their conclusions. Unfortunately, control is often obtained only at the expense of realism. In a dynamic business setting, it is very difficult to totally control all of the variables. Remember the Hawthorne experiments and the difficulty the researchers had in determining what was happening and why it was happening.

Scope refers to the range of research. A field study is usually much broader in scope than a laboratory experiment. The former is often used to collect information on an issue or area that is too complex for a lab experiment. On the other hand, when the researcher wants to study a cause-and-effect relationship in depth, the narrow scope provided by the lab experiment may be ideal.

Cost refers to the expenditure of time and money necessary to design the study and gather and analyze the data. For example, a laboratory experiment often has relatively low setup costs. There are few resource needs, and the expense associated with hiring subjects is often minimal. On the other hand, field studies and field experiments often require large research organizations, a great many subjects, and computation facilities for analyzing the data.

These five aspects of major designs all affect the final choice of the behavioral scientist. There must be a trade-off between them.

Data Collection

As we noted earlier, there are many ways of collecting data in a behavioral study. Some of the most common are observation, secondary sources, questionnaires, and interviews.

Observation. One of the easiest ways to collect data is to observe people's behavior. If a production manager wants to know whether some of his workers are leaving early and being clocked out by fellow workers, he can wait near the time clock at the end of the shift and observe who punches two cards.

The major problem with the observation method is that the observer can only infer the causes of behavior. For example, Bob may be clocking Andy out so that the latter can leave early, avoid the traffic tie-up that occurs around the plant at the end of every shift, and get to the hospital in time to visit his sick wife. The manager, however, may interpret the situation as one in which Bob and Andy are breaking the rules because they want to see how much they can get away with.

Secondary sources are a popular data collection method.

Secondary Sources.   Another way to gather data about people is to consult secondary sources such as company records. If productivity in a manufacturing firm is down 7 percent from its level at this time last year, it is appropriate to ascertain which departments or units are now less efficient. The problem area may be pinpointed and then followed up with closer study.

Other secondary sources include industry reports and academic journals. For example, if an organization wants to increase work output, what type of motivation should it offer? One way to decide is to determine what other organizations are doing and what results they are having. Such information can often be found in industry or academic journals. In fact, a great deal of data can be collected from secondary sources.

On the positive side, such data are often inexpensive and easily accessible to the investigating organization. On the negative side, careful consideration must be given to interpreting these data. For example, productivity may be down because the management and union are disputing a new contract, or because some departments are reacting against new work procedures that they believe discriminate against them. These causes cannot be discovered by simply consulting internal secondary sources. Meanwhile, in the case of external secondary data, if a competitive organization gave its workers a 15 percent salary increase and achieved a 25 percent rise in productivity, it does not mean that the same thing will happen if the investigating organization offers the same salary increase. The management has to be careful about the conclusions it draws from secondary sources.

Questionnaires.   Sometimes organizations want to gather a great deal of information as quickly and easily as possible. In such cases the questionnaire can be very helpful. There are two general types of questionnaires, objective and descriptive.

Objective questionnaires are close-ended.

In the *objective questionnaire* the person is given a question and a choice of answers. The individual replies by noting the appropriate response. One of the major advantages of the objective questionnaire is the ease with which responses can be collected and fed into a computer for statistical analysis. One of the major disadvantages is that respondents are restricted in their replies—they cannot explain their answers.

Descriptive questionnaires are open-ended.

The *descriptive questionnaire* presents the respondent with a series of questions and lets the person respond in his or her own words. Typical questions related to various aspects of organizational climate would be the following: Are the fringe benefits good? Are you being paid an equitable salary? Does your job make you feel important? How can the organization communicate more effectively with your department? This approach has more leeway than the objective questionnaire. On the positive side, it can provide information not obtainable with objective questions; on the negative side, it takes more time for respondents to fill out the questionnaire and for the researcher to read and interpret the answers.

Interviews are commonly used in data collection.

Interviews.   One of the most commonly used methods of data collection is the interview. In this face-to-face situation, the interviewer asks questions and the respondent answers them. Interviews have one of three general purposes. First, they can be used as exploratory devices to help understand the variables in question. For example, if a manager were in the process of hiring engineers for an overseas assignment, he or she might ask the first four or five candidates what they are looking for in their work. Based on their answers, the manager would be able to determine how best to create job interest among the applicants.

Second, interviews can be used as major research instruments. For example, a manager may want to know why some people are terminating their employment with the firm while others are not. One way to understand the causes of termination would be to interview people from both groups and compare their responses. Perhaps it is the work they are assigned, their financial remuneration, or the social setting in which the work is done. In any event, it may be possible to identify (or at least get an idea about) their reasons for leaving.

Third, interviews can supplement other methods of data collection. For example, an objective questionnaire restricts respondent replies; an interview would allow respondents to explain why they answered as they did.

STOP

Review your answer to Question 3 and make any changes you would like before continuing.

3. What form(s) of data collection should the individual use? Why?

_____

There are a number of forms of data collection that would be useful to the individual. Observation and interviews would be the two primary forms. Questionnaires would be a third important form. Secondary sources would also be useful because they would provide the researcher with additional data.

Timing of Data Collection

Data can be collected at different times. The three most frequently used methods are the single-time, after-only, and before-and-after measures.

Single-time data collections do not use test or control groups.

Single-time data collections are used to gather information about the attitudes, performance, or other characteristics of the subjects at only one time. There is no test group or control group. The researcher is interested only in current practices or events. An excellent example is student evaluations of teachers, which are used only once, typically at the end of the semester or quarter. Their purpose usually is to obtain feedback from the students regarding the professor, the book, and the course in general. In business firms it is common to use single-time data collections to determine the relevance of certain practices or trends. In some cases the information is used to investigate relationships between two or more groups of data. For example, if the company gave out an attitude survey, it could compare the results of the survey with current job performance to determine the relationship between satisfaction and performance.

After-only data collection is used with test and control groups. After the former has been given a particular treatment, such as managerial training, the two groups are tested to see if there is any difference in their performance. The problem with this type of data collection is that without a profile of both groups before the training was given, it is difficult to determine the effect of the training. Nevertheless, this method is popular and in some cases it is a good choice. For example, suppose that Group A has just returned from a one-week management training program but that Group B was not sent because of budgetary constraints. Did the training do any good? The best way to answer this question is by tracking the performance of Group A for the next couple of months. If it is higher than that of Group B, we can infer that the training was the cause. Keep in mind, however, that we do not have initial data regarding the performance of both groups, so it is possible that Group A was always more productive than Group B. This possibility is a drawback of the after-only data collection method.

Before-and-after data collection begins by gathering baseline data on both the test and the control group. Then, after the test group is given the treatment, measurements are again taken to determine the effect of the treatment. This research design is the closest that organizational behavior has come to demonstrating cause and effect. Unfortunately, sometimes data about the key issues cannot be collected by this method. For example, a company may be thinking of totally revamping its production process and may want to know if the idea will be well received by the personnel. The firm does not want to invest millions of dollars and then find out it made a mistake. In this case, the best method would be single-time data collection. Other times there are no baseline data on the targeted area. In this case an after-only approach is the best management can do.

Ethics in Research

An aspect of behavioral science that we have not yet examined is the ethical responsibility of the researcher to the people who participate in the research study.

Sometimes the information being solicited is of a confidential nature. For example, few subordinates would be happy to have their boss learn how they answered these questions: What do you see as your superior's biggest weakness? If you were in charge of this department, what changes would you make? Overall, how would you rate your boss in contrast to other bosses you have had? The researcher has a moral obligation to maintain the confidentiality of such data, thereby ensuring the anonymity of the respondents.

In other cases the research involves naive subjects who are unaware of, or have been deliberately misinformed about, the researcher's real objectives. In Milgram's study, for example, the subjects did not know the true purpose of the experiment. They thought they were helping the behavioral scientist gain insights into the effect of punishment on learning, whereas in fact it was *their* behavior that was being studied. Yet Milgram believed it was necessary to mislead them, at least initially, if he was to achieve his goal of studying the effect of authority on obedience.

When such studies are complete, however, the subject should be told what was really being done. Experimenters have to be very careful about affecting the lives of their subjects. Primary concern must be for the welfare of the participants, not the

---

Margin notes:

After-only methods can be used to evaluate the effect of training.

Before-and-after measures help establish causal relationships.

The behavioral scientist has an ethical responsibility toward those who participate in the research.

results of the study. In Milgram's case, all of his subjects were informed of the actual nature of the experiment. Those who obeyed all the orders were told that their behavior was perfectly normal and that many other subjects had done the same. Those who disobeyed by refusing to continue shocking the learner were given support for their actions. Then when the study was complete, the participants learned what had actually been going on. Follow-up research among the subjects revealed that only 1 percent were sorry that they had participated in the study, suggesting that Milgram had handled the subjects quite well.

In some major academic institutions subjects have to sign a consent agreement. In addition, they are promised an explanation of the procedures to be followed and a description of the study and the outcomes to be expected. Researchers also offer to answer any inquiries about the procedures, and they accord subjects the right to discontinue participation at any time. Developments such as these are important for maintaining the optimal level of ethics in research.[15]

SUMMARY

1. The three primary behavioral sciences are psychology, sociology, and anthropology. Psychology is the study of human behavior. Sociology is the study of social behavior, particularly within and among groups. Anthropology is the science of man, and its most important subfield, regarding the study of organizational behavior, is cultural anthropology, which is concerned with the impact of culture on behavior.

2. Modern behavioral scientists are empirical in their approach to their respective fields. In particular, they are careful not to confuse common sense and scientific findings. In conducting their scientific inquiries, they begin by formulating a research design. This design consists of a plan, a structure, and a strategy of investigation. The plan is the overall scheme or program of the research. The structure contains the variables to be measured and the relationships that exist between or among those variables. The strategy includes the methods to be used in gathering and analyzing the data, as well as a determination of how the research objectives will be attained and how any problems encountered along the way will be resolved. Some of the fundamentals used in a research design are hypothesis formulation and the formation of experimental and control groups.

3. There are a number of research designs commonly used in the study of organizational behavior. One is the field study, which is employed to simply gather information from the respondents. A second is the laboratory experiment, which is designed to observe the effects of an independent variable on a dependent variable. A third is the field experiment, which is designed to apply the laboratory method to a real-life situation.

4. There are many ways of collecting data in a behavioral study. Some of the most popular include observation, secondary sources, interviews, and questionnaires. Each has advantages and limitations.

5. The behavioral scientist has an ethical responsibility toward those who participate in a research study. Since the information gathered by researchers is often confidential, the anonymity of the respondents must be ensured. Moreover, in cases in which subjects are deliberately misled, as in the Milgram study, researchers have an obligation to tell the participants what was actually taking place.

KEY TERMS

psychology	culture	hypothesis
sociology	research design	field study
primary groups	research design plan	laboratory experiment
anthropology	research design structure	field experiment
cultural anthropology	research design strategy	

REVIEW AND STUDY QUESTIONS

1. Explain the field of psychology in your own words.
2. What kinds of problems or issues does the modern sociologist study? Explain.
3. The most important subfield of anthropology is cultural anthropology. What problems or issues do cultural anthropologists study? Explain.
4. A research design contains a plan, a structure, and a strategy. What is involved in each?
5. What are some of the design fundamentals used in behavioral science research? Describe them.
6. All research should embody, to some degree, the six characteristics of an ideal science. What are these six characteristics?
7. How does a field study differ from a field experiment? How does a field experiment differ from a laboratory experiment?
8. In what way is a laboratory experiment more rigorous than a field study? Be sure to include a full description of a field study in your answer.
9. If you were interested in measuring the effect of a speed-reading course on college freshmen, which of the three research designs described in this chapter would you use? Why?
10. When would observation be a useful method of data collection? When would secondary sources be most beneficial?
11. What are the benefits and drawbacks of the objective questionnaire? The descriptive questionnaire? Explain.
12. In which of the three research designs described in this chapter would you expect interviews to be most helpful? Explain. What about questionnaires? Secondary sources? Observation?
13. What kinds of ethical responsibility do modern behavioral scientists have to those participating in their research studies?

CASES

What, No Lecture?

At State University the basic economics course is taught on a lecture basis. The professor who coordinates the course gives a 9 A.M. lecture to the first group and a 1 P.M. lecture to the second group. The average size per group is 225 students.

Last year one of the research professors at the university suggested to the University Senate that the effectiveness of large lecture sessions should be measured. This professor envisioned offering these courses in a number of versions, including conventional lectures, videotaped lectures, and home study. The economics department volunteered its basic course for the pilot study.

After several meetings, the research professor and the economics department faculty agreed that the basic course would first be videotaped. This part of the project was accomplished by the research professor, the economics professor, and the university's multimedia division in five weeks of intensive work.

The research design called for one-third of the economics students to be randomly assigned to this videotape section. These students would read the text, attend showings of the videotaped lectures, and would address any questions to the teaching assistant assigned to the class, who would meet with them one day a week for a lab session.

One-third of the total group was to be randomly assigned to the "text-only" section. These people would not attend any lectures. They would read the assigned material, and all would meet one day a week with their teaching assistant, who would answer any questions they had. However, the assistant would not lecture on the text material and would discourage the students from trying to find out what was going on in the other two sections. (Some of the people in this text-only section were not content with their situation, however, and occasionally tried to sneak into the lecture section. Such actions were common just prior to the midterm and final exams. Teaching assistants had to stand by the door checking student ID cards to ensure that only those scheduled for the lecture section entered the room. On one occasion several students from the other two sections had to be forcibly denied entrance.)

The last group attended a lecture by the professor and a lab session with their teaching assistant. This group was to be the control group, taking the course in the traditional manner.

At the end of the semester in which the pilot study was conducted, the results were analyzed and conclusions were drawn. To the surprise of many, those taking the course on a text-only basis had the highest average scores on the multiple-choice exams. The second highest grades were achieved by the lecture group, whereas the scores of those who attended the videotaped sessions ranked a close third. Overall, however, there was no statistically significant difference among the three groups. As a result, the economics department decided to go back to teaching the course the traditional way.

1. What type of research design was used in this study? Explain.

2. Was it all right to assign the students to the groups on a random basis, or should they have been allowed to choose their own sections? Give your reasoning.

3. Based on the results, was the economics department justified in going back to the traditional way of presenting the course?

Looking for the Cause

The Bunting Corporation is a large manufacturing company located in the northeastern part of the United States. A year ago Bunting was acquired by a large conglomerate, which is in the financial field and knows very little about manufacturing. Nevertheless, in accord with its philosophy of management, the conglomerate replaced some of the top manufacturing personnel with its own employees. These people have a strong financial background and know quite a bit about cost cutting. Their objective is to keep expenditures in line and to maintain the highest levels of efficiency.

Unfortunately, things do not seem to be working out very well. Over the last eight months the ratio of the firm's production costs to its sales has risen from 72 percent to just under 80 percent. The conglomerate would like to know why.

The old management at Bunting believes the cost-cutting procedures of the people brought in by the conglomerate have backfired, resulting in poor attitudes, a decline in employee satisfaction, and a general feeling of apathy among the workers. The Bunting people would like to see the conglomerate move its personnel out of their key administrative jobs and let the manufacturing people run things the way they did before Bunting was taken over.

On the other hand, the financial personnel who were put in by the conglomerate argue that they arrived on the scene in the nick of time. They claim that everything they have done has been to improve efficiency and cut costs and that without their efforts the manufacturing firm would now be close to bankruptcy. As one of them put it, "How can you say that we are the cause of increased inefficiency? If anything, we have improved things around here. We have streamlined the purchasing function, improved payroll procedures, and negotiated a more advantageous long-term loan for the firm. I can only wonder what the state of affairs would have been by now had we not arrived when we did."

The president of Bunting thinks that the conglomerate's people are overstating their contributions to efficiency. In fact, he believes that they are the cause of many current problems. In particular, the workers are concerned that the conglomerate is using these financial people to identify areas where the work force can be cut. These fears are resulting in increased inefficiency. The big question for the president is, can he prove that the new managers are causing the effectiveness problems? The president realized that the only way to identify the true cause(s) of the rising production costs is to bring in some outside experts to study the situation. In particular, he wants to hire a behavioral scientist to investigate job satisfaction and determine the relation of employee behavior and attitudes to rising costs. If this can be done, and the conglomerate's financial personnel are found to be causing the problem, the president is convinced that he can get the conglomerate to remove its people and allow the manufacturing firm to operate the way it did before acquisition. If the cause(s) of the problem proves to be the manufacturing personnel, of course, then it is likely that some of the current manufacturing personnel will have to be let go and the financial people will remain. The president does not think this is likely to happen. However, as he said to his assistant yesterday, "I'm willing to let the chips fall where they may. My primary objective is to find out the cause of our problem. Once that's done, we'll deal with whatever situation we have to face."

1. What type of research design would you suggest that the behavioral scientist use? Explain.

2. What kind of data collection method(s) would the researcher employ? Why? Be complete in your answer.

3. If the researcher does uncover apathy and declining job satisfaction, how can these attitudes be directly related to the changes introduced by the conglomerate? How can the researcher establish a cause-and-effect relationship between the cost-cutting procedures and the rising production costs? Explain.

SELF-FEEDBACK EXERCISE

What Do You Know About Human Behavior?

In this chapter we discussed the importance of collecting and analyzing behavioral data. Modern behavioral scientists do not use intuition; they get the facts so their findings are empirically based. Yet much of what we "know" about the world is not based on empirical data. We have opinions, biases, hunches, and misinformation that we use both in making statements about others and in deciding what we do. The following twenty-five choices are designed to provide you with some feedback regarding what you "know" about human behavior. Read each statement and mark T (true) or F (false) next to it. Answers are provided at the end of the quiz.

True/False

_____ 1. People who graduate in the upper third of their college class tend to make more money during their careers than do average students.

_____ 2. Genius is very closely related to insanity.

_____ 3. Exceptionally intelligent people tend to be physically weak and frail.

_____ 4. Most great athletes are of below-average intelligence.

_____ 5. Silent people are often deep thinkers.

_____ 6. On average, men are better auto drivers than women.

_____ 7. As far as friendships are concerned, opposites tend to attract.

_____ 8. On average, women are slightly more intelligent than men.

_____ 9. After you learn something, you forget more of it in the next few hours than in the next several days.

_____ 10. In small doses, alcohol facilitates learning.

_____ 11. Left-handed people are better athletes than right-handed people.

_____ 12. Forty-year-old people are more intelligent than twenty-year-olds.

_____ 13. In most U.S. presidential elections, the winner was taller than the loser.

_____ 14. A person's IQ score can be affected by the particular test that is being used.

_____ 15. Short women are more likely to marry tall men than they are to marry average or short men.

_____ 16. People who do poorly in academic work are superior in mechanical ability.

_____ 17. High-achieving people are high risk takers.

_____ 18. Blind people have excellent hearing.

_____ 19. Highly cohesive groups are also highly productive ones.

_____ 20. Experiences as an infant tend to determine behavior in later life.

_____ 21. Famous people are born of poor but hard-working parents.

_____ 22. Politicians have a strong desire to persuade and influence others.

_____ 23. A daily exercise program can help relieve work tension and reduce the chance of heart attacks.

_____ 24. University professors have higher self-esteem than members of virtually any other occupational group.

_____ 25. Most university professors are not very intelligent but they are highly educated.

1. T	6. F	11. F	16. F	21. F
2. F	7. F	12. F	17. F	22. T
3. F	8. F	13. T	18. F	23. T
4. F	9. T	14. T	19. F	24. T
5. F	10. F	15. F	20. T	25. F

Check your answers with those given. How well did you do? Most people get between fifteen and twenty right. Did you beat the average? In any event, the point is that some of what you know about human behavior is erroneous. No matter how you got that information, it is incorrect. So as we move on to Chapter 3 and begin our formal study of organizational behavior, remember that this subject encompasses more than "common knowledge." We study behavior in organizations because the information we need about that behavior is not intuitively available. Organizational behavior may be a soft science in comparison with mathematics or physics, but it is a science!

NOTES

1. James V. McConnell, *Understanding Human Behavior,* 4th ed. (New York: Holt, Rinehart & Winston, 1983), pp. 10–14.

2. Marilyn E. Gist, "Self-Efficacy: Implications for Organizational Behavior and Human Resource Management," *Academy of Management Review,* July 1986, pp. 472–485.

3. Charles Horton Cooley, *Social Organization* (New York: Charles Scribner's Sons, 1901), p. 23.

4. James B. McKee, *Introduction to Sociology* (New York: Holt, Rinehart & Winston, 1969), p. 55.

5. William Ouchi, *Theory Z: How American Business Can Meet the Japanese Challenge* (Reading, MA: Addison-Wesley Publishing Co., 1981).

6. *Ibid.*

7. Richard M. Hodgetts and Fred Luthans, *International Management* (New York: McGraw-Hill Book Co., 1991), p. 37.

8. *Ibid.*, Chapter 2.

9. Fred N. Kerlinger, *Foundations of Behavioral Research,* 2nd ed. (New York: Holt, Rinehart & Winston, 1973), p. 300.

10. *Ibid.*

11. Bernard Berelson and Gary A. Steiner, *Human Behavior: Shorter Edition* (New York: Harcourt, Brace and World, 1967), p. 7.

12. Stanley Milgram, "Some Conditions of Obedience and Disobedience to Authority," *Human Relations,* February 1965, pp. 57–75.

13. See *Psychology Today,* June 1974, p. 77.

14. For more on this topic see Edward E. Lawler, III, "Challenging Traditional Research Assumptions," in Edward E. Lawler, III, Alan M. Mohrman, Jr., Susan A. Mohrman, Gerald E. Ledford, Jr., and Thomas G. Cummings (eds.), *Doing Research That Is Useful for Theory and Practice* (San Francisco: Jossey-Bass, 1985); Kenneth W. Thomas and Walter Tymon, Jr., "Necessary Properties of Relevant Research: Lessons from Recent Criticisms of the Organizational Sciences," *Academy of Management Review,* July 1982, pp. 345–352; and James R. Meindl, "The Abundance of Solutions: Some Thoughts for Theoretical and Practice Solution Seekers," *Administrative Science Quarterly,* December 1982, pp. 670–685.

15. For more on this topic see "Ethical Standards of Psychologists," *American Psychologist,* January 1963, pp. 56–60; and Mary von Glinow, *et al.,* "Ethical Issues in Organizational Behavior," *Academy of Management Newsletter,* March 1985, pp. 1–3.

PART II
INDIVIDUAL BEHAVIOR
IN ORGANIZATIONS

Conceptual Model for this Book

Individual behavior
Personality and
perception
Attitudes and
job satisfaction
Learning and
reinforcement
Motivation

Group behavior
Group dimensions
Group dynamics
Leadership
Power, organizational
politics, and
conflict

Organizational structure
Organizational design
Job design
Stress and work

Organizational processes
Decision making
Communication
Organizational climate
and culture
Organizational change
and development

Organizational behavior

O ur study of organizational behavior starts with an examination of the role of the individual in organizations. The unique behavior of people in organized settings defines much of what happens and permits us to make predictions about what might occur. Further, understanding individual processes aids a manager in his or her attempt to develop an effective organization.

This part of the book will help you understand why people do what they do. Although it would be presumptuous to claim that behavioral science research has solved all the mysteries of human nature, there is much we do know, and in the next four chapters we present some of the concepts that clarify the dynamics of life in organizations.

In Chapter 3 we examine two important components of human behavior: personality and perception. Personality consists of an individual's characteristics and behaviors, organized to reflect the unique adjustment that person makes to his or her environment. Perception is an individual's view of reality. These two components help explain why people act as they do.

In Chapter 4 attitudes and job satisfaction are the focal points of consideration. Attitudes reflect how individuals feel about other people or things, the beliefs they have about them, and their reactions to them. Job satisfaction is an emotional response to a job situation. Employee satisfaction is related to age, gender, and hierarchical level. There are a variety of causes and outcomes of job satisfaction, and they will be examined in this chapter.

Chapter 5 addresses learning and reinforcement theory. To a great degree, people do things, or refrain from doing them, based on the rewards or punishments that their actions elicit. In short, behavior is a function of its consequences. Learning theory and reinforcement theory provide insights into how behavior is strengthened, weakened, or altered.

Chapter 6 explores the motivation process, the nature of needs, and goal-directed behavior. It focuses on a basic model of individual behavior that is useful not only in organizations but also in our personal lives. Then the specific nature of needs is examined by applying the content theories of Maslow, McClelland, Alderfer, and Herzberg. Alternative explanations of motivation are discussed in the context of process theories, most specifically goal setting, equity theory, and expectancy-valence theory.

The primary objective of these chapters is to explain how and why people act as they do at work. When you have finished reading this part of the book, you should have a solid understanding of the major components of individual behavior, as well as knowing what some of the major modern motivation theories are. ◆

CHAPTER 3
Personality and Perception

GOALS OF THE CHAPTER

This chapter begins our study of individual behavior in organizations. It is well known that human behavior has a significant effect on virtually every phase of an organization's existence. Our purpose here is to develop an understanding of some of the *whys* of human behavior.

What follows is not a blueprint specifying what people will do in every situation, because nobody really knows all the answers. However, we will describe two of the basic components of individual behavior and present examples of how people behave in different ways, seemingly because of these components. We begin by considering selected ways of viewing individuals. Then we examine specific components of behavior, including personality and perception. When you have finished reading this chapter, you should be able to:

1. identify and describe contrasting models of individual behavior;
2. define the term *personality* and discuss four factors influencing personality development;
3. discuss those factors that influence the perceptual process.

Until four months ago, work output in Roger Rothman's company had not been a major problem. The company typically had a twenty-day backlog of orders, which is standard in this industry.

However, ninety days ago the firm landed a large subcontract from a major aerospace firm and it became necessary to institute overtime and weekend work. This new contract had to be completed in fifty work days. In an effort to encourage his people to work longer hours, Roger instituted a productivity incentive program. In addition to the hourly wage, workers were paid a bonus based on how much work they produced. This payment was in direct proportion to output. For example, an individual who did 10 percent more work than required by his or her job assignment received a 10 percent increase in salary, etc. Since most of the employees at Roger's company are production workers, the plan was easy enough to create and implement, and it seemed to work quite well. Productivity increased 14 percent, and the new contract was completed in the agreed-upon time. When asked about his approach to getting the extra work out of the employees, Roger made the following statement.

My plan worked well because it was tied to money, and let's face it: Money motivates. That's a fact of life. It motivates me, and it motivates the people who work for me. Everyone wants to have a better life, and one way of getting it is through higher earning power. Of course, there's a price to be paid for this. For example, I make everyone clock in and clock out around here, and I don't stand for any fooling around. I've got rules and regulations, and I expect everyone to abide by them. Anyone who doesn't toe the mark is fired. I've got to run the place this way. After all, we've got a lot of important contracts that have to be completed within agreed-upon times, and I can't be running late on any of them. My success in filling that aerospace contract shows that my approach was the right one.

Roger's success with the aerospace contract is likely to land him more business with this firm. In the interim, he has done away with the productivity bonus plan. To his surprise, however, work productivity is remaining 14 percent higher than before. If this continues, it means that Roger's backlog of orders will soon be gone and he will have to either secure more new contracts or begin laying off some of the workers.

1. Which model of human behavior best describes the way Roger sees people: the economic or self-actualizing model? Also, is Roger a Theory X or Theory Y manager?
2. In what way does Argyris's immaturity-maturity theory help explain Roger's view of the employees?
3. How does Roger use stereotyping and projection in forming a perception of his employees?

Write down your answers to these questions and put them aside. We will return to them later.

THE NATURE OF INDIVIDUALS

Although human beings are known to be complex creatures, many people seem disposed to compress their counterparts into reductive cliches: People are basically good; The average person is out to make a fast buck; or If you give people a chance to prove themselves, you'll be pleasantly surprised.

Behavioral theorists, on the other hand, attempt to describe individuals by setting up models designated by contrasting pairs of adjectives. Some of the most popular formulations of individual differences include models such as rational-emotional, behavioristic-humanistic, economic-self-actualizing, and Theory X and Theory Y. These comparisons all contain some degree of accuracy, and most people fall somewhere between the extremes of each. In examining these comparisons, remember that they are presented as antithetical pairs primarily for the purpose of emphasis and examination.

Rational and Emotional Models

Some theorists see the individual as a highly rational entity having computer-like characteristics. According to this view, whenever faced with a decision, a person will gather all of the available information about the subject, analyze it, evaluate every course of action, determine the cost-benefit ratio associated with each action, and then choose the one that offers the greatest benefit. The **rational model** presents human beings as deliberative, serious, and computational.

At the opposite extreme is the **emotional model** of the human being. Scholars of the Freudian persuasion place great faith in this model, which sees individuals as primarily controlled by their emotions, many of which are unconscious responses. This viewpoint is directly tied to what Freudians consider the three major subsystems of an individual's personality: the id, the ego, and the superego. The *id* is the core of the unconscious. Consisting of raw, primitive, instinctual drive, it continually seeks gratification and pleasure. The *ego* is the conscious and logical part of the Freudian person. It uses intellect and reason in interpreting reality. The *superego* is often depicted as the conscience, which provides guidelines for determining right and wrong.[1]

Freudians see human beings as basically irrational because of the constant conflicts that prevail among these three major personality subsystems. These inner conflicts, according to Freudians, cause individuals to be subject to their emotions.

Behavioristic and Humanistic Models

Some scholars believe that the individual can be described solely in terms of behavior. These theorists are interested only in *observable* behavior, as contrasted with thoughts or feelings. In its most radical form, the **behavioristic model** holds that all behavior is environmentally determined. One of the most famous statements by an adherent of the behavioristic view was that of John B. Watson:

> Give me a dozen healthy infants, well-formed, and my own specified world to bring them up in and I'll guarantee to take any one at random and train him to become any type of specialist I might select—doctor, lawyer, artist, merchant-

Some theorists see the individual as highly rational.

Other theorists see the individual as controlled by emotion.

Some theorists describe individuals solely in behavioral terms.

chief and, yes, even beggar-man and thief, regardless of his talents, penchants, tendencies, abilities, vocations and the race of his ancestors.[2]

Today, these basic ideas are echoed in the works of the well-known psychologist B. F. Skinner. We will expand upon this view when we discuss learning theory in Chapter 5.

The **humanistic model** of the person is more philosophical than scientific. Humanists see the individual as capable of surmounting irrational impulses through conscious reasoning. In their view, people control their own destiny to a great degree, and their potential cannot be underestimated. The belief that "anyone in America can succeed through hard work" is an example. This model offers a great deal of hope and comfort to many, although to date empirical research has failed to substantiate many of its tenets. In contrast to the behavioristic view, however, humanists argue that people are complicated beings, and mere analysis of observable phenomena is an inadequate approach to the study of individual behavior.

Some see people as controllers of their own destiny.

Economic and Self-Actualizing Models

Another way of describing individual differences is that of the economic-self-actualizing contradistinction. The **economic model** of the human being conceptualizes the individual as totally economic in orientation. This model was central to the emergence of scientific management during the late 1880s. As we saw in Chapter 1, at the heart of this movement was a concern for standardizing jobs, specializing work functions, and offering economic incentives to those who could produce at standard or above standard levels.

Some theorists believe people are totally economic in orientation.

The antithesis of the economic model is found in the **self-actualizing model**. Many psychologists see people as motivated by the opportunity to grow, mature, and become all they are capable of becoming. They believe that the individual cannot be adequately described by economic or physiological considerations alone. People strive for loftier goals, like self-fulfillment and self-actualization. Adherents of this model see the individual as craving personal growth, job competence, and self-fulfillment. Although individuals may be temporarily sidetracked in this quest, they eventually will return to it. The challenge of the organization, therefore, is to provide the proper conditions for self-actualization.

Some see the individual as seeking self-actualization.

Theory X and Theory Y Models

The attitudes of management also tend to be dualistic, as the basic tenets of McGregor's famous Theory X and Theory Y views of human beings attest:

Theory X and Theory Y provide contrasting views of people.

Theory X	Theory Y
1. People have an inherent dislike of work and will avoid it when possible.	1. Work is as natural as rest or play, and people do not inherently dislike it.
2. To get them to work, it is necessary to use coercion and threats of punishment.	2. Coercion and threats of punishment are not the only ways to get people to work.

3. Individuals actually like to be directed.

4. The average person has little ambition and above all else seeks security.

3. Under the right conditions, individuals not only seek responsibility but willingly pursue organizational goals.

4. The ability to exercise a relatively high degree of imagination, ingenuity, and creativity in the solution of organization problems is widely distributed in the population.

Theory X sees the individual as lazy, uncreative, and in need of constant prodding. **Theory Y** views the individual as having tremendous potential, which effective management can channel toward organizational goals.[3] Obviously, depending on the individual manager's philosophy of human behavior, there may be a divergence of managerial practices in the same organization.

Comments on the Dualistic Theories

Each of the preceding eight models (see Figure 3–1) has some measure of validity. For example, some people are basically logical decision makers (rational model), but in some cases even they make impulsive choices (emotional model). Some may often be described in terms of behavior (behavioristic model), but at times require a more philosophical description (humanistic model). Some people are motivated by money (economic model), but are also interested in doing work that they find challenging and rewarding (self-actualization model). Likewise, some managers believe that the average person works best under conditions of loose control (Theory Y), but when pressure for higher output is exerted by top management they will begin instituting close control procedures (Theory X). As a result, all of the models are partly accurate and partly inaccurate.

A person's behavioral characteristics are the result of the interaction of various human attributes under different conditions. One of the most important of these attributes is personality.

FIGURE 3–1

Models of Individual Behavior

Rational ——————————————— Emotional
Behavioristic ——————————————— Humanistic
Economic ——————————————— Self-Actualizing
Theory X ——————————————— Theory Y

STOP

Review your answers to Question 1 and make any changes you would like before continuing.

1. Which model of human behavior best describes the way Roger sees people: the economic or self-actualizing model? Also, is Roger a Theory X or Theory Y manager?

The economic model best describes the way Roger sees people. Notice the way he believes that people are motivated by money. The self-actualizing model views people as motivated by the opportunity to grow, mature, and become all they are capable of becoming.

Roger is a Theory X manager. He believes that it is necessary to carefully monitor and control employee activities. If anyone disobeys the rules, he or she may be fired. Roger relies heavily on coercion and threats of punishment to help keep the workers in line.

PERSONALITY

An awareness of the significance of personality is fundamental to understanding human behavior. The study of personality is quite detailed and encompasses a wide variety of topics, many of which are beyond the scope of this chapter. Nevertheless, it is useful to remember that every person is in certain respects: (a) like all other people; (b) like some other people; and (c) like no other people.

Each person has features that result from biological and environmental factors, yet each person is also unique as a result of the interaction of numerous encounters, stresses, ideas, skills, abilities, attitudes, and experiences. Since no two people are exactly alike, it is not surprising that behavior patterns differ over a wide range.

Personality is an individual's characteristics and behaviors, organized in a way that reflects the unique adjustment the person makes to his or her environment. It is generally believed that an individual's personality remains relatively stable over time, but behavior will vary from situation to situation.

Some psychologists have attempted to identify those factors that can be used to measure an individual's personality. One researcher, employing factor analysis, came up with a list of sixteen bipolar traits that can be used to describe individuals in objective, measurable terms. Among the characteristics were the following:[4]

Personality helps an individual adjust to his or her environment.

aloof, cold	warm, sociable
emotional, unstable	mature, calm
mild	aggressive
timid, shy	adventurous, thick skinned
tough, realistic	sensitive
trustful	suspecting
simple, awkward	sophisticated, polished
unshakable	insecure

accepting   critical
composed   excitable

In order to understand how personality affects behavior, however, we need to know more than just some of the adjectives that can be used to describe personality. A knowledge of the factors that influence the development of personality is required.

Factors Influencing Personality Development

A number of theories have been developed that attempt to explain the differences in personalities, but none is definitive. The major influences common to all theories are shown in Figure 3–2.

People are born with certain traits and characteristics.

Genetics. Certain traits and characteristics of people are inherited through the genetic process. These traits form at least one basis for future personality development. Typically, characteristics inherited by all people include physical structure, reflexes, innate drives, and intelligence.

Thus, how large or small a person is, the pattern of direct responses to stimuli, impulses, ability to learn, and emotional constitution are all determined genetically. Further, each of these characteristics influences people's behavior. For example, a 5 ft., 10 in. professional basketball player will behave differently than a 7 ft., 2 in. player on the court. Likewise, differences in intelligence levels clearly manifest themselves in different behavioral patterns.

Environment helps shape personality.

Environment. Although people are born with certain characteristics, they also develop habits through their interaction with others and with the culture around them as they grow up. The effect of a person's environment is quite strong. The experiences and interactions of a black man raised in a ghetto differ markedly from those of a white man raised in an upper-class community. As a result, their self-perceptions and their methods of coping with the world, including such things as attitudes toward work, are influenced in different ways, leading to different behavioral response patterns.

FIGURE 3–2
Factors Influencing Personality

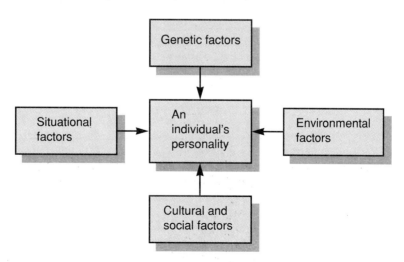

Cultural and Social Factors. Cultural and social factors also contribute to an individual's personality. **Culture** consists of those beliefs and values shared by a group of people. This culture is transmitted from one generation to the next. Some elements of a culture are language, skills, art, religion, laws, and customs. Thus, culture can help guide people's behavior. Furthermore, because their perspectives and behaviors differ, people who live in one cultural milieu (for example, the Western world) often have different personalities from those who live in other cultures (such as the Far East).

Cultural and social factors affect personality.

Culture can also refer to a narrow range of society, or subculture. A **subculture** consists of people whose ways of behaving are peculiar to their particular group within the larger society. Typical examples include professional athletes, hippies, artists, college students, and international managers.[5] The term can even be extended to comprise organizational subcultures: assembly-line workers, staff personnel, and top managers.[6]

Several sociocultural factors enter into personality development. The most important are imposed during the socialization process, when cultural values and role patterns are transmitted.

The people and groups an individual is associated with help shape his or her personality. A person acquires behavior patterns in relation to others through the process known as socialization.

Socialization conditions behavior.

Socialization is the conditioning of an individual's behavior in ways that are customary and acceptable to the individual's social environment. Socialization begins in early childhood, when the young person learns acceptable behavior for fulfilling physical needs. Later, needs for affection emerge, and behavior oriented toward satisfying this and other learned needs continues to develop.[7] It seems clear that family, religious affiliation, ethnic background, immediate work group,[8] and social class are all important elements in personality development.

The situation can influence personality.

Situational Factors. Situational factors are spontaneous or unpredictable events that have a significant influence on future behavior. These events may be cultural, social, or environmental and have a major impact on the person.

Examples of such events are numerous. A student who is undecided about a career, or who is equally drawn to several different vocations, may happen to sit down in an airplane next to a lawyer who is an engaging and persuasive advocate of the legal profession. This encounter may be decisive in shaping the student's personality by stimulating interest in a course of study that would not otherwise have been considered.

Hence, chance can present opportunities so significant that personality change may result. A related idea is that there are predictable crises in adult life that affect personality development.[9] Such events as the birth of a child, a move to a new city, the death of a parent, or a divorce may alter an individual's personality because of the disruptive impact on an otherwise stable life.

Personality and the Workplace

Personality formation has also been examined in terms of the workplace. One of the best known works has been that of Chris Argyris.

Individuals mature over time, but organizations often encourage the opposite type of behavior.

Immaturity-Maturity Theory. An interesting model has been developed by Chris Argyris (Figure 3–3) to explain the relationship between human personality development and place of employment. Argyris makes the case that the normal stages of human development start with an infant, who is dependent on others for need fulfillment and reactive in behavior, whereas adults are ideally independent, autonomous, and proactive in behavior. Formal organizations, however, as they grow and develop generally assume pyramidal structures in which information is centralized, work divided, and jobs specialized. Managing such organizations requires order giving, evaluation of performance, rewards and punishment, and efforts to ensure conformity and the perpetuation of membership. In effect, as the company becomes larger and more formal, it prefers employees whose behavior is more consistent with infant characteristics (dependent, passive, reactive). There is a conflict, then, between the goals and capabilities of the healthy, striving adult and the needs of the organization, since inconsistent behavior patterns are required at some levels.

For example, the lower an employee is in the organizational hierarchy, the less control he or she has over working conditions and the less likely it is that he or she will be able to fully employ his or her abilities. The more directive the leadership, the more dependent the employee becomes, and frustration-reducing responses on the part of the worker are likely to occur. Some employees will fight the organization to gain more control; others may join a union. Some will leave the organization permanently, while some will leave psychologically by becoming apathetic and indifferent. Finally, some will downgrade the importance of the job and substitute higher pay as a reward for meaningless work.

Argyris has tested his model and found support for it in various cultures, at different organizational levels, and within different types of organizations. He states that the results indicate that the overall impact of the formal organization on the individual is

to decrease his control over his immediate work area, decrease his chance to use his abilities and increase his dependence and submissiveness; second, that to the extent to which the individual seeks to be autonomous and functions as an adult he adapts by reactions ranging from withdrawal and noninterest, to aggression or perhaps to the substitution of instrumental money rewards for intrinsic rewards. The weight of the deprivations and the degree of adaptation increase as we descend the hierarchy. Formal structures, alas, are unintentionally designed to discourage the autonomous and involved worker.[10]

Argyris suggests several techniques for changing this situation, including job enrichment, job redesign, and methods for better integrating the individual into the

FIGURE 3–3
Argyris's Immaturity–Maturity Continuum

Immaturity characteristics	Maturity characteristics
Passivity———————————————▶	Activity
Dependence———————————————▶	Independence
Few ways of behaving———————▶	Many ways of behaving
Shallow interests————————————▶	Deep interests
Short-run time perspective—————▶	Long-run time perspective
Subordinate position————————▶	Superordinate position
Lack of self-awareness————————▶	Self-awareness and self control

Organizational Behavior In Action

YES, THEY CAN!

Numerous studies have been conducted to determine the personal qualities and characteristics of successful entrepreneurs. Some of the most commonly cited include commitment, perseverance, a drive to achieve, initiative, persistent problem solving, a tolerance for ambiguity, calculated risk taking, a tolerance for failure, and the need for power. Most entrepreneurs have some of these characteristics but few have all of them. However, there is one that is universal: internal locus of control. Successful entrepreneurs believe that they can achieve success through their own efforts; and they are convinced that if they work hard and stay on top of things, they will come out ahead. Commenting on this characteristic, two researchers recently noted that:

> Successful entrepreneurs believe in themselves. They do not believe that the success or failure of their venture will be governed by fate, luck, or similar forces. They believe that their accomplishments and setbacks are within their own control and influence and that they can affect the outcome of their actions. This attribute is consistent with high-achievement motivation drive, the desire to take personal responsibility and self-confidence.
>
> Related to this idea, and equally important, is the successful entrepreneur's view of failure. Research shows that many of them have failed in their first (and sometimes second and third) business efforts, but they pushed on with a new venture. They are not afraid of failing, and many of them admit that they learn more from their failures than from their successes.
>
> Why are they so positive in their attitudes and convinced that they will end up on top? The primary reason is because they believe that success or failure is dictated by circumstances that they can control. These people are characterized by internal locus of control.

Source: Donald F. Kuratko and Richard M. Hodgetts, *Entrepreneurship: A Contemporary Approach* (Chicago: Dryden Press, 1989), pp. 66–73.

organization. Holland has gone even further and suggested that people's personalities play a key role in the careers they choose.[11]

Locus of Control

Locus of control influences behavior.

Behavioral scientists interested in the influence of personality dimensions on behavior have focused their attention on some of the areas identified by Argyris. One of these is **locus of control,** a term that refers to the extent to which individuals believe that events that occur to them are (or are not) basically under their control. A person with an internal locus of control believes he or she can influence events. A person with an external locus of control believes that what happens to him or her is a matter of luck or fate. Internals like to participate in decision making and have input regarding what is going on. They believe they can influence things in the workplace, for example, and in so doing improve their working conditions and/or chances for raises or promotions. (See "Organizational Behavior in Action: Yes, They Can!"). Externals let things happen without any attempt to influence things because they believe such behaviors will have no effect. What is meant to happen will happen. This personality dimension helps explain why some people act very differently away from the job than they do at work.[12]

Authoritarianism

Authoritarian and dogmatic personalities are character- ized by rigidity.

Another area of interest is authoritarianism and dogmatism. People with **authoritarian personalities** rigidly adhere to conventional values. These individuals obey recognized authority, are concerned with such things as power and toughness, and look unfavorably on the use of subjective feelings. **Dogmatism,** a closely related term, refers to the rigidity of a person's beliefs. Highly dogmatic people see the world as a threatening place, commonly regard established authority as absolute, and accept or reject other people on the basis of their agreement or disagreement with accepted authority or doctrine. "High dogmatic" people are typically unreceptive to new ideas, in contrast to "low dogmatic" people who are often open-minded. Commenting on high dogmatic (HD) and low dogmatic (LD) people, Hellriegel, Slocum, and Woodman point out that

> there is some evidence that HDs depend more on authority figures in the orga- nization and are more easily influenced by them. In addition, the authoritarian personality probably is subservient to authority figures and may even prefer a highly directive, structured leadership style from supervisors. Also, there ap- pears to be some relationship between the degree of dogmatism and interper- sonal and group behavior. For example, HDs typically need more group struc- ture than LDs to work effectively with others. This means that the performance of HDs on task forces, committee assignments, and so on may vary somewhat depending on how the group goes about doing its task. Some evidence also suggests that a high degree of dogmatism is related to limited search for information in decision situations and, perhaps as a result, some- times to poor managerial performance.[13]

STOP

Review your answers to Question 2 and make any changes you would like before continuing.

2. In what way does Argyris's immaturity-maturity theory help explain Roger's view of the employees?

Argyris's immaturity-maturity theory holds that most organizations keep their peo- ple in a state of immaturity by treating them like children and never giving them the opportunity to mature and develop. Certainly Roger does this in the way he attempts to monitor and control employee behavior and keep the workers in a state of dependency. Everyone has to obey the rules and do as they are told. There is little opportunity for independence or self-control.

PERCEPTION

A second fundamental component in understanding why people behave the way they do is perception. *Perception* is the way stimuli are selected and grouped by a person so they can be meaningfully interpreted. It is a person's view of reality. The process of perception enables us to understand and cope with the environment in which we live.

Factors Influencing Perception

A number of factors influence a person's perception. Four of the most important are: (a) the selection of stimuli; (b) the organization of stimuli; (c) the situation; and (d) the person's self-concept.

Selection of Stimuli.   While people are surrounded by many stimuli, they focus on only a small number. This process is known as selection and is one reason why individuals perceive things differently—each selects specific cues and filters, or screens, out the others.[14] For example, a person may be so intently watching a movie that he is oblivious to the noises caused by people shifting in their squeaky seats, popcorn boxes falling to the floor, latecomers being seated nearby, and talkers in the lobby. These distractions are screened out and do not interfere with the person's viewing.

If someone were to stand up and yell during the movie, however, the individual would notice. This is because we all have thresholds. We continue to filter out cues until they become too distracting to ignore any longer; then we take action based on this more obtrusive information. People have different threshold levels.

Organization of Stimuli.   A second factor influencing perception is organization. After information has undergone the screening process, it must be arranged to become meaningful. The mind tries to bring order out of the chaotic onslaught of sensory data by selecting certain items and putting them together in a meaningful way that is based on experience.

For example, there are a few principles that determine how we interpret visual stimuli. One is differentiation. The simplest visual differentiation is that of a figure from its background. The figure can appear well defined, at a definite location, solid, and in front of the ground, or it can appear amorphous or indefinite.

Figure 3–4 shows two examples in which figure and ground change places. In these figures the same visual stimuli are perceived alternately as figure and ground, as the viewer's mind changes the way it interprets what is observed. In Figure 3–4(a), you may see the fronts of five black cubes with white tops. If you continue looking at the sketch, however, you will see three black cubes with white bottoms. (Stare at the lowest white square.) In Figure 3–4(b), do you see a goblet or the twins? (The twins are facing each other.) Whichever you see, try to find the other. When you have found it, try to change your perception back to what it was at first.

A second organizing principle is closure, which means the perceiver's mind supplies the elements needed to form a recognizable whole. Frequently, we see only parts of an object, but the mind completes the image so that what is seen becomes meaningful. Figure 3–5 shows two examples of closure. Figure 3–5(a) is a dog, not 20

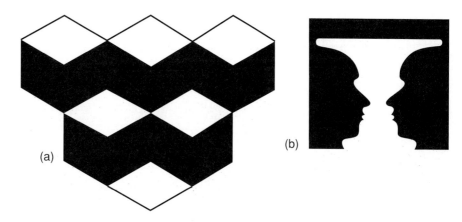

FIGURE 3–4
Perceptual Organization by Differentiating between Figure and Ground: (a) Reversing Blocks;
(b) Peter–Paul Goblet

discrete blotches; Figure 3–5(b) is an image of a man with a beard. The latter is difficult for most people to see.

Now that you have refined your perceptual skills, look at Figure 3–6. Which bar in Figure 3–6(a) is the tallest? In Figure 3–6(b), which center circle is larger?[15]

The perceptual organization of information helps people categorize sensory inputs. The central function of the categorization process is to reduce initially complex information into simpler categories. This categorization occurs not only with objects but also with people. We take familiar cues and translate them into meaningful wholes.

The situation also affects perception.

The Situation. Another factor influencing perception is the situation. A person's familiarity with, or expectations about, a situation, as well as his or her past ex-

FIGURE 3–5
Perceptual Organization by Closure

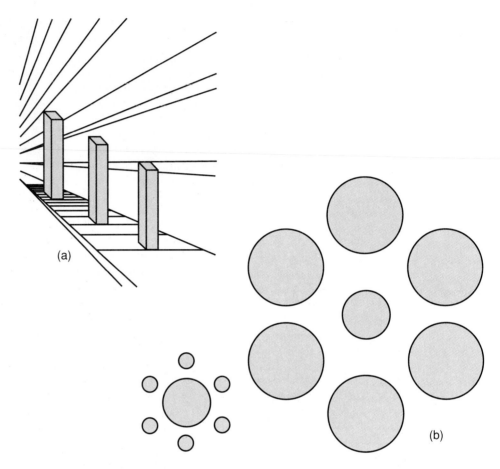

FIGURE 3–6
Perception Pictures

periences, affect what that person perceives. For example, in 1986 President Reagan was riding a wave of popularity and was perceived as one of the nation's strongest presidents. The next year, caught in the middle of the Iran-Contra affair, his leadership was being seriously questioned by the public.[16]

Self-Concept.   A fourth factor influencing perception is the self-concept. The way people feel about and perceive themselves is known as their **self-concept**. You might see yourself as well-liked, honest, patient, or intelligent, or as all of the foregoing. The self-concept is important because your mental picture of yourself determines much of what you perceive and do. If you do not see yourself as a competitive person, you will not be as likely to attend to those stimuli in the environment that relate to opportunities to be competitive.

In most cases, an individual's self-concept changes as the person matures. If only for purposes of psychological well-being, people try to maintain a relatively stable, positive self-concept. They try to avoid pain and to enhance the self. Whether or not a

An individual's self-concept influences his or her perception of the environment.

self-concept is "accurate" is not the critical issue. We have all seen people who seem to have inflated self-concepts, possibly because of a poor self-image, or who accuse others of being narrow when in fact it is they themselves who are. In each case the self-concept is striving to be internally logical. If it is not, an identity crisis may result.

Factors Creating Perceptual Difficulty

Perception often results in different people responding to the same stimuli in different ways. These differences can cause interpersonal difficulty. Four factors that contribute to this difficulty are stereotyping, the halo effect, perceptual defense, and projection.

Stereotyping. **Stereotyping** is the process of categorizing people or things based on a limited amount of information. It is widely used by decision makers in simplifying complex stimuli. The bases for such stereotyping may be derived from a wide number of sources, from the mass media to past experience. All provide input for generalized conclusions. This is especially true when individuals attempt to describe people on the basis of nationality or occupation. For example, one group of researchers asked one hundred Princeton students to take a list of eighty-four attributes and assign those that were most applicable to ten ethnic groups. They found that almost every ethnic group was assigned at least three traits by over 20 percent of the students, and one trait by over 50 percent of the students. Americans were identified as materialistic (67 percent), Germans as industrious (59 percent), English as conservative (53 percent), and Chinese as loyal to family ties (50 percent).[17] In short, the students had stereotyped views of the ethnic groups.

Nor is stereotyping limited to any geographic region. After conducting a review of multi-cultural studies, Hodgetts and Luthans found that many international managers had stereotypical perceptions of themselves. For example, in contrast to the other two groups, Dutch managers saw themselves as very willing to delegate authority, Indian managers viewed themselves as having a high concern for rules, and West German managers perceived themselves as very willing to tolerate conflict.[18]

Stereotyping can be very useful because it helps the decision maker simplify the situation, and since most people lack either the ability or the desire to deal with complex facts and alternatives, it is common to find individuals using it. Keep in mind, however, that some people are able to deal with complexity and abstractness, and under such conditions will still attempt to carry out environmental surveillance and comparative analysis of the alternatives. People who are nondogmatic,[19] or who have a high tolerance for ambiguity,[20] fit into this category; but they tend to be the exception rather than the rule.

Halo Effect. Closely related to the idea of stereotyping is the halo effect. The **halo effect** refers to the use of a known particular trait as the basis for an overall evaluation. For example, the job applicant who arrives for an interview and finds a friendly recruiter may decide that the company, no matter how large, offers a friendly work environment. A junior executive who performs well on his or her first task may be adjudged competent in all respects and be placed on a "fast track" for promotion. In reality, the task may have been one with which the junior executive had a great deal of experience.

Stereotyping is the process of categorizing people based on limited information.

The halo effect can cause perceptual problems.

Personal descriptions can also entail a halo effect. For example, Asch has conducted research to determine the effect of one personality trait on the description of an individual. In his study, two people with identical personality traits were evaluated. However, one was identified to the evaluators as being "warm," whereas the other was described as "cold." People evaluated the person identified as warm much more positively than the one described as cold.[21]

Perceptual Defense.   Another difficulty in the perception process is known as **perceptual defense,** which refers to screening out or distorting information that is personally disturbing or that we do not care to acknowledge. People have a tendency to select or attend to information that supports their viewpoints, and concurrently to ignore or fail to perceive information that is contrary to their opinions. For example, an argument over political preference near election time may find two people elaborating on only those characteristics of a candidate that are consistent with their own beliefs. Another example is the actions of a manager after he or she has decided, because of poor performance, not to promote a subordinate. The manager may actively seek out negative information to support the decision but largely ignore the positive. Data are distorted to preserve the simple categorization. In other words, people develop ways to keep from having to change their perceptions.

Projection.   A fourth difficulty in the perceptual process is **projection,** which is attributing one's own undesirable traits or characteristics to others. For example, Joe justifies keeping his desk locked by saying, "People around here will walk off with anything they can," where in fact Joe often picks up materials that belong to others and conceals them in his desk.

Perceptions may also be distorted by emotions we are experiencing or by personality traits we possess. For example, a manager who is frightened by rumors of impending organizational changes often judges others to be more frightened than they actually are. People rated high in personality traits such as stinginess, obstinacy, and disorderliness are more likely to rate others high on these traits than are those rated low in these personality traits. We often see others in a less favorable light than ourselves by projecting some of our shortcomings or feelings onto them.

Attribution Theory

When people observe the behavior of others, they seek to develop explanations of why these individuals behave as they do. **Attribution theory** provides explanations of how individuals observe behavior and then attribute causes to it.[22] The theory suggests that when we observe behavior, we decide whether the behavior has been internally or externally caused. This decision is heavily based on three factors: consistency, consensus, and distinctiveness.

Internally-caused behaviors are those that are seen as being under the personal control of the individual. For example, if an individual turns in a report late, this might be viewed as a result of an internally-caused behavior such as laziness or general lack of concern over preparing the report in a timely manner. Externally-caused behaviors are a result of outside causes. If the individual turned in the report late because the

People tend to screen out disturbing information.

Projection occurs when one attributes his or her feelings to others.

accounting department was tardy in providing the necessary financial data, this might be viewed as the result of an externally-caused behavior.

Consistency is the extent to which the same person behaves in the same way at different times. For example, if the individual in the previous paragraph always turns reports in late, the observer is likely to attribute these results to internal causes. If the individual is seldom late, the observer is likely to attribute the results to external causes.

Consensus is the extent to which others in the same situation behave in the same way. If everyone in this department is late with their reports (high consensus), it is likely that the observer will attribute these results to internal causes (the group might not care about submitting timely reports). If most people are never late with their reports, the observer would probably attribute the results to external causes (the accounting department held things up).

Distinctiveness is the extent to which the person behaves in the same way in different situations. Is the individual being observed often late in submitting work projects? If so, the situation would be seen as having low distinctiveness and the cause would be internally attributed. Conversely, if the person is almost always timely in submitting work, the situation would be seen as having high distinctiveness and the cause would be externally attributed.

Attribution theory is important to the study of organizational behavior because it helps explain how people go about attributing causes to perceived behaviors. The theory is also proving useful to researchers in a variety of fields, including communication, motivation, leadership, and performance appraisal.[23]

> Consistency is the extent to which the same person behaves in the same way at different times.

> Consensus is the extent to which others in the same situation behave in the same way.

> Distinctiveness is the extent to which the person behaves in the same way in different situations.

Review your answers to Question 3 and make any changes you would like before continuing.

3. How does Roger use stereotyping and projection in forming a perception of his employees?

Roger uses stereotyping in that he categorizes all of the workers into one overall group. For example, his productivity bonus plan was based on everyone doing more work and the plan was uniformly applied. Roger perceives all of the workers as motivated by money, and he has formed general impressions which he uses in dealing with the workers. He does not individualize the employees in his mind or try to deal with them on a one-on-one basis. He uses projection in that he is motivated by money and assumes that they are, too.

SUMMARY

1. The behavior of individual human beings is complex. Psychologists have developed various models in an effort to explain why people do what they do. These models are based on assumptions about human nature that are usually expressed as dichotomies. The rational-emotional, behavioristic-humanistic, economic-self-actualizing, and Theory X-Theory Y formulations are some examples. These formulations, however, serve only as starting points for understanding human behavior, which also is comprised of such specific components as personality and perception.

2. Personality is the composite of behavioral and emotional characteristics that distinguishes one person from another. Although there is much debate regarding the precise effect of various factors on personality development, most psychologists agree that genetic, environmental, cultural, social, and situational variables are most significant. Understanding these factors provides a better understanding of behavioral patterns. In the context of the workplace, for example, when a maturing personality that strives to function more autonomously finds itself in an organization that requires passivity and dependence, a conflict ensues. Beliefs such as those relating to locus of control and characteristics such as authoritarianism and dogmatism also have a significant effect on organizational behavior.

3. Perception is a person's view of reality, and through the perceptual process people cope with their environment. For many reasons, however, people can and do perceive even the same object or event differently, and this disparity can lead to misunderstanding and difficulty. The factors influencing perception are selection, organization, situation, and self-concept. Common problems resulting from perceptual differences are stereotyping, the halo effect, perceptual defenses, and projection.

KEY TERMS

rational model	**culture**	**stereotyping**
emotional model	**subculture**	**halo effect**
behavioristic model	**socialization**	**perceptual defense**
humanistic model	**locus of control**	**projection**
economic model	**authoritarian personalities**	**attribution theory**
self-actualizing model	**dogmatism**	**consistency**
Theory X	**perception**	**consensus**
Theory Y	**self-concept**	**distinctiveness**
personality		

REVIEW AND STUDY QUESTIONS

1. What are the differences between the behavioristic and humanistic models of behavior?

2. Theory X and Theory Y are popular ways of categorizing managers. Why do you think this is the case? Why does the behavior of a Theory Y manager differ from that of a Theory X manager?

3. "She's got a lousy personality—she'll never get anywhere in this organization." What does a statement like this really mean? Can you change someone's personality?

4. What are four factors that help determine personality? Identify each, indicate the one you believe is most important, and explain why.

5. "One of the functions of schooling is socialization." What does this statement mean?

6. What is the nature of the conflict between personality and organization? Explain.

7. How do locus of control and dogmatism affect organizational behavior? Explain.

8. What is meant by perceptual selection and organization? Give an example of each.

9. Evaluating a subordinate's performance is always a difficult job. One of the barriers to objective evaluation is stereotyping. Another problem is the halo effect. What is the reason for each?

10. What is attribution theory? What role does perception play in attributing behavior?

CASES

Anti-union Sentiment

The management and union at Drusterg Manufacturing have had poor relations for over thirty years. During this period each side had used its power to achieve gains at the other's expense. For example, when the economy was good and management wanted to avoid labor problems so as to maximize output and profit, the union held out on a new contract and ended up getting 12 percent more in wages and fringe benefits than the company had initially offered. Conversely, during the severe economic slump of the late 1970s, the firm prevailed during the labor negotiations and forced the union to sign a three-year contract providing salary increases equal to 75 percent of the cost of living but no increases in fringe benefits.

Each side had fixed perceptions of the other, and any time a new employee entered their ranks he or she was quickly indoctrinated in the respective group's point of view. As a result, two years after joining the firm as a supervisor, Bill Jackens gave every indication that he was anti-union.

Two months ago, one of the women who worked in Bill's department requested a day off because her father was having surgery and she wanted to be with the family that day. The day she requested was a Friday, always the busiest one for the firm. As a result, Bill turned down her request. He told his supervisor, "If I give her this day, my overall output is going to suffer. Look, she can spend the whole weekend with her father. She doesn't need Friday as well. Besides, she already has taken her two personal days this year for vacation with her family. The company recommends that these days be kept for emergencies. If she had done this, I would have been required to grant her request and would have been provided backup assistance from the floating labor pool. If she takes a nonpaid day now, I won't get anyone to replace her and the problem will be mine entirely. Why should the company have to suffer because she has personal problems? We go out of our way to assist the work force around here. Once in a while, though, they have to pitch in and help us out. I've turned down her request because it is unreasonable."

Bill's boss did not challenge his decision. "If you think this is the right thing," he said, "I'll stand behind you. However, I think it only fair to tell you that the union is threatening to fight this thing to the top and I have no doubt that they will. This woman has been with us for over twenty-five years, and she has a lot of friends in both the union and top management. On the other hand, we've got to do what's best for the company and can't allow ourselves to be dictated to by the employees every time they have a personal problem and want a special favor. Go ahead and stand your ground. If there is a fight, we'll take it head on."

Bill's boss actually understated the situation. The union was incensed over the decision. Its representatives took the matter right to the top, indicating that if the woman was not granted her request, they would call for a walkout on that Friday. When the matter was finally resolved, the woman was given the day off. Bill was angry when he heard about top management's decision since he felt that it undermined his authority as a supervisor. Additionally, he felt confused over the decision since he believed he had done exactly what management had encouraged him to do over the past two years, namely, adopt an anti-union stance.

1. Using the rational model of human behavior that was discussed in this chapter, explain Bill's behavior. Do the same thing using the emotional model of human behavior discussed in this chapter. Which is most descriptive of Bill? Explain.

2. Is Bill a Theory X or Theory Y manager? Explain.

3. Many people think that Bill has perceptual difficulties when it comes to understanding the workers. What particular factors might be accounting for these difficulties? Explain.

The Pushy Chairperson

Richard Whiting is a member of one of the largest fraternities at Private University. Richard is currently in his junior year and has a 3.89 grade point average. Very few people who know him believe that he will have much trouble getting into medical school. Richard is very close to his father, a well-known surgeon in the city where Private University is located, and both father and son hope to practice together in future years.

Although the fraternity brothers all have a great deal of respect for Richard, he has never been elected to an office in the organization, and it seems as if he never will. Perhaps the major reason is that Richard has trouble getting along with the other members of this social group. For example, last semester he was appointed to a committee that was to raise funds for the annual muscular dystrophy drive. Richard got everyone in the house who was interested to sign up. The national organization then sent the fraternity more than 500 canisters to place in stores and restaurants around the city. Richard assigned some of the members of his committee to the task of calling on these stores and asking if they would help by placing the containers at places where they would be visible to customers. The rest of the members he assigned to the task of actually distributing the containers.

During the middle of the campaign midterm exams came up, and some of the brothers did not get their jobs done. This resulted in a heated argument between Richard and these individuals. Some of them said he was too pushy to be an effective committee chairperson. Others said that he demanded too much of them. "Just because he doesn't have to study six hours a day doesn't mean we don't," one of them said.

Despite such problems, the fraternity's effort was a tremendous success. They collected over 80 percent more money than they had the previous year. As the spring semester drew to a close and the fraternity took nominations for high offices, Richard's name was put up. However, he was beaten. The argument that was most impressive against him was by a brother who said, "He's going to make a great doctor with his dogmatic, rigid personality. However, I really don't know if he'll ever be much of a human being."

1. If the above description of Richard is accurate, what factors influencing personality might account for it?

2. What would you expect the typical behavior of the other fraternity members to be? In what ways would this behavior differ from Richard's?

3. If Richard were told what the individual had said about him during the fraternity meeting, would he agree or disagree? Explain.

SELF-FEEDBACK EXERCISE

Insights to Your Own Personality

The following statements are designed to provide insights regarding how you see yourself. In the blank space next to each statement, write the number which best describes how strongly you agree or disagree with the statement, or how true or false the statement is as it applies to you. The numbers represent the following:

5 = Strongly agree, or definitely true
4 = Generally agree, or mostly true
3 = Neither agree nor disagree, neither true nor false
2 = Generally disagree, or mostly false
1 = Strongly disagree, or definitely false

_____ 1. In some past circumstances, you have taken the lead.

_____ 2. Everyone should trust in a supernatural force whose decisions he or she always obeys.

_____ 3. You like to perform activities involving selling or salesmanship.

_____ 4. As a rule, you assess your previous actions closely.

_____ 5. You often observe those around you to see how your words and actions affect them.

_____ 6. What you earn depends on what you know and how hard you work.

_____ 7. Generally, those in authority do their share of the unpleasant jobs without passing them on to others.

_____ 8. The remedy for social problems depends on eliminating dishonest, immoral, and mentally inferior people.

_____ 9. Most people earn their income through their own work.

_____ 10. The highest type of person is the one who loves and respects his or her parents.

_____ 11. There are two kinds of people: the weak and the strong.

_____ 12. You tend to look into and analyze yourself.

_____ 13. All children should be taught obedience and respect for authority.

_____ 14. Taking on important responsibilities like starting your own business is something you would like to do.

_____ 15. In a meeting you will speak up when you disagree with someone you are convinced is wrong.

_____ 16. You enjoy thinking about complex problems.

_____ 17. It is better to work for yourself than for a good boss.

_____ 18. You often would like to know the real reasons why people behave as they do.

_____ 19. In the long run, everyone gets what they deserve.

_____ 20. Getting ahead is based more on your performance than your politics.

Enter your answers in the appropriate spaces following. Where there is an asterisk before the number, use *reverse scoring* by subtracting your score from 6, i.e., a 1 becomes a 5, a 4 becomes a 2, etc.

Group 1	Group 2	Group 3	Group 4
6. _____	1. _____	*2. _____	4. _____
7. _____	3. _____	*8. _____	5. _____
9. _____	14. _____	10. _____	12. _____
19. _____	15. _____	*11. _____	16. _____
20. _____	17. _____	*13. _____	18. _____
Total _____	Total _____	Total _____	Total _____

Now take each of your totals and divide by the number of answers so as to obtain your average responses, i.e., 2.3, 3.2, 4.1, etc. On a scale of 1–5, this measures how you see yourself in each of these four areas.

Average Score	The four areas, represented by Groups 1–4 respectively are:
_____	1. Fair—this score measures the extent to which you see the world as treating you fairly.
_____	2. Assertive—this score measures the extent to which you see yourself as aggressive.
_____	3. Equalitarian—this score measures the extent to which you see yourself as nonauthoritarian.
_____	4. Introspective—this score measures the extent to which you see yourself as thinking about things that go on around you and trying to determine why they occur.

NOTES

1. James V. McConnell, *Understanding Human Behavior,* 4th ed. (New York: Holt, Rinehart & Winston, 1983), p. 485.

2. J. B. Watson, *Behaviorism* (Chicago: Univ. of Chicago Press, 1930), p. 104.

3. Douglas McGregor, *The Human Side of Enterprise* (New York: McGraw-Hill Book Co., 1960), Chapters 3 and 4.

4. For more on this subject, see McConnell, *Understanding Human Behavior,* pp. 513–514.

5. Nancy J. Adler, *International Dimensions of Organizational Behavior,* 2nd ed. (Boston: PWS/Kent, 1991).

6. Manfred F. R., Kets de Vries, and Danny Miller, "Personality, Culture, and Organization," *Academy of Management Review,* April 1986, pp. 266–279.

7. For more on this see John P. Wanous, Arnon E. Rei-

chers, and S. D. Malik, "Organizational Socialization and Group Development: Toward an Integrative Perspective," *Academy of Management Review,* October 1984, pp. 670–683.

8. Gareth R. Jones, "Socialization Tactics, Self-Efficiency, and Newcomers' Adjustments to Organizations," *Academy of Management Journal,* June 1986, pp. 262–279.

9. Gail Sheehy, *Passages: Predictable Crises of Adult Life* (New York: E. P. Dutton, 1976).

10. Chris Argyris, "Personality vs. Organization," *Organizational Dynamics,* Fall 1974, p. 10.

11. John L. Holland, *Making Vocational Choices: A Theory of Vocational Personalities and Work Environments,* 2nd ed. (Englewood Cliffs, NJ: Prentice-Hall, 1985).

12. Paul E. Spector, "Behavior in Organizations as a Function of Employee's Locus of Control," *Psychological Bulletin,* May 1982, pp. 482–497.

13. Don Hellriegel, John W. Slocum, Jr., and Richard W. Woodman, *Organizational Behavior,* 4th ed. (St. Paul, MN: West Publishing Co., 1986), p. 73.

14. See for example Georgia T. Chao and Steve W. J. Kozlowski, "Employee Perceptions on the Implementation of Robotic Manufacturing Technology," *Journal of Applied Psychology,* February 1986, pp 70–76.

15. All three bars are the same size, and both center circles are the same size.

16. Jonathan Alter, "Has Reagan Changed?" *Newsweek,* November 23, 1987, p. 20.

17. Marvin Karlins, Thomas L. Coffman, and Gary Walters, "On the Fading of Social Stereotypes: Studies in Three Generations of College Students," *Journal of Personality and Social Psychology,* September 1969, pp. 1–16.

18. Richard M. Hodgetts and Fred Luthans, *International Management* (New York: McGraw-Hill Book Co., 1991), p. 39.

19. Barbara H. Long and Robert C. Ziller, "Dogmatism and Predecisional Information Search," *Journal of Applied Psychology,* October 1965, pp. 376–378.

20. Jerry D. Dermer, "Cognitive Characteristics and the Perceived Importance of Information," *Accounting Review,* July 1973, pp. 511–519.

21. S. E. Asch, "Forming Impressions of the Personality," *Journal of Abnormal and Social Psychology,* July 1946, pp. 258–290.

22. H. H. Kelley, "Attribution in Social Interaction," in E. Jones, *et al., Attribution: Perceiving the Causes of Behavior* (Morristown, NJ: General Learning Press, 1972).

23. For some examples see Brendan D. Bannister, "Performance Outcome Feedback and Attribution Feedback: Interactive Effects on Recipient Responses," *Journal of Applied Psychology,* May 1987, pp. 203–210; and Dennis A. Gioia and Henry P. Sims, Jr., "Cognition-Behavior Connections: Attribution and Verbal Behavior in Leader-Subordinate Interactions," *Organizational Behavior and Human Decision Processes,* April 1986, pp. 197–229.

CHAPTER 4
Attitudes and Job Satisfaction

This chapter continues our study of individual behavior in organizations by examining attitudes and job satisfaction. While these are often linked, we shall discuss them separately by first examining the nature and components of attitudes and looking at how attitudes can be changed. Then we will study how job satisfaction can be measured and examine some of the influences on and outcomes of job satisfaction. When you have finished reading this chapter, you should be able to:

1. identify the components of individual attitudes;
2. explain the concept of cognitive dissonance;
3. define the term *job satisfaction* and relate some of the typical ways of measuring satisfaction;
4. discuss the influences and outcomes of job satisfaction.

OPENING CASE: FINDING OUT WHAT'S WRONG

Over the past six months, turnover at Abrams & Yarrell (A&Y) has reached a new high. The company has had to replace 106 of its 1,734 employees. Most of those who have left were in the middle and lower ranks of the organization. The largest percentage have been supervisors with less than three years of seniority.

It is common for the personnel/human resources management (P/HRM) department to conduct exit interviews with all personnel, and through this source the company has learned that most of the supervisors are taking jobs with other firms that are paying more money. "Over 60 percent of the people we interviewed," the P/HRM director told the president, "have mentioned salary and fringe benefits as major reasons for their decision to leave." The company has always paid less than industry average and has never before had trouble keeping people. Most felt the work was interesting and challenging, and they were unwilling to give this up for an increase in wages and benefits. However, the company now believes that it may be necessary to close the gap between itself and the competition and offer an across-the-board increase of 18 percent. This would bring it directly into line with the industry average.

Before doing so, however, A&Y would like to learn more about the attitudes and job satisfaction of the personnel, especially those at the lower ranks. As a result, the human resources department is in the process of constructing an attitude survey that will be given to everyone at the supervisory level or below. Based on the results, the firm will then decide on a course of action.

1. In gathering information on employee attitudes, would it be useful to conduct an attitude survey? Would this provide the firm with the desired feedback?
2. If management were to increase salaries and benefits, might the workers still suffer dissonance? Why or why not?
3. Would it be possible for management to measure job satisfaction in any way other than with a questionnaire?
4. If worker satisfaction increases, will productivity also increase? Explain.

Write down your answers to these questions and put them aside. We will return to them later.

ATTITUDES

Attitudes are a person's feelings about objects, events, or other people.

In the previous chapter, two important components of individual behavior were examined: personality and perception. A third major component is attitudes. **Attitudes** are a person's relatively enduring disposition toward people, objects, events, or activities. These feelings can be either positive or negative, are typically learned over a period of time, and may change.[1]

Although the terms *attitudes* and *opinions* are often used interchangeably, they differ slightly in meaning. Opinions are expressions of attitudes, are more susceptible to change than attitudes, and generally are of shorter duration. For example, John's opinion that Sue is an ineffective manager may be an expression of an antifemale attitude, an antimanagement attitude, or an attitude of dissatisfaction with Sue as a manager. The opinion may change, but not as quickly as the attitude ("Sue is effective, but other female managers are not").

Components of Attitudes

Attitudes are multidimensional because they manifest the simultaneous operation of several factors. The factors most researchers agree on are the affective, cognitive, and conative components of attitudes.

There are three components of attitudes.

Affective Component. The **affective component** is the emotional response triggered by the object of the attitude. It typically refers to whether we like or dislike, are happy or sad about, love or hate the attitude object.

Cognitive Component. The **cognitive component** refers to the beliefs a person has about the object or event. These beliefs are developed from thought, knowledge, observation, and the logical interrelationship among them. A person may believe that accountants are narrow-minded, their boss is spiteful, or that their colleagues are smart. These beliefs may be, in reality, accurate or inaccurate; to this individual, however, they are accurate, having been developed through a learning process. It makes no difference that the data sources are unverified; the person is convinced!

Conative Component. The **conative component** is the behavioral disposition a person exhibits toward an attitude object. Some psychologists believe that a certain attitude will lead to predictable behavior.[2] Thus they hold that if you have a very positive attitude toward your organizational behavior class, you are likely to attend class regularly, keep up with your reading, and do a good job on your assignments.

However, it would be premature to conclude that attitudes determine behavior. This hypothesis has not been adequately demonstrated, and in fact, there is evidence that behavior may give rise to attitudes, or at least to changes in attitudes. Lieberman studied and noted the attitudes of a group of workers and found that some of them joined the ranks of management by becoming foremen.[3] Their attitudes were then resurveyed and found to be more like those of management. Other workers became union officials, and their attitudes changed from those of the original group of workers and became more like those of other union officials. In these cases, the individuals' attitudes changed to become consistent with the work each did. Other researchers have reached similar conclusions. For example, Fishbein reports that

> after more than seventy-five years of attitude research, there is little, if any, consistent evidence supporting the hypothesis that knowledge of an individual's attitude toward some object will allow one to predict the way he will behave with respect to the object. Indeed, what little evidence there is to support any relationship between attitude and behavior, comes from studies showing that a person tends to bring his attitudes into line with his behavior rather than from studies demonstrating that behavior is a function of attitude.[4]

Since considerable doubt exists about the specific relationship between attitudes and behavior, a manager must exercise caution in making assumptions that relate worker performance to a particular set of attitudes.

Attitudes combine feelings, thoughts, and actions.

Attitudes are often thought of as a combination of feelings (affective), thoughts (cognitive), and actions (conative). Usually, the three components tie together.[5] For example, liking something, believing it to be useful, and working to promote it would seem to go together, as would disliking something, believing it harmful, and working against it. Nonetheless, many times when we compare people's feelings, beliefs, and stated intentions with what they actually do, we find startling inconsistencies. In short, attitudes and actions sometimes conflict.[6]

Several studies illustrate this inconsistency. For example, Campbell has reported that although institutionalized religions foster strong beliefs about right and wrong, these beliefs seem to have little effect on the morality of a churchgoer's actual behavior.[7] Meanwhile, Kothandapani found that people's feelings and beliefs about the morality of birth control did not provide very good predictors of actual use of contraceptives.[8]

Attitudes and Organizational Behavior

We mentioned earlier the difficulty in drawing conclusions about the relationship between a person's attitudes and his or her behavior.[9] Yet we similarly observed many instances in which attitudes seem to have a profound influence on how people behave in organizations.[10] For example, research shows a negative relationship between organizational commitment and both absenteeism and turnover.[11] Comments like "If he only had a better attitude, he would be more effective" or "Her positive attitude makes it easy to work with her" reflect this belief. In addition, there is such strong interest in knowing how people feel in various organizational situations that it is reasonable to discuss two major issues related to this interest: (a) how can attitudes be measured? and (b) if we do not like what we find after measurement, how can we change attitudes to make them more constructive?

Measuring Attitudes.   The desire of people to understand attitudes and the role they play in organizational behavior has led to frequent attempts to measure them. Although it is difficult to quantify and still capture the dynamics of a group's attitudes about something, a number of inventories and scales have been developed for this purpose.

The method most often used in industry is an attitude survey similar to that illustrated in Figure 4–1. Such surveys usually employ an attitude questionnaire in which the employee is asked to indicate feelings toward a variety of job-related areas.[12] Examples include current pay, promotion opportunities, relations with supervisors, and relations with co-workers.[13] The results of such questionnaires are usually averaged

---

INSTRUCTION: This survey is designed to obtain job-related information from all salaried employees. All responses will remain *confidential*. What we are interested in are your attitudes and opinions regarding your job and working conditions here at the XYZ company. The value of this survey will depend on how accurately your answers reflect the way you feel. We would like to make XYZ the best company in the industry, but we need your help in doing so. Please complete all parts of the survey. Then fold up the questionnaire so that the Human Resource Department's address is on the outside, remove the protective tape, use the flap to seal the survey, and then drop it in the nearest suggestion box. These boxes are located near the elevators on every floor. THANK YOU FOR YOUR COOPERATION.

PART I: SALARY AND FRINGE BENEFITS

The statements below are related to salary and fringe benefits here at XYZ. Read each statement carefully and then circle the response number that best describes how you feel about the statement. Use the following scale:

1	Strongly Disagree
2	Disagree
3	Undecided
4	Agree
5	Strongly Agree

	Strongly Disagree	Disagree	Undecided	Agree	Strongly Agree
My salary is at about the right level for the type of work I do..................	1	2	3	4	5
People who do the same basic job as I do receive about the same pay.........	1	2	3	4	5
Most people in this firm get paid at least what they deserve...............	1	2	3	4	5
My pay allows me to keep up with the cost of living.........................	1	2	3	4	5
I understand the way in which my salary is determined....................	1	2	3	4	5
Overall, I am satisfied with the salary I receive............................	1	2	3	4	5
I am fully aware of the fringe benefit package at XYZ......................	1	2	3	4	5
The fringe benefit package provides very good coverage....................	1	2	3	4	5
Overall, I am satisfied with the fringe benefit package	1	2	3	4	5

FIGURE 4–1
An Example of an Attitude Survey Questionnaire (Partial Form)

over a number of employees to obtain an aggregate measure of group or departmental attitude.

As measures of job satisfaction, attitude surveys can be useful tools. Extreme caution must be exercised, however, since a survey that is not properly designed can easily give misleading or distorted information. The construction of individual survey items and the administration of the survey itself are matters best left to professionals who have been trained in survey research. Even if the test itself is well designed, the way the survey is conducted can lead to dysfunctional results, especially if the purpose of the survey is not made clear or if respondents fear reprisals from those who see the results.

Another method used to collect information about attitudes is the interview. Attitudes can be elicited from employees through guided questions that probe for feelings about work situations. Although the potential for more robust responses exists in interviewing, employees frequently resist exposing their negative feelings if they themselves can be easily identified. For this reason, interviewers should be from outside the organization. In addition, several companies require exit interviews for all employees leaving the organization in order to gather information about attitudes toward the work, workplace, and management.

Surveys and interviews can be used to measure attitudes.

Review your answers to Question 1 and make any changes you would like before continuing.

1. In gathering information on employee attitudes, would it be useful to conduct an attitude survey? Would this provide the firm with the desired feedback?

It would indeed be useful to employ an attitude survey. This instrument should provide management with some important insights regarding how the workers feel about such things as salary and fringe benefits. It might also give management information regarding other important areas such as salary equity, promotion opportunities, and leadership behaviors that could help identify and address areas that are causing negative attitudes.

Changing Attitudes. If a manager believes that the attitudes of certain workers hamper their effectiveness, he or she may attempt to change those attitudes (see "Organizational Behavior in Action: It Can Be a Matter of Attitude"). There are many ways to affect attitude changes, including persuasion and consistency theory. While examining them, however, we note that attitudes result from a variety of influences, both positive and negative. Changing attitudes essentially involves shifting the balance of these influences so that the individual can take on new attitudes.

Persuasion. One way to change attitudes is through the use of persuasion. For the persuasive process to succeed there must be: (a) willingness on the part of the attitude holder to change; (b) trust in the persuasive message or its source; and (c)

Organizational
Behavior
In Action

IT CAN BE A MATTER OF ATTITUDE

How important is attitude to success? Dennis Conner, the only man to win the America's Cup three times (and the only one to ever lose it) has referred to attitude as one of the five most important elements in winning. According to him, a positive attitude can be developed by following five simple steps.

First, a commitment must be made. The individual has to decide that he or she wants to attain a particular goal. Once this has been done, many other decisions will fall into line.

Second, the individual has to see himself or herself winning the race or attaining the objective. This self-image has to be strong, positive, confident, and optimistic before the person ever gets started. Then as progress is made toward the objective, the individual's confidence will begin to grow even more.

Third, progress has to be made in an incremental way. Each day the person has to move closer to the main goal. Then, after weeks or months of progress, the individual can compare where he or she was initially and where he or she is now.

Fourth, the individual has to eliminate all excuses for losing. For example, if the person does not have the necessary equipment to accomplish the objective, this material must be purchased. If the person has not trained sufficiently, a more rigorous training schedule has to be formulated. In short, all reasons that can result in losing have to be eliminated. Once this is done, attention can be focused on winning.

Fifth, and finally, the individual has to be willing to come back from any failure. When Dennis Conner lost the America's Cup in 1983, that was the first defeat for a country that had held the cup for 132 years. Commenting on this event, Conner noted, "But losing the '83 Cup taught me some of the greatest lessons I've learned—how to put together a design team, raise money, manage people more efficiently, keep closer watch over the competition, and motivate people to participate in a great campaign. Defeat tastes awful, but you must find the upside, consider a change of tactics, give yourself a reality check, and plan your comeback." In the final analysis, attitude plays a major role.

Source: Dennis Conner and Edward Claflin, "The Art of Winning," *Success*, January-February 1989, p. 74.

a strong, convincing message.[14] If employees are not willing to listen, change attempts will be difficult. Similarly, if employees do not trust the manager or if the message itself is not convincing, there will be no disposition to change.

With regard to the foregoing points it is important to realize that the more significant the communicator is, the more validity listeners will attribute to the message and the more likely a change of attitude is. A manager with high prestige is likely to be more effective in getting employees to change than a manager with little prestige.

Persuasion depends in part on prestige and likability.

Also important is whether the manager is well liked. People tend to identify with people they like, and this can lead to changes in attitudes. For example, if you believe smoking marijuana is terrible but your friend says it is great, an inconsistency is created.

One way of creating consistency is to change your attitude about smoking marijuana and agree with your friend. In contrast, if someone you dislike has an attitude different from yours, there is no imbalance and no pressure to change your attitude.

Individuals are also more readily influenced by people who are similar to them than by people who are different. This is partly because of the tendency to like people who are similar to you, and vice versa. Groups with whom people identify also exert pressure to conform to commonly shared attitudes through supporting those that hold them.

Of course, a highly trusted and prestigious source would have little hope of affecting attitude change if the message that source delivers is weak or was presented in an unconvincing manner. Both the strength and the logic of the message, as well as the form in which it is transmitted, are important. The more the message varies from what the attitude holder believes, the less likely it is that change will occur. Business firms spend great sums of money on advertising in order to present logical arguments through mass media (television, radio, magazines, and the like) in the hope of developing favorable consumer attitudes toward products or services.

Finally, a caution: Even if the manager is trusted and well liked and presents a strong message in an influential way, there is no guarantee that attitude change will occur. This is because the strength of the affective component of an attitude is also important. A worker who refuses a transfer because of a commitment to a particular geographic region may be unmoved by attempts to persuade him or her to relocate. Especially when attitudes have been expressed publicly, it is more difficult to change because of the show of commitment and reluctance to admit a mistake. This may also help explain why research reveals that male MBA students continue to hold more negative attitudes toward women executives than do female MBAs. Apparently the education process is ineffective in persuading male MBAs to change their attitude. Commenting on the results of an eight-year research effort, Dubno reports:

> This longitudinal study of male and female MBA students' attitudes toward women executives has shown that a wide discrepancy exists between these two groups. Men are much more negative toward women executives than are women. Furthermore, over an eight year period, the data collected showed no discernible trends in either a positive or a negative direction. Apparently, men and women are polarized in their attitudes regarding women executives, and tended to remain so during the past decade. Because a large proportion of the MBA sample members are expected to enter business organizations as managers, women executives may expect to continue to suffer from discrimination and stereotyping for some time to come.[15]

People strive to see the world as orderly and consistent.

Consistency Theory. Another set of ideas about how attitudes change is provided by consistency theory. **Consistency theory** is based on the notion that people strive to see the world as orderly and consistent, and they adjust their attitudes to maintain this consistency. Although there are many consistency theories, we will confine our discussion to the most prominent, Festinger's theory of cognitive dissonance.[16]

The theory of **cognitive dissonance** is based on the idea that people seem to need to maintain consistency among their attitudes, opinions, beliefs, knowledge, and values, and there is a limit to the amount of inconsistency people can tolerate. When one of our cognitions (ideas, thoughts, knowledge) follows from or is implied by another ("good work performance leads to promotion"), we refer to this relation as consonance. However, if one of our ideas follows from or is implied by an opposite idea, we experience dissonance. Table 4–1 presents examples of consonant and dissonant ideas.

Cognitive dissonance is generally found to be more intense when any of the following conditions exist:

1. The decision is an important one psychologically or financially.
2. There are a number of foregone alternatives.
3. The foregone alternatives have many favorable features.[17]

For example, a manager may be given his first major hiring responsibility and proceeds to recruit a person for a new position. The decision is psychologically important because the choice may have a significant effect on how this manager handles additional responsibility, or it may be important for his or her reputation. It may also be important financially, to both the organization and the manager, if the cost of a poor decision is considered. Now, assume that the labor market is such that there are a number of attractive candidates for the job. No matter whom the manager selects, it is likely he or she will experience some dissonance after making the decision.

Typically, the manager will attempt to reduce this dissonance. Four methods are most often used for this purpose:

1. The individual seeks information that confirms the wisdom of the decision.
2. The individual selectively perceives (distorts) information in a way that supports the decision.

TABLE 4–1
Consonant and Dissonant Relationships

Case	Basic Cognition	Consonant Cognition	Dissonant Cognition
1. Logically consistent or inconsistent	If one pencil costs 5¢, a dozen pencils will cost 60¢.	The college bookstore wants 60¢ for a dozen nickel pencils.	The college bookstore wants 98¢ for a dozen nickel pencils.
2. Consistent or inconsistent with social mores	According to the campus honor code, thou shalt tell the truth, and nothing but the truth.	I told the instructor frankly that I didn't take her exam because I wasn't prepared for it.	I told the instructor that I didn't take her exam because my grandmother died—but I didn't mention that it happened on October 3, 1981.
3. Consistent or inconsistent with encompassing rules or principles	The less you eat, the more weight you lose.	I cut out bread, beer, potatoes, pie, and butter and lost 20 pounds.	I cut out bread, beer, potatoes, pie, and butter and still gained weight.
4. Consistent or inconsistent with past experiences	I've found exchange students from Samaria to be selfish and inconsiderate.	At the conference some Samarian students parked their cars in such a way that I couldn't get mine out of the lot.	After the conference some Samarian students gave my car a push after the battery went dead.

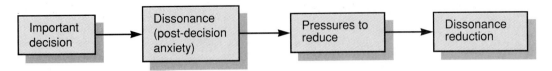

FIGURE 4–2
Sequence of Events in Postdecision Dissonance Reduction

3. The person adopts a less favorable attitude toward the foregone alternatives.

4. The person downplays the importance of any negative aspects of the choice and magnifies the positive elements.[18]

If dissonance exists, people are motivated to reduce it.

In the example given, dissonance may be reduced by gathering additional information that indicates that the person selected really did have the best track record or by disregarding one negative letter of recommendation. Other ways to reduce the dissonance would be to choose to believe that the other candidates were not really that good or to decide that the selected candidate's two successful years of experience were much more significant than that person's five years of mediocre results.

The process of cognitive dissonance reduction is illustrated in Figure 4–2. The magnitude of a person's experienced dissonance is directly related to the pressure the person feels to reduce it. In turn, this dissonance reduction leads to attitude change.

Review your answers to Question 2 and make any changes you would like before continuing.

2. If management were to increase salaries and benefits, might the workers still suffer dissonance? Why or why not?

The workers might suffer dissonance because they would wonder what management was up to. Is the company attempting to manipulate them by suddenly offering better wages and benefits? Would they be better off looking for a job with another company? Or is the firm sincere in its efforts to reduce turnover, and is this an example of the steps they are willing to take to ensure that workers remain with the company? Until these questions are answered, dissonance might be a problem.

JOB SATISFACTION

Employee attitudes are related to job satisfaction, and if workers are satisfied with their jobs they are more likely to remain with the organization than if they are not. For this reason, job satisfaction is an important consideration in the study of organizational behavior.

Nature of Job Satisfaction

Job satisfaction has been described in a number of ways. Locke sees it as "a pleasurable or positive emotional state resulting from the appraisal of one's job or job experience."[19] Luthans sees it as "a result of employees' perception of how well their job provides those things that are viewed as important."[20] This undoubtedly helps explain why job satisfaction is the most important and frequently studied attitude.[21]

Job satisfaction is an emotional response to a job situation.

Job satisfaction is an emotional response to a job situation. It is typically influenced by how well outcomes meet or exceed personal expectations. For example, a group of employees that work hard and are given a 10 percent salary increase are more likely to have high job satisfaction than another group that has higher output but is given only a 5 percent raise.

Job satisfaction represents several related attitudes. Smith and her associates have suggested that there are five job dimensions that represent the most important job characteristics about which people have affective responses. These include: pay, promotion opportunities, supervisors, coworkers, and the work itself.[22] More recently, Glisson and Durick have found that job satisfaction is most influenced by role clarity and variety of skills required by the job, while leadership, employee education, and age of the organization affect employee commitment.[23] Overall, three groups of factors influence job satisfaction: organizational, group, and personal. Figure 4–3 illustrates this.

Job satisfaction is influenced by organizational, group, and personal factors.

Organizational factors relate to the job and its surrounding environment and include such things as pay, promotion, working conditions, and the work itself. Group

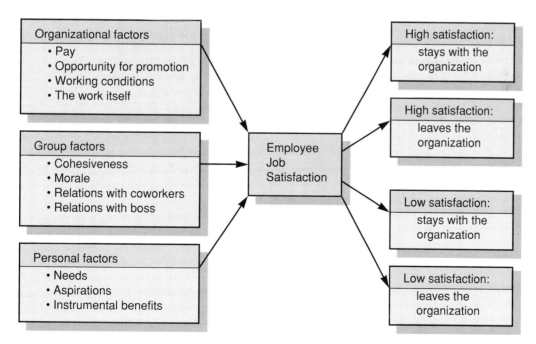

FIGURE 4–3
Causes and Outcomes of Job Satisfaction

factors relate to the cohesiveness and morale that exists in the group as well as the individual's relations with coworkers and the boss. Personal factors relate to the individual's needs, future aspirations such as a desire for promotion, and instrumental benefits such as the extent to which the current job provides the person with the experience and training necessary to secure a more desirable job. In turn, satisfaction may be high or low and can result in the individual remaining with the organization or leaving. Notice from Figure 4–3 that not everyone who is satisfied with his or her job will remain with the organization, and not everyone who is dissatisfied will leave. However, it is likely that those who are satisfied will stay and those who are not will look for employment elsewhere.

Measurement of Job Satisfaction

There are a variety of ways to measure job satisfaction. Some of the most common include rating scales, critical incidents, interviews, and action tendencies.

Rating Scales.   The most frequently used approach in measuring job satisfaction is the use of rating scales. Figure 4–1 is one illustration. Another is provided in Figure 4–4, which provides sample items from the Minnesota Satisfaction Questionnaire. This instrument is designed to provide feedback on specific examples of employee satisfaction and dissatisfaction.

> **Rating scales are a common method of measuring job satisfaction.**

Rating scales provide a number of advantages in measuring job satisfaction. One is that they are typically short and can be filled out quickly and easily. A second is that they are often constructed in general language, so that the instrument used with the workers in the manufacturing area can also be used in measuring job satisfaction among accounting employees. A third is that the data can be quantified by giving a score of five, for example, for a response of very satisfied on down to a score of one for a response of very dissatisfied. This quantification allows comparisons to be made between departments and units as well as on a time basis, such as this year's responses compared to last year's responses. On the other hand, there are some disadvantages associated with rating scales. One is the assumption that everyone is going to be honest and forthright when filling out the instrument. A second is whether the questions really do measure job satisfaction (the instrument is valid) and whether the questionnaire items do so consistently (the instrument is reliable).

> **Critical incidents can provide specific job-related information.**

Critical Incidents.   Critical incidents are another common method of assessing job satisfaction. In this process, the employees are asked to focus on some situation or incident that is related to job satisfaction, such as asking individuals to relate what they particularly like or dislike about their jobs. This provides specific job-related information that can be content analyzed to identify factors that are causing or preventing job satisfaction. One of the primary benefits of this approach is that the respondents can say anything they like; their choices are not restricted as they are in the case of rating scales. On the other hand, this approach is time consuming, and there is always the likelihood of bias on the part of the respondents. For example, when individuals are asked to relate what they like about their job, there tends to be a bias toward making comments that are internally focused such as: I like the chance to succeed. I enjoy the opportunity to use my skills. I like the chance to use my

Ask yourself: How satisfied am I with this aspect of my job?
VS means I am very satisfied with this aspect of my job.
S means I am satisfied with this aspect of my job.
N means I can't decide whether I am satisfied or not with this aspect of my job.
DS means I am dissatisfied with this aspect of my job.
VDS means I am very dissatisfied with this aspect of my job.

On my present job, this is how I feel about:	VDS	DS	N	S	VS
1. Being able to keep busy all the time	☐	☐	☐	☐	☐
2. The chance to work alone on the job	☐	☐	☐	☐	☐
3. The chance to do different things from time to time	☐	☐	☐	☐	☐
4. The chance to be "somebody" in the community	☐	☐	☐	☐	☐
5. The way my boss handles his men	☐	☐	☐	☐	☐
6. The competence of my supervisor in making decisions	☐	☐	☐	☐	☐
7. Being able to do things that don't go against my conscience	☐	☐	☐	☐	☐
8. The way my job provides for steady employment	☐	☐	☐	☐	☐
9. The chance to do things for other people	☐	☐	☐	☐	☐
10. The chance to tell people what to do	☐	☐	☐	☐	☐
11. The chance to do something that makes use of my abilities	☐	☐	☐	☐	☐
12. The way company policies are put into practice	☐	☐	☐	☐	☐
13. My pay and the amount of work I do	☐	☐	☐	☐	☐
14. The chances for advancement on this job	☐	☐	☐	☐	☐
15. The freedom to use my own judgment	☐	☐	☐	☐	☐
16. The chance to try my own methods of doing the job	☐	☐	☐	☐	☐
17. The working conditions	☐	☐	☐	☐	☐
18. The way my co-workers get along with each other	☐	☐	☐	☐	☐
19. The praise I get for doing a good job	☐	☐	☐	☐	☐
20. The feeling of accomplishment I get from the job	☐	☐	☐	☐	☐

FIGURE 4–4

Sample Items from the Minnesota Satisfaction Questionnaire (Source: *Manual for the Minnesota Satisfaction Questionnaire*. Used by permission of the Industrial Relations Center, University of Minnesota).

creative abilities. Conversely, when asked what they dislike about their jobs, most people are externally focused and make comments such as: The salary is too low. The boss does not provide sufficient direction and assistance. The working conditions are poor. People tend to like those things over which they have control and tend to dislike those things that are environmentally related and over which they have little, if any, control. As a result, the responses are often biased.

Interviews are another means of measuring job satisfaction.

Interviews.   Interviews are more open-ended than critical incidents and allow the individual wider latitude of response. Another benefit is that the interviewer has the opportunity to ask questions and obtain more information about comments that are unclear or need further explanation. One of the biggest drawbacks, however, is that the process is time consuming. Another shortcoming is that the interviewer may be biased in interpreting the results, either because the individual misunderstands the gist of the comments or has preconceived ideas of what the respondents will say and fits their comments into this predetermined conclusion.

Action tendencies are the inclinations to approach or to avoid certain things.

Action Tendencies.   **Action tendencies** are "the inclinations people have to approach or to avoid certain things."[24] Examples include how anxious people are to go to work in the morning, whether they would choose the same career if they were starting over, and whether they would recommend their current job to a friend who had similar interests and education. By gathering information about how workers feel with regard to their jobs, job satisfaction can be measured. However, this approach does have a number of shortcomings. One is that respondents may lack self-insight and thus give erroneous answers. A second is that because the approach allows for a wide variety of responses, the approach can be time consuming.

Review your answers to Question 3 and make any changes you would like before continuing.

3. Would it be possible for management to measure job satisfaction in any way other than with a questionnaire?

There are a number of ways in which job satisfaction could be measured, although questionnaires are certainly the most frequently used. Other methods include critical incidents, interviews, and action tendencies. Of the latter, interviews are the most popular. However, depending on the situation, any one of the three could be useful to management, and some firms rely on these as methods of supplementing information that is gathered through job satisfaction questionnaires.

Employee Satisfaction

How satisfied are employees with their jobs? The answer will depend on the individual, because research has uncovered two important facts about job satisfaction. First, under certain working conditions some people will be satisfied while others are not, and it is possible that nothing management does will create high job satisfaction among the latter. This is illustrated in Figure 4–5 where job satisfaction and the work environment are examined. Notice that under unfavorable working conditions all four people were dissatisfied with their jobs. However, as the favorableness of the work environment increased, the job satisfaction of individuals 1 and 2 increased sharply while individuals 3 and 4 had only minor increases in satisfaction. This figure illustrates the accuracy of the cliche, "You can't make everyone happy." Management must realize that the larger the organization, the more likely it is that some of the personnel will be dissatisfied.

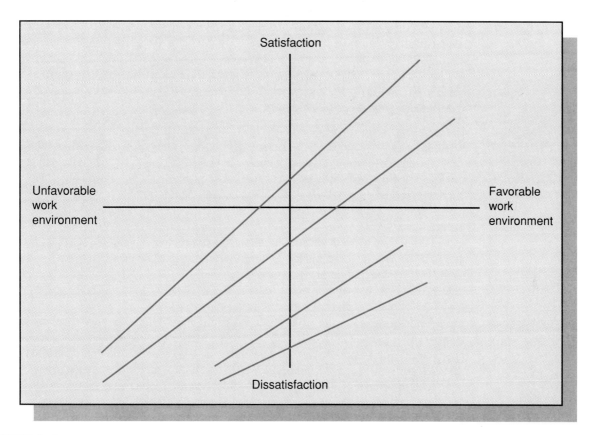

FIGURE 4—5
The Work Environment and Job Satisfaction: Some Possible Relationships

Second, job satisfaction often varies, depending on age, sex, or hierarchical level. For example, young workers, women, or those at the lower ranks of the hierarchy often have different levels of job satisfaction than older workers, men, or those at higher hierarchical levels.

Older workers are usually more satisfied with their jobs than are younger workers.

Age. Research shows that younger workers tend to be less satisfied with their jobs than are older workers. A number of reasons have been found for this. One is that younger employees often enter the work place with high expectations and become dissatisfied when their aspirations are not fulfilled. This is particularly true among college graduates who find that jobs are often boring and undemanding. A second reason is the lack of control that young employees are given over their work. A third is the lack of authority they have for decision making.

Women are less satisfied with their jobs than are men.

Sex. Women also report greater job dissatisfaction than men. Some of the major reasons include low pay, limited promotion opportunities, and sexual harassment. Women also report that many managements do a poor job of running their organizations. Some of the specific areas that are criticized include the ability to (a) set goals; (b) eliminate red tape; (c) make employees feel important; (d) assign reasonable work loads; and (e) provide feedback on job performance.[25] Of 7,800 women polled by *Working Woman,* over 60 percent of those looking for another job mentioned these five reasons. Simply put, if management wants to improve job attitudes among female employees, it is going to have to change the way things are being done and create a climate that provides greater psychological satisfaction and more feedback on work performance.

Hierarchical Level. Research reveals that many blue-collar workers are dissatisfied with their jobs. One reason is because they see themselves as falling economically farther and farther behind. Moreover, a blue-collar cycle is beginning to emerge, with the children of blue-collar workers also becoming blue-collar employees. The upward job mobility of earlier generations, characterized by blue-collar parents and white-collar children, is starting to diminish. Perhaps most disheartening of all, blue-collar workers today are better educated than ever, with half of their ranks filled with high school graduates in comparison to 25 percent in 1960. In short, the educational level is increasing but the opportunities for higher-level, better-paying jobs are not increasing. During the 1980s blue-collar purchasing power declined and, if this trend continues, it is likely that job satisfaction at the lower ranks will continue to remain low during the 1990s.

Job satisfaction is higher among white-collar than blue-collar workers.

Job satisfaction in the managerial and white-collar ranks is higher than among the blue-collar ranks, but even here there has been a decline. One of the major reasons has been massive organizational layoffs and cutbacks at the middle and upper-middle ranks. As firms such as IBM, USX, and AT&T trimmed their work forces, individuals who had been with the company for decades suddenly found their jobs being eliminated and their careers terminated. Many of them, now in their mid- to late-40s or early 50s, found that their age and experience worked against them. Some companies were unwilling to hire them because there were looking for younger people (even though such actions are clearly a violation of Age Discrimination in Employment Act) while other firms turned them down because their experience made them a threat to some of the current personnel. On the other hand, research shows that middle and upper-middle managers who have been laid off often find new, better jobs. *Fortune* reports that while 80 percent of the managers they surveyed took over three months to find employment, 45 percent of them landed jobs with higher salaries, and only 35 percent had to settle for less than their previous job pay.[26]

Common Causes of Job Satisfaction

There are a number of factors that influence job satisfaction.

What are the specific influences on job satisfaction? What result can be expected from such satisfaction? These are two of the most commonly asked questions about job satisfaction. The following provides answers to each by noting that a number of factors influence job satisfaction. These tend to be related to rewards, the work itself, supervision, the work group, and working conditions.

Pay and Benefits. Pay and benefits are one of the major causes of job satisfaction. Individuals who feel that they are underpaid are likely to be dissatisfied with their jobs, and those who feel they are being paid equitably tend to be satisfied (or at least not as dissatisfied). Employees use pay and benefits to gauge how well they are doing, and they compare what they are getting to what competitors are paying for similar work. They also compare their financial rewards to others who are doing similar work in their own company as a way of determining whether they are being paid equitably. For example, employees who feel that they are doing more work than others in their group but are not being paid more are likely to be dissatisfied.

Promotions. Promotions can be based on a number of factors. Two of the most common are seniority and merit. In an organization where longevity is critical to promotion, individuals expect to be promoted when it is "their turn." If management fails to do this, job satisfaction is likely to suffer. More important to satisfaction is promotion based on merit. If individuals with superior production records are passed over for promotion in favor of those with poorer records, job satisfaction among the former group is likely to suffer. Moreover, the final outcome is often that these individuals will leave the firm, and management will find that it must make up their output by relying more heavily on individuals who are not as effective or productive. So promotions not only help build and maintain job satisfaction, they help the firm develop a cadre of qualified personnel.

The Job. There are a number of job-related factors that help increase job satisfaction. One of these is **skill variety** or the degree to which the job allows the worker to use a number of different abilities or talents in carrying out tasks. A second is the amount of interest and challenge provided by the work. Individuals tend to be more satisfied with jobs that tap their talent than those that are boring and routine. A third is the lack of role ambiguity. The more clearly an individual understands what he or she is supposed to be doing and how the job is to be performed, the greater the likelihood of high job satisfaction.[27]

Leadership. The way in which the boss leads subordinates will influence their job satisfaction. There are two approaches, typically complementary, that managers use in leading their people. One is an emphasis on the work to be done. The other is an emphasis on the people who are doing the work. The first is task-centered and takes such forms as ensuring that the personnel have the equipment and the materials needed to do the work and are given any guidance necessary in performing these chores. This includes technical instructions, advice, and feedback on performance. The second is people-centered and takes such forms as communicating with the people regarding what is going on, getting feedback from them about problems they are having doing the work, encouraging and praising them for completing tasks correctly and on time, and allowing them to participate in decision making. In regard to the latter, research shows that creation of a participative environment has a positive effect on job satisfaction.[28]

Work Group. The people with whom an individual works will also have an effect on the person's job satisfaction. Cooperative coworkers, for example, are a modest source of satisfaction because of the support and assistance they provide to the individual. However, the effect of good work groups is felt more in their absence than in their presence. Research has not confirmed that this factor is essential to job satisfaction, but if conditions are negative job satisfaction is likely to suffer. So intragroup working relationships and climate tend to be more important in preventing job dissatisfaction than in creating job satisfaction.

Working Conditions.   The physical environment in which people work is similar to that of the work group environment. Research shows that working conditions have a moderate effect on job satisfaction. If people are dissatisfied with the working conditions there is likely to be low job satisfaction, but if they are satisfied with working conditions job satisfaction will not automatically be high. This is because most people expect working conditions to be acceptable, and they are dissatisfied when these conditions are not. Moreover, some researchers have noted that complaints about working conditions are often manifestations of other problems.[29] For example, an individual may have been denied a promotion and upon returning to his office complains that it is difficult to work in a small office that is never properly cleaned. It appears that the individual is dissatisfied with working conditions, but the person is actually upset over not receiving the promotion.

Results of Job Satisfaction

If job satisfaction is high, will employees do more and better work? If it is low, will there be morale problems and high turnover? Surprisingly, the linkage between job satisfaction and outcomes such as productivity, turnover, and absenteeism is not as clear-cut as many people think. The following examines some of these linkages.

Productivity and satisfaction are not positively related.

Satisfaction and Productivity.   Are highly satisfied workers more productive than less satisfied workers? This "satisfaction leads to performance" linkage has been a matter of interest for many years. Certainly the idea has intuitive appeal; it would seem logical that productivity and satisfaction are positively related. However, research shows that this linkage, at best, is relatively low. Iaffaldano and Muchinsky, for example, conducted a meta-analysis of the relation between satisfaction and performance and found that they are only slightly related to each other; i.e., satisfied workers were not necessarily high performers and vice versa. They concluded that:

> Our results indicate, similar to the findings reported by the earlier reviewers published over 20 years ago, that satisfaction and performance are only slightly related to each other. The amount of empirical support for the satisfaction-performance relation does not approximate the degree to which this relation has been espoused in theories of organizational design. It is almost as if the satisfaction-performance relation is itself . . . an illusory correlation, a perceived relation between two variables that we logically or intuitively think should interrelate, but in fact do not.[30]

There is a moderate relationship between satisfaction and employee turnover.

Satisfaction and Turnover.   Research reveals a moderate relationship between satisfaction and employee turnover. Individuals who are satisfied with their jobs are less likely to leave the organization than are those who are dissatisfied.[31] Simply put, high job satisfaction can help reduce turnover, and low job satisfaction will result in increased turnover. This is particularly true among young people who, if they are dissatisfied with their jobs, will seek employment elsewhere.

As job tenure increases, however, the turnover rate tends to decline regardless of job satisfaction. For example, workers with eighteen years on the job may not be as satisfied with their work as they were ten years earlier, but it is unlikely that they will leave. A number of reasons can be cited including: (a) they are close to qualifying for twenty-year retirement; (b) they know their job so well that work demands are minimal; (c) they cannot visualize themselves doing any other kind of work; and (d) at their age it is difficult to find another job with the same benefits and work demands. These reasons help illustrate the linkage between satisfaction and commitment. Some people stay with their organization because they are satisfied; some remain because they are committed to the enterprise; and still others stay because of both satisfaction and commitment.

Earlier it was noted that skill variety and lack of role ambiguity are directly related to job satisfaction. Research shows that leadership, organizational age, and worker education all help account for commitment. Effective leadership helps develop and strengthen employee commitment. Organizational age is important because it helps the worker understand what the enterprise will and will not do and thus provides predictability and assurances regarding the future. Worker education is important because well-educated people are less committed than poorly educated people. One reason may well be that education increases the individual's self-esteem and self-reliance and makes him or her less reliant on the organization for job security or meaningful employment. Given the individual's credentials, the person may feel that he or she can find employment elsewhere should the need arise.[32]

There is an inverse relationship between satisfaction and absenteeism.

Satisfaction and Absenteeism.   Researchers have found a basically inverse relationship between satisfaction and absenteeism. When satisfaction is low, absenteeism tends to be high and vice versa.[33] However, this relationship is not linear. While low satisfaction will bring about high absenteeism, high satisfaction will not guarantee low absenteeism.[34] Additionally, there are moderating variables that will influence this relationship. For example, individuals who believe their work is important are less likely to leave the organization than are those who feel that their jobs are mundane and routine. Similarly, those who have the opportunity to use a variety of skills and whose job objectives are clear are more likely to be satisfied than those who have low skill variety and high role ambiguity. Additionally, workers who like their boss and their work group are more likely to remain with the company than are those who do not like their boss or coworkers.

Job satisfaction can influence mental and physical health.

Other Outcomes.   Job satisfaction also tends to bring about outcomes other than those discussed. One is improved mental and physical health. Individuals who like their jobs and are satisfied with what they are doing tend to have more positive mental attitudes and better health. This, in turn, translates into lower absenteeism and turnover as well as fewer on-the-job accidents and, in the case of union employees, fewer grievances. High job satisfaction can be also be useful in attracting new people. One of the first questions that prospective employees ask is: What type of organization is this? They want to learn whether it is friendly or hostile, whether promotions are based on merit or political clout, and whether people remain with the organization for a long time or there is rapid turnover.

Job satisfaction is an important topic in the study of organizational behavior. However, unlike many areas its importance seems to be tied more to the effects of low satisfaction than high satisfaction. If an organization does not provide a minimum level of job satisfaction, then absenteeism, turnover, productivity, and morale will decline. However, if there is high satisfaction, there is no empirical proof that productivity will reach new heights and stay there while absenteeism and turnover decline markedly and remain low. Rather, the importance of job satisfaction appears to be more clearly revealed by its absence than its presence. This basic idea is also crucial in understanding another important organizational behavior area, motivation, which is the focus of the next chapter.

STOP

Review your answers to Question 4 and make any changes you would like before continuing.

4. If worker satisfaction increases, will productivity also increase? Explain.

Productivity might increase, but it is unlikely to be a direct result of improved work satisfaction. Research has failed to establish a direct linkage between satisfaction and productivity. The company is likely to find that as turnover goes down, productivity goes up. However, this would be a result of the company's ability to retain experienced workers who know how to do their job well. If the firm continues to have high turnover, its productivity will drop or be lower than it should be because many of the new personnel will need time to master their jobs and learn the shortcuts to increased productivity.

SUMMARY

1. Attitudes are a person's feelings about something or someone. They are composed of affective (emotions), cognitive (thoughts), and conative (behaviors) components. Attitudes are usually measured through questionnaires or interviews or both. If the results of attitude evaluation in an organization indicate that change is necessary, there are techniques for bringing about the needed change. Among them are persuasion and the application of consistency theory. Consistency theory is based on the idea that people try to maintain consistency between their attitudes and their perception of the world around them. When inconsistencies develop, people may change their attitudes. Festinger's theory of cognitive dissonance explains one way to expedite the process of change.

2. Job satisfaction is an emotional response to a job situation. There are three groups of factors that influence job satisfaction: organizational, group, and personal.

3. There are a number of ways in which job satisfaction can be measured. Four of the most common are rating scales, critical incidents, interviews, and action tendencies.

4. Job satisfaction often varies depending on age, sex, and hierarchical level. Young workers tend to be less satisfied with their jobs than older workers. Women are more dissatisfied than men. Blue-collar workers are less satisfied than white-collar workers.

5. Some of the specific factors influencing job satisfaction include pay, benefits, promotions, the job, leadership, the work group, and working conditions. Research shows that job satisfaction is only slightly related to productivity. However, there is a moderate relationship between satisfaction and employee turnover and an inverse relationship between satisfaction and absenteeism. Job satisfaction also has an effect on mental and physical health.

KEY TERMS

attitudes	**conative component**	**job satisfaction**
affective component	**consistency theory**	**action tendencies**
cognitive component	**cognitive dissonance**	**skill variety**

REVIEW AND STUDY QUESTIONS

1. What is meant by the term *attitudes*? What are the three components of attitudes? Describe each.

2. How can attitudes be measured? Give an example.

3. How would you suggest trying to change someone's attitudes about his or her work? Explain your answers.

4. What is the attitude of male MBAs regarding female executives? Explain.

5. What is cognitive dissonance? How is such dissonance reduced?

6. In your own words, what is meant by job satisfaction?

7. Job satisfaction relates to three factors: organizational, group, and personal. What is meant by this statement?

8. How can job satisfaction be measured? Identify and describe three ways.

9. What is meant by the statement, "You can't make everyone happy"? How does your answer relate to job satisfaction?

10. How do the following relate to job satisfaction: age, sex, hierarchical level.

11. What are some causes of job satisfaction? Identify and describe four.

12. Are satisfied workers also productive workers?

13. In what way is satisfaction related to turnover? How is it related to absenteeism?

CASES

Bad and Getting Worse

Over the last nine months Jill Wadberg has had to make a number of difficult decisions. One of these involved a cutback in the workforce. Her company's end of the insurance business has seen a dramatic increase in competitiveness, which has brought about lower premium rates and sharply reduced profits. As revenues began to fall off and rates dipped, Jill started cutting back overhead. Her first move was to reduce some of the travel and entertainment budget and to eliminate all new hiring. When things continued to decline, cutbacks were started.

Except among salespeople, every department has seen a 15 to 20 percent reduction in personnel. Jill estimates that it will take about six more months before things turn around, and during that time another 10 percent of the workforce is likely to be laid off. In the interim, her biggest concern is that job attitudes will decline and people will begin doing less work. They will simply reason, "Why should I care what happens around here? I'm going to get laid off shortly, so I might as well take it easy while I'm waiting for the ax to fall."

Jill would like to know the current status of job attitudes in the company. She would also like to learn if job satisfaction is being affected by the cutbacks or if the personnel understand that these measures are necessary to save the firm. Jill also wants to find out which departments are most affected in terms of satisfaction. Here is how she explained it to the head of the human resources department.

> We're going through some pretty rough times, and things are likely to continue this way for at least another six to nine months. The worst thing that can happen to us now is to learn that people are dissatisfied with their work situation and are starting to give up. I want to find out the current state of job attitudes and see if we can work to keep everyone's morale high. I know this isn't going to be easy, but it's an important step. I want you to determine how to measure current job attitudes and then report back to me with this information. Then I'll decide what should be done next.

1. How can job satisfaction be measured? What methods might be used? Identify and describe two.

2. If the human resources manager tells the president, "Job attitudes are declining," what does this mean? What conclusions can Jill draw from this information?

3. If job satisfaction is declining, is productivity also going down? Defend your answer.

Dick's Game Plan

When Dick Elling took over the helm at Skyway Shipping, the company was just coming out of a major recession. During this period, one-third of the personnel had been laid off and salaries had been frozen. Fortunately for Dick, the previous chief executive officer had stuck to his guns and kept spending money for training, developing, new equipment, and maintenance. When the turnaround came, Skyway was in an ideal position to get the jump on its competitors.

Over the last four months sales have been increasing at an annual rate of 41 percent. Some of the people who were let go have been rehired, and there are plans to bring back more of them if things continue to improve. In addition, salaries have now been unfrozen and there has been a 9 percent, across-the-board raise. Further salary increases are scheduled over the next ninety days, and if this plan is carried out, Skyway salaries will be the highest in the local area.

Dick believes that one of the most important things right now is to ensure that a sharp downturn does not seriously affect the company's recovery. He has therefore decided not to rehire everyone who was laid off. Only 80 percent of these people will be brought back. The 20 percent with the poorest performance records will be left out. Earlier this week, he explained his reasoning at a meeting of the management team:

This industry is becoming more competitive than ever, and cost control is going to be a major determinant in separating the survivors from the casualties. I need people who can pull their own weight and more. In the past we had too much overhead, and that included individuals who had been with the firm for a long time and had retired on the job. We can't afford the luxury of keeping these people around. From now on, we are going to bear down and get maximum performance from everyone. In turn, I intend to pay the best wages in the industry and make sure that layoffs occur only after I've exhausted all other avenues of cost cutting.

1. If Dick were to conduct a job satisfaction survey, would he find that satisfaction had gone up? Explain.

2. Is productivity at the company likely to rise over the next ninety days? Is job satisfaction likely to play any role in what happens? Why or why not?

3. What is likely to happen to turnover and absenteeism over the next ninety days? Is this related in any way to job satisfaction? Explain.

SELF-FEEDBACK EXERCISE

How Satisfied Are You with Your Job?

Think of your current job or one that you held recently. Then respond to these 20 statements by noting your satisfaction with each. Use the following scale in answering:

    5   Highly accurate
    4   Fairly accurate
    3   Indifferent
    2   Fairly inaccurate
    1   Highly inaccurate

_____ 1. I am being paid fairly.

_____ 2. My boss provides me with a great deal of assistance.

_____ 3. Promotions in this firm are based strictly on performance.

_____ 4. Most of my coworkers are very productive, and this makes things enjoyable.

_____ 5. My work is boring.

_____ 6. I am never praised by my boss no matter how well I do my work.

_____ 7. Most companies have a better benefit package than we do.

_____ 8. My job is challenging.

_____ 9. Promotions are based on merit, and that is the way it should be.

_____ 10. My work is interesting.

_____ 11. My boss knows his job and does it well.

_____ 12. Most of my coworkers are not very competent, and this puts an unfair advantage on the rest of us.

_____ 13. Opportunities for promotion are not very good.

_____ 14. My coworkers are far too slow in getting things done.

_____ 15. The fringe benefits are very good.

_____ 16. I do not really care for my job.

_____ 17. My boss is biased and rewards people based on how well he or she likes them rather than on their ability.

_____ 18. Most people in my work group are good people.

_____ 19. I'm worth a lot more money than I'm getting.

_____ 20. Regrettably, seniority is the only factor in the promotion decision, and I have little seniority.

Place your answers below. In those cases where there is an asterisk (*) next to the number, use reverse scoring by subtracting your answer from 6, i.e., a 2 becomes a 4, and a 5 becomes a 1.

Salary and benefits	Supervision	Opportunity for promotion
1. _____	2. _____	3. _____
*7. _____	*6. _____	9. _____
15. _____	11. _____	*13. _____
*19. _____	*17. _____	*20. _____
Total _____	Total _____	Total _____

Group members	Work itself
4. _____	*5. _____
*12. _____	8. _____
*14. _____	10. _____
18. _____	*16. _____
Total _____	Total _____

Interpretation

For each category, the interpretation of scores is the following:

17–20	You are highly satisfied with this aspect of your job.
13–16	You are moderately satisfied with this aspect of your job.
9–12	You are moderately dissatisfied with this aspect of your job.
8 or less	You are highly dissatisfied with this aspect of your job.

NOTES

1. Charles P. Bird and Terri D. Fisher, "Thirty Years Later: Attitudes Toward the Employment of Older Workers," *Journal of Applied Psychology,* August 1986, pp. 515–517.

2. Martin Fishbein, "Attitude and the Prediction of Behavior," in Martin Fishbein (ed.), *Readings in Attitude Theory and Measurement* (New York: John Wiley & Sons, 1967), p. 477.

3. Seymour Lieberman, "The Effects of Changes in Roles on the Attitudes of Role Occupants," *Human Relations,* April 1966, pp. 385–402.

4. Fishbein, *Readings in Attitude Theory,* p. 47.

5. Martin Fishbein and Icek Aizen, "Attitudes toward Objects as Predictors of Single and Multiple Behavior Criteria," *Psychological Review,* January 1974, pp. 59–74.

6. Albert A. Harrison, *Individuals and Groups* (Monterey, CA: Brooks/Cole, 1976), p. 193.

7. Ernest Q. Campbell, "Adolescent Socialization," in David A. Goslin (ed.), *Handbook of Socialization Theory and Research* (Chicago: Rand McNally & Co., 1969), pp. 851–854.

8. Virupaksha Kothandapani, "Validation of Feeling, Belief, and Intention to Act as Three Components of Attitude and Their Contribution to Prediction of Contraceptive Behavior," *Journal of Personality and Social Psychology,* September 1971, pp. 321–333.

9. Cynthia D. Fisher, "On the Dubious Wisdom of Expecting Job Satisfaction to Correlate with Performance," *Academy of Management Review,* October 1980, pp. 607–612.

10. M. M. Petty, Gail W. McGeen, and Jerry W. Cavender, "A Meta-Analysis of the Relationship Between Individual Job Satisfaction and Individual Performance," *Academy of Management Review,* October 1984, pp. 712–721.

11. James L. Price and Charles W. Meuller, *Handbook of Organizational Measurement* (Marshfield, MA: Pitman Publishing, 1986), pp. 223–227.

12. H. Angle and J. Perry, "Organizational Commitment: Individual and Organizational Influence," *Work and Occupations,* May 1983, pp. 123–146; and J. Pierce and R. B. Dunham, "Organizational Commitment: Pre-Employment Propensity and Initial Work Experiences," *Journal of Management,* Spring 1987, pp. 163–178.

13. See for example L. Reibstein, "A Finger on the Pulse: Companies Expand Use of Employee Surveys," *The Wall Street Journal,* October 27, 1986, p. 27.

14. Jonathan L. Freedman, J. Merrill Carlsmith, and David Sears, *Social Psychology,* 3rd ed. (Englewood Cliffs, NJ: Prentice-Hall, 1978), Chapter 9.

15. Peter Dubno, "Attitudes Toward Women Executives: A Longitudinal Approach," *Academy of Management Journal,* March 1985, p. 238.

16. Leon Festinger, *A Theory of Cognitive Dissonance* (Stanford, CA: Stanford University Press, 1957).

17. *Ibid.,* Chapter 1.

18. W. J. McGuire, "Cognitive Consistency and Attitude Change," *Journal of Abnormal and Social Psychology,* May 1960, pp. 345–353.

19. E. A. Locke, "The Nature and Cause of Job Satisfaction," in M. D. Dunnette (ed.), *Handbook of Industrial and Organizational Psychology* (Chicago: Rand McNally & Co., 1976).

20. Fred Luthans, *Organizational Behavior,* 5th ed. (New York: McGraw-Hill Book Co., 1989), p. 176.

21. Terence R. Mitchell and James R. Larson, Jr., *People in Organizations,* 3rd ed. (New York: McGraw-Hill Book Co., 1987), p. 146.

22. P. C. Smith, L. M. Kendall, and C. L. Hulin, *The Measure of Satisfaction in Work and Retirement* (Chicago: Rand McNally & Co., 1969).

23. Charles Glisson and Mark Durick, "Predictors of Job Satisfaction and Organizational Commitment in Human Service Organizations," *Administrative Science Quarterly,* March 1988, pp. 61–81.

24. Luthans, *Organizational Behavior,* p. 180.

25. Jane Ciabattari, "The Biggest Mistake Top Managers Make," *Working Woman,* October 1986, p. 54.

26. Peter Nulty, "Pushed Out at 45—Now What?" *Fortune,* March 2, 1987, p. 29.

27. Glisson and Durick, p. 74.

28. Katherine I. Miller and Peter Monge, "Participation, Satisfaction, and Productivity: A Meta-Analytic Review," *Academy of Management Journal,* March 1986, p. 748.

29. Luthans, *Organizational Behavior,* p. 186.

30. Michell T. Iaffaldano and Paul M. Muchinsky, "Job Satisfaction and Job Performance: A Meta-Analysis," *Psychological Bulletin,* Volume 97, 1985, p. 270.

31. For more on this see Thomas W. Lee and Richard T. Mowday, "Voluntarily Leaving an Organization: An Empirical Investigation of Steers and Mowday's Model of Turnover," *Academy of Management Journal,* December 1987, pp. 721–743.

32. For more on this see Glisson and Durick, "Predictors of Job Satisfaction."

33. K. Dow Scott and G. Stephen Taylor, "An Examination of Conflicting Findings on the Relationship Between Job Satisfaction and Absenteeism: A Meta-Analysis," *Academy of Management Journal,* September 1985, pp. 599–612.

34. Chris W. Clegg, "Psychology of Employee Lateness, Absence, and Turnover: A Methodological Critique and an Empirical Study," *Journal of Applied Psychology,* February 1983, pp. 88–101.

CHAPTER 5
Learning and Reinforcement Theory

GOALS OF THE CHAPTER

In this chapter we are going to look at another major component of individual behavior: learning. In addition to discussing the relevance of learning to organizational behavior, we are going to examine how, through the use of reinforcement theory, behavioral modification programs can be developed and successfully used in modern organizations.

The first goal of this chapter is to examine how learning takes place. The second objective is to study the various types of learning strategies that can be employed in this process. The third objective is to look at the role of reinforcement schedules. The final objective is to review the successes of some organizations that have developed learning-based programs for retraining and motivating their personnel. When you have finished reading this chapter, you will be able to:

1. discuss how individuals learn;
2. distinguish between classical and operant conditioning;
3. describe how learning intervention strategies work;
4. explain how reinforcement schedules work;
5. describe some of the successes that organizations have had in their use of behavior modification.

OPENING CASE: THEY JUST SEEM TO DO MORE WORK

Over the past six months Jean Conway has noted a dramatic increase in employee tardiness. Although the work day begins at 8:30 A.M., many of the employees were arriving between 8:45 and 8:50 A.M. In an effort to eliminate this growing practice, Jean decided to have a desk placed near the entrance to the department and to spend the first thirty minutes of the day working at this location. This gave her the opportunity to see who came in on time and who was late. She then made it a practice to greet everyone who was on time and exchange a few congenial words with them. However, beginning at 8:31 A.M., she ignored everyone who came in late by pretending to be very busy, although it was obvious to these people that Jean was aware of their tardiness.

Within two weeks of the time she began this practice, Jean noticed that tardiness has dropped sharply. Prior to her moving to the front of the office, approximately 45 percent of the personnel were coming late. At the present time less than 5 percent are late, and Jean is thinking about moving her workplace back to her assigned office for the entire day.

Jean has also started using MBWA (management by walking around) and dropping into people's offices unannounced. If she finds the individuals working hard, she talks to them about what they are doing and often asks questions that indicate a strong interest in their projects. She then urges them to keep up their efforts. If she finds them doing very little, she simply asks them how things are going and then leaves.

Jean makes it a practice to walk through the workplace three days a week, although the specific days vary from week to week. Additionally, she takes between four and six trips a day, although the pattern varies and it is difficult to know when she is coming. In the beginning it seemed that Jean was more likely to walk around during the morning, but just last week she made all of her trips during the afternoon. In any event, no one seems to know for sure when she will be coming around, but everyone is trying very hard to be busy with some project should she suddenly drop by.

Jean believes that her approaches to dealing with tardiness and in encouraging people to do more work are useful. "I feel that my presence is an important motivator in getting people to work longer and harder," she says. "When I'm around people just seem to do more work."

1. What two learning intervention strategies does Jean use? Explain.
2. What type of reinforcement schedule is Jean using in implementing MBWA? Explain.
3. Which of the two critical behaviors would it be most difficult to measure: tardiness or working hard?
4. On what types of jobs might Jean find it easier to use behavior modification? Explain.

Write down your answers to these questions and put them aside. We will return to them later.

LEARNING

Learning is a relatively permanent change in behavior potentiality that results from reinforced practice or experience.[1] This behavioral change can be a result of direct or indirect experience. It can be acquired through such means as reading, observing, or doing. Whether or not a person will actually perform a learned response, however, is determined by the reinforcing consequence (such as a reward or punishment) that follows from the action. Four other facts to remember about the learning process are the following:

Four facts about the learning process are important.

1. Learning involves a change, although not necessarily an improvement, in behavior. For example, prejudices, stereotypes, and poor habits are all learned.

2. A change in behavior must be relatively permanent in order for it to be considered learning. Behavioral changes due to fatigue or temporary adaptations do not qualify as learning.

3. Some form of experience or practice is necessary for learning to occur.

4. Some form of reinforcement is necessary for learning to take place. Without reinforcement, the learned behavior will eventually disappear.

A second fundamental learning principle is that reinforcement given immediately after the performance of an act is more likely to produce repetition of that behavior than reinforcement given at a later time. This is because individuals seem to be better able to associate behavior and reward if the two follow in close sequence. In addition, the person knows that repeat behavior will lead to repeat positive reinforcement, so there is greater motivation to perform the act again.

Not all learning, however, occurs in the same way. Different types of learning acquisition curves are illustrated in Figure 5–1.

Much of what an individual learns can be represented by the curve in Figure 5–1a. At first learning is very pronounced, but as the behavior is perfected, it progresses at a decreasing rate. Finally, a point is reached at which practically no learning occurs and behavior continues in an effective mode. Learning associated with routine jobs often follows this pattern.

There are various types of learning curves.

Some learning, however, is the reverse of the foregoing (Figure 5–1b). The individual starts very slowly and then spurts. These increasing returns do not continue indefinitely, but they do carry the individual to the necessary level of proficiency. People who are being trained to handle difficult or unfamiliar tasks often show very slow progress at first, followed by giant learning strides.

Figure 5–1c is a combination of the first two curves. An individual learning a new job will often start slowly, spurt, and then experience diminishing returns. Many psychologists feel that the S-shaped curve represents the most accurate description of learning.

Figure 5–1d shows that some learning progresses for a time, but then reaches a plateau at which nothing new is learned. This situation commonly occurs with menial or very simple jobs in organizations, and the dead-end nature of this work can be one reason for poor motivation.

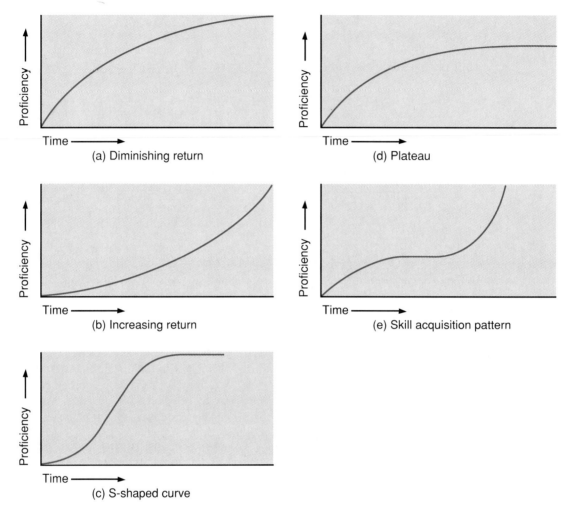

FIGURE 5–1
Learning Curves

Figure 5–1e presents the most complex pattern for learning which is often associated with skill acquisition and combines many of the sequences shown in the other curves. The first three parts of the curve illustrate increasing returns, decreasing returns, and the plateau. Note, however, that learning does not end at that point. The plateau is followed by increased proficiency. There is a breakthrough in learning that allows the individual to further improve his or her performance. In the case of many workers, practice does indeed make perfect.

There are two categories of learning (or conditioning, as it is sometimes called): classical and operant. The following subsections examine each of these.

Classical Conditioning

Classical conditioning deals with stimulus-response learning.

Classical conditioning was discovered by the famous Russian physiologist Ivan Pavlov. While studying the automatic reflexes associated with digestion, he noticed that when a piece of meat was presented to his laboratory dog, the animal salivated. Pavlov called the food an unconditioned stimulus and the salivation an unconditioned response because the relationship between the two was unlearned. Whenever the dog saw the meat, it salivated. On the other hand, when Pavlov rang a bell (neutral stimulus), the dog did not salivate. It perceived no relationship between the ringing of the bell and the presentation of meat.

Pavlov wanted to determine if he could induce the dog to salivate to a learned, or conditioned, stimulus such as the bell. To find out, he began having the bell rung immediately before the food was placed in the dog's mouth. After this had been done several times, the bell was rung but meat was not given to the dog. Nevertheless, the animal salivated. Pavlov had conditioned the dog to respond to a learned stimulus. The formerly neutral stimulus (the bell) was now able to elicit a physiological response (salivation). Pavlov's procedure for conditioning the dog is outlined in Figure 5–2.

Classical conditioning experiments have been very important in supporting stimulus-response (S-R) theories of learning. Nevertheless, classical conditioning is of limited relevance in an organizational context, where complex behaviors of employees that are learned through reinforcers such as money, praise, and recognition are at issue. This type of learning is called operant conditioning.

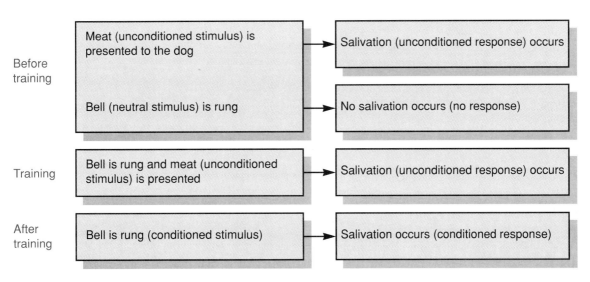

FIGURE 5–2
Pavlov's Classical Conditioning Process

Operant Conditioning

Operant conditioning is learning that occurs as a consequence of behavior. This is quite different from classical conditioning. The major differences between the two are the following:

1. In classical conditioning, a change in the stimulus (unconditioned stimulus to conditioned stimulus) will elicit a particular response. In operant conditioning, one particular response out of many possible ones occurs in a given stimulus situation. The stimulus situation serves as a cue in operant conditioning. It does not elicit a response but serves as a cue for a person to emit a response. The critical aspect of operant conditioning is what happens as a consequence of the response. The strength and frequency of classically conditioned behaviors are mainly determined by the frequency of the eliciting stimulus (the environmental event that precedes the behavior). The strength and frequency of operantly conditioned behaviors are mainly determined by the consequences (the environmental event that follows the behavior).

2. During the classical conditioning process the unconditioned stimulus, serving as a reward, is presented every time. In operant conditioning, the reward will occur only if the organism performs the correct response. The organism must operate on the environment in order to receive a reward. The response is instrumental in obtaining the reward.[2]

Operant conditioning deals with learned behavior.

In general terms, operant conditioning explains much of organizational behavior.[3] A great deal of what an individual learns is a result of reinforcement. For example, a manager who turns in the monthly cost control report early and is praised by the boss is likely to turn in future reports early if he or she finds the praise satisfying. On the other hand, if the manager turns in the report and is reprimanded for not waiting and submitting it as scheduled, he or she is unlikely to turn in future reports early. Additionally, feedback should be immediate and specific.[4]

If the manager wants the subordinate to continue giving a particular response, some form of positive reinforcement must be accorded the person. Conversely, if the manager wants to stop the subordinate from doing something, a strategy designed to extinguish the behavior must be devised. These approaches are sometimes called learning intervention strategies. Before examining them, however, an understanding of social learning theory is important.

Social Learning Theory

Social learning theory is an important complement to operant conditioning. **Social learning theory** holds that learning can take place via modeling and self-control processes. This theory extends beyond operant conditioning and provides additional insights into the learning process. Albert Bandura, who is most closely associated with social learning theory, has explained that:

> Although behavior can be shaped into new patterns to some extent by rewarding and punishing consequences, learning would be exceedingly laborious and hazardous if it proceeded solely on this basis. . . . [I]t is difficult to imagine a

socialization process in which the language, mores, vocational activities, familial customs and educational, religious and political practices of a culture are taught to each new member by selective reinforcement of fortuitous behaviors, without benefit of models who exemplify the cultural patterns in their own behavior. Most of the behaviors that people display are learned either deliberately or inadvertently, through the influence of example.[5]

By watching how others act and noting the rewards or penalties that result, an individual can learn how and what to do (or avoid doing). A growing body of literature on this subject suggests that a modeling strategy can be used to improve performance. The strategy would likely include steps such as:

1. Precisely identify the goal or target behavior that will lead to performance improvement.
2. Select the appropriate model and modeling medium (for example, a live demonstration, a training film, or a videotape).
3. Make sure the employee is capable of meeting the technical skill requirements of the target behavior.
4. Structure a favorable learning environment that increases the probability of attention and reproduction and that enhances motivation to learn and improve.
5. Model the target behavior and carry out supporting activities, such as role playing. Clearly demonstrate the positive consequences of the modeled target behavior.
6. Positively reinforce reproduction of the target behavior, both in training and back on the job.
7. Once it is reproduced, maintain and strengthen the target behavior, first with a continuous schedule of reinforcement and later with an intermittent schedule.[6]

Whether behavior is a result of operant conditioning or social learning, one thing is certain: reinforcement is the key to learning.

Learning Intervention Strategies

In order to manage organizational behavior effectively, some knowledge of the effect that consequences have on future responses is necessary. For example, feedback enhances performance,[7] and specific feedback is more important than nonspecific feedback.[8] If the manager rewards someone for high output and the individual strives for high performance in the future, the consequence (reward) has led to desired behavior (continued effort for high performance).

Sometimes, however, the manager may want to reduce or eliminate (extinguish) a given behavior. Tardiness and poor workmanship are illustrations. How do we increase or decrease response frequency? In general, there are four learning intervention strategies that have been found useful for this purpose: (a) positive reinforcement; (b) negative reinforcement; (c) extinction; and (d) punishment. There are also combination strategies.

A positive reinforcer is a reward that strengthens a behavior.

Positive Reinforcement. **Positive reinforcement** uses rewards to strengthen a behavior. With money as an example, the process of positive reinforcement can be

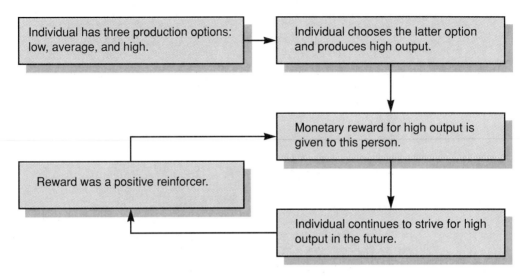

FIGURE 5–3
When a Reward Serves as a Positive Reinforcer

diagrammed as shown in Figure 5–3. Note in the figure that there is a feedback arrow from the behavioral outcome (high future output) to the monetary reward. This indicates that the payoff (sometimes called a contingent consequence) was favorably viewed by the individual. However, not all payoffs or rewards are positive reinforcers. If the company gives individuals with high output two extra days off a year, this may not be regarded as much of a reward. The workers might prefer a monetary reinforcer. If they do, then the days off will not lead to the desired behavioral outcome. (Figure 5–4 illustrates this idea.)

Additionally, in the successful application of reinforcement procedures: (a) the reinforcers that are selected should be sufficiently powerful to maintain the desired response; (b) reinforcement should be contingent upon the desired behavior; and (c) the contingencies should be designed in such a way that the desired responses are elicited. There needs to be a balance between the ease and difficulty of the task and the rewards or payoffs that are given. If something is extremely difficult, it may be necessary to reward the person every time he or she does a task (or subtask) correctly. If something is extremely easy, a more long-run or varied reward pattern may be best in motivating the individual.

A negative reinforcer also strengthens a desired behavior.

Negative Reinforcement. **Negative reinforcement** increases the frequency of a desired behavioral event while bringing about the termination or withdrawal of some aversive condition. For example, students who come to class late and are criticized by the professor (the aversive condition) will often make an effort to get there on time. Salespeople who are continually urged by the vice-president of sales to make more customer calls may do so just to avoid their superior's badgering. In both of these cases, the frequency of the desired behavioral event increases.

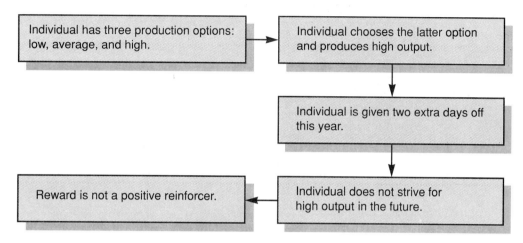

FIGURE 5—4
When a Reward Does Not Serve as a Positive Reinforcer

Extinction can reduce undesirable behavior.

Extinction. **Extinction** is a strategy for eliminating undesirable behavior. Some people have difficulty understanding how extinction can be a behavioral strategy, since it involves doing nothing. However, when we remember that responses must be reinforced if they are to recur, it becomes obvious that if behavior does not result in reinforcement, the person's response rate will decline. Individuals who perform well are often praised by their superiors. If these workers begin to slack off, however, or start turning out shoddy work, the manager may try to modify this undesirable behavior by withholding praise. Note that the person is not criticized or threatened with dismissal; he or she is simply denied any feedback whatsoever. If the individual starts to improve, the manager may return to praise (positive reinforcement), but if poor performance recurs, nonreinforcement (extinction) will again be used.

Punishment will reduce undesirable behavior.

Punishment. With **punishment,** when an individual does something that is regarded as wrong or improper, an aversive stimulus follows immediately. Punishment reduces the response frequency; it weakens behavior. For example, a subordinate who continually drops by the boss's office to relate the latest worker complaints may soon find the manager criticizing him or her for providing this feedback. The boss may be tired of hearing nothing but bad news. The objective of the boss's criticism is to reduce the subordinate's visits. The problem with this and other forms of punishment, however, is that this strategy has a number of undesirable side effects,[9] and many behavioral theorists make a case against its use.

Combination Strategies. Combination strategies are often used when there are two incompatible responses, one desirable and the other undesirable. For example, an individual works very hard (desirable), but always arrives late for work (undesirable). A combination strategy is used to reinforce the desirable behavior and reduce or extinguish the other.

An **extinction-positive reinforcement strategy** is one example. Consider the case of a subordinate who continually asks the boss for assistance on routine matters. Since the worker should be able to handle these minor problems without any help, the manager will want to extinguish this behavior. In the past the boss may have encouraged it by providing the requested help. Now a reversal of this procedure is in order. This about-face can be made by not giving the desired assistance. Every time the individual asks for help, the manager suggests that the subordinate work out the problem for him- or herself. Additionally, if the worker does so, the manager encourages this independent problem-solving behavior through praise and other positive reinforcers.

A second combination approach is a **punishment-positive reinforcement strategy**. This method is similar to the previous strategy except that it entails punishing undesirable responses. Consider the case of an employee who works with flammable materials. Any horseplay or violation of the safety rules by this person can have serious consequences. Therefore, if the worker does break one of these rules, punishment (a reprimand or days off without pay) may be imposed to discourage this behavior in the future. On the other hand, if the individual follows the rules and there are no violations, the manager may encourage this behavior with positive reinforcers.

A third combination method is a **punishment-negative reinforcement strategy**. In this rather complex strategy, the undesirable behavior is punished (punishment), and this is not terminated (negative reinforcement) until the undesirable response is replaced by a desirable one. The manager who nags one of his or her subordinates until the latter gets back to work is using a punishment-negative reinforcement strategy.

> **Combination strategies are often used when there is both an undesirable and a desirable response.**

 STOP   Review your answers to Question 1 and make any changes you would like before continuing.

1. What two learning intervention strategies does Jean use? Explain.

Jean is using positive reinforcement with those who are coming to work on time and extinction with those who are coming late. Notice that she ignores the latter by pretending to be busy at work and not having time to talk to them. However, at the same time, they realize that she is aware of their tardiness.

REINFORCEMENT SCHEDULES

If certain types of individual behaviors (high productivity, promptness in turning in reports, quality workmanship) are to be encouraged, and other types (absenteeism, tardiness, shoddy workmanship) are to be discouraged, some kind of reinforcement schedule must be developed. In essence, there are two types of reinforcement schedules: continuous and intermittent.[10] Under a **continuous reinforcement schedule** the individual receives a reward every time he or she performs a desired behavior. An illustration is the case of salespeople who received a fixed commission (reward) on every sale (desired behavior). There are two major problems, however, with continuous reinforcement. First, in most organizations the manager is simply unable to reinforce desired behavior every time. Most managers do not have time to praise their subordinates every time they do something right. Second, although learning is very rapid under continuous reinforcement, if the schedule is terminated, learning will be rapidly extinguished as well.

Under an **intermittent reinforcement schedule,** the individual does not receive a reward after each instance of desired behavior; rather, the reward is administered on a variable or random basis. Intermittent reinforcement usually leads to a behavior being maintained for a longer period after the rewards have been discontinued.[11]

Four types of intermittent reinforcement schedules are typically used to bring about desired behavior: fixed ratio, fixed interval, variable ratio, and variable interval.

Fixed Ratio Schedule

A fixed-ratio reinforcement schedule gives rewards after a specific number of correct responses.

Under a **fixed-ratio schedule,** reinforcement is given after a specific number of responses. Although this can be in a ratio of one reinforcement per correct response (continuous reinforcement), it is more common to find organizations shifting the ratio as learning progresses. Thus, for the first week, a one-to-one (1:1) ratio might be used, but the reinforcement schedule would then be changed. For the second week, it might be two correct responses per reward (2:1); for the third week, 4:1, and on up to 10:1, where it would remain indefinitely.

A fixed-ratio schedule tends to produce a response rate that is both vigorous and steady. The individual soon realizes that reinforcement is received only after a specific number of responses, and so he or she tends to work as quickly as possible. A common illustration of a fixed-ratio schedule is the piece-rate incentive system, in which the individual receives a reward on the basis of how many pieces are produced. For example, the worker receives $1 for every ten pieces he or she processes.

Fixed-Interval Schedule

A fixed-interval reward is based on a fixed passage of time.

In a **fixed-interval schedule** rewards are administered after a fixed passage of time rather than in relation to a specific response. Paying employees on a biweekly basis is an illustration: everyone who is on the payroll at the end of the two-week period receives a check.

In contrast to a fixed reinforcement ratio with its steady and vigorous response rate, with a fixed-interval schedule the response pattern varies. As soon as the employees receive their reward (paycheck), responses tend to decline. People do not work as hard. The reason may well be that they know that they will not be rewarded again for two weeks. As the time for the next paycheck draws near, however, productivity tends to increase. A similar example of this activity pattern can be observed among students who may be very lethargic during a lecture but begin to revive as the period draws to a close. When the bell rings, virtually everyone is energized for departure.

Because of the time interval between fixed rewards, many behaviorists think that fixed-interval scheduling is of limited value to industry. Some, for example, believe that the time interval is generally too long to be an effective form of reinforcement for work-related behavior.

Variable-Ratio Schedule

A variable-ratio schedule varies the reward so that the person does not know when it is coming.

A **variable-ratio schedule** is similar to a fixed-ratio schedule because the individual's reward is based on the number of right responses. In this case, however, the ratio varies randomly. That is, whereas on a fixed schedule the person may have been rewarded for every tenth correct response, now the individual may be rewarded after the third, the twelfth, and the fifteenth right responses. If we average them out, the person is being rewarded on a 10:1 basis (the same as in the fixed), but the person does not know when the next reinforcement is scheduled. Since the person does not know when the reward is coming, a variable-ratio reinforcement is very effective in promoting steady work output.

Variable-Interval Schedule

A variable-interval schedule provides reinforcement at the end of randomly determined time intervals.

A **variable-interval schedule** is similar to a variable-ratio schedule in that reinforcement is given on a random basis. In this case, however, the reward is given at the end of randomly determined intervals of time. This schedule tends to produce a high response rate that is steady, vigorous, and resistant to extinction. An example is the case of the boss who takes random walks through the workplace an average of twice a day, approving outstanding performance. During a one-week period this individual makes ten trips. On some days, however, the manager may come by three times, and on other days not at all. No one knows for sure when the individual will be around. Since the time of reinforcement is unpredictable, performance tends to be higher and to fluctuate less than with, for example, the fixed-interval schedule.

Rules for Using Reinforcement Theory

Over the years, researchers have formulated a number of rules that can be helpful in using behavior reinforcement ideas. Some of these rules are mere common sense, although many managers, based on the way they arrange the contingencies, seem unaware of them. Hamner has identified six of them.[12]

First, do not reward all people the same. Rewards should be different, based on performance. Managers who give everyone the same reward end up punishing their best performers and rewarding their poorest ones. When this happens, the former are likely to slow up their output or move to another organization. In either event, the manager loses their full efforts.

Second, a failure to respond has reinforcing consequences. Managers are constantly shaping the behavior of their subordinates by what they fail to do as well as what they actually do. For example, failure to correct a worker's tardiness may be viewed as a sign that it is all right to come late to work. Managers have to be careful to examine the performance consequences of their nonactions as well as of their actions.

Third, be sure to tell subordinates what they can do to be rewarded. By making reinforcement contingencies clear to the workers, the manager can actually increase their job freedom. The individuals now have a built-in feedback system that allows them to make judgments about the quantity and quality of their work output.

Fourth, tell subordinates what they are doing wrong. This information helps them understand how to make the necessary changes in their work habits. Without such feedback, they are likely to misunderstand why rewards are being withheld or why punishment or extinction strategies are being used.

Fifth, do not punish subordinates in front of their peers. This punishes the individual twice. The result may be a subordinate whose self-image is so badly damaged that he or she begins looking for ways of getting even with the management. The outcome usually is bad for all parties involved.

Sixth, make the consequences equal to the behavior. This rule calls for the manager to be fair with subordinates. If an individual is doing a good job, the person should be rewarded appropriately. Those who get less than they deserve will often limit their effort and output. Those who get more than they deserve often see no reason to increase their effort and output. In the final analysis, the organization loses out. Perhaps Skinner said it best when he wrote that people "are happy in an environment in which active, productive and creative behavior is reinforced in effective ways."[13]

There are six useful rules for using reinforcement theory.

STOP — Review your answers to Question 2 and make any changes you would like before continuing.

2. What type of reinforcement schedule is Jean using in implementing MBWA? Explain.

Jean is using a variable-interval schedule. The employees do not know on what days of the week she will be walking around to look in on them. Neither do they know how many times she will be coming by that day nor whether these visits will occur during the morning, afternoon, or throughout the work day.

USING BEHAVIOR MODIFICATION

The application of operant conditioning principles is known as **behavior modification,** and these principles have been successfully applied in many organizations. The process (see Figure 5–5) comprises five specific steps. The following subsections examine each of these.

Identification of Critical Behaviors

The first step in using behavior modification is identifying the behaviors that are most important to the organization—the critical behaviors. Many enterprises find that 5–10 percent of all behaviors can account for 60–80 percent of all work output.

One of the most common ways of identifying critical behaviors is by having the person closest to the job in question, typically the supervisor or the actual jobholder, determine them. Another approach is to conduct a behavioral audit, in which internal

FIGURE 5—5
The Behavior Modification Process

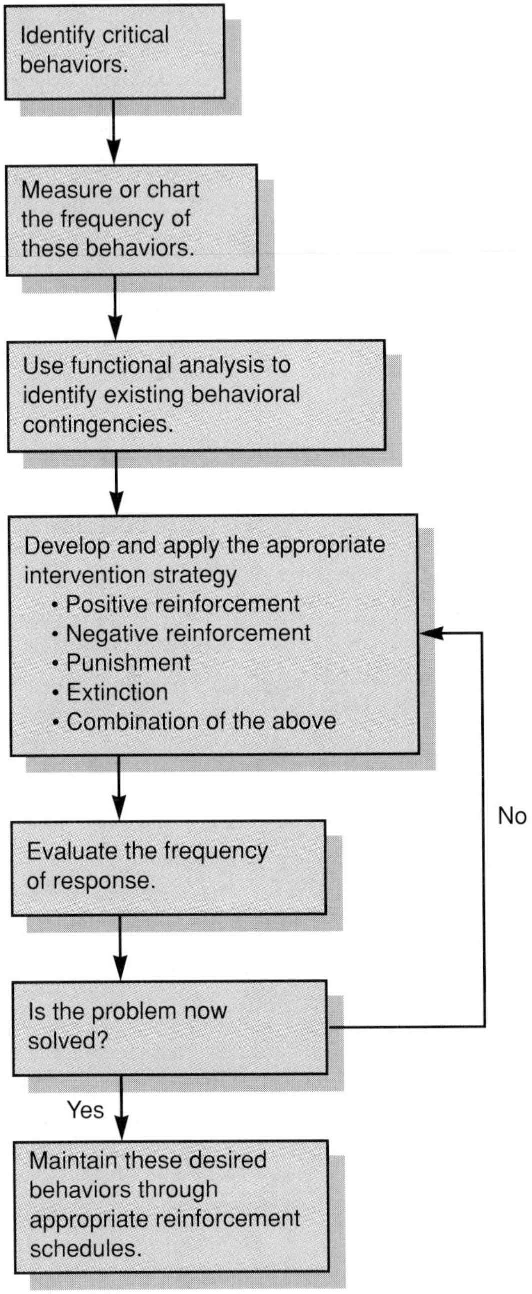

```
┌─────────────────────┐
│ Identify critical   │
│ behaviors.          │
└─────────────────────┘
          │
          ▼
┌─────────────────────┐
│ Measure or chart    │
│ the frequency of    │
│ these behaviors.    │
└─────────────────────┘
          │
          ▼
┌─────────────────────┐
│ Use functional      │
│ analysis to         │
│ identify existing   │
│ behavioral          │
│ contingencies.      │
└─────────────────────┘
          │
          ▼
┌──────────────────────────────┐
│ Develop and apply the        │
│ appropriate intervention     │◄────────┐
│ strategy                     │         │
│   • Positive reinforcement   │         │
│   • Negative reinforcement   │         │
│   • Punishment               │         │
│   • Extinction               │         │
│   • Combination of the above │         │
└──────────────────────────────┘         │
          │                           No │
          ▼                              │
┌─────────────────────┐                  │
│ Evaluate the        │                  │
│ frequency of        │                  │
│ response.           │                  │
└─────────────────────┘                  │
          │                              │
          ▼                              │
┌─────────────────────┐                  │
│ Is the problem now  │──────────────────┘
│ solved?             │
└─────────────────────┘
          │ Yes
          ▼
┌─────────────────────┐
│ Maintain these      │
│ desired behaviors   │
│ through appropriate │
│ reinforcement       │
│ schedules.          │
└─────────────────────┘
```

staff specialists, outside consultants, or both analyze the jobs in question and determine which behaviors are critical. Some experts believe that a combination approach, in which consultants examine the jobs and get feedback from those who are responsible for them on a day-to-day basis, is best. The consultants usually know how to gather analytical information, and the jobholders are best equipped to provide substantive descriptions regarding the data being collected.

Behaviors must be observable.

The behaviors that are identified must all meet certain guidelines. For example, one guideline is that they be observable and measurable. Such behaviors as a bad attitude, a poor personality, or a lack of motivation are not directly measurable and are not considered critical behaviors. However, their outcomes (tardiness, absenteeism, low productivity) are.

Measurement of the Behaviors

Baseline data must be obtained.

Having identified the critical behaviors, the next step is to measure them by getting baseline data.[14] This information shows how often the critical behaviors are occurring. The data provide objective frequency information. Sometimes, to the amazement of the manager, some of the critical behaviors that were designated as worthy of change are really not.

> In some instances the baseline measure may cause the "problem" to be dropped because its low (or high) frequency is now deemed not to need change. For example, attendance may have been identified . . . as a critical behavior that needs to be changed. The supervisor reports that the people "never seem to be here." The baseline measure, however, reveals that there is 96 percent attendance, which is deemed to be acceptable. In this example, the baseline measure rules out attendance as being a problem.[15]

Behaviors can be measured with tally sheets. These sheets record the number of times a critical behavior occurs. For purposes of simplicity, it is common to find notebook paper used for recording behaviors. On the pad there is generally a column for "yes" and a column for "no," as well as a place for recording the number of times the critical behavior occurs. Then the individual collecting the data has only to check the appropriate box. If the company is interested in every time the behavior occurs, as in the case of employee tardiness, this information is recorded. If the behavior can be measured on a random basis, such as when the number of items workers are producing each hour is sought, the data can be collected by using a time sampling approach. Then the information is often transferred from tally sheets to charts or graphs so that it is easier to follow changes in the frequency of behaviors. Perhaps the biggest problem at this stage of the process is that the presence of the observer who is collecting information may distort the behaviors being measured; that is, people may change their work habits when the observer is around.

Functional Analysis of the Behaviors

Behavioral consequences should be identified.

Once data have been collected and plotted, attention is focused on why the critical behaviors are occurring and what their consequences are. For example, in one reported case the production supervisor found that the workers were taking unscheduled breaks, which was having a negative effect on their output. The baseline data revealed that the workers were leaving their work stations twice in the morning (at 9 and 11 A.M.) and twice in the afternoon (at 2 and 4 P.M.) in addition to their 10 A.M. and 3 P.M. work breaks. Functional analysis revealed that the clock was cueing this behavior. By taking these breaks, the workers were able to get away from a boring job and socialize with each other. This consequence reinforced their behavior, and the workers continued taking the unscheduled breaks.[16] Once the company was aware of the cue that brought about the behavior and the consequence that followed, it could decide how to deal with the situation.[17]

Development of an Intervention Strategy

Interventions must then be formulated.

The three steps we have just discussed are preliminary ones; development of an intervention strategy is the beginning of the action phase of the process. The goal of whatever intervention is used is always the same: to weaken behaviors that are undesirable and strengthen those that are desirable. Here is where the strategies discussed earlier in the chapter come into play. The main ones are positive reinforcement, punishment-positive reinforcement, and extinction-positive reinforcement. When possible, positive reinforcers are employed. How does the organization know what the personnel consider to be a positive reinforcer? The easiest way to find out is by asking the individuals who are to be reinforced. There are two basic types of reinforcers, contrived and natural.

Contrived reinforcers come in many forms. Four of the most common are: (1) consumables, such as coffee breaks, free lunches, and company picnics; (2) manipulatables, such as wall plaques, a company car, and country club privileges; (3) visual and auditory rewards, such as piped-in music, an office with a window, and a redecoration of the work environment; and (4) tokens, such as money, stock, stock options, and profit sharing. **Natural reinforcers** are heavily social, such as verbal praise, friendly greetings, and solicitations of advice.[18]

What we have to remember about contrived and natural reinforcers is that behavior modification experts prefer to use the latter because contrived rewards are often not closely tied to performance. Except in the case of salespeople or those on piece-rate incentive plans, pay is generally not contingent on the performance of critical behaviors. On the other hand, natural reinforcers often are tied directly to performing critical behaviors, and (as is often overlooked by many managers) such reinforcers are often quite effective.

Evaluation and Monitoring of Performance Improvement

Ongoing behavior must be monitored.

One of the most interesting things about behavior modification programs is that they are set up to monitor ongoing behavior. This is in contrast to many programs, especially training and development, where nothing is done after the program is completed. It is assumed that the training given to the participants will be taken back and applied to job-related problems or, if the training took place on the job, that it will continue to be used in solving job-related problems. Behavior modification programs take into account that new problems may arise or old ones may no longer be solved with the same reward

Organizational Behavior In Action

POSITIVE REINFORCEMENT WINNERS

Positive reinforcement is extremely important to organizational success both among individuals and enterprises. Recent research, for example, shows that people who have a positive attitude have a greater chance of succeeding than do those who lack this attitude. Martin Seligman, a psychologist at the University of Pennsylvania, has proven that optimists are more successful than equally talented pessimists in a variety of activities ranging from business to sports to politics. In fact, relying exclusively on this theory of optimistic thinking, Seligman was able to identify George Bush and Michael Dukakis as their 1988 presidential race party nominees long before the primary process was complete and the formal presidential campaign had begun. Seligman has also found that optimists tend to make better salespeople than pessimists, typically outselling the latter by 20 percent the first year and 50 percent the second. His Seligman Attributional Style Questionnaire is now being used by Metropolitan Life in choosing salespeople.

Another important characteristic of successful people is that they are able to visualize themselves winning prior to the event taking place. This puts them in a positive frame of mind and better prepares them for the contest to come. In particular, such mental training is now becoming a major step in preparing athletes for competition.

"The next frontier in sports will be mental training," predicts Nort Thornton, coach of the men's swimming team at the University of California, one of the top teams in the nation and a consistent training ground for Olympians. "Top athletes train physically about as much as they possibly can. Significant improvements in performance in the future will come from mental training."

Successful people know the benefits of positive reinforcement, and they do not wait for others to give it to them. Instead, they provide personal reinforcement, and in the process better prepare themselves for victory. They end up being the primary forces in modifying their own behavior.

Source: "Beyond Positive Thinking," *Success,* December 1988, pp. 32–34.

contingencies. By continually monitoring behavior, it is possible to identify what is going wrong and to design new behavioral strategies for handling the problem(s).[19] This is true not only for organizations but individuals as well (see "Organizational Behavior in Action: Positive Reinforcement Winners").

STOP   Review your answers to Question 3 and make any changes you would like before continuing.

3. For which of the two critical behaviors would it be most difficult to measure: tardiness or working hard?

It would be most difficult to measure whether the personnel are working hard because this would require Jean to draw some conclusions that might not be accurate. For example, if she came upon two workers busily engaged in putting together a report, would she be correct in concluding that they were working hard? Perhaps they are, but the reason may be that they are running late on a project because they have delayed in getting all of the data they needed. So instead of reinforcing them for hard work, she should be asking why this work was not completed earlier. On the other hand, it would be easier to measure tardiness because this can be done on a day-to-day basis by simply noting who is coming in late.

RESULTS FROM POSITIVE REINFORCEMENT PROGRAMS

There have been a number of successful programs.

Have organizations had much success with behavior modification or positive reinforcement programs? The answer is a qualified yes. A number of firms, including Emery Air Freight, Michigan Bell-Operator Services, General Electric, and Weyerhaeuser, have reported success.[20] Table 5–1 provides a brief overview of the results of their programs. Success has also been reported in not-for-profit organizations such as hospitals.[21] The following subsections present a short discussion of these programs.

Emery Air Freight

Emery uses positive reinforcement and has reported very favorable results over the years. The program is heavily self-instructional. All managers and supervisors are trained through the use of programmed instructional texts. One of these texts teaches them the principles of reinforcement; the other instructs them in the principles of feedback. No formal off-the-job training is used. Once a supervisor has finished reading the books, he or she is encouraged to begin applying the learning on the job.

One of Emery's greatest successes with the program came in the container area. The firm realized that one critical behavior vital to the success of the company was ensuring that the dock workers used air-freight containers to the fullest advantage. If each container were sent out full, the firm stood to make a great deal of money; if many containers were sent out only partially full, the firm would lose a great deal of money. Both management and the workers estimated that all containers were about 90 percent full when they were shipped. However, a performance audit team found that the effective utilization rate was only 45 percent. Through the use of feedback and social reinforcers this situation was turned around. Within a year of the time the program was

TABLE 5–1
Results of Positive Reinforcement Programs in Selected Organizations

Organization	Number of Employees Involved	Type of Employees	Specific Goals	Frequency of Feedback	Reinforcers Used	Results
Emery Air Freight	500	Entire work force	(a) Increase productivity (b) Improve the quality of service	Immediate to monthly, depending on task	Previously only praise and recognition; others now being introduced	Cost savings directly attributed to the program
Michigan Bell-Operator Services	2,000	Employees at all levels in operator services	(a) Decrease turnover and absenteeism (b) Increase productivity (c) Improve union-management relations	(a) Lower level: weekly and daily (b) Higher level: monthly and quarterly	(a) Praise and recognition (b) Opportunity to see oneself become better	(a) Attendance performance improved by 50% (b) Productivity and efficiency continued to be above standard in areas where positive reinforcement was used
General Electric	1,000	Employees at all levels	(a) Meet Equal Employment Opportunity objective (b) Decrease absenteeism and turnover (c) Improve training (d) Increase productivity	Immediate; uses modeling and role playing as training tools to teach interpersonal exchanges and behavior requirements	Social reinforcers (praise, rewards, and constructive feedback)	(a) Cost savings directly attributed to the program (b) Productivity increased (c) Worked extremely well in training minority groups and raising their self-esteem (d) Direct labor cost decreased
Weyerhaeuser	500	Clerical, production (tree planters), and middle-level management and scientists	(a) To teach managers to minimize criticism and to maximize praise (b) To teach managers to make rewards contingent on specified performance levels (c) To use optimal schedule to increase productivity	Immediate; daily and quarterly	(a) Pay (b) Praise and recognition	(a) With money, a 33% increase in productivity was obtained with one group of workers, an 18% increase with a second group, and an 8% decrease in a third group (b) Firm is currently experimenting with goal setting and praise or money (or both) at various levels in the organization (c) With a lottery-type bonus, the cultural and religious values of workers must be taken into account

Source: Adapted from W. Clay Hamner and Ellen P. Hamner, "Behavior Modification on the Bottom Line," *Organizational Dynamics* (Spring 1976), 12–14.

instituted the company saved $600,000, and over the next five years an additional $1.4 million was saved. Since this initial program, the firm has had additional successes.

Michigan Bell-Operator Services

The operator services division of this utility found that when standards and feedback were not provided to the workers, the latter generally felt that their performance was at about the 95 percent level. When performance data were gathered, however, it turned out that the performance was at the 50 percent mark. When the company began providing the workers with feedback on performance, output went up almost immediately and remained at 90 percent or more. Through the use of positive reinforcement the company was able to maintain it at this level. Commenting on one specific experiment, the general manager for operator services reported that:

> Michigan Bell found that when goal setting and positive reinforcement were used in a low-productivity inner-city operator group, service promptness (time to answer call) went from 94 percent to 99 percent of standard, average work time per call (time taken to give information) decreased from 60 units of work time to 43 units of work time, the percentage of work time completed within ideal limits went from 50 percent to 93 percent of ideal time (standard was 80 percent of ideal), and the percentage of time operators made proper use of references went from 80 percent to 94 percent. This led to an overall productivity index score for those operators that was significantly higher than that found in the control group, where positive reinforcement was not being used, even though the control group of operators had previously (six months earlier) been one of the highest producing units.[22]

General Electric

General Electric uses positive reinforcement and feedback in many areas, including employee training. At first, the programs centered on teaching male supervisors how to interact and communicate with female and minority employees and on teaching those employees how to improve their self-image. Later programs have focused on the relationship between supervisors and employees in general. These programs use **behavior modeling**.[23] During the program the trainee is shown a videotape of a person with his or her characteristics (sex, race, superior, subordinate) who is performing in a proper manner. Through the process of role playing, the employee is then encouraged to act in the same manner as the successful role model shown on the film. The result has been an increase in employee self-esteem and a rise in their productivity.

Weyerhaeuser

Weyerhaeuser has had a long history of using positive reinforcement. The company is particularly interested in finding ways to improve employee productivity through the use of goal setting and positive reinforcement feedback.

> Weyerhaeuser is currently applying reinforcement principles with tree planters in the rural South as well as with engineers and scientists at their corporate

headquarters. In the latter case, they are comparing different forms of goal setting (assigned, participative, and a generalized goal of "do your best") with three different forms of reinforcement (praise or private recognition from a supervisor, public recognition in terms of a citation for excellence, and a monetary reward). . . . The purpose of the program is to motivate scientists to attain excellence. Excellence is defined in terms of the frequency with which an individual displays specific behaviors that have been identified by the engineers/scientists themselves as making the difference between success and failure in fulfilling the requirements of their job. [24]

B. F. Goodrich Chemical

Goodrich introduced into one of its production sections a positive reinforcement program that incorporated goal setting and feedback about scheduling, costs, problem areas, and targets. At the time, the production section was in poor shape. Under the new program, the foremen were given information each week on how well their group was doing. This was the first time that the foremen and the employees had ever been told about the costs that were actually incurred by their group. Additionally, charts were published showing achievement in areas such as sales, productivity, and costs. Films were also made showing top management what the employees were doing, and these films were shown to the workers so that they would know what management was being told about the program and their performance. This positive reinforcement program actually turned the plant's performance around. Productivity, over a five-year period, went up 300 percent and costs dropped.

A Large Hospital

Positive reinforcement programs have not been restricted to private enterprises. Municipalities have used them successfully (as in the case of Detroit's sanitation workers) and so have health care institutions. The results of one study of the effects of behavior modification in a large hospital are reported by Snyder and Luthans in Table 5–2. Their behavior modification program incorporated personnel from virtually every area of the hospital, including supervisors from the emergency room, equipment repair, medical records, radiology, and admitting. The supervisors were given training in behavior modification (as described earlier in the chapter and summarized in Figure 5–5). All supervisors were encouraged to select employee problems and behaviors that could be measured, analyzed, and altered by behavior modification. Then intervention strategies were chosen and applied. The results clearly indicate that behavior modification principles had a very positive impact on performance at the hospital (see Table 5–2). Behavior modification techniques, long restricted in health care to mental health areas, are also useful in health care organizations in general.

BEHAVIOR MODIFICATION: POINT-COUNTERPOINT

Although the use of behavior modification in organizations has been successful in many cases, there are critics who make important behaviorally-based attacks on the method.

TABLE 5–2
Productivity Changes in a Large Hospital after the OB Mod Training Program

Unit	Measure(s)	Preintervention	Postintervention	Percent Change
Emergency room clerks	Registration errors (per day)	19.16	4.580	76.10
Hardware engineer group, HIS	Average time to repair (minutes)	92.53	33.250	64.06
Medical records file clerks	Errors in filing (per person per audit)	2.87	.078	97.30
Medical records	Complaints	8.00	1.000	875.00
Transcriptionists	Average errors	2.07	1.400	33.00
	Average output	2,258.00	2,303.330	2.00
Heart station	EKG procedures accomplished (ave.)	1,263.00	1,398.970	10.76
	Overdue procedures	7.00[a]	4.000	42.85
Eye clinic	Daily patient throughput	19.00	23.000	21.05
	Daily patient teaching documentation	1.00	2.800	180.00
	Protocols produced	0.00	2.000	200.00
Pharmacy technicians	Drug output (doses)	348.80	422.100	21.00
	Posting errors	3.67	1.480	59.70
	Products waste (percent)	5.80	4.350	25.00
Radiology technicians	Average patient throughput (procedural)	3,849.50	4,049.000	5.20
	Retake rate (percent)	11.20	9.950	11.20
Patient accounting	Average monthly billings	2,561.00	3,424.500	33.70
Admitting office	Time to admit (minutes)	43.73	13.570	68.97
	Average cost	$ 15.05	$ 11.730	22.00
Data center operations	Systems log-on (time)	1:54	1:43	9.7

Note: All averages are arithmetic means.

[a] Estimate.

Source: Charles Snyder and Fred Luthans, "The Application of O.B. Mod. to Increase the Productivity of Hospital Personnel." Reprinted with the permission from *HRMagazine* (formerly *Personnel Administrator*), August 1982, p. 72, published by the Society for Human Resource Management, Alexandria, VA.

In this section we present both the criticisms and the replies made by the proponents of behavior modification.

Many of the criticisms of behavior modification have been addressed.

Critics argue, first, that behavior modification ignores individual differences. For example, when a program is designed to reward with praise all who do a job well, it is assumed that praise is a positive reinforcer for all of the workers. Proponents of behavior modification assert that this is not the case at all—that reinforcement is based on what is actually rewarding to the individual and will be changed if the worker does not respond to praise.

Second, critics contend that behavior modification ignores prevailing work-group norms. They say the program is established with little regard for current group practices. Such a program, for example, often establishes higher rates of output with no corresponding increase in pay. Proponents admit that group norms can prove to be a serious problem. In fact, when a suitable organizational climate cannot be developed they believe it is often best not to attempt a behavior modification program.

Third, behavior modification, argue the critics, ignores the fact that employees can be intrinsically motivated. They contend that behavior modification relies on the use of extrinsic (external) rewards. Actually, they are wrong on this point. Although extrinsic rewards are often employed, experts in behavior modification realize that these are contrived reinforcers, and where possible natural rewards are used to supplement and, it is hoped, replace them.

Fourth, behavior modification is said to assume that all behaviors must be externally reinforced in order to be learned. By this, the critics mean that people do not learn new responses by observing other people being reinforced for the desired response. They say that there is no vicarious learning. This is not true; behavior modification experts have demonstrated that not all behaviors have to be externally reinforced. Role modeling is an important part of learning.

Fifth, critics claim that behavior modification is not a new technique for motivating employees. In fact, some point out that it may be nothing more than the application of scientific management concepts. For example, at Emery Air Freight it was claimed that behavior modification helped container use jump from 45 percent to 95 percent in a single day. Since genuine conditioning is supposed to be a gradual process, how can we account for these spectacular results? Critics say that what happened at Emery was merely a redefining of the jobs, resulting in new standards and more accurate feedback about performance in relation to these standards. Proponents argue that this is not true and the critics are exaggerating their point.

Behavioral modification does have shortcomings.

Overall, behavior modification proponents have successfully responded to many of their critics' comments. This is not to say, however, that such an approach to training, development, and general supervision is the wave of the future. Behavior modification has some important shortcomings that limit its use. One is that it works best on jobs where output is measurable and quantifiable. This means that its use at the middle and upper levels of an organization is at best marginal. Second, it requires constant data collection to identify changes in desired behavior (such as a decrease in output or an increase in tardiness) and then taking steps to correct the situation, which often results in organizations abandoning their behavior modification efforts. The time and expense associated with maintaining the program is considered too great. Third, some organizations treat the concept as a short-run method for increasing output or reducing problem areas. The minute things improve, the program is abandoned. Many of these shortcomings are less the fault of the technique itself than of the organization and its personnel. Nevertheless, in order to put behavior modification into perspective, it is important to understand why its application is limited.

STOP

Review your answers to Question 4 and make any changes you would like before continuing.

4. On what types of jobs might Jean find it easier to use behavior modification? Explain.

Jean would find it easier to use behavior modification on jobs where it is easiest to identify the critical behaviors and to measure them. Second, the behaviors should respond to external reinforcement. Third, it must be possible to develop intervention strategies that are individually tailor-made so that if a person does not respond to one strategy, it is possible to develop another.

SUMMARY

1. Learning is a relatively permanent change in behavior that results from reinforced practice or experience. It can be a result of direct or indirect experience. Learning can be acquired in a number of different ways. Figure 5–1 illustrates some of these learning curves.

2. In essence, there are two types of learning: classical conditioning and operant conditioning. Classical conditioning relies on the relationship between an unconditional stimulus and an associated response. Operant conditioning is the result of a reinforcement process and is far more useful to the study of organizational behavior. Types of reinforcement strategies include positive reinforcement, negative reinforcement, extinction, punishment, and combinations of these strategies. These strategies, to be successful, are typically applied according to some schedule. A continuous reinforcement schedule will reward an individual for desired behavior each time the behavior is exhibited. Since this is often impractical, intermittent reinforcement schedules, such as fixed-ratio, fixed-interval, variable-ratio, and variable-interval schedules, are usually employed. These techniques can be successful in improving organizational performance.

3. Over the years researchers have formulated a number of rules that can be helpful in arranging reinforcement contingencies: Do not reward all people the same; a failure to respond has reinforcing consequences; be sure to tell subordinates what they can do to get reinforced; tell subordinates what they are doing wrong; do not punish subordinates in front of their peers; and make the severity of the consequences equal to the behavior.

4. The application of operant conditioning principles is known as behavior modification, and these principles have been successfully applied in many organizations. The process by which this is done is presented in Figure 5–5. A number of organizations, including Emery Air Freight, Michigan Bell-Operator Services, General Electric, Weyerhaeuser, and B. F. Goodrich Chemical, have successfully employed these ideas in in-house behavior modification programs.

5. Some critics claim that behavior modification has significant shortcomings. Although many of these claims are exaggerated or false, behavior modification does have limitations. In particular, it works best on jobs where output is measurable and quantifiable—something that many organizations are unwilling to commit themselves to on an ongoing basis, and its value at the middle and upper level of the hierarchy is marginal. Despite these limitations, however, it does offer modern organizations an excellent behavioral science tool to use in their efforts to attain such objectives as increased productivity and reduced absenteeism and turnover.

KEY TERMS

learning
classical conditioning
operant conditioning
social learning theory
positive reinforcement
negative reinforcement
extinction
punishment
extinction-positive
   reinforcement strategy

punishment-positive
   reinforcement strategy
punishment-negative
   reinforcement strategy
continuous reinforcement
   schedule
intermittent reinforcement
   schedule
fixed-ratio schedule
fixed-interval schedule

variable-ratio schedule
variable-interval schedule
behavior modification
contrived reinforcers
natural reinforcers
behavior modeling

REVIEW AND STUDY QUESTIONS

1. What is learning? How does your answer relate to organizational behavior?

2. What kind of learning curve best describes a student who crams for an exam and does well? How about a student who crams for an exam and does poorly? Explain.

3. How does classical conditioning differ from operant conditioning? Compare and contrast the two.

4. How do each of the following learning strategies work: positive reinforcement, negative reinforcement, extinction, punishment? Describe each.

5. How does a combination learning strategy work? Give an example.

6. A series of "pop quizzes" during the term is an example of what type of reinforcement schedule? Explain your answer.

7. When is a continuous reinforcement schedule most effective? Under what conditions is each of the four types of intermittent reinforcement schedules most effective? Be complete in your answer.

8. Are there any rules that are useful in operant conditioning? State and explain four.

9. How are behavior modification programs conducted? Use Figure 5–5 in your description.

10. Has behavior modification been used successfully by any organizations? Cite at least three examples.

11. Have any criticisms been made of behavior modification? What are they? In your answer, include counter-arguments as well.

CASES

No More Help

Janet Karems is a supervisor in a large insurance company. Janet works in the claims section, and the 15 people in her department are responsible for processing hospitalization and medicine claims. Much of the work is routine and involves keeping an active file on everyone who files for reimbursement of medical expenses. Most of the policies require the individual to pay the first $100 personally, and after this there is an 80-20 percent division, with the insurance company picking up the larger part of the bill.

Sometimes people will file a bill twice; other times, people who have not met their deductible will file for reimbursement. In either case, it is the responsibility of the people in this department to figure out what the individual is doing wrong and send a form letter explaining why they cannot be reimbursed.

Occasionally, one of Janet's people will receive a host of bills or letters that is so confusing that it is difficult to determine what the individual is trying to say. When this

happens, Janet will sit down with her subordinate and together the two of them will figure out what the problem is
and how it should be resolved. However, this occurs so
rarely that Janet finds she can devote most of her energies
to other matters.

Four months ago a new woman, Mary Quigley, was
assigned to Janet's department. Mary is industrious but has
a very low threshold for ambiguity. The minute she feels
that something is wrong with a claim, she goes in to see
Janet. In the past, Janet has talked with her and tried to
show her how to expedite the situation. Over the past eight
weeks, however, Janet has concluded that Mary is still no
further along than when she first joined the department. As
a result, Janet has advised her secretary that when Mary
comes by she is to be told that Janet is "in conference" and
encouraged to "handle the matter as best you can." As a
follow-up strategy, Janet has begun checking Mary's work,
and when she sees some difficult matter that has been handled properly, she goes out of her way to call Mary and
praise her.

In the past two weeks, Mary has begun calling on
Janet less and less. In fact, the average number of daily calls
has dropped from five a day to just over one. Janet, meanwhile, has talked to Mary about her improved performance
three times last week and twice this week. In each case,
Mary had handled a difficult matter very well and Janet
wanted her to know that this job performance was not going
unnoticed. Janet believes that in three or four weeks, Mary
will not be calling on her at all. At this point, Janet intends to
check Mary's work every two to three weeks and praise her
accordingly.

1. What type of combination strategy has Janet used to
   reduce Mary's dependence on her? Explain your answer.

2. What type of ratio schedule did Janet use with Mary last
   week? Defend your answer.

3. If Janet wants to be as effective as possible, what type of
   ratio schedule should she use with Mary when the latter
   stops calling on her for help? Explain.

A Mod Proposal

Metropolitan Hospital does not have a great deal of money
for training and development or consulting. Thus, most of
its management improvement efforts are a result of inside
programs put together by the human resources (HR) department or by individuals who are specialists in a particular
area and are willing to offer their services to the hospital in
the form of a "free" program. From time to time, the hospital does have outside speakers talk on management-
related topics, but this is done rarely because the fee has to
be approved by the Board of Trustees, and they usually do
so only if the small amount of training and development
funds has not been expended on other activities.

This year, the hospital's budget for training and consulting is larger than it has ever been. The new administrator fought hard to get more funds, and the board went along
with her request. The major question confronting the HR
department, which handles these funds, is how to spend
them. After making a systematic analysis of the types of
training that could be offered, the head of the department
has decided to bring in the president of a local consulting
firm that specializes in behavior modification. Most of the
personnel in the hospital are familiar with the basics of "behavior mod." The hospital has a very large psychiatric clinic
where the concept is widely used. However, the human
resources department manager is unfamiliar with how behavior modification can be used for training and development

purposes. It was always his impression that the concept was
limited in use to mental patients or individuals with various
psychiatric problems. Upon talking to the president of the
consulting firm, however, he has learned that this company
has been conducting behavior modification seminars all
around the country and has three programs currently in
place in major health care institutions.

The HR manager's greatest concern is that the consultants will cost him most of his budget while providing
training that is either superficial or useless. The head of the
consulting firm has tried to alleviate these fears by spelling
out exactly how a behavior modification program works.
The part about identifying, charting, and following critical
behaviors is of great interest to the manager. He also likes
the fact that the program is an ongoing one that can be used
to continually identify problems and deal with them.

The head of the consulting firm has suggested that he
come to the hospital and make a presentation to the Board
of Trustees and the top administrative staff. "In this way,"
he said, "you'll get a chance to learn what we do and why we
do it. Then if there are any questions, you can have them
answered. If you are not completely satisfied, don't use us.
Also, please remember that our contracts are always written so that you can terminate them at any time by merely
paying us for all the work done. So if you find that your
budget is suddenly reduced, you can cut back or stop all

work at once. On the other hand, if things proceed to your satisfaction, we will continue our training of your management personnel in the ways to use behavior modification so that it is of benefit to them. We will start at the supervisory level and work our way right up to the top." The head of the human resources department likes what he hears, but he wants to reserve judgment until the board and the top staff have had a chance to evaluate the program for themselves.

1. In your own words, how does a behavior modification program work? Be complete in your answer.

2. Of what value would such a program be to Metropolitan Hospital? What would it do for the hospital? Give some examples of how it would help.

3. Based on what the consultant has told the head of the human resources department, how well does his firm understand behavior modification? What problems are they likely to have if they engage this group? Be specific in your answer.

SELF-FEEDBACK EXERCISE

How Effective Are You in Using Reinforcement Principles?

Below are a dozen situations with which you might be confronted on the job. In each case there are four (and only four) responses you can make to the situation. (In some cases you may have to reword the response a little to give it the right meaning.) In choosing one, keep in mind the principles of reinforcement theory as well as your general understanding of organizational behavior. Here are the four responses:

a. I'd praise him (or her) for what he (or she) did and make it a point to include it in his (or her) performance evaluation.

b. I'd praise him (or her) for doing a good job.

c. I'd ignore the situation. A lot of times this is the best approach. If I talked to him (or her) it would be about something else.

d. I'd chew him (or her) out good and proper and bring formal sanctions against him (or her) if it happened again.

Read each of the following situations carefully and then decide which one of the four responses is appropriate. Put your answer to the left of the number.

_____ 1. Andy has come in late for the third day in a row. You talked to him about it yesterday and he promised it would not happen again. It has.

_____ 2. Mary has just submitted a detailed, complex report on time. It looked like she would be late with it, but she stayed at the office until 8 P.M. yesterday to ensure that it got in on time.

_____ 3. Although most salespeople in his region have barely made quota, Paul's sales were 10 percent over quota. This is the third year in a row he has done better than expected.

_____ 4. Usually Eileen does an excellent job. Last week, however, 3 percent of her assembled products were defective. The maximum defective rate is 2 percent.

_____ 5. You were tied up in the president's office and missed a lunch meeting with one of your biggest clients. Your assistant, Jay, realized what was happening and assumed the initiative, taking the client to your club, entertaining him, and having him back in your office by 2 P.M., when the individual was scheduled to hear your group's sales presentation. The client signed a large order on the way out. Going past Jay's office, you stick your head in to talk to him.

_____ 6. Bob and Steve work in an area where chemicals are loaded onto trucks. There is a strict no smoking rule in this area. You showed up there unexpectedly to talk to them about a special order and found both of them smoking.

_____ 7. For the third day in a row Jeanne is waiting to see you about the same problem. The air conditioning unit in her office is broken, and it will be the end of the week before maintenance can get to it. You informed her of this on both of her previous visits.

_____ 8. You've just received a memo that Karl's suggestion regarding how to reorganize the office work flow will save the firm $10,000 this year. He is being sent a check for $500 and the memo is to inform you of his good work.

_____ 9. During the weekly departmental meeting, Tim was not prepared to present his report. This is the fourth week in a row that he has been un-prepared.

_____ 10. Roberta has been working toward reducing tardiness in her department by 7 percent. The latest quarterly figures show that her tardiness rate is down by 12 percent.

_____ 11. Carol was on the West Coast yesterday closing a business deal. Although you would have liked her support at this morning's meeting, you realized that the West Coast deal had priority. To your surprise, she took the red eye special, arrived five minutes before the meeting, and made an excellent defense of your long-range proposal, which was accepted by top management.

_____ 12. You have just received a call from a regional sales manager who informs you that Hank, a reliable salesperson, is supposed to be making a sales presentation to a customer in his region. As you hang up the phone, you see Hank in the outer office. He tells you he is terribly upset, but he simply forgot about the scheduled presentation.

Scoring

Notice that the four responses available to you offer three types of reinforcement: positive, negative, and extinction. Undoubtedly you employed all of these in handling the twelve situations. How well did you do? In answering this question, compare your responses to the answers of 125 business people who created the scoring key below. In each case, circle the number under your answer to each question.

Question	A	B	C	D
1	−2	−1	+1	+2
2	+2	+1	−1	−2
3	+2	+1	−1	−2
4	−2	−2	+2	0
5	+1	+2	0	−2
6	−2	−2	0	+2
7	−2	−2	+2	+1
8	+1	+2	−1	−2
9	−2	−2	0	+2
10	+2	+1	−2	−2
11	+2	+2	−2	−2
12	−2	−2	+2	−2
	+	+	+	=
	___	___	___	___

Here is the scoring key:

20–24	Excellent
16–19	Good
12–15	Average
8–11	Poor
7 or less	Reread the material on reinforcement theory

NOTES

1. W. Clay Hamner, "Reinforcement Theory and Contingency Management in Organizational Settings," in Richard M. Steers and Lyman W. Porter (eds.), *Motivation and Work Behavior* (New York: McGraw-Hill Book Co., 1983), p. 118. Also see Gib Akins, "Varieties of Organizational Learning," *Organizational Dynamics,* Autumn 1987, pp. 36–48.

2. Fred Luthans, *Organizational Behavior,* 5th ed. (New York: McGraw-Hill Book Co., 1989), p. 294.

3. See for example Judith L. Komaki, "Toward Effective Supervision: An Operant Analysis and Comparison of Managers at Work," *Journal of Applied Psychology,* May 1986, pp. 270–279.

4. Fred Luthans, Richard Hodgetts, and Stuart A. Rosen-kranz, *Real Managers* (Cambridge, MA: Ballinger, 1988), pp. 141–142.

5. Albert Bandura, "Social Learning Theory," in T. J. Spence, R. C. Carson, and J. W. Thibaut (eds.), *Behavioral Approaches to Therapy* (Morristown, NJ: General Learning, 1976), p. 5.

6. Fred Luthans and Robert Kreitner, *Organizational Behavior Modification and Beyond,* (Glenview, IL: Scott, Foresman & Co., 1985), p. 157.

7. D. M. Prue and J. A. Fairbank, "Performance Feedback in Organizational Behavior Management: A Review," *Journal of Organizational Behavior Management,* Spring 1981, pp. 1–16.

8. Robert C. Linden and Terence R. Mitchell, "Reactions to Feedback: The Role of Attributions," *Academy of Management Journal,* June 1985, pp. 291–308.

9. Richard Arvey and John M. Ivancevich, "Punishment in Organization: A Review of Propositions and Research Suggestions," *Academy of Management Review,* April 1980, pp. 123–132.

10. For more on reinforcement schedules see Thomas C. Mawhinney, "Reinforcement Schedule Stretching Effects," in Edward A. Locke (ed.), *Generalizing From Laboratory to Field Settings* (Lexington, MA: Lexington Books, 1986), pp. 181–186.

11. Luthans and Kreitner, *Organizational Behavior Modification and Beyond,* p. 157.

12. W. Clay Hamner, "Reinforcement Theory and Contingency Management in Organizational Settings," in Richard M. Steers and Lyman W. Porter (eds.), *Motivation and Work Behavior* (New York: McGraw-Hill Book Co., 1983), pp. 128–131.

13. B. F. Skinner, *Contingencies of Reinforcement* (New York: Appleton-Century-Crofts, 1969), p. 64.

14. See for example Joseph R. Ferrari and Charles H. Baldwin, "From Cars to Carts," *Behavior Modification,* January 1989, pp. 51–64.

15. Luthans, *Organizational Behavior,* p. 324.

16. For more on this process see V. Mark Durand, "Employee Absenteeism: A Selective Review of Antecedents and Consequences," *Journal of Organizational Behavior Management,* Spring/Summer 1985, p. 157.

17. Luthans, *Organizational Behavior,* p. 328.

18. Fred Luthans and Robert Kreitner, *Organizational Behavior Modification* (Glenview, IL: Scott, Foresman & Co., 1975), p. 101.

19. See for example Garry L. Martin and E. Rosemarie Hrydowy, "Self-Monitoring and Self-Management Reinforcement Procedures For Improving Work Productivity of Developmentally Disabled Workers," *Behavior Modification,* July 1989, pp. 322–339.

20. Luthans and Kreitner, *Organizational Behavior Modification and Beyond,* Chapter 8.

21. For additional examples see Fred Luthans, Walter S. Maciag, and Stuart Rosenkrantz, "O.B.Mod.: Meeting the Productivity Challenge with Human Resource Management," *Personnel,* March-April 1983, pp. 28–36; Fred Luthans, Robert Paul, and Lew Taylor, "The Impact of Contingent Reinforcement on Salespersons' Performance Behaviors: A Replicated Field Study," *Journal of Organizational Behavior Management,* Spring/Summer 1985, pp. 25–35; and Kirk O'Hara, C. Merle Johnson, and Terry A. Beehr, "Organizational Behavior Management in the Private Sector: A Review of Empirical Research and Recommendations for Further Investigation," *Academy of Management Review,* October 1985, pp. 848–864.

22. W. Clay Hamner and Ellen P. Hamner, "Behavior Modification on the Bottom Line," *Organizational Dynamics,* Spring 1976, p. 16.

23. Kenneth E. Hultman, "Behavior Modeling for Results," *Training and Development Journal,* December 1986, p. 60.

24. *Ibid.,* p. 18.

CHAPTER 6
The Motivation Process

GOALS OF THE CHAPTER

Every organization depends on its managers to motivate personnel. Yet motivation is a very difficult process because people respond so differently to the same stimuli. For some, money is a prime motivator; for others, it seems to have little effect. For some, praise and other psychological rewards are very important; for others they hold little motivational force. The goals of this chapter are to examine the nature of motivation and to review some of the most important theories in the area. When you have completed this chapter you should be able to:

1. define the term *motivation;*
2. discuss psychological and managerial approaches to motivation;
3. explain and evaluate four important content theories of motivation;
4. describe three of the major process theories of motivation and tell why they are so popular with modern behaviorists.

When Henry White started working for Liddell, Inc., he set a target for himself: sales manager of western operations within six years. In the past no one had ever been promoted from salesperson to sales manager in less than ten years. There seemed to be an unwritten rule at Liddell that it should take a person a decade to master the selling function, and only the best salespeople were ever promoted to sales management positions. The sales manager for eastern operations, for example, had been in the field for twenty-two years before his promotion. The sales manager for southern operations had eighteen years of field experience.

While Henry was aware of the company's past history regarding sales manager jobs, he was also convinced that he could secure this position if he could prove he was the best salesperson in the firm. It took Henry two years to become the number one salesman in his territory and another twelve months before he was the top salesman in the entire firm.

Every year at its annual sales dinner, the president presents a special award to the top five salespeople throughout the country. The first time Henry won this award, everyone was surprised. Typically the honor went to someone with ten to fifteen years of field experience. When Henry won it for the third time, the president could hardly contain his admiration. It was obvious to everyone at the dinner that Henry was going to be promoted to some managerial position. Last month the sales manager of western operations announced his retirement and two weeks later Henry was named to the job.

Henry's new position guarantees him $100,000 annually, plus 1 percent of all commissions earned by people in his territory. This means that even though he was making a very large commission, as sales manager Henry's overall gross earnings will be about 15 percent more than they were last year. In addition, Henry will be included in the executive benefit program and will be given five weeks of paid vacation, two more than he had as a salesperson. Commenting on his success, Henry noted:

> I knew that I could succeed if I just set the right goals for myself

and kept striving. There was no way I could fail. I knew that the firm always promoted the best salespeople and I was convinced that with hard work, I could become the best. It was just a matter of hard work.

1. In terms of Maslow's need hierarchy, what needs are satisfied by Henry's increased salary? Explain.
2. Is Henry a high achiever? Defend your answer.
3. In terms of the two-factor theory of motivation, what hygiene factors has the firm given to Henry? Are there any motivators in his new job? What are they?
4. How did goal setting help Henry succeed?
5. In what way did expectancy, valence, and instrumentality enter into Henry's strategy for getting the sales manager job? Explain.

Write down your answers to these questions and put them aside. We will return to them later.

THE NATURE OF MOTIVATION

The word **motivation** is derived from the Latin verb *movere,* which means to move. Today, of course, the term means a lot more than this. Robbins defines motivation as "the willingness to exert high levels of effort toward organizational goals conditioned by the effort's ability to satisfy some individual need."[1] Luthans says it is "a process that starts with a physiological or psychological deficiency or need that activates behavior or a drive that is aimed at a goal or incentive."[2] Moorhead and Griffin see it as "the forces that cause people to behave in certain ways."[3]

These descriptions refer, implicitly or explicitly, to three common aspects of the motivation process: (a) what energizes human behavior; (b) how this behavior is directed or channeled; and (c) how the behavior can be maintained. These ideas can be diagrammed as shown in Figure 6–1. To illustrate the figure, we can use the case of a thirsty person. Thirst, as a need, results in the individual seeking water (goal-directed behavior). Having drunk water, the person has satisfied the need, and his or her inner state of disequilibrium has been modified. Keep in mind, however, that Figure 6–1 is only a general model of the motivation process. In reality, motivation is a very complex process. Five reasons can be cited.

1. The primary cause, or motive, a person has for a particular action cannot be seen; it can only be inferred.
2. Individuals may have a host of needs or expectations that are continually changing and, in some cases, in conflict with each other, so it can be very difficult to either observe or measure motivation.
3. People satisfy their needs in many different ways.
4. Satisfaction of a particular need may actually lead to an increase in its intensity; for example, a raise in salary sometimes results in a person wanting even more money, and one promotion sometimes brings about a desire for still another.
5. Goal-directed behavior does not always lead to need satisfaction.

Thus our model in Figure 6–1 is subject to many complications.

There are three common aspects of the motivation process.

People satisfy their needs in many different ways.

FIGURE 6–1
A Simple Model of the Motivation Process

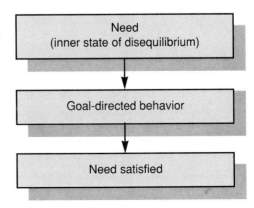

APPROACHES TO MOTIVATION

The study of motivation in organizations typically involves consideration of psychological and managerial approaches. The following subsections examine both.

Psychological Approaches

One way to examine motivation is through the use of psychological theories. All of these, to some degree, have their roots in **hedonism,** which holds that individuals will tend to seek pleasure and avoid pain. This theory, although intuitively appealing, does not explain how people actually determine which events are pleasurable or painful, nor how the source of pleasure or pain might be modified by experience. However, efforts to fill this void have resulted in the emergence of several empirically based theories of motivation. One of these early efforts was instinct theory.

Some psychologists see behavior as instinctual.

Instinct Theory.   Some early psychologists believed that instincts were prime determinants of behavior. **Instinct theory** held that these predispositions, as influenced by internal and external cues, caused the person to behave in a given way. Freud added to this approach by bringing in the concept of unconscious behaviors, claiming that people often did things for reasons that they did not consciously understand. Thus a major factor in motivation was seen to be forces that were unknown even to the individual experiencing them.

Instinct theory began to lose its popularity during the 1920s because it could not withstand certain attacks. One was that the list of human instincts was so long that it was difficult to deal with all of them. A second was that some researchers found little relationship between the strengths of certain motives and subsequent behavior. A third was that some psychologists began to question whether unconscious motives such as those described by Freud were instinctive or actually learned.

Some psychologists explain behavior in terms of drive or reinforcement, or both.

Drive and Reinforcement Theories.   A second psychological approach to motivation, **drive and reinforcement theories,** holds that decisions about present behavior are largely based on the consequences or rewards of *past* behaviors. One of the earliest comprehensive drive theories was formulated as Effort = Drive × Habit × Incentive. **Drive** is the intensity of behavior; **habit** is the strength of the relationship between past stimulus and response; **incentive** is the anticipatory reaction to future goals.[4] Notice the relationship between this drive theory and our discussion of behavior modification in the previous chapter.

Others see behavior as purposeful and goal directed.

Cognitive Theories.   A third psychological approach to motivation is provided by cognitive theories, which can best be described in relation to drive theories. **Cognitive theories** view behavior largely as a function of what will happen in the future; drive theories view behavior largely as a function of what has happened in the past. Cognitive theories hold that "a major determinant of human behavior is the beliefs, expectations, and anticipations individuals have regarding future events."[5] Behavior is thus seen as purposeful, goal-directed, and based on conscious intentions. Three of the most popular cognitive theories are goal setting, equity theory, and expectancy-valence theory, which will be discussed later in the chapter.

Managerial Approaches

Motivation has not remained a subject solely for theoretical analysis and discussion. Practicing managers have been interested in applying motivational concepts in the workplace. Perhaps the most comprehensive approach to the subject is that of Miles, which served as the basis for Table 1–1. A review of this table shows that there are different managerial approaches to motivation. The human resources model presents a philosophy that is accepted by modern behavioral scientists, and much of the research in the field today supports the tenets of this approach. Inherent in this philosophy are four basic assumptions about the nature of people.

The human resources model represents one managerial approach.

1. People want to contribute on the job and are somewhat premotivated to perform.
2. Through proper job design and an increase in such factors as job autonomy, feedback, and variety of task, work can be made more motivational.
3. Employees are quite capable of making both significant and rational decisions affecting their work, and giving them greater latitude in the decision-making process can actually be in the best interests of the organization.
4. Increases in self control and self direction can help influence the level of satisfaction.

Pulling together the basic concepts of motivation into an understandable framework can be very difficult. There are many different theories and approaches. When they are grouped into major categories, however, two emerge: content theories and process theories. The following sections examine both.

SELECTED CONTENT THEORIES OF MOTIVATION

Content theories of motivation attempt to explain the subject in terms of *what* arouses, energizes, or initiates behavior. Four of the most representative content theories are those of Maslow, Alderfer, McClelland, and Herzberg.

Maslow's Need Hierarchy

Maslow's hierarchy contains five basic needs.

Abraham Maslow has postulated that everyone has five basic needs, which constitute a **need hierarchy**. In ascending order, starting with the most basic, the hierarchy comprises: (a) physiological; (b) safety; (c) social; (d) esteem; and (e) self-actualization needs (Figure 6–2).

Physiological needs consist of such requirements as food, clothing, and shelter. Maslow contended that if people were deprived of all their needs, the drive to satisfy physiological needs would be greater than that to satisfy any other. Such things as the salary people earn on the job help them to fulfill this need.

Safety needs include the desire for security, stability, and the absence of pain. These needs are often satisfied in organizations by such things as medical insurance, retirement programs, and the disbursement of safety equipment to employees working in hazardous areas.

Social needs involve the "need to feel needed." They are often satisfied through social interaction in which people give and receive friendship and affection. In organizations, informal groups play a key role in satisfying these needs.

FIGURE 6–2
Maslow's Need Hierarchy

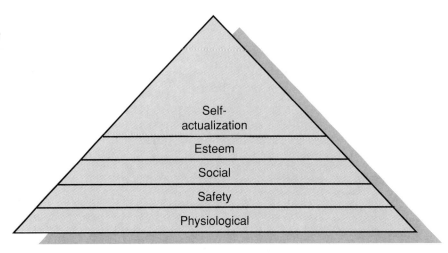

Esteem needs are twofold in nature: Individuals need to feel important, and they must receive from others recognition that supports these feelings. Such reinforcement leads to feelings of self-confidence and prestige. Positive feedback of this nature is often given by one's organizational peers.

Self-actualization needs were defined by Maslow as "the desire to become more and more what one idiosyncratically is, to become everything that one is capable of becoming."[6] At this level the individual attempts to realize his or her full potential in terms of self-development and creativity in the broadest sense of the word. Although less is known about this need than about any other, we do know that competence and achievement are closely related motives. As a result, individuals attempt to satisfy their self-actualization needs by mastering their environment through learning what they are and are not capable of doing, and by striving to achieve as much as they can by pursuing moderately difficult but potentially achievable goals.[7]

The hierarchy is based on a number of assumptions.

The need hierarchy theory of motivation includes a number of basic assumptions. One is that lower level needs (physiological, safety) must be satisfied before upper level needs (esteem, self-actualization) are sufficiently activated and begin to energize behavior. A second assumption is that once a need is satisfied, it no longer serves as a motivator. Thus a person whose need for food is basically sated will then move on to higher levels (safety and then social) of the hierarchy. A third assumption is that, in most cases, a number of needs affect the behavior of an individual at any one time. A fourth is that there are more ways to satisfy higher level needs than lower level needs.[8] The theory also postulates the relationship between need satisfaction and motivation, holding that only unfulfilled needs energize behavior, and that in the case of equal need strength, the lower level need must be sated first. These concepts, if valid, could be very useful to managers in predicting organizational behavior. Unfortunately, research related to the theory has raised several questions.

Problems with the Need Hierarchy.   One of the basic problems with the need hierarchy is that very little evidence exists to support the contention that there are five levels of needs. Furthermore, there is disagreement about whether the satisfaction of one need automatically activates the next need in the hierarchy. In addition, there is no definitive proof that once a need has been satisfied, its strength diminishes.[9]

A second problem with Maslow's model is that some outcomes satisfy more than one need. For example, an increase in salary will help an executive fill physiological needs. The raise will now allow the purchase of such things as higher grade meat, more expensive clothing, more health insurance, and a better home. At the same time, however, the raise will help satisfy upper level needs such as social needs and self-esteem.

The theory has a number of shortcomings.

A third problem derives from the differences that exist among people. Some individuals have a great, and continuing, need for safety. Many people who work in bureaucracies, for example, prefer jobs in which their tenure is assured to positions in highly competitive industries where salaries, promotions, and other rewards are much greater, but so too is the likelihood of dismissal or replacement. Other differences can be tied to age. Research shows that young workers (twenty-five years old or under) have greater esteem and self-actualization deficiencies than do older workers (over thirty-five years of age).[10] Race is also important, with some research reporting that black managers have a greater lack of need fulfillment than their nonblack counterparts in almost every category.[11]

Size of the firm is another causal variable. Porter, for example, found that managers in small companies who operated at the lower managerial levels were less deficient in their needs than counterpart managers who worked in large companies, and vice versa.[12] And the effect of individual differences goes on and on. Urban workers are reported to be less concerned with higher level need satisfaction on the job than are rural workers; Mexican workers attribute more importance to need fulfillment in the workplace than do Americans.

Despite these drawbacks, Maslow's need hierarchy remains very popular as a motivation theory. Another, which is similar in content but offers some important new insights regarding needs and motivation, is Clayton Alderfer's ERG theory.[13]

 STOP

Review your answers to Question 1 and make any changes you would like before continuing.

1. In terms of Maslow's need hierarchy, what needs are satisfied by Henry's increased salary? Explain.

This is not clear from the case, but an argument could easily be made that the increased salary will satisfy all levels of the hierarchy: physiological, safety, social, esteem, and self-actualization. The money will help fulfill both physical and psychological needs.

ERG Theory

Alderfer's hierarchical theory has three need categories: existence (E), relatedness (R), and growth (G). It also integrates the concepts of frustration and satisfaction.

Existence needs are related to the lowest level of Maslow's hierarchy: physiological and certain safety needs. These include the need for food, clothing, shelter, physical working conditions, money, and benefits.

Relatedness needs parallel those at the middle of Maslow's hierarchy: safety needs, social needs, and some esteem needs. These include, in particular, the need for interpersonal, social relationships.

Growth needs are those related to the upper levels of Maslow's hierarchy: esteem and self-actualization. These include, in particular, the need for personal growth and a chance to be creative on the job.

Although these explanations attempt to match Alderfer's concepts with those of Maslow, it is important to remember that ERG needs do *not* have strict lines of demarcation and that there is only a general fit between the two theories.

ERG theory is based on three major propositions. The first proposition is that the less each level of need has been satisfied, the more it will be desired. For example, if an individual's need for a specific salary is not satisfied, the individual will strive to increase his or her pay. The second proposition is that as lower-level needs are satisfied, there is a greater desire for higher-level need satisfaction. For example, as a person satisfies his or her existence needs, there will be an increase in the desire for relatedness needs. The third proposition is that the more higher-level need satisfaction is frustrated, the more the individual will seek lower-level need satisfaction. (This last proposition is diagrammed in Figure 6–3.)

There are some important differences between Maslow's need hierarchy and ERG theory. One, just referred to, is that although people will seek higher-level need satisfaction as their lower- level needs are basically sated, they will regress to a lower-level need component if they encounter frustration. Thus while there is an acceptance

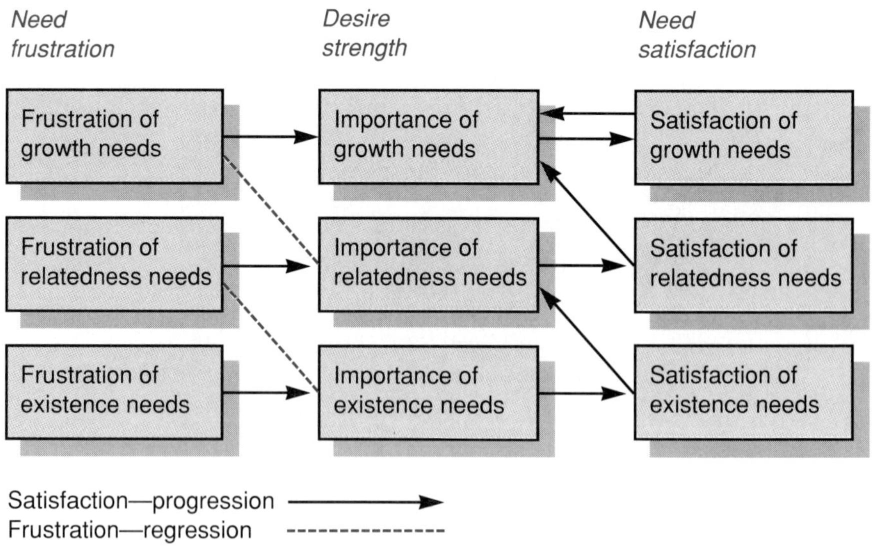

ERG theory is based on three major propositions.

ERG theory differs from Maslow's need hierarchy.

Need frustration	Desire strength	Need satisfaction
Frustration of growth needs	Importance of growth needs	Satisfaction of growth needs
Frustration of relatedness needs	Importance of relatedness needs	Satisfaction of relatedness needs
Frustration of existence needs	Importance of existence needs	Satisfaction of existence needs

Satisfaction—progression ⟶
Frustration—regression - - - - - - -

FIGURE 6–3
Two Key Components of ERG Theory: Satisfaction-Progression and Frustration-Regression

of Maslow's satisfaction-progression idea, there is also a frustration-regression concept that describes what happens when progression is not possible. As Figure 6–3 illustrates, if a person seeks to fulfill growth needs and is successful, then need satisfaction occurs. If the individual is unsuccessful, however, ERG theory postulates that the person will, because of this frustration, have an increased desire for relatedness needs. Yet, the figure shows that the individual does not remain here indefinitely. The person, having satisfied relatedness needs, will again strive for growth and may be successful this time. The same logic applies in moving from existence needs to relatedness needs.

A second major difference is that ERG holds that *more* than one need may be operative at the same time. Rather than progressing up the hierarchy, the person may be at all levels (although to differing degrees) *simultaneously.*

Current Status of the Theory. ERG theory is a recent addition to the content theories. Reported studies among managers, bank employees, and students have found stronger support for ERG than for Maslow's theory.[14] More recently, however, questions have been raised regarding whether the theory is as applicable in some organizations as it is in others.[15] Perhaps the biggest argument in its favor is that ERG provides a more workable approach to motivation than do most other content theories, and its satisfaction-progression and frustration-regression components constitute a very clear explanation of human behavior at work.[16]

Need Achievement Theory

Another content theory is that of David McClelland, who has spent decades studying the desire to achieve.[17] While similar to other content theories, **need achievement theory** is much more "applied."

In an effort to measure people's need achievement strength, McClelland uses the Thematic Apperception Test (TAT), which contains a number of projective pictures. In these pictures some activity is going on. In one of them, for example, a man with a series of blueprints in front of him is looking at a desk picture of his wife and family. McClelland asks the respondent to look at the picture briefly (10–15 seconds) and then write a story about what is going on in it. From the person's responses an analysis is made of whether the individual has high need achievement.

Characteristics of High Achievers. Through years of empirical research, McClelland and his associates have identified three characteristics that describe **high achievers**.

High achievers take personal responsibility.

First, high achievers like situations in which they take *personal* responsibility for finding solutions to problems. These people want to play an active role in determining the outcome rather than to rely on chance or luck. They want to make their own opportunities. We also know from research that they are willing to assume responsibility for their actions rather than pass the buck. In a business setting they make personal decisions rather than assign difficult problems to a committee or delegate authority for their solution to subordinates. They have self-confidence.

High achievers tend to be moderate risk takers.

Second, high achievers tend to take *moderate* risks rather than high or low risks. If they take a low risk, there is little satisfaction in the accompanying success. If they take a high risk, there is likely to be little satisfaction because the chance of success is so remote. In addition, failure to achieve may prove to be a source of frustration and anxiety. The best chance for maximizing a sense of personal achievement and the likelihood of success occurs with moderate risks.

Third, high achievers want *concrete feedback* on their performance. They like to know how well they are doing. Business people who are high achievers, for example, continually examine feedback in the form of production, sales, and profit figures to see how they are doing. This is one reason why high achievers choose business careers. Many are also doctors, who can evaluate a patient's progress, note how well the person is doing, and take corrective action as required. A third illustration is trial lawyers, who can measure their achievement by how many cases they take on and win.[18]

Developing High Achievement.   In addition to identifying characteristics of high achievers, McClelland has worked to develop the drive to achieve in people. In particular, he has suggested four steps. First, the individual should strive to attain feedback. By doing so, he or she secures reinforcement for successes, thereby strengthening the desire to achieve more. Second, the individual should choose models of achievement—people who have performed well—and try to emulate them. Third, the individual should seek to modify his or her self-image by imagining himself or herself as someone who needs success and challenge. Fourth and finally, the individual must control daydreaming by thinking and talking to himself or herself in positive terms.[19]

Power and Affiliation.   In his need achievement theory McClelland does not overlook other needs. In particular, he has investigated the power motive and the affiliation motive.

The **power motive** is the need to manipulate others or be superior to them. It is the need to feel in charge. In recent years McClelland has begun to believe that power is perhaps the most important factor in motivation.[20] There are, however, two sides to power, negative and positive. Negative power is associated with heavy drinking, gambling, and aggressive impulses. Positive power is social power and is characterized by a concern for group goals, helping people formulate direction, and providing the members with a feeling of strength and competence as they seek to attain their objectives.

The **affiliation motive** is equated with social motives or group dynamics, or both. Of the three motives McClelland has studied, affiliation has received the least attention. McClelland found that many successful managers do not have a high affiliation motive because it gets in the way of doing things. Those who have high affiliation needs tend to go along with the group and, rather than wanting to lead, prefer to be one of the members. As a person moves up the organizational hierarchy, the need for affiliation tends to decline.

Achievement Theory in Perspective.   Achievement theory research does not fully explain why people desire to achieve. This is its biggest shortcoming. Most research conducted on the theory has focused on identifying or on trying to develop a desire to achieve.[21] On the other hand, achievement motivation research has proven very useful in helping us to understand the characteristics of high achievers and how managers can try to develop this need in subordinates. However, how do managers motivate these people who are not high achievers? In addition, what specific factors, such as money, working conditions, and recognition, should the manager offer in order to really motivate personnel? Frederick Herzberg has sought to answer questions such as these in his two-factor theory of motivation.

STOP

Review your answers to Question 2 and make any changes you would like before continuing.

2. Is Henry a high achiever? Defend your answer.

He certainly is a high achiever. Notice how he set goals for himself and then proceeded to achieve them. These goals were realistic and Henry undoubtedly used the feedback from his sales efforts to help him modify his approaches and increase his performance. It took him two years to become the best salesperson in his territory and another year to become first in the entire company. This success is certainly a result of Henry's high achievement drive.

Herzberg's Two-Factor Theory

One of the most controversial theories of motivation is that of Frederick Herzberg. Originally based on research that he and his associates conducted among 200 engineers and accountants,[22] it is commonly referred to as the **two-factor theory of motivation,** or the motivation-hygiene theory.

Motivation and Hygiene Factors.   In their research, Herzberg and his associates sought to examine the relationship between job satisfaction and productivity. Using semistructured interviews, they asked their respondents to recall a time when each felt exceptionally good about his or her job and a time when he or she felt exceptionally negative about his or her job.

From the results, the researchers concluded that motivation derived from two sets of factors. The first, associated with positive feelings about the job and related to the content of the work itself, they called **motivators.** Illustrations included achievement, recognition, the work itself, responsibility, advancement, and growth. The factors in the second set, which they labeled **hygiene,** did not bring about satisfaction; they simply prevented dissatisfaction. These factors are external to the work itself. Illustrations included company policies, supervision, interpersonal relations, working conditions, and salary.

Hygiene does not cause satisfaction.

As seen in Figure 6–4, which relates factors affecting job attitudes as reported in twelve investigations, those factors labeled motivators usually led to extreme satisfaction. Conversely, those factors labeled hygiene characterized events that usually led to extreme dissatisfaction. The overall factors in the figure total more than 100 percent because two factors were sometimes attributed to a single event. For example, advancement often accompanied the assumption of responsibility.

Herzberg and those who support his theory believe that hygiene creates a zero level of motivation. If employees are given such factors as good supervision, adequate

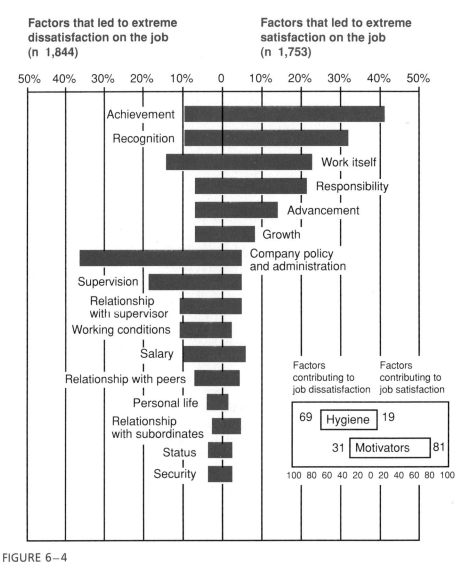

FIGURE 6−4
Factors Affecting Job Attitudes (Adapted from Frederick Herzberg, "One More Time: How Do You Motivate Employees?" *Harvard Business Review,* January−February 1968, p. 57.)

Motivators do cause satisfaction.

salaries, and a chance to interact with their peers, this will not create motivation, but it will prevent dissatisfaction. If they are given factors such as recognition, increased responsibility, and a chance for advancement and growth, this will result in motivation. Thus the two-factor theory sees satisfaction and dissatisfaction as separate and distinct concepts. Hygiene factors, at best, result in no satisfaction, and may bring about dissatisfaction. Motivators, meanwhile, can bring about satisfaction and, at worst, result in no satisfaction.

The Two-Factor Theory Under Attack. The two-factor theory is a matter of controversy. On the one hand, there have been successful replications of the original findings. Filley, House, and Kerr report that in ten studies designed to test Herzberg's theory:

> 17 different populations of employees were interviewed. . . . Of 51 significant differences reported for 6 satisfiers, every one was in the predicted direction. For 57 dissatisfiers, 54 were in the predicted direction. In sum, when theoretical predictions were made for each study separately, the predictions were found to be valid in more than 97 percent of the cases.[23]

Solimon has found that in seventeen of twenty studies that used Herzberg's methodology, results supportive of the two-factor theory were obtained,[24] and Hodgetts and Luthans report a number of successful international replications of the theory.[25]

On the other hand, critics argue that the storytelling critical-incident method, in which the interviewee relates extremely satisfying and dissatisfying job events, accounts for the results. People tend to give socially acceptable responses when asked questions such as those used by Herzberg and his associates. In short, they tell the interviewer what they think the individual would like to hear. The theory is thus regarded as being *methodologically bound,* which means that the method used to measure the factors determines the results. Such a criticism, of course, strikes at the very heart of the theory because it challenges the value of the data collection method.

A second major criticism is that the research is fraught with procedural deficiencies. One of these is that interviewee responses sometimes had to be interpreted by the researcher. Thus there was a chance of interviewer bias and contamination. Additionally, the operational definitions used by Herzberg and his associates to identify satisfiers and dissatisfiers are criticized as being inadequate. In particular, critics have questioned the mutual exclusiveness of the dimensions, resulting in individuals responding in the same manner to similarly worded statements.

Pulling together criticisms such as these, researchers like House and Wigdor have concluded that the two-factor theory does not withstand empirical scrutiny.

> Our secondary analysis of the data presented by Herzberg . . . yields conclusions contradictory to the proposition of the Two-Factor theory that satisfiers and dissatisfiers are unidimensional and independent. Although many of the intrinsic aspects of jobs are shown to be more frequently identified by respondents as satisfiers, achievement and recognition are also shown to be very frequently identified as dissatisfiers. In fact, achievement and recognition are far more frequently identified as dissatisfiers than working conditions and relations with the superior.
>
> Since the data do not support the satisfier-dissatisfier dichotomy, the . . . proposition of the Two-Factor theory, that satisfiers have more motivational force than dissatisfiers, appears highly suspect. This is true for two reasons. First, any attempt to separate the two requires an arbitrary definition of the classifications satisfier and dissatisfier. Second, unless such an arbitrary separation is employed, the proposition is untestable.[26]

Critics also note that for many people money is a motivator[27] as seen by the fact that pay-for-performance plans often boost productivity[28] and result in pay satisfaction.[29] Yet Herzberg claims it is a hygiene factor.

In summary, then, the theory is at best controversial. It has been consistently supported when the critical-incident storytelling method is employed but not consistently supported when other measures are used. Thus the findings appear to be a result of the methodology, which is biased in favor of the theory.

 STOP   Review your answers to Question 3 and make any changes you would like before continuing.

3. In terms of the two-factor theory of motivation, what hygiene factors has the firm given to Henry? Are there any motivators in his new job? What are they?

The salary, commissions, benefits, and vacation are all hygiene factors. The case does not relate anything directly about motivators. However, there are some that can be easily assumed, including increased responsibility, advancement, growth, achievement, recognition, and the work itself. A review of Figure 6–4 should make this clearer.

Comparison of Content Theories

The four content theories examined in this section, all of which can be explained in terms of needs, are summarized in Figure 6–5. By using Maslow's theory as the reference point, we can compare the other three models to his. All of them provide

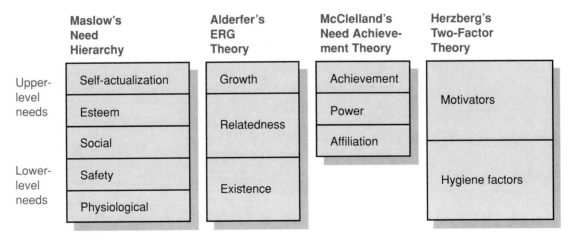

FIGURE 6–5
Comparison of Selected Content Theories

Organizational Behavior In Action

A TOUGH ACT TO FOLLOW

How do you motivate people? Typical approaches include kindness, understanding, and concern for others. However, there are many managers who seem to totally disregard such humanistic approaches and run their firms with an iron fist. Moreover, some of these individuals are top executives at major firms. Here are three examples.

Frank Lorenzo, who resigned as Chairman of Texas Air just as this book was going to press, put together one of the largest commercial airlines in the world by acquiring carriers such as Continental and Eastern. In the process, he had more than his share of troubles from both the pilots and the machinists who viewed him as a "loose cannon." Lorenzo was famous for undermining his own managers, making abrupt changes in air fares, and diverting planes from one of the company's airlines to another. Lorenzo was regarded as incredibly impulsive and was widely mistrusted both inside and outside the organization. On the other hand, he proved himself an excellent dealmaker and was a major force in the commercial airline business for almost a decade.

Richard Mahoney, Chief Executive of Monsanto, set a goal of 20 percent return on equity, which is extremely high for the industry. He managed to approach this goal by cutting both unwanted business and excess costs. He is known for unilaterally adjusting targets before they are reached, so that executives who thought they were going to achieve their goals now found them being revised upward. He is also tough on his managers, lecturing them unceasingly. One manager recalls a time when he made a mistake, and all the way back on the plane Mahoney harped on him for not living up to his potential. Mahoney is regarded as having a big ego, little empathy, and an inability to believe that he is ever wrong.

Jim Manzi, Chairman of Lotus Development, often labels ideas that do not please him as "dumb" or "stupid." If an individual's explanation is too long, he cuts the person short. When he gets bored in meetings, he sets a clock for two minutes and tells the individual to "finish up." Many subordinates claim that the easiest way to communicate with him is through computer mail and to limit the message to just a few sentences.

Are these individuals exceptions to the rule, or are we likely to see even more of them in the future? Commenting on this, *Fortune* magazine reports:

> The outlook for CEO temperaments? Toughness . . . will probably become more prevalent. . . . As global competition heats up and turmoil rocks more industries, tough management should spread. So look for more bosses who are steely, superdemanding, unrelenting, sometimes abusive, sometimes unreasonable, impatient, driven, stubborn, and combative. And have a nice day.

Source: Peter Nulty, "America's Toughest Bosses," *Fortune,* February 27, 1989, pp. 40–54.

important insights into the subject of motivation, albeit from different points of view. However, a need theory approach is not the only way to examine motivation. Another way is offered by process theories.

SELECTED PROCESS THEORIES OF MOTIVATION

While content theory approaches the study of motivation from the standpoint of *what* it is that motivates people, **process theories of motivation** focus on *how* behavior is initiated, redirected, and halted. In recent years, a number of important process theories have been developed. Three of these are goal setting, equity theory, and expectancy-valence theory.

Goal Setting

Goal setting influences work behavior.

The basic premise in **goal setting** is that an employee's conscious objectives will influence his or her work behavior. Some of the most important work in goal setting has been done by Latham and Locke.[30] One research study, conducted among independent loggers in the South, found that the groups that were most productive had supervisors who stayed on the job with the men, provided training, gave instructions and explanations, and—most importantly, and in contrast to the other work groups—set *specific* production goals for the day or the week. These goals were high, but the group was able to attain them.

Latham and Locke decided to follow up their research and find out if goal setting was the causal factor in productivity. Twenty independent logging crews, identical in size, productivity, and attendance, were chosen for the study. Half the crews were randomly selected to receive training in goal setting; the other half served as the control group. Performance was measured for twelve weeks, and the productivity of the goal-setting group was found to be significantly higher than that of the control group, whereas absenteeism was significantly lower. This led the researchers to note that

> harvesting timber can be a monotonous, tiring job with little or no meaning for
> most workers. Introducing a goal that is difficult, but attainable, increases the
> challenge of the job. In addition, a specific goal makes it clear to the worker
> what it is he is expected to do. Goal feedback . . . provide(s) the worker with
> a sense of achievement, recognition, and accomplishment. He can see how
> well he is doing now as against his past performance and, in some cases, how
> well he is doing in comparison with others. Thus the worker not only may ex-
> pend greater effort, but may also devise better or more creative tactics for
> attaining the goal than those he previously used.[31]

Other researchers also have reported positive results. For example, White conducted a study in two high-technology plants.[32] He found that four events—(a) pursuing a specific goal; (b) working under a deadline; (c) having a large amount of work to do; or (d) having an uninterrupted routine—accounted for more than half of the high-productivity events among those being studied. Conversely, he found that such events as having a small amount of work to do, suffering goal blockage, not having a deadline, and suffering work interruptions accounted for nearly 60 percent of the low-productivity events.

Goal-Setting Theory in Perspective

From studies such as those cited here and others that investigated the importance of goal setting, a number of conclusions have been reached. Some of the most important are the following:

1. Setting clear and specific goals has a greater positive impact on performance improvement than does "do the best you can" goal setting.[33]

2. Employee goals that are seen as difficult but attainable lead to higher performance than do easy goals, as long as the worker accepts the particular goals.[34]

3. When a goal is unique or novel and the individual is unsure of how to proceed, effort may increase but accuracy may decline.[35]

4. Support has been reported for the superiority, in terms of performance improvement, of participative goal setting over the use of assigned goals[36]

5. The use of frequent feedback in the goal-setting process brings about higher individual performance than when such feedback sessions are not employed.[37]

A number of conclusions have been reached about goal setting.

Conclusions such as these have led goal-setting theorists to construct their own models of motivation theory. One example is provided in Figure 6–6. Notice that these theorists see goal setting as a simple, straightforward technique that can result in high

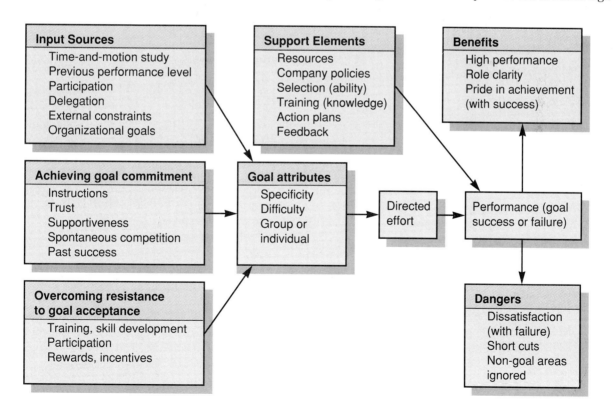

FIGURE 6–6
Goal–Setting Model

motivation and productivity. As is evident in the model, however, there is more to the approach than the mere setting of objectives. Attention must also be focused on rewards, incentives, supportiveness and trust on the part of management, full instructions regarding what is to be done, and direction of the work where required. If the goals are unfair or arbitrary, poor performance may result. If pressure for short-run results is applied without concern for how things are to get done, long-run efficiency may suffer. As Latham and Locke put it, "Like any other management tool, goal setting works only when combined with good managerial judgment."[38] Research in this area continues today.[39]

STOP

Review your answers to Question 4 and make any changes you would like before continuing.

4. How did goal setting help Henry succeed?

Goal setting helped Henry because he set objectives that were difficult but attainable. Remember that no one had ever become a sales manager as fast as Henry did. This was accomplished by setting the right goals, i.e., higher sales than anyone else in the territory and, then, in the company. These goals were tied directly to the company's promotion philosophy, so Henry's strategy was right in line with the company's thinking.

Equity Theory

Equity theory involves social comparison.

A second process approach to motivation is **equity theory,** which holds that if people see a discrepancy between the rewards they are receiving for their efforts when compared to others (the reward-to-work ratio), they will be motivated to do more (or less) work. In essence, equity theory is a *social comparison* theory, because people use it to compare themselves with others to answer the question, "How well am I doing in comparison to others in this organization?" Obviously, people tend to compare themselves with others who are doing similar work or holding similar positions.

The answer to the comparative question can be any one of three: (a) the reward-to-work ratio is lower than that of others; (b) the reward-to-work ratio is the same as that of others; or (c) the reward-to-work ratio is greater than that of others. When the first conclusion is reached, the individual will feel he or she is not being properly rewarded and will take steps to bring the reward-to-work ratio back into line. This often takes the form of securing more rewards or doing less work.[40] Of course, if neither of these two alternatives is feasible, the individual may simply stop making comparisons with these other people because there is nothing the person can do to bring about equity (at least in his or her own mind). Or the individual may quit or get a job elsewhere in the organization, where the perceived reward-to-work ratio is equitable.

Personal perception influences equity considerations.

Equity theory involves *personal perception*. A manager may actually be receiving higher pay than his fellow managers but believe that he is worth even more. In this case, the reward-to-work ratio is still out of balance.[41] Another manager may be receiving the same pay as her fellow managers but, because there is pay secrecy, think that she is getting less. In both cases, the managers believe they are being treated inequitably, although many observers would question their judgment.

Current Status of the Theory.   Over the past decade, a great deal of research and writing has been generated on equity theory.[42] Perhaps the most relevant research has focused on equity theory predictions of employee reactions to pay. These predictions typically distinguish between two conditions of pay (underpayment and overpayment) and two methods of compensation (hourly rate and piece rate). The predictions are listed in Table 6–1.

Research supports equity theory predictions.

Current research findings support many equity theory predictions.[43] This is particularly true regarding underpayment. For example, Lord and Hohenfeld investigated the effect of equity on the performance of major league baseball players. They focused their attention on those players who began the season without contracts and elected to play out their option (at a rate of pay not less than 80 percent of their previous salary) and became free agents. It was believed that these players would view themselves as undercompensated vis-à-vis other players, and that such perceptions would produce lower performance. This hypothesis was found to be true in the case of such performance measures as batting average, home runs, and runs batted in.[44]

On the other hand, Berkowitz and his colleagues have found that satisfaction with one's pay was influenced by whether this pay was regarded as equitable, but it was not influenced by social comparison with others.[45] So there is evidence to indicate that social comparison may not be as universally applied as some theorists would have us believe. Additionally, some researchers have suggested that time lags affect inequity and these need to be more closely studied.[46]

Overall, equity theory is useful to the study of motivation because it helps us better understand human behavior at work. The theory also helps explain why management can redesign someone's job, give the person more autonomy and feedback on performance, and still not motivate the individual.[47] The reason may be found in the

TABLE 6–1
Equity Theory Predictions Regarding Employee Reactions to Inequitable Payment

	Underpayment	Overpayment
Hourly payment	Subjects underpaid by the hour produce less or poorer quality output than equitably paid subjects.	Subjects overpaid by the hour produce more or higher quality output than equitably paid subjects.
Piece-rate payment	Subjects underpaid by piece rate will produce a large number of low-quality units in comparison with equitably paid subjects.	Subjects overpaid by piece rate will produce fewer units of higher quality than equitably paid subjects.

Source: Richard T. Mowday, ''Equity Theory Predictions of Behavior in Organizations,'' in Richard M. Steers and Lyman W. Porter (eds.), *Motivation and Work Behavior* (New York: McGraw-Hill Book Co., 1983), p. 95.

reward-to-work ratio. The worker may feel that management should also raise his or her pay. Motivation is a multifaceted area, and changes in one job factor may require changes in others. Finally, equity theory encourages managers to continually reevaluate the bases on which they distribute available rewards. What is considered equitable today may not be regarded that way tomorrow.

Expectancy-Valence Theory

The most popular process theory is **expectancy-valence theory**. This theory can actually be traced to early work by Tolman[48] and Lewin,[49] but it is most closely associated with such current researchers as Vroom,[50] Lawler,[51] and Hackman and Porter.[52] Expectancy theory postulates that individuals are thinking, reasoning beings who have beliefs and anticipations about future events in their lives. In analyzing what motivates them, therefore, we have to examine what people want from the organization and how they believe they can get it. In doing so there are three major concepts that must be understood: instrumentality, valence, and expectancy.

Instrumentality, Valence, and Expectancy. People are motivated to do things to the extent that they see something in it for themselves. For example, the company wants George to have a good sales year. But what is in it for George? What will he get for achieving high sales? Suppose for a moment that he perceives a positive correlation between high sales and a big raise. Given this assumption, there are two outcomes: the first-level outcome, which is high sales; and the second-level outcome, which is a big raise. The relationship an individual perceives between a first-level and a second-level outcome is known as **instrumentality**.

Next we have to consider George's **valence** or preference for achieving high sales. In doing so, we could list other alternatives as well, including average sales and low sales, as seen in Figure 6–7. If George wants a big raise, there is only one way to get it: He will have to produce high sales, which should have positive valence for him because high sales are instrumental to his obtaining a big raise.

Finally, we have to consider whether George feels he is capable of attaining this sales goal. With a lot of effort and drive, does he believe he can make high sales? The perceived probability of attaining a first-level outcome is called **expectancy**. This probability of success will range from 0 (no chance) to 1 (certainty). If George believes that he can achieve high sales with hard work, his expectancy will be very high (1.0, 0.9, or 0.8).

In this model, there are two specific types of expectancy. The first is the $E \rightarrow P$ expectancy, representing a belief that effort will lead to desired performance. The second is the $P \rightarrow O$ expectancy or instrumentality. Some researchers prefer to use the $E \rightarrow P$ for all level outcomes, first, second, third, and so forth, and to confine themselves to just two concepts, expectancy and valence which are the beliefs the individual has regarding the likelihood that performance will lead to a particular outcome. An individual's motivational force is determined by multiplying the $E \rightarrow P$ expectancy times the $P \rightarrow O$ expectancy times the outcome valence. To illustrate how this can be done, we'll assign probabilities to George, the salesman whose expectancy-valence model is presented in Figure 6–7.

Instrumentality is the relationship between a first- and second-level outcome.

Valence is a person's preference for something.

Expectancy is the perceived probability of attaining a first-level outcome.

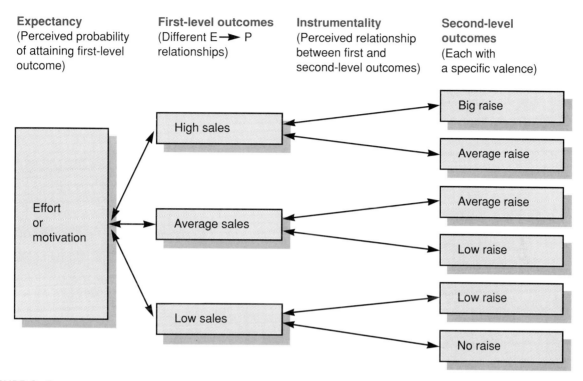

Expectancy
(Perceived probability of attaining first-level outcome)

First-level outcomes
(Different E → P relationships)

Instrumentality
(Perceived relationship between first and second-level outcomes)

Second-level outcomes
(Each with a specific valence)

Effort or motivation

High sales

Average sales

Low sales

Big raise

Average raise

Average raise

Low raise

Low raise

No raise

FIGURE 6–7
Vroom's Expectancy–Valence Model

Motivational force can be measured.

Let us assume that George believes that with hard effort he can attain high sales. We'll put this probability at 0.9 (a 90 percent chance); he has a high E → P expectancy. Furthermore, George believes that high sales will definitely result in a big raise. This P → O expectancy is 1.0, or certainty. Finally, George very much wants a big raise, and places a valence of 0.9 on this reward. In this case his effort would be computed as follows: $0.9 \times 1.0 \times 0.9 = 0.81$, a very high motivational force. On the other hand, if George believed that high sales had a low relationship with a big raise (such as 0.2), then the motivation force would drop dramatically ($0.9 \times 0.2 \times 0.9 = 0.16$). Expectancy theorists see all three concepts—instrumentality, valence, and expectancy—as vitally important to motivation.

Motivation research continues today.

Current Status of the Theory. At present, research on expectancy theory continues.[53] Some of it has been very beneficial in validating at least parts of the theory.[54] For example, it has been found that incentive-pay workers with high expectancy perceptions were significantly higher producers than those with low expectancy perceptions.[55] And pay has generally proved to be an important outcome. Despite these results, however, there are problems.

In particular, researchers would like to know more about the E → P relationship. Some of the factors influencing it include self-esteem, the actual situation, past experiences in similar situations, and communication with others. However, what other causal factors are there? Likewise, the P → O relationship is affected by such factors as the attractiveness of outcomes, E → P expectancies, past experience in similar situations, and the actual situation. Once again, however, what other causal variables are there? Finally, more work needs to be done in determining how expectancies and instrumentalities develop and what influences them. Yet even allowing for these current shortcomings, expectancy theory is very popular among modern behavioral scientists, who: (a) see it as a theory that can be subjected to empirical validation; and (b) like it because it helps shed light on individual motivational factors.

On a more applied basis, expectancy theory provides some useful input for management. First, with regard to E → P expectancies, it is becoming increasingly evident that job training, coaching, managerial guidance, and participation in job-related decisions can all help clarify the relationship. Through such managerial actions, employees are better able to see that high levels of performance are actually within their reach and thus will strive to attain them.

It is also becoming evident that P → O expectancies can be clarified by showing employees that reward systems are based on actual performance. Efforts toward this end not only strengthen the relationship but also help management deal with equity issues. Developments such as these are important in clarifying how expectancy theory can be applied on the job.

STOP

Review your answers to Question 5 and make any changes you would like before continuing.

5. In what way did expectancy, valence, and instrumentality enter into Henry's strategy for getting the sales manager job? Explain.

Expectancy entered into Henry's strategy because he believed that he had the ability to achieve high sales. Valence played a role because he placed a high value on both sales and on the second-level outcome, promotion to sales manager. Instrumentality was important because Henry perceived a strong relationship between high sales and the sales manager job. He was convinced that if he became the leading salesperson in the firm, he would get a sales manager job.

Comparison of Process Theories

As in the case of content theories, the process theories we have examined all approach the study of motivation in a slightly different way. Goal-setting theory puts strong emphasis on difficult but attainable objectives. Equity theory suggests that people are motivated by how well they feel they are being treated vis-à-vis others performing similar work. Expectancy-valence theory recognizes the importance of peer influence, but allows for situations where people make decisions irrespective of others. On the other hand, there are also similarities among the three theories. All three focus on the

TABLE 6–2
Key Motivation Questions

1. Can performance be defined in individual, behavioral terms? If not, develop a separate measure of motivation.
2. Is motivation important for performance, or are abilities and situational factors more important? If motivation is important, but not the same as performance, develop a separate measure of motivation.

If one cannot meet the requirements of questions 1 and 2, it may not be worth it to proceed further. If, however, motivation is important for performance and performance is a good reflection of motivation or a good measure of motivation exists, then proceed with the analysis.

3. Is the reward system rigid and inflexible? In other words, are people and tasks grouped into large categories for reward purposes?
4. Is it difficult to observe what people are actually doing on the job?
5. Is an individual's behavior dependent heavily on the actions of others?
6. Are there lots of changes in people, jobs, or expected behavior?
7. Are social pressures the major determinants of what people are doing on the job?

If questions 3 through 7 are answered with a no, then some system combining a needs analysis with goal setting, operant, expectancy, and equity ideas should be effective.

Source: Terence R. Mitchell, "Motivation: New Directions for Theory, Research and Practice," *Academy of Management Review,* January 1982, p. 86. Reprinted by permission of the author and publisher.

motivation process. They also recognize individual and situational differences that affect the outcomes. Finally, all three are concerned with how people will behave; that is, they are futuristic in their orientation.

What is the future of motivation theory? Researchers like Mitchell believe that more attention needs to be focused on integrating the various approaches.[56] For example, goal setting and equity theory can actually be incorporated into expectancy-valence theory. Second, more attention needs to be directed toward developing contingency types of motivation models that can be developed and tested. Some of Mitchell's ideas are incorporated in Table 6–2. Third, since most jobs are interdependent, social, and subject to change, more theory and research need to be generated toward discovering how group processes affect motivation. Until steps such as these are carried out, a substantial inadequacy will remain in our ability to understand and influence motivation on the job.[57]

SUMMARY

1. Three common denominators characterize the motivation process. They deal with: (a) what energizes human behavior; (b) how this behavior is directed or channeled; and (c) how it can be maintained. Study of motivation in organizations typically involves consideration of psychological and managerial approaches.

2. Content theories reveal a great deal about motivation. Maslow's need hierarchy assumes the existence of levels of needs: physiological, safety, social, esteem, and self-actualization. Although still well received by some, this theory has several shortcomings, including: (a) very little evidence exists to support the contention that there are five

levels of needs; and (b) because people are so different, it is impossible to apply Maslow's theory in a general way to the populace at large.

3. Alderfer's ERG theory explains motivation in terms of existence, relatedness, and growth needs. Although there is some concern about the universality of its application, its satisfaction-progression and frustration-regression components are very useful in explaining human behavior at work.

4. McClelland has also used human needs as a basic unit of analysis in developing need achievement theory. He has found that high achievers: (a) like situations in which they take personal responsibility for finding solutions to problems; (b) tend to be moderate risk takers; and (c) want concrete feedback on their performance.

5. Based on research conducted among 200 engineers and accountants, Herzberg and his associates concluded that motivation is based on two sets of factors. One set, which does not cause satisfaction but prevents dissatisfaction, they called hygiene. It comprises factors external to the work itself, such as company policies, supervision, and salary. The other set, which can cause satisfaction, they called motivators. This set includes achievement, recognition, and the work itself. Although this theory has been highly popularized, it has come under severe attack as being methodologically bound and fraught with procedural deficiencies.

6. Whereas content theories approach the study of motivation from the standpoint of what has been done, process theories focus on how behavior is initiated, redirected, and halted. One such theory is goal setting, which holds that an individual's objectives will influence his or her behavior. If these objectives are clear, difficult but attainable, set in conjunction with the superior, and feedback on performance is provided, high motivation and output often result.

7. A second popular process theory is equity, or social comparison, theory. According to this theory, people compare themselves to others in the organization by using a reward-to-work ratio to determine how well they are being treated. Although the conclusion involves personal perception and may well be wrong, it does influence the individual's motivation. Current research findings support many equity theory predictions, although in and of itself the approach is incomplete in helping to explain the motivation process.

8. A third popular process theory is expectancy-valence theory. Based on the concept that individuals are thinking, reasoning beings who have beliefs and anticipations, the theory approaches motivation from the standpoint of instrumentality, expectancy, and valence. Using this approach, it is possible to compute an individual's motivational force. Research has validated some parts of the theory, and work is continuing on the rest.

KEY TERMS

motivation	safety needs	two-factor theory of motivation
hedonism	social needs	motivators
instinct theory	esteem needs	hygiene
drive and reinforcement theories	self-actualization needs	process theories of motivation
drive	existence needs	goal setting
habit	relatedness needs	equity theory
incentive	growth needs	expectancy-valence theory
cognitive theories	need achievement theory	instrumentality
content theories of motivation	high achievers	valence
need hierarchy	power motive	expectancy
physiological needs	affiliation motive	

REVIEW AND STUDY QUESTIONS

1. What is meant by the term *motivation*? Put it in your own words.

2. In what way can Maslow's need hierarchy help us understand the motivation process?

3. What are some of the basic problems associated with Maslow's need hierarchy?

4. How does ERG theory help us understand motivation? Explain.

5. What are the three characteristics that describe high achievers? Explain each.

6. How can a person develop high achievement drive? Discuss the four steps McClelland suggests.

7. What does Herzberg mean by hygiene factors? Motivators? Give illustrations of each.

8. How does goal-setting theory explain motivation? How accurate is the theory?

9. In what way is equity theory a social comparison theory? How complete is this theory in describing the motivation process?

10. In expectancy-valence theory terms, what is meant by instrumentality, valence, and expectancy?

11. What is meant by the following statement? An individual's motivational force is determined by multiplying the $E \rightarrow P$ expectancy times the $P \rightarrow O$ expectancy times the outcome valence.

12. Why is the expectancy-valence theory so well liked by modern behavioral scientists?

CASES

Strictly a Fixed Salary

Carl Bettman was not an outstanding student in college. Majoring in English, he felt quite lucky to have secured a sales position with a large regional wholesaling firm in New England. The pay was competitive with that of business administration majors, and best of all, he believed, was the company policy of paying the salespeople a fixed salary rather than putting them on an incentive plan.

During his first two years with the firm Carl's performance was anything but impressive. However, as he learned the job and how to make retail contacts, his sales began to rise gradually. By the end of the third year Carl believed he was in the top 20 percent in sales among the company's seventy-five salespeople. The following year, based on discussions with co-workers, Carl concluded that he was now number one. Since the company never gave out sales data and discouraged the comparing of sales information among the personnel, Carl could not be certain he was the leading salesman, but he was reasonably certain that this was the case.

Last year, Carl had an exceptional sales year. His quota, which was 25 percent higher than the previous year, was met by early August. Although he did not say anything to any of the other salespeople, Carl had no indication from any of them that they were even close to fulfilling their own quotas. Additionally, Carl's boss called him in for a brief meeting in late September and congratulated him on the fine year he was having. On the way out, he said to Carl, "I wish we had more people like you around here. It sure would be nice to have two or three superstars." Carl said nothing; he just smiled. However, he took this to mean that he was far and away the best salesperson in the firm.

This year, the company again increased Carl's sales quota by 25 percent. Although he is not off to as fast a start as last year, he is running ahead of expectations. Carl believes that by early October he should be able to meet his quota. At the same time, however, he is finding himself having motivational problems. He is most troubled by the lack of feedback provided by the firm. He has heard that many of the competitors have sales contests and awards that they give out at banquets. There are also in-house newspapers that carry sales information around the firm, letting everyone know who is the best salesperson of the month or year. Carl has been thinking about the way things are done at this firm, and he finds himself getting upset. Initially, of course, when he was not doing well, he had little interest in his sales rank, but now it has grown in importance for him. Furthermore, he is starting to feel that it is unfair to pay salespeople a fixed salary; pay should be tied to sales performance. Last month when he broached this idea with his boss, however, he was quickly rebuffed. Yesterday, to the company's surprise, Carl resigned to go to work for a competitive firm that operates on an incentive plan.

1. Why did Carl disapprove of the firm's fixed-salary payment plan?

2. Is Carl a high achiever? Explain, incorporating into your answer the characteristics of a high achiever.

3. If Carl wants to develop high achievement drive (above and beyond any he might have currently), how might he go about doing so? Explain.

Betting On the Best Horses

A controversy is currently under way at a major midwestern university. A minority of the faculty there have recently banded together and sent the president of the university a letter requesting that 50 percent of all future salary raises be awarded on the basis of annual measurable performance. Specifically, these faculty members have asked the president to use such quantifiable measures as: (a) number of students taught per year; (b) student evaluations; (c) evaluations by departmental chairmen; (d) community service; (e) university committee service; (f) master's and doctoral committees served on and chaired; (g) articles written; and (h) books published. Using this approach, they are proposing that half of all the money allocated for raises be divided among the faculty, with everyone except those being promoted getting a standard across-the-board increase such as 3 percent. After faculty receiving promotions are given an extra raise, the remainder is to be shared by the top 20 percent of the faculty in each college as determined by the quantifiable measures.

Most professors have voiced extreme opposition to this plan, calling it both arbitrary and subjective, since some of the proposed criteria cannot be easily measured. Furthermore, many of the opponents have stated that effective teaching involves more than mere committee work, research, and writing. Much of a professor's value is intangible and thus cannot be reduced to quantifiable measures.

The head of the faculty union has also come out against the plan. She believes that there are so many faculty who are currently underpaid that any attempt to reward one group at the expense of the others is self-defeating. "If we begin giving out merit raises on this basis, we are going to lose faculty, and it costs a lot more to hire replacements. We should be working to keep our faculty by offering the most competitive salaries rather than figuring out ways of dividing them against each other."

On the other hand, a number of the younger professors (among others) have come out in favor of the plan. They argue that there are too many teachers who have retired on the job. They use old lecture notes, come to class late and leave early, and are never around to counsel or assist the students. Yet because they have been in the system for a long time, their salaries are relatively high and an across-the-board increase would be much more beneficial to them than it would be to new professors.

The president of the university has promised to examine the merits of both arguments. Although he believes the plan is controversial, he has made two comments that the sponsors have found supportive. First, the president says that he would like some system for tying pay to performance. Second, he says that without merit pay, the faculty will degenerate into mediocrity. "We should consider giving a large share of our money to our best people, since they are the ones most likely to build us a national reputation. I see nothing wrong with betting on our best horses, as opposed to spreading our bets across the board."

1. What are the benefits of tying pay to performance?

2. Is the proposed plan feasible? Explain.

3. If the plan does not go through, how can a dean of a college go about motivating his or her faculty? What types of rewards are there available to this person?

SELF-FEEDBACK EXERCISE

Identifying What Motivates You

There are many factors that motivate people at work. Below is a list of thirty factors. Read each one and decide how important it is to you. Use the following key to distinguish between those factors that are extremely important and those that hold little motivational appeal:

5   Extremely important
4   Important
3   Indifferent
2   Not very important
1   Of no importance

_____ 1. Interesting work

_____ 2. Impressive job title

_____ 3. Good retirement program

_____ 4. A challenging task

_____ 5. Increased responsibility

_____ 6. Recognition for a job well done

_____ 7. Extra days off with pay

_____ 8. Bonus plan

_____ 9. Job autonomy ✓				7. _____	20. _____	5. _____	22. _____
_____ 10. Good wages ✓				8. _____	24. _____	6. _____	23. _____
_____ 11. A company car				10. _____	25. _____	9. _____	26. _____
_____ 12. Job feedback on performance				11. _____	28. _____	12. _____	27. _____
_____ 13. Feeling of importance				15. _____	30. _____	13. _____	29. _____
_____ 14. A chance to achieve				17. _____	Total _____	14. _____	Total _____

_____ 9. Job autonomy ✓
_____ 10. Good wages ✓
_____ 11. A company car
_____ 12. Job feedback on performance
_____ 13. Feeling of importance
_____ 14. A chance to achieve
_____ 15. Office parties
_____ 16. A feeling of competence
_____ 17. Guaranteed cost of living increase
_____ 18. Good working conditions
_____ 19. Generous expense account
_____ 20. Large office
_____ 21. Pride in the job
_____ 22. Job freedom
_____ 23. A feeling of self-worth ✓
_____ 24. Carpeting on the floor
_____ 25. Health insurance coverage ✓
_____ 26. Social power
_____ 27. A chance to help others
_____ 28. A large desk
_____ 29. A chance to exercise personal initiative
_____ 30. Window in the office

Take each of your answers (1-5) and enter them in the scoring key below. Then total each group.

Group A		Group B	
2. _____	18. _____	1. _____	16. _____
3. _____	19. _____	4. _____	21. _____

Interpretation

Remember that you gave a 5 to a factor that was extremely important and a 1 to a factor that was of no importance, so the group with the *highest* total is the one that includes the factors that have the greatest overall motivational appeal for you. Group A consists of physical rewards (money, working conditions, and job security), while group B consists of psychological rewards (interesting work, job challenge, and a feeling of competence). Group A reflects the importance that physiological, safety, and social need satisfaction have for you. Group B indicates the importance that esteem and self-actualization need satisfaction have for you. If the total of your two lists is close, you have an equal need for both lower and upper level need satisfaction. Most people have a higher total in Group B than in Group A. In further analyzing your own responses, look at those factors to which you gave a 5. This will help you identify the types of things that have the greatest motivational appeal to you. You might also compare your totals with those of other students in the class to see what other patterns of response were elicited by this exercise.

NOTES

1. Stephen P. Robbins, *Organizational Behavior,* 4th ed. (Englewood Cliffs, NJ: Prentice-Hall, 1989), p. 147.

2. Fred Luthans, *Organizational Behavior,* 5th ed. (New York: McGraw-Hill Book Co., 1989), p. 231.

3. Gregory Moorhead and Ricky W. Griffin, *Organizational Behavior,* 2nd ed. (Boston: Houghton Mifflin Co., 1989), p. 103.

4. Clark L. Hull, *Principles of Behavior* (New York: Appleton-Century-Crofts, 1943); Clark L. Hull, *A Behavior System: An Introduction to Behavior Theory Concerning the Individual Organism* (New Haven, CT: Yale Univ. Press, 1952).

5. Richard M. Steers and Lyman W. Porter (eds.), *Motivation and Work Behavior,* 3rd ed. (New York: McGraw-Hill Book Co., 1983), p. 10.

6. Abraham H. Maslow, *Motivation and Personality,* 2nd ed. (New York: Harper & Row, 1954), p. 46.

7. Richard M. Hodgetts, *Management: Theory, Process and Practice,* 5th ed. (Orlando, FL: Academic Press, 1990), p. 470.

8. Howard S. Schwartz, "Maslow and Hierarchical Enactment of Organizational Reality," *Human Relations,* October 1983, pp. 933–955.

9. Edward E. Lawler, III and J. Lloyd Suttle, "A Causal Correlation Test of the Need Hierarchy Concept," *Organizational Behavior and Human Performance,* April 1972, p. 268.

10. Cyrus A. Altimus, Jr. and Richard T. Tersine, "Chronological Age and Job Satisfaction: The Young Blue Collar Worker," *Academy of Management Journal,* March 1973, pp. 53–66.

11. John W. Slocum, Jr. and Robert H. Strawser, "Racial Differences in Job Aptitudes," *Journal of Applied Psychology,* February 1972, pp. 28–32.

12. Lyman W. Porter, "Job Attitudes in Management: IV. Perceived Deficiencies in Need Fulfillment as a Function of a Size of Company," *Journal of Applied Psychology,* December 1963, pp. 386–397.

13. Clayton P. Alderfer, *Existence, Relatedness, and Growth* (New York: Free Press, 1972).

14. Benjamin Schneider and Clayton P. Alderfer, "Three Studies of Measures of Need Satisfaction in Organizations," *Administrative Science Quarterly,* December 1973, pp. 489–505.

15. John P. Wanous and A. Zwany, "A Cross-Sectional Test of Need Hierarchy Theory," *Organizational Behavior and Human Performance,* February 1977, pp. 78–97.

16. Clayton P. Alderfer, "A Critique of Salancik and Pfeffer's Examination of Need-Satisfaction Theories," *Administrative Science Quarterly,* December 1977, pp. 658–669.

17. David C. McClelland, *The Achieving Society* (Princeton, NJ: Van Nostrand Reinhold Co., 1961).

18. For more information about the characteristics of high achievers see David C. McClelland, "Business Drive and National Achievement," *Harvard Business Review,* July-August 1962, pp. 99–112.

19. For more on this see David McClelland, "Achievement Motivation Can Be Learned," *Harvard Business Review,* November-December 1965, pp. 6–24; and Rob-

ert L. Helmreich, Linda I. Sawin, and Alan S. Carsrud, "The Honeymoon Effect in Job Performance: Temporal Increases in the Predictive Power of Achievement Motivation," *Journal of Applied Psychology,* May 1986, pp. 185–188.

20. David C. McClelland and David H. Burnham, "Power Is the Great Motivator," *Harvard Business Review,* March-April 1976, pp. 100–110.

21. Stephen X. Doyle and Benson P. Shapiro, "What Counts Most in Motivating Your Sales People?" *Harvard Business Review,* May-June 1980, pp. 133–140; Michael J. Stahl and Adrian M. Harrell, "Evolution and Validation of a Behavioral Decision Theory Measurement Approach to Achievement, Power, and Affiliation," *Journal of Applied Psychology,* December 1982, pp. 744–751.

22. Frederick Herzberg, Barnard Mausner, and Barbara Bloch Snyderman, *The Motivation to Work* (New York: John Wiley & Sons, 1959).

23. Alan C. Filley, Robert J. House, and Steven Kerr, *Managerial Process and Organizational Behavior,* 2nd ed. (Glenview, IL: Scott, Foresman & Co., 1976), p. 197.

24. Hanafi M. Solimon, "Motivator-Hygiene Theory of Job Attitudes: An Empirical Investigation and An Attempt to Reconcile Both the One- and Two-factor Theories of Job Attitudes," *Journal of Applied Psychology,* October 1970, pp. 452–461.

25. Richard M. Hodgetts and Fred Luthans, *International Management* (New York: McGraw-Hill Book Co., 1991), pp. 379–382.

26. Robert J. House and Lawrence A. Wigdor, "Herzberg's Dual-Factor Theory of Job Satisfaction and Motivation: A Review of the Evidence and a Criticism," *Personnel Psychology,* Winter 1967, pp. 385–386.

27. Connie Wallace, "The Fine Art of Using Money as a Motivator," *Working Woman,* January 1990, pp. 126–139.

28. Jerold R. Bratkovich, "Pay for Performance Boosts Productivity," *Personnel Journal,* January 1989, pp. 78–86.

29. Robert L. Heneman, David B. Greenberger, and Stephen Strasser, "The Relationship Between Pay-For-Performance Perceptions and Pay Satisfaction," *Personnel Psychology,* Winter 1988, pp. 745–759.

30. See, for example, Gary P. Latham and Edwin A. Locke, "Goal-Setting—A Motivational Technique That Works," *Organizational Dynamics,* Autumn 1979, pp. 68–80.

31. *Ibid.,* p. 72.

32. *Ibid.,* pp. 75–76.

33. Sam E. White, Terence R. Mitchell, and Cecil H. Bell, Jr., "Goal-Setting, Evaluation Apprehension, and Social Cues as Determinants of Job Performance and Job Satisfaction in a Simulated Organization," *Journal of Applied Psychology,* December 1977, pp. 665–673.

34. Gary P. Latham and Gary A. Yukl, "A Review of Research on the Application of Goal-Setting in Organizations," *Academy of Management Journal,* December 1975, pp. 824–845; and Dov Eden, "Pygmalion, Goal-Setting, and Expectancy: Compatible Ways to Boost Productivity," *Academy of Management Review,* October 1988, pp. 639–652.

35. P. Christopher Earley, Terry Connolly, and Goran Ekegren, "Goals, Strategy Development, and Task Performance: Some Limits on the Efficacy of Goal Setting," *Journal of Applied Psychology,* February 1989, pp. 24–33.

36. John M. Ivancevich, "Effects of Goal Setting on Performance and Job Satisfaction," *Journal of Applied Psychology,* October 1976, pp. 605–612; and Miriam Erez, P. Christopher Earley, and Charles L. Hulin, "The Impact of Participation on Goal Acceptance and Performance: A Two-Step Model," *Academy of Management Journal,* March 1985, pp. 50–66.

37. Jay S. Kim and W. Clay Hamner, "Effect of Performance Feedback and Goal Setting on Productivity and Satisfaction in an Organizational Setting," *Journal of Applied Psychology,* February 1976, pp. 45–57.

38. Gary P. Latham and Edwin A. Locke, "Goal-Setting—A Motivational Technique That Works," *Organizational Dynamics,* Autumn 1979, p. 80.

39. John R. Hollenbeck and Howard J. Klein, "Goal Commitment and the Goal-Setting Process: Problems, Prospects, and Proposals for Future Research," *Journal of Applied Psychology,* May 1987, pp. 212–220; A. J. Mento, R. P. Steele, and R. J. Karren, "A Meta-Analytic Study of the Effects of Goal Setting on Task Performance: 1964–1984," *Organizational Behavior and Human Decision Processes,* Volume 39, 1987, pp. 52–83; and Edwin L. Locke, Gary P. Latham, and Miriam Erez, "The Determinants of Goal Attainment," *Academy of Management Review,* January 1988, pp. 23–29.

40. For more on equity theory see J. Stacy Adams, "Toward an Understanding of Inequity," *Journal of Abnormal and Social Psychology,* November 1963, pp. 422–436; and J. Stacy Adams, "Inequity in Social Exchange," in L. Berkowitz (ed.), *Advances in Experimental Social Psychology* (New York: Academic Press, 1965).

41. See for example Richard C. Huseman, John D. Hatfield, and Edward W. Miles, "A New Perspective on Equity Theory: The Equity Sensitivity Construct," *Academy of Management Review,* April 1987, pp. 222–234.

42. P. S. Goodman, "Social Comparison Processes in Organizations," in B. M. Staw and G. R. Salancik (eds.), *New Directions in Organizational Behavior* (Chicago: St. Clair Press, 1977), pp. 97–131; Richard T. Mowday, "Equity Theory Predictions of Behavior in Organizations," in Richard M. Steers and Lyman W. Porter, *Motivation and Work Behavior,* 3rd ed. (New York: McGraw-Hill Book Co., 1983), pp. 91–111.

43. Rodger W. Griffeth, Robert P. Vecchio, and James W. Logan, Jr., "Equity Theory and Interpersonal Attraction," *Journal of Applied Psychology,* June 1989, pp. 394–401.

44. Robert G. Lord and Jeffrey A. Hohenfeld, "Longitudinal Field Assessment of Equity Effects on the Performance of Major League Baseball Players," *Journal of Applied Psychology,* February 1979, pp. 19–26.

45. Leonard Berkowitz, Colin Fraser, F. Peter Treasure, and Susan Cochran, "Pay, Equity, Job Gratifications, and Comparisons in Pay Satisfaction," *Journal of Applied Psychology,* November 1987, pp. 544–551.

46. Richard A. Cosier and Dan R. Dalton, "Equity Theory and Time: A Reformulation," *Academy of Management Review,* April 1983, pp. 311–319.

47. Keep in mind, however, that despite complaints about inequity, most workers regard their job as a source of personal satisfaction and pride, as reported in research such as William Rabinowitz, Kenneth Falkenback, Jeffrey R. Travers, C. Glenn Valentine, and Paul Weener, "Worker Motivation: Unsolved Problem or Untapped Resource," *California Management Review,* January 1983, pp. 45–56.

48. Edward C. Tolman, *Purposive Behavior in Animals and Men* (New York: Century Company, 1932).

49. Kurt Lewin, *A Dynamic Theory of Personality* (New York: McGraw-Hill Book Co., 1935).

50. Victor H. Vroom, *Work and Motivation* (New York: John Wiley & Sons, 1964).

51. Edward E. Lawler, III, *Motivation in Work Organizations* (Monterey, CA: Brooks/Cole, 1973).

52. Richard Hackman and Lyman W. Porter, "Expectancy Theory Predictions of Work Effectiveness," *Organizational Behavior and Human Performance*, November 1968, pp. 417–426.

53. See for example D. F. Parker and L. Dyer, "Expectancy Theory as a Within Person Behavioral Choice Model: An Empirical Test of Some Conceptual and Methodological Refinements," *Organizational Behavior and Human Performance*, October 1976, pp. 97–117; and H. J. Arnold, "A Test of the Multiplicative Hypothesis of Expectancy-Valence Theories of Work Motivation," *Academy of Management Journal*, March 1981, pp. 128–141.

54. Michael J. Stahl and Adrian M. Harrell, "Using Decision Modeling to Measure Second Level Valences in Expectancy Theory," *Organizational Behavior and Human Performance*, August 1983, pp. 23–34.

55. John E. Sheridan, John W. Slocum, Jr., and Byung Min, "Motivational Determinants of Job Performance," *Journal of Applied Psychology*, February 1975, pp. 119–121.

56. Terence R. Mitchell, "Motivation: New Directions for Theory, Research and Practice," *Academy of Management Review*, January 1982, pp. 80–88.

57. Also see Lynn E. Miller and Joseph E. Grush, "Improving Predictions in Expectancy Theory Research: Effects of Personality, Expectancies, and Norms," *Academy of Management Journal*, March 1988, pp. 107–122; and Howard J. Klein, "An Integrated Control Theory Model of Work Motivation," *Academy of Management Review*, April 1989, pp. 150–172.

PART III
GROUP BEHAVIOR IN ORGANIZATIONS

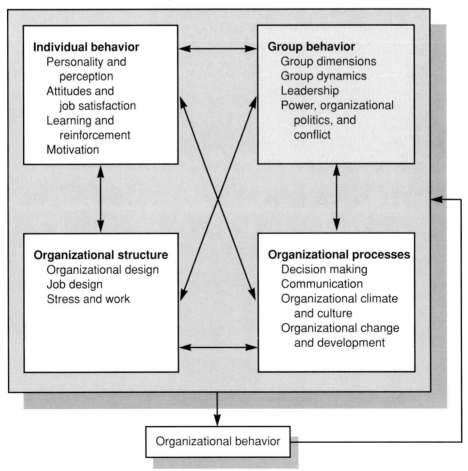

Conceptual Model for this Book

Individual behavior
Personality and
 perception
Attitudes and
 job satisfaction
Learning and
 reinforcement
Motivation

Group behavior
Group dimensions
Group dynamics
Leadership
Power, organizational
 politics, and
 conflict

Organizational structure
Organizational design
Job design
Stress and work

Organizational processes
Decision making
Communication
Organizational climate
 and culture
Organizational change
 and development

Organizational behavior

In an organizational setting, no individual functions alone. All are members of at least one informal group. As a result, our study of organizational behavior would be incomplete without consideration of group behavior in organizations.

The major goal of this part of the book is to study the nature and dynamics of group behavior. In this study, primary attention will be given to the structural components of groups, intragroup behavior, intergroup behavior, and the role of leadership.

In Chapter 7 we will examine the basic dimensions of a group. In so doing we will begin by defining the term *group* and examining the kinds of groups people join, as well as why they join them. Then we will study the structural components of groups: composition, norms, status, roles, cohesiveness, and leadership (both formal and informal).

In Chapter 8 we will examine group dynamics—the ways in which individual members interact in a group and the ways groups interact with each other. We will begin by analyzing some of the characteristics that individuals bring to groups and the ways these characteristics help determine each member's influence on the group. We will then study intragroup behavior, giving primary attention to communication networks and decision making. Finally, we will examine intergroup behavior by focusing on intergroup performance and intergroup power.

In Chapter 9, we will study the leadership process. This process involves influencing people to direct their efforts toward achieving particular goals. As such it is a key variable in the study of group behavior. Our examination of leadership will begin with trait theory and continue on to behavioral theory and contingency theory. We will see where leadership theory research has been, currently is, and seems to be heading. Finally, before concluding our discussion of leadership, we will carefully examine the topic of leader effectiveness and explore an integrative model of leadership.

In Chapter 10, we will consider power and organizational politics. This chapter will examine the five bases of power and the ways in which people use these forms of power to accomplish their objectives. Attention will also be focused on the tactics used to gain individual, intragroup, and intergroup power, as well as some of the most commonly used political tactics.

When you have finished reading this part of the book, you should know how groups are formed and why people join them. You should also know the structural components of a group, how individuals influence a group (and are influenced in turn), the major variables affecting intergroup performance, strategies that are useful in managing intergroup performance, the ways in which groups gain power over other groups, and some of the cooperative strategies often used for power acquisition. Most important, you should have a solid understanding of group behavior and its importance to the study of organizational behavior. ◆

CHAPTER 7
Group Dimensions

Groups are an important component in the study of organizational behavior. This chapter's goals are to introduce and to explain the dimensions of groups. First, we will investigate why people join groups. Then we will define the term and discuss the three major kinds of groups. Finally, we will examine the structural components of groups, including group composition, norms, status, roles, cohesiveness, and leadership. When you have finished reading this chapter you should have a solid understanding of how groups are formed and what the structural components of groups are. You should also be able to:

1. define what is meant by the term *group;*
2. give some of the major reasons that people join groups;
3. identify and compare the three different kinds of groups found in organizations: functional groups, task and project groups, and interest and friendship groups;
4. discuss the structural components of groups, including group composition, norms, roles, status, cohesiveness, and leadership;
5. describe the four distinct phases that groups go through as they develop and grow.

OPENING CASE: A CLOSE-KNIT GROUP

Maria Delgado is a new member of the customer accounts group at a large regional chain. The group's job is to contact customers whose accounts are delinquent and get these individuals to pay their bills. Each member of the group is supposed to call an average of ten people an hour and to generate $1,000 a day in collections. The work is stressful, and the group members admit that if it were not for the high salary ($12 an hour plus benefits) they would quit.

Within the first week, Maria showed that she was a very effective worker. A number of accounts that were judged uncollectible were turned over to her, and she managed to contact 80 percent of these people and get partial payments from all of them. Maria is also very helpful to her co-workers. In a number of cases she has gotten on the line with a fellow worker and helped convince the customers to pay the bill. As a result,

Maria is well liked by the group.

Because it is so important for all of the members to be productive, anyone who fails to carry his or her share of the work is soon let go. In the interim, however, everyone else is expected to make up this slack by placing more calls per hour and generating more payments. The group of ten workers is usually able to attain its objective of $10,000 daily because there is a great deal of joint cooperation. "If it weren't for the high amount of teamwork, we'd never be able to reach our daily targets," one of the group members said recently. "It's a group effort."

Last week one of the members of the group heard that the company intends to raise the daily goal to $1,100 per person. "If they do that," the woman said, "I'm not going along. It's tough enough getting $1,000 a day." From the comments made by the other group members, Maria

could tell they were in agreement with these sentiments.

1. Why are the individuals in this group so supportive of each other?
2. What type of group is this? Explain.
3. Is this a homogeneous or a heterogeneous group? Are there any norms that govern behavior in the group?
4. How do people in this group gain status? What explains Maria's status in the group?
5. Does this group have high cohesion? If the group members decide to oppose management's efforts to raise the daily work quota to $1,100, what will be the result? Explain.

Write down your answers to these questions and put them aside. We will return to them later.

WHAT IS A GROUP?

There is no universally accepted definition of a group. A cursory review of the literature reveals that most authors tend to define a **group** on the basis of one or more specific characteristics. Some of these characteristics include perception, motivation, organization, interdependency, and interaction.[1]

Those who define a group in terms of group member perceptions believe the individuals have to be aware of their relationships to others. This usually occurs in face-to-face meetings, but this is not a necessary condition.

Another way to define a group is from the standpoint of motivation: People join a group because it will satisfy some need. In this case, the group provides some form of reward to the participants. This is true even if the individual contributes very little and, in fact, gets a "free ride."[2]

There are various definitions of a group.

One common definition, especially in the sociological literature, emphasizes organizational characteristics. Students of group behavior who are impressed by the structural elements of groups (norms, roles, statuses) and the relationships among them also fall into this category. Others feel that the essential aspect of a group is the interdependency of its members. Still others see interaction as the primary characteristic of a group. In an effort to incorporate these ideas into this book but not give any one preeminence over the others, we will use the following definition:

> A group is a collection of two or more interdependent and interactive individuals who are seeking to attain common objectives.

WHY DO PEOPLE JOIN GROUPS?

There are many reasons that people join groups. One of the most obvious is need satisfaction, a topic we examined in Chapter 5. Other reasons include: (a) proximity, interaction, and influence; (b) similarity; and (c) group goals and activities.

Proximity, Interaction, and Influence

One of the most common reasons why people join groups is because they work near each other. Informal groups often seem to spring up among those who are in close work proximity. Additionally, when people have frequent interaction or contact with one another there is a strong likelihood that they will form a group. Finally, if the behavior of one individual influences that of others, they are all likely to form a group.

Similarity

People also join groups because they are attracted to individuals who are similar to themselves. This similarity can take numerous forms. People with the same attitudes and beliefs often end up in the same group. This is as true when we explain why workers join a union as it is in describing why a particular individual belongs to one church rather than to another. Research shows that other similarity factors include personality, economic position, race, sex, and perceived ability.[3] In short, people tend to associate with others who have similar characteristics and beliefs. For example, in a math class where everyone is convinced that the professor is out to fail them, the students are likely to constitute a closely knit group. In this case, the basis of attraction is misery, and we know that misery loves company.

Group Activities and Goals

Individuals are also attracted to groups because they want to participate in certain activities or pursue particular goals. For example, if a group of workers has a bridge game going during lunch hour, a person may join the informal group because he or she enjoys playing bridge. The same analogy holds true in the case of formal groups. For example, if a group of engineers is being assembled to work on a project, those interested in the type of activity required for this project's success are most likely to apply for admission to the group.

Although it is difficult to separate the activities of a group from its goals, an individual may be particularly attracted to a group because of its overall purposes. For example, many people join fund-raising groups because they want to support the group's cause. In fact, some may not know any of the other members of the group before joining (and may not care to develop friendships with them during the campaign), but this does not stop them from wanting to contribute their time and effort. Also, we must not overlook the fact that some projects cannot be achieved by one person alone, so those who are interested in the objective must be prepared to join the group.

STOP

Review your answers to Question 1 and make any changes you would like before continuing.

1. Why are the individuals in this group so supportive of each other?

The individuals are highly supportive of each other because they work in close proximity, and this tends to encourage interaction and support. Second, they all face the same situation, i.e., collect $1,000 per day, and this common goal draws them together if only because misery loves company.

KINDS OF GROUPS

Many different kinds of groups are found in organizations. For purposes of classification, however, they can be reduced to three: (a) functional groups; (b) task or project groups; and (c) interest and friendship groups.

Functional Groups

A functional group is determined by the organization's
structure.

A **functional group** is one determined by the organization's structure. In a typical national manufacturing firm, for example, there is a marketing department, within which we would find sales groups. These groups are each headed by a district sales manager who has been assigned authority over the personnel by higher management. This manager supervises the salespeople and is responsible for seeing that the group meets its sales quota.

In a university setting there are analogous functional groups. For example, people in the College of Business who are behavioral scientists are commonly found in the management department, while those who teach advertising are in the marketing department, and those who teach auditing are assigned to the accounting department. In each case, a department chairperson is responsible for supervising these people and seeing that they are helping to meet the formal goals of the college.

Functional groups can also be found in hospitals. For example, the head nurse of a hospital ward is responsible for the care of ward patients. This individual, in turn, translates the directions of the physicians into tasks, which are then assigned to the members of the functional group (registered nurses, licensed practical nurses, and nurses' aides) who work in the ward. It is the responsibility of these people to carry out the assignments.

Functional groups are usually classified as formal organizational groups, and they tend to remain in existence for an indefinite period of time. The objectives, interactions, interdependencies, and performance levels of these groups are determined by the organization itself.

Task or Project Groups

A task or project group is temporary in nature.

Some groups are created to accomplish a particular objective, and once it has been done they are disbanded. These are called **task groups** or **project groups**.

One of the widest uses of such groups is in the aerospace industry, in which workers are assigned to a specific project. Working within this group the members design, build, and test specific hardware, such as a missile or an aircraft. The organization assigns a project manager to head the undertaking, and reporting to this individual are people responsible for research and development, engineering, manufacturing, testing, and controlling. Following a prepared master plan, the manager strives to complete the project within the specified time, cost, and quality parameters. Analogous illustrations can be found in the construction, chemical, and oil industries, in which heavy use is also made of project teams.

Such groups are not limited to a specific industry, however. In addition to helping build things, task and project groups are widely used for problem identification and resolution. For example, in hospitals task groups made up of individuals may investigate ways to reduce administrative overhead and cut costs. In universities task groups may study curriculum development and make recommendations regarding new courses to offer or old ones to drop.

Task or project groups consist of individuals whose common goal is to attain some specific objective. Thus, the relationships of the members revolve around goal attainment. In most cases there is a superior-subordinate relationship within the group, although it is much more informal in the university committee, for example, than in the aerospace industry group. In any event, these groups are generally considered to be formal groups.

Interest and Friendship Groups

Interest and friendship groups are formed on the basis of common concerns, beliefs, or activities.

Many people form **interest groups** and **friendship groups** on the basis of common concerns, beliefs, or activities. For example, a functional group in a commercial loan department may also be a friendship group when the individuals are out on the golf links (Figure 7–1). However, the informal leader, or person with the highest recognition and status, on the golf course may not be the leader when the group is back in the office.

Many times, however, the interest and friendship groups to which a person belongs do not have the same membership as the formal groups of which that person is a member (see Table 7–1). People from different departments may be on the same bowling team, serve together on the United Way campaign, or play bridge every day during lunch hour, or may do all three. In short, organizational personnel tend to belong to many different and overlapping formal and informal groups. Furthermore, the goals of informal groups and those of the organization are *not* always in agreement. When they are not, this can mean trouble for management. Before we have finished our discussion of groups in the next chapter, we will have examined some of the ways in which these potential problems can be resolved.

	Functional Group: Commercial Loan Department	Friendship Group: Golfing Foursome	
Highest recognition, most status, greatest autonomy	*George Anderson* Can make loans of up to $300,000 without clearing it with the committee	*Phil Boulding* 5 handicap	Recognized as best golfer
	Dick Ludlam Can make loans of up to $100,000 without clearing it with the committee	*Bob Whitney* 12 handicap	
	Phil Boulding Can make loans of up to $25,000 without clearing it with the committee	*Dick Ludlam* 18 handicap	
Least recognition, least status, least autonomy	*Bob Whitney* Can make loans of up to $10,000 without clearing it with the committee	*George Anderson* 22 handicap	Recognized as poorest golfer

FIGURE 7–1
Functional and Friendship Groups

TABLE 7–1

Types and Characteristics of Groups

Type	Characteristics
Functional groups	1. Relationship of the members is determined by the organization structure. 2. Purpose of the group is to carry out ongoing tasks. 3. There is a superior-subordinate relationship between the members. 4. The group is generally considered a formal one.
Task or project group	1. Relationship between the members is geared toward the attainment of some specific objective. 2. Life of the group is limited, with a phaseout occurring when the goal is accomplished. 3. The group can involve superior-subordinate relationships. 4. It is usually considered a formal group.
Interest or friendship groups	1. Relationship between the members is based on some common characteristics, such as personal interests or political beliefs. 2. The goals of the group may be congruent with those of the organization, but not always. 3. Depending on the situation, the group can be either a formal or an informal one.

Committee Organization

No discussion of groups would be complete without a consideration of the committee form of organization. The committee form transcends the various types of groups because functional, task, project, interest, and friendship groups often use the committee form.

There are two basic types of committees: ad hoc and standing. An **ad hoc committee** is formed for a particular reason, and when the objective has been accomplished, the group is disbanded. A product development group is an example of an ad hoc committee. Once the group has completed designing or developing the product or its commercial success is ensured, the committee is disbanded and functional personnel (manufacturing and marketing) take over.

A **standing committee** is one that exists indefinitely. The most common example is a corporation's board of directors. Personnel and finance committees in large firms are other examples.

Advantages and Disadvantages. The committee has a number of advantages. Three of the most commonly cited include: (a) the opportunity it provides for collective judgment; (b) the benefits it offers in coordinating planning activities and transmitting information throughout the organization; and (c) the motivational value it creates among the personnel, who often derive from it both support and enthusiasm for their own decisions.

There are two basic types of committees.

Committees also have a number of drawbacks. These include: (a) they can be a waste of time and money; (b) they often compromise by opting for an alternative that pleases no one but is acceptable to all; and (c) they often are used when the matter can be best handled by an individual manager.

Committee Effectiveness. How can committees be employed effectively? There are a number of useful guidelines. One rule is that only the best-qualified individuals should be chosen to serve on the committee. The choice of people should be tied directly to the objectives of the group. If the goal is to review personnel policies, the membership should be familiar with these policies and be knowledgeable regarding the personnel area. If the objective is to improve production efficiency, the members should know how the organization produces its products and the types of bottlenecks that exist in the process.

A second useful rule is to have a specific agenda drawn up and delivered to each of the members prior to the meeting. In this way everyone is more likely to come to the meeting prepared to discuss the issues and to make recommendations that are both practical and cost effective.

A third important rule is to have enough committee members that the assigned tasks can get done, but not so many that people on the committee get in each other's way or sit around doing nothing. There is a balance between understaffed and over-staffed, and the chairperson should strive to achieve this balance.

A fourth important rule is for the chairperson to keep the meeting headed toward its stated objectives. Occasionally discussion will wander off the main point. However, the chairperson must then gently but firmly steer the group back to its purpose.

These guidelines will not guarantee committee success. However, they are designed to improve committee performance because they deal directly with some of the most common pitfalls in committee operations.[4]

A number of guidelines exist for improving committee effectiveness.

Review your answers to Question 2 and make any changes you would like before continuing.

2. What type of group is this? Explain.

This is a functional group because all of the individuals perform the same activity, collecting money from customers who are delinquent in paying their bills. It is an interest group because everyone has the same concerns. It is also a friendship group because the members help out each other.

THE STRUCTURAL COMPONENTS OF GROUPS

In order to understand group behavior fully, we have to examine the structural components of a group. These components include: (a) group composition; (b) norms; (c) roles; (d) status; (e) cohesiveness; and (f) leadership.

Group Composition

Group behavior is a function of the individuals who compose the group. Sometimes these people have similar needs, motives, and personalities, in which case they constitute a **homogeneous group**. Other times the needs, motives, and personalities of the members are greatly varied, constituting a **heterogeneous group**.

Homogeneous groups are similar in composition; heterogeneous groups are diverse.

Homogeneous groups have been found to be very effective at handling simple, routine tasks. Since everyone in the group is highly compatible, group cooperation and communication are good, and the members usually have few interpersonal problems. This harmonious environment is conducive to high group effectiveness on routine matters.[5] However, such compatibility often results in overconformity, making it very difficult for the individuals to deal with nonroutine matters.

Heterogeneous groups, on the other hand, have been found to be very effective at handling complex tasks, especially those requiring innovative approaches to problem solving. The members often have different training and knowledge so that what one person does not know, another does. Additionally, because their personalities are so different the members do not hesitate to ask questions and challenge the thinking or conclusions of other members. The result is an active interchange of ideas, often resulting in highly innovative solutions. On the negative side, of course, heterogeneous groups have great potential for conflict.

Many organizations have a need for homogeneous groups because the work is basically simple and coordination is a high priority. Banks, insurance companies, utilities, and manufacturing firms all require personnel to handle routine, everyday activities. Homogeneous groups are ideal for this purpose. At the same time these firms also need heterogeneous groups to handle major problems and develop creative and innovative ideas that can be turned into new goods and services for the consumer. Thus, every organization requires groups with both kinds of composition.

Norms

Norms are behavioral rules of conduct.

Norms are behavioral rules of conduct that have been established by members of the group. These norms provide each individual with a basis for predicting the behavior of other members, thereby helping the person anticipate the actions of others and prepare an appropriate response. Norms relate how the group member ought to act.

In understanding how norms develop and influence group behavior, it is important first to realize that a group does not establish norms to cover every conceivable situation, but only those that have significance for it. Second, some norms apply to everyone, as in the case of how much work each person ought to do, whereas others apply to select individuals, as in the case of the person located nearest the window who can see the supervisor approaching and alert the rest of the group.

Third, norms vary in the degree to which they are accepted by the group. Some workers may be willing to restrict their output to 90 percent of that required by management, while others will do as much as 105 percent of this standard. Finally, norms vary in range of permissive deviation. When people do deviate, some form of sanction is usually directed toward them. If the deviation is considered small, it may result in the other members verbalizing mild disapproval. ("If you don't slow down your output, George, you're going to make the rest of us look bad and probably get someone fired.") If the deviation is considered major, it may result in the group's ganging up on the individual and trying to get him fired or transferred. ("I told the foreman that George is in such a hurry to get his work done that he's causing bottlenecks in the rest of the line. The foreman is going to reprimand George and probably recommend that he be moved over to Department F.")

Conformity to Norms.   There are many reasons why individuals conform to group norms. Among the major ones are personal factors, ambiguity, situational factors, and intragroup relationships.

Personal factors include such things as age, sex, intelligence, and authoritarianism. Research shows, for example, that conformity tends to increase to a maximum level at ages thirteen to fifteen and to decrease thereafter.[6] Females, meanwhile, tend to be more conforming than males at all age levels. One researcher has offered the following explanation:

> Sex differences in conformity behavior may simply reflect cultural differences in sex roles . . . or they may reflect other cultural influences. . . . It has been suggested that there exists in our society a stereotypical belief that men are superior to women in certain areas. . . . If men are seen as more competent then it is not surprising that they conform less than women. In line with these expectations, Tuddenham et al. reported that women were more conforming when they were concerned about their answers not appearing peculiar to others, whereas men conformed more when they were concerned about completing the task quickly. This becomes especially significant in explaining sex differences in conformity behavior when the different orientations of men and women are considered.[7]

Intelligence, however, tends to be negatively related to conformity. Individuals with high intelligence are usually less conforming than are those with low intelligence. Likewise, people who are heavily nonauthoritarian tend to be less willing to conform than are those who are highly authoritarian.

Ambiguity can cause conformity.

A second major factor accounting for conformity is *ambiguity.* If people do not understand instructions or the choice of alternatives is unclear, they are likely to conform to the lead of those who seem to know what is going on.

Group size can also influence conformity.

Situational factors include such variables as group size, unanimity of the majority, and structure of the group. Size is important because conformity tends to increase as group size grows, and then, after some point, remains essentially constant.[8] Conformity will also vary depending upon the responses of the other group members. If one of the other people answers correctly while the rest give a unanimously wrong answer, the naive subject is much less likely to conform. One obvious reason is that the subject is encouraged that someone else agrees with him or her. A second reason, demonstrated by Shaw and colleagues, is that the simple lack of unanimity among the other members leads the person to reject conformity pressures.[9] Finally, group structure is an important variable in that conformity is generally greater in a decentralized communication network than in a centralized one.[10] In overall terms, the social context in which group interaction occurs has a marked effect on the conformity behavior of the members.

Intragroup relationships are the relations between members of the group. Included are such variables as the kind of pressures exerted, the composition of the group, how successful the group has been in achieving past goals, and the degree to which the person identifies with the group.[11] Numerous illustrations of these variables can be cited. One of the most interesting, in which all three variables are brought together, has been provided by Arthur Schlesinger, one of the advisers to President Kennedy during the Bay of Pigs invasion.

> In the months after the Bay of Pigs I bitterly reproached myself for having kept so silent during those crucial discussions in the Cabinet Room, though my feelings of guilt were tempered by the knowledge that a course of objection would have accomplished little save to *gain me a name as a nuisance.* I can only explain my failure to do more than raise a few timid questions by reporting that one's impulse to blow the whistle on this nonsense was simply undone by the circumstances of the discussion.[12]

Norms have a great impact on how group members act. People "need to be needed," and if attainment of this goal requires them to abide by behavioral rules of conduct formulated by the group at large, in most cases they are willing to comply.

Review your answers to Question 3 and make any changes you would like before continuing.

3. Is this a homogeneous or a heterogeneous group? Are there any norms that govern behavior in the group?

This is basically a homogeneous group because members are handling routine tasks and they have similar needs, motives, and personalities. Of course, to the extent that some of the individuals use highly creative approaches in getting customers to remit payment, the group is somewhat heterogeneous as well.

The primary norm that governs behavior is collecting $1,000 a day from delinquent customers. A complementary norm is helping out the other members of the group. Notice how Maria pitches in and assists coworkers.

Roles

Roles are expected behaviors.

Everyone in a group is expected to behave in particular ways; these expected behaviors constitute a **role.** Quite often this role is a function of the individual's job description. The head of advertising is expected to review the proposals and plans of the subordinates, vetoing those that will not effectively promote company products and giving approval to those that will. The principal of a school is expected to supervise the teachers, plan and organize the academic program, deal with parent-teacher relations, and engage in other school-related activities. The hospital administrator is expected to provide direction to the associate administrators, interact with the general public, and keep the board of directors apprised of what is going on, in addition to being responsive to their directives.

When the concept of role is examined in depth, however, it becomes obvious that there are three types of roles. The first, which we have just illustrated, is the **expected role**. The second is the **perceived role,** which consists of those activities or behaviors the individual believes are required to fulfill the expected role. The new manager who learns that the job requires the approval of annual budgets for the group members will schedule a meeting with each person in the department. From the expected role, the individual will develop a perceived role.

Finally, from the perceived role comes an **enacted role,** which is the way the person actually behaves. During the meeting, the manager will ask many questions about the individual's proposed budget, discuss some minor changes, and encourage the person to develop further support for some of the largest requests ("so I can defend it to my boss and ensure smooth sailing for your whole budget"). Many of the things a manager says and does during this meeting will be determined by his or her interpretation of the proper way to carry out the perceived role.

In moving from an expected to a perceived role, the greatest problem is role ambiguity. In moving from a perceived to an enacted role, the biggest problem is role conflict (Figure 7–2).

Role Ambiguity.   **Role ambiguity** occurs when an individual is uncertain about his or her authority, responsibility, or job duties, or all three. Regardless of the hierarchical level, very little guidance may be provided by either the job description or the superior. The person is simply told, "Okay, you're the new supervisor. You start Monday." Implied in the announcement is that the individual knows what he or she is supposed to do.

A second situation giving rise to role ambiguity is promotion up the management ranks. There may be job descriptions for supervisors, but there are none (of any substantive nature) for the top person in the organization. The farther up the line a person goes, the less likely it is that the person can define all of the duties for which he or she is responsible.

For example, in a hospital study they conducted, Sims and Szilagyi found that head nurses had clearly specified rules and practices to guide them in carrying out their duties. At the next hierarchical level, however, associate director of nursing, there was significant role ambiguity, which resulted in confusion, conflict, and lower performance.[13]

Role Conflict.   **Role conflict** occurs whenever an individual must perform two roles simultaneously, and the performance of one precludes performance of the other. For example, a person's superior tells the individual that the latter's

Role ambiguity is a result of unclear authority.

FIGURE 7–2
Role Relationships

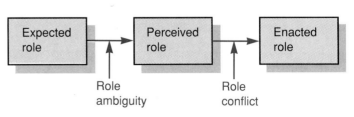

subordinates are to adhere strictly to company rules. One of these rules requires that everyone wear safety equipment in the work area. However, the subordinates have not only taken off some of this safety equipment in the past, claiming that it impedes their ability to do a good job, but they have also told their boss that most of the company's safety regulations are "Mickey Mouse" rules and they appreciate that the individual has not been after them to put the equipment back on. This type of conflict is known as **intrarole conflict,** because it involves the receiving of different and conflicting messages by someone playing one role.

A second form of role conflict, known as **inter-role conflict,** occurs when an individual has a number of roles to play and they conflict with each other. Many managers find themselves in this position when they have to evaluate the performance of subordinates. The role of judge—and the potential role of punisher—interferes with the ability to fulfill the role of trainer, developer, or teacher.

There are five types of role conflict problems.

A third form of role conflict is **intrasender conflict**. This occurs as a result of individuals' *role sendings*. For example, the materials manager tells a purchasing agent to buy a certain raw material from whatever source has it available and at whatever cost is necessary, but to order only from previously approved suppliers, none of which has the required material. In this case, obviously, the purchasing agent cannot behave in a manner consistent with the role assignment.

A fourth common form of role conflict is **person-role conflict,** which arises when the behavior appropriate to a role is incompatible with a person's own values. For example, the salesperson who is told that she can expect an increase of 300 percent in orders from Company A if she agrees to kick back 25 percent of her commission to Company A's purchasing manager may be caught between conflicting pressures. On the one hand, she wants to sell more products; on the other, she is unwilling to engage in unethical practices.

Finally, there is **role overload conflict,** which occurs when a person has so much work to do that it is impossible to fulfill the expected role. For example, a high school principal has to finish writing a speech that is to be delivered to the graduating class later in the day, meet with some irate parents in fifteen minutes, return a phone call from some alumni who phoned earlier, and deal with a desk full of paperwork. In these circumstances, the principal is clearly overwhelmed by role functions and must give some of them priority in order to handle them adequately.[14]

Resolving Role Problems. There are a number of ways of resolving role ambiguity and role conflict problems. One is to simply live with them. However, this approach is often unsatisfactory. People faced with role problems for any extended period of time will often either succumb to the stress and resign from the organization or withdraw from certain interactions and activities and thereby become less productive.

Individuals confronting role ambiguity need to confer with their superiors in order to identify at least those key areas where performance is required. Closer interaction with subordinates can also help in this process.

Meanwhile, in the case of role conflict, a number of approaches are feasible.

1. If you are experiencing intrarole conflict, you can evaluate the situation on its merits, put one of the conflict groups ahead of the other(s), and stick with your choice.

2. If you are experiencing inter-role conflict, you can recognize the need to wear more than one hat and seek the support of your superior and advice of others in the organization in fulfilling those roles that are uncomfortable to you.

3. If you are experiencing intrasender conflict, you can adhere to the rules and regulations of the organization and tell the sender that deviation from them is forbidden by organizational directive.

4. If you are experiencing person-role conflict, you might hide behind the organization's code of ethics, if there is one; otherwise, simply refuse to comply and acknowledge to yourself that a clear conscience is more important than conforming to someone else's ethical code.

There are a number of ways to solve role conflict problems.

5. If you are experiencing role overload, you can set priorities on the tasks to be done and delegate the portions you cannot complete.

Status

Status refers to the relative ranking of an individual in an organization or group. Some people have high status and, as a result, are treated with respect (and perhaps fear) by the members. Others have very little status and, as a result, tend to be taken for granted by the members. Since status plays such a key role in how people are treated, it is common to find group members trying both to acquire and to maintain some minimum level of status.

Status Determinants.   There are a number of dichotomies that are helpful in explaining how status is obtained. One is the *ascribed-achieved* pairing. Sometimes an individual will obtain status through birthright (ascribed), as in the case of a Rockefeller or a Du Pont. More important in the study of organizational behavior is achieved status, in which the individual attains a specific position in the social system through education or skill, or both. The "self-made person" is a classic illustration.

A second status pairing is *scalar-functional.* Sometimes an individual will obtain status through his or her position in the hierarchy (scalar), as in the case of a president or top-level administrator. In some organizations, the jobs people do (functional) play a major role in determining their status. For example, in some companies accountants are considered more important than sales managers. As a result, although a particular accountant may be no higher in the organization structure than a specific sales manager, the former is more highly regarded by his or her peers and by the personnel in general than is the sales manager.

There are a number of ways to achieve status.

A third status pairing is *positional-personal.* Status is often accorded to a position, no matter who occupies it. The president of the United States has status simply because of the office. Similar analogies can be drawn for doctors, lawyers, and university professors. Then there is status based on personality. Some people are outgoing, friendly, cooperative, and always ready to listen and offer a kind word. Individuals with both position and personality, of course, have the best chance of acquiring status.

The final pairing is *active-latent.* Some forms of status are active on the job while others are latent. For example, a supervisor's managerial role is active while the individual's role as a Little League coach is latent. Off the job these two forms of status are reversed.

Status is supposed to provide stability and predictability in personal relations. However, there are some status problems.

Status Problems.   Two of the most common status problems are status incongruency and status discrepancy. **Status incongruency** occurs whenever there is disagreement among group members regarding an individual's status. Lack of status symbols can cause such an incongruency. For example, if a new executive is given an office that is clearly inferior (no thick rug, no expensive furniture) to those of the other executives, there is an incongruency between the individual's position and the status symbols being provided. This may lead the other executives to conclude that the new person is "not really top management timber." It certainly will create some confusion in interpersonal relations, since the executives will be unsure of how much respect and deference to accord to this individual.

Status discrepancy occurs when people do things that do not accord with their status ranking in the group. For example, the hospital administrator who eats lunch with the nurses may be looked at askance by other key administrators. People are expected to stay within their own reference groups, those groups with which members identify and whose values and behavior they have adopted. In some organizations, full professors do not ask advice from assistant professors; vice-presidents do not socialize with supervisors; line people do not act impressed by recommendations from staff people. Conversely, if individuals of lower status attempt to improve their relative positions by associating with those of higher status, the latter tend to rebuff them. If those with high status continually associate with people outside their reference groups, they may find their own status suffering.

In understanding group behavior, then, it is important to remember that people are expected to act "properly." Individuals who do too much work, act bossy, or fail to help out other members who are having work problems not only may find their status changing but also may eventually be excluded from group membership.

> *Two common status problems are status incongruency and status discrepancy.*

  Review your answers to Question 4 and make any changes you would like before continuing.

4. How do people in this group gain status? What explains Maria's status in the group?

There are two ways that people in this group gain status. One is through achievement, and the other is through personality. Maria has status because she attains her goal of $1,000 a day. She also helps out her coworkers, and she undoubtedly is friendly and persuasive when talking customers into paying their bills.

Cohesiveness

Cohesiveness denotes the closeness or interpersonal attractions that exist between members of a group. When cohesion is high, the members are motivated to remain in the group; when it is low, members will often leave the group. Moreover, this commitment can exist with regard to organizations with nonidentical objectives such as employer and unions.[15] Two major variables in group cohesion are interaction and group productivity.

Cohesiveness and interaction tend to be related.

Cohesion and Interaction.   Cohesion is an important factor in group interaction.[16] Research shows that in groups with high cohesiveness there tends to be a great deal of verbal interaction.[17] French's work also reveals that cohesion and quality of interaction are related.[18] In fact, the overall behavior of high- and low-cohesive groups is markedly different. Shaw and Shaw illustrated this disparity by forming schoolchildren into three-person groups. Each group had a varying degree of cohesiveness and was formed on the basis of the children's preferences for working partners. The groups were then assigned the task of learning to spell lists of words. The teacher, who did not know the cohesiveness scores of the groups, observed and recorded the behavior of each. In high-cohesive groups, the members were cooperative, friendly, and laudatory to one another. Low-cohesive groups, meanwhile, were hostile, aggressive, and quick to express delight when one of their members made an error. Additionally, high-cohesive groups decided on a plan of study at the very beginning and stuck to it throughout, whereas those with low cohesion usually began to immediately test each other without any preliminary planning. Finally, a strong leader emerged in both the high- and low-cohesive groups, but in the former the leader functioned in a democratic manner, whereas in the latter the individual was bossy and autocratic. As the experiment continued, the high-cohesive groups began engaging in more nontask activities (social), whereas the low-cohesive groups developed interpersonal conflicts and tended to break up and study as individuals.[19]

> In summary, it is clear that cohesiveness is related to both quantity and quality of group interaction. Members of high-cohesive groups communicate with each other to a greater extent, and the content of group interaction is positively oriented. Members of high-cohesive groups are cooperative, friendly, and generally behave in ways designed to promote group integration, whereas low-cohesive group members behave much more independently, with little concern for others in the group.[20]

Cohesion and Productivity.   Members of a highly cohesive group will work hard to attain group goals. One common result is high productivity. A good example is provided by Japanese auto plants in the United States, which have created very high cohesion within their work forces.[21] (See "Organization Behavior in Action: Maintaining High Productivity.") However, this is not always the case, for a high-cohesive group may have low productivity goals, resulting in low output. Research by Schachter and colleagues has made this very clear.[22]

Using college coeds as subjects, Schachter and his associates told roughly half the girls that they would be members of an extremely congenial group, and there was every reason to believe they would like the other members and vice versa. The second half of the subjects, however, were told that scheduling difficulties had made it impossible to assemble a congenial group, and that "there is no particular reason to think that you will like them or that they will care for you."[23] By giving this information to the girls, the researchers thereby created high- and low-cohesive groups.

Organizational Behavior In Action

MAINTAINING HIGH PRODUCTIVITY

When it comes to productivity, there are few firms that can match the record of Japanese auto manufacturers. Whether they are operating in the United States or in Japan, productivity is extremely high. For example, the Toyota-General Motors joint venture, New United Motor Manufacturing, Inc., or Nummi for short, is able to assemble a car in nineteen hours as compared to a typical GM plant where it takes thirty-one hours. Moreover, the cars produced by Nummi have ranked second in consumer quality surveys of new cars sold in the United States, while no GM car has ranked in the top fifteen during this same time period. Similar statistics are cited for other Japanese-run car plants in the United States.

What accounts for the success of the Japanese? One of the overriding causes is the high group cohesion that is nurtured and developed. Not only do the Japanese carefully select their personnel, but they train them and work hard on building and maintaining group morale. This results in greater work effort, lower absenteeism, and lower turnover. Nissan, for example, currently has the best attendance record in the industry, and Nummi's absenteeism is 78 percent below that of the average GM plant. Turnover typically averages 2 percent a year for Japanese-run firms, far lower than that of the Big Three automakers.

There are a number of ways that the Japanese have managed to attain these goals. One is by getting the workers more actively involved in the production process by consulting with them and encouraging feedback regarding how operations can be streamlined. A second is by requiring everyone to give 100 percent. One way this has been accomplished is by group members taking up the slack for employees who are ill. Another is by encouraging assembly workers to quickly correct any mistakes without stopping the line. In a typical assembly plant, if something goes wrong the line is usually stopped until the problem is corrected. Some workers object to the strong emphasis given to work productivity and claim that the Japanese approach results in high worker stress. Yet there are many employees who believe that the efficiency of the plants ensures that they will continue to have a job even if the American auto industry encounters bad times. Additionally, they point to the fact that they often make twice as much money on the assembly line as they would working in an office. Overall, most employees feel that the benefits far outweigh the drawbacks, and they are willing to pitch in and work as a cohesive team in getting things done.

Source: Louis Kraar, "Japan's Gung-Ho U.S. Car Plants," *Fortune,* January 30, 1989, pp. 98–108; John Holusha, "No Utopia, But to Workers It's a Job," *New York Times,* January 29, 1989, Section 3, pp. 1, 10; and James P. Womack, Daniel T. Jones, and Daniel Roos, "How Lean Production Can Change the World," *New York Times Magazine,* September 23, 1990, pp. 20–23, 34–38.

The subjects were then given their assignments. Each was to be a member of a three-person assembly-line operation making cardboard checkerboards. The three functions of each group consisted of cutting out pieces of cardboard, mounting and pasting them on heavier stock, and then painting through with a stencil. All of the subjects were made cutters, who would pass their work to the other two members of their group (the paster and the painter) in the next room. All communication between the three was to be carried out via written notes.

Unknown to the subjects, however, there were no pasters or painters. The researchers intercepted all notes from the subjects and, in turn, sent them prewritten messages. The purpose of the messages was to test the impact of positive induction ("let's go faster!") and negative induction ("let's slow up!") on the subjects.

For the first sixteen minutes each person received five notes from her nonexistent fellow workers. These messages made no attempt to influence productivity. In the last sixteen minutes of the experiments, however, half of the subjects in the high-cohesive groups and half in the low-cohesive groups received notes encouraging them toward higher production. The other subjects received negative notes urging them to slow down. As a result of such manipulations, four experimental groups were created:

high cohesive, positive induction
low cohesive, positive induction
high cohesive, negative induction
low cohesive, negative induction

High cohesion will not guarantee high productivity.

The findings of the study revealed that both of the groups that received notes encouraging higher productivity did increase their output. Of those receiving negative notes, however, only the high-cohesive groups reduced their output significantly.[24] Thus we return to our earlier statement regarding the effect of group goals on productivity. Highly cohesive groups that have high output objectives will be very productive, whereas those with low output goals will be very unproductive.

 STOP

Review your answers to Question 5 and make any changes you would like before continuing.

5. Does this group have high cohesion? If the group members decide to oppose management's efforts to raise the daily work quota to $1,100, what will be the result? Explain.

The group certainly does have high cohesion, so if they decide to oppose management's efforts to raise the daily work quota to $1,100 they are likely to be successful. Of course, one or two members of the group may break ranks, but these individuals will tend to be denied assistance by the others, and such assistance is apparently very important to meeting daily goals. In short, the group at large has high cohesion and if they also have low induction, work output is likely to suffer.

Group Leadership

Leadership is often regarded as one of the most important structural characteristics of a group. There are two types of group leaders: formal and informal.

A *formal leader* is one who has been assigned authority over a group by the management. This authority is commonly conferred by the person's superior, and with it comes the right to reward and punish. Those who comply with the leader's directives can expect to receive pay raises and promotions. Those who do not comply can expect to receive reprimands, days off without pay, and in some cases outright dismissal from the organization.

An *informal leader* is one who has been given authority over the group by the members themselves. They often choose this person to be their leader because the individual reflects their values, can help them in attaining mutual goals, assists them in resolving group conflict, and serves as their spokesperson in interacting with management or other groups.

Sometimes the formal and informal leaders are the same person, although this is not usually so. Additionally, while the formal leader will remain indefinitely, the informal leadership role often changes, depending on the situation. If the person lacks the necessary knowledge or skills to lead the group, it will be impossible to maintain the group's respect and status, and a new informal leader will emerge.

There are two types of leaders: formal and informal.

GROUP DEVELOPMENT

As we have just noted, informal groups will change leaders whenever they feel that the current leader is unable to fulfill the expected role. Formal groups, however, retain the same leader indefinitely, and for this person to be effective, he or she needs to be aware that as formal groups develop and grow they go through four distinctive phases: (a) mutual acceptance; (b) communication and decision making; (c) growth and productivity; and (d) control and organization.[25]

During the mutual acceptance stage the individuals come together for the first time. Initial communication patterns are established; interdependencies between the members begin to develop; everyone starts becoming familiar with the structure; the goals of the group and expectations of individual members are often verbalized; and the people begin mutually to accept each other. This is a "feeling-out" phase.

The next stage is concerned with communication and decision making. It is characterized by a need to clarify the rules, goals, and relationships that will exist among the group members.[26] Many times people have deeply ingrained feelings about authority, power, and leadership in a group setting. If these feelings are not identified and the potential for interpersonal conflict reduced, the performance of the group may be adversely affected.

The third phase of group development is the growth and productivity stage. Having identified its goals, the group develops communication channels for both providing and receiving information; interpersonal relations are good, cohesion is high, and efforts toward goal attainment are often very satisfactory.

Control and organization constitute the final stage in group development. During this period the group leader will try to facilitate tasks and provide feedback and eval-

There are four stages of group development and growth.

uation. The group, meanwhile, will revise and renew its interdependencies and continue to exhibit strong motivation toward goal attainment.

If there are any changes in the group's structure or processes, such as a change in leadership or the introduction of interpersonal conflict, the group may revert to an earlier stage. For example, a change in leadership can move a group from the control and organization stage to the communication and decision-making stage. By knowing which stage of development the group is in, the manager can determine the most effective type of leadership style. This individual is also in a good position to judge how prepared the group is to assume its tasks. For example, if interpersonal conflict, role ambiguity, or problems related to role clarification exist, the manager can work to resolve these issues before leading the group into its next project. Knowledge of these group developmental stages helps the manager gauge the proper leadership style to employ.[27]

As you can see, an analysis of these development stages reveals how dynamic group behavior can be.[28] Now that we have examined the foundations and structural components of group behavior, we are ready to take a close look at group dynamics in the next chapter.

SUMMARY

1. A group is a collection of two or more interdependent and interactive individuals who are seeking to attain common objectives. In all, there are three different kinds of groups: (a) functional; (b) task; and (c) interest and friendship. Functional groups are determined by the organization's structure and are permanent groups. Task groups are also determined by the specific needs of the organization but are temporary in nature. Interest and friendship groups are basically informal in nature and are formed on the basis of common concerns, beliefs, or activities. Organizational personnel tend to belong to many different and overlapping formal and informal groups. They also end up on various types of committees, both ad hoc and standing.

2. People join groups for many reasons, including need satisfaction, proximity, interaction, similarity, and group goals and activities. In order to understand group behavior fully, however, it is necessary to examine the structural components of a group, including group composition, norms, status, roles, cohesiveness, and leadership. Groups can be either homogeneous or heterogeneous. The former are extremely effective in handling routine matters, whereas the latter excel at complex problem solving.

3. Norms are behavioral rules of conduct that relate to the way group members ought to act. There are many factors that determine whether or not an individual will conform to group norms, including intelligence, sex, ambiguity of the situation, group size, responses of the other members, and intergroup relations.

4. Roles are the expected behaviors of individuals. There are three types of roles: expected, perceived, and enacted. In moving from an expected to a perceived role, the greatest problem is role ambiguity. In moving from a perceived to an enacted role, the biggest problem is role conflict.

5. Status refers to the relative ranking of an individual in an organization or group. Some of the dichotomies that are helpful in explaining how status is obtained include ascribed-achieved, scalar-functional, positional-personal, and active-latent. The purpose of status is to provide stability and predictability in interpersonal relations. However, there are some status problems, the most common of which are status incongruency and status discrepancy.

6. Cohesiveness is a term used to describe the closeness or interpersonal attractions that exist between members of a group. Highly cohesive groups tend to have high interaction. However, their productivity will not be high unless this is one of the group's goals.

7. Group leadership is another important structural component. Groups can have both formal and informal leaders, each playing an important role in the life of the group. In the case of the former, in particular, the leader needs to be aware of the group's current stage of development to gauge more effectively the proper leadership style to employ.

KEY TERMS

group	personal factors	inter-role conflict
functional group	ambiguity	intrasender conflict
task groups	situational factors	role sendings
project groups	intragroup relationships	person-role conflict
interest groups	role	role overload conflict
friendship groups	expected role	status
ad hoc committee	perceived role	status incongruency
standing committee	enacted role	status discrepancy
homogeneous group	role ambiguity	cohesiveness
heterogeneous group	role conflict	
norms	intrarole conflict	

REVIEW AND STUDY QUESTIONS

1. What is a *group*? Define it in your own words.

2. Why do people join groups? List and explain at least four reasons.

3. What are the similarities and differences between functional, task, interest, and friendship groups?

4. What are the advantages and disadvantages of the committee form of organization? Discuss three of each.

5. "Organizational personnel tend to belong to many different and overlapping formal and informal groups." Explain this statement.

6. When would a homogeneous group's performance be superior to that of a heterogeneous group? When would the reverse be true? Explain.

7. Why do people conform to group norms? In your answer be sure to include personal factors, ambiguity, situational factors, and intragroup relations.

8. When the concept of role is examined in depth, it becomes obvious that there are three types of roles: expected, perceived, and enacted. What is meant by each?

9. Some of the problems associated with roles include role ambiguity and role conflict. Describe these problems and suggest solutions for remedying each.

10. What is meant by the term *status*? What are some of the major status determinants? Explain.

11. Are cohesiveness and interaction related in any way? Explain.

12. How are cohesiveness and productivity related? Based on your answer, what challenges or opportunities does this relationship present to management?

13. How does a formal leader differ from an informal leader?

14. What are the four phases of group development? If the manager of the formal group knows what stage the group is in, how can this information be of value in leading the group?

CASES

Slow Progress

Six months ago, a large aerospace firm was awarded a contract to build a communications satellite. When this satellite has completed all ground tests, it will be launched into earth's orbit from the Kennedy Spacecraft Center at Cape Canaveral. The satellite is to contain the latest communications technology and will cost almost three times that of the last orbited communications satellite. Because of the high technology and costs involved, the company has assembled a project team consisting of the best available technical and management personnel. The team has been given seven months to complete the project and have the satellite shipped to the Cape.

At first, the project went smoothly. The engineering and research and development people coordinated their efforts with the manufacturing personnel, and the test and control people reviewed the plans and provided substantive input. In fact, cohesiveness among these people, all with diverse backgrounds, was very high, and the project progressed well. By the end of the fourth month, the team was nine days ahead of schedule.

As the group has entered the last phases of the project, however, management has been noticing a slow-down in progress. Absenteeism and turnover have begun to increase, and work output as measured on a daily basis is down to approximately 75 percent of what it was a month ago. During the last ten days the project actually fell four days behind. As a result, instead of being nine days ahead of schedule, the project is now only five days ahead. With one more month to go, it is critical that the project remain on schedule. If slippage continues at its present rate, however, the project manager estimates that the undertaking will come in approximately three days late. This means that the firm will not earn any extra "early time" money. When the project was conceived it was believed that the undertaking could be finished early, and for this reason extra personnel were assigned to the group. If the bonus money for being early is not earned, the company's return on investment will be much lower than expected. The project manager must do everything he can to ensure that the project comes in at least six days ahead of schedule.

In an effort to straighten out the situation and get everything back on schedule, the project manager has been talking to his people. He has learned that only 20 percent of them have been contacted by the management and told that they are going to be given new assignments when the cur-

rent project is completed. Most of the remaining 80 percent believe that they will be laid off when the project is over, and so they are in no hurry to finish. The company grapevine says that last week the management received a confidential memo from the Department of Defense. In essence the memo told the company that it had been unsuccessful in its bid for a large military contract. The company's primary competitor won the bid. Management was quite certain that it was going to get the new contract. The top research and design people felt that their design of the proposed aircraft was superior to that of any other bidder. The management would have to lay off a large number of people if the bid were unsuccessful, and they believed this fact would help a great deal in ensuring that the Department of Defense would award the contract to them. The grapevine also reports that cutbacks will start next month except in the case of personnel who currently are assigned to projects. The status of these individuals will be determined as their projects wind down to the last month. The project manager does not know whether or not to believe the grapevine, but the story does seem to make a lot of sense. In any event, the project manager does not know what to say or do to motivate the team to complete the undertaking on time.

1. Is this project team a homogeneous or heterogeneous group? Explain.

2. How have group norms changed from when the project team was formed until now? Defend your answer.

3. As of the end of the case, is group cohesion high or low? What effect is this having on group productivity? Is there anything the project manager can do?

A Case Of Uncertainty

Last year Chet Bernstein received his Ph.D. in English from an Ivy League school and immediately accepted his first full-time job, a position with a large state university in the southwest. The summer before he began, Chet received a call from the dean asking him to become chairperson of the English department. The position carried an eleven-month appointment and paid much better than the original contract Chet signed. Additionally, the job offered the possibility for future advancement into the administrative ranks of the university. Chet accepted at once.

By the end of his first year, however, Chet was sorry he had accepted. From the moment he came on board he encountered problems. The ex-department chairperson had only two years until retirement and had been forced out by a vote of the department, which felt he was not doing the job properly. The individual now came to the university only to

teach class. Chet could get no information from him regarding the duties of the English department chairperson. The other college chairpeople tried to help out, but they were unable to answer many questions directly affecting the English department. The departmental faculty, meanwhile, looked to Chet to get things done and not bother them with administrative details or questions.

At the first departmental meeting he called, Chet found himself in an awkward position. He was younger than all the rest of the English faculty and unsure of the role he was supposed to play. In several instances, some of the older faculty took control of the meeting, voicing their opinion on various matters that were not on the agenda. Chet was unsure how to handle the meeting and, when it was over, felt it had gone badly.

Later in the year he was required to meet with each faculty member and discuss his or her performance. This, too, left him uneasy, since he was not sure how to do it. One female faculty member had three refereed articles accepted for publication during the year, but her teacher ratings were poor. Chet felt awkward talking to her about improving her teaching, since she had ten more years of experience than he, and he felt she knew her shortcomings. Nevertheless, he did make an effort to discuss improved teaching. In another case, meanwhile, a faculty member was being considered for tenure. If he did not receive it, he would be terminated. Chet offered him some advice on presenting his record to the tenure committee and even wrote a letter in support of the individual. When the man was not tenured, Chet worked to help him find a position elsewhere. Once again, however, Chet was unsure of himself.

At the end of the academic year, the faculty, as was customary, voted on whether to keep the chairperson or select another. Chet felt he had done a poor job and looked forward to moving over to full-time teaching. However, after the dean had counted the votes, he told Chet that nine of the faculty rated him excellent, the other two rated him very good, and all wanted him to remain chairperson. Chet was delighted with the news and agreed to stay on. "I hope next year is easier," he told the dean. "This year I really didn't know where I stood." The dean told him not to worry. "As the second year progresses, you'll find the faculty opening up more with you. For the moment, be content that you've proven your competence. This was your first job, and they didn't know what to make of you. From here on, it should be smooth sailing."

1. What type of group is an English department—functional, task, interest, or friendship? Is it a homogeneous or heterogeneous group? Explain.

2. What types of role problems did Chet have? Why did they arise, and how could he have resolved them?

3. From what you know of the department, what did they like about Chet? Why were they pleased with his leadership of the group? Explain.

SELF-FEEDBACK EXERCISE

You and Your Work Group

The statements below are designed to provide you feedback on your work group situation. Some questions relate to your particular job. Others deal with your work group including yourself, others, the boss to whom you report and the organization at large. If you do not work currently, think of the last job you had and use this as a point of reference. The numbers represent the following:

5 = Definitely true, or strongly agree
4 = Mostly true, or generally agree
3 = Neither true nor false, or neither agree nor disagree
2 = Mostly false, or generally disagree
1 = Definitely false, or strongly disagree
0 = Does not apply

_____ 1. Your work is influenced by laws or regulations from outside your organization.

_____ 2. In your enterprise, feelings between managers and subordinates are good.

_____ 3. Everyone in your work group is fully committed to help the group.

_____ 4. In order to do their jobs properly, members of your work group must work closely together.

_____ 5. You know clearly what someone in your job should accomplish.

_____ 6. Group members let very little interfere with their progress.

_____ 7. In your enterprise, most people are friendly and approachable.

_____ 8. People in your work group rely on work done by others in the group in order to get their own jobs accomplished.

_____ 9. Your work is influenced by outside economic events such as inflation and interest rates.

_____ 10. No one in your work group really cares what happens.

_____ 11. You are often told how well or poorly your work is done.

_____ 12. Things seem to be pretty disorganized in your enterprise.

_____ 13. When you have a problem outside your own group, you never know whom to go to about it.

_____ 14. Your group works together as a team.

_____ 15. People in your enterprise do not trust each other.

_____ 16. Your organization spells out exactly what it expects from its work groups.

_____ 17. Your work is influenced by public opinion, business associations, chambers of commerce, community groups, or other social groups outside the organization.

_____ 18. There is a lot of confusion about the meaning of organizational policies and procedures.

_____ 19. You cannot get help from other people in your work group.

_____ 20. Your work is influenced by political events that occur outside your organization.

_____ 21. People of your work group have little need to work with each other.

_____ 22. You do not know if you are doing a good job.

_____ 23. Policies and rules of the organization are clear.

_____ 24. Your enterprise's productivity sometimes suffers from lack of orderliness and planning.

_____ 25. Group members continually grumble about the work they do.

_____ 26. Most people in your organization are hard to get to know.

_____ 27. The assignments in your organization are clearly and sensibly arranged.

Scoring:

Transfer your answers from the above questionnaire to the scoring key below. In so doing, look closely at those numbers in the key which have an asterisk in front of them. These call for reverse scoring, which means that you are to subtract your answer from 6. In this way an initially high score (such as 5) would end up as a low score (1) and vice versa. Then obtain an average score in each category for all of those statements to which you gave a ranking of 1-5 (omit all zeros from consideration).

External Influences	Warmth	Commitment to the Group
1. _____	2. _____	3. _____
9. _____	7. _____	6. _____
17. _____	*15. _____	*10. _____
20. _____	*26. _____	*19. _____
Total _____	Total _____	*25. _____
Average _____	Average _____	Total _____
		Average _____

Interdependence	Clarity of Objectives	Order
4. _____	5. _____	*12. _____
8. _____	11. _____	*24. _____
14. _____	*22. _____	27. _____
*21. _____	Total _____	Total _____
Total _____	Average _____	Average _____
Average _____		

Clarity		
*13. _____		
16. _____		
*18. _____		
23. _____		
Total _____		
Average _____		

Place each of your average scores to the left of the descriptions below. Here is what each of your scores mean.

_3.75_ External Influences—This measures your perception of how much influence external events and groups have on your particular work group.

_4_ Warmth—This measures your perception of the degree of friendliness and trust that exists in your work group.

_4.8_ Commitment to the Group—This measures your perception of how much everyone is committed to the progress and success of the group.

_4.5_ Interdependence—This measures your perception of how much group members have to depend on each other in order to achieve group goals.

_3.6_ Clarity of Objectives—This measures your perception of how clear your job is and how clear that of others in the work group is.

_4_ Order—This measures your perception of how well things are organized and arranged in your organization.

_4.75_ Clarity—This measures your perception of how clear the rules, policies, and procedures are in your organization.

NOTES

1. Marvin E. Shaw, *Group Dynamics: The Psychology of Small Group Behavior* (New York: McGraw-Hill Book Co., 1971), p. 5.

2. Robert Albanese and David D. Van Fleet, "Rational Behavior in Groups: The Free-Riding Tendency," *Academy of Management Review,* April 1985, pp. 244–255.

3. Shaw, *Group Dynamics,* p. 84.

4. For more on this see Jane W. Gibson and Richard M. Hodgetts, *Organizational Communication: A Managerial Perspective,* 2nd ed. (New York: Harper Collins, 1991), Chapter 14.

5. Sharon Tziner and Dov Eden, "Effects of Crew Composition on Crew Performance: Does the Whole Equal the Sum of Its Parts?," *Journal of Applied Psychology,* February 1985, pp. 85–93.

6. Philip R. Costanzo and Marvin E. Shaw, "Conformity as a Function of Age Level," *Child Development,* December 1966, pp. 967–975.

7. Shaw, *Group Dynamics,* p. 164.

8. See for example S. E. Asch, "Effects of Group Pressure Upon the Modification and Distortion of Judgments," in H. Guetzkow (ed.), *Groups, Leadership and Men* (Pittsburgh, PA: Carnegie Press, 1951), pp. 177–198.

9. Marvin E. Shaw, Gerald H. Rothschild, and John F. Strickland, "Decision Processes in Communication Nets," *Journal of Abnormal and Social Psychology,* May 1957, pp. 323–330.

10. S. C. Goldberg, "Influence and Leadership as a Function of Group Structure," *Journal of Abnormal and Social Psychology,* July 1955, pp. 119–122.

11. Shaw, *Group Dynamics,* p. 252.

12. Arthur M. Schlesinger, Jr., *A Thousand Days* (Boston: Houghton Mifflin Co., 1965); p. 255. Italics added.

13. Henry P. Sims, Jr. and Andrew D. Szilagyi, "Leader Structure and Subordinate Satisfaction for Two Hospital Administrative Levels: A Path Analysis Approach," *Journal of Applied Psychology,* April 1975, pp. 194–197.

14. For additional insights into these two areas see Susan E. Jackson and Randall S. Schuler, "A Meta-analysis and Conceptual Critique of Research on Role Ambiguity and Role Conflict in Work Settings," *Organizational Behavior and Human Decision Processes,* August 1985, pp. 16–78.

15. Edward J. Conlon and Daniel G. Gallagher, "Commitment to Employer and Union: Effects of Membership Status," *Academy of Management Journal,* March 1987, pp. 151–162.

16. William E. Piper, Myriam Marrache, Renee Lacroix, Astrid M. Richardsen, and Barry D. Jones, "Cohesion as a Basic Bond in Groups," *Human Relations,* February 1983, pp. 93–108.

17. Gary Moran, "Dyadic Attraction and Orientational Consensus," *Journal of Personality and Social Psychology,* July 1966, pp. 94–99.

18. John R. P. French, Jr., "The Disruption of Cohesion of Groups," *Journals of Abnormal and Social Psychology,* July 1941, pp. 361–377.

19. Marvin E. Shaw and Lilly May Shaw, "Some Effects of Sociometric Grouping Upon Learning in a Second Grade Classroom," *Journal of Social Psychology,* August 1962, pp. 453–458.

20. Shaw, *Group Dynamics,* p. 197.

21. Louis Kraar, "Japan's Gung-Ho U.S. Car Plants," *Fortune,* January 30, 1989, pp. 98–108.

22. Stanley Schachter, Norris Ellertson, Dorothy McBride, and Doris Gregory, "An Experimental Study of Cohesiveness and Productivity," *Human Relations,* August 1951, pp. 229–239.

23. *Ibid.,* p. 232.

24. *Ibid.,* pp. 234–236.

25. Bernard M. Bass, *Organizational Psychology* (Boston: Allyn & Bacon, 1965), pp. 197–198.

26. John P. Gustafson and Lowell Cooper, "Unconscious Planning in Small Groups," *Human Relations,* December 1979, pp. 1039–1064.

27. For more on this topic see John P. Wanous, Arnon E. Reichers, and S. D. Malik, "Organizational Socialization and Group Development: Toward An Integrative Perspective," *Academy of Management Review,* October 1984, pp. 670–683.

28. Gibson and Hodgetts, *Organizational Communication,* pp. 143–144.

CHAPTER 8
Group Dynamics

GOALS OF THE CHAPTER

Now that you are familiar with the basic dimensions and components of a group, we want to look at how groups function, from both an intragroup and an intergroup standpoint. The first goal of this chapter is to examine the individual characteristics each member brings to the group and determine how these can affect group behavior. The second goal is to study the ways in which group members interact among themselves. The final goal is to examine how groups interact with each other. As you read this chapter, keep in mind that much of what we are saying relates to both formal and informal groups. When you have finished reading this chapter you should be able to:

1. identify and describe the three major individual characteristics that explain a member's influence on the group;
2. discuss the types of communication networks often found in small groups;
3. relate why groups are often greater risk takers than individuals are;
4. compare and contrast interacting, delphi, and nominal groups;
5. describe how intergroup performance can be affected by task certainty, group goals, and interdependency, and relate some of the strategies that can be useful in managing intergroup performance.

Phil Hartack is sales manager of a group that sells audiovisual equipment in the north central part of the United States. This nine-state region is one of the fastest growing, and Phil and his group of eighteen salespeople have set new sales records for each of the last eleven quarters. Most of the salespeople are on the road four days a week and in the office the other day, so when Phil receives directives from headquarters, he typically communicates these to his people on a one-to-one basis either by phone or in person. However, on the last Friday of every month there is a general office meeting of all salespeople. At this time Phil has the opportunity to discuss headquarter's directives with the salespeople and to get individual and collective feedback from them. Quite often these sessions give everyone a chance to talk both to Phil and to each other about the directives and their effect on sales strategies.

In a meeting last year Phil discussed headquarter's suggestion that three new states be added to Phil's territory. Phil thought that this was a bad idea because it would put too much responsibility on the group and require too much work. However, the salespeople talked him out of it. "We can do it," they said. "Stop worrying about whether we're going to fall on our face and look at the bright side of things. We've got a lot of talent around this table, and we'll surprise a lot of those guys at headquarters." Phil agreed to adding the three states, and last quarter his group had the highest average sales of any sales group in the company.

Phil has recently been asked to help out headquarters in two different ways. The first is to complete a sales forecast questionnaire related to three new products the firm will be offering next year. The company wants his guesstimate regarding how well each product will sell. His anonymous responses and those of other sales managers around the country will then be sent back to the participants, and he will be asked to revise his forecast based on the range of responses obtained from all sales managers. This process will continue for five rounds, after which the company will make a formal sales forecast projection for the new products.

The second is a request to coordinate his group's efforts with the central marketing research department. The latter is going to be conducting research in four states in Phil's sales region, and the company president wants Phil to use this information in drawing up a special marketing campaign. "I want better coordination between marketing research and our sales offices," the president told Phil, "and I'd like to start with your region." Phil told the president that he would have his full support.

1. What type of communication network does Phil use in passing information to his people, and what type of net is used during the general office meeting? Explain.
2. How does this case illustrate the risky-shift phenomenon in action?
3. What type of group is being used to collect sales forecast information on the three new products? Explain.
4. What type of interdependence will there be between Phil's group and the marketing research department?

Write down your answers to these questions and put them aside. We will return to them later.

THE INDIVIDUAL AND THE GROUP

Individual characteristics
help determine behavior in
groups.

The group is more than the sum of the individual members. For example, each person working alone may be able to produce six pieces an hour, but when the individuals are put into a highly cohesive group with high output norms, production may rise to an average of ten pieces an hour. Nevertheless, in our study of groups it is important to remember that the goals, interactions, and performance of groups are largely determined by the individual characteristics of the members.

Individual Characteristics

There are three major clusters of individual characteristics that explain a member's influence on the group. These three clusters of traits determine what the person *can* contribute to the group, what he or she *wants* to contribute to the group, and the extent to which the individual *will* interact with the other members in goal attainment. The components of these three determinants are: (a) biographical circumstances and physical attributes; (b) abilities and intelligence; and (c) personality.

Biographical Circumstances and Physical Attributes. Included among biographical circumstances and physical attributes are such factors as age, sex, size, height, and weight. Research shows that the chronological age of a group member is related to several aspects of group interaction. In particular, as individuals grow older there tends to be an increase in the degree and selectivity of contact with others. However, there is a decreasing tendency on the part of adults (over twenty-one years of age) to conform readily to group norms.

Sex is an important characteristic in that females tend to be more conforming to group norms than males, a result often attributed to cultural values.[1] Finally, physical size (height, weight) tends to be a factor in a person's becoming a group leader.[2] Keep in mind, however, that although physically superior people have a slightly better chance of becoming leaders, there is no evidence that size is related to the performance of leaders.[3]

Abilities and Intelligence. Intelligence is important in determining what an individual can do for the group. Evidence indicates that more intelligent people tend to be more active and less conforming in groups than their less intelligent counterparts. More important, however, are the person's specific abilities. Individuals with abilities related to the group task tend to be more active in the group, make more contributions toward task completion, and have greater influence on the group's decisions. Such people tend to bring about higher performance and are likely to emerge as group leaders. They also are more satisfied with the group's cooperation and performance because of their place in the group and the fact that the group has been successful because of their efforts.

Personality. Personality traits influence how the individual will interact and behave with the other group members. Many of these traits, including authoritarianism, self-reliance, unconventionality, anxiety, and adjustment, have been the focus of research efforts. Findings to date reveal that there is good, although limited, evidence that behaviors in groups are at least partly the result of personality characteristics.

Fundamental Interpersonal Relations Orientation

Personal characteristics help determine an individual's interpersonal needs. This is one major variable in group behavior. The second major variable is the interpersonal needs of the other group members. Schutz has provided an interesting theory for studying these two interpersonal dimensions of group behavior. Popularly known as **FIRO (fundamental interpersonal relations orientation),** the theory, which focuses on two-person relationships, is based on two concepts: behavioral expression and interpersonal needs (Figure 8–1).[4]

Behavioral expression consists of two types of behavior. The first is **expressed behavior,** which is behavior people initiate or show to others. The second is **wanted behavior,** which is how people want others to act toward them.

The second basic concept is interpersonal needs. In all, there are three basic interpersonal needs. The first is a need for inclusion, or interaction. Some people have a great need to be included in group activities, whereas others prefer less contact and more privacy. Note in Figure 8–1 that this need can be either high or low and reflects both expressed and wanted behaviors.

The second interpersonal need is for affection, or friendship. Some people desire close personal relationships, whereas others prefer more distant and impersonal contact.

		Behavioral expression	
		Expressed *(Behavior one initiates or* *expresses to others)*	*Wanted* *(Behavior one prefers others to* *generate or express them)*
Interpersonal needs	*Inclusion or interaction*	High: Individual initiates action with others. Low: Individual does not initiate action with others.	High: Individual needs to be included by other people. Low: Individual does not need to be included by other people.
	Affection or friendship	High: Individual wants to act in a close, personal way with others. Low: Individual does not want to act in a close, personal way with others.	High: Individual wants others to act in a close, personal way with him or her. Low: Individual does not want others to act in a close, personal way with him or her.
	Control or influence	High: Individual needs to control others. Low: Individual does not need to control others.	High: Individual wants people to control him or her. Low: Individual does not want people to control him or her.

FIGURE 8–1
FIRO: A Theory of Interpersonal Behavior

Individuals have three interpersonal needs: inclusion,
affection, and control.

The third interpersonal need is for control, or influence. Some people need to control their environment, including the individuals with whom they interact. Other people want neither to control others nor to be controlled by them. They prefer independence and autonomy.

The FIRO framework provides insights into human behavior in a given situation. For example, an individual with high inclusion needs would tend to dislike a job that entails little social interaction. A person with high affection needs would not do well in a job where the workers are isolated and discouraged from talking. An employee with high control needs would tend to dislike a group in which the members have high inclusion and affection needs but low control needs.

Keep in mind, however, that FIRO focuses on two-person relationships. When groups consist of more than two people and the composition of the group and the environment in which it operates are often changing, it can be difficult to use FIRO to predict the compatibility of individual behavior in groups.[5] To do so requires a deeper understanding of intragroup behavior, especially in the areas of communication and decision making.

INTRAGROUP BEHAVIOR

Intragroup behavior is behavior which occurs within groups. There are two major areas of intragroup behavior that are important in the study of group dynamics: communication networks and decision making. A **communication network** is a pattern or flow of communication between people in a group. Groups tend to have specially designed communication nets through which the members pass and receive information. Additionally, depending on the size and composition of the group, members display varying degrees of risk acceptance and participation and employ different types of political tactics.[6]

Communication Networks

Theoretically, every member of a group is able to communicate with all of the other members. In reality, this is not so. When people transmit information they usually exercise great care with regard to who receives the message. People are selective in their transmissions. Some individuals in the group are deliberately excluded. Norms, status, roles, and other formal and informal characteristics are used in determining who is to be part of the communication network.

There are five types of communication networks.

Types of Networks.   At least in principle, as the number of people in a group increases arithmetically, the number of possible interrelationships increases geometrically. For ease of discussion, therefore, we will use a five-person group. For purposes of analysis, we will examine the five basic communication networks (or *nets*), which are the ways group members communicate with each other, shown in Figure 8–2. These networks illustrate the major conformations that might be found in a five-person group. These five nets are known as the *wheel,* the *Y,* the *chain,* the *circle,* and the *all-channel network*. Each two-headed arrow between pairs of names in the figure represents a two-way communication channel. An inspection of

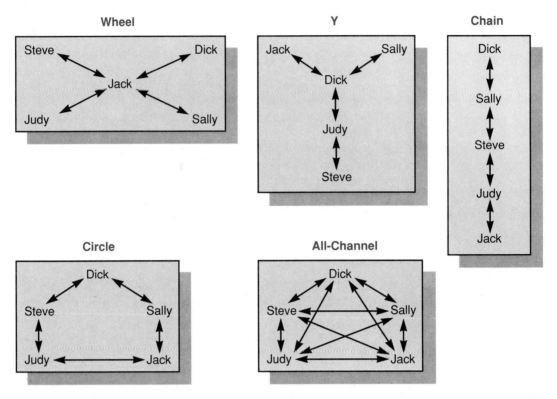

FIGURE 8–2
Communication Networks in a Five-Person Group

these nets reveals that the order in which they are presented in Figure 8–2 ranges from high restriction (the wheel) to low restriction (all-channel network). In the wheel, all communications must flow between Jack and each of the other members. In the all-channel network, meanwhile, the members are able to communicate with each other simultaneously.

Comparison of Networks. Analysis of the five nets reveals that each provides varying potential for predicting efficiency, effectiveness, member satisfaction, and group leaders. The first characteristic in Table 8–1, degrees of centralization, refers to the degree to which some group members have access to more communication channels than other group members. The wheel network is most centralized because all communications flow to and from one individual. The all-channel net is least centralized because each member can communicate with any or all of the others at any time.

The second characteristic, number of possible communication channels, is basically the reverse of the degree of centralization characteristic. In the wheel network the number of channels for members as a whole is at a minimum, whereas in the all-channel network it is at a maximum.

TABLE 8–1

Basic Characteristics of Communication Networks

Characteristic	NETWORK				
	Wheel	Y	Chain	Circle	All-Channel
Degree of centralization	Very high	High	Moderate	Low	Very low
Number of possible communication channels	Very low	Low	Moderate	Moderate	Very high
Average group-member satisfaction	Low	Low	Moderate	Moderate	High
Range in individual-member satisfaction	High	High	Moderate	Low	Very low
Leadership predictability	Very high	High	Moderate	Low	Very low

The third and fourth characteristics, average group-member satisfaction and range in individual-member satisfaction (see Table 8–1), provide some interesting insights into small groups. In the wheel network, average member satisfaction is low in contrast to what prevails in most of the other nets. However, the range of individual-member satisfaction is often high in relation to that of the other nets. A close look at Figure 8–2 should make this relationship clear. In the wheel net, Jack is the center of attention and will undoubtedly be very satisfied with the communication net. The other members, however, are likely to be much less satisfied, so the average group satisfaction is going to be low. Since one person is very satisfied and the others are not, the range of satisfaction is quite high. The reverse is true for the all-channel net: On the average, everyone in the group has high satisfaction, so the range is not very great.

The fifth characteristic, leadership predictability, refers to our ability to identify the individual most likely to emerge as the group leader. As applied to Figure 8–2, we can make the following predictions: Jack in the wheel net, Dick in the Y net, and Steve in the chain will become the leader of their respective groups.

Our predictions are based on the fact that the individual with the greatest amount of control or centrality, or both, is most likely to emerge as the group leader. Since no one has major control in the circle or all-channel nets, our chances of predicting the group leader in such networks are not very good.

Networks and Task Accomplishment. Which type of network is most effective? This will depend on the demands of the situation. The wheel appears to be most effective in solving simple problems, whereas the all-channel net is often most effective in handling complex problems. In the rare case in which a complex problem does not require a great deal of member interdependence, the matter can be resolved through one of the more centralized communication nets (Y or chain). Keeping in mind that some nets are most effective in certain situations but not others, we note the following managerial implications:

There are managerial implications of communication networks.

1. No single network is likely to be effective for a work group confronting a variety of tasks and objectives. Even the wheel net, with its simplicity and efficiency, can be dysfunctional if member satisfaction becomes so low as to affect motivation.

2. Complex problems requiring high member interdependence may be ineffectively handled as a result of inadequate sharing of information and inadequate consideration of alternatives.

3. There are always trade-offs or opportunity costs to be considered. A work group that prefers an all-channel net will be less than totally effective in handling simple problems for which little member interdependence is required. Conversely, a work group that prefers the wheel net will have great difficulty handling a complex task.

Review your answers to Question 1 and make any changes you would like before continuing.

1. What type of communication network does Phil use in passing information to his people, and what type of net is used during the general office meeting? Explain.

In passing information to his people, Phil uses the wheel. He is the sole communicator who tells them the news, whether this is done over the phone or on a face-to-face basis. During the general office meeting, an all-channel net is used. The salespeople talk directly to Phil and vice versa, as well as to each other. There is a free flow of communication all around.

Decision Making

Another important area of group dynamics is intragroup decision making. Although there are many topics that can be addressed in this context,[7] we will limit our discussion to four: (a) group versus individual decision making; (b) the risky-shift phenomenon; (c) groupthink; and (d) interacting, delphi, and nominal groups.

Group Decisions versus Individual Decisions.   Are group decisions superior to individual decisions? Although many people believe they are, it actually depends on the situation. Research suggests that one of the key situational variables is the nature of the problem. For example, when it comes to generating ideas (especially unique ones), recalling information accurately, estimating and evaluating uncertain or ambiguous situations, or in any combination of these objectives, the group appears to be superior to the individual. On the other hand, when it comes to thinking out problems that require long chains of decisions, the individual is often superior to the group.[8]

Additionally, all successful groups are likely to employ both individual and group decision making. However, it is important to remember that although groups perform at a level that is generally better than the competence of its average members, they rarely do as well as the most efficient members.[9] Yetton and Bottger, for example, have found that groups who have adopted the decisions of the individual member who was judged to have the "best member" strategy did as well as teams that talked over their strategy and collectively decided what to do.[10] Moreover, training individuals can improve overall group performance.[11]

The Risky-Shift. One of the characteristics of group decision making that has long intrigued behavioral scientists is that of the risky-shift phenomenon. When making decisions as individuals, people tend to be more conservative than when they make decisions in a group. Most studies investigating the level of risk in individual versus group decisions have used measures in which the individual is asked to choose or recommend a course of action from among five or six alternatives. The individual is then placed in a group, which is given the same task to perform. The group members tend to be greater risk takers. A number of explanations have been offered for this **risky-shift phenomenon.**[12] Of these, five have received the greatest attention:

There are various reasons for the risky-shift phenomenon.

1. Making a decision in a group allows for diffusion of responsibility in the event of a wrong decision.

2. Risky people are more influential in group discussions than conservative people and so are more likely to bring others to their point of view.

3. Group discussion leads to deeper consideration of, and greater familiarization with, the possible pros and cons of a particular decision. In turn, greater familiarization and consideration lead to higher levels of risk.

4. Risk taking is socially desirable in our culture, and socially desirable qualities are more likely to be expressed in a group rather than alone.

5. According to a modification of the fourth explanation, a moderate risk is valued in our culture on certain kinds of issues, while on other kinds of issues moderate caution is valued. When the value of risk is engaged, people will choose a risk level which they believe is equal to or greater than the risk the average person will take. When a decision-making group is formed, members discovering that they are more conservative than the average will become riskier. . . . Likewise . . . those discovering that they are more risky than the average will shift in a conservative direction.[13]

Additionally, there is the effect of pressure.[14] For example, if the organization wants a unanimous opinion from the group, the minority may be pressured by the majority to go along with the decision. On the positive side, this pressure can also bring about organizational creativity, as in the case of subordinates who push their superior toward riskier and more creative results. This influence-response mechanism can be depicted as shown in Figure 8–3.

Many modern behavioral scientists believe that the key to the risky-shift rests in the composition of the group. By carefully selecting and placing group members, or in some cases by simply recognizing the implications of the current group composition,

FIGURE 8–3
Group Pressure and Creativity

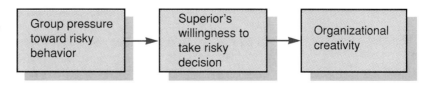

management may be able to influence creativity, generate the types of decisions it desires, and increase employee motivation.

Before concluding our discussion of the risky-shift, it should be noted that there is still a great deal of misunderstanding regarding the willingness of managers to take risks. For example, many people believe that managers in the public sector are risk avoiders. Actually, research shows that these individuals are no more likely to shun risk than those in the private sector. For example, Barton and Waldron surveyed the risk preferences of 118 managers in the private sector and 96 in the public sector. They found that private-sector managers were more willing than public-sector managers to see the organization use severe penalties, such as dismissal, salary reduction, loss of status, and reduced opportunity for promotion, against those who did not measure up. On the other hand, both private- and public-sector managers saw risk taking as potentially rewarding and were willing to accept these risks in order to improve performance.[15] Both groups also reported that they did not see jeopardizing their careers as a strong deterrent to risk taking. Overall, reported the researchers, "The results of this analysis clearly suggest that generalizations regarding differences between public and private administrators may frequently be overstated, particularly where attitude toward risk assumption in association with decision making is concerned."[16]

Most managers are not risk avoiders.

There are many other reported examples of the willingness of leaders to take risks. In fact, report Frost, Fiedler, and Anderson, personal risk taking can actually be a part of the job. For example, they have found that effective military combat leaders demonstrate more personally endangering acts than their less-effective counterparts, and effective fire combat leaders in urban fire departments show more personal bravery than less-effective fire combat leaders.[17] Pulling together the results of their study, they have concluded that "the willingness to expose oneself to danger is associated with effective leadership in potentially life-threatening situations and . . . factors found in studies of motivation in organizations may account for such acts of personal bravery."[18]

STOP

Review your answers to Question 2 and make any changes you would like before continuing.

2. How does this case illustrate the risky-shift phenomenon in action?

This case illustrates that individuals often take greater risks when they are in groups than when they are acting alone. Notice how the sales group influenced Phil to allow the increase in the sales territory. Their support for the idea removed Phil's fear that it might prove to be too much responsibility and work.

Groupthink is social conformity to group ideas.

Groupthink.   Another group phenomenon related to decision making is that of **groupthink,** or social conformity to group ideas. Popularized by Janis,[19] this designation denotes a concept that is useful in explaining why groups "collectively" make poor decisions.[20] Some classic examples of groupthink include the recommendation by President Kennedy's advisers to go ahead with the Bay of Pigs invasion, the decision by President Johnson and his advisers to bomb North Vietnam, and the National Security Council's involvement in the Iran arms-for-hostages agreement.[21]

In retrospect, these decisions are generally considered to have been bad ones. Yet how could groups of well-intentioned, well-informed people have been so wrong? The answer is found in groupthink, a phenomenon that is characterized by the failure of the group participants to challenge the thinking of the group. Some of the primary symptoms of groupthink include: (a) a belief that the group's decision cannot be wrong (whether this belief is ever expressed is irrelevant); (b) a belief that everyone in the group is in agreement with the decision(s) being made; (c) a feeling that the group leader, as well as the other members of the group, should be protected from information that might disturb the complacency that is shared by all; (d) a rationalizing away of any indications that the group's action might be wrong; (e) the placing of pressure on any person in the group who expresses doubts; and (f) an overriding desire to keep all disagreement within acceptable bounds.

The ultimate result of groupthink is that the group members become isolated from the world around them. They read positive signs as a reaffirmation of their goals and intentions; they read negative signs as an indication that there are individuals who do not understand what they are doing and that these individuals should be ignored (and perhaps even punished). During this entire process, it is common to find the group clinging to a belief that its ideals are humanitarian and based on high-minded principles. As a result, no attempt is made by the members to challenge or question the ethics of the group's behavior. A second common observation is high esprit de corps and amiability among the members. This often leads them to believe that those who question their approach or intentions are acting irrationally.

Quite often groupthink is only recognized after a group has made a disastrous decision. When this occurs, the members are apt to ask, "How could we have been so blind? Why didn't anyone call attention to our errors?" Unfortunately, at the time the group was making its decision(s), it is unlikely that any criticism or questioning of its actions would have been given serious consideration.

How can groupthink be overcome or dealt with effectively? There are a number of useful rules that can be employed.

There are ways of preventing groupthink.

First, the manager must encourage the open airing of objections and doubts. Second, one or more outsiders should be invited into the group to challenge the views of the members. Third, one member of the original group should be appointed to function as a lawyer who is challenging the testimony of the other members. Finally, after reaching a preliminary decision, the group should hold a "second chance" meeting at which every member expresses, as vividly as possible, all his or her doubts and the group thinks through the entire issue again before making a final decision.[22]

Investigation of group behavior has also led modern behavioral scientists to study the ways in which three basic types of groups—interacting, delphi, and nominal groups—differ. Which is superior to the others and under what conditions?

Interacting, Delphi, and Nominal Groups. One of the overriding concerns of contemporary administrators is that of finding effective decision-making methods when a number of people with different backgrounds and perspectives are involved in the problem-solving process. Three formats for group decision making are interacting, delphi, and nominal groups.

Interacting groups are the most common type.

An **interacting group** is one in which the members come into contact with each other. It is the most widely used of the three. The typical format involves a group leader's statement of the problem and general discussion or interaction of the members for the purpose of generating ideas and pooling judgments. The meeting usually concludes with a majority vote on how to resolve the problem.

Delphi members never see each other.

A **delphi group** consists of individuals who do not meet face to face. Instead, each isolated member is presented with the same problem, usually in the form of a structured questionnaire, and asked for his or her answer. All responses are then tabulated and sent back to the members, who can see the range and types of answers given. After looking them over, each member is again asked for an answer to the original problem. Additionally, if anyone's response (as in a quantitative problem) is higher or lower than the mid-range of the group, the person is asked to qualify it. After three or four delphi rounds, it is common to find the responses converging toward some central answer or range.

The nominal group technique uses structured decision making.

In a typical **nominal group** the members all sit around a table and employ a structured decision-making format known as a nominal group technique (NGT). This technique proceeds as follows:

1. Individual members first silently and independently generate their ideas on a problem or task in writing.

2. This period of silent writing is followed by a recorded round-robin procedure in which each group member (one at a time, in turn, around the table) presents one of his or her ideas to the group without discussion. The ideas are summarized in a terse phrase and written on a blackboard or sheet of paper on the wall.

3. After all the individuals have presented their ideas, there is a discussion of the recorded ideas for the purposes of clarification and evaluation.

4. The meeting concludes with a silent independent voting on priorities by individuals through a rank ordering or rating procedure, depending upon the group's decision rule. The "group decision" is the pooled outcome of individual votes.[23]

In a study they conducted, Van de Ven and Delbecq formed all three types of groups (twenty interacting, twenty delphi, and twenty NGT, all composed of seven heterogeneous members) and had each work on the same problem. The groups were asked to specify the job description of part-time student dormitory counselors who reside in and supervise student living units of university-owned or approved housing. A preliminary survey of students, faculty, administrators, and parents was conducted to validate the premise that the problem was indeed: (a) very difficult; (b) had no solution equally acceptable to all interest groups involved; and (c) would evoke highly emotional and subjective responses. The objective of the study was to compare the decision-making effectiveness of the three groups in terms of: (a) quantity of ideas developed; and (b) the perceived satisfaction of the groups with the decision-making process in which they were involved.

A comparison of intragroup dynamic factors is presented in Table 8–2. It shows that in this study there were great differences among the three groups. Overall, how-

TABLE 8–2
Comparison of Interacting, Delphi, and Nominal Groups

	Interacting Groups	Delphi Groups	Nominal Groups
Method	Unstructured face-to-face meeting; high variability in member and leader behavior from group to group	Structured series of questionnaires and feedback; low variability in member and leader behavior from group to group	Structured face-to-face meeting; low variability in member and leader behavior from group to group
Orientation of the groups	A lot of effort directed toward maintaining social and emotional relationships, little attention given to performance of the task	High emphasis given to performing the task	A balanced focus between social relationships and task orientation
Relative quantity of ideas	Low	High	Higher
Search behavior	Reactive search behavior characterized by short periods of attention to the problem; a tendency to avoid the task; much tangential discussion and many efforts to establish social relationships and generate social knowledge	Proactive search behavior characterized by high task centeredness	Proactive search behavior characterized by high task centeredness
Normative behavior	Pressures to conform inherent in face-to-face discussions	Since the members were anonymous, there was the freedom not to conform	Tolerance for nonconformity through independent search and choice activity
Equality of participation	Some members tended to dominate the process at one phase or another	Member equality	Member equality
Method of problem solving	Person centered; people tended to smooth things over or withdraw from the situation	Problem centered, with a majority rule of pooled independent judgments	Problem centered, with confrontation and problem solving used to resolve the issues
Feeling of accomplishment	Low	Medium	High
Resources utilized	Low administrative time and cost; high participative time and cost	High administrative time and cost	Medium administrative time and cost; high participative time and cost
Time to obtain group ideas	1½ hours	Five months	1½ hours

Source: Adapted from Andrew H. Van de Ven and Andre L. Delbecq, "The Effectiveness of Nominal, Delphi, and Interactive Group Decision Making Processes," *Academy of Management Journal,* December 1974, p. 615.

ever, Delbecq and Van de Ven found that the interacting groups generated the lowest number of unique ideas and had the lowest perceived satisfaction of the three. The NGT and delphi groups were superior and, depending on the situation, offered some very positive benefits to managers.

> This research suggests that, when confronted with a fact finding problem that requires the pooled judgment of a group of people, the practitioner can utilize two alternative procedures: (a) the . . . nominal group technique for situations where people are easily brought together physically, and for problems requiring immediate data, and (b) the . . . delphi technique for situations where the cost and inconvenience of bringing people together face to face is very high, and for problems that do not require immediate solution. Both the nominal group technique and the delphi method are more effective than the conventional discussion group process.[24]

The implications of this study are quite clear. When managers form task or project groups for problem-solving purposes, interacting groups commonly offer the least advantage of the three groups under consideration. Yet they are the most widely used of the three. An understanding of intragroup behavior can help the manager evaluate the pros and cons of each group and choose the one that will work best for all involved.[25]

Review your answers to Question 3 and make any changes you would like before continuing.

3. What type of group is being used to collect sales forecast information on the three new products? Explain.

A delphi group is being used to collect the sales forecast information. Notice that the questionnaire is anonymous, the data are collected and fed back to the participants, and the process continues for a series of rounds before a final answer is determined. These are all characteristics of the delphi process in action.

INTERGROUP PERFORMANCE

Intergroup behavior consists of behavioral interactions between two or more groups. These groups may be in the same major department, as in the case of purchasing and production, or they may come from different major departments, as in the case of sales and quality control. In either event, it is important to the manager that the interactions and performance of these groups result in the attainment of organizational goals.[26] In this section we are going to examine those factors that influence intergroup performance and note some of the strategies for managing such performance.

Intergroup performance can be affected by any of three variables: task certainty, group goals, and interdependence (Figure 8–4).

FIGURE 8–4
Causes of Intergroup Performance

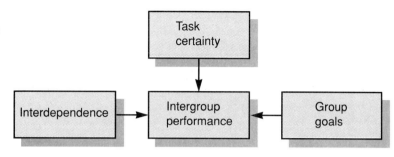

Task Certainty

Groups that know exactly what they are supposed to be doing are much more likely to have higher performance than those that lack such knowledge. Feedback, for example, can be very helpful.[27] However, task uncertainty cannot be avoided.

Task certainty depends on the clarity of the work and on the environment itself.

One of the factors on which task certainty depends is the clarity of the work, or the degree to which the responsibilities and requirements of the group are both stated and understood. Groups involved in the physical manufacture or sale of goods or services usually face little task uncertainty. They know what they are supposed to do and how to go about getting it done. However, those who are creating new products or thinking up new advertising campaigns often experience considerable uncertainty, since there are no fixed rules to guide them.

A second factor that affects task certainty is the environment, both internal and external, with which the group must interact. If this environment is dynamic, the task may prove much more difficult than if the environment is stable. For example, when a manufacturing department interacts with the accounting department regarding some new cost control forms, the problem may be minor. However, when the department interacts with its outside suppliers, it may find prices rising, materials in short supply, and delivery dates continually changing. Since manufacturing depends on these suppliers for its inputs, changes in this environment directly affect the department and impede its performance.

Group Goals

Every group in an organization has goals. For example, the marketing department wants to increase sales by 30 percent during the next year; the production department wants to reduce the cost per unit of Product A from $4.00 to $3.85; and the finance department wants to cut short-term debt by 20 percent and long-term debt by 50 percent. Each of these goals, in turn, is a subgoal of one of the organization's overall objectives, namely, a 22 percent increase in profit.

Group goals may be incompatible.

The major problem, from a group dynamics standpoint, is that the goals of these three groups may be incompatible. For example, if marketing increases its sales by 30 percent, the production department may be able to cut cost per unit of Product A back to $3.90. To get it to $3.85, however, the marketing people will have to increase sales by 40 percent, and this will require a greater marketing effort. Meanwhile, the finance department may be reluctant to provide the funds for such an effort since it wants to reduce overall debt. Clearly we have a situation in which not every department can attain its goals. Some trade-offs must be made.

A related dilemma is the time orientation of these different organizational groups. Some have very short-run time perspectives, as in the case of manufacturing and marketing. They are often most concerned with the next three, six, and twelve months. This contrasts with their counterparts in finance, who have to look farther ahead in evaluating changes in the interest rates and forecasting economic trends for the next three to five years. Time orientation differences can affect intergroup performance when each group develops tunnel vision and is concerned only with the information or results needed for performing its own tasks.

Interdependence

Closely related to group goals is interdependence, the degree to which groups have to coordinate their activities in order to attain the desired level of performance.[28] Thompson has noted three distinct types of interdependence: pooled, sequential, and reciprocal (Table 8–3).[29]

There are three types of interdependency: pooled, sequential, and reciprocal.

Pooled interdependence occurs whenever groups are relatively independent of each other, but each has some effect on the overall organization. For example, the physical therapy, pharmacy, and medical records departments of a hospital may seldom interact with each other. However, if any one of them is highly inefficient, it may result in the hospital failing to meet one or more of its overall objectives, such as covering its expenses or providing the highest quality medical services in the community.

TABLE 8–3
Intergroup Interdependence

Type of Interdependence	Degree of Dependence	Illustration
Pooled	Low	A⟶ These three departments are relatively independent of B⟶ each other, but their goals contribute C⟶ to those of the overall organization
Sequential	Medium	A⟶B⟶C The output of one department is an input for the next
Reciprocal	High	A⟷B⟷C The output of each department becomes input for the others, as well as for possibly still other groups

Sequential interdependence occurs when the outputs of one group become inputs for other groups. For example, research and development often provides the products for the manufacturing department, which in turn provides the outputs that the marketing department sells. Likewise, in an academic setting there is sequential interdependence between the various grade levels. Those groups in the third grade will become inputs for next year's fourth grade; high school graduates are inputs for college freshman classes; and college graduates are inputs for master's programs.

Reciprocal interdependence occurs when the outputs of each group become inputs for the other groups. For example, the maintenance department of an airline provides an input for operations in the form of a serviceable aircraft. Conversely, the operations department flies the craft and in so doing provides input to the maintenance department in the form of an airplane that needs maintenance. Each feeds off the other.

When we discuss intergroup performance, it is important to realize that as we progress from pooled to sequential and then to reciprocal interdependence the amount of interaction between groups becomes increasingly more difficult to achieve. Unless groups are aware of the effect of their output on the other groups in the organization, intergroup performance may be less than desirable (Table 8–3). Conversely, when the members trust each other and openly exchange information, productivity increases,[30] although increased interaction is no guarantee of intergroup cooperation.[31]

Review your answers to Question 4 and make any changes you would like before continuing.

4. What type of interdependence will there be between Phil's group and the marketing research department?

There will be sequential interdependence. The output from the marketing research department will become input for the sales department. Of course, if the marketing research people follow up and use sales results to help refine their forecasts and then send this information back to Phil, this would be an example of reciprocal interdependence because the output of each group would start becoming input for the other.

Achieving Desired Intergroup Performance

So far we have presented some of the challenges that confront the manager in achieving intergroup performance. Now we want to examine some of the strategies that can be helpful in managing this performance (also see "Organizational Behavior in Action: Employee Ownership Can Really Pay Off").

Organizational Behavior In Action	**EMPLOYEE OWNERSHIP CAN REALLY PAY OFF**

EMPLOYEE OWNERSHIP CAN REALLY PAY OFF

A few years ago Avis, the well-known car rental firm, was acquired by its 12,500 members through the use of an employee stock option plan (ESOP) strategy. Now all of the workers at Avis are part owners of the firm. Recent operating results indicate that the employees are quite happy with the arrangement, and internal measures of service quality are setting new records. For example, on-time arrivals of airport buses have risen from 93 percent to 96 percent, service-related customer complaints are down 35 percent, and the firm is paying off in record time the loan it floated for the purchase of the company. Additionally, Avis's market share is beginning to edge up while Hertz's (its major competitor) is beginning to slip.

In particular, industry analysts are pointing to the high degree of intergroup performance. Cooperation between all levels of the hierarchy and operating units is at an all-time high. Participative decision making, for example, is widely disseminated, and everyone is playing a role in helping run his or her area of operations. Some employees are even suggesting that the company tighten up its performance standards and start demanding more out of everyone.

This desire to increase productivity has gotten to the point where employees literally take their work home with them. *Fortune* magazine reports:

> Employees don't just make suggestions—they follow up. Says Avis Fort Lauderdale district manager Dan Falvey: "In many cases people will go out on their own time and get prices on materials for some ideas they've had and come back to the committee and say, 'Hey, should we do it?' And we make the decisions as a group. We're not sitting there as managers and employees. We're sitting there as a group of employees in Fort Lauderdale, asking how we can provide better service." They must be coming up with good answers. Since the ESOP purchase Avis has beaten Hertz in Fort Lauderdale market share for the first time ever.

Moreover, the employees are now so actively involved in decision making that the firm is starting a new program for managers on how to deal with people. Group performance has never been higher, and the company wants to maintain this initiative in every way possible. Maintenance of effective group interaction is one of the items at the top of this list.

Source: David Kirkpatrick, "How the Workers Run Avis Better," *Fortune,* December 5, 1988, pp. 103–114.

Rules and procedures can improve intergroup performance.

Rules, Procedures, and the Hierarchy. One of the most basic approaches to managing intergroup performance is to spell out the required activities and behavior of group members in the form of rules and procedures. Such an approach can help resolve incompatible goals and task uncertainty while promoting the necessary interaction for ensuring desired performance.[32] For example, if a manufacturing firm finds that its major supplier cannot handle a rush order and there is a rule covering this

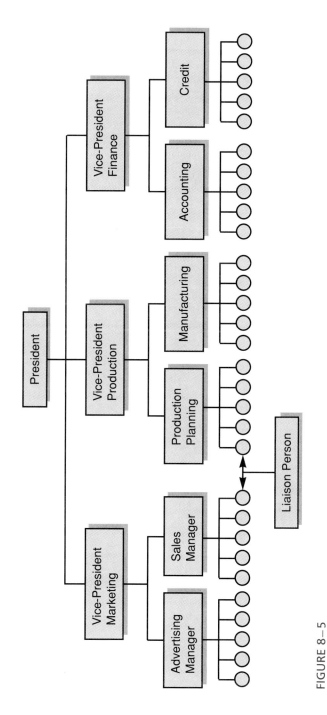

FIGURE 8–5
The Sales and Production Liaison Person

situation, all the manager need do is follow the guideline that has been set forth, such as placing the order with a competitive supplier.

Sometimes, however, rules and procedures do not cover a particular occurrence. In these cases it may be possible to use the hierarchy and have a common supervisor decide the issue. For example, there is a conflict between the marketing department and management department of a business college regarding where the international management courses should be taught. Each department claims that this area is within its province. The dean of the college, the common boss for both departments, can resolve the issue by making the final decision.

Planning and Liaison.   Another way of achieving desired intergroup performance is to determine the role and responsibilities of all groups in advance through forward planning. For example, when we see people building a house, we do not see carpenters, painters, and bricklayers bumping into each other. Each group knows what it is supposed to do and, via a master plan, the contractor coordinates the efforts of all.

Sometimes, however, when the interactions between two or more units or groups become very frequent, organizations will make use of liaison, or coordinating, personnel. The job of these people is to facilitate the flow of information between the groups, resolving any difficulties before they get out of hand.

Planning and liaison also enhance intergroup performance.

Liaison people can be used to coordinate the efforts of many groups in the organization. Figure 8–5 illustrates the liaison role between people in the sales department and those in the production planning department. Such coordination helps ensure a balance between the number of products being sold and those available for sale.

SUMMARY

1. The group is more than the sum of the individual members. Nevertheless, its goals, interactions, and performance are largely determined by the individual characteristics of its members. The three major clusters of characteristics that explain a member's influence on the group are: (a) biographical and physical characteristics; (b) abilities and intelligence; and (c) personality.

2. Individual characteristics help determine the interpersonal needs of the individual. This is one major variable in group behavior. The second is the interpersonal needs of the other group members. In the form of his FIRO, or fundamental interpersonal relations orientation, Schutz has provided an interesting theory for studying these two interpersonal dimensions of group behavior. In particular, the FIRO framework can be very helpful in providing insights into why people behave as they do in given situations. However, it is difficult to use FIRO to predict the compatibility of individual behavior in groups. To fully understand how people in a group interact, it is necessary to examine intragroup behavior.

3. One major area of intragroup behavior that is important in the study of group dynamics is communication networks. People are selective in their communication transmissions. An analysis of these nets among five-person groups reveals that the most common are the wheel, the Y, the chain, the circle, and the all-channel network. Some basic characteristics of each are degree of centralization, number of possible communication channels, average group satisfaction, range in individual/member satisfaction, and leadership predictability. Depending on the situation, any one of these five networks can be most effective.

4. Intragroup decision making is another major area of group dynamics. Groups tend to be better than individuals at handling some decisions, but not all. The individual is sometimes superior to the group. Regardless of the decision, however, it seems that people are greater risk takers when in groups than when operating alone. Yet this does not mean that group decisions are always superior to individual ones. Groupthink, in particular, can be the cause of very poor results.

5. The kind of group that is most effective also depends on the situation. Recent evidence reveals that delphi and nominal groups are often superior to interacting groups in handling fact-finding problems, one of the most common of all group goals. Both within and between groups, individuals use all sorts of tactics to improve their position and standing. The specific tactics employed in organizational politics are often determined by hierarchical level.

6. Intergroup behavior—interactions that occur between two or more groups—is of interest as regards intergroup performance, which depends on task certainty, group goals, and interdependence. Some ways of achieving desired intergroup performance include rules, procedures, the hierarchy, planning, and liaison personnel.

KEY TERMS

FIRO (fundamental interpersonal relations orientation)	communication network	nominal group
expressed behavior	risky-shift phenomenon	intergroup behavior
wanted behavior	groupthink	pooled interdependence
intragroup behavior	interacting group	sequential interdependence
	delphi group	reciprocal interdependence

REVIEW AND STUDY QUESTIONS

1. In what way can an individual's biographical and physical characteristics determine his or her influence on the group? What influence will intelligence and abilities have? What about personality traits?

2. Of what value is FIRO in the study of group behavior? Explain.

3. What are the most common types of small-group networks? Describe each.

4. Compare and contrast the five networks described in this chapter along the following lines: degree of centralization, number of possible communication channels, average group satisfaction, range in individual-member satisfaction, and leadership predictability.

5. What kinds of decisions or situations can a group handle better than an individual? When is an individual superior to a group? Explain.

6. Are groups greater risk takers than individuals? Explain, incorporating into your answer the concept of the risky-shift.

7. How does groupthink work? What negative effects does it have? How can groupthink be dealt with effectively? Explain.

8. How does an interacting group function? A delphi group? A nominal group? In what kinds of situations would you expect each to be superior to the others?

9. How can uncertainty of the task affect intergroup performance? What about goal incompatibility? Time orientation?

10. In what way can interdependence of tasks affect intergroup performance? Include in your answer the three types of interdependence: pooled, sequential, and reciprocal.

11. In what way can rules and procedures help the manager achieve desired intergroup performance? What about planning? Liaison?

CASES

Passing It On

There are five people in Work Group 6 at the Ponsky Plant, but only one, Tony DiBiasi, is responsible for seeing that all work-related changes are communicated to the other members. Tony is the straw boss of the group and is the direct interface with the supervisor.

Work-related changes are communicated to the other

members within a day of when Tony gets them. This usually is handled one-on-one, with Tony explaining to each person what he or she is supposed to do.

Other matters such as discussion of bottlenecks and related production problems are handled in a plenary session with all five members of the group talking directly to each other. This approach has been very useful in helping identify where productivity is being lost and formulating suggestions about how to correct the problem. Tony then takes these ideas, writes them up in memo form, and submits them to his supervisor for action by higher-level management.

A third common communication pattern is a round-robin format that is often used when there is no time for a group meeting. Tony will pass along something that he has learned from the supervisor such as the fact that all vacations must be taken during the months of June to September and everyone in the group must go out during the same month. Tony recently conveyed the information to Diane Hartwicker. "I, personally, prefer August for a vacation,"

he said. "What about you?" Diane agreed. "Well, why don't you talk to Bob, see what he wants, and have him talk to Jenny. Jenny can then talk to Pete, who can get back with me." When Pete and Tony met, it turned out that two of the group wanted their vacation in August and the other three preferred September. "We better have a general meeting on this one," Tony said. "We're going to have to iron it out face-to-face."

1. What three types of communication nets were described in this case? Identify each.

2. Which of the three nets is likely to be highest in terms of: centralization, average group member satisfaction, leadership predictability? Explain.

3. Which of the three is likely to be lowest in terms of: number of possible communication channels, range in individual member satisfaction, leadership predictability? Explain.

The Proposed Expansion

Barry Roberts came to the attention of the board of directors of Mercy General Hospital soon after the administrator announced her decision to retire. Barry was the administrator of a medium-sized hospital located approximately 250 miles from Mercy General. During Barry's five years at the helm, that hospital had increased its bed capacity by 21 percent, paid off 62 percent of its long-term debt, and gained a reputation as the finest hospital in its area. After interviewing Barry, the board offered him the position of hospital administrator at Mercy General, and Barry accepted.

Mercy General was founded in 1917 and had not had a major expansion since 1958. The accountant and the associate administrators had all been after the former administration to recommend a building program to the board. However, they had been unsuccessful. "The board has always been conservative in its approach to fiscal matters," she had told the group, "and that is why the hospital has been able to survive for so long. We don't want to make any drastic changes that might lead to financial disaster."

Barry echoed these basic feelings. He believed that Mercy General was in a good financial position, but not strong enough to undertake any vigorous building program. "In fact," he told the accountant, "that's one reason why the board hired me—to maintain the status quo and not get them involved in some expensive building program." Despite such comments, the accountant and the other admin-

istrators kept working on Barry. Six months later he capitulated, "All right, you win," he told them, "I'll make the request to the board. I now see that an expansion program is much more feasible than I initially thought; moreover, if you guys are willing to back me up on this proposal, I'm willing to sponsor it."

The board was surprised at Barry's recommendations. They felt that the hospital might need some renovations over the next few years, but nothing extensive. However, after Barry explained what needed to be done, how much it would cost, and why he felt the risk was acceptable, the board began to change its mind. Over the next month Barry sent each of them a series of reports addressing various questions they had raised during the meeting. At the next board meeting, the directors voted to go along with the proposed expansion program. As the meeting adjourned, one director turned to the other and said, "If you had told me six months ago I'd be voting approval of a major building program, I'd have said you were crazy."

1. Why did Barry change his mind about the building program? Why did the board change its mind?

2. Do groups always make riskier decisions than individuals? Explain.

3. What is the lesson we can learn from this case about the risky-shift phenomenon?

SELF-FEEDBACK EXERCISE

Risk Taking and You

Instructions: Read each of the following scenarios very carefully. Then decide whether or not you would (a) do nothing, or (b) take a risk. If you choose the latter, then indicate the minimum odds you would be willing to accept. Be sure to answer each scenario by placing an "X" next to your choice.

1. You are a college basketball coach and your team is ranked number two nationally. You are playing the number one-ranked team in the NCAA finals and are two points behind with five seconds to go. You call a time out in order to set up a play. You have two choices. One is a very safe one that is sure to get you two points, tie the game, and send it into overtime. The other is a tricky play that involves your player's being fouled on a lay-up, but if it works it will produce three points and give you the victory. Following are the probabilities or odds that the risky play will succeed. Check the lowest probability that you would consider acceptable for the risky play to be attempted.

_____ The chances are 1 in 10 that the play will work.

_____ The chances are 3 in 10 that the play will work.

_____ The chances are 5 in 10 that the play will work.

_____ The chances are 7 in 10 that the play will work.

_____ The chances are 9 in 10 that the play will work.

_____ You would not try the risky play regardless of the probabilities of success.

2. You have just been to the doctor and learned that you have a very bad heart. You have two alternatives. One is to have an operation and take the risk of dying. The other is to refuse the operation, in which case you will live approximately ten more years but no longer since your problem can only be cured with this operation. Check the lowest probability you would consider acceptable regarding your surviving the operation.

_____ The chances are 1 in 10 that you will survive.

_____ The chances are 3 in 10 that you will survive.

_____ The chances are 5 in 10 that you will survive.

_____ The chances are 7 in 10 that you will survive.

_____ The chances are 9 in 10 that you will survive.

_____ You would not submit to the operation regardless of the probabilities associated with survival.

3. You want to be a writer. There are two colleges on which you have had your eye. One is local, and although it is not very well ranked academically, you have been offered a scholarship and can live at home. The other, where you have also been accepted, is considered one of the finest schools in the country for aspiring writers. The problem with the latter, however, is that the flunk-out rate is very high. Less than one-third of those entering the freshman class actually graduate. What is the lowest probability of graduating that you would consider acceptable before registering at the nationally ranked school?

_____ The chances are 1 in 10 that you would graduate.

_____ The chances are 3 in 10 that you would graduate.

_____ The chances are 5 in 10 that you would graduate.

_____ The chances are 7 in 10 that you would graduate.

_____ The chances are 9 in 10 that you would graduate.

_____ You would not accept admission to the nationally ranked school regardless of the probability of graduation.

4. You have saved $10,000 and intend to invest it in the stock market for a period of one year. You have decided on one of two stocks. Stock A is a blue chip and will provide you a return of between 7 and 10 percent. Stock B is a speculative issue that, if things go well for the firm, will double in value over the next year. If

things do not go well, however, it is likely that you will lose your entire investment. What is the lowest probability that you would consider acceptable before investing in Stock B?

_____ The probability of the firm doing well is 1 in 10.

_____ The probability of the firm doing well is 3 in 10.

_____ The probability of the firm doing well is 5 in 10.

___ℓ___ The probability of the firm doing well is 7 in 10.

_____ The probability of the firm doing well is 9 in 10.

_____ You would not invest in the speculative issue regardless of the probability of success.

5. You are in the process of buying a new car and have reduced your choices to two: a domestic auto and a foreign one. The domestic one will have average resale value and its performance has been rated as good by a consumer service. The foreign one, which costs a little more, has received mixed reviews. Its performance is superior to that of most cars on the road, but those who have had mechanical difficulty report it is tough to get parts and service from the dealers, the car is in the shop for one to two weeks at a time, and repair costs are high. Those who have had no trouble with their foreign care report that its resale value is extremely high (provided you can prove to the buyer that yours is not one that has had trouble), and they intend to purchase another one in the future. What is the lowest probability you would consider acceptable before buying the foreign car?

_____ 1 chance in 10 that the car will have no major problems.

_____ 3 chances in 10 that the car will have no major problems.

_____ 5 chances in 10 that the car will have no major problems.

_____ 7 chances in 10 that the car will have no major problems.

_____ 9 chances in 10 that the car will have no major problems.

___ℓ___ You would not buy the foreign car regardless of the probability that you would have no major problems.

6. You are going to buy a house. One that is acceptable to you and within your budget is located in a good neighborhood. The other, which is much more expensive and currently too high for your budget, is located in an excellent neighborhood. A friend of yours is the loan officer at the local savings and loan and is willing to help you buy the more expensive house should you want it. Her plan is to give you a five-year escalating interest rate that will start two percentage points below the current average rate and will rise to two percentage points above the current average rate by the end of five years. If you opt for the larger house, you will have to get high performance appraisal ratings at work so as to get merit raises. If you fail to get these raises (an average of 10 percent a year) you will lose the house. What is the lowest probability of your getting high performance appraisal ratings over each of the next five years that you would accept before agreeing to buy the more expensive house?

_____ 1 chance in 10 of getting high ratings for five years.

_____ 3 chances in 10 of getting high ratings for five years.

_____ 5 chances in 10 of getting high ratings for five years.

_____ 7 chances in 10 of getting high ratings for five years.

_____ 9 chances in 10 of getting high ratings for five years.

___ℓ___ You would not purchase the more expensive house regardless of the probability of getting high ratings for five years.

7. Your company is going to expand its operations. Two final choices are being considered and the decision is yours. One is to open a new plant in Seattle. The expected return on this investment is 14 percent. The other is to open a new plant in a South American country. The expected return on this investment is 25 percent, although there is a chance that after the next national elections (next year) your operations will be nationalized and the overall result will be an 80 percent loss of your total investment. What is the lowest possible probability of the nationalization's not occurring that you would consider acceptable before investing in this country?

_____ The chances are 1 in 10 that nationalization will not occur.

_____ The chances are 3 in 10 that nationalization will not occur.

_____ The chances are 5 in 10 that nationalization will not occur.

_____ The chances are 7 in 10 that nationalization will not occur.

_____ The chances are 9 in 10 that nationalization will not occur.

___✓___ You would not recommend expansion into this country regardless of the likelihood of nationalization.

8. You have just written a novel that could become a national best seller. On the other hand, it could end up as just another book. You have offers from two publishers. One will give you a fixed amount of money for your rights to the book. All revenues from the sale of the novel will then belong to the publisher. The other firm will not directly give you any money, but it will give you 15 percent of the sales price of all copies sold. If the book does not sell well at all, the first offer will provide you more money. If the book becomes a best seller, the second offer is your best one. What is the lowest probability of the book's becoming a best seller that you would accept before agreeing to sign with the second publisher?

_____ 1 chance in 10.

_____ 3 chances in 10.

_____ 5 chances in 10.

___✓___ 7 chances in 10.

_____ 9 chances in 10.

_____ You would not sign with the second publisher regardless of the probability that the book would become a best seller.

9. You are having trouble with your car. If you take it in to the dealer it will cost you $700. However, the individual will warranty the work, and if something goes wrong it will be fixed free of charge. The local service station will also fix your car for a price of $225 but will not warranty the work. Check the lowest probability that you would consider acceptable before taking the car to the service station to have the work done.

_____ 1 chance in 10 that it will be done right.

_____ 3 chances in 10 that it will be done right.

___✓___ 5 chances in 10 that it will be done right.

_____ 7 chances in 10 that it will be done right.

_____ 9 chances in 10 that it will be done right.

_____ You would not take the car to the service station regardless of the probability of success.

10. You have two one-year job offers. One is a guaranteed $24,000. The other is for $5,000 plus 5 percent of all sales that you make. Check the lowest probability of your making over $24,000 that you would consider acceptable before taking the second offer.

_____ 1 chance in 10.

_____ 3 chances in 10.

_____ 5 chances in 10.

_____ 7 chances in 10.

_____ 9 chances in 10.

___✓___ You would not accept the second offer regardless of the probability of making over $24,000.

Scoring:

Go back to each of your answers and note the probability that you checked. If you checked 1 chance in 10, your score on that situation is 1; if you checked 5 chances in 10, your score on that situation is 5, and so on. If you said that you would not take the chance, your score for that situation is 10. Notice that the lower your risk-taking willingness in a particular situation, the higher your score. Now enter your ten scores below and total them.

1. _____5_____

2. _____7_____

3. _____7_____

4. _____7·_____

5. _____10_____

6. _____10_____

7. _____10_____

8. _____7·_____

9. _____5_____

10. _____10_____

Total _____78_____

Are you a high risk taker? Are you basically a risk avoider? The answer will depend on how low (or high) your score is. Based on all of those who have taken this exercise, the following provides a general picture of willingness to take risk:

Low risk takers	71–100
Moderate risk takers	41– 70
High risk takers	10– 40

Are individuals willing to assume more risks when they are operating as a member of a group than when they are making the same decision by themselves? The answer is generally yes. One way to check and find out if you fall into this category is to sit down with two to four of your classmates and, without telling each other how you scored this exercise, decide collectively how you would vote on each situation. Then total your score and compare it to the one already calculated. Over 80 percent of all participants find that they are greater risk takers in a group situation than when acting alone.

NOTES

1. Marvin E. Shaw, *Group Dynamics: The Psychology of Small Groups* (New York: McGraw-Hill Book Co., 1971), pp. 162–165.

2. Ralph M. Stogdill, "Personal Factors Associated with Leadership: A Survey of the Literature," *Journal of Psychology,* January 1948, pp. 35–71.

3. Shaw, *Group Dynamics,* p. 165.

4. Will Schutz, *FIRO Awareness Scales Manual* (Palo Alto, CA: Consulting Psychologists Press, Inc., 1978); William C. Schutz, *Interpersonal Underworld* (Palo Alto, CA: Science and Behavior Books, 1967); and William C. Schutz, *A Three-Dimensional Theory of Interpersonal Relations* (New York: Holt, Rinehart & Winston, 1958).

5. William W. Lidell and John W. Slocum, Jr., "The Effects of Individual-Role Compatibility Upon Group Performance: An Extension of Schutz's FIRO Theory," *Academy of Management Journal,* September 1976, pp. 413–426.

6. Also see Gregory P. Shea and Richard A. Guzzo, "Group Effectiveness: What Really Matters?," *Sloan Management Review,* Spring 1987, pp. 25–31.

7. See for example Stuart L. Hart, "Toward Quality Criteria for Collective Judgments," *Organizational Behavior and Human Decision Processes,* October 1985, pp. 209–228.

8. For more information on this subject see Bertram Schoner, Gerald L. Rose, and G. C. Hoyt, "Quality of Decisions: Individual Versus Real and Synthetic Groups," *Journal of Applied Psychology,* August 1974, pp. 424–432.

9. John Rohrbaugh, "Improving the Quality of Group Judgment: Social Judgment Analysis and the Delphi Technique," *Organizational Behavior and Human Performance,* August 1979, pp. 73–92; Kaoru Ono and James H. Davis, "Individual Judgment and Group Interaction: A Variable Perspective Approach," *Organizational Behavior and Human Decision Processes,* April 1988, pp. 211–232; and Preston C. Bottger and Philip W. Yetton, "An Integration of Processes and Decision Scheme Explanations of Group Problem Solving Performance," *Organizational Behavior and Human Decision Processes,* October 1988, pp. 234–249.

10. Philip W. Yetton and Preston C. Bottger, "Individual Versus Group Problem Solving: An Emperical Test of a Best-Member Strategy," *Organizational Behavior and Human Performance,* June 1982, pp. 307–321.

11. Preston C. Bottger and Philip W. Yetton, "Improved Group Performance by Training in Individual Problem Solving," *Journal of Applied Psychology,* November 1987, pp. 651–657.

12. Dorwin Cartwright, "Risk Taking by Individuals and Groups: An Assessment of Research Employing Choice Dilemmas," *Journal of Personality and Social Psychology,* December 1971, pp. 361–378; Russell D. Clark, III, "Group Induced Shift Toward Risk: A Critical Appraisal," *Psychological Bulletin,* October 1971, pp. 251–270; and Dean G. Pruitt, "Choice Shifts in Group Discussion: An Introductory Review," *Journal of Personality and Social Psychology,* December 1971, pp. 339–360.

13. Earl A. Cecil, Larry L. Cummings, and Jerome M. Chertkoff, "Group Composition and Choice Shift: Implications for Administration," *Academy of Management Journal,* September 1973, pp. 413–414.

14. Deborah L. Gladstein and Nora P. Reilly, "Group Decision Making Under Threat: The Tycoon Game," *Academy of Management Journal,* September 1985, pp. 613–627.

15. M. Frank Barton, Jr. and Darryl G. Waldron, "Differences in Risk Preference Between the Public and Private Sectors," *Human Resource Management,* Winter 1978, pp. 2–4.

16. *Ibid.,* p. 4.

17. Dean E. Frost, Fred E. Fiedler, and Jeff W. Anderson, "The Role of Personal Risk-Taking in Effective Leadership," *Human Relations,* February 1983, pp. 185–202.

18. *Ibid.,* p. 185.

19. Irving Janis, "Group Think," *Psychology Today,* November 1971, pp. 43–46; 74–76.

20. See also Glen Whyte, "Groupthink Reconsidered," *Academy of Management Review,* January 1989, pp. 40–56.

21. See *The Tower Commission Report* (New York: New York Times, 1987) and *Taking the Stand* (New York: Simon & Schuster, 1987).

22. Richard M. Hodgetts, *Modern Human Relations At Work,* 4th ed. (Hinsdale, IL: Dryden Press, 1990), pp. 1, 3, 4.

23. Andrew H. Van de Ven and Andre L. Delbecq, "The Effectiveness of Nominal, Delphi, and Interacting Group Decision Making Processes," *Academy of Management Journal,* December 1974, p. 606.

24. *Ibid.,* p. 620.

25. For more on nominal grouping see Jim Grepson, Mark J. Martinko, and James Belina, "Nominal Group Techniques," *Training and Development Journal,* September 1981, pp. 78–83.

26. See for example Kenwyn K. Smith and David N. Berg, "A Paradoxical Conception of Group Dynamics," *Human Relations,* October 1987, pp. 633–658.

27. Tamao Matsui, Takashi Kakuyama, and Mary Lou Uy Onglatco, "Effects of Goals and Feedback on Performance in Groups," *Journal of Applied Psychology,* August 1987, pp. 407–415; and Tony E. Gear, Nicholas R. Marsh, and Peter Sergent, "Semi-Automated Feedback," *Human Relations,* August 1985, pp. 707–721.

28. See for example Karen A. Brown and Terence R. Mitchell, "Influence of Task Interdependence and Number of Poor Performers on Diagnoses of Causes of Poor Performance," *Academy of Management Journal,* June 1986, pp. 412–424.

29. Leigh L. Thompson, Max H. Bazerman, and Elizabeth A. Mannix, "Negotiation in Small Groups," *Journal of Applied Psychology,* 1989, pp. 508–517.

30. Dean Tjosvold, "Cooperative and Competitive Dynamics Within and Between Organizational Units," *Human Relations,* June 1988, pp. 425–436.

31. Gillian Oaker and Rupert Brown, "Intergroup Relations in a Hospital Setting: A Further Test of Social Identity," *Human Relations,* August 1986, pp. 767–778.

32. See for example Reed E. Nelson, "The Strength of Strong Ties," *Academy of Management Journal,* June 1989, pp. 377–401.

CHAPTER 9
The Leadership Process

GOALS OF THE CHAPTER

A successful manager must be capable of leading his or her group of subordinates. The goals of this chapter are to study the nature of the leadership process and to examine some of the major approaches for analyzing and examining what leadership is all about. The first objective of this chapter is to review the general area of leadership. Then attention will be focused on trait theory, behavioral theory, and contingency theory, the three basic approaches that have been taken by researchers in their study of this area. Finally, additional leadership perspectives will be explored. When you have finished reading this chapter you should be able to:

1. define the term *leadership* and explain the nature of leadership;
2. identify the contributions made to leadership theory by the Ohio State University and University of Michigan researchers;
3. describe some of the modern contingency models of leader effectiveness;
4. discuss additional perspectives that will be the focal point of attention during the 1990s.

OPENING CASE: DOING IT HER WAY

There were six finalists for the vice-president, industrial sales position of a large New England-based high tech firm. The final choice, Angela Barberi, was an outside candidate with a very successful track record. However, the main reason she was given the job was that she impressed the committee members more than any other candidate did. "She looks more like a vice-presidential person than the other people we interviewed," one of the selection committee members noted. Another said Angela was "more self-assured and had better presence than any of the others."

Angela took over her new assignment within thirty days and immediately began holding meetings with her people to get feedback regarding industrial sales problems and how they could be resolved. Angela then set out a plan for dealing with these matters. Soon thereafter sales started

going up. This continued until eighteen months ago when the industry suffered a tremendous sales slump. The company began cutting back, and Angela started spending two days a week in the field working with the salesforce. She soon found that the salespeople fell into two groups. One was very hard working and determined to turn things around. The other was content to ride out the industry slump. Angela soon recommended a change in compensation policy that would result in the first group's making greater incentive pay and the second group's making very little. She also wrote very favorable evaluations for the members of the first group and poor evaluations for those in the second group.

The industry is still having a difficult time, but Angela's group is doing quite well. Sales are up 37 percent in the last six months while industry sales during this period have declined

8 percent. Angela believes that a major reason for this success is that she has been able to reward the high performers and encourage the others to "get on the band wagon or get out."

1. Did management use trait theory in choosing Angela for the job? Explain.
2. How would you describe Angela in terms of the Ohio State leadership grid?
3. What type of leadership style would Fred Fiedler recommend Angela use when things got bad? Explain.
4. In what way does leader-member exchange theory help explain Angela's leadership style?
5. Is Angela a charismatic leader? Why or why not?

Write down your answers to these questions and put them aside. We will return to them later.

THE NATURE OF LEADERSHIP

For the last ninety years the area of leadership has been the object of analysis and study.[1] During this time, behavioral scientists and practicing managers alike have sought to analyze and define what leadership is. Today the literature is replete with both theories and definitions,[2] although there is still a great deal we do not know about the subject.

In beginning our study of this area it is important to distinguish between management and leadership. Management is the process of getting things done through other people. **Leadership** is the process of influencing people to direct their efforts toward the achievement of some particular goal(s). This influence comes from two basic sources: (a) the leader's **position power,** or the formal authority that accompanies a particular job; and (b) the subordinate's willingness to comply.[3]

Leadership is the process of influencing people.

Thus we have the leader and the led, and in order to be effective the former must solicit and obtain cooperation from the latter in both formal and informal ways.[4] This usually requires the leader to prove himself or herself, for example, by demonstrating competence, providing job-related assistance, giving moral and psychological support, and securing greater economic benefits for the followers. Leader-subordinate relationships always involve some kind of psychological or economic exchange.[5] In some cases, this results in leaders trying to turn their own personnel into leaders.[6]

The task of the leader is to determine which method of leadership will work best given: (a) his or her personality, experience, and knowledge; (b) the background, training, and expectations of the followers; and (c) the environment in which everyone is functioning.

Over the years there has been a great deal of speculation about leadership. Some of the most commonly raised questions include: What traits do leaders have in common that other people do not? What kinds of leadership behavior are more effective than others? How important is it for a leader to analyze each situation and then "play it by ear"? These three questions are fundamental to leadership theory because, from first to last, they relate to the three basic approaches that have been taken to study this area: trait theory, behavioral theory, and contingency theory.

LEADERSHIP-TRAIT THEORY

Much early leadership research was based on **leadership-trait theory,** which sought to identify those traits or characteristics that distinguish successful leaders from unsuccessful leaders. For the most part, however, the results of these studies were inconclusive. For example, Byrd analyzed trait theory research up to 1940 and found that only 5 percent of the traits identified in any one study were common to four or more investigations.[7] Stogdill reviewed 124 studies in this area and also found mixed results.

There is no universal list of traits for successful leaders.

However, Stogdill did discover some characteristics that leaders seemed to have in common. These included intelligence, dependability, responsibility, social activity, high originality, and high socioeconomic status. Over the years, other researchers have also produced some positive findings on leadership traits. One of these studies, conducted by a group of researchers from the University of Minnesota, contained data from thirteen Minnesota firms ranging in size from 100 to 4,000 employees. The researchers found that many successful managers enjoyed interacting with other people and were more intelligent, better educated, and more highly motivated than their less successful counterparts. These managers also showed a marked preference for business-related activities.[8] The problem with both the Stogdill and the Minnesota results, however, was that the common characteristics did not hold true for all successful managers; there were many exceptions to the general pattern.

Today there is still interest in leadership-trait theory, as reflected in the research of E. E. Ghiselli.[9] Ghiselli's data show that cognitive skills and self-assurance are much more important than some of the traits commonly believed to be important to leaders, such as initiative or a need for power over others. Other researchers have uncovered supportive results, thus indicating Ghiselli is on the right track.[10]

Similarly, in reviewing the characteristics that consistently separate the effective from the ineffective leader, Bass has concluded that the effective leaders can be described in terms of certain characteristics.

> The leader is characterized by a strong drive for responsibility in task completion, vigor and persistence in pursuit of goals, venturesomeness and originality in problem solving, drive to exercise initiative in social situations, self-confidence and sense of personal identity, willingness to accept the consequences of his or her decision and action, readiness to absorb interpersonal stress, willingness to tolerate frustrations and delay, ability to influence other people's behavior and the capacity to structure social interaction systems to the purpose at hand.[11]

Nevertheless, most researchers do not focus on traits, undoubtedly because no universal list has been forthcoming. While trait theory research continues,[12] many in the field have turned their attention to leadership-behavior theory.[13]

 STOP

Review your answers to Question 1 and make any changes you would like before continuing.

1. Did management use trait theory in choosing Angela for the job? Explain.

It certainly did. Notice from the comments by the selection committee members that the traits they saw in Angela were apparently more important than her previous track record or the fact that she had the ability to do the job.

LEADERSHIP-BEHAVIOR THEORY

Leadership studies from a behavioral theory perspective focus on exploring the relationships between the behavior of leaders and work-group performance and satisfaction. In contrast with trait theory, which attempts to describe leadership on the basis of the personal characteristics that leaders possess, **leadership-behavior theory** seeks to explain leadership in terms of what leaders do (see "Organizational Behavior in Action: Effective Leadership Guidelines").

EFFECTIVE LEADERSHIP GUIDELINES

How do effective leaders behave? Research shows that they tend to follow seven basic guidelines. Depending on the situation, of course, some will be more important than others, but all are critical at one time or another.

The first important guideline is to trust subordinates. Effective leaders push authority down the line and rely on the energy and talent of their people to get the work done. They develop a mutual trust between themselves and their people. As the president of Johnson & Johnson put it, "Leaders are developed by challenges."

Second, leaders have a vision of where they want to take their organization. For example, Ray Kroc, who made McDonald's what it is today, continually stressed quality, service, cleanliness, and value, four characteristics that represented his vision of what McDonald's should offer. These characteristics continue to represent the company's vision.

Third, effective leaders keep cool under pressure. For example, when someone slipped poison into a Tylenol package, the company president kept his cool and quickly withdrew all capsules from the market. He was calm when appearing in front of the press, and he even allowed TV cameras into the boardroom to film meetings in which strategies for dealing with the situation were discussed.

Fourth, effective leaders encourage risk and allow failure. For example, when Fred Smith started Federal Express no one thought that he would be successful because the demand for overnight air delivery service was too small. Nevertheless Smith risked the several million dollars his father had left him and took the plunge. Today Federal Express has revenues in excess of $4 billion annually.

Fifth, effective leaders are experts in critical areas that require job knowledge and competence. For example, when John Sculley left his position at PepsiCo to become president of Apple Computer, he did not know the computer business. However, he quickly learned because without this expertise he knew he would be unable to interact effectively with stockholders, investors, organizational personnel, or customers.

Sixth, effective leaders invite dissent. They allow their people to disagree or to voice concerns. In fact, they often use this feedback to help them shape their strategies and revise their plans. As the president of Xerox's U.S. marketing group put it, "The higher you get in an organization, the more important it is to have people who will tell you when you are right or wrong."

Seventh, effective leaders provide simple answers to complex questions. They zero in on the essential parts of the answer and present them in understandable fashion. When they are done giving an answer, the listener(s) understands what has been communicated. For example, when Drew Lewis of the Union Pacific Railroad was asked to help produce a plan for reducing the massive annual federal deficits, he cut right to the bottom line and recommended cuts in those areas that would produce the most savings: military spending, interest payments, and entitlement programs. While his advice is unlikely to be heeded, no one is in doubt regarding his message.

Source: Kenneth Labich, "The Seven Keys to Business Leadership," *Fortune,* October 24, 1988, pp. 58–66.

Over the last thirty-five years a number of behavioral models have emerged. Most of them incorporate two main dimensions: (a) the leader's interest in getting work done; and (b) the leader's concern for the people themselves. In other words, to what extent is the leader task oriented and people oriented?

Continuum of Leadership Behavior

One of the simplest ways of examining leadership behavior is to look at the various styles that can be used. This can be done via a leadership-behavior continuum ranging from heavily boss-centered leadership to heavily subordinate-centered leadership, as seen in Figure 9–1. On the left side of the continuum are the **authoritarian leaders** who delegate very little authority, preferring to make the bulk of the decisions themselves. As one progresses across the continuum, the delegation of authority increases, the trust of the managers in the subordinates goes up, and the freedom of subordinate personnel to exercise their own initiative in work-related matters rises. At the far right side of the continuum are the **democratic leaders** who delegate a great deal of authority to their subordinates.

The participative approach is not always better.

Authoritarian Styles versus Democratic Styles.   While most people acknowledge that effective leadership behavior is a function of the situation, many also believe that participative leaders are superior to authoritarian ones. However, research does not substantiate the universal superiority of the participative approach. For example, McCurdy and Eber investigated the effects of autocratic and democratic styles on

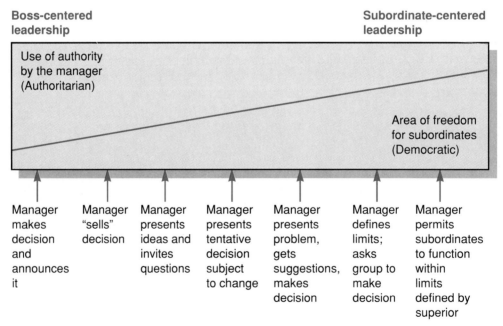

FIGURE 9–1

Continuum of Leadership Behavior (Based on Robert Tannenbaum and Warren H. Schmidt, "How to Choose a Leadership Pattern," *Harvard Business Review*, May–June 1958, p. 183.)

three-person groups involved in problem-solving activities. The teams working under authoritarian leaders were told to simply obey orders, while those working under democratic leaders were told to offer suggestions and not follow orders blindly. The researchers found no difference in productivity between the two groups.[14]

Other investigations have found that democratic leadership often results in higher job satisfaction, but autocratic leadership (especially in the short run) can bring about greater productivity. Finally, it is important to note that some individuals seem to prefer autocratic leadership. Vroom, for example, has found that participative leadership has a positive effect only on those individuals with strong nonauthoritarian values or a high need for independence.[15]

Shortcomings. The basic problem with the continuum approach to studying leadership behavior is that it seems to support "trade-offs". A boss-centered leader is seen as being heavily interested in task-related activities but not very concerned about people. A subordinate-centered leader is seen as being greatly concerned about people but not very interested in the work. Research, however, has revealed that this need not be the case. This has been illustrated by, among others, the Ohio State studies.

The Ohio State Studies

The Ohio State Leadership Studies began shortly after World War II. Conducted among military aircraft crews by the Bureau of Business Research at The Ohio State University, one of the primary objectives of these studies was to investigate situational determinants of leadership behavior. In particular, the researchers sought to answer the following questions: What types of behavior do leaders display? What effect do these leadership styles have on respective work-group performance and satisfaction?

During these studies a **Leader Behavior Description Questionnaire (LBDQ),** consisting of a list of descriptive statements about leadership behavior, was developed. Items on the questionnaire related to the leader's interest in people, such as: (a) the leader finds time to listen to the group members; (b) the leader is willing to make changes; and (c) the leader is friendly and approachable. Items related to the leader's interest in the work included: (a) the leader assigns group members to particular tasks; (b) the leader asks the group members to follow standard rules and regulations; and (c) the leader lets group members know what is expected of them. From this analysis came four dimensions that, based on the responses of participants, characterized the behavior of their commanders.

1. **Consideration factor**: leadership behaviors indicative of friendship, respect, mutual trust, and warmth.
2. **Initiating structure factor**: leadership behaviors that enable the aircraft commander to organize and define the relationship between himself and his crew.
3. *Production emphasis*: leadership behaviors by which the commander attempts to motivate the crew to greater activity by emphasizing the mission or job to be done.
4. *Sensitivity* (social awareness): leadership behaviors that indicate the aircraft commander's sensitivity to and awareness of social relationships and the pressures existing both inside and outside the crew.[16]

Consideration and initiating structure are independent dimensions of leadership.

Consideration and initiating structure may have different effects on satisfaction and performance.

After evaluating the results, the researchers eventually dropped the third and fourth factors. The end result was a two-dimensional leadership model composed of the consideration factor and the initiating structure factor. These dimensions were found to be independent, thereby resulting in four leadership styles as illustrated in Figure 9–2. Many research studies have been conducted, both at Ohio State and elsewhere, to determine the effects of these four styles on subordinate performance and satisfaction. The high consideration-high initiating structure style has been found to result in high satisfaction and performance more frequently than any of the other styles.[17] However, some studies have revealed dysfunctional consequences accompanying these positive results. In one study, for example, consideration was negatively related to the performance ratings of the leader by his or her superiors.[18] In another, initiating structure was associated with decreased subordinate satisfaction and increased grievance rates.[19] Thus high consideration and high structure do *not* always bring about positive outcomes.

Situational factors must be considered in order to understand initiation of structure and consideration.

It seems appropriate to conclude that the effects of both consideration and initiating structure are situationally determined.[20] This is undoubtedly why researchers have been unable to demonstrate clearly how these behaviors are related to subordinate performance and satisfaction in a host of different leadership settings. Nevertheless, the goal of the Ohio State researchers was attained because they were able to identify and describe the two primary behaviors displayed by leaders: consideration and initiating structure. Current researchers have altered their position, placing greater emphasis on situational factors.[21] As a result, the value of the Ohio State model has improved.

 STOP

Review your answers to Question 2 and make any changes you would like before continuing.

2. How would you describe Angela in terms of the Ohio State leadership grid?

In terms of the Ohio State leadership grid, Angela started off with a style characterized by high structure and high consideration. When things got bad, she maintained the high structure but became less considerate, at least in regard to certain individuals.

The Michigan Studies

At the same time the Ohio State studies were under way, leadership research was in progress at the University of Michigan. Early studies were conducted among clerical workers in a large insurance firm.[22] While the results were not statistically significant, effective supervisors seemed to delegate more authority, use general (as opposed to close) supervision, and express concern for the personal lives and well-being of their people more often than their less effective counterparts. Similar results were obtained in other studies, resulting in the initial conclusion that employee-centered leadership was superior to production-centered leadership.

FIGURE 9–2
Ohio State Leadership Grid

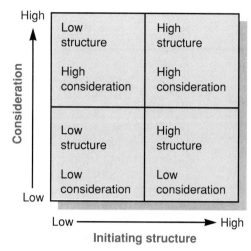

FIGURE 9–3
A Production-Centered/Employee-Centered Leadership Continuum

The Michigan researchers uncovered styles similar to those found by the Ohio State people.

These findings seem to refute the Ohio State research because they place leadership on a continuum such as that shown in Figure 9–3 and conclude that the further to the right that leaders go, the better off they are. While there are some theorists who seem to accept this general proposition,[23] further research has indicated that employee and work orientations are two separate dimensions and that a leader can be either high or low on one or both.[24] Thus the two styles uncovered by the Michigan researchers were similar to those of the Ohio State people. The production-centered leadership factor and the initiating-leadership structure factor both measured work orientation, while the employee-centered factor and the consideration factor both measured people orientation.

As with the Ohio State studies, however, the Michigan studies found no universally superior leadership style. The best approach still remained a function of the situation. So once again we return to contingency-determined leadership. Many modern behavioral scientists are advocates of this approach.

CONTINGENCY-DETERMINED LEADERSHIP THEORY

For more than thirty years researchers have been conducting studies on various aspects of contingency theory. From their work, leadership styles have been shown to be effective when associated with a variety of factors, including the kind of job the leader holds,[25] the size of the group,[26] the degree to which group-member cooperation is required,[27] the quality of leader-member relations,[28] and subordinate maturity.[29]

Contingency theory attempts to put realism into the study of leadership.

When viewed as a composite, these studies offer dramatic evidence that the contingency approach is a very realistic way of examining leadership. However, it must be noted that contingency-determined leadership theory has to identify both the specific critical variables in the situation under analysis and the relationship among these variables, leadership traits, and behaviors. In this section, we are going to examine four theories that do this.

Fiedler's Contingency Theory of Leadership Effectiveness

The best known contingency-determined leadership theory is that of Fred Fiedler. His **contingency theory of leadership effectiveness** is a result of years of research effort.[30]

The least preferred co-worker scale (LPC) measures a leader's degree of task and people orientation.

The Theory. Beginning in 1951, Fiedler started conducting research on the relationship between organizational performance and leader attitudes. He was particularly interested in determining whether leaders who were less discriminating in evaluating their associates were more (or less) likely to have effective, high-producing groups than their counterparts who were highly demanding or discriminating in evaluating their people. To measure these attitudes Fiedler and his associates developed the **least preferred co-worker scale (LPC),** which measures how favorably a leader evaluates the least preferred co-worker. The LPC questionnaire contains from sixteen to twenty items, depending upon the version used (see Figure 9–4). The respondent is asked to think of the individual with

FIGURE 9–4
Least Preferred Co-Worker Scale

Pleasant	8 :	7 :	6 :	5 :	4 :	3 :	2 :	1	Unpleasant
Unfriendly	1 :	2 :	3 :	4 :	5 :	6 :	7 :	8	Friendly
Accepting	8 :	7 :	6 :	5 :	4 :	3 :	2 :	1	Rejecting
Frustrating	1 :	2 :	3 :	4 :	5 :	6 :	7 :	8	Helpful
Enthusiastic	8 :	7 :	6 :	5 :	4 :	3 :	2 :	1	Unenthusiastic
Tense	1 :	2 :	3 :	4 :	5 :	6 :	7 :	8	Relaxed
Close	8 :	7 :	6 :	5 :	4 :	3 :	2 :	1	Distant
Cold	1 :	2 :	3 :	4 :	5 :	6 :	7 :	8	Warm
Cooperative	8 :	7 :	6 :	5 :	4 :	3 :	2 :	1	Uncooperative
Hostile	1 :	2 :	3 :	4 :	5 :	6 :	7 :	8	Supportive
Interesting	8 :	7 :	6 :	5 :	4 :	3 :	2 :	1	Boring
Quarrelsome	1 :	2 :	3 :	4 :	5 :	6 :	7 :	8	Harmonious
Self-Assured	8 :	7 :	6 :	5 :	4 :	3 :	2 :	1	Hesitant
Inefficient	1 :	2 :	3 :	4 :	5 :	6 :	7 :	8	Efficient
Cheerful	8 :	7 :	6 :	5 :	4 :	3 :	2 :	1	Gloomy
Guarded	1 :	2 :	3 :	4 :	5 :	6 :	7 :	8	Open

whom he or she had the greatest difficulty in getting a job done and describe this person on the LPC scale.

Originally the researchers hypothesized that high LPC scores would be associated with effective group performance. However, the research yielded both mixed and conflicting findings. Fiedler and associates thus hypothesized that the "right" type of leadership behavior depends upon whether the group situation is favorable or unfavorable to the leader. The three dimensions that determine situational favorableness are these:

There are three situational dimensions of leadership.

1. The **leader-member relations** dimension refers to the quality of the relationship between the leader and the group. It is measured by such things as how well the individual is liked and trusted and how warm and friendly a relationship he or she has with the members.

2. The **task-structure** dimension refers to the degree to which the task is programmed or spelled out via established procedures. It is measured by such things as how clearly stated the goals are, the number of solutions that can be used in reaching each of these goals, and the degree to which the correctness of the solution or decision can be demonstrated by appeal to authority, logical procedures, or feedback.

3. The position-power dimension refers to the degree to which the position itself enables the leader to get the members to comply with and accept his or her direction and leadership. Some of the measures of position power include the authority to recommend punishments and rewards, affect promotion or demotion, and tell or direct members concerning what to say or do.[31]

Taking these three dimensions, Fiedler then constructed eight group-task situations. Each represented a different combination of the dimensions (see Table 9–1). Finally, Fiedler related the favorableness of each situation to LPC scores (Figure 9–5).

TABLE 9–1
Classification of Situation Favorableness

Situation	Leader-Member Relations	Task Structure	Leader Position Power	Situational Favorableness
1	Good	High	Strong	Favorable
2	Good	High	Weak	Favorable
3	Good	Weak	Strong	Favorable
4	Good	Weak	Weak	Moderately favorable
5	Moderately poor	High	Strong	Moderately favorable
6	Moderately poor	High	Weak	Moderately unfavorable
7	Moderately poor	Weak	Strong	Moderately unfavorable
8	Moderately poor	Weak	Weak	Unfavorable

Source: Adapted from Fred E. Fielder, *A Theory of Leadership Effectiveness* (New York: McGraw-Hill Book Co., 1967), p. 34.

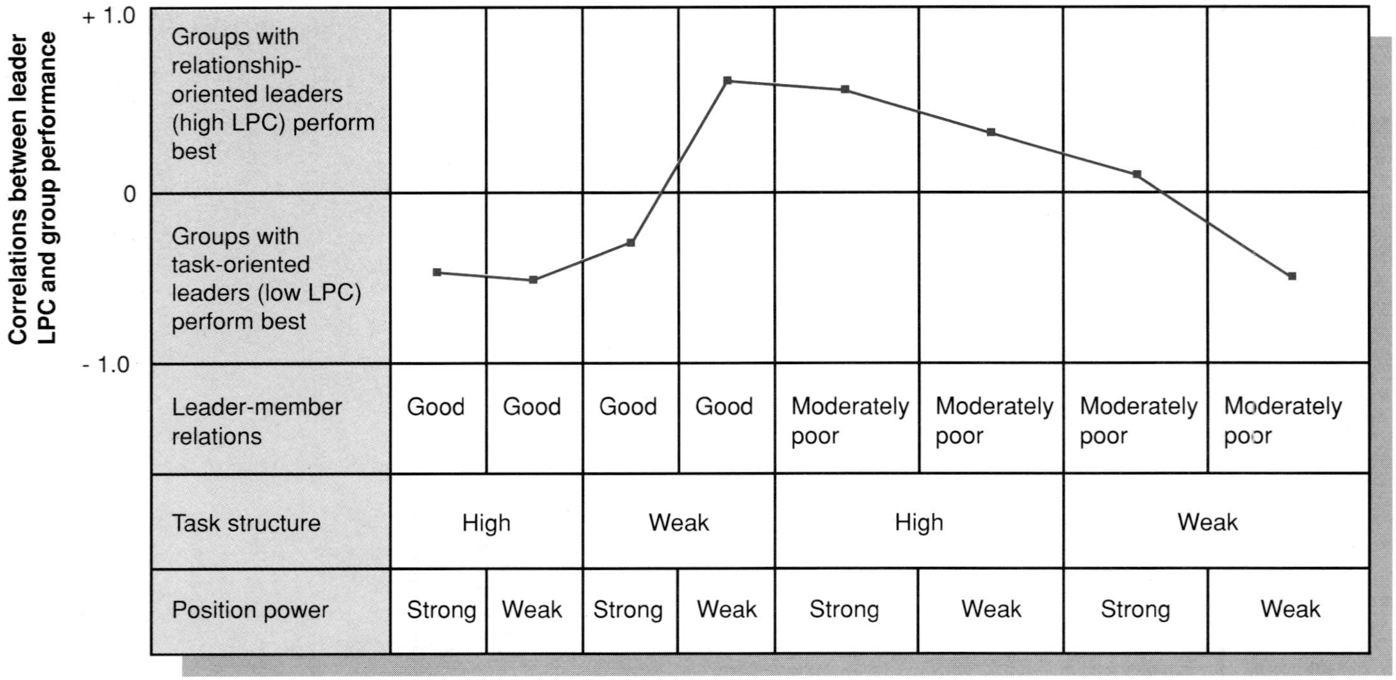

Correlations between leader LPC and group performance

+1.0 — 0 — −1.0

Groups with relationship-oriented leaders (high LPC) perform best

Groups with task-oriented leaders (low LPC) perform best

Leader-member relations	Good	Good	Good	Good	Moderately poor	Moderately poor	Moderately poor	Moderately poor
Task structure	High		Low		High		Low	
Position power	Strong	Weak	Strong	Weak	Strong	Weak	Strong	Weak

Note: The point for octant VI was determined by extrapolation, as little data are available. The other points are based on actual data.

FIGURE 9–5
Fiedler's Contingency Leadership Research Results (Source: Adapted from Fred Fiedler, *A Theory of Leadership Effectiveness* (New York: McGraw-Hill Book Co., 1967), p. 146.)

Research Findings. Fiedler contends that the appropriate leadership style for maximizing group performance is based on the favorableness of the group-task situation. When the situation is either very favorable or unfavorable (see Table 9–1), a task-oriented leader is appropriate. When the dimensions are mixed and the situation is moderately favorable, a relationship-oriented leader is more effective.

> Group performance, then, is related to both the leadership style and the degree to which the situation provides the leader with the opportunity to exert influence. Task-oriented . . . leaders perform best in situations which are highly favorable for them or in those which are relatively unfavorable. Considerate, relationship-oriented leaders tend to perform best in situations in which they have only moderate influence, either because the task is relatively unstructured or because they are not too well accepted although their position power is high and the task is structured.[32]

Fiedler believes that there should be a match between the leader and the situation, and this will result in leadership effectiveness. Based on this, he has developed a leader match training program that operationalizes his ideas.[33]

Criticism and Evaluation of the Theory. While Fiedler's theory provides some interesting insights into the area of leadership, it has also been the object of criticism. For example, Graen and colleagues have objected to Fiedler's use of the same completed studies to both refashion and support his findings. Some claim that rather than testing his theory with new research, Fiedler shapes his theory to fit known results.[34] There is also concern over what LPC actually measures.

Other criticisms appear even more damaging. One is that Fiedler's conceptualization of the components of situational favorableness is incomplete. For example, Kerr and colleagues have identified a number of situational modifiers affecting the relationship among leader behavior, subordinate performance, and satisfaction that were not considered by Fiedler. These include subordinate expectations of leader behavior, congruence of leadership style among organizational levels, and the ability of the leader to influence his or her superior.[35] A second criticism of the contingency model is that it does not explain how situational favorableness affects the relationship between leader behavior and subordinate performance.[36]

Thus, the contingency theory of leadership contains shortcomings and flaws. On the negative side, Fiedler may not really have a theory in the true sense of the word. A theory suggests explanations for why certain phenomena occur and proposes the causes of these phenomena. In Fiedler's case, then, we can ask, why should the same leadership style work equally well in favorable and unfavorable situations (see Figure 9–5)? Fiedler has not sufficiently answered questions such as this. As a result, he may have less of a theory and more of an empirical generalization. For the moment, we will have to wait for further research before deciding which it is.[37] On the positive side, however, contingency theory is seen by many as providing the best available description of the leadership process. Additionally, Fiedler and his co-workers have begun dealing with some of the above-mentioned problems.

Some people see this theory as providing the best available description of the leadership process.

STOP   Review your answers to Question 3 and make any changes you would like before continuing.

3. What type of leadership style would Fred Fiedler recommend Angela use when things got bad? Explain.

Fred Fiedler would recommend that she start becoming much more task-oriented. This is exactly what she did do; her actions were right in line with his theory.

Path-Goal Theory

A second contingency theory is the **path-goal theory of leadership** originally proposed by House[38] and later refined and extended in collaboration with Dessler.[39] The model is based on Vroom's expectancy theory of motivation, incorporating such key concepts as expectancy, valence, and instrumentality, although these specific terms are not used. The leader's job is seen as being one of: (a) clarifying the tasks to be performed by the subordinates; (b) clearing away any roadblocks that prevent goal attainment; and (c) increasing the opportunity for the subordinates to obtain personal satisfaction. In accomplishing these three activities, the "best" style of leader behavior is seen as a function of the individuals and the task.

Subordinates see the behavior of leaders as acceptable if it is an immediate source of satisfaction.

The Individuals.   Path-goal theory holds that subordinates will view the behavior of leaders as acceptable to the extent that they see such behavior either as an immediate source of satisfaction or as needed for future satisfaction. For example, if the leader sits down to help a subordinate fill out the monthly cost control report, this is an immediate source of satisfaction. If the leader provides information that will be useful in later reports, this is a source of future satisfaction. In addition, some subordinates have a high need for affiliation or esteem. Supportive leaders help fill this need. Other subordinates have high needs for autonomy or self-actualization. Leaders who are less directive are often most successful in helping these individuals.

Subordinates want clarification of path-goal relationships.

The Task.   To the extent that leaders help clarify path-goal relationships, their behavior is seen as acceptable. When the task is highly unstructured, a directive leader is more likely to have satisfied employees. Unsure of how to handle the situation, subordinates welcome guidance and direction. However, when tasks and goals are readily evident and the work is basically routine, any attempt to further explain the job is seen as unnecessarily close control.

Effective leadership behavior, therefore, is based not only on the willingness of the leader to help out his or her followers, but also on the needs of the subordinates for such assistance. If the leader wants to have highly satisfied subordinates, he or she usually needs to employ high direction on unstructured tasks and low direction on structured ones.[40]

Evaluation of the Theory. Not a great deal of research has been conducted on the path-goal theory. However, what has been done is encouraging. For example, some researchers report that workers performing highly structured tasks have high job satisfaction when their immediate supervisor uses a supportive style.[41] Conversely, individuals performing in unstructured task environments often work best under a directive leadership style, although this style does not always result in high job satisfaction. It has also been found that when subordinates have more ambiguity in their jobs, more considerate supervision is associated with high job satisfaction.[42]

However, more research needs to be done to overcome current problems. In particular, some individuals find the entire theory to be sketchy in nature, requiring further clarification and expansion. A second complaint is that the path-goal theory, like Fiedler's contingency model, was constructed post hoc, so that some of the evidence supporting the theory was also used to build it. Thus, while path-goal theory does offer promise as a contingency model of leadership, more research will be needed before its true value can be fully determined.[43]

Leader Participation Theory

Another contingency theory, first proposed by Victor Vroom and Philip Yetton and recently expanded by Vroom and Arthur Jago, relates leadership and decision making.[44] This **leader participation theory** prescribes a leadership style appropriate to a given situation.

The theory is based on two assumptions: (a) subordinates should participate in decision making; and (b) no one decision-making process is ideal for all situations, but each must be judged on its own merits.

There are actually four decision trees, two for group-level decisions and two for individual-level decisions. One of each is used when time is important; the others are used when time is not important. The model for a time-driven decision is illustrated in Figure 9–6. In using the model, the manager starts by asking the first question at the top of the figure: How important is the technical quality of the decision? Based on the answer, the individual continues moving from branch to branch through the tree. The decision styles at the end of the branches represent the following actions:

AI: The manager should make the decision alone.

AII: The manager should ask for information from subordinates but make the decision alone. Subordinates may or may not be informed about the situation.

CI: The manager should share the situation with individual subordinates and ask for information and evaluation. Subordinates should not meet as a group, and the manager should make the decision.

CII: The manager and the subordinates should meet as a group to discuss the situation, but the manager should make the decision.

GII: The manager and subordinates should meet as a group to discuss the situation, and the group should make the decision.

QR	**Quality requirement:**	How important is the technical quality of this decision?
CR	**Commitment requirement:**	How important is subordinate commitment to the decision?
LI	**Leader's information:**	Is there sufficient information for making a high-quality decision?
ST	**Problem structure:**	Is the problem well structured?
CP	**Commitment probability:**	If you were to make the decision by yourself, is it reasonably certain that your subordinate(s) would be committed to the decision?
GC	**Goal congruence:**	Do subordinates share the organizational goals to be attained in solving this problem?
CO	**Subordinate conflict:**	Is conflict among subordinates over preferred solutions likely?
SI	**Subordinate information:**	Do subordinates have sufficient information to make a high-quality decision?

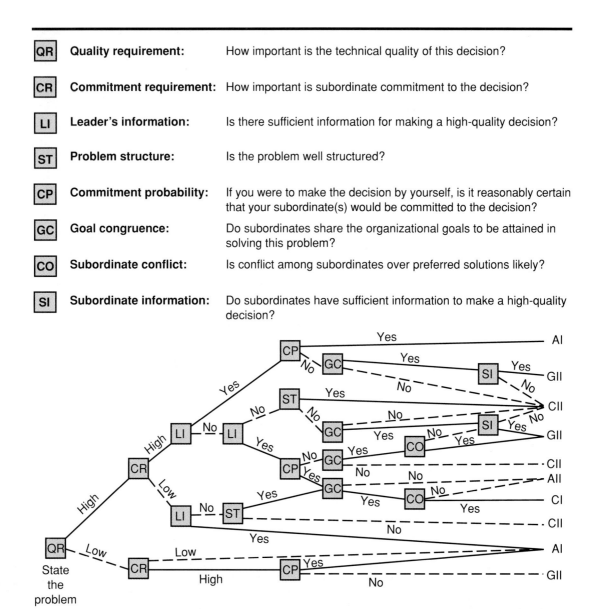

FIGURE 9–6
One Version of the Vroom-Yetton-Jago Model

230

The latest model is much more complex than its predecessor. However, a special computer software package has been developed so the increase in the number of options and situations can be easily accommodated.

The current Vroom-Yetton-Jago model has not been scientifically tested. However, the original model was generally supported by research.[45] For example, leaders who made decisions that were consistent with the model were more effective than those who did not.

Leader-Member Exchange Theory

Leadership is explained in terms of superior-subordinate interaction.

Leader-member exchange (LMX) **theory,** also known as vertical-dyad theory, explains leadership in terms of the interaction between superior and subordinate.[46] LMX theory holds that there is a relationship between the leader and each subordinate, which can be viewed as a vertical dyad. This dyad, or two-way relationship, is based on whether the leader views the follower as a member of the in-group or the out-group (see Figure 9–7). LMX theory predicts that if the leader sees the subordinate as part of the in-group, the latter will receive higher performance ratings and have greater satisfaction with the superior and vice versa. Research shows that in-group subordinates tend to have personal characteristics, such as age, sex, or personality, that are compatible with the leader and/or a higher level of competence.[47]

LMX research continues as investigators attempt to identify and refine an understanding of how and why leaders choose in-group members. However, the theory is useful in providing insights into the leadership process.[48] It also serves as a point of departure for researchers studying the linkage between climate and leadership and their effect on subordinate perception and performance.[49]

 STOP

Review your answers to Question 4 and make any changes you would like before continuing.

4. In what way does leader-member exchange theory help explain Angela's leadership style?

Leadership exchange theory states that leaders will tend to divide their subordinates into an in-group and an out-group, and the former will have higher performance evaluations and greater satisfaction with the leader than will the latter.

ADDITIONAL PERSPECTIVES

During the 1990s, contingency leadership will continue to be a focal point for both research and analysis. For example, some researchers have been examining the linkage of attribution theory and leadership. As noted in Chapter 3, attribution theory suggests that people observe the behavior of others and then attribute causes to it. For example, if a leader attributes poor employee performance to a lack of effort, the individual might

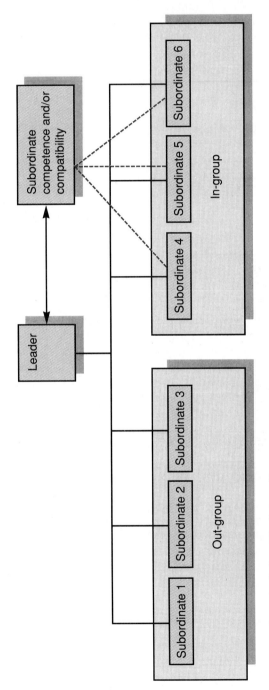

FIGURE 9-7
Leader-Member Exchange Theory

——— formal relationships/interactions

------- interactions based on trust, high
interaction, perceived competence, etc.

Leader

Subordinate competence and/or compatibility

In-group

Subordinate 4

Subordinate 5

Subordinate 6

Out-group

Subordinate 1

Subordinate 2

Subordinate 3

reprimand the worker. However, if performance is attributed to a lack of proper training, the leader might schedule the employee for a training course.[50] Other areas of interest will be charismatic leadership, inquiry regarding whether leadership is important to overall organizational performance, and attempts to synthesize the nature of leadership.

Charismatic Leadership

Charismatic leaders inspire devotion and extraordinary effort.

Charismatic leaders are individuals who lead by virtue of their ability to inspire devotion and extraordinary effort from their followers. A number of researchers have examined the nature of charismatic leadership. Weber perceived it as a "devotion to the specific and exceptional sanctity, heroism, or exemplary character of an individual person, and of the normative patterns of order revealed or ordained by him."[51] Political scientists and sociologists have spent decades examining the phenomenon. Based on in-depth case studies, Willner has concluded that charismatic leadership is neither personality based nor contextually determined. Rather it is relational and perceptional. He notes, "It is not what the leader is but what people see the leader as that counts in generating the charismatic relationship."[52]

More recently, Conger and Kanungo[53] have sought to create a behavioral framework for studying how charismatic leaders act. They found ten behavioral differences that they believe account for the differences between charismatic and noncharismatic leaders (see Table 9–2). Are these comparisons accurate? Only additional research will tell, but one thing is clear. During the upcoming decade more and more leadership researchers are going to seek answers to the question: How does a charismatic leader act? The answer should help provide a fuller understanding of the leadership process.

STOP

Review your answers to Question 5 and make any changes you would like before continuing.

5. Is Angela a charismatic leader? Why or why not?

She is a charismatic leader in that she has some of the characteristics found in these types of leaders. However, she is not totally charismatic, as can be seen by comparing her behavior to the behavior characteristics presented in Table 9–2.

Are Leaders Necessary?

Some researchers have found that leadership is not always a significant variable.

Can people perform well without leaders? Do leaders really contribute much to the overall efficiency or effectiveness of an organization? When Lieberson and O'Connor obtained data on sales, profits, profit margins, and periods of leader incumbency for 167 publicly owned U.S. corporations over a twenty-year period, they found that leadership did not seem to make much difference in terms of organizational performance.[54] Salancik and Pfeffer examined the effect of mayoral leadership on city budgets and concluded

TABLE 9-2
Behavioral Components of Charismatic and Noncharismatic Leaders

	Noncharismatic Leader	Charismatic Leader
Relation to Status Quo	Essentially agrees with status quo and strives to maintain it	Essentially opposed to status quo and strives to change it
Future Goal	Goal not too discrepant from status quo	Idealized vision which is highly discrepant from status quo
Likableness	Shared perspective makes him/her likable	Shared perspective and idealized vision makes him/her a likable and honorable hero worthy of identification and imitation
Trustworthiness	Disinterested advocacy in persuasion attempts	Disinterested advocacy by incurring great personal risk and cost
Expertise	Expert in using available means to achieve goals within the framework of the existing order	Expert in using unconventional means to transcend the existing order
Behavior	Conventional, conforming to existing norms	Unconventional or counternormative
Environmental Sensitivity	Low need for environmental sensitivity to maintain status quo	High need for environmental sensitivity for changing the status quo
Articulation	Weak articulation of goals and motivation to lead	Strong articulation of future vision and motivation to lead
Power Base	Position power and personal power (based on reward, expertise, and liking for a friend who is a similar other)	Personal power (based on expertise, respect, and admiration for a unique hero)
Leader-Follower	Egalitarian, consensus seeking, or directive Nudges or orders people to share his/her views	Elitist, entrepreneur, and exemplary Transforms people to share the radical changes advocated

Source: Jay A. Conger and Rabindra N. Kanungo, "Toward a Behavioral Theory of Charismatic Leadership in Organizational Settings," *Academy of Management Review*, October 1987, p. 641.

that these leaders accounted for only about 10 percent of the effect on organizational performance.[55] Similarly, at a lower organizational level some researchers have noted that personnel have been trained to take over many of the functions commonly performed by supervisors.[56] The result was an increase in the supervisor's span of control coupled with higher employee job satisfaction. These studies all seem to point to the fact that leadership does not make much of a difference.[57]

On the other hand, there are many researchers who point to studies which have found that leadership is an important variable. For example, Weiner replicated the Lieberson and O'Connor study and found that the order in which the data were analyzed helped account for the results.[58] So the initial study may have understated the importance of leadership. Thomas conducted a similar study among twelve British firms and also concluded that leadership was far more important than Lieberson and O'Connor had found.[59] These mixed findings help indicate why the relevance of leadership will continue to be a focal point for research during the 1990s.

Integration of Leadership Concepts

A third area of interest among leadership researchers is the integration of leadership ideas into an overall composite. An example is provided in Figure 9–8, which incorporates the three major areas of leadership: the leader, the subordinates, and the work environment.

The leader needs to be competent in his or her work, be able to reward subordinates when they do things well, and have influence with upper management. Yet competence alone is insufficient. The subordinates want to be compensated for their efforts, and if the leader can demonstrate a direct relationship between performance and monetary rewards, subordinate task-related effort often increases. In addition, the leader needs to have influence with his or her own superior and represent and negotiate the best possible rewards for subordinates.

The subordinates have values they bring with them to the job. Some want to satisfy upper-level needs; others are primarily interested in lower-level need satisfaction. Some want a leader who is supportive; others prefer a task-centered boss. The subordinates also have perceptions of the leader and the work. If they see tasks as relatively simple and the boss as highly directive, most will be dissatisfied with this leadership style. Conversely, if they see the work as complex, most will welcome a task-oriented leader and will not be satisfied with an individual with a high people orientation but a low task concern. Finally, there is the homogeneity of the work group. If the entire group must rely on each other and work as a cohesive unit, as in the case of an assembly line, a surgical team, or even a football team, a highly considerate, people-oriented leader is often best. If everyone is going his or her own way and coordination and direction are required, a task-oriented leader is often best.

In the work environment the leader must be concerned with the nature of the work. Routine structured jobs usually require supportive or considerate leadership if one hopes to achieve high job satisfaction and performance. Complex jobs require task-oriented leaders. The leader must also take into account the size of the work group. In small groups, leaders tend to be more like technical specialists, emphasizing interpersonal functions. In large groups in which individuals are relatively autonomous,

Leaders need to be able to reward subordinates.

Subordinates have needs that a leader should satisfy.

A leader must be able to diagnose the work environment in order to select an effective style of leading.

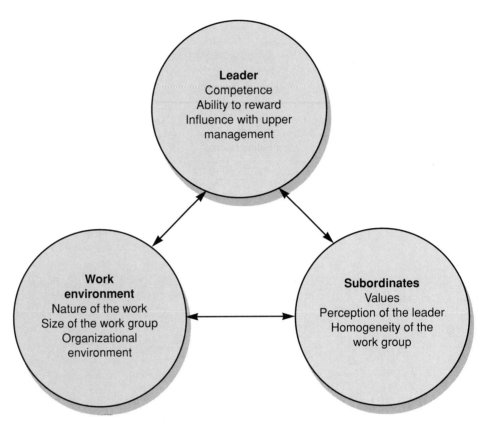

FIGURE 9–8
An Integrative Model of Leadership

effective leadership behavior tends to emphasize task accomplishment and conflict resolution between the individuals in the group. Finally, there is the organizational climate.
If the management or the leader insists on the enforcement of many rules and regulations, an autocratic style may be required. If people are free to make their own
decisions—that is, if autonomy and decentralization are encouraged—a democratic
style will work best.

While additional research on the integration of leadership concepts continues,[60]
Figure 9–8 provides a state-of-the-art picture. The specific importance of each variable
under changing conditions, however, will be a continued focal point for research during
this decade.

SUMMARY

1. Leadership involves influencing people to direct
their efforts toward the achievement of some particular
goal(s). This influence comes from two basic sources: position power and the willingness of subordinates to comply.

2. In an effort to further study this process, three
basic approaches have been taken. The first approach is
leadership-trait theory, in which an attempt is made to identify those traits or characteristics that distinguish successful

from unsuccessful leaders. For the most part, however, no universal list of traits has been forthcoming.

3. Leadership-behavior theory seeks to explain leadership in terms of what leaders do. One of the most popular behavioral approaches is the leadership continuum, in which various leadership styles ranging from boss-centered to subordinate-centered are examined. The basic problem with the continuum approach is that it seems to imply a trade-off situation and views leader behavior as one-dimensional.

4. The Ohio State and Michigan studies have demonstrated that leadership is actually two-dimensional, and leaders can be either high or low in regard to concern for work and concern for people. Which combination of these two is best? This will depend on the situation, which undoubtedly explains why so much current interest has switched to contingency-determined leadership theory.

5. Contingency theory identifies both the specific critical variables in the situations under analysis and the relationship among these variables, leadership traits, and behaviors. Two theories that have sought to do this are Fiedler's contingency theory of leadership effectiveness and House's path-goal theory of leadership. Fiedler's theory holds that the right type of leadership style is dependent upon three situational dimensions: (a) leader-member relations; (b) task structure; and (c) position power. From these three dimensions, eight group-task situations were constructed. Depending upon the overall favorableness of each situation, Fiedler recommends a particular leadership style. In situations that are either very favorable or unfavorable, a task-orientation is advised. In those that are moderately favorable, a relationship-oriented style is suggested. While criticized as failing to consider all critical components of situational favorableness and for continually shaping the theory to fit known results rather than testing it with new research, the contingency model still represents the best available description of the leadership process. House's path-goal theory postulates that the leader's job is one of clarifying subordinate tasks, clearing away roadblocks preventing goal attainment, and increasing the opportunity for subordinates to obtain personal satisfaction. The theory offers promise as a contingency model of leadership.

6. The leader participation theory proposed by Vroom, Yetton, and Jago prescribes a leadership style appropriate in a variety of decision-making situations. Leader-member exchange theory explains leadership in terms of the interaction between superior and subordinate. Both of these theories are useful in shedding light on the leadership process.

7. There currently are additional areas of attention among leadership researchers. These include a closer analysis of charismatic leadership, the importance of leadership to organizational performance, and integrative models for describing the leadership process.

KEY TERMS

leadership	consideration factor	task structure dimension
position power	initiating-structure factor	path-goal theory of leadership
leadership-trait theory	contingency theory of leadership	leader participation theory
leadership-behavior theory	effectiveness	leader-member exchange theory
authoritarian leaders	least preferred co-worker scale	charismatic leaders
democratic leaders	(LPC)	
Leader Behavior Description	leader-member relations	
Questionnaire (LBDQ)	dimension	

REVIEW AND STUDY QUESTIONS

1. What is meant by the term *leadership*?

2. Are there traits that appear to be related to successful organizational leadership? Explain.

3. Why are most behavioral scientists not very interested in trait theory?

4. How does a continuum approach help explain leader behavior?

5. In what way did the Ohio State studies help us better understand leader behavior?

6. How did the Michigan studies complement the Ohio State studies?

7. What are the three main situational dimensions in Fiedler's leadership theory? Explain each.

8. When does Fiedler believe a task-oriented leader is superior to a relationship-oriented leader? When is a relationship-oriented leader superior to a task-oriented leader? Explain.

9. What are the major criticisms of Fiedler's theory? Explain them.

10. In your own words, what is the path-goal theory of leadership?

11. According to the path-goal theory, what relationship exists between leader directiveness, job satisfaction, and the degree of job structure?

12. In what way is the Vroom-Yetton-Jago leader participation model of value in understanding contingency leadership? Explain.

13. What is leadership exchange theory all about?

14. What is meant by the statement, "An integrative model of leadership has three major parts: (a) the leader; (b) the followers; and (c) the situation"?

CASES

Butt Out

When Paula Cartwright began working for Randing Motors, she found herself greatly confused. As a purchasing manager she was expected to read invoices, give direct approval on purchases under $100, evaluate and discuss with her boss all purchase requests ranging between $100 and $500, and send those in excess of $500 directly to her superior with her views on whether or not to okay them. The paperwork was astounding!

However, Paula found her boss, Al Davidson, to be a very helpful individual. During the first ninety days Al helped her out of numerous trouble spots. His seventeen years of experience had provided him with a wealth of information about purchasing, and he used it to show Paula all types of shortcuts and rules of thumb that could be used in expediting purchase requests.

Under his direction, Paula began to develop a series of systematic procedures. First, she would clear away all the minor purchase orders and initial all those between $100 and $500 that had proper support. Then around 2 P.M. every day she and Al would spend an hour going over all the requests over $100. During this time Paula would take notes on why Al felt some requests should be turned down and the types of supporting data that needed to be obtained on others.

As Paula learned more about the job and the procedures involved, she found that it was not as difficult and complex as it first appeared. She began to develop her own methods for getting the work done on the simpler orders and found that they worked well. Paula found that she felt good about being able to work out her own methods for doing the job and actually enjoyed doing the work.

At the end of her fourth month Paula found that she had only one or two purchase requests that needed to be discussed. This is when she noticed a problem developing. Once she and Al were finished with the requests she brought to his office, he would ask her what else she had done that day. Paula would show Al the other requests she had okayed or sent back for further information. Usually Al would agree with her decisions, although he would occasionally make minor suggestions. Paula found this frustrating in that she felt Al was second-guessing her. "I like to get help when I need it," she told a fellow worker, "but if I know what I'm doing, I'd like to be left alone to do it my way. I wish Al would butt out."

While Paula found herself getting upset with Al, she had second thoughts about saying anything to him. There were two reasons for her ambivalence. First, without him she would never have learned the job as fast as she did. Second, she did not want to hurt his feelings.

1. In terms of a behavioral leadership model, is Al a work-centered or an employee-centered leader? Explain.

2. Using Figure 9–6 in your book, what predictions can you make about Al's effectiveness and Paula's job satisfaction over the next six months?

3. What would you recommend Paula do about the situation? Explain.

A No-Nonsense Person

Things at General Hospital have not been going well. At the quarterly meeting of the board of trustees last week, it was revealed that expenditures are running 14 percent ahead of budget and some of the nursing staff have threatened to quit if they are not given their scheduled raise. This raise of 7 percent had been promised to them eight months ago, effective two months from now, but the grapevine in the hospital says that due to the large deficit, there will be no raises.

To make matters worse, a local newspaper has been running a story about conditions at General Hospital. While the newspaper is apparently exploiting a few mistakes made at the hospital, the board is afraid that the overall reputation of the institution will suffer. In particular, the paper has reported that people in the emergency room sometimes wait up to two hours before receiving treatment. (The hospital has tried to point out that the incident to which the paper is referring occurred one night when there were seven car accidents in the area, and all of the injured were brought to General. The doctors in the emergency room had to dispense treatment on the basis of need. None of the people who waited two hours was badly hurt, and all declined to bring suit against the hospital despite pressure from some local attorneys.) Another complaint reported in the paper is that an elderly lady fell from her bed and lay on the floor for over an hour. (The hospital has verified the accuracy of the report but notes that this woman had a protective railing on her bed and was asked to call for nurse assistance before attempting to leave her bed. The lady attempted to climb over the railing and slipped. She has admitted blame for her fall and has refused to sue the hospital.)

At its meeting the board of trustees discussed ways to find a solution to the budget and publicity problems. One trustee said that the solution to the problems required a change of leadership, namely, replacing the hospital administrator. The majority of board members are particularly keen on bringing in a "no-nonsense" individual who will keep the budget in line, fire any people who are not doing their jobs properly, and maintain a good public relations image with the community, thereby off-setting these newspaper stories. In particular, the majority believes that by changing administrators now, they can create the image of cleaning house. "We think the current administrator has done a good job, but the present situation will only get worse if we don't seek new leadership," one of them said. While a majority of the trustees seemed to agree, some wonder if the problems are not due to conditions over which the administrator has little influence. A new administrator would find the same problems and the lack of influence to do anything about them. The three minority members are even more wary about bringing in a "no-nonsense" administrator. They feel this move may create more problems than it solves.

1. What are the benefits of bringing in a no-nonsense manager? What are the drawbacks?
2. Drawing on Fiedler's contingency theory of leader effectiveness, what type of leader would be most effective? Explain.
3. Drawing together the ideas contained in Figure 9–7 of this chapter, describe the type of leader the hospital needs.

SELF-FEEDBACK EXERCISE

What Type of Leader Are You?

The following statements are designed to provide insights regarding how you see yourself. In the blank space next to each statement, write the number that best describes how frequently you engage or would engage in the behavior described if you were in a leadership position. The numbers represent the following:

5 = Always

4 = Very often

3 = Fairly often

2 = Occasionally

1 = Never

Example:

__4__   I ask for suggestions from the group. (The respondent's "4" next to the statement indicates that the respondent feels he or she very often asks for suggestions from the group.)

_____ 1. I delegate decision-making authority to others.

_____ 2. I tell my subordinates what is expected of them.

_____ 3. The decisions I make reflect prior consultations with my people.

_____ 4. I do personal favors for my personnel.

_____ 5. I make no final decisions until subordinates are in general agreement with them.

_____ 6. I alone make the final decisions, but I get my subordinates' opinions before doing so.

_____ 7. I often change my behavior to fit the occasion.

_____ 8. My subordinates and I jointly analyze problems in reaching decisions.

_____ 9. I set deadlines by which my subordinates must finish their work.

_____ 10. I sell my decisions to others through effective persuasion.

_____ 11. I get subordinates' ideas regarding tentative decisions before making them final.

_____ 12. I show confidence and trust in my personnel.

_____ 13. I specify definite standards of performance that are expected of my personnel.

_____ 14. I let subordinates have as much responsibility for final decisions as I do.

_____ 15. I use rewards and promises of rewards to influence my people.

_____ 16. I lead with a firm hand.

_____ 17. My people have as much a voice in decision making as I do.

_____ 18. I give suggestions but leave members free to follow their own course of action.

_____ 19. Before I make a decision I look for individual subordinates' opinions.

_____ 20. I like to let subordinates make their own decisions.

Take your answers to the above questions and enter them below in the appropriate space, and then compute the average for each group.

Group 1	Group 2	Group 3	Group 4	Group 5
2. __	4. __	3. __	5. __	1. __
9. __	7. __	6. __	8. __	12. __
13. __	10. __	11. __	14. __	18. __
16. __	15. __	19. __	17. __	20. __
Total __	Total __	Total __	Total __	Total __
Avg. __	Avg. __	Avg. __	Avg. __	Avg. __

On a scale of 1 to 5, this measures how you see yourself in each of these five areas.

Average Score — The five areas, represented by Groups 1 to 5 are:

_____ 1. Directive—The higher the score, the more you see yourself as a task-oriented leader.

_____ 2. Negotiative—The higher the score, the more you see yourself as a leader who gets things done by making deals with subordinates.

_____ 3. Consultative—The higher the score, the more you allow subordinates to have inputs to the decision you eventually make.

_____ 4. Participative—The higher the score, the more you share decision-making authority with your subordinates.

_____ 5. Delegative—The higher the score, the more you let subordinates obtain results in their own way.

NOTES

1. See for example "Leaders of the Most Admired," *Fortune,* January 29, 1990, pp. 42–54.

2. See Bernard M. Bass, *Bass and Stogdill's Handbook of Leadership* (New York: Free Press, 1990) for incisive and detailed discussion; Barbara Kellerman (ed.), *Leadership: Multidisciplinary Perspectives* (Englewood Cliffs, NJ: Prentice-Hall, 1982) for a multifaceted examination; and James R. Meindl, Sanford B. Ehrlich, and Janet M.

Dukerich, "The Romance of Leadership," *Administrative Science Quarterly,* March 1985, pp. 78–102.

3. G. Ronald Gilbert and Albert C. Hyde, "Followership and the Federal Workers," *Public Administrative Review,* November–December 1988, pp. 962–967; and Robert E. Kelley, "In Praise of Followers," *Harvard Business Review,* November–December 1988, pp. 142–148.

4. Louis B. Barnes and Mark P. Kriger, "The Hidden Side of Organizational Leadership," *Sloan Management Review,* Fall 1986, pp. 15–25.

5. See for example Dennis W. Organ, "Social Exchange and Psychological Reactance in a Simulated Superior-Subordinate Relationship," *Organizational Behavior and Human Performance,* August 1974, pp. 132–142; and Walter Kiechel III, "How to Manage Your Boss," *Fortune,* September 17, 1984, pp. 207–210.

6. Virginia J. Vanderslice, "Separating Leadership From Leaders: An Assessment of the Effect of Leader and Follower Roles in Organizations," *Human Relations,* September 1988, pp. 677–696.

7. Charles Byrd, *Social Psychology* (New York: Appleton-Century-Crofts, 1940).

8. Thomas A. Mahoney, Thomas H. Jerdee, and Allan N. Nash, "Predicting Managerial Effectiveness," *Personnel Psychology,* Summer 1960, pp. 147–163.

9. Edwin E. Ghiselli, *Explorations in Management Talent* (Pacific Palisades, CA: Goodyear, 1971).

10. See for example Gregory H. Dobbins and Stephanie J. Platz, "Sex Differences and Leadership: How Real Are They?," *Academy of Management Review,* January 1986, pp. 118–127; Dafne N. Izraeli and Dov Izraeli, "Sex Effects in Evaluating Leaders: A Replication Study," *Journal of Applied Psychology,* August 1985, pp. 540–546; Craig Eric Schneier and Kathryn M. Bartol, "Sex Effects in Emergent Leadership," *Journal of Applied Psychology,* June 1980, pp. 341–345; and Johanne Trempe, Andre-Jean Rigny, and Robert R. Haccoun, "Subordinate Satisfaction with Male and Female Managers: Role of Perceived Supervisory Influence," *Journal of Applied Psychology,* February 1985, pp. 44–47.

11. Bass, *Bass and Stogdill's Handbook,* p. 87.

12. See for instance David A. Kenny and Steven J. Zaccaro, "An Estimate of Variance Due to Traits in Leadership," *Journal of Applied Psychology,* November 1983, pp. 678–688.

13. For research that spans both trait and leadership behavior theory see Janet R. Goktepe and Craig Eric Schneier, "Role of Sex, Gender Roles, and Attraction in Predicting Emergent Leaders," *Journal of Applied Psychology,* February 1989, pp. 165–167.

14. Harold G. McCurdy and Herbert W. Eber, "Democratic versus Authoritarian: A Further Investigation of Group Problem-solving," *Journal of Personality,* December 1953, pp. 258–269. Also see Jan C. Muczyk and Bernard C. Reimann, "The Case for Directive Leadership," *Academy of Management Executive,* November 1987, pp. 301–311.

15. Victor H. Vroom, "Some Personality Determinants of the Effects of Participation," *Journal of Abnormal and Social Psychology,* November 1959, pp. 322–327.

16. A. W. Halpin and B. J. Winer, "A Factorial Study of the Leader Behavior Descriptions," in R. M. Stogdill and A. D. Coons (eds.), *Leader Behavior: Its Descriptions and Measurement* (Columbus, OH: The Ohio State Univ., Bureau of Business Research, 1957), pp. 42–44.

17. Orlando Behling and Chester Schriesheim, *Organizational Behavior: Theory, Research and Application* (Boston: Allyn & Bacon, 1976), p. 299.

18. Edwin A. Fleishman, Edwin F. Harris, and Harold E. Burtt, *Leadership and Supervision in Industry* (Columbus: The Ohio State Univ., Bureau of Educational Research, 1955), p. 7.

19. Edwin A. Fleishman and Edwin F. Harris, "Patterns of Leadership Behavior Related to Employee Grievances and Turnover," *Personnel Psychology,* Spring 1982, pp. 43–56.

20. Steven Kerr, Chester A. Schriesheim, Charles J. Murphy, and Ralph M. Stogdill, "Towards a Contingency Theory of Leadership Based upon the Consideration and Initiating Structure Literature," *Organizational Behavior and Human Performance,* August 1974, pp. 62–82.

21. Bruce M. Fisher, "Consideration and Initiating Structure and Their Relationships with Leader Effectiveness: A Meta-Analysis," *Academy of Management Proceedings,* 1988, pp. 201–205.

22. D. Katz, N. Maccoby, and N. Morse, *Productivity, Supervision and Morale in an Office Situation* (Ann Arbor, MI: Univ. of Michigan, Survey Research Center, 1950).

23. See for example Rensis Likert and Jane Gibson Likert,

New Ways of Managing Conflict (New York: McGraw-Hill Book Co., 1976).

24. D. Katz and R. Kahn, "Human Organization and Worker Motivation," in R. L. Tripp (ed.), *Industrial Productivity* (Madison, WI: Industrial Relations Research Association, 1952).

25. Ralph M. Stogdill, Robert J. Wherry, and William E. Jaynes, "A Factorial Study of Administrative Performance," in Ralph M. Stogdill and Carroll L. Shartle (eds.), *Patterns of Administrative Performance* (Columbus: The Ohio State Univ., Bureau of Business Research, 1956), pp. 39–108.

26. John K. Hemphill, "Relations between the Size of the Group and the Behavior of 'Superior' Leaders," *Journal of Social Psychology,* August 1950, pp. 11–22.

27. Thomas M. Lodahl and Lyman W. Porter, "Psychometric Score Patterns, Social Characteristics, and Productivity of Small Industrial Work Groups," *Journal of Applied Psychology,* April 1961, pp. 73–79.

28. Jon P. Howell, Peter W. Dorfman, and Steven Kerr, "Moderating Variables in Leadership Research," *Academy of Management Review,* January 1986, pp. 88–102.

29. Robert P. Vecchio, "Situational Leadership Theory: An Examination of a Prescriptive Theory," *Journal of Applied Psychology,* August 1987, pp. 444–451.

30. Fred E. Fiedler, *A Theory of Leadership Effectiveness* (New York: McGraw-Hill Book Co., 1967).

31. *Ibid.,* pp. 22–32.

32. *Ibid.,* p. 147.

33. See Fred E. Fiedler, Martin M. Chemers, and Linda Mahan, *Improving Leadership Effectiveness: The Leader Match* (New York: John Wiley & Sons, 1976).

34. George Graen, Kenneth Alvares, James Burdeane Orris, and Joseph A. Martella, "Contingency Model of Leadership Effectiveness: Antecedent and Evidential Results," *Psychological Bulletin,* October 1970, pp. 285–296.

35. Steven Kerr, Chester Schriesheim, Charles J. Murphy, and Ralph M. Stogdill, "Towards a Contingency Theory of Leadership Based upon the Consideration of Initiating Structure Literature," *Organizational Behavior and Human Performance,* August 1974, pp. 62–82.

36. Also see Arthur G. Jago and James W. Ragan, "The Trouble with Leader Match is that it Doesn't Match Fiedler's Contingency Model," *Journal of Applied Psychology,* November 1986, pp. 555–559; and S. Schi-

flett, "Is There a Problem with the LPC Score in Leader Match?" *Personnel Psychology,* Winter 1981, pp. 765–769.

37. For some additional insights see Fred E. Fiedler and Joseph E. Garcia, *New Approaches to Effective Leadership: Cognitive Resources and Organizational Performance* (New York: John Wiley & Sons, 1987).

38. Robert J. House, "A Path-Goal Theory of Leader Effectiveness," *Administrative Science Quarterly,* September 1971, pp. 321–338.

39. Robert J. House and Gary S. Dessler, "The Path-Goal Theory of Leadership: Some Post-Hoc and A Priori Tests," in James G. Hunt and Lars L. Larson (eds.), *Contingency Approaches to Leadership* (Carbondale, IL: Southern Illinois Univ. Press, 1974), pp. 29–55.

40. For more on this theory see Robert J. House, "Retrospective Commentary," in Louis E. Boone and Daniel D. Bowen, *The Great Writings in Management and Organizational Behavior,* 2nd ed. (New York: Random House, 1987), pp. 354–364.

41. Robert T. Keller, "A Test of the Path-Goal Theory of Leadership with Need for Clarity as a Moderator in Research and Development Organizations," *Journal of Applied Psychology,* April 1989, pp. 208–212.

42. Enzo R. Valenzi and Gary S. Dessler, "Relationships of Leader Behavior, Subordinate Role Ambiguity, and Subordinate Job Satisfaction," *Academy of Management Journal,* December 1978, pp. 671–678.

43. See for example Andrew D. Szilagyi and Henry P. Sims, Jr., "An Explanation of the Path-Goal Theory of Leadership in a Health Care Environment," *Academy of Management Journal,* December 1974, pp. 622–634; H. Kirk Downey, John E. Sheridan, and John W. Slocum, Jr., "Analysis of Relationships Among Leader Behavior, Subordinate Job Performance and Satisfaction: A Path-Goal Approach," *Academy of Management Journal,* June 1975, pp. 253–262; John E. Stinson and Thomas W. Johnson, "The Path-Goal Theory of Leadership: A Partial Test and Suggested Refinement," *Academy of Management Journal,* June 1975, pp. 242–252; and Gary S. Dessler and Enzo R. Valenzi, "Initiation of Structure, and Subordinate Satisfaction: A Path-Goal Theory," *Academy of Management Journal,* June 1977, pp. 251–259.

44. Victor H. Vroom and Philip H. Yetton, *Leadership and Decision Making* (Pittsburgh, PA: Univ. of Pittsburgh Press, 1973); and Victor H. Vroom and Arthur G. Jago,

The New Leadership (Englewood Cliffs, NJ: Prentice-Hall, 1988).

45. Madeline E. Heilman, Harvey A. Hornstein, Jack H. Cage, and Judith K. Herschlag, "Reactions to Prescribed Leader Behavior as a Function of Role Perspective: The Case of the Vroom-Yetton Model," *Journal of Applied Psychology,* February 1984, pp. 50–60; and R. H. George Field, "A Test of the Vroom-Yetton Normative Model of Leadership," *Journal of Applied Psychology,* October 1982, pp. 523–532.

46. George Graen and J. F. Cashman, "A Role-Making Model of Leadership in Formal Organizations: A Developmental Approach," in J. G. Hunt and L. L. Larson (eds.), *Leadership Frontiers* (Kent, Ohio: Ohio State Univ. Press, 1975), pp. 143–165; and Fred Danserau, George Graen, and W. J. Haga, "A Vertical Dyad Linkage Approach to Leadership With Formal Organizations: A Longitudinal Investigation of the Role-Making Process," *Organizational Behavior and Human Performance,* February 1975, pp. 46–78.

47. Dennis Duchon, Stephen G. Green, and Thomas D. Taber, "Vertical Dyad Linkage: A Longitudinal Assessment of Antecedents, Measures, and Consequences," *Journal of Applied Psychology,* February 1986, pp. 56–60.

48. Mark J. Martinko and William L. Gardner, "The Leader/Member Attribution Process," *Academy of Management Review,* April 1987, pp. 235–249; Terri A. Scandura, George B. Graen, and Michael A. Novak, "When Managers Decide Not to Decide Autocratically: An Investigation of Leader-Member Exchange and Decision Influence," *Journal of Applied Psychology,* November 1986, pp. 579–584; and Richard M. Dienesch and Robert C. Liden, "Leader-Member Exchange of Leadership: A Critique and Further Development," *Academy of Management Review,* July 1986, pp. 618–634.

49. Steve W. J. Kozlowski and Mary L. Doherty, "Integration of Climate and Leadership: Examination of a Neglected Issue," *Journal of Applied Psychology,* August 1989, pp. 546–553.

50. For more on this topic see Martinko and Gardner, "The Leader/Member Attribution Process," pp. 235–249.

51. S. N. Eisenstadt, *Max Weber: On Charisma and Institution Building* (Chicago: Univ. of Chicago Press, 1968), p. 46.

52. A. R. Willner, *The Spellbinders: Charismatic Political Leadership* (New Haven, CT: Yale Univ. Press, 1984), p. 14.

53. Jay A. Conger and Rabindra N. Kanungo, "Toward a Behavioral Theory of Charismatic Leadership in Organizational Settings," *Academy of Management Review,* October 1987, pp. 637–674.

54. Stanley Lieberson and James F. O'Connor, "Leadership and Organizational Performance: A Study of Large Corporations," *American Sociological Review,* April 1972, pp. 117–130.

55. Gerald R. Salancik and Jeffrey Pfeffer, "Constraints on Administrator Discretion: The Limited Influence of Mayors on City Budgets," *Urban Affairs Quarterly,* June 1977, pp. 475–498.

56. Thomas O. Taylor, Donald J. Friedman, and Dennis Couture, "Operating Without Supervisors: An Experiment," *Organizational Dynamics,* Winter 1987, pp. 26–29.

57. For more on this see Steven Kerr and John M. Jermier, "Substitutes for Leadership: Their Meaning and Measurement," *Organizational Behavior and Human Performance,* December 1978, pp. 375–403; Charles C. Manz and Henry P. Sims, Jr., "Leading Workers to Lead Themselves: The External Leadership of Self-Managing Work Teams," *Administrative Science Quarterly,* March 1978, pp. 106–129; and Edward L. Deci, James P. O'Connell, and Richard M. Ryan, "Self-Determination in a Work Organization," *Journal of Applied Psychology,* August 1989, pp. 580–590.

58. Nan Weiner, "Situational and Leadership Influences on Organizational Performance," *National Academy of Management Proceedings,* San Francisco, 1978, pp. 230–234. Also see Nan Weiner and Thomas A. Mahoney, "A Model of Corporate Performance as a Function of Environmental, Organizational, and Leadership Influences," *Academy of Management Journal,* September 1981, pp. 453–470.

59. Alan Berkeley Thomas, "Does Leadership Make a Difference to Organizational Performance?," *Administrative Science Quarterly,* September 1988, pp. 388–400.

60. See Richard M. Hodgetts and Fred Luthans, *International Management* (New York: McGraw-Hill Book Co., 1991), Chapter 12.

CHAPTER 10
Power, Organizational Politics, and Conflict

GOALS OF THE CHAPTER

Power, organizational politics, and conflict are closely linked with leadership, for leaders wield power, often engage in organizational politics, and need to understand how to resolve conflicts. The overriding objectives of this chapter are to examine the nature of power, the ways in which people both gain and use power, the role of organizational politics in influencing behavior, and the ways of managing conflict. When you have finished reading this chapter, you will be able to:

1. define the term *power* and describe five bases of power;
2. describe how people use the various types of power;
3. identify some of the common tactics used to gain individual and intragroup power;
4. discuss some of the most common methods used in gaining intergroup power;
5. define the term *organizational politics* and describe some of the commonly used political tactics;
6. explain some of the common forms of organizational conflict and effective ways of resolving these problems.

When Les Handon was hired as production head, profits at the Everling Corporation were at a five-year low. Les spent the first couple of months examining the situation and identifying major problem areas. Then he made a series of critical decisions. He fired 20 percent of the production staff and reorganized the rest. The latter, whom he believes are capable of collectively making up the loss of production brought about by the work force reduction, were then divided into two groups. One group was given a 22 percent raise; the other was given a 14 percent raise. These raises were designed to bring these people into line with current market wage rates.

The initial reaction to Les's decisions was hard to gauge. Some people seemed thoroughly surprised; others appeared pleased. However, there was very little open discussion. Over the six months since the action, however, things have changed dramatically at Everling. Productivity is at an all-time high, profits are rising, and labor turnover, which used to run around 16 percent annually, is down to 2 percent. In particular, the workers seem to like Les's style. He continually walks around the production area talking to people, encouraging them, listening to their concerns, and making decisions designed to remove roadblocks. Although production deadlines are tighter than ever, Les has explained the reasons for them, and there appears to be agreement among the personnel that these deadlines can be met.

A few people have not approved of Les's approach, and they have voiced their concern with higher-level management. However, unknown to them, Les had first presented his plan to this group and, through a process of give-and-take, had it approved. So the disgruntled employees have found no support for their concerns. As one of them put it, "It looks like we're stuck with him, like it or not."

1. What types of power did Les use? Identify and describe them.
2. How did Les go about gaining power? Explain.
3. What organizational political tactics did Les use? Identify and describe three.
4. What conflict resolution method did Les use? Explain.

Write down your answers to these questions and put them aside. We will return to them later.

POWER

Power is the ability to influence someone to do something that he or she would not otherwise do.

Power is the ability to influence someone to do something that he or she would not otherwise do. For example, a subordinate sends her boss a memo detailing the fact that the purchase of new photocopiers for the department will result in an annual savings of $11,500 for the organization. The superior, acting on this information, orders the machines. The subordinate has influenced the superior to take action that would not otherwise have been taken.

There are many ways in which individuals use power. Sometimes the person will use one of these sources or bases of power, while other times the individual will use a combination of them.[1]

Bases of Power

There are five commonly cited bases of power: reward, coercive, legitimate, referent, and expert[2] (See Figure 10–1). The following examines each of these and then looks at supplemental bases of power.[3]

Reward power is based on a follower's expectation of receiving a desired outcome.

Reward Power. **Reward power** is based on a follower's expectation of receiving something that he or she wants. For example, in many organizations those individuals who comply with company rules and are productive members of the work group are given annual salary raises. Notice that reward power, like all other forms of power, is based on follower expectation. If the members of the work group do not believe that they will be rewarded for their efforts or output, the person attempting to influence them will not be successful using reward power. Also note that the person giving the rewards does not have to be the formal manager. If one member of the group is well-liked by the others, they may be willing to comply with the individual's requests because they want to remain friends with this person. In this

FIGURE 10–1
Five Bases of Power

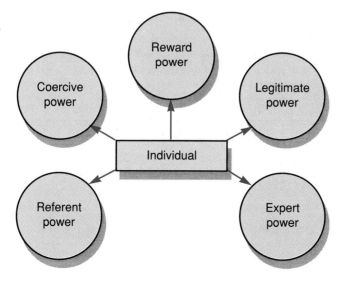

case the individual has informal power (not directly sanctioned by management), and it is reward based.

Reward power is secured whenever someone can dispense rewards that are desired by others and the latter are willing to obey this person in order to get this payoff. Typically the payoff is materialistic such as a pay increase, a promotion, or a desired work assignment, but it can be psychological as in the case of praise or encouragement.

Coercive Power. **Coercive power** is power based on fear. It is present when followers believe that the leader has the power to punish them and the person is willing to use it. Coercive power is often viewed as the opposite of reward power.

Coercive power is based on fear.

Coercive power can take many forms. In everyday life, an individual who threatens to use force on another is employing coercive power. In an organizational setting coercive power typically takes the form of discipline or punishment. Examples include giving someone a poor performance evaluation, docking the individual's pay, demoting the person, or firing the individual.

Coercive power typically is used only after other forms of power have proven unsuccessful. One reason is because the overuse of coercion can lead to fear and distrust. However, if it is employed prudently coercive power can be useful in ensuring necessary compliance. For example, during a crisis situation many managers find that using coercive power ensures that those who do not obey orders and pitch in for the overall good can be quickly sanctioned, brought into line, or dismissed.

Legitimate Power. **Legitimate power,** sometimes called position power, is power vested in the manager's position or role in the hierarchy. For example, senior-level managers have more legitimate authority than middle-level managers, and the latter have more legitimate authority than lower-level managers. When followers obey because of legitimate power, they are responding to the manager's position and not to the individual's personality, knowledge, past performance record, or other personally-related factors.

Legitimate power is vested in the manager's position or role in the hierarchy.

Referent Power. **Referent power,** sometimes referred to as charismatic power, is based on the follower's identification with the leader. When a person has referent power, followers comply with requests or orders because of who issued them. Before doing so, they might ask, "Who said (or asked for) this?" Once they learn, they obey. Referent power is tied closely to factors such as trust, similarity, affection, and acceptance.

Referent power is based on the follower's identification with the leader.

Expert Power. **Expert power** is power based on competence. A leader who is seen as capable of analyzing, implementing, and controlling tasks that have been assigned to the group will often have expert power. The followers will look to the individual to provide them with the competence or direction needed to get the job done. Expert power can be acquired in many different ways.[4] One is experience; a second is formal training.

Expert power is based on competence.

Additional Bases of Power. While the above five bases of power are the most commonly accepted ones, there are additional ways of examining the area of power. These include subordinate power, work design power, and extraneous power.[5]

Subordinate Power.   Subordinate power can take a number of different forms. For example, subordinates have power based on legislation such as equal pay laws and antidiscrimination legislation. The leader is prohibited from discriminating against the followers on the basis of race, color, creed, sex, or national origin.

Subordinates also have collective power based on the potential they have to refuse to obey the leader's directives. Unionized employees have used this power to force management to consider contract demands. Individual employees have also been able to "persuade" management to follow their directives. A good example was provided by "Magic" Johnson of the Los Angeles Lakers. A few years ago he announced that he could not continue to play under his coach, Paul Westhead. He wanted to be traded. The next day management made its decision: They fired the coach. Why? Because Magic had a lucrative financial, twenty-five-year contract with the team and it would have been very difficult to trade him since no other team would pick up his contract. Caught on the horns of this dilemma, management made an economic decision and released one of the finest coaches in the league. Magic used what is often called **affluence power,** which is based on an organization needing an employee more than he or she needs the organization.

Affluence power is based on the organization needing an employee more than he or she needs the organization.

Work Design Power.   Sometimes the leader's power is diminished by the design of the work. For example, in highly automated plants the leader has little control over the workers; their activities and pace are established by the assembly line. Likewise, if the workers are geographically dispersed as in the case of traveling salespeople, international airline captains, or field geologists, the leader's power is affected. The same is true if the subordinates are far more educated or experienced than the leader, as in the case of research and development (R & D) scientists who are being supervised by an R&D manager. The scientists are much more knowledgeable about their work than is the manager, and so the latter's leadership influence is limited.

Extraneous Power.   **Extraneous power** consists of those sources that are outside the leader's direct work environment. One example is organizational policies and procedures that are established by higher-level management and which limit the leader's power to do such things as reward or punish subordinates. A second is the organizational structure, which establishes reporting relationships. These will limit the leader's influence. A third is the unwillingness of superiors to delegate power to their people, thus minimizing the latter's influence. A fourth is pressure from outside powers such as the general public, as in the case of environmentalists or other citizen action groups. These sources will often tie a leader's hands in terms of the types of decisions the individual can make.[6]

Extraneous power consists of sources outside the leader's direct work environment.

Uses of Power

One method of analyzing power use is in terms of commitment, compliance, and re-sistance. Commitment exists when the follower is willing to strongly support the leader and do whatever is asked. When commitment is high, the leader's power can be successfully employed. Compliance is a willingness to follow the leader's request just as long as it does not take extra time or effort to do so. Resistance is the unwillingness to comply with requests. When each of the five types of power discussed earlier are used under these three conditions (commitment, compliance, resistance), different outcomes will result. Table 10–1 provides an example.

Rewards must be fair and equitable.

Using Reward Power.   Many leaders like to use reward power because it involves giving followers positive reinforcement. However, leaders need to understand some things about the use of this power. One is that the rewards must be fair and equitable. If subordinates feel that they are not being given adequate rewards, they will see the leader as unfair, and the individual's power base will begin to erode. Among other things, this means that the leader must verify everyone's performance and not simply give out rewards indiscriminately. The leader must also be careful not to promise anything that cannot be delivered. A third guideline is to give rewards that have value to the subordinates. A leader who gives an individual a promotion but no salary increase may find that the subordinate is not motivated. Finally, rewards must not be seen as payment for unethical behavior or as inducements to encourage such behavior.

Coercive power should be used sparingly.

Using Coercive Power.   Coercive power should be used sparingly and judiciously because it can create more problems than it solves. For example, leaders who

TABLE 10–1
Use of Power Under Varying Conditions

Type of Power Used	OUTCOME AS A RESULT OF SUBORDINATE:		
	Commitment	Compliance	Resistance
Reward	If the follower believes that the request is important to the leader, the person will respond appropriately.	If the reward is given in an impersonal way, it is likely that the followers will comply.	If the reward is applied in a manipulative or arrogant way, the followers are likely to resist.
Coercive	The individual is unlikely to commit under the threat of coercion.	If applied in a helpful and nonpunitive way, it is possible that the followers will go along with directive.	If used in a hostile or manipulative way, the followers are likely to resist.
Legitimate	The follower is likely to go along if the request is viewed as appropriate and is politely presented.	If the order is viewed as legitimate, the followers are likely to comply.	If the request does not appear to be proper, it is possible that the leader will encounter resistance.
Referent	If used in a subtle and personal way, the follower is likely to go along with the request.	If the request is viewed as important to the leader, it is possible that the followers will comply.	If the followers believe that the request will bring harm to the leader, they are likely to resist.
Expert	If the request is persuasive and the followers share the leader's desire for goal attainment, they are likely to be committed.	If the request is persuasive and the followers are apathetic about the goals, it is possible that they will comply.	If the leader is arrogant or insulting, the followers are likely to oppose the directive.

arbitrarily use coercive power often erode their referent power because followers no longer identify with them. One of the best rules to follow in using coercive power is to make the penalty fit the infraction. If someone has broken a minor regulation, give the individual a minor penalty such as a verbal reprimand. If things get progressively worse, the leader can then increase the severity of the punishment.[7] In carrying out this approach, two steps are particularly helpful. First, followers should have the rules communicated to them so that they know what is expected of them. Second, when there is an infraction information should be collected regarding what happened and why. If the leader waits until this information is gathered, he or she avoids that all-too-common problem of penalizing someone and then finding it necessary to modify the punishment. This procedure also reduces the likelihood that the leader will assign a penalty that is totally uncalled for and end up losing the respect and trust of the followers.

Orders should be viewed as fair.

Using Legitimate Power. Orders given in one's formal managerial role automatically carry some degree of influence. In fact, research shows that during crisis situations effective leaders are accorded more legitimate power than they actually hold.[8] The leader must ensure that the orders are conveyed politely and are viewed as fair. For example, when communicating with employees who are older than he or she, the leader should be courteous. When communicating with followers who are nervous or anxious about what is going on, the individual should convey confidence and calm. The leader should also be prepared to explain the reasons for the order or request. Subordinates often find themselves unsure of why they are being asked to do certain things. Sometimes they will feel that it is not part of their job or believe that the assignment can wait for a couple more days. The leader must be prepared to back up the order by justifying the rationale.

Similarity can promote referent power.

Using Referent Power. The primary requirement for referent power is that the followers identify with the leader. This can be accomplished in a number of ways. One of the most common is by choosing subordinates who have similar backgrounds, education, or training. People tend to identify with individuals who remind them of themselves, i.e., similarity can promote referent power. In using this power leaders have to be sensitive to the needs of their people and be prepared to defend the subordinates' needs and feelings. They also need to provide good role models because the followers will emulate the leaders.

Using Expert Power. Leaders typically use expert power by promoting an image that conveys knowledge, wisdom, and experience. This is often done by making others aware of the leader's academic or business achievements. Typically this can be as subtle as dropping a remark such as, "When I worked in the Zurich office, we had a special way of expediting these requests." The comment lets those in attendance know that the individual has international business experience. Another common approach is to use the title "Doctor" when one has an M.D. or Ph.D. in an applicable field of study.[9] For example, many directors of training and development with a Ph.D. in behavioral science believe this title increases their credibility among both followers and peers. Of course, if the individual were doing some work in the marketing area, he or she might not use the title because it would not promote the person's expertise. The individual is out of his or her field.

Expert power should be
used judiciously.

When leaders use expert power, they have to be careful not to intimidate those with whom they interact. If they are perceived as arrogant or "know-it-alls," this will negatively affect their ability to influence others. It also is important for them to stay abreast of their field so that they are continually regarded as knowledgeable. To the extent that they can accomplish these objectives, they will be able to effectively use expert power.

STOP Review your answers to Question 1 and make any changes you would like before continuing.

1. What types of power did Les use? Identify and describe them.

Les used a number of different types of power. First, he used coercive power by firing some of the personnel. Second, he used reward power by giving salary increases to the remainder. Third, he used legitimate power by exercising the authority that came with his position.

GAINING POWER

There are a wide variety of ways in which power can be gained. Some of these are more commonly used by individuals operating alone or within groups; others tend to be employed between groups. The following examines both.

Individual and Intragroup Power

Individuals desire power for many different reasons. One of the most common is because it gives them control over their environment. Physicians, for example, are often perceived to be irreplaceable by other health care professionals, which helps ensure them smooth sailing in carrying out their duties.[10] This explains their need for creating and maintaining expert power. Many working women have a high need for **social power** which is characterized, among other things, by a concern for others.[11] Successful top managers also exhibit this type of power. Another common form is **personalized power** which is characterized by personal aggrandizement. Individuals who flaunt their wealth or success strive for this type of power. Yet regardless of the specific kind of power being sought, there are many tactics that individuals use in their quest.

Social power is characterized
by a concern for others.

Personalized power is characterized by personal ag-
grandizement.

Tactics. One of the most comprehensive lists of tactics used in the pursuit of individual power was compiled by Kipnis, Schmidt, and Wilkinson. Drawing upon data from a two-part study that involved over 900 participants, they found eight different types of influence tactics: assertiveness, ingratiation, rationality, sanctions, exchange, upward appeals, blocking, and coalitions.[12]

Assertiveness was measured by such tactics as continually checking up on the other individual to see if he or she would agree to do what was requested, telling the other person what to do, or bawling out the individual for doing things wrong. Other examples of this tactic, as well as the others described here, are presented in Table 10–2.

Ingratiation was measured by behaviors designed to make the other person feel empathetic or agreeable toward compliance. Examples of ingratiating behavior included praising the other person, acting in a friendly manner prior to asking for the favor, and inflating the importance of what was being requested. (Again, see Table 10–2.)

Rationality tactics were characterized by attempts to be logical and to present a detailed, well-formulated request. Examples included writing detailed plans that justified the request, presenting information in support of the request, and using logic to sway the other person.

Sanctions took the form of coercive power. Examples included giving the other individual no salary raise, preventing the person from getting a raise, and threatening the person with a loss of promotion.

Exchange tactics involved various forms of reciprocity. Examples included doing personal favors for the other person, offering to exchange favors with the individual, and reminding the person of favors that had been done for him or her in the past by the individual now asking for help.

Upward appeals consisted of efforts to secure support from people further up the hierarchy. This included such tactics as getting informal support of higher-ups and making a formal appeal to higher levels to back up the request.

Blocking involved efforts to prevent the other person from carrying out some action. Examples included tactics such as threatening to stop working with the individual until he or she gave in to the request and engaging in work slowdowns until the other person complied.

Coalitions consisted of getting assistance from other parties. Examples included tactics such as rounding up support from co-workers and from subordinates.

In addition to the above, the researchers found tactics that did not fit into any of these eight categories. These unclassified items included actions such as: (a) kidding the individual until he or she did what was desired; (b) ignoring the person and going ahead and doing what was desired; (c) pretending not to understand what needed to be done so that the other person would volunteer to do it; and (d) concealing some of the reasons for trying to influence the other person.

Other researchers have uncovered additional tactics that are used in gaining individual power. For example, after studying how school principals tried to gain power, Mowday found that highly effective principals were more likely to use manipulation than were their less successful counterparts.[13] Another common tactic is to prove one's ability to do a job and thus encourage the superior to delegate more decision-making control.[14] Yet regardless of what approach is used, research also shows that the specific tactic used to gain power is contingency based.

Intergroup Power

Intergroup power is a function of influence and dependence. Groups that can influence other groups, as in the case of a board of directors that can tell the top management team the long-range goals they are to pursue, have intergroup power. Similarly, groups

There are a wide variety of influence tactics.

TABLE 10–2
Examples of Influence Tactics Used by People at Work to Get Their Way

Assertiveness

Set a deadline by which time the other individual is to comply.

Tell the individual that the work has to be done as ordered or the individual will have to propose a better way.

Become a nuisance by pestering the individual until the person does as requested.

Ingratiation

Make the person feel important, i.e., only you have the brains, talent to do this.

Act humbly while asking the individual for what is desired.

Wait until the individual is in a receptive mood and then make the request.

Rationality

Explain the reasons for the request.

Write a memo that describes what is wanted.

Demonstrate personal competence before asking the individual for the request.

Sanctions

Threaten to fire the individual.

Threaten to get the individual fired.

Threaten to give the individual an unsatisfactory performance appraisal.

Exchange

Offer to work longer hours.

Offer to produce more work.

Offer to do the other person's share of the work.

Upward Appeal

File a report about the other person with a higher-up, e.g., the superior.

Send him or her to your superior.

Blocking

Threaten to notify an outside agency if he or she does not give in to the request.

Distort or lie about reasons why the other person should comply with the request.

Coalitions

Have the other person come to a formal conference at which time the request is made.

Obtained the support of subordinates to back up the request.

Source: David Kipnis, Stuart M. Schmidt, and Ian Wilkinson, "Intraorganizational Influence Tactics: Explorations in Getting One's Way," *Journal of Applied Psychology*, August 1980, pp. 445–446. © by the American Psychological Association. Reprinted by permission.

that provide goods or services to other groups have the latter in a state of dependence and can exercise some degree of control over them. In a university setting, for example, the professors decide the textbooks their classes will use, and the bookstore is dependent on this information for its sales orders. The professors thus have some control over the bookstore.

Intergroup power is a function of three determinants: (a) a group's ability to absorb uncertainty for other groups; (b) the degree to which the group can substitute inputs from alternative courses for the inputs from other groups; and (c) the group's importance as an integrating mechanism with other interacting groups.[15]

Uncertainty Absorption.   One way a group gains power over other groups is by absorbing some of the uncertainty that faces the latter. For example, in many large organizations the accounting department devises procedures for handling travel expenses. Whenever people go somewhere for the organization, they have to fill out a travel form. By providing a ready-made form, the accounting department absorbs some of the uncertainty facing these people, and whenever there are problems associated with filing travel expenses, everyone is likely to defer to the judgment of the accounting group.

Absorption of uncertainty can give one group power over others.

Furthermore, the greater the uncertainty, the more willing groups are to let those with the necessary expertise take care of the situation. For example, in many large manufacturing firms that have a number of production plants one centralized industrial relations department usually interfaces with the union in negotiating contracts, handling major worker grievances, and interpreting contractual issues. This industrial relations department also negotiates the final contract with the union, since to let each individual plant negotiate its own would lead to chaos. When handling union disputes, the production plants generally turn the matter over to the central industrial relations department, which has a much better view of the overall picture. In turn, this department often encourages the plants to "let us handle any union problems you have, since we do this on a full-time basis." By absorbing the uncertainty associated with handling union problems, the industrial relations department gains a degree of power over the production plants.

If one group is needed by another, the former has bargaining power with the latter.

Substitutability.   If one group is dependent on another to provide it with needed inputs, the latter has some control over the former. Conversely, if the first group can find a substitute for the goods or services being provided, it can reduce or eliminate this intergroup power. For example, in the illustration just cited, if the production plants brought in their own industrial relations expert to handle union-management problems, they would not have to rely very heavily on the central industrial relations department. In many organizations, however, such a strategy is not possible. Organizational rules require that groups employ internal sources before going outside. When examined from an intergroup power standpoint, the rule also ensures that those groups that have some degree of control over others will be able to keep it.

Integrative importance also gives a group power.

Integrative Importance.   A third determinant of intergroup power is the group's degree of integrative importance. How much do the other groups need this one? If the answer is a lot, then this group cannot be bypassed or ignored. Conversely, if the answer is not very much, then the group's input may be substituted or reduced. In either event, some groups have a very large degree of intergroup power because they play a key role in intergroup performance, whereas others have relatively little power. For example, in a university organization the computer department has a great amount of control over the other departments on campus since most other departments, either directly or indirectly, depend on the computer people for processing information. Class rosters (both beginning and final) and grade rosters are both generated by the computer. So, too, are the professors' paychecks. Without the computer department, the university would almost cease to function.

On the other hand, some groups have very little intergroup power. The college curriculum committee is an illustration. This committee can refuse to approve a course proposed by a particular department in the college, but this is about the extent of its power. The committee cannot require a department to teach a particular course (unless they put it to the vote of the entire college), and they cannot demand that a course that is approved by their committee be put into the college catalog, for in many universities the university curriculum committee screens all college offerings before they go into the catalog, and this group can veto the college committee's suggestions. Thus the college curriculum committee is important, but it has much less intergroup power than the computer department.

Sometimes groups try to expand their power by developing cooperative strategies for power acquisition. Three of the most common are contracting, co-opting, and coalescing.[16]

Contracting. **Contracting** involves negotiating an agreement between two or more groups for the purpose of controlled exchange or guaranteed interaction. For example, in order to reduce the likelihood that they will spend the next three years trying to undermine each other's efforts, a union and a company's management will sign a contract spelling out the terms of agreement and cooperation between them. This agreement relates what each will do (and not do) for the other. Of course, contracting need not involve a legally binding document. It can be an informal agreement, as in the case of a doctor who tells the local hospital administrator that all of his patients who need to be hospitalized will be sent to the administrator's hospital. Relying on such promises from the doctors in the community, the administrator then tells the board of directors that there will be sufficient demand to justify adding a new wing to the hospital. Contracting thus reduces uncertainty and ambiguity.

Co-opting. **Co-opting** is the process of absorbing new groups into the leadership or policy-making structure of an organization in order to avert threats to stability or survival.[17] For example, in recent years the students at some universities have claimed that the board of governors was not concerned with their well-being. In order to avert the possibility of student problems, many boards voted to increase their membership by adding some student body representatives. These boards resolved the problem by taking into the policy-making structure representatives of a group that threatened their stability. By giving the students a chance to help run the university, the boards hope that the student representatives will report to their peers that the governing body is indeed looking after student interests.

Another common illustration of co-opting is when the board of directors of a company gives a few seats on the board to officers of the bank that has just lent it $10 million. By taking in the banking group as part of the policy-making structure, the company helps reduce the threat of the bank's recalling its loan. After all, how can the bank say the company is not being run properly when some of its members are helping operate it?

Coalescing involves a joint venture between two or more groups.

Coalescing. **Coalescing** refers to a joint venture between one group and another. This strategy is used regularly by political parties. For example, when none of them have sufficient strength to win an election, two or more of them will band together into a coalition. By combining their efforts instead of directing them against each other, the coalition is able to win the election. However, coalescing is not restricted to the political arena. We find it used in executive committees in organizations, management groups in hospitals, and administrative groups in colleges. As long as the coalition and its members represent and promote the main objectives of the organization, the coalition will remain in existence. Otherwise, the coalition will be disbanded and a new one formed.[18]

STOP

Review your answers to Question 2 and make any changes you would like before continuing.

2. How did Les go about gaining power? Explain.

Les gained power in a number of different ways. First, he used ingratiation by visiting with the personnel, listening to their concerns, and encouraging them to do their best. Second, he used assertive and rational tactics by setting deadlines for them and explaining why it was important to meet these deadlines. Third, he used sanctions to remove those whom he felt were not productive employees. Fourth, he used upward appeal by getting top management support for his position.

ORGANIZATIONAL POLITICS

Organizational politics is the management of influence in order to obtain objectives.

Organizational politics is managing influence in order to obtain objectives that either are not sanctioned by the organization or are being pursued through nonsanctioned means.[19]

How prevalent is organizational politics in the workplace? When Gandz and Murray surveyed 365 organizational personnel, they found that three statements about workplace politics received strong support: (a) the existence of workplace politics is common to most organizations; (b) successful executives must be good politicians; and (c) the higher one goes in an organization, the more political the climate becomes. On the other hand, they also found strong support for the statement "Powerful executives do not act politically."[20] Quite obviously, while there may be a great deal of political behavior, not everyone engages in it. Those who do, however, tend to rely on similar tactics, and these individuals have similar personal characteristics.[21]

Tactics and Personal Characteristics

Attacking or blaming others is common.

Allen and his associates have investigated political tactics used in organizations through a series of personal interviews.[22] Polling managerial personnel from the supervisory, staff, and chief executive officer ranks of thirty different organizations, they asked each manager to discuss the tactics of organizational politics of which they were aware. A summary of their findings is presented in Table 10–3, which lists eight categories of political tactics that were most frequently mentioned by each group. Over half of the respondents admitted that they attacked or blamed others for problems. Attacking tactics involved making rivals look bad in the eyes of influential organizational members and was typically used to reduce competition for scarce resources. Blaming tactics involved scapegoating in an effort to minimize personnel association with an undesirable situation or result.

Selective use of information is a popular tactic.

Over half of all respondents, on average, also used information as a political tool. In most cases this involved withholding data that might be personally detrimental, avoiding individuals and situations that might require an explanation that would reflect badly on the manager, and selectively disclosing information about individuals or events that would create a desired effect.

Image creation is also widely used.

A third popular tactic was creating and maintaining a favorable image. This involved such things as developing a reputation of being well liked, enthusiastic, honest, thoughtful, and the like, and dressing and acting in accord with organizational norms.

Upper-level managers build a base of support.

The fourth most frequently cited tactic, developing a base of support, was most common among upper-level managers. It involved getting others "to understand one's ideas before a decision is made, setting up the decision before the meeting is called, and

TABLE 10–3
Managerial Perception of Organizational Political Tactics
(Percent of Respondents Mentioning Tactics)

Tactic	Combined Groups	Chief Executive Officers	Staff Managers	Supervisors
Attacking or blaming others	54.0	60.0	50.0	51.7
Use of information	54.0	56.7	57.1	48.3
Image building/ impression	52.9	43.3	46.4	69.0
Support building for ideas	36.8	46.7	39.3	24.1
Praising others, ingratiation	25.3	16.7	25.0	34.5
Power coalitions, strong allies	25.3	26.7	17.9	31.0
Associating with the influential	24.1	16.7	35.7	20.7
Creating obligations/ reciprocity	12.6	3.3	14.3	30.7

Source: Robert W. Allen, Dan L. Madison, Lyman W. Porter, Patricia A. Renwick, and Bronston I. Mayes, "Organizational Politics." © 1989 by The Regents of the Univ. of California. Reprinted from the *California Management Review*, vol. 22, no. 1 (Fall 1979, p. 79). By permission of The Regents.

Organizational Behavior In Action

LIKE IT OR NOT

In 1972 less than 1 percent of all MBAs were awarded to women. By 1977 this percentage had increased to 5 percent and today it stands at 20 percent. Women know that if they are to get ahead in the business world, an advanced degree is an important educational credential. However, their power strategies involve a lot more than this. In describing how women are learning to win the corporate game, *Fortune* magazine recently noted:

> They are gutsy and gritty women in a man's world who refuse to let the feeling of being out of place become an obstacle. Most compete while retaining their femininity. Rather than try to change the corporation, they learn its rules, and they play by them.

Today women make up 45 percent of the work force and they hold 38 percent of all nonfarm, executive, administrative, and managerial jobs. They also account for 2 percent of all senior-level positions, and over the past 16 years they have almost doubled the percentage of management jobs they hold. How are they doing it? What power tactics do they use? Three are particularly dominant.

One is that successful women have taken on many of the values and life patterns of career males. They think and make decisions in a similar manner, and this helps them fit into the corporate world.

A second is that successful women are able to compete well. They learn their jobs and they welcome new challenges because this is one of the easiest ways to separate themselves from the average manager and show their superior that they are promotable.

A third is that successful women try to gain as much experience as possible. They will accept the management of new projects or go to geographic locales where no one else wants to go and work their way back to the home office. Along the route they learn the business so well that they become indispensable to the firm.

These are not the only power tactics that women use, but they do illustrate the basic pattern. And over the next two decades, there are going to be even more women in the executive suite. One reason is that during the next twenty years there is going to be a severe shortage of management talent. This gap is going to have to be filled by bringing more women and other minorities into the management ranks. So whether male managers like it or not, women are becoming an integral part of the executive management team.

Source: Monci Jo Williams, "Women Beat the Corporate Game," *Fortune,* September 12, 1988, pp. 128–138.

getting others to contribute to the idea (possibly making them feel it is theirs) to assure their commitment."[23]

Many of the other tactics mentioned involved some form of reciprocal relationship. Rewards, coercion, and threats (not shown in Table 10–3) were mentioned by less than 10 percent of the respondents. Top managers cited them more than any other group. Allen *et al.* noted that "it appears that promises and threats may be more instrumental to individuals at higher levels than to those at lower levels. The latter may have little to promise and be quite sensitive to the personal dangers involved in making threats."[24] (See "Organizational Behavior in Action: Like It or Not".)

Each managerial group has a distinct profile.

The researchers also investigated the personal characteristics of effective managers. Their list is presented in Table 10–4. Notice that each group of managers, on average, had a distinct type of profile. The chief executive officers felt that a successful top manager had to be sensitive to other individuals, situations, and opportunities. They also felt that the manager had to be articulate, ambitious, intelligent, and a good team player.

Staff managers agreed with the chief officers regarding the importance of being articulate. They also felt that successful managers had to be socially adept, ambitious, competent, sensitive, logical, and self-confident.

Supervisors provided a different picture of the successful politician in the organizational setting. They saw the individual as having to be aggressive, popular, competent, and devious.

TABLE 10–4
Personal Characteristics of Effective Political Actors
(Percent of Respondents Mentioning Characteristic)

Personal Characteristics	Combined Groups	Chief Executives	Staff Managers	Supervisors
Articulate	29.9	36.7	39.3	12.8
Sensitive	29.9	50.0	21.4	17.2
Socially adept	19.5	10.0	32.1	17.2
Competent	17.2	10.0	21.4	20.7
Popular	17.2	16.7	10.7	24.1
Extroverted	16.1	16.7	14.3	17.2
Self-confident	16.1	10.0	21.4	17.2
Agressive	16.1	10.0	14.3	24.1
Ambitious	16.1	20.0	25.0	3.4
Devious	16.1	13.3	14.3	20.7
"Organization man"	12.6	20.0	3.6	13.8
Highly intelligent	11.5	20.0	10.7	3.4
Logical	10.3	3.3	21.4	6.9

Source: Robert W. Allen, Dan L. Madison, Lyman W. Porter, Patricia A. Renwick, and Bronston I. Mayes, "Organizational Politics." © 1989 by The Regents of the Univ. of California. Reprinted from the *California Management Review*, vol. 22, no. 1 (Fall 1979, p. 80). By permission of The Regents.

The viewing lens of supervisors tended to focus on a political actor striving for popularity. They agreed with the higher levels on his aggressiveness but not on the commendability of this behavior. The supervisors also said that political actors are competent, but saw them as more devious than did the higher levels. The responses of chief executive and staff officers referred to and favored politically effective individuals at their levels in the organization, while the supervisors referred to these same, but less favorably.[25]

Using the appropriate tactics is important.

Findings such as those just reported illustrate that organizational politics is an important aspect of group behavior. They also help explain why some people are successful in their efforts to make it up the organizational ladder and others are not. The former are often using the "right" tactics, whereas the latter are not. As a person begins to play organizational politics, it is important to remember the rules of the game regarding how to act in a group setting. A supervisor who is not popular with his or her subordinates may not get the next promotion. However, as a person approaches the middle and upper levels of the hierarchy more sensitivity and polish in dealing with others is required. In fact, as a person enters top management positions the distinction between the manager as a leader and the manager as a politician often begins to blur. The extent to which this happens can greatly influence an individual's job effectiveness.[26]

Benefits and Drawbacks

Organizational politics is a two-edged sword.

Do organizational politics energize and motivate the personnel and result in greater goal attainment, or do they deplete the enterprise's energies and waste company resources? Research shows that there are both benefits and drawbacks. Madison and his associates interviewed managers from thirty different organizations.[27] Each was asked a series of questions related to the frequency of organizational politics in the organization and how their occurrence can be helpful or harmful to the individual and the organization. The results showed that most managers regard organizational politics as a two-edged sword. There are both advantages (career advancement, recognition, status, goal attainment, organizational survival, effective coordination) and drawbacks (loss of credibility, demotion, feelings of guilt, misuse of resources, divisiveness, negative climate) to the use of these tactics. Additionally, the researchers found that power was strongly related to perceived political activity. Those who had power typically engaged in organizational politics. Thus the two main topics of this chapter, power and politics, are interrelated.[28]

Ethical behavior is a current area of concern.

Another current area of concern regarding organizational politics is ethical behavior.[29] Does such political activity result in unethical practices? Are people willing to lie and cheat in order to get ahead? Do organizational politics encourage such activity by rewarding those who carry out these activities? Some of the current news stories such as insider trading on Wall Street and contractor kickbacks in the defense industry make people wonder if companies are willing to enforce ethical standards or will overlook them as long as the company is making money.[30] While such activity must not be condoned by the enterprise, and effective managers refuse to allow such behavior, the area will continue to be a focal point of interest during the 1990s.[31]

STOP

Review your answers to Question 3 and make any changes you would like before continuing.

3. What organizational political tactics did Les use? Identify and describe three.

Les used a number of different organizational tactics. One was the use of information to find out what was going on; he did this before he took any major steps. A second was praising others. A third was forming a power coalition with higher level management.

CONFLICT

Conflict is closely related to power and organizational politics, and it can occur at both the individual and the group level. However, if properly managed, conflict can be a source of increased organizational effectiveness.

Conflict at the Individual Level

Whenever the needs of the individual and the organization are at odds, conflict can develop. Two of the most common forms are frustration and role conflict.

Frustration. Individuals experience **frustration** whenever they are prevented from reaching a desired goal. An example is the case in which three managers are in line for a promotion, but only one can receive it. When the final decision is announced, the two managers who do not get the promotion will undoubtedly experience some form of frustration. Similarly, in organizational life there are many situations in which people can succeed only at the expense of others. Management cannot totally prevent the ensuing frustration; it must learn to deal with it.

Role Conflict. Everyone has a number of roles or expected behavior patterns. A male adult may be a husband and father at home, a manager at the office, and a golf partner at the country club. Sometimes the expected behavior patterns of one role will affect the others, resulting in **role conflict**. This same analogy holds in the work place. A classic illustration is the first-line supervisor. Management expects this individual to be part of their team, while the workers typically believe that the supervisor should represent them and serve as their link with management. Trying to serve in both of these roles leaves the supervisor caught in the middle. So, too, are those workers who are expected by their fellow employees to adhere to group norms, while simultaneously receiving pressure from management to increase their output. Such developments create a state of inner conflict for those personnel who want to meet all of their work expectations.

Problems such as these can result in conflict because the individual is trying to fill role expectations from two different (and sometimes opposing) groups. While there are various ways of managing this individual conflict, it is important to realize that such conflict is often inevitable and should not be regarded as inherently bad.

Frustration occurs when goal-directed behavior is unsuccessful.

The supervisor is the person in the middle.

Conflict at the Organizational Level

When viewed from the organizational level, conflict can often be categorized into two groups: institutionalized and emergent. Each can present problems.

Institutionalized conflict is inherent in organizations.

Institutionalized Conflict. **Institutionalized conflict** often results from organizational attempts to structure work assignments. This is clearly seen in the case of departmentalization, in which organizations group their personnel into major departments such as finance, marketing, and production. Once assigned to such a bailiwick, it is common to find the personnel becoming highly concerned with the needs of their own particular department and relatively unconcerned with those of the others. Budget time finds everyone fighting for increased departmental allocations. Since this is a win-lose situation, those who get percentage increases achieve them only at the expense of the other departments.

A similar type of institutionalized conflict emerges from the organization's creation of a hierarchy. Low-level managers have short-run problems related to work schedules and quotas. Top managers have long-run concerns related to the future course of the total organization. Each hierarchical level tends to be in some degree of conflict with the one above.[32]

Each of these institutionalized conflicts is caused by the creation of a formal organization. Management cannot sidestep them; they are inherent in a hierarchical structure. All the organization can do is try to manage them properly.

Emergent Conflict. *Emergent conflict* arises from personal and social causes. One of the most common is *formal-informal organizational conflict*. When the goals of these two groups are incompatible, problems can result. For example, the objectives of the formal organization may call for more output than the members of the informal organization are willing to give.

Emergent conflict is personal and social in nature.

A second form of emergent conflict arises from *status incongruency*. Some people in the organization may feel that they know a great deal more than their superiors do about how to improve efficiency. However, status is often accorded on the basis of rank. Additionally, line managers often suffer status incongruency when staff advisors have the boss's ear and can convince the latter to implement their recommendations. In such cases the line personnel are reduced to taking orders, while the staff people call the shots.

Managing Conflict

Since conflict is inevitable, the organization needs to consider ways of managing it. In doing so, the management must ensure that conflict does not become an end in itself. Those conflict situations that are disruptive or counterproductive must be resolved, while the others are channeled in constructive directions. Some of the common methods for handling conflict include mutual problem solving, superordinate goals, expansion of resources, avoidance, smoothing, and compromise.

Mutual problem solving encourages cooperation and productive action.

Mutual Problem Solving. One method for resolving conflict is through *mutual problem solving*. In this method, all of the parties are required to come face-to-face with each other and discuss the issues. For example, the production manager who believes that the department can increase its efficiency by introducing new technology may be fighting resistance from the workers who feel threatened by these proposed changes. Through sharing and communicating their differences, it is often possible to accentuate the positive by highlighting the commonly held views of the parties and identifying similarities that can serve as a basis for cooperative effort.

The use of superordinate goals encourages coopera-tion and productive action.

Superordinate Goals.   This method involves introducing an objective requiring the cooperation of all parties identified. In a manufacturing firm, for example, profit depends upon coordinating all departmental activities. No one department can go off on its own without hurting the overall profitability of the entire organization. Thus profit is a superordinate goal, and management attempts to resolve interdepartmental conflict by getting everyone to put aside his or her individual differences and work toward this shared goal.

If resources can be ex-panded, conflict can be re-duced.

Expansion of Resources.   Sometimes conflict is based upon the scarcity of resources. There may be only so much money available to meet budget requests, so an increase in one department's allocation may mean less for another. Or there may be only one promotion available and three highly qualified people in line for it. These win-lose situations can sometimes be avoided if the organization can resort to the *expansion of resources.* For example, by delaying capital expenditures and putting the money into the current budget, the organization may be able to meet all of the departmental requests. Likewise, by reorganizing the structure the top management may be able to create three positions for the three available people.

Avoidance takes two forms: withdrawal and suppression.

Avoidance.   When individuals find themselves in conflict with each other, one way to deal with the situation is through *avoidance* of the other party. This can take two forms: withdrawal and suppression. In the case of *withdrawal,* for example, when the marketing department finds that it cannot deal with the manufacturing people, it may withdraw from interaction with them by sending its reports directly to the president, who will then forward them to manufacturing. Meanwhile, intradepartmental withdrawal often takes the form of "staking out a territory." Each party to the conflict decides what it will do, and no one interferes with the work of the others. In situations in which close coordination is unnecessary, such a resolution technique can work well. In the case of *suppression,* each party merely withholds information or feelings that will upset the other. This evasion tactic does not really address the cause of the conflict, but it does prevent a win-lose situation. This effective resolution technique may indeed be one of the primary factors holding together many organizational relationships.

Smoothing plays down dif-ferences.

Smoothing.   **Smoothing** plays down differences between individuals and groups while emphasizing their common interests. Since it is only a superficial resolution, smoothing is used primarily as a temporary solution. In the long run, these dissimilarities will arise again, and more long-run solutions will have to be implemented.

With compromise there are no distinct winners or losers

Compromise.   In this process there is no distinct loser or decisive winner because each party is required to give up something. Many illustrations of compromise can be cited, with perhaps one of the best known being union-management negotiations.

During contract talks it is typical to find each side giving up something if the other will do likewise. Of course, the amount given up by each party will be in direct relation to its strength. For example, if the union feels it has management at a disadvantage, it will give up less than the latter. Overall, conflict resolution is usually only temporary, and the conflict that initiated the compromise situation will often recur.

STOP — Review your answers to Question 4 and make any changes you would like before continuing.

4. What conflict resolution method did Les use? Explain.

Les used a mutual problem-solving approach. He met with the top management committee and, using a give-and-take process, he hammered out an agreement that was acceptable to the group. In this way, Les anticipated problems at the lower levels of the hierarchy that could result in conflict, and he worked to eliminate the negative impact.

SUMMARY

1. Power is the ability to influence someone to do something that he or she would not otherwise do. There are five commonly cited bases of power. Reward power is based on the follower's expectation of receiving something that he or she wants. Coercive power is based on fear. Legitimate power is vested in the manager's position or role in the hierarchy. Referent power is based on the follower's identification with the leader. Expert power is based on competence. In addition there are supplemental bases of power. Three of the most important are subordinate power, work design power, and extraneous power. Effective ways of using each of the five basic types of power were described in the chapter.

2. Individuals use a variety of tactics in gaining personal and intragroup power. Some of the most common include assertiveness, ingratiation, rationality, sanctions, exchange, upward appeals, blocking, and coalitions. Groups also use a variety of tactics in gaining power over other groups. Examples include uncertainty absorption, substitutability, and integrative importance. In addition there are cooperative strategies for power acquisition, including contracting, co-opting, and coalescing.

3. Organizational politics is managing influence in order to obtain objectives that either are not sanctioned by the organization or are being pursued through nonsanctioned means. Common tactics include blaming others, image building, praising others, using power coalitions, and creating obligations. Some of the most common characteristics of effective political managers include the ability to articulate, sensitivity, social adeptness, and competence. There are benefits and drawbacks to using organizational political tactics, as illustrated in Tables 10–4 and 10–5. Another current area of concern regarding organizational politics is ethical behavior, which will continue to be a point of interest during the 1990s.

4. Conflict can occur at the individual and group levels. At the individual level, it often takes the form of frustration or role conflict. At the group level, it commonly presents itself in the form of institutionalized or emergent conflict. Some of the most effective ways of dealing with conflict include mutual problem solving, superordinate goals, expansion of resources, avoidance, smoothing, and compromise.

KEY TERMS

power
reward power
coercive power
legitimate power
referent power
expert power

affluence power
extraneous power
social power
personalized power
contracting
co-opting

coalescing
organizational politics
frustration
role conflict
institutionalized conflict
smoothing

REVIEW AND STUDY QUESTIONS

1. In your own words, what is meant by the term *power*?

2. How would a manager use each of the following types of power: reward, coercive, legitimate, referent, expert?

3. There are supplemental bases of power, including subordinate power, work design power, and extraneous power. What is meant by this statement? Be complete in your answer.

4. How should effective managers use each of the following types of power: reward, coercive, legitimate, referent, expert? In each case, give an example.

5. How do individuals go about gaining power? In your answer be sure to identify and describe at least four common tactics.

6. "Research shows that the specific tactic used to gain individual power is contingency based." What does this statement mean?

7. How do groups attempt to gain power over other groups? Identify and describe two methods.

8. What are some types of cooperative strategies for power acquisition? Identify and describe two.

9. What is meant by the term *organizational politics*? How common is organizational politics? Defend your answer.

10. What are some of the common tactics used in organizational politics? Identify four of them. What are some of the personal characteristics of those who engage in organizational politics? Identify and describe five of them.

11. Are there any benefits to organizational politics? Are there any drawbacks? Explain.

12. Why is ethical behavior in organizational politics likely to continue to be an area of concern for the 1990s? Explain.

13. What are some of the most common forms of conflict at the individual and the group level? Identify and describe two of each.

14. How can conflict be managed? Identify and describe three useful methods.

CASES

Score One For Rita

When her company landed a new account last year, Rita Roberts was appointed as the company's direct liaison. Along with her work group, Rita's job was to examine the client's insurance needs, recommend coverages to keep and drop, and propose new forms of insurance that would be in the client's best interests. Since taking over the account, Rita has done an outstanding job. In fact, all of her accounts have generated at least 30 percent more revenue than was forecasted. "I look over my client's insurance needs very

carefully," Rita explains, "and I often find loopholes that the average insurance person doesn't. Closing those gaps can be important to the client and, of course, it earns us greater commissions."

A week ago Rita learned that the firm was about to sign a new major client. This company is headquartered in Europe and is looking for an American insurance brokerage to handle its stateside business. Rita very much wanted this account, and she began politicking to get it. First, she had her people compare forecasted and actual revenue from each account that had been given to the group over the last three years. Second, she called four of the people who are on the assignment committee and expressed an interest in handling this new account. Third, she personally met with the president of the firm, told this individual how well she was doing with her other accounts, and asked for "increased responsibilities that will further develop the talents of my work team."

Last week the committee made its decision: Rita's group was assigned the new account. In discussing the matter among themselves, the committee members referred to

Rita as "hard working, intelligent, articulate, confident, and ambitious." They also concluded that she will do an excellent job with the account.

1. What political tactics did Rita use in pursuing her objective? Identify and describe three of them.

2. Which primary political tactic did Rita avoid using? Why do you think she did this? Explain.

3. What personal characteristics does Rita have that may have helped account for her effectiveness in politicking for the account? Identify and describe two of them.

Computer Fear

At Easling International the name of the game is profit. Every week, two weeks, or month, depending on the area, a computerized financial printout is sent to each manager. For example, the manufacturing people receive production output data every week, cost per unit information every two weeks, and "budget versus actual expenditures" data each month.

Each department analyzes these printouts very carefully in an effort to identify where costs can be cut or output increased, or both. Those managers who show the greatest profit and efficiency are most likely to be promoted. As a result intergroup competition has become so great that many managers spend the first couple of hours of each week comparing their latest performance against their previous performance and asking their peers, "How did you do?"

The central computer department is directly responsible for collecting the data, processing it, and seeing that the printouts are delivered to the various departments by 9 A.M. every Monday morning. Some departments in the organization, however, have been complaining about this entire process. Their arguments can be reduced to three.

First, since the computer department is charged with the responsibility of processing the data, it has the final word in deciding the format in which this information is to be submitted. On three different occasions over the last two years the computer people have designed new data forms and required all the departments to use them. The managers consider these changes to be power plays, but they are reluctant to complain openly because they do not want to incur the wrath of the computer department.

Second, the grapevine says that some managers are being given copies of computer printouts destined for other departments. This allows them to see how others are doing, resulting in those with poor performance ganging up on those with higher performance. For example, if Department A was very efficient last month, the department upon which A is dependent will slow their support and thereby reduce A's efficiency. Additionally, those managers who are friendly with key computer personnel are the ones, it is said, who are getting these additional printouts. Top management has categorically denied these rumors, but last week extra copies were found in the offices of four managers who were not supposed to have them.

Third, the computer department has become so important in the organization that some key managers are predicting that the head of this department will become the next president. "The guy's not only running all over us," said one manager, "but he's most likely to get the president's job when Harry retires next year. After all, who's going to say anything bad about the computer department? We're all scared @#$! of it."

1. Upon which of the three determinants of intergroup power is the computer department relying in achieving its influence?

2. How is the current situation causing intergroup performance problems?

3. If you were president of the organization, how would you resolve the problem? Explain.

SELF-FEEDBACK EXERCISE

Power and You

Read each of the following five situations and decide what you would do in each case by placing a 5 next to the action you would most likely follow, a 4 next to your second favorite choice, on down to a 1 next to your least favorite choice. Then enter your answers on the answer sheet and total the columns. An interpretation of the exercise is provided at the end.

1. Someone from your work crew must be transferred to the Buffalo office. You know that no one wants this assignment, but since it must be done you are determined to send the best qualified employee, Julia Wilson. You know that Julia is going to object to the assignment, but you are determined to stick to your guns. Indicate your order of preference for each of the following approaches to this problem.

_____ a. Remind Julia that this job pays 20 percent more than she currently is making and could be an important step in her promotion into higher-level management.

_____ b. Point out that you have analyzed the abilities, talents, and performance evaluations of all the personnel and feel she is best qualified for the job.

_____ c. Tell her that if she does not take the job, her future career at the firm could be in jeopardy.

_____ d. Remind her that you have always given her good advice in the past, and then recommend that she take this appointment.

_____ e. Point out that as the manager it is your job to make these decisions, and this is your decision.

2. Because of the increasing effectiveness of your store's advertising program, you are now having to stay open on Saturdays. You need more people to staff the store this day and, as a result, some of those who have been working a Monday-to-Friday shift are going to have to work an extra day. You intend to rotate this assignment beginning with Bill Shapiro, who will have to work this Saturday. Bill is not going to be pleased because he enjoys spending weekends with his family. Indicate your order of preference for each of the following approaches to this problem.

_____ a. Tell Bill that Saturday assignments are part of the job, and if he does not like it he can secure employment elsewhere.

_____ b. Tell Bill that your job is to make staffing decisions, and you have just done so.

_____ c. Point out to Bill that Saturday work will result in increased store profits and thus greater profit-sharing for him.

_____ d. Explain that you have examined the situation carefully and rotating Saturday assignments is the only way to handle the situation, at least until you are able to hire more people.

_____ e. Remind Bill that you would never ask him to give up a Saturday with his family if there were other ways of resolving the problem.

3. The district manager is going to be in your office a week from today. You would like to have a special presentation designed to inform the manager about how well your office is doing. The best qualified person for writing and presenting this report is Harvey Kahil. What approach would you use in getting Harvey to write this report?

_____ a. Tell Harvey that you are delegating this job to him, and ask him to have the report ready to discuss with you within five days.

_____ b. Remind Harvey that you often made these types of presentations and that they were important in helping you get where you are today.

_____ c. Tell Harvey precisely what you would like him to present to the district manager, review the data with him, and then ask him to give you a preliminary presentation the day before the district manager arrives so that you can offer any suggestions for improvement.

_____ d. Tell Harvey when you want the report ready, and point out that if the presentation is not effective it could be bad for his career.

_____ e. Explain to Harvey what needs to be done, thank him for his help, and tell him that you will write a special memo acknowledging his contribution and put it in his personnel file.

4. You need extra funding for equipment in your department. If you get it, you will be able to increase your output by 15 percent. However, your boss has very little discretionary money and will be reluctant to buy this equipment. How would you go about persuading him to do so?

_____ a. Remind him that you have built a reputation as a highly productive manager, and this purchase is a wise decision.

_____ b. Focus your presentation on the fact that those senior-level managers such as himself who are unable to achieve productivity increases are being let go.

_____ c. Remind your boss that you were hired to increase departmental productivity, and this request is directly in line with the authority that has been delegated to you.

_____ d. Point out that if your unit's productivity goes up, the boss's chances for promotion will also rise.

_____ e. Explain that you have examined a wide variety of ways of increasing productivity, and this is the most efficient of all.

5. You want Roberta Garcia to apply for a company-sponsored training program. You have not yet talked to her about it, but you believe this will be good for her career. How would you go about selling her on this idea?

_____ a. Explain that you have evaluated her performance and believe that this training will be helpful to her in carrying out her assignments.

_____ b. Remind her that promotion out of her current position requires additional training such as the program you are recommending.

_____ c. Point out that you would never recommend training that you yourself have not had.

_____ d. Note that you are required to periodically choose people for these training programs, and you have chosen her.

_____ e. Tell her if she does not take this training she is likely to be laid off the next time the company has a cut-back.

Answer Sheet

Transfer your answers to the answer sheet below by placing the number for each choice next to the appropriate letter. For example, if you placed a 5 next to choice "a" in Situation 1, put a 5 next to the "a" in Row 1. If you placed a 3 next to choice "b" in Situation 1, put a 3 next to the "b" in Row 1. After you have entered all of your answers to Situation 1, go on to Situation 2, etc. In each case, your row should contain a 5, 4, 3, 2, and 1. When you finish entering all of your answers, add each of the five columns. An interpretation is provided.

	Col I	Col II	Col III	Col IV	Col V
Situation 1	— a	— b	— c	— d	— e
Situation 2	— c	— d	— a	— e	— b
Situation 3	— e	— c	— d	— b	— a
Situation 4	— d	— e	— b	— a	— c
Situation 5	— b	— a	— e	— c	— d
Totals	══	══	══	══	══

Interpretation: The first column indicates your use of reward power. Columns II through V represent expert, coercive, referent, and legitimate power, respectively. The higher the column number, the greater your preference for the particular type of power. Research shows that most managers use reward and expert power the most and coercive power the least. Referent and legitimate power are of moderate importance.

NOTES

1. See for example Paul Magnusson and Blanca Riemer, "Carla Hill, Trade Warrior," *Business Week,* January 22, 1990, pp. 50–54.

2. John R. P. French, Jr. and Bertram Raven, "The Bases of Social Power," in Dorwin Cartwright (ed.), *Studies in Social Power* (Ann Arbor, MI: Institute for Social Research, 1959), pp. 155–164; Virginia E. Schein, "Individual Power and Political Behaviors in Organizations: An Inadequately Explored Reality," *Academy of Management Review,* January 1977, pp. 64–72; and Hugh R. Taylor, "Power at Work," *Personnel Journal,* April 1986, pp. 45–46.

3. For more on this topic see Timothy R. Hinkin and Chester A. Schriesheim, "Development and Application of New Scales to Measure the French and Raven (1959) Bases of Power," *Journal of Applied Psychology,* August 1989, pp. 561–567.

4. See for example Warner P. Woodworth, "Managing From Below," *Journal of Management,* Fall 1986, pp. 391–402.

5. See for example, James A. Lee, "Leader Power for Managing Change," *Academy of Management Review,* January 1977, pp 73–80.

6. For additional insights into the various aspects of power, see Jay A. Conger and Rabindra N. Kanungo, "The Empowerment Process: Integrating Theory and Practice," *Academy of Management Review,* July 1988, pp. 471–482; David B. Greenberger and Stephen Strasser, "Development and Application of a Model of Personal Control in Organizations," *Academy of Management Review,* January 1986, pp. 164–177; and Richard S. Blackburn, "Lower Participant Power: Toward a Conceptual Integration," *Academy of Management Review,* January 1981, pp. 127–131.

7. Richard M. Hodgetts, *Modern Human Relations at Work,* 4th ed. (Hinsdale, IL: Dryden Press, 1990), Chapter 10, pp. 399–404 .

8. Mauk Mulder, Rendel D. de Jong, Leendert Kippelaar, and Jaap Verhage, "Power, Situation, and Leaders' Effectiveness: An Organizational Field Study," *Journal of Applied Psychology,* November 1986, pp. 566–570.

9. Joseph S. Fiorelli, "Power in Work Groups: Team Member's Perspectives," *Human Relations,* January 1988, pp. 1–12.

10. Bruce J. Field, "Power Acquisition in a Health Care Setting: An Application of Strategic Contingencies Theory," *Human Relations,* December 1988, p. 924.

11. Leonard H. Chusmir, "Personalized vs. Socialized Power Needs Among Working Women and Men," *Human Relations,* February 1986, pp. 149–159.

12. David Kipnis, Stuart M. Schmidt, and Ian Wilkinson, "Intraorganizational Influence Tactics: Explorations in Getting One's Way," *Journal of Applied Psychology,* August 1980, pp. 440–452.

13. Richard T. Mowday, "The Exercise of Upward Influence in Organizations," *Administrative Science Quarterly,* March 1978, pp. 137–156.

14. Carrie R. Leana, "Power Relinquishment Versus Power Sharing: Theoretical Clarification and Empirical Comparison of Delegation and Participation," *Journal of Applied Psychology,* May 1987, pp. 228–233.

15. D. J. Hickson, C. R. Hinings, C. A. Lee, R. E. Schneck, and J. M. Pennings, "A Strategic Contingencies' Theory of Interorganizational Power," *Administrative Science Quarterly,* June 1971, pp. 216–229.

16. James D. Thompson, *Organizations in Action* (New York: McGraw-Hill Book Co., 1967), pp. 34–36.

17. *Ibid.,* p. 35.

18. For additional insights into intergroup power see Cathy A. Enz, "The Role of Value Congruity in Intraorganizational Power," *Administrative Science Quarterly,* June 1988, pp. 284–304.

19. Bronston T. Mayes and Robert W. Allen, "Toward a Definition of Organizational Politics," *Academy of Management Review,* October, 1977, p. 675.

20. Jeffrey Gandz and Victor V. Murray, "The Experience of Workplace Politics," *Academy of Management Journal,* June 1980, p. 244.

21. For more on this topic see Dan Farrell and James C. Petersen, "Patterns of Political Behavior in Organizations," *Academy of Management Review,* July 1982, pp. 403–412.

22. Robert W. Allen, Dan L. Madison, Lyman W. Porter, Patricia A. Renwick, and Bronston I. Mayes, "Organizational Politics," *California Management Review,* Fall 1979, pp. 72–83.

23. *Ibid.,* p. 80.

24. *Ibid.*

25. *Ibid.,* p. 81.

26. For more on organizational politics, tactics, and strategies see Donald J. Vredenburgh and John G. Maurer, "A Process Framework of Organizational Politics," *Human Relations,* January 1984, pp. 46–66.

27. Dan L. Madison, Robert W. Allen, Lyman W. Porter, Patricia A. Renwick, and Bronston T. Mayes, "Organizational Politics: An Exploration of Managers' Perceptions," *Human Relations,* February 1980, pp. 79–100.

28. For more on organizational politics, especially the use of coalitions, see Kathleen M. Eisenhardt and L. J. Bourgeois III, "Politics of Strategic Decision Making in High-Velocity Environment: Toward a Midrange Theory," *Academy of Management Journal,* December 1988, pp. 737–770.

29. Gerald F. Cavanagh, Dennis J. Moberg, and Manuel Velasquez, "The Ethics of Organizational Politics," *Academy of Management Review,* July 1981, pp. 363–374.

30. Gary Weiss, Christopher Power, and Stan Crock, "Insider Trading: Business as Usual," *Business Week,* August 24, 1987, pp. 20–21.

31. For additional insights to power and politics see Henry Mintzberg, *Mintzberg On Management* (New York: Free Press, 1989), pp. 236–252.

32. For other examples see Richard M. Hodgetts, *Management: Theory, Process, and Practice,* 5th ed. (San Diego: Harcourt, Brace Jovanovich, 1990), p. 154.

PART IV
ORGANIZATIONAL STRUCTURE AND ORGANIZATIONAL BEHAVIOR

Conceptual Model for this Book

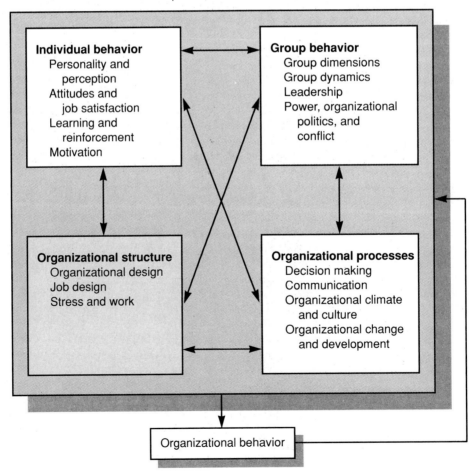

In the previous two parts of this text, we examined the individual and the group. Now we turn our attention to organizational structure and organizational behavior. Since both individuals and groups function within the confines of organizations, it is important to understand the interface that occurs between the people and the structure of organizations. In this part of the book we will be examining three specific topic areas.

First, in Chapter 11, we will study the basic structural factors found in organizational design. Our objective is to identify and describe the four factors present in all structures: job definition, departmentalization, span of control, and decentralization and delegation of authority. In this part of the chapter, our emphasis will be on *how* organizations are structured.

We will then examine *why* organizations are designed the way they are by analyzing contingency factors found in organizational design. The internal factors we will study include organization size and employee characteristics. The external factors that will receive consideration include dependence on the external environment, turbulence of the environment, and technology. After examining these factors, some of the guidelines used in attaining the "right fit" between an organization and its environment will be reviewed.

In Chapter 12 we will study job design. No matter what an organization's structure looks like, in the final analysis the people and work must be brought together in an efficient manner. Therefore, it is necessary for us to bring our study of structure down to the level of the individual job. In this chapter, we will study some of the most popular job design techniques and examine a job characteristics model that has proved to be very useful in redesigning jobs. Key job enrichment principles that are of value in job redesign will also be considered. Finally, some of the current trends in quality of work life will be identified and discussed.

Chapter 13 examines the nature of work and stress. Specific stressors will be identified and their effects discussed. Attention will also be focused on individual differences and how these help explain people's ability to cope with high levels of anxiety and tension. The last part of the chapter will set forth some of the most useful approaches for managing stress.

The overall objective of this part of the book is to provide an understanding of organization and job design. In particular, you will learn how and why specific structures emerge and what an organization can do to obtain the necessary congruence, or fit, between the person and the job. Keep in mind that the structure will affect organizational behavior in that restrictions and demands will be placed on the activities of the people; conversely, the personnel will affect the structure by bringing their values, attitudes, knowledge, beliefs, and norms to the work place. Each must accommodate the other. ◆

CHAPTER 11
Organizational Design

GOALS OF THE CHAPTER

The purpose of the organizational structure is to coordinate the people and the work in a harmonious fashion. The goal of this chapter is to examine the basic structural factors and contingency factors that influence organizational design. Our primary interest will be in examining how structures are designed and in examining some of the behavioral effects associated with these designs. Then we will examine internal and external contingency factors that affect organization structure. When you have finished reading this chapter you should be able to:

1. identify the basic characteristics of an ideal bureaucracy and explain the impact of universal design theory on modern organizational structures;
2. discuss the impact of span of control on structure;
3. relate the structural and behavioral effects of decentralization;
4. note the relationship between an organization's dependence on external forces and the type of structure it employs;
5. compare and contrast mechanistic organizational structures with organic organizational structures;
6. describe the impact of technology on organizational design.

OPENING CASE: CARL'S IDEAS

Over the past five years the Conflux Corporation has increased its sales by 440 percent. In the process, the firm has more than doubled the number of personnel and has opened four large branch offices in addition to its headquarters. The president, Carl Adamecki, believes that now is the time for the company to consider a major reorganization. "We've gotten so large over the last five years," he says, "that we have to revamp our structure to help us do a better job of responding to our environment. In particular, I am very much concerned that we are going to turn into a bureaucracy that is incapable of responding to external demands. When we were much smaller, we had no trouble getting things done. However, today I feel we have too much red tape and are getting ourselves bogged down in rules and procedures." Carl has set forth a number of suggestions that he believes will be useful in improving organizational performance and ensuring that the firm remains competitive. Three of his suggestions are these:

1. Reorganize the structure and eliminate some of the middle levels by increasing the average span of control. This will result in a flatter organization design and, in Carl's opinion, a more efficient one.
2. Delegate more authority to the personnel. This will create a feeling of importance among the personnel and result in higher morale and work output.
3. Reduce the number of people in each locale by creating more branch offices. This will help reduce the amount of red tape and improve overall employee satisfaction.

Carl intends to make these suggestions to the board of directors next week. If the board agrees, the suggestions will be implemented within the next six months.

1. Is a flat structure more efficient than a tall structure? Explain.
2. What problems might be encountered as the company attempts to delegate more authority to the personnel? Identify and briefly describe three.
3. If the company establishes more branch offices so that there are fewer people at each locale, is this likely to reduce red tape and improve overall employee satisfaction?
4. If competitiveness in the industry increases, is Carl wise to change the organization structure and reduce the amount of bureaucracy, or would he be better off trying to create a more bureaucratic design? Explain.

Write down your answers to these questions and put them aside. We will return to them later.

BASIC STRUCTURAL FACTORS AFFECTING ORGANIZATIONAL DESIGN

Research shows that many successful firms first formulate their strategy and then determine the organization structure needed to implement the plan.[1] This "strategy to structure" pattern, however, typically results in a closed-loop process with structure affecting decision making and these decisions then affecting strategy.[2] So a reciprocal relationship often exists between strategy and structure. Nevertheless, organizations strive to create the structure that will be most efficient for them.

There are many theories about how to structure an organization. In his description of the ideal **bureaucracy,** for example, Max Weber set forth the following five characteristics:

There are five characteristics of an ideal bureaucracy.

1. A clear-cut division of labor, resulting in a host of specialized experts in each position.

2. A hierarchy of offices, with each lower one being controlled and supervised by the one immediately above it.

3. A consistent system of abstract rules and standards, which assures uniformity in the performance of all duties and the coordination of various tasks.

4. A spirit of formalistic impersonality in which officials carry out the duties of their office.

5. Employment based on technical qualifications and protected from arbitrary dismissal.[3]

However, Weber's bureaucratic characteristics merely provide us with a point of departure. The needs of the organizational personnel and the demands of the external environment have to be accommodated. In doing so, there are four basic factors that warrant attention: (a) job definitions; (b) departmentalization; (c) span of control; and (d) decentralization and delegation of authority. Before examining these, however, it is important to note that every organization will be different even though many modern organization concepts had their roots in classical or universal design theory.[4]

Universal Design Theory

Advocates of **universal design theory** believed that there were a series of principles around which work and organizations should be structured. Some of these principles related to job design; others applied to the structure itself. Scientific managers such as Frederick Taylor suggested the following principles:

Scientific management principles focused on job design and structure.

1. Develop a science for each element of an individual's work, thereby replacing the old rule-of-thumb method.

2. Scientifically select and then train, teach, and develop the worker, as opposed to having the individual do all this on his own.

3. Cooperate with the workers so as to ensure that all of the work is done in accordance with the principles of science that have been developed.

4. Divide the work and responsibility equally between management and the workers, with each doing that for which he is best suited.[5]

Through the development of work specialization and physiological principles, the scientific managers hoped to extract the greatest amount of efficiency from the workers.

Meanwhile, in the matter of organizational design, a series of classical principles emerged. The best-known list was presented by Henri Fayol. Five of his principles are directly related to structure. Stated succinctly, they are:

Principles of organizational design related to structure.

1. *Division of labor.* Work specialization can bring about efficiency increases.
2. *Authority and responsibility.* To as great a degree as possible, authority and responsibility must be delegated equally. No person should have one without the other.
3. *Unity of management.* There should be one manager and one plan for all operations having the same objective.
4. *Centralization.* In every situation there is an optimal balance between centralization and decentralization of authority.
5. *The hierarchy.* Throughout the organization there is a scalar chain of authority running from top to bottom.[6]

Principles such as these have been criticized because they are too general and view the personnel as "a given rather than a variable in the system."[7] Nevertheless, these basic concepts can be of value if properly employed.

The four basic structural factors that will be examined in this chapter have their roots in this classical theory. However, modern organizations employ them in a flexible manner. Additionally, there is more to the structure of organizations than the mere application of classical organizational principles. The remainder of this chapter will examine *how* modern organizations are designed and *why* they are structured in a particular way.

Job Definitions

Job definitions can improve efficiency.

A **job definition** is a summary of the tasks to be carried out by an individual performing a particular job. Much of the attention given to job definitions has been concentrated at the lower levels of the hierarchy. However, economic and technical benefits can also be achieved at the managerial level. For example, by establishing a position of director of public relations, a large corporation can reduce the amount of time other executives need to spend on disseminating information to the press. Likewise, by appointing an associate administrator for medical services, a hospital administrator can ensure that such vital services as radiology, physical therapy, and electrocardiography are provided to the patients.

Departmentalization

Once individual tasks have been identified and defined, it is necessary to start combining them into groups. This process is known as **departmentalization**. The following examines some of the major departmentalization arrangements.

Functional Departmentalization. The most common form of departmentalization is **functional departmentalization**. In this arrangement the organization identifies those basic, or *organic,* activities that must be performed and organizes all work around them. In a typical manufacturing firm these activities might consist of marketing, production, and finance. Many other organizations are also organized by function. For example, Figure 11–1 shows a large hospital that is organized into three major areas—nursing division, medical services, and supportive services—as well as a number of auxiliary areas, such as finance, computer services, public relations, and employee relations. Departments typically consist of homogeneous groups. The major advantage of functional departmentalization is that it allows the organization to place primary attention on the organic functions. The major disadvantage is that specialists in each area often become more interested in the goals of their own department than in those of the overall organization. This tunnel vision can be detrimental to interdepartmental cooperation.

Product Departmentalization. Many organizations have found that as they grow in size, a functional structure no longer serves their needs. This is especially true for multiline, large-scale enterprises like Ford, DuPont, and Coca-Cola. For these types of organizations **product departmentalization** works best. These departments often have heterogeneous groups. Figure 11–2 presents the organizational chart for this form of departmentalization in a communications corporation.

One of the major advantages of this structural arrangement is that it permits the organization to bring together all the activities associated with a particular production line, thereby facilitating coordination and specialization. It also allows the company to establish each product line as a semi-autonomous profit center. Since all revenues and costs can be differentiated and assigned to a particular product line, high-profit lines can be cultivated, and unprofitable ones can be dropped. The major drawback to this design is that the product divisions may try to become too autonomous, thereby presenting top management with a control problem. In addition, product departmentalization, because of the emphasis on semiautonomy, works well only in those organizations that have a sufficient number of personnel with general management ability.

Territorial Departmentalization. When an organization is physically dispersed, as in the case of a nationwide retail chain, **territorial departmentalization** is common. (see Figure 11–3). The major benefit to such an arrangement is that it allows the firm to cater to the specific needs of a geographic locale. Another advantage is that it provides a training ground for managers by familiarizing them with field operations. On the other hand, it is often difficult for top management to control things because of the great amount of authority the units have over their own operations. In addition, in order to do a good job running one of the units, managers need general management skills; however, it is often difficult to find people with these abilities.

Customer Departmentalization. **Customer departmentalization** structures are designed to meet the needs of specific customer groups. For example, some major universities have the usual departments for handling the needs of day students and then have an extension division for providing night and off-campus courses. Similarly, in a business setting there are meat packing firms with major departments for dairy and poultry, beef, lamb, and veal; retail stores have major departments for men's clothing, women's apparel, and children's wear; and banks offer commercial

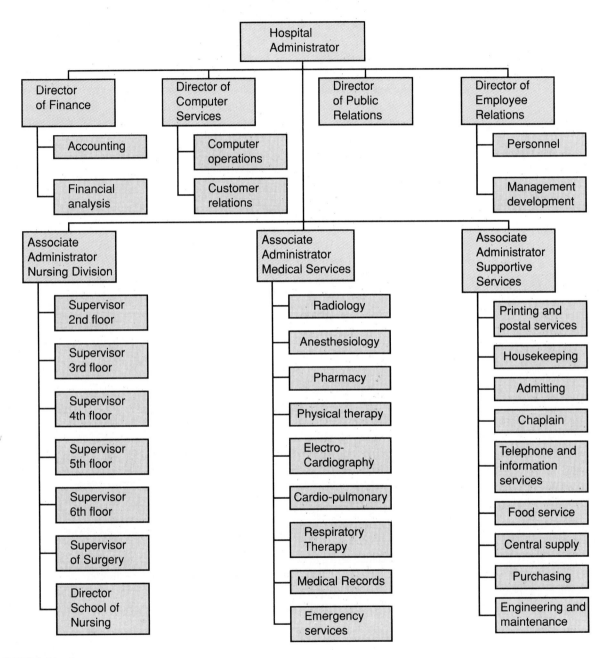

FIGURE 11–1
Organizational Chart for a Hospital

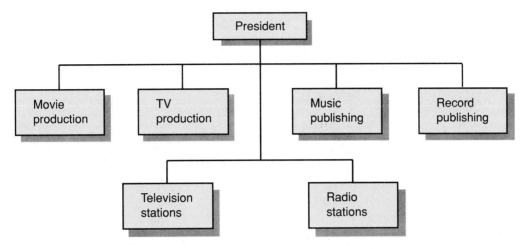

FIGURE 11–2
Product Departmentalization in a Major Communications Corporation

and retail banking services (see Figure 11–4). The major advantage of this structure is that it provides primary attention to the needs of the customer. The major disadvantage is that the personnel often develop tunnel vision and become unconcerned with developments in other departments or units.

Matrix Departmentalization. **Matrix departmentalization** is a hybrid organizational form that allows operational responsibilities to be divided into *two* parts. One part contains all of the responsibilities associated with the management of a business and is given to an individual who can be aptly titled a business-results manager. The other part contains all of the responsibilities related to the management of facilities, personnel, and other resources needed to get the job done. This person is the

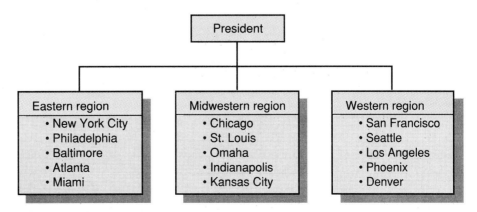

FIGURE 11–3
Territorial Departmentalization Arrangement in a National Retail Chain

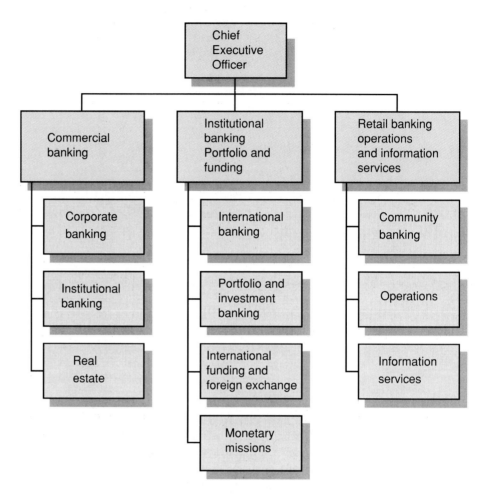

FIGURE 11–4
Organizational Chart for a Large Bank

resource manager. The matrix is built around a "cooperative relationship between the 'business-results manager,' *who directs the work but who does not deploy the people,* and the 'resource manager,' *who does the hiring, training, paying, and terminating of the people who actually do the work but who does not determine what work they do.*"[8] An excellent example is provided by the product-region matrix used by multinational manufacturers. As depicted in Figure 11–5, the product managers determine what is to be sold in each geographical locale, and the resource managers are responsible for production planning, scheduling, and output. The primary advantage of the matrix design is that it places emphasis on *both* output (what is to be produced) and results[9] (seeing that the output is sold and the customer is happy). The major disadvantage is the difficulty of achieving full cooperation among all involved parties.[10]

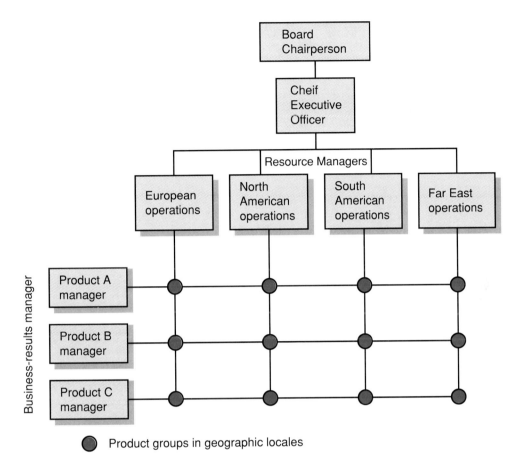

FIGURE 11–5
A Product-Region Matrix

Span of Control

While departmentalization serves as a basis for grouping jobs, it is still necessary to determine how many people will be included in each group. The answer will depend on the manager's effective **span of control,** or the number of individuals he or she can effectively supervise. This concept has a significant effect on both organizational design and behavior. This becomes evident when enterprises with different average spans of control are compared. Figure 11–6 illustrates the hierarchical structure of an organization with an average span of control of two. This narrow span of control results in a four-level hierarchy. Figure 11–7 illustrates the hierarchical structure of an organization with an average span of control of fourteen. This wide span of control results in a two-level hierarchy. Close control will be more easily accomplished in the **tall organizational structure** (Figure 11–6), while vertical communication (from top to bottom) will be faster in the **flat organizational structure** (Figure 11–7). Since there

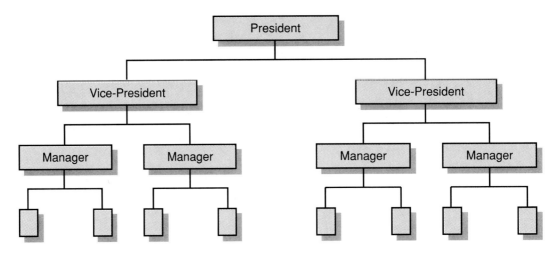

FIGURE 11–6
A Narrow Span of Control

are advantages and disadvantages to both wide (many subordinates) and narrow (few subordinates) spans of control, it is important to broach the question, how can the optimal span be determined?

Classical management theorists believed that narrow spans were superior to wide ones because they permitted close supervision. Many of them felt these spans should vary from three at the upper levels to six at the lower ranks.[11] The overriding problem with this line of reasoning, however, is that it makes the a priori assumption that narrow spans are *always* superior to wide ones. This is too sweeping a generalization to be accepted at face value.

In order to test this classical proposition, a number of research efforts have been undertaken. One of the earliest and most extensive was by Worthy, a consultant for Sears, Roebuck and Company. After comparing the results of tall and flat structures, he concluded that "flatter, less complex structures . . . tend to create a potential for improved attitudes, more effective supervision, and a greater individual responsibility and initiative among employees."[12]

The optimal span depends on the situation.

However, not all researchers agree. Carzo and Yanouzas, for example, tested the relative efficiency of the two types of structures under controlled conditions and found

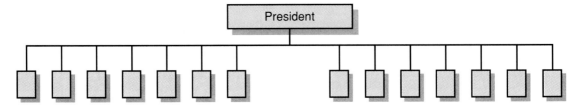

FIGURE 11–7
A Wide Span of Control

that, once the groups learned their tasks, those operating under a tall structure had both higher profits and higher rates of return. This result, they concluded, "was explained by the fact that the tall structure, with a great number of levels, allowed group members to evaluate decisions more frequently, and that the narrow span of supervision provided for a more orderly decision process."[13]

Meanwhile, other researchers have found that the value of a flat versus a tall structure can somewhat depend on the size of the firm. For example, Porter and Lawler surveyed over 1,500 managers to determine if there was any relationship between flat or tall organizations and managerial satisfaction.[14] They discovered that, among organizations of less than 5,000 people, perceived managerial satisfaction was higher in flat structures. Conversely, among organizations of 5,000 or more people, perceived managerial satisfaction was higher if the company had a tall structure. A follow-up of this research was conducted by Porter and Siegel.[15] Replicating the previous study with a sample of 3,000 managers from thirteen countries, they found evidence supporting the first research: flat structures seemed to be superior in firms of less than 5,000 employees; tall structures seemed to be superior in organizations with 5,000 or more personnel.

Still other work in the field indicates that the span, especially of the individual manager, will vary depending on the work to be done, the skill and training of the subordinates, and the personality and leadership ability of the manager.[16] Overall, however, there has been little empirical study of this topic. After conducting a thorough review of the literature, Dalton and his associates have reported:

> Conflicting reports and a paucity of empirical work in the area make it difficult to summarize this research. . . . It is probably safe to say that there is no evidence concerning the relationship of span of control and performance of blue collar, nonmanagerial, or nonprofessional employees.[17]

Nevertheless, research interest in the area continues.[18]

Review your answers to Question 1 and make any changes you would like before continuing.

1. Is a flat structure more efficient than a tall structure? Explain.

There is no empirical research to prove that a flat structure is always more efficient than a tall one. In Carl's case this form of reorganization might be helpful, but it would not be a result of simply increasing the span of control. If Carl wants to increase the amount of authority being delegated to the personnel or wants to give them greater autonomy, a flat structure could help promote these objectives. However, if done simply for the sake of efficiency, a flat structure may not be any more efficient than the current one.

Decentralization and Delegation of Authority

While decentralization and delegation of authority are often used interchangeably, **decentralization** of authority is more encompassing in nature and reflects a philosophy of management regarding the types of decisions that should be pushed down the line and those that should be made at the upper levels. Dale has pointed out that decentralization increases in relation to the following factors:

A series of factors influence decentralization.

1. The greater the number of decisions made lower down the management hierarchy.
2. The more important the decisions made lower down the management hierarchy.
3. The more functions affected by decisions made at lower levels.
4. The less checking required on the decision.[19]

   Delegation of authority is a process the manager uses in distributing work to the subordinates. In functional departmentalization, for example, the president will often decentralize most manufacturing decisions and place them in the production department. From this point, then, the authority will be delegated down the line, beginning at the vice-president's level and continuing on to the lowest-level employee. This same basic procedure will be used in decentralizing decisions in the marketing and finance departments. Similarly, in product departmentalization the president will decentralize authority down to the product division and let it be delegated from there. The same is true for the other departmentalization forms we examined.

Research Findings.   In the early 1960s Chandler published his findings from an intensive study of American business corporations.[20] Equating decentralization with divisionalization, he found that companies placing heavy emphasis on research and development or expansion through diversification tended to favor decentralization. In the case of Westinghouse Electric, for example, the firm realized that expansion by diversification created a myriad of administrative difficulties. Westinghouse therefore decided to experiment with autonomously integrated operating divisions in which authority was decentralized. Chandler found similar decisions being made by such firms as General Electric, International Harvester, Allis-Chalmers, Borg Warner, Ford Motor, General Motors, and the Chrysler Corporation. In each case, he reported, decentralization resulted in a structure more capable of meeting competitive challenges.

   On the other hand, many firms did not move toward more decentralized structures. Companies in industries such as copper, nickel, aluminum, and steel tended to remain basically centralized. Illustrations included Kennecott Copper, International Nickel, Alcoa, Bethlehem Steel, and Jones and Laughlin. Basically, Chandler found that decentralization seemed to be affected by the degree of dynamism in the external market place.

   Other researchers have reached similar conclusions. For example, Negandhi and Reimann gathered data from thirty manufacturing firms in India representing a host of industries, including heavy equipment, pharmaceuticals, chemicals, typewriters, cosmetics, and soft drinks. After studying the degree of market competitiveness measured by variables such as price competition and alternative product lines, they concluded:

> We cannot say that organization effectiveness requires decentralization under dynamic or competitive market conditions and centralization under stable, noncompetitive conditions. Rather we would suggest that dynamic, competitive market conditions make decentralization *more important* to organizational effectiveness than do stable conditions.[21]

A good example is found in the case of General William Creech, who reorganized the Tactical Air Command (TAC) and changed it from a highly centralized to a highly decentralized structure. In the process he turned TAC into the best-run command in the Air Force.[22]

However, the external environment is not the only variable affecting decentralization.[23] Dale surveyed one hundred large and sixty-six medium-sized firms and found organizational size and decentralization to be related. As companies become larger, they tend to decentralize more authority.[24] These findings have been supported in studies by Child and by Pugh and associates.[25]

From the standpoint of performance, there is some problem in establishing causal relationships. Dalton and his associates note that much of the research on this topic has not used hard performance criteria, and those that did have focused on the performance of professionals.

> The lack of hard criteria reduces confidence in generalizing an overall reported inverse association and, again, it is not clear that managers and professionals react as blue collar or nonprofessional employees to centralization. Nonetheless, the limited evidence tends to support a negative relationship between centralization and performance for managers and professionals in studies using hard performance criteria. Otherwise, little is known of the association between centralization and performance.[26]

Other Key Factors. In examining decentralization, it is also important to consider internal variables. One of these is the philosophy of top management. Some firms are highly centralized and others highly decentralized because that is what the top executives in the firm want.

A second key factor is the philosophy of the subordinate managers. If these individuals want to participate in important decision making, top management may feel there is little to be gained from a centralized structure. Conversely, if subordinate managers shun increased responsibility, centralization may be necessary.

A third key variable is cost. There tends to be a direct relationship between cost and centralization. Decisions involving a great deal of money are made at the top; other decisions are decentralized to varying degrees, depending on the firm.

Decentralization is also determined to some degree by internal factors.

Finally, in functional departmentalization in particular, the specific functional area should be considered. For example, production and sales activities are often decentralized so that decision making rests at the operating level. After all, who knows more about these activities than the people carrying them out? On the other hand, finance, advertising, pricing, and market-research problems, areas in which costs are high or the need for control is paramount, tend to be much more centralized, regardless of the overall organization philosophy on decision making.

Problems and Shortcomings of Decentralization and Delegation. From what has been said so far, it is evident that decentralization is a vital organizational concept. However, it is not without problems. One of the most obvious is that as authority is delegated, organizational control may suffer. In addition, there are the behavioral problems often associated with delegation of authority. Sometimes these are brought about by a supervisor's reluctance to delegate. Five of the most common reasons for this reluctance are:

1. some executives get themselves trapped in the "I can do it better myself" fallacy;
2. a lack of ability to direct;
3. a lack of confidence in subordinates;
4. an absence of selecting controls designed to warn of impending problems;
5. a temperamental aversion to taking a chance.

Meanwhile, subordinates sometimes try to avoid responsibility, for such reasons as:

1. subordinates find it easier to ask the boss to make the decision rather than deal with it themselves;
2. the fear of criticism in the case of errors;
3. a lack of the necessary information and resources to do a good job;
4. too much work already;
5. a lack of self-confidence;
6. inadequate incentives.

 STOP

Review your answers to Question 2 and make any changes you would like before continuing.

2. What problems might be encountered as the company attempts to delegate more authority to the personnel? Identify and briefly describe three.

The most likely problems would be those related to acceptance of increased responsibility by the personnel. Many of the subordinates might be unwilling to take more authority (and the accompanying responsibility). Some of the most common reasons include: (a) a fear of making mistakes; (b) a willingness to let the boss continue to make these decisions; (c) a lack of time to get all of this additional work done; (d) a lack of self-confidence; and (e) a lack of incentive in the form of rewards.

CONTINGENCY FACTORS AFFECTING ORGANIZATIONAL DESIGN

Why are no two organizational structures identical? The answer is that each organization faces a different environment (no matter how slight) and must be organized in a manner that best accommodates these internal and external forces to accomplish the organization's goals.[27] In recent years, a great deal of attention has been directed toward studying contingency factors in organizational design. These factors can be grouped under two headings: the internal environment and the external environment.

Internal Contingency Factors

There is no universal agreement on those internal factors that ultimately determine an organization's design. However, two of the most important appear to be: (a) the size of the organization; and (b) the characteristics of the employees.

Size of the Organization. Organization size has long been recognized as an important contingency design variable. Research suggests that as the number of people at a given location increases, one is likely to find more formalization. No longer can the personnel interact on a casual, face-to-face basis and still get all the work done efficiently. It now becomes necessary to introduce rules, polices, procedures, and other formal methods.[28]

Some organizations have cut back their work forces.

Some organizations have attempted to deal with this drift toward bureaucracy by geographically spreading out the personnel and thus reducing the negative effects of having many people at the same locale. Others have begun downsizing by reducing the size of their corporate staff.[29] In recent years, for example, IBM has cut its work force by 7 percent; AT&T has let 32,000 employees go; and United Airlines has trimmed its Chicago headquarters staff by over 25 percent.[30] "Organizational Behavior in Action: Small Is Beautiful" provides additional examples.

There also is a tendency to assign more and more people to specialized roles, have more standard procedures, and delegate authority farther down the hierarchy.[31] Additionally, Child reports that those organizations that become more formalized as they grow tend to be more effective than those that do not.[32] This helps explain why large, successful corporations are far more bureaucratic than are their smaller counterparts.[33]

Employee Characteristics. A second internal variable influencing organization design is employee characteristics.[34] Some individuals prefer (or need) a highly structured environment, while others rebel against it. We can attribute this behavior to many causes. One is the age (and the accompanying values of that age) of the employees. For example, many young people want to be included in the decision-making process at an earlier age than did their parents and grandparents. Many are also reluctant to accept the rigid rules and regulations employed by formal organizations.

Another important employee characteristic is education. The better educated the personnel, the more likely they will want some input into the decision-making and control processes. Among highly educated personnel, a more flexible organizational structure is likely, with less attention paid to the enforcement of rules and regulations and more to reliance on ad hoc groups and informal cooperation to get the work done.

A third major employee characteristic is intelligence. The higher the individual's intellect, the less likely he or she will be to accept bureaucratic rules. One obvious reason is that such people often formulate shortcuts which circumvent the rules but get the work done more efficiently. As a result, they are continually at loggerheads with the bureaucrats, who want things done by the book.

Employee characteristics will influence organization design.

Another important employee characteristic is experience. When people are unsure of work rules or procedures, they welcome guidance. In the case of new employees, close control is often an effective technique. Once an individual begins to master the job, however, less control is required. As a result, the more experienced an individual, the more likely that a flexible structure will be effective.

Of course, once we start mixing some of these characteristics the profile is likely to change. For example, will a highly educated person from an authoritarian family do as well in an unstructured environment as a person of average intelligence who was raised in a permissive atmosphere? This is difficult to say. Certainly more research about the impact of employee characteristics on organization structure is needed. We do know, however, that characteristics such as those discussed here constitute important contingency design factors.

STOP   Review your answers to Question 3 and make any changes you would like before continuing.

3. If the company establishes more branch offices so that there are fewer people at each locale, is this likely to reduce red tape and improve overall employee satisfaction?

Yes, it is likely to reduce red tape and improve overall employee satisfaction. If the number of people at a particular locale is reduced by half it is easier for these individuals to work together as a team, and the amount of red tape is usually reduced because people can get things done without having to resort to excessive rules and regulations. Employee satisfaction is also likely to increase because the personnel will prefer this new environment to the old one. Research shows that locations with fewer employees tend to have higher employee satisfaction than those with many employees.

External Contingency Factors

External contingency factors are also very important in organizational design. These include: (a) dependence on external forces; (b) volatility of the environment; and (c) technology.

Dependence on External Forces. Since organizations are open systems, they must respond to their external environments.[35] The forces that make up these environments can be categorized under two headings: (a) the general environment;

Organizational
Behavior
In Action

SMALL IS BEAUTIFUL

In recent years there has been a trend toward reducing organization size. Some of the largest firms are now finding that they can operate more efficiently by trimming their work forces as well as the number of people in each locale. The 3M Company is a good example.

> The company makes a conscious effort to keep its work units as small as possible, because its officers think it helps keep them flexible. The 52,000 U.S. employees . . . are divided among 37 divisions and 9 subsidiaries. Among the company's 91 manufacturing plants, only 5 employ 1,000 persons or more, and the average company installation has 270. Many of the recent successes of 3M are attributed to its strategy of "multiplication by division."

> The auto industry is another good example. Prior to the 1970s the Big Three automakers (General Motors, Ford, Chrysler) were vertically integrated. Most of what they needed to produce their cars was provided by company-owned sources. When they did go outside, there was vigorous bidding by suppliers, and the one with the lowest price was awarded the contract. Sometimes a million dollar contract was won on the basis of a bid that was only $100 less than the next bid. However, today this approach has all but disappeared. The Big Three have reduced their in-house supply capability and moved away from heavy reliance on vertical integration. The auto firms have also lengthened their contracts with suppliers from one year to three to five years. Cutthroat supplier competition has now been replaced by cooperative agreements that are resulting in higher quality and more on-time delivery.

> Although the new arrangement makes the auto makers more reliant on their suppliers, the manufacturers have been able to reorganize their operations to accommodate the change. In the process, they are finding that their hierarchical structures are now giving way to flexible designs that are more efficient and more profitable.

Source: Walter W. Powell, "Hybrid Organizational Arrangements: New Form Or Transitional Development?" *California Management Review,* Fall 1987, pp. 67–87.

and (b) the task environment. Both are described in Table 11–1 and presented in visual form in Figure 11–8.

General environmental forces can affect every organization. Depending on the organization, however, some of these forces have no direct effect, while others are never fully accommodated. *Task environmental forces,* on the other hand, are more specific and relevant to design making and organization design.

By analyzing its external setting and determining the effects of these general and task forces, an organization can design a viable structure. For example, if the economic environment is a primary concern, as in the case of a bank, an economic forecasting department can be created. If the physical-natural environment is a concern, as in the case of an oil company, an exploration department for determining new oil drilling sites

TABLE 11–1
General and Task Environmental
Characteristics of Organizations

General	Task
Demographic: nature of the human population, including age, sex, family size, income, occupation, and education	*Competition:* other buyers and sellers in the same market niche
Physical-natural: climatic and other conditions, as well as the type, quantity, and availability of natural resources	*Customer and client:* demand for the organization's goods and services, customer loyalty, and product differentiation
Political-legal: nature of the political system and the specific laws governing the behavior of organizations	*Suppliers:* labor supply, equipment, machinery, materials, and parts suppliers
Sociocultural: class structure, mobility, norms, values, and ideologies of the society	
Technological: development and application of scientific knowledge for the betterment of society, as reflected in consumer, industrial, and commercial goods	
Economic: the country's monetary and fiscal policies, economic cycles, employment, investment in plant and equipment, and consumer spending	

can be established. If the customer-client environment presents problems, the organization can establish a special department or unit for resolving these dilemmas. In short, structures tend to be modified to accommodate environmental forces.

Volatility of the Environment. Volatility of the environment is measured by the amount and predictability of change faced by an organization. Those in highly volatile environments will often have a different type of structure from those in highly stable, predictable environments. This has been made particularly clear through two important research studies, the first of which was conducted by Tom Burns and G. M. Stalker.[36]

Burns and Stalker's Research. Burns and Stalker investigated twenty industrial firms in the United Kingdom to determine how changes in the technological and market environment affected management processes. The companies in this study came from a variety of industries with different rates of technological and market change. At one extreme there was a rayon manufacturer operating in a very stable environment. At the other extreme was a newly created electronics development company conducting business in a highly volatile and unpredictable environment. By carefully examining the settings in which all twenty firms operated, Burns and

FIGURE 11–8
The Organization and Its Environment

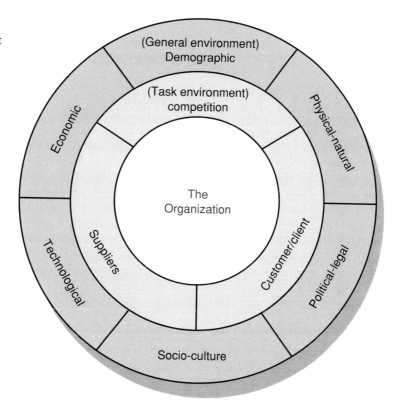

Stalker were able to distinguish five different kinds of environments, ranging from "stable" to "least predictable." They were also able to identify the management processes and structures used by each. A summary of their findings is presented in Table 11–2. Based on their results, the researchers reported:

> There seemed to be two divergent systems of management practice. Neither was fully and consistently applied in any firm, although there was a clear division between those managements which adhered generally to the one, and those which followed the other. Neither system was openly and consciously employed as an instrument of policy, although many beliefs and empirical methods associated with one or the other were expressed. One system, to which we gave the name *"mechanistic,"* appeared to be appropriate to an enterprise operating under relatively stable conditions. The other, *"organic,"* appeared to be required for conditions of change.[37]

A mechanistic-organic construct was developed.

The most important contribution of the Burns and Stalker study is the **mechanistic organization** versus **organic organization** construct it provides for analyzing organizations. Placed on a continuum, it looks like this:

A MECHANISTIC-ORGANIC CONTINUUM
Mechanistic ————————————— Organic

TABLE 11–2
Firms and Their Environments in Burns and Stalker's Study

STABLE		TYPE OF ENVIRONMENT		LEAST PREDICTABLE
Rayon Mill	Electrical Engineering	Radio and TV Manufacturing	Other Electronics Firms	Electronics Development Manufacturer
Highly structured Standing plans Carefully defined roles and tasks	Somewhat flexible structure Contingency plans for meeting special eventualities	Relatively flexible structure No organizational charts No great degree of role definition or job specialization	Flexible No organizational charts Deemphasis on job descriptions Reliance on informal cooperation and teamwork	Very flexible No organizational charts No job descriptions Emphasis on teamwork and interpersonal interaction to ensure goal attainment

In classifying organizational structures, each can be placed somewhere on this continuum. To the left would be highly structured, bureaucratic forms of organization; to the right would be highly unstructured, flexible forms. Those companies moving into dynamic environments or finding their present one becoming more turbulent would have to make a transition from a mechanistic to an organic design, and vice versa.

Another important research study related to volatility of the environment was conducted by Paul Lawrence and Jay Lorsch. Their study has provided important insights into the way in which departments in a structure relate to their environments.

Lawrence and Lorsch Research. Stimulated by the work of Burns and Stalker, Lawrence and Lorsch attempted to go one step further by seeking to answer the question: What kind of organization does it take to deal with various economic and market conditions? Specifically, they wanted to determine how particular firms organize to meet environmental demands. They did this by looking not only at the overall structure but also at the way in which specific departments within the firms are organized.

Their research was carried out in two distinct but related phases. The first was a detailed study of six firms operating in the plastics industry. The second phase entailed the study of a highly effective and less effective competitor in each of two other industries: food and containers. In particular, Lawrence and Lorsch sought to answer the following questions:

1. How are the environmental demands facing various organizations different, and how do environmental demands relate to the internal functioning of effective organizations?

2. Is it true that organizations in certain or stable environments make more exclusive use of the formal hierarchy to achieve integration, and if so, why? Because less integration is required, or because in a certain environment these decisions can be made more effectively at higher organizational levels or by fewer people?

3. Is the same degree of differentiation in orientation and in departmental structure found in organizations in different industrial environments?

4. If greater differentiation among functional departments is required in different industries, does this influence the problems of integrating the organization's parts? Does it influence the organizational means of achieving integration?[38]

These questions summarize the basic thrust of their research. They also introduce two concepts that were central to the study: differentiation and integration.

Differentiation is the process by which units respond to their environments.

By **differentiation** Lawrence and Lorsch meant that within the overall organization or system there are subsystems or subenvironments, each of which tends to develop a specific posture in regard to its own relevant external environment. For example, managers at the upper levels might be highly concerned with external developments such as new pollution control legislation or a rapid increase in the rate of inflation. Meanwhile, at the lower levels the managers might be most concerned with developing new work-flow procedures. Divisions, departments, and personnel will often behave differently because of the demands of their own *particular* environment.

Integration is the quality of the state of collaboration.

Of course, in a highly differentiated organization each unit might end up going its own way. However, companies that require interdepartmental teamwork in order to be effective would undoubtedly prevent this by developing techniques for overcoming any built-in conflicts of interest. Lawrence and Lorsch called this **integration** and defined it as "the quality of the state of collaboration that exists by the demands of the environment."[39] Sometimes these techniques, as in the case of mechanistic structures, take the form of rules, policies, and procedures that govern the behavior of organizational members. Other times, as in the case of organic structures, integration is achieved through mutual cooperation and teamwork on the part of the personnel.

In their analysis of the six firms in the plastics industry, Lawrence and Lorsch found the three major departments (corresponding to the subenvironments) in each—research, sales, and production—to be diverse. The research units were continually confronted with pressure for new ideas and product innovations. Their scientific subenvironment was the most dynamic of any of the three departments in the firm. At the other extreme were the production departments, which faced fairly stable and predictable technical and economic subenvironments. Their time horizons were short-range, with primary concern given to quality control and product delivery time. In the middle were the sales units. They operated in a moderately unstable market subenvironment. Thus there was differentiation between the major departments, although the degree varied from firm to firm, with four having high differentiation and two having low differentiation.

Successful plastics firms had high differentiation and high integration.

If an organization's units are highly differentiated, will this not make integration difficult? Lawrence and Lorsch found that it did not. They reported that "the two organizations with the most successful performance records had, in fact, achieved the highest degree of integration of the six and were also among the most highly differentiated"[40] (see Table 11–3). Thus in the plastics industry, the most effective structure was one that permitted high differentiation *and* integration. This means that the most effective structures in the specific units such as research, sales, and production were those that allowed each unit to interact most effectively with its own particular subenvironment, while *at the same time* allowing people in the organizational system to interact on an interdepartmental basis to resolve conflict and achieve integration between their department's efforts and those of other units.

Conversely, the firms in the container industry operated in the most stable environment. As a result, major departments were all similar in structure, and there was a low level of differentiation. The food industry firms fell in between the plastic and container industry companies in regard to the need for differentiation. Surprisingly perhaps, the container industry required a high level of integration for success.

Lawrence and Lorsch's study has provided us with a great deal of insight on the effects of contingency factors and environmental demands on organizational design. In particular, they have proven that *high-performing organizations come nearer to meeting the demands of their specific environment than do their less effective competitors*. Of course, the *right amount* of differentiation and integration will differ by industry, so both will be vital to success. In addition, it is important to reemphasize that Lawrence and Lorsch were concerned not only with how an overall organization interacts with its external environment but also with the way in which the individual units interact with their own subenvironments. Thus contingency organizational design factors are relevant in structuring *all* levels of the hierarchy.

Technology.   Most researchers who are interested in the effects contingency factors have on organizational design seem to believe that *technology,* the application of knowledge to practical purposes, has a major effect on organizational structure.[41] Two of the most important technology studies that merit close attention are those of Joan Woodward and Richard Hall.

The Woodward Studies.   The Woodward studies took place in South Essex, England. In all, one hundred firms were surveyed. From each, information was gathered regarding:

1. the history, background, and objectives of the company;
2. a description of the firm's manufacturing processes;

TABLE 11–3

Differentiation, Integration, and Performance in Six Firms in the Plastics Industry

Firm	Differentiation Score	Integration Score	Effectiveness Score
1	High	High	High
2	High	High	High
3	Low	High	Medium
4	High	Low	Medium
5	High	Low	Low
6	Low	Low	Low

3. forms and routines relating the way in which the company was organized and operated;

4. facts and figures that could be used in making an assessment of the company's commercial success.[42]

The researchers then identified interorganizational differences between structure, management, and operating processes and the relative profitability of the firms. However, they met with little success until they investigated the relationship between technology and the firms' organizational structures. In an effort to determine the relationship, the researchers devised a system for categorizing the companies along technological lines. The three basic groups into which they classified the firms were:

There were three basic technological classifications.

1. *unit and small-batch production* used by firms making prototypes, "one of a kind" items, or a small number of units produced to customer specifications;

2. *large batch and mass production* used by companies producing large numbers of goods, often with the use of standardized, interchangeable parts;

3. *process production* used by firms producing a continuous flow of the same product, as in the production of liquids, gases, and crystalline substances.

This classification system ranged from the oldest and simplest form of production (unit and small-batch) to the most modern and sophisticated (process production).

When the firms were classified according to this three-part scheme, the researchers found a strong relationship between organizational structure and success within each group. Unit-production firms that were above average had organizational characteristics in common with one another. The same was true for both successful large-batch firms and successful process-production firms.

Table 11–4 provides a comparison of some of the organizational characteristics that existed among the successful firms in each of the three categories. Although companies in the unit and process-production categories did not resemble each other in every conceivable way, there were many similarities between the two groups. For example, both were organized organically, in contrast to the mechanistic structures of the large-batch and mass-production firms.

Additionally, in contrast to the two extremes, the large-batch and mass-production firms made the most rigid application of line-staff organization; clearly distinguished, at least on paper, between executive and advisory responsibility; and made the greatest use of written communication, such as interdepartmental memoranda, operating instructions, and policy directives.

Technology was found to be a causal organizational design variable.

Follow-up research was conducted by the investigators. Twenty firms, each employing more than 250 people, were selected for additional study. Companies representing each of the three technological groups (unit, mass production, and process) and each success category were included. Using interviews and observational methods, the researchers gathered information on how each firm's current organizational structure had emerged and the way in which decision making and other operational processes were carried out. An assessment was also made concerning the appropriateness of the existing structure in meeting the situational demands arising from its technology. In addition, three firms that employed between 2,000 and 4,000 people and in which

TABLE 11–4

Comparison of Organizational Characteristics among the Firms in Woodward's Study

Organizational Characteristics	Unit and Small-Batch Production	Large-Batch and Mass Production	Process Production
Number of employees controlled by first-line supervisors	Small	Large	Small
Relationship between work groups and supervisor	Informal	Formal	Informal
Basic type of workers employed	Skilled	Semiskilled and unskilled	Skilled
Definition of duties	Often vague	Clear-cut	Often vague
Degree of delegation of authority	High	Low	High
Use of participative management	High	Low	High
Type of organizational structure	Flexible	Rigid	Flexible

manufacturing methods were mixed or changing were chosen for intensive study. Each of the case studies not only confirmed the link between technology and organizational characteristics but also demonstrated that it was *causal rather than coincidental.*[43]

The Hall Study. While the Woodward studies examined the impact of technology *among* organizations, other researchers have been concerned with the effect of technology *within* organizations. One of the most significant studies in this area was conducted by Richard Hall.[44] His research was carried out among personnel from ten organizations: five profit-making companies and five government agencies. It was designed to test two hypotheses: (a) departments dealing with uniform events and traditional skills, such as assembly-line work or routine administrative tasks, will require different organizational arrangements than those engaged in nonroutine events, such as advertising and research; and (b) hierarchical organizational levels that perform routine jobs will require an organizational arrangement different from those performing nonroutine tasks. In addition, Hall postulated that those departments and levels that performed routine work could be described by characteristics from Weber's bureaucratic model, including:

1. a well-defined hierarchy of authority;
2. a division of labor based on functional specialization;
3. a system of rules covering the rights and responsibilities of the personnel;
4. a system of procedures for handling work situations;

5. impersonality in interpersonal relationships;

6. selection for employment and promotion based on technical competence.[45]

Hall examined the degree to which each of these six characteristics was present in different departments and hierarchical levels of the ten organizations in the study. After comparing responses from sixteen departments, he found the first hypothesis to be basically accurate. In terms of a hierarchy of authority, division of labor, and procedures for dealing with work situations, nonroutine departments were seen as being significantly different.

Hall also found a great deal of support for his second hypothesis. After administering a questionnaire to 116 executives and 187 nonexecutives, he reported that people performing nonroutine jobs required a different type of structure than those carrying out routine work. This statement was true for four of the six dimensions listed above, including hierarchy of authority, division of labor, procedures for handling work situations, and impersonality of interpersonal relationships.

Hall's study complements that of Woodward in that it provides an insight into *intraorganizational* design, while Woodward dealt most heavily with analyzing *interorganizational* variation in structure. His study also reinforces the research of Burns and Stalker, since in the main Hall has shown that mechanistic (bureaucratic) designs are more appropriate for routine work, and organically designed structures are more effective for nonroutine work.

STOP

Review your answers to Question 4 and make any changes you would like before continuing.

4. If competitiveness in the industry increases, is Carl wise to change the organization structure and reduce the amount of bureaucracy, or would he be better off trying to create a more bureaucratic design? Explain.

Carl is wise to change the structure and make it more flexible and adaptive. Some of his suggestions will move the firm from a bureaucratic to a more organic structure, and this is good. Carl would make a big mistake were he to try creating a more bureaucratic design. This will actually reduce efficiency and profit and make it more difficult to get things done in a speedy and productive manner.

DESIGNING THE "RIGHT" STRUCTURE

The five contingency factors we have just examined modify the basic ones presented early in the chapter. For example, as an organization in a static environment grows larger, we can expect it to start structuring job definitions, employing standard forms of departmentalization (functional, product, territorial), moving toward narrower spans of control, and introducing decentralization of authority in selected areas. Sometimes the final result will be a semibureaucratic structure; other times an *adhocratic* design will emerge in which units and project groups will be created and disbanded as necessary. Highly innovative organizations such as Johnson & Johnson, Proctor & Gamble, and 3M are good examples.[46] It also is common to find enterprises using hybrid arrangements that involve a mix of different organizational structure patterns.[47] This is particularly true in high-tech firms and those conducting international operations.[48]

In short, by studying the environment in which the organization operates, we can modify the basic factors to fit the needs of the situation. Based on the data in this chapter, we can classify the contingency factors favoring both a mechanistic and an organic structure as follows:

Mechanistic	Organic
Many people in one locale	Few people in one locale
Not well trained	Highly trained
Older people	Younger people
Low intellect	High intellect
Low experience	High experience
Perceived simple, static environment	Perceived dynamic, complex enivironment
Independent of external forces	Dependent on external forces
Stable environment	Volatile environment
Low technology	High technology
Routine work	Nonroutine work

In closing our discussion of organizational design, it should now be obvious that the best structure will be a function of both behavioral and nonbehavioral forces. Yet there is more to this entire area of organizational design than the mere structuring of divisions, departments, and groups. There is also the individual work unit. Are highly structured jobs superior to loosely structured ones? Under which do workers respond best? Questions such as these bring us into the area of job design, which will be the subject of attention in the next chapter.

SUMMARY

1. There are four basic organizational design factors: job definitions, departmentalization, span of control, and decentralization and delegation of authority. The basis of job definition is found in division of labor and work specialization. However, the major problem confronting the modern organization is that of determining the optimum point along the continuum of specialization.

2. Departmentalization is the process of forming individual tasks into groups. Some of the most common forms of departmentalization include functional, product, territo-

rial, customer, and matrix. Span of control refers to the number of people a manager can effectively handle. There is no universally optimal span; it depends on the situation. Decentralization is present to some degree in all organizations. While managers cite many advantages associated with it, decentralization is a function of numerous factors, including competitive market conditions, size, philosophy of management, and cost. Additionally, it is important to note that there are various problems associated with decentralization, perhaps the most important of which is loss of control.

3. Contingency factors affect organizational design. In the internal environment one of the most important factors is the size of the organization. Research to date suggests that as the number of people at a given location increases one is likely to find more mechanistic structures. A second important internal variable is that employees with characteristics such as high education, intelligence, and experience tend to favor less structure than do their counterparts who are not as educated, intelligent, or experienced.

4. In the external environment, dependence on external forces is a key contingency factor. The more dependent the organization is on the external environment, the more likely that it will need a responsive, flexible design, and vice versa. The volatility of the environment is a second external contingency factor. As one moves from stable environments to dynamic ones, there is a trend toward a more flexible design, eventually culminating in a highly organic structure. A third external contingency factor is technology. Research indicates that the link between technology and organizational characteristics is causal rather than coincidental. Firms in unit, small-batch, and process production tend to use organic designs, while those in large-batch and mass-production industries commonly employ mechanistic structures.

KEY TERMS

bureaucracy	territorial departmentalization	decentralization
universal design theory	customer departmentalization	delegation of authority
job definition	matrix departmentalization	mechanistic organization
departmentalization	span of control	organic organization
functional departmentalization	tall organizational structure	differentiation
product departmentalization	flat organizational structure	integration

REVIEW AND STUDY QUESTIONS

1. What are the basic characteristics of an ideal bureaucracy? Are any of these contained in modern organizational structures?

2. How has universal design theory contributed to modern organizational design?

3. In the area of job definitions, what are the basic problems that confront most organizations? Discuss them.

4. How does a functional departmentalization structure differ from a product departmentalization arrangement?

5. How does matrix departmentalization work? Put it in your own words.

6. In what way can the span of control affect a manager's relationship with his or her subordinates?

7. How can one determine whether or not an organization is decentralized?

8. What are some of the key factors that help determine the right amount of decentralization? Does decentralization have any effect on organizational behavior? Explain.

9. How does organization size affect organizational design?

10. In what way do employee characteristics help determine the formality-informality of an organizational structure? Explain.

11. What are some of the key general environmental forces affecting organizational design? What are some of the key task environmental forces affecting organizational design? Describe each group.

12. How does dependence on external forces affect organizational design? Explain.

13. What are some of the generally accepted propositions related to organizational design and the organization's dependence on external forces? Identify and discuss five.

14. How does an organic structure differ from a mechanistic structure? Compare and contrast the two.

15. If, on an overall basis, an organization employs a mechanistic structure, will all departments or units within the

organization have mechanistic designs? What if the situation is reversed and the overall design is an organic one?

16. One of the findings from the Lawrence and Lorsch study was that "high-performing organizations come nearer to meeting the demands of their specific environment than do their less-effective competitors." What does this statement mean?

17. According to Woodward, what impact does technology have on structure?

18. How can the contingency factors described in this chapter be of value in designing a viable organizational structure? Explain.

CASES

Changing Conditions

Rogret Food is a medium-size food wholesaler. When the firm was started by Paul Rogret in 1955, it sold dry goods such as coffee, tea, sugar, and cereal to institutional buyers, including local grammar schools, private academies, and health care institutions. Over the past thirty-five years, the population of the local area has increased by 200 percent and the firm's sales are now twenty times what they were in 1955. During this same period, Paul has turned the company over to his son Andrew. Along the way, operations have been reorganized.

In the beginning the company had three major departments: sales, purchasing, and warehousing. The primary department was sales, which serviced current accounts and tried to land new ones. During the past three decades the salespeople have been very successful. They have won large contracts with most of the grammar schools and high schools in the local metropolitan area, and they have also become the main food supplier for three junior colleges and one large university located near their headquarters. They have also secured a large portion of the dry goods business with many local hotels and restaurants, as well as with hospitals and health care facilities. The management is currently thinking about expanding its operations from the current ten-mile radius out to fifty miles. "This will make us a $900 million firm by 1999," notes the president, "and would put us in an ideal position to expand throughout this five-state region."

As the company expanded, it began to reorganize operations. The following figure shows the structure that is used currently. The marketing function has been divided among three different managers. Each is directly responsible for one primary target group. The other two major departments are responsible for providing support services. Purchasing is charged with buying the goods that are needed to fill customer contracts. Warehouse and shipping is responsible for storing the goods until they are to be delivered and then seeing that the merchandise arrives on time and in proper condition. The latter is particularly important since Rogret has added frozen foods to its offerings. Customers can now purchase a wide variety of vegetables, meats, and fish. This marketing decision opened up a major market for the firm and resulted in sales increasing dramatically over the last five years.

The president believes that the firm has now reached an important crossroads and a decision must be made regarding whether to expand rapidly or continue growing at the current 18 percent rate. If the firm expands into a five-state region, it will be necessary to reorganize into a geographic arrangement. If it decides to remain with a ten-mile radius, the current structure should be adequate.

1. What departmentalization structure does the firm now use? Is it a better one than the previous structure? Why?

2. If the company expanded into a geographic arrangement, how would the structure change? Would decentralization of authority become more important under this new arrangement? Why or why not?

3. Regardless of the specific structure, would Rogret operate more efficiently under an organic or mechanistic design? Defend your answer.

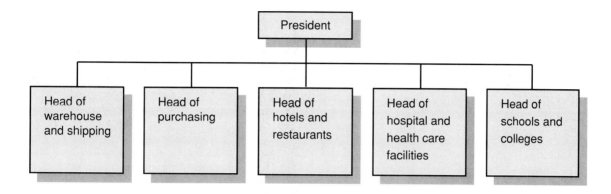

A Turbulent Move

A west coast manufacturer has been expanding its sales at an average annual rate of 21 percent over the last five years. A good portion of these sales has come from the firms the manufacturing company has been acquiring. All, however, have one common characteristic—they are producing durable goods.

While the company believes its current growth rate is very good, the president of the organization feels that the real action in the mid-1990s will be in the electronics field. "Those firms that do well here are going to be the big winners," he has stated. As a result, the president has been urging his top management to begin thinking about products the firm could manufacture that would provide it a base in the electronics field.

One area in which the president believes there is going to be a very large market is that of microcomputers. He has noticed that over the last three years a large number of firms have begun offering all types of micros, including portable models. Many of these are IBM or Apple-compatible, meaning that the buyer who already owns hardware or software from these giant manufacturers can use these compatible models without having to change anything. Since firms like IBM tend to price higher than the competition, companies that offer compatible equipment at a lower price stand a good chance of attracting business from small- and medium-size firms that cannot afford the luxury of paying extra for the IBM name. The president has also discussed the possibility of offering portable micro-computers like the Compaq, which weigh around twenty pounds and can be taken on the road by executives who want to work in their hotel rooms. Last week the president read an article in a leading business journal that said the microcomputer market would generate sales in excess of $10 billion over the next three years. "We can bite off a big piece of that action," he told his executives, "if we act now. We have the manufacturing expertise. All we need to do is develop the technology, or buy it, and then start producing the products. In this market, a great product will sell itself, and everyone knows that we are a quality manufacturer."

A number of the top managers, however, are opposed to this line of thinking. They feel the company will be getting into a market about which they know very little. In particular, they cite the turbulent environment of the computer industry and the need to keep abreast of technological developments. One of the top managers expressed her concern over the proposed expansion this way:

What do we know about the microcomputer field? Why, the environmental variables there are far more dynamic than those we currently face. If we get into this field we will confront all types of problems that will put immense pressures on us. First, we will have to adopt a more flexible organizational structure to accommodate market changes. Second, we will have to bring on board individuals who can thrive in this environment, since most of our current staff will probably not like the increased pressure. Third, we will be more at the mercy of the environment than we are now. We are going to be biting off a lot more than we can chew, if you ask my opinion.

1. If the company decides to go into the computer industry, which of the contingency factors discussed in this chapter will be most crucial in maintaining a viable organizational structure?

2. What types of structural changes would you expect if the firm decides to go ahead with its expansion plans?

3. If you were an outside consultant and the firm told you

that it wanted to proceed with its expansion plans, what advice would you give it regarding how to organize for this new environment? Explain.

SELF-FEEDBACK EXERCISE

Identifying an Organizational Design That Is Ideal for You

Think of the type of organization for which you would like to work. Then read each of the fifteen A and B statements given below and score each using the following scales:

If the A statement is totally descriptive of the organization for which you would like to work, give yourself 5 points.

If the A statement is much more descriptive of the organization for which you would like to work than is statement B, give yourself 4 points.

If the A statement is slightly more descriptive of the organization for which you would like to work than is statement B, give yourself 3 points.

If the B statement is slightly more descriptive of the organization for which you would like to work than is statement A, give yourself 2 points.

If the B statement is much more descriptive of the organization for which you would like to work than is statement A, give yourself 1 point.

If the B statement is totally descriptive of the organization for which you would like to work, give yourself 0 points.

1. _____ A. Job descriptions should be detailed and complete so that the personnel know exactly what they are supposed to be doing.

   B. Job descriptions are not really necessary. A general verbal description of the work to be done will get the personnel into the ballpark, and that should be enough.

2. _____ A. Organization charts should be constructed for every unit and department as well as for the enterprise as a whole so that everyone knows where they fit in the total structure.

   B. Organization charts are unnecessary. At best they merely serve to provide a general scheme of things, but since operations are in a continual state of flux, they really never reflect things as they truly are.

3. _____ A. Authority should be reflected in the position. For example, in every department or unit,

personnel who are in higher-level positions should have authority over those in lower-level positions.

   B. Authority should be a function of knowledge. Regardless of formal job descriptions and authority, the person who knows the most about the problem or solution should be the one who decides what should be done.

4. _____ A. Goal setting should be done from the top down, with managers setting objectives for their people and then communicating them to the personnel.

   B. Goal setting should be a participative process, with managers and subordinates getting together to mutually set objectives for the latter.

5. _____ A. The general nature of the work should be routine and repetitive.

   B. The general nature of the work should be nonroutine and challenging.

6. _____ A. The focus of the planning process should be on the formulation and implementation of long-term goals.

   B. The focus of the planning process should be on the formulation and implementation of short-term goals.

7. _____ A. The environment in which the organization operates should be a predictable one.

   B. The environment in which the organization operates should contain a great deal of uncertainty.

8. _____ A. Interpersonal relations should be formal in nature.

   B. Interpersonal relations should be informal in nature.

9. _____ A. Motivation should come basically in the form of extrinsic rewards.

B. Motivation should come basically in the form of intrinsic rewards.

10. _____ A. The technology in the industry should be stable and not subject to much change.

B. The technology in the industry should be dynamic and subject to much change.

11. _____ A. The general nature of the industry should be calm.

B. The general nature of the industry should be turbulent.

12. _____ A. Control procedures, tools, and techniques should be basically impersonal in nature.

B. Control procedures, tools, and techniques should be basically interpersonal in nature.

13. _____ A. The pervading values of the organization should be efficiency, predictability, and security.

B. The pervading values of the organization should be effectiveness, adaptability, and risk taking.

14. _____ A. The decision-making process should entail only standard, routine decisions.

B. The decision-making process should include many nonstandard, nonroutine decisions.

15. _____ A. Organizational emphasis should be on bottom-line performance.

B. Organizational emphasis should be on problem solving.

Place each of your answers below and total them.

1. _____	9. _____
2. _____	10. _____
3. _____	11. _____
4. _____	12. _____
5. _____	13. _____
6. _____	14. _____
7. _____	15. _____
8. _____	

TOTAL _____

Interpretation:

0–15   You would feel most comfortable working in an organization that is highly organic.

16–30   You would feel most comfortable working in an organization that is basically organic.

31–45   You would feel most comfortable working in an organization that is a blend of organic and mechanistic characteristics.

46–60   You would feel most comfortable working in an organization that is basically mechanistic.

61–75   You would feel most comfortable working in an organization that is highly mechanistic.

NOTES

1. Alfred D. Chandler, *Strategy and Structure* (Cambridge, MA: MIT Press, 1962).

2. James W. Fredrickson, "The Strategic Decision Process and Organization Structure," *Academy of Management Review,* April 1986, pp. 280–297.

3. Peter M. Blau, *Bureaucracy in Modern Society* (New York: Random House, 1956), pp. 28–33.

4. For an interesting contrast with internationally operated firms see "Organizing International Operations," in Richard M. Hodgetts and Fred Luthans, *International Management* (New York: McGraw-Hill Book Co., 1991), pp. 149–169.

5. Frederick W. Taylor, *Principles of Scientific Management* (New York: Harper & Brothers Publishers, 1911), pp. 36–37.

6. Henri Fayol, *Industrial and General Administration,* trans. J. A. Coubrough (Geneva: International Management Institute, 1929), pp. 19–33.

7. James G. March and Herbert A. Simon, *Organizations* (New York: John Wiley & Sons, 1958), p. 29.

8. Allen R. Janger, *Matrix Organization of Complex Businesses* (New York: The Conference Board, Inc., 1979), p. 2.

9. For more insights on matrix management see Lawton R. Burns, "Matrix Management in Hospitals: Testing Theories of Matrix Structure and Development," *Administrative Science Quarterly,* September 1989, pp. 349–368.

10. For more on this see Erik W. Larson and David H. Gobeli, "Matrix Management: Contradictions and Insights," *California Management Review,* Summer 1987, pp. 126–138; Jay R. Galbraith and Robert K. Kazarijian, "Organizing to Implement Strategies of Diversity and Globalization: The Role of Matrix Designs," *Human Resource Management,* Spring 1986, pp. 37–54; and William F. Joyce, "Matrix Organization: A Social Experiment," *Academy of Management Journal,* September 1986, pp. 536–561.

11. Sir Ian Hamilton, *The Soul and Body of an Army* (New York: George H. Doran Co., 1921), p. 230.

12. James C. Worthy, "Organizational Structure and Employee Morale," *American Sociological Review,* April 1950, p. 179.

13. Rocco Carzo, Jr. and John N. Yanouzas, "Effects of Flat and Tall Organization Structure," *Administrative Science Quarterly,* June 1969, p. 191.

14. Lyman W. Porter and Edward E. Lawler III, "The Effects of 'Tall' Versus 'Flat' Organization Structures on Managerial Job Satisfaction," *Personnel Psychology,* Summer 1964, pp. 135–148.

15. Lyman Porter and Jay Siegel, "The Effects of Tall Versus Flat Organization Structures on Managerial Satisfactions in Foreign Countries," University of California, Berkeley, 1964 (photocopy).

16. Robert J. House and John B. Miner, "Merging Management and Behavioral Theory: The Interaction Between Span of Control and Group Size," *Administrative Science Quarterly,* September 1969, pp. 461–462.

17. Dan R. Dalton, William D. Todor, Michael J. Spendolini, Gordon J. Fielding, and Lyman W. Porter, "Organization Structure and Performance: A Critical Review," *Academy of Management Review,* January 1980, p. 55.

18. See David Van Fleet, "Span of Management Research and Issues," *Academy of Management Journal,* September 1983, pp. 546–552.

19. Ernest Dale, *Planning and Developing the Company Organization Structure,* Research Report No. 20 (New York: American Management Association, 1952), p. 107.

20. Alfred D. Chandler, Jr., *Strategy and Structure* (Cambridge, MA: MIT Press, 1962).

21. Anant R. Negandhi and Bernard C. Reimann, "A Contingency Theory of Organization Reexamined in the Context of a Developing Country," *Academy of Management Journal,* June 1972, p. 144.

22. Jay Finegan, "Four-Star Management," *Inc.,* January 1987, pp. 48, 51.

23. Mahnaz Azma and Roger Mansfield, "Market Conditions, Centralization, and Organizational Effectiveness: Contingency Theory Reconsidered," *Human Relations,* February 1981, pp. 157–168.

24. Ernest Dale, *Organization* (New York: American Management Association, 1967), pp. 118–130.

25. John Child, "Predicting and Understanding Organization Structure," *Administrative Science Quarterly,* June 1973, pp. 168–185; D. S. Pugh, D. J. Hickson, C. R. Hinings, and C. Turner, "Dimensions of Organization Structure," *Administrative Science Quarterly,* June 1968, pp. 65–105.

26. Dan R. Dalton, *et al.,* "Organizational Structure," p. 59.

27. Henry Mintzberg, "Organization Design: Fashion or Fit," *Harvard Business Review,* January–February 1981, pp. 103–116.

28. John Child, "Predicting Organization Structure."

29. Thomas Moore, "Goodby, Corporate Staff," *Fortune,* December 21, 1987, pp. 65–76.

30. George Russell, "Rebuilding to Survive," *Time,* February 16, 1987, p. 44.

31. See for example Peter M. Blau and Richard A. Schoenherr, *The Structure of Organizations* (New York: Basic Books, 1971); and John H. Cullen and Kenneth S. Anderson, "Blau's Theory of Structural Differentiation Revisited: A Theory of Structural Change or Scale," *Academy of Management Journal,* June 1986, pp. 203–229.

32. John Child, "Managerial and Organizational Factors Associated with Company Performance—Part II. A Contingency Analysis," *The Journal of Management Studies,* February 1975, p. 20.

33. Also see Elliott Jacques, "In Praise of Hierarchy," *Harvard Business Review*, January–February 1990, pp. 127–133.

34. Dennis R. Briscoe, "Organizational Design: Dealing with the Human Constraint," *California Management Review*, Fall 1980, pp. 71–80.

35. Tom Peters, *Thriving on Chaos* (New York: Alfred A. Knopf, Inc., 1987).

36. Tom Burns and G. M. Stalker, *The Management of Innovation* (London: Tavistock Publications, 1961).

37. *Ibid.,* p. 4 (italics added).

38. Paul R. Lawrence and Jay W. Lorsch, *Organization and Environment* (Homewood, IL: Richard D. Irwin, 1967), p. 16.

39. *Ibid.,* pp. 9–10.

40. *Ibid.,* p. 49.

41. R. Dennis Middlemist and Michael A. Hitt, "Technology as a Moderator of the Relationship between Perceived Work Environment and Subunit Effectiveness," *Human Relations,* June 1981, pp. 517–532.

42. Joan Woodward, *Industrial Organization: Theory and Practice* (London: Oxford Univ. Press, 1965), p. 11.

43. *Ibid.,* p. 185.

44. Richard H. Hall, "Intraorganizational Structural Variation: Application of the Bureaucratic Model," *Administrative Science Quarterly,* December 1962, pp. 295–308.

45. *Ibid.,* p. 297.

46. Kenneth Labich, "The Innovators," *Fortune,* June 6, 1988, pp. 51–64.

47. Walter W. Powell, "Hybrid Organizational Arrangements: New Form or Transitional Development?" *California Management Review,* Fall 1987, pp. 67–87.

48. See for example Homa Bahrami and Stuart Evans, "Stratocracy in High-Technology Firms," *California Management Review,* Fall 1987, pp. 51–66; and Christopher A. Bartlett and Sumantra Ghoshal, "Organizing for Worldwide Effectiveness: The Transnational Solution," *California Management Review,* Fall 1988, pp. 54–74.

CHAPTER 12
Job Design

In the previous chapter, we examined organizational design. Now we want to turn our attention to the work itself by investigating the area of job design. **Job design** consists of job content, the methods to be used on the job, and the manner in which the particular job will relate to others in the organization. Today job design presents a major challenge to organizations. The goals of this chapter are to examine these challenges, to review some of the common methods of redesigning jobs, to study the role of a job characteristics model in this process, and to examine current trends in the quality of work life. By the end of this chapter you should be able to:

1. define what is meant by the term *job design* and describe the two dimensions of all jobs: job range and job depth;

2. relate the three most popular job design techniques: job rotation, job enlargement, and job enrichment;

3. describe the four conditioning factors that affect job design;

4. outline a job characteristics model useful in redesigning jobs and present five key job-enrichment principles of value in job redesign;

5. discuss some of the current trends in quality of work life.

OPENING CASE: DOING IT DIFFERENTLY

When Frances O'Herley was hired two years ago she was assigned to a large secretarial typing pool. In this job Frances typed all kinds of correspondence, from office memos and letters to sales releases to cost control reports. She started work at 8:30 A.M. and finished at 4:30 P.M. and was allowed to leave her desk only for lunch, coffee breaks (midmorning and midafternoon), and short rest periods.

When Frances completed one assignment, she would immediately go on to another. The work was simple and boring, and Frances found herself daydreaming quite a bit. Sometimes a report would be returned to her with a note saying, "Would you please make the following changes in this material." Frances would not remember having typed the report until she booted up her computer and found the report in memory.

Six months ago the company decided to break up the secretarial pool and assign the personnel to individual departments. Frances was assigned to a senior manager in public relations. Her job is now quite different. Frances takes dictation and types correspondence, reporting directly to this person and no one else. She also sits in on key meetings and takes notes for the manager. While her work hours are the same, she is free to take her coffee breaks and lunch whenever she wants.

Frances was recently contacted by one of the people in the human resources department and asked how well she liked her new job. Frances explained some of the main reasons why she was happier under the new arrangement. The man told her that most of the people from the typing pool felt the same way and that the company was thinking about making other similar organizational changes. First, however, they wanted to get feedback regarding what might be done. "Since you've been through an organizational change, we felt that you would be able to help us identify those things that you like about your new job. Then we could try to incorporate these types of factors into other newly created jobs. We're going to have a meeting next Tuesday at 10 A.M. Could you join us?" Frances assured him that she would be there.

1. How is Frances's new job different from her old one in terms of variety, wholeness, human interaction, and freedom?
2. Are the changes that took place in Frances's job an example of job enlargement or job enrichment? Explain.
3. How were the core job dimensions associated with her job changed? What types of principles were employed in this process?
4. Is the company's decision to get feedback from Frances and her associates a wise one? Will this information help the firm do a better job of redesigning work? Explain.

Write down your answers to these questions and put them aside. We will return to them later.

JOB DIFFERENCES

Research shows that while many lower-level workers do not like their jobs, most upper-level managers have no such problem. Although there is *not* a direct relationship between hierarchical position and job satisfaction,[1] upper-level managers usually derive greater satisfaction from their jobs than do lower-level personnel. One of the major reasons for differences in job satisfaction can be seen clearly by contrasting the job characteristics of various positions. Eight of the most common job characteristics are the following:

These are common job characteristics.

1. *Variety*: Some jobs are narrow and routine, requiring the performance of a few rote tasks, while others demand a series of more sophisticated procedures.

2. *Wholeness*: Some work requires the person to carry out only one or two tasks, such as putting a bolt on a car and doing some minor wiring. Other work calls for the individual to do the whole job, such as a salesperson who opens the sale, makes the pitch, and then closes things out by getting the customer's order.

3. *Human interaction*: Some jobs allow for little social interaction, while others permit the workers to talk and develop mutual friendships.

4. *Freedom*: Some jobs are highly programmed, and the individual has no real freedom of action. Others allow the worker to decide what to do, when to do it, and how to do it, as long as the job is completed within the assigned time and quality parameters.

5. *Physical fatigue*: Some jobs demand a great deal of physical effort; others require very little.

6. *Job environment*: Some individuals work in noisy, dark, hot, or smelly environments; others carry out their jobs in very pleasant surroundings.

7. *Work locale*: Some individuals, such as secretaries, are confined to one location; others, such as salespeople, move about during the day.

8. *Work time*: Some jobs, especially blue-collar ones, require people to be at work by 8 A.M. and not leave before 5 P.M. Other jobs have more flexible time schedules, as in the case of an insurance salesperson who chooses his or her own hours, often making evening calls but not coming into the office before 10 A.M.

If we take two extreme illustrations, such as assembly-line worker and the president of the organization, and contrast them according to the eight above characteristics, we would end up with the profile shown in Figure 12–1. In every case in which the assembly-line job has a low rating (variety, wholeness, human interaction, freedom, job environment, multiple work locales, and flexible work times), the president's job has a high one. Conversely, where the assembly-line job has a high rating (physical fatigue, single work locale, and inflexible work time), the president's job has a low one. When we realize that many of the characteristics found in top management jobs are not present in lower-level jobs and managers have fewer problems adjusting to their work, it is easier to understand why job design is a more critical factor at the lower end of the hierarchy.

Before examining routine, repetitive work, however, we should note that in comparing jobs it is not always necessary to go through a long list of job characteristics. Work can often be examined in terms of two job dimensions.

Job Dimensions

Job range refers to the number of operations or tasks an individual performs.

All jobs consist of two dimensions: job range and job depth. **Job range** refers to the number of operations or tasks an individual performs. An assembly-line worker has a low range. Consider, for example, the worker who described his job in this way: "There's a lot of variety in the paint shop. You clip on the color hose, bleed out the old color, and squirt. Clip, bleed, squirt, think; clip, bleed, squirt, yawn; clip, bleed, squirt, scratch your nose."[2] A company president, on the other hand, has a high range. On a particular day, the individual may perform such diverse tasks as meeting people, discussing long-range planning, listening to advice, and deciding where to hold the annual stockholders' meeting. Figure 12–1 shows how variety and wholeness relate to job range.

Job depth refers to the amount of power an individual has over the job or surrounding environment.

Job depth refers to the amount of power an individual has to alter or influence either the job or the surrounding environment. The assembly-line worker cannot really

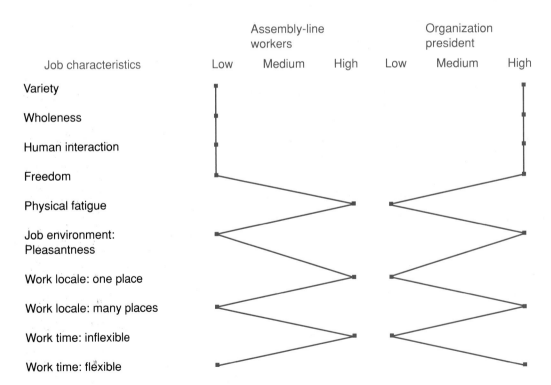

FIGURE 12–1
Comparison of Job Characteristics

control either the job or the environment. The individual is at the mercy of the line: the faster the pace, the quicker the operations have to be performed. Research reveals that blue-collar assembly-line workers suffer high stress because of this mechanical pacing.[3] This is in direct contrast to the president of an organization who has control over operations, deciding what will be done and when. If there are some things the individual does not want to do, there is a high likelihood that he or she will simply delegate them to subordinates.

Most jobs fall between the two extremes described above. For example, a maintenance repairperson will usually have high range but low depth. The individual has many tasks that he or she can perform, but the proper way to do them is limited; that is, there are standard procedures for repairing a television, and some parts of the set have to be fixed before work on other parts can begin. Control of operations is thus limited.

Conversely, a plant security officer has low range and high depth. The individual is responsible for performing only a small number of functions, but in doing so the person has quite a bit of autonomy. For example, the officer may be charged with keeping people out of a particular locale unless they have security clearance. Aside from employing excessive force, the individual is usually free to handle the matter as he or she sees fit. All four of the illustrations we have just discussed are presented in Figure 12–2. Every job can be placed somewhere in this figure.

FIGURE 12–2
Job Dimensions

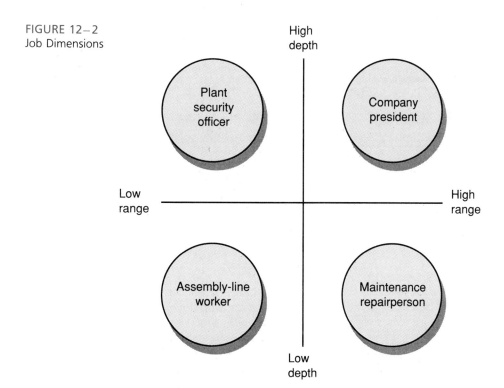

Review your answers to Question 1 and make any changes you would like before continuing.

1. How is Frances's new job different from her old one in terms of variety, wholeness, human interaction, and freedom?

The new job offers much more variety, wholeness, human interaction, and freedom. Note that Frances now carries out a greater variety of tasks, and there is more wholeness to the job. Instead of just being a producer of typed material, she serves as a secretary and assistant to an important manager. Frances also gets to interact more with people and has greater job freedom as seen by the fact that she has control over much of her work routine.

JOB DESIGN TECHNIQUES

How can the organization deal with lower-level jobs that workers find to be boring, repetitive, stressful, or unchallenging? Three of the most popular job design techniques are job rotation, job enlargement, and job enrichment.

Job Rotation

Job rotation involves moving a person to another job.

Job rotation involves moving an individual from one job to another to reduce boredom (see Figure 12–3). For example, an individual who is wiring a television set might switch jobs with someone who is testing the finished product. By moving to another task, the worker develops other skills and, in many cases, acquires a perspective on how his or her activity fits into the overall work flow. In the process, it is hoped, the individual's identification with the final output also increases.

Upon close analysis, job rotation is not a true job-design method, because neither the work nor the individual is altered in any way. Furthermore, once the person becomes familiar with the new task, the job may again prove boring. As a result, some critics charge that job rotation merely exposes the worker to other boring and monotonous jobs.

Job Enlargement

Job enlargement increases the job range.

Job enlargement involves an increase in the range of a job by giving an individual more to do. As applied to the workers in Figure 12–3, for example, each would now do two or more jobs, such as assembling and wiring the television set or soldering and testing it. Job enlargement moves in the opposite direction from job specialization or work simplification.

Research on job enlargement has provided mixed results. Positive findings have been reported from job enlargement programs for clerical work at the Colonial Insur-

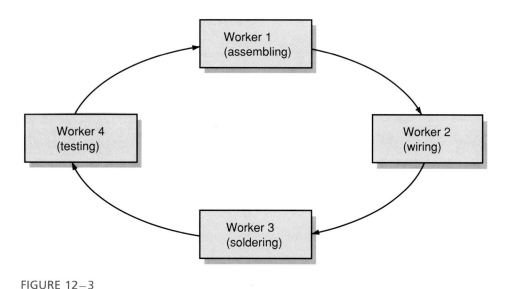

FIGURE 12–3
Job Rotation

ance Company,[4] the Social Security Administration, the Internal Revenue Services,[5] and the Maytag Company.[6]

On the other hand, critics note that some workers prefer repetitive tasks or, at worst, express no real preference for changing things. For example, when Kilbridge asked assembly-line workers in a television receiver manufacturing plant about hypothetical changes in their jobs, over 50 percent expressed a preference for changes resulting in *more* repetitive jobs. The second largest group expressed no preference either way. Less than 12 percent wanted a reduction in repetitive work.[7] In another study, Reif and Schoderbek found that some workers liked routine jobs. In particular, repetitive work gave them time to daydream or socialize without impairing their productivity.[8]

The biggest argument raised against job enlargement, however, is that it may give the worker more to do but does not necessarily introduce any psychological motivators, such as variety, increased responsibility, or the chance for accomplishment. In short, there is a big difference between enlarged jobs and enriched jobs.

Job Enrichment

Job enrichment attempts to build psychological motivators into the work.

Job enrichment attempts to build into a job the psychological motivators described by Herzberg in his two-factor theory. Some of the characteristics of enriched jobs include the authority to: (a) plan the work by organizing and scheduling the tasks, solving any problems that arise, and developing methods that will increase efficiency; and (b) control the job by taking care of such follow-up functions as inspecting, testing, repairing, evaluating, and recording the output.

In recent years many job enrichment programs have been reported in the literature. Two of the most famous involve the Swedish automakers Saab and Volvo. In the case of Saab, annual turnover at their assembly plant stood at 70 percent, while absenteeism was close to 20 percent. Replacing the traditional assembly line with production groups ranging in size from five to twelve people and allowing each the autonomy to do the job his or her way (as long as 470 engines were assembled every ten days), the firm increased its productivity, lowered employee turnover, and improved product quality. Similar results have been obtained by Volvo.[9] (See also "Organizational Behavior in Action: The Volvo Way".)

American companies have also reported success with job enrichment. Some of the best-known programs have been those conducted by AT&T, Corning Glass, Honeywell, Travelers Insurance, and Topeka Pet Foods, although these are but a handful. Alber, for example, conducted a national survey and gathered job enrichment information from over seventeen private and governmental organizations[10] (see Table 12–1). His results show that production output, job satisfaction, improved quality as measured by a decrease in items failing to meet quality standards, reduced turnover rates, and reductions in the size of the work force were some of the reported benefits.

On the negative side some researchers report less than great success with job enrichment. Robert Ford, who was primarily responsible for implementing job enrichment at AT&T, rated nine of their nineteen enrichment programs as only moderately successful and called one a complete flop.[11] Meanwhile, Reif, Ferazzi, and Evans report that some of the major problems encountered by workers in adjusting to enriched jobs include: (a) reluctance to accept increased authority and responsibility; (b) difficulty in

TABLE 12–1
Impact on Performance Caused by Job Enrichment Changes

Item	Unfavorable Change	No Change	Favorable Change
Quality			
Number of items produced that were rejected for failure to meet quality standards	1	5	28
Amount of work that had to be recycled	2	3	22
Resource Utilization			
Labor force idle time	2	9	18
Production output	1	9	40
Operating Benefits			
Accident rate	1	10	4
Order expediting	1	7	8
Grievance rates	1	11	12
Absenteeism	1	11	26
Turnover	4	15	28

Source: Antone F. Alber, "The Real Cost of Job Enrichment," *Business Horizons,* February 1979, p. 67. Reprinted with permission.

Organizational Behavior In Action

THE VOLVO WAY

When Volvo built its Kalmar auto plant on the east coast of Sweden in 1975, the factory was radically different from that of the typical assembly line. Instead of having the workers standing along a line and the car passing between them, the Kalmar plant organized the personnel into work groups and had each individually assemble a car. Every member of the group was taught a number of different assembly tasks so that the workers could trade jobs or easily fill in for anyone who was absent. This approach to building cars was revolutionary, and it also proved to be highly successful. After shaking out all the problems often associated with a new corporation, Volvo's Kalmar plant became the most productive in the industry.

This success convinced the firm to build a second plant, which will soon be opened in Uddevalla on the west coast of Sweden. The principles introduced at Kalmar are being employed at Uddevalla. The plant will use "standstill" production whereby the workers are stationed around the car and parts and materials are brought to the work stations. However, there will be even more changes designed to move the operation further away from the typical assembly line operations found in Detroit and Tokyo. The workers will have a greater opportunity to control their jobs and work at their own pace, just as long as they finish the assigned amount of work for the week. Pointing out the importance of the team approach to building cars, one consultant has noted:

> One advantage of this team approach is that it affords greater flexibility. For example, with certain areas of production more labor-intensive, it becomes easier to substitute a new part or make a small design change in the middle of a model year. In a highly automated operation, making these changes would require a major system change.

> Under this new arrangement, quality is also carefully monitored by the workers and tracked by a central computer. Problems can be pinpointed in anywhere from twenty minutes to two hours. In a typical assembly plant it often takes up to two weeks to uncover these types of problems.

It is still too early to tell whether the Uddevalla plant will have even greater efficiency than the Kalmar operation. However, one thing is certain. This new approach to building cars is highly motivational and one that will receive a good deal of attention during the 1990s as auto makers seek to effectively bring together the workers and the work.

Source: Steve Lohr, "Making Cars the Volvo Way," *New York Times*, June 21, 1987, pp. 29, 33.

adapting to changes in work content; (c) a suspicion of management's motives; and (d) difficulty in adjusting to self-supervision and self-control.[12]

The majority of firms currently practicing job enrichment also seem to have a limited understanding of the concept, being unsure of exactly how, when, and where to apply it. For example, many organizations have assumed that work teams are a natural adjunct to job enrichment, so they have emphasized team projects as opposed to individual projects. The personnel are given enriched group jobs in which they interact and work with others. However, researchers have *not* found that team approaches are better. In fact, Alber and Blumberg report that in a survey study they conducted team approaches were inferior to individual approaches in terms of products rejected for failure to meet quality standards, work requiring recycling, production output, accident rates, order expediting, grievance rates, and absenteeism.[13]

Moreover, regardless of which job redesign technique is used, important behavioral considerations must be taken into account. Among the most important are the conditioning factors that influence the design.

STOP

Review your answers to Question 2 and make any changes you would like before continuing.

2. Are the changes that took place in Frances's job an example of job enlargement or job enrichment? Explain.

They are an example of job enrichment because Frances is psychologically motivated by the new working conditions. True, she has been given more work than before, but the fact that it is not as simple or boring as it was before helps explain why she likes the new arrangement better than the previous one.

JOB DESIGN: CONDITIONING FACTORS

Perhaps the most important thing to remember when discussing job design is that there is no universally good design for work. A well-designed job is a function of the work itself and the circumstances within which it is performed. As such there are four conditioning factors that can substantially affect the impact of a job on employee satisfaction and productivity: (a) individual differences among the employees; (b) the social and interpersonal context of the job; (c) the organizational climate; and (d) the technology of which the work is a part.[14]

Individual Differences

There must be a congruence between the person and the job. Both have demands that must be met and specific resources to contribute to this individual job interaction. This congruence is illustrated in Figure 12–4.

FIGURE 12–4
People and Job Congruence

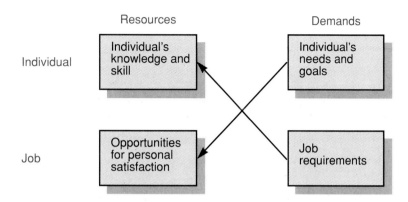

Probably the most important moderator of how a person reacts to a job is the level of knowledge and skill the individual possesses for performing the work. A related problem is the assumption that the job itself is properly designed, so the organization need only concentrate on identifying people who can do the work. If the job design is poor, as reflected in work that is either excessively simple and routine or overly complex and stressful, it may be almost impossible to find a well-suited individual.

A second important moderator is the degree to which the job allows the individual to satisfy important personal needs while working productively at the job. One of these is the need for personal growth and development. A second is the need for meaningful social relationships. Workers with strong social needs should respond positively to jobs permitting interpersonal interaction. At present, however, not enough research has been conducted to determine what constitutes an optimum level of social interaction. It may turn out that "trade-offs between satisfaction and work productivity will be encountered when job changes deal solely with the social aspects of work."[15]

Social and Interpersonal Relationships

Job redesign can alter interpersonal relationships.

If jobs are altered or redesigned in such a way as to change interpersonal relations, it is likely that productivity, motivation, and satisfaction will be affected. For example, if a job is redesigned but the interaction of the individuals is reduced, productivity may suffer. On the other hand, if interpersonal relations are not adversely affected, the redesign effort may be quite successful. Careful attention to the social consequences of work change is warranted, even among those changes intended to affect the job only.

Organizational Climate

Organizational climate is an important job-design variable.

A third conditioning variable is organizational climate and style. Porter, Lawler, and Hackman have formulated the contingency model shown in Figure 12–5. In this model, the interactions among organizational climate and style (mechanistic and organic structures), job design (simple versus enriched work), and employee growth need (low versus high) are considered.

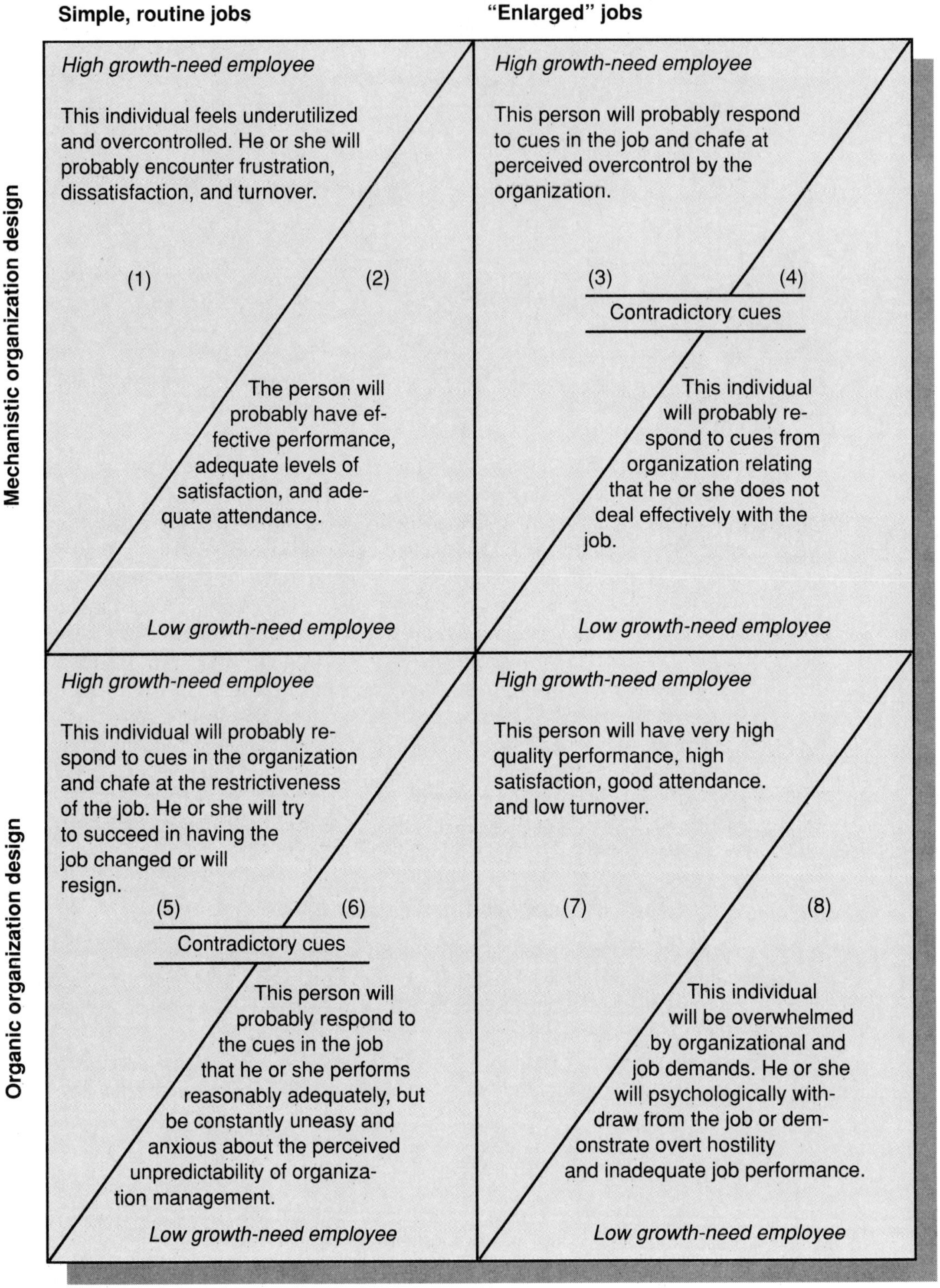

Simple, routine jobs   **"Enlarged" jobs**

High growth-need employee

This individual feels underutilized and overcontrolled. He or she will probably encounter frustration, dissatisfaction, and turnover.

(1)   (2)

The person will probably have effective performance, adequate levels of satisfaction, and adequate attendance.

Low growth-need employee

High growth-need employee

This person will probably respond to cues in the job and chafe at perceived overcontrol by the organization.

(3)   (4)
Contradictory cues

This individual will probably respond to cues from organization relating that he or she does not deal effectively with the job.

Low growth-need employee

High growth-need employee

This individual will probably respond to cues in the organization and chafe at the restrictiveness of the job. He or she will try to succeed in having the job changed or will resign.

(5)   (6)
Contradictory cues

This person will probably respond to the cues in the job that he or she performs reasonably adequately, but be constantly uneasy and anxious about the perceived unpredictability of organization management.

Low growth-need employee

High growth-need employee

This person will have very high quality performance, high satisfaction, good attendance. and low turnover.

(7)   (8)

This individual will be overwhelmed by organizational and job demands. He or she will psychologically withdraw from the job or demonstrate overt hostility and inadequate job performance.

Low growth-need employee

Mechanistic organization design (left side vertical label)

Organic organization design (left side vertical label)

FIGURE 12–5
Organizational Climate, Style, and the Employee

The most congruent cells are numbers 2 and 7. In the former are low growth-need employees performing simple, routine jobs in a mechanistic organization. In the latter are high growth-need employees working at enriched jobs in an organic design. The most incongruent cells are numbers 1 and 8. In cell 1, high growth-need employees are confronted with simple jobs and mechanistic structures, while in cell 8 low growth-need employees face enriched jobs and an organic design.

All of the other cells (3 through 6) are characterized by contradictory cues. This has led Porter, Lawler, and Hackman to postulate that in these cells the workers will respond to those cues that are consistent with their own need states and ignore those that are not.[16] Research by Zierden, however, has cast some doubt on this hypothesis.[17] While he confirmed the Porter, Lawler, and Hackman predictions for those cells involving employees with strong growth needs (cells 1, 3, 5, and 7) and found some support for cell 2 (low growth need, simple job, mechanistic design), he did not confirm their findings for those cells in which low growth-need workers faced an enriched job or an organic environment, or both (cells 4, 6, and 8). Porter and his colleagues predicted negative outcomes for these cells, but Zierden found moderate to high satisfaction among these employees. He has explained his results in terms of the level of expectation people have about their work. Low growth-need employees may have low expectations about the amount of satisfaction that can be derived from their jobs. Not expecting much, they are not overly disconcerted by the work and report general feelings of satisfaction.

Technology

Technology is an important job-design variable.

As noted in the Woodward studies, technology can affect organizational structure, and to the extent that the structure impacts on interpersonal relations and organizational climate, it is a job-design variable. Since this topic of technology has already been discussed, we shall note but one point: Job redesign is sometimes affected by technology. For example, auto assembly lines employ a special type of technology that provides little opportunity for workers to identify with the task or to secure autonomy, two key motivation factors. Thus job design can be limited by technology, and in some cases people will not end up with enriched jobs no matter what is done.

JOB CHARACTERISTICS MODEL

In recent years diagnostic tools and principles for enriching jobs have emerged. One of these tools, proposed by Hackman and Oldham, is a **job characteristics model,** which has proved very useful in redesigning individual jobs.

Nature of the Model

According to these authors, there are five **core job dimensions** (as seen in Figure 12–6) that bring about three critical psychological states and result in a number of personal and work outcomes.[18] The three psychological states are:

There are three critical psychological states.

1. Experienced meaningfulness of work: The individual has to feel that the work is important and worthwhile.

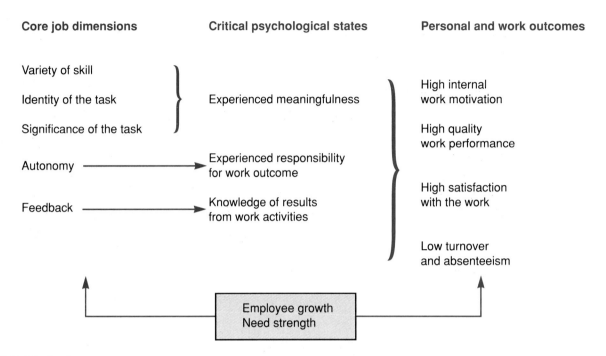

FIGURE 12–6
Job Characteristics Model of Work Motivation (Adapted from J. Richard Hickman and J. Lloyd Suttle [eds.], *Improving Life at Work: Behavioral Science Approaches to Organizational Change* [Santa Monica, CA: Goodyear Publishing Co., 1977], p. 129.)

2. Experienced responsibility for work outcome: The worker has to feel personally responsible for the work he or she performs.

3. Knowledge of results from work activities: The individual has to receive fairly regular feedback on how well he or she is doing.

When these three conditions are present, people feel good about themselves when they perform well. If these critical psychological states are not present, the individual may try harder to obtain these internal reinforcing rewards.

There are five core job dimensions.

    Of the five core job dimensions in Figure 12–6, three contribute to the experienced meaningfulness of the work:

1. Variety of skill: the degree to which the job calls for activities involving different talents and skills.

2. Identity of the task: the degree to which the job allows for completion of a whole and identifiable piece of work.

3. Significance of the task: the degree to which the job has an impact on the lives or work of other people, as in the case of an aircraft mechanic who knows that any error on his or her part can result in a serious plane crash.

The characteristic related to "experienced responsibility for work outcome" is autonomy—the degree to which the job allows the individual freedom and discretion in scheduling and carrying out the work. Finally, feedback, which fosters knowledge of results from work activities, is the degree to which job performance information is available.

Drawing on Figure 12–6, Hackman and Oldham have proposed a model for reflecting the overall potential of the job to bring about self-generated work motivation (Figure 12–7). Jobs that are high on motivating potential must be high on at least one of the "experienced meaningfulness" states, as well as on both autonomy and job feedback. The latter statement is true given the fact that autonomy and job feedback are multiplicative functions, so a near-zero score on either autonomy or job feedback will reduce the MPS to nearly zero.

The part of Figure 12–6 dealing with the strength of the employee growth need postulates that: (a) high growth-need people are more likely to experience the three psychological states when their jobs are enriched than are their low growth-need counterparts; and (b) individuals with high growth need will respond more positively to the psychological states than will their low growth-need counterparts. The personal and work outcomes part of Figure 12–6 is predicted to be positively affected by a job that is high in motivating potential.

At present, the job characteristics model is still being tested.[19] Results to date, however, are generally supportive. For example, Hackman and Oldham have reported the following:

1. People who work on jobs with high core job dimensions are more motivated, satisfied, and productive than those who do not.

2. People with strong growth needs respond more positively to jobs that are high in objective motivating potential than do those with weak growth needs.

3. As predicted by the model, job dimensions operate through the psychological states in influencing personal and work outcome variables rather than influencing them directly.[20]

Job Enrichment Principles. **Job enrichment principles** can be used in creating core job dimensions. Samples of five principles and their relation to the core job dimensions are illustrated in Figure 12–8.[21]

$$\text{Motivating potential score (MPS)} = \left(\frac{\text{Variety of skill} + \text{Identity of the task} + \text{Significance of the task}}{3} \right) \times \text{Autonomy} \times \text{Job feedback}$$

FIGURE 12–7
Computing a Motivating Potential Score

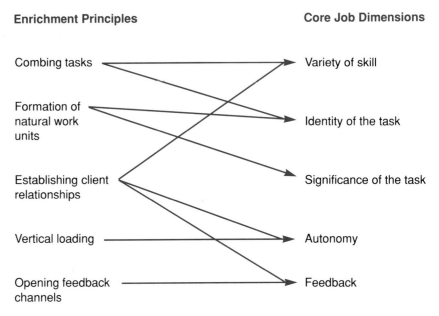

FIGURE 12–8
Job Enrichment Principles for Attaining Core Job Dimensions

Job enrichment principles
create core job dimensions.

First, where possible, tasks should be combined. For example, a person who is performing one of five tasks on a product could be assigned the job of doing all five. In this way the person's skill is increased, and there is greater task identity.

Second, natural work units should be formed. For example, instead of placing typists in a secretarial pool and assigning each work on a random basis, work ownership can be created by assigning specific departmental typing to specific secretaries. This method allows the secretaries to identify with the task and see the importance the job has on the well-being of other people (task significance).

Third, client relationships should be established. There should be contact between the worker and client whenever possible. If the worker is an engineer designing a product for the client, the two should get together to discuss progress, problems, and future direction. This type of face-to-face contact provides autonomy, feedback, and the opportunity to increase skill variety because of the necessity for developing and exercising one's interpersonal skills in maintaining the client relationship.

Fourth, vertical loading should be used if possible. **Vertical loading** gives workers greater authority for planning and controlling their work. When a job is vertically loaded, there is an inevitable increase in autonomy.

Fifth, feedback channels should be opened to provide information on how well people are doing. Some of the ways this can be done include establishing direct client relationships, giving individuals responsibility for checking their own work, and, when the latter is not possible, providing performance-related feedback to them.

STOP Review your answers to Question 3 and make any changes you would like before continuing.

3. How were the core job dimensions associated with her job changed? What types of principles were employed in this process?

One of the best ways to answer this question is by referring to Figure 12−8. Notice that Frances's new job combined a number of different tasks (typing, taking dictation, sitting in on meetings and taking notes) so there was an increase in the variety of skill, the identity of the task, and the significance of the task. Frances was also given more job autonomy. By examining the enrichment principles associated with these job dimensions (again, see Figure 12−8) it is possible to establish the linkage between the dimensions and the principles.

QUALITY OF WORK LIFE: CURRENT TRENDS

Quality of work life (QWL) programs are designed to help meet the sociotechnical problems currently facing many organizations. Bringing together the people (socio) and the machinery and equipment (technical) in a harmonious fashion can be a major challenge. Work-design techniques such as job enrichment and the use of the job characteristics model are important elements of many QWL programs.

However, some current trends do not fit directly within the areas we have been discussing but, nevertheless, do warrant consideration. One of these is quality circles. A second is the current participative management movement.

Quality Circles

Quality circles are very popular today.

Quality circles (QC) are team approaches to identifying and resolving work-related problems. The QC concept is quite simple: a group of eight to ten workers and a supervisor or team leader meet regularly to identify and solve job-related problems. The idea has gained a large following in manufacturing firms where QC groups analyze and evaluate the way the work is done and then make recommendations regarding how things can be improved.[22] Can such an approach really increase productivity? The answer is yes.

The QC concept actually began many years ago in the United States, but in the early 1960s the Japanese popularized the approach. Determined to overcome the label "made in Japan," Japanese manufacturers worked to increase the quality and reliability of their products. The auto producers, in particular, began using quality circles, and their rejection rate dropped dramatically. Today QC circles can be found in almost all Japanese manufacturing firms, from large heavy equipment producers to minicomputer firms.

In the United States many firms are also using QC teams. Most of these are in manufacturing, but the concept is also being used for handling service-related problems.

The QC idea appears easy to understand and employ. However, behavioral scientists are currently reporting some difficulties with its implementation. Klein notes that it is easy "to overestimate the ease and speed with which a quality circle program can be initiated and installed."[23] There is a need to secure the support and involvement of workers, and in many cases the union as well. These individuals may have questions or preferences regarding the new organizational job design, as well as a concern with the outcome of the program. Metz warns about the potential of quality circles becoming another fad that will then be tossed onto the organizational trash heap along with other productivity and cost improvement schemes.[24]

How can these problems be avoided? Four of the most important steps are the following:

Four steps help implement
quality circles.

1. *Assess the managerial and organizational readiness for quality circles.* The culture of the organization must support a participative managerial approach.

2. *Carry out adequate start-up and implementation planning.* The support of both the workers and the union, if there is one, must be secured. Additionally, the use of a steering committee that provides program goals and support is important. A long-run plan must be developed for tracking both the costs and the benefits of the circle.

3. *Use care in selecting a quality circle facilitator.* This individual is responsible for training the quality circle leaders, initiating new circles, attending circle meetings, counseling leaders on how to improve their skills, and keeping all levels of management apprised of what is going on. These facilitators need a high level of knowledge of interpersonal skills.

4. *Recognize the organizational development implication of quality circles.* The quality circle concept is more than just a productivity program. As a management philosophy, it reflects a trust in the workers and a commitment of resources to the growth and development of both employees and teamwork. It is a conscious decision to manage by participative principles.

As a job design concept, quality circles offer a great deal of promise.[25] The fact that so many organizations currently use them is some indication of their value. The real issue now is whether they will prove as beneficial as many hope. Griffin recently reported that over a three-year period the attitudes, behaviors, and effectiveness of the quality circles under study increased and then dropped back to previous levels.[26] Tang, Tollison, and Whiteside have found that participation at QC meetings and the size of the group can affect motivation and productivity.[27] Cole, director of the Center for Japanese Studies at the University of Michigan, reports that only about one-third of the circles in Japan are doing well.[28] So the overall value of QCs must be measured on an individual basis.

A Participative Management Movement

Another current QWL trend is a move from representative democracy to participatory democracy. Naisbitt explains it this way:

For at least the past three decades, American management consultants and behavioral scientists have been trying to push the idea [of participative management] here, to no avail. American managers thought the idea mushy and unmeasurable and felt certain it would have no impact on the almighty bottom line.

Meanwhile, U.S. productivity gains slid, high-quality imports gained a greater and greater U.S. market share, and American companies finally had to ask themselves: "What are we doing wrong?" Only at that point was the door opened for increased worker participation. This follows the established pattern for social change.[29]

There is also talk of looking more closely at the overall management system to see how it can be aligned with the needs of modern workers.[30] One of the most interesting theses, which will have a profound effect on the way management interacts with personnel, has been offered by Ouchi.[31] Noting that the Japanese have been very successful during the last decade, he postulates that part of this success is a result of their approach to managing personnel. Ouchi recommends that American firms integrate Japanese concepts into their management practices. This approach, called **Theory Z,** is offered as a means of dealing with many current organizational behavior challenges.

What makes such a theory useful? Ouchi believes the answer is found in society itself. When Americans lived in an environment in which family, church, neighborhood, voluntary organizations, and long-term friendships were common, there was a great deal of stability. Workers were able to develop ties outside of work to complement the impersonal nature of participation in the firm. As these traditional relationships were weakened by people moving to large cities and up-and-coming managers finding themselves being transferred to other parts of the country every three to five years, individuals began feeling the need for a sense of belonging. Inside the firm, they had no roots; outside the firm the situation was the same. Theory Z concepts help bring about some of the sense of belonging needed in American society.

Does Theory Z also help improve organizational efficiency and effectiveness? Ouchi reports that it does. In one case he cited, the Brookhaven Packard Division created a task force to design a sociotechnical system for the plant. Its purpose was to improve the quality of working life and effectiveness through employee involvement. The plan called for addressing areas such as work design, work responsibility, plant layout, and facility design. In line with this plan, teams of eight to twenty people were formed. Each team was responsible for all activities related to its job, including quality control, die setting, and maintenance. As the members learned to work together, the company gave each team more responsibility, including selecting of the team leader, performance evaluation, scrap control, time and absenteeism control, calculations of internal efficiencies, and job-knowledge evaluation to be used for determining pay raises. Each team was also charged with electing a representative to a plant-wide committee that dealt with broader issues than day-to-day work arrangements.

More recently, the Nissan Motor Company plant in Smyrna, Tennessee has been introducing Japanese techniques wherever it feels they are appropriate. These include minimizing the typical trappings of rank and corporate status. For example, all employees eat at one of two company cafeterias; there are no separate dining rooms for executives. The company also spent several million dollars to bring more than 375 American employees to Japan to work alongside their Japanese counterparts at Nissan factories so that they could learn how the Japanese system works.[32]

Results such as these help explain why many firms are now looking into more participative job design approaches.[33] Industrial democracy is a formal, usually legally sanctioned arrangement of worker representation at various levels of management decision making.[34] In contrast, participative management is an informal style of face-to-face leadership. The former is a structural approach to organizational and job design; the latter is a behavioral approach. The former is much more common in industrialized firms in Europe; the latter is much more common in America. Yet the two do seem to offer opportunities for a more effective quality of work life.

A majority of American managers now see themselves as institutional stewards who are seeking optimum solutions that meet the diverse interests of their organizational personnel. As a result, in the years to come it is likely that increasing attention will be paid to industrial democracy and participative management as ways to achieve such optimization.[35]

 STOP   Review your answers to Question 4 and make any changes you would like before continuing.

4. Is the company's decision to get feedback from Frances and her associates a wise one? Will this information help the firm do a better job of redesigning work? Explain.

It certainly is a wise decision. In redesigning jobs, input from the personnel is extremely important. Notice, for example, that in quality circles the workers decide the changes that should be implemented to increase output and reduce costs. This form of participative management helps to effectively pinpoint problem areas and to direct the group's effort. Employee involvement is critical in job redesign efforts for, in the final analysis, it is the workers who generally best know the way jobs should be redesigned in order to increase their intrinsic motivation and to make them more meaningful.

SUMMARY

1. Over the last decade a number of reports have been published about people in the work place. Many of these reports indicate widespread apathy, absenteeism, and even industrial sabotage among blue-collar workers and poor morale among white-collar workers. In an effort to deal with the problem, more and more organizations are beginning to examine the design of the job.

2. For purposes of analysis, all jobs can be reduced to two dimensions: job range and job depth. Job range refers to the number of operations or tasks an individual performs;

job depth relates to the amount of power an individual has to alter or influence either the job or the surrounding environment.

3. Three of the most commonly used job-design techniques are job rotation, job enlargement, and job enrichment. Job rotation moves a person from one job to another to relieve some of the boredom. Job enlargement increases the range of the job by giving the individual more to do. Job enrichment builds psychological motivators, such as increased responsibility and autonomy, into the work. Each of

these methods of job modification has both strengths and weaknesses.

4. In an effort to obtain congruence between the person and the job, recent efforts have been made toward determining conditioning factors that influence this congruence: (a) individual differences among the employees; (b) the social and interpersonal context of the job; (c) the climate and managerial style of the organization; and (d) the technology of which the work is a part. Hackman and Oldham have developed a job characteristics model that takes these factors into consideration. According to this model, variety of skill, identity of the task, significance of the task, autonomy, and feedback can result in experienced meaningfulness of the work, experienced responsibility for work outcome, and knowledge of results from work activities, resulting in high internal work motivation, high-quality work performance, high satisfaction, and low turnover and absenteeism. Research to date reveals that this model can be very helpful in helping achieve work-worker congruence.

5. One of the most popular current trends in quality of work life is quality circles, which are widely used in Japan and are gaining a strong following in the United States. The biggest problem with the QC concept appears to be implementing the program without proper planning and thought. Another QWL development is the participative management movement. Concepts such as Theory Z are being espoused as examples of how organizations can involve the personnel in greater decision making and also help them meet their needs for belonging.

KEY TERMS

job design	job enlargement	job enrichment principles
job range	job enrichment	vertical loading
job depth	job characteristics model	quality circles (QC)
job rotation	core job dimensions	Theory Z

REVIEW AND STUDY QUESTIONS

1. What is meant by the term *job design*? Put it in your own words.

2. Some of the most common job characteristics are variety, wholeness, human interaction, freedom, physical fatigue, job environment, work locale, and work time. How does each of these affect quality of life on the job?

3. "All jobs consist of two dimensions: job range and job depth." Explain this statement.

4. How can job rotation reduce boredom among the workers? What is the major drawback to its use?

5. How does job enlargement work? Why do all organizations not introduce job enlargement and thereby eliminate boring tasks?

6. How does job enrichment differ from job enlargement? What are some of the problems involved in using job enrichment? Explain.

7. What are the four conditioning factors that influence how a job is designed? Explain each.

8. In Figure 12–5, cells 3 to 6 are characterized by contradictory cues. Can job design help in resolving such contradictions? Explain.

9. Of what value is the job characteristics model to work motivation?

10. What is the logic behind the motivation potential score formula? How can this score help in job design?

11. How are the job enrichment principles related to the core job dimensions?

12. What is a quality circle? Of what value are these circles to modern organizations? Be complete in your answer.

13. Are participative management practices likely to increase in use during the next decade? Why?

14. How useful are Theory Z ideas to modern management? Explain.

CASES

A Change in Work

For the last two and a half years, Carl Wentworth has worked on an auto assembly line. In the beginning, he liked the job. There were a lot of things Carl did not know about assembly-line work and learning them proved to be fun. Additionally, he and his work team would often change jobs, so if one task became boring, he could switch to another. During the first year on the line, Carl learned how to do all of the jobs of his work group. The next year he was switched to another place on the line, and he again found himself learning new tasks. As before, he and his team rotated tasks in an effort to overcome the boredom. During these two years, Carl was neither absent nor late for work one time.

Over the past six months, however, Carl has found himself becoming bored with the work. Even when the company agreed to pay the workers a premium salary for allowing the line to be sped up to accommodate sixty cars an hour, as compared to the average of fifty cars an hour, the boredom remained. In fighting it, Carl found himself daydreaming a lot, letting himself get behind on work and then racing to keep up, and engaging in memorization activities. (During one eight-hour block, he memorized the names of all of the presidents of the United States, as well as the top ten best sellers on both the fiction and nonfiction list of national magazines.)

Despite all of these attempts to deal with his working conditions, Carl found himself disliking the work more and more. He thought that if he could tolerate the problem for a couple of months, it would go away. However, it actually intensified to the point where he mentioned it to some of the other fellows on the shift. They all expressed the same feelings, although Carl could tell that they intended to hang on for as long as it took to get their pensions. "Where else," one of them asked, "can you get the type of pay, benefit package, and retirement plan that's available here? We've got it made! Sure, working on the line is no fun. But that doesn't worry me. I wait until I leave the job to have fun." Everyone in the group agreed and thought Carl felt the same way. To their surprise, however, he tendered his resignation. When asked why he was leaving, Carl said that he had landed a job in a specialized, pattern-maker shop. The work is demanding and requires a fair amount of creativity and ingenuity, but the owner of the seven-employee operation has promised to teach Carl the business.

Upon hearing of the resignation, one of the supervisors expressed surprise. "I don't understand that guy. He's giving up a high-paying job for one that pays only about two-thirds of what he'll get here. And as far as security goes—forget it. Why, that pattern shop is going to have very little, if anything, to offer in way of a retirement plan. And when you consider the seasonality of that work and the fact that half of those guys will be out of jobs the next time we have a recession, Wentworth is giving up an awful lot for nothing. If you ask me, he's a real jerk."

1. What type of conditions was Carl working under? Using Figure 12–2 in this chapter, describe the work.

2. Why did Carl decide to leave? Explain, incorporating into your discussion the job characteristics model in Figure 12–6.

3. Evaluate the arguments of the supervisor. Do you agree or disagree with the individual's point of view? Why?

A New Design

The Jackson Company makes many different kinds of consumer products. One of these is a small hair dryer, compact enough to fit into a traveling case so that individuals can take it with them on out-of-town trips. The dryer comes in five different parts and can be easily assembled by five workers, each putting together one of the subunits. Assembly time is five minutes per dryer.

The company recently decided to change these jobs by introducing some job-design modifications. In particular, the firm believed that it could reduce assembly time and improve output by giving the workers a twelve-minute rest break after every twelve units were assembled. While output might decline initially, the company felt that this approach would eventually lead to an increase in productivity. Additionally, the firm decided to let each worker assemble an entire unit. The management hoped that this decision would result in each assembler taking greater pride in his or her work and feeling more autonomy and responsibility for the finished product; moreover, since the units did not have to be moved from assembler to assembler, it would reduce the amount of overall assembly time to under four minutes.

Three months after initiating these changes, the company reverted to the old assembly technique. The new job design program had simply not worked. Several causes were cited. First, while the workers admitted they liked the opportunity for increased autonomy and responsibility, they said they had to work harder under this new system. Second, some of the assemblers were easily able to turn out the required twelve units an hour, but others had difficulty. In fact, 20 percent of the assemblers never averaged over seven an hour; they were simply unable to master some of the more difficult parts of the assembly process. Their co-workers, realizing their dilemma, began to slow down their output, and the supervisor noticed that some workers, on occasion, would finish a unit and give it to one of the slower assemblers. When the workers heard that management was going back to the old assembly method, they expressed their approval. One of them said, "Oh, great. Now maybe we can once again concentrate on working together as a team instead of a bunch of competitors trying to outdo each other."

The first-line supervisors also thought that management's decision was a good one. However, many of them wondered why the company did not concern itself with job design problems at their level. "Just because the assemblers like things the way they are," one supervisor said, "doesn't mean we do. There's a lot management could do to improve our situation. But like in everything else, we're the group that's always forgotten."

1. When management changed the job so that each worker assembled a complete unit, was it introducing job enlargement or job enrichment? Explain.

2. In redesigning this work, which of the four conditioning factors discussed in this chapter did management fail to consider? Explain.

3. When asked about the redesign of the work, management said that it had attempted to ensure that the five core job dimensions in the job characteristics model were all taken into consideration. Why, then, did the program fail to achieve the desired results?

4. What kinds of work-related problems do supervisors have? What can management do to help them adjust to these problems? Be specific in your answer.

SELF-FEEDBACK EXERCISE

Evaluating the Motivating Potential Score of Your Own Job

Answer the questions in this self-feedback quiz based on the job you currently hold. If you are not employed, think of the last job you held. If you have never worked, think of the job you would like to get upon completion of your education. (Be realistic in your choice.)

Part I

Answer each of these statements as objectively as possible. Use the following continuum in choosing your response.

1	2	3	4	5	6	7

Very little   A moderate amount   A great deal

_____ a. How much autonomy does your job allow you in terms of deciding how to do your work?

_____ b. To what degree does your job involve doing a whole or identifiable piece of work, as opposed to a small part of an overall piece of work that is then completed by someone else?

_____ c. To what degree does your job allow you to use a variety of skills and talents, as opposed to doing the same routine over and over again?

_____ d. How important or significant is your job in terms of its effect on the lives or well-being of other people?

_____ e. To what degree does your job itself (as opposed to other workers or your boss) provide you with feedback regarding how well you are doing?

Part II

Read each of the statements below and indicate the degree to which each is an accurate or inaccurate description of your job. Use the following scale in making the description.

1 Very inaccurate   5 Slightly accurate
2 Mostly inaccurate   6 Mostly accurate
3 Slightly inaccurate   7 Very accurate
4 Uncertain

_____ 1. My job requires me to use a number of different complex or high-level skills.

_____ 2. My job is set up so that I have the opportunity to do an entire piece of work from beginning to end.

_____ 3. The work I do provides me the opportunity to determine how well I am doing.

_____ 4. My job is complex and nonrepetitive.

_____ 5. My job performance affects a lot of other people.

_____ 6. My job allows me the opportunity to use personal initiative and judgment in doing the work.

_____ 7. My job provides me the chance to completely finish the work I begin.

_____ 8. My job provides me a large amount of feedback regarding how well I am doing.

_____ 9. My job gives me considerable opportunity for both independence and freedom in carrying out the work.

_____ 10. My job is very important and/or significant in the broader scheme of things.

Go back and make sure you have answered each question or statement. Then enter your answers below in the appropriate place noting that the letters refer to your answers to Part I and the numbers refer to your answers to Part II.

A. Skill Variety   B. Task Identity   C. Task Significance

c. _____	b. _____	d. _____
1. _____	2. _____	5. _____
4. _____	7. _____	10. _____
Total _____	Total _____	Total _____

D. Autonomy   E. Feedback

a. _____	e. _____
6. _____	3. _____
9. _____	8. _____
Total _____	Total _____

The descriptions of each of the above five core job dimensions were provided in the chapter. If you are unsure of what any of them mean, go back and reread them. Now compute your motivating potential score (MPS) by first averaging the above scores by dividing each total by three. The highest total you can now have for each area is seven. Use your five averaged numbers to complete the following MPS formula:

$$MPS = \left[\frac{Skill\ Variety + Task\ Identity + Task\ Significance}{3} \right] \times (Autonomy) \times (Feedback)$$

$$MPS = \left[\frac{\_\_\_ + \_\_\_ + \_\_\_}{3} \right] \times (\quad) \times (\quad)$$

The national average MPS score for all jobs is approximately 130. How high is yours in relation to this?

Now plot your five core job dimension scores on the graph on page 333. Notice that we have placed the national average for all jobs on the graph, so you have a point of reference in determining how each of your scores compares.

NOTES

1. Jon S. Ebeling and Michael King, "Hierarchical Position in the Work Organization and Job Satisfaction: A Failure to Replicate," *Human Relations*, July 1981, pp. 567–572.

2. Barbara Garson, "Luddites in Lordstown," *Harper's*, June 1972, p. 69.

3. Ena Naunton, "Blue-Collar Work: On-the-Job Stress," *The Miami Herald*, March 14, 1977, Section C, p. 1.

4. Robert H. Guest, "Job Enlargement—A Revolution in Job Design," *Personnel Administration*, March–April 1957, pp. 13–15.

5. Raymond F. Pelissier, "Successful Experience with Job Design," *Personnel Administration*, March–April 1965, pp. 12–16.

6. M. D. Kilbridge, "Do Workers Prefer Larger Jobs?" *Personnel*, September–October 1960, pp. 45–48.

7. *Ibid.*

8. William E. Reif and Peter P. Schoderbek, "Job Enlargement: Antidote to Apathy," *Management of Personnel Quarterly*, Spring 1966, pp. 16–23.

9. Steve Lohr, "Making Cars the Volvo Way," *New York Times*, June 23, 1987, pp. 29, 33.

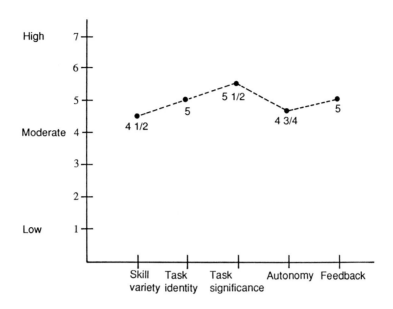

10. Antone F. Alber, "The Real Cost of Job Enrichment," *Business Horizons,* February 1979, pp. 60–72.

11. Robert N. Ford, "Job Enrichment Lessons From AT&T," *Harvard Business Review,* January–February 1973, p. 106.

12. William E. Reif, David N. Ferrazi, and Robert J. Evans, Jr., "Job Enrichment: Who Uses It and Why," *Business Horizons,* February 1974, p. 76.

13. Antone Alber and Melvin Blumberg, "Team vs. Individual Approaches to Job Enrichment Programs," *Personnel,* January–February 1981, p. 74.

14. J. Richard Hackman, "Work Design," in J. Richard Hackman and J. Lloyd Suttle (eds.), *Improving Life at Work: Behavioral Science Approaches to Organizational Change* (Santa Monica, CA: Goodyear Publishing Co., 1977), p. 115.

15. *Ibid.,* p. 119.

16. Lyman W. Porter, Edward E. Lawler III, and J. Richard Hackman, *Behavior in Organizations* (New York: McGraw-Hill Book Co., 1975), p. 310.

17. W. E. Zierden, "The Person, the Manager, the Job: Interactive Effects on Job-Related Satisfaction," Ph.D. dissertation, Yale Univ., 1975.

18. J. Richard Hackman and Greg R. Oldham, "Development of the Job Diagnostic Survey," *Journal of Applied Psychology,* April 1975, p. 162.

19. Moses N. Kiggundu, "An Empirical Test of the Theory of Job Design Using Multiple Job Ratings," *Human Relations,* May 1980, pp. 339–351; and Karlene H. Roberts and William Glick, "The Job Characteristics Approach to Task Design: A Critical Review," *Journal of Applied Psychology,* April 1981, pp. 193–217.

20. Hackman, "Work Design," pp. 132–133.

21. For more on this subject see John W. Slocum, Jr. and Henry P. Sims, Jr., "A Typology for Integrating Technology Organization and Job Design," *Human Relations,* March 1980, pp. 192–212.

22. Larry R. Smeltzer and Ben L. Kedia, "Training Needs of Quality Circles," *Personnel,* August 1987, pp. 51–55.

23. Gerald D. Klein, "Implementing Quality Circles: A Hard Look At Some of the Realities," *Personnel,* November–December 1981, p. 15.

24. Edmund J. Metz, "Caution: Quality Circles Ahead," *Training and Development Journal,* August 1981, p. 72.

25. Murray R. Barrick and Ralph A. Alexander, "A Review of Quality Circle Efficacy and the Existence of Positive Findings Bias," *Personnel Psychology,* Autumn 1987, pp. 579–592.

26. Ricky W. Griffin, "Consequences of Quality Circles in an Industrial Setting: A Longitudinal Assessment," *Academy of Management Journal,* June 1988, pp. 338–358.

27. Thomas Li-Ping Tang, Peggy Smith Tollison, and Harold D. Whiteside, "The Effect of Quality Circle Initiation on Motivation to Attend Quality Circle Meetings and on Task Performance," *Personnel Psychology,* Winter 1987, pp. 799–814.

28. Metz, "Caution," p. 72.

29. John Naisbitt, *Megatrends: Ten New Directions Transforming Our Lives* (New York: Warner Books, 1982), pp. 181–182.

30. See Newton Margulies and Stewart Black, "Perspectives on the Implementation of Participative Approaches," *Human Resource Management,* Fall 1987, pp. 385–412; Don Nichols, "Taking Participative Management to the Limit," *Management Review,* August 1987, pp. 28–32; and James W. Thacker and Mitchell W. Fields, "Union Involvement in Quality-of-Worklife Efforts: A Longitudinal Investigation," *Personnel Psychology,* Spring 1987, pp. 97–111.

31. William Ouchi, *Theory Z: How American Business Can Meet the Japanese Challenge* (Reading, MA: Addison-Wesley Publishing Co., 1981).

32. Steve Lohr, "Nissan Uses Japan's Ways in Tennessee," *New York Times,* April 4, 1983, p. 27.

33. Manuel London and John Paul MacDuffie, "Technological Innovations: Case Examples and Guidelines," *Personnel,* November 1987, pp. 26–38; Charles C. Manz and Henry P. Sims, Jr., "Leading Workers to Lead Themselves: The External Leadership of Self-Managing Work Teams," *Administrative Science Quarterly,* March 1987, pp. 106–128; Lori Henry, "Reorganization at McCormack & Dodge: Getting Everybody into the Act," *Personnel,* November 1987, pp. 48–52; and Ron Zemke, "Scandinavian Management—A Look at our Future?" *Management Review,* July 1988, pp. 44–47.

34. Bernard M. Bass and V. J. Shackleton, "Industrial Democracy and Participative Management: A Case for a Synthesis," *Academy of Management Review,* October 1979, p. 393.

35. Also see Jan P. Muczyk and Bernard C. Reimann, "Has Participative Management Been Oversold?" *Personnel,* May 1987, pp. 52–56.

CHAPTER 13
Stress and Work

GOALS OF THE CHAPTER

In recent years, there has been an increasing interest in studying how stress and work are related and the ways to moderate the negative effects of excessive stress. The first goal of this chapter is to examine the nature of stress. The second goal is to study those factors that cause stress. The third is to examine the effects of stress and explain why some people are more affected by it than are others. The fourth is to review the way in which individuals and organizations can manage employee stress.

When you have read all of the material in this chapter, you will be able to:

1. define the term *stress* and explain how stress works;
2. identify specific factors that cause stress, including individual, group, organizational, and extraorganizational stressors;
3. discuss the effects of stress and relate why stress has a greater impact on some individuals than on others;
4. explain how stress can be managed.

OPENING CASE: SHE'S HANGING IN THERE

Until six months ago June Grady's firm had been producing two major product lines: consumer goods and high tech goods. At that time the company decided to phase out its consumer goods line and focus exclusively on high tech products. "This is where the greatest profit is," the president said, "and it's where our best growth potential rests. So we're going to change our product emphasis and go high tech all the way."

Since then June, a regional manager, has found herself working thirteen to fourteen hours a day, six days a week. There are a number of reasons for these long hours. One is that a large number of regional managers and salespeople who used to sell consumer goods have quit. As a result, June is now coordinating the sales activities for two regions and is having to spend much more time in the field. A second reason is that those salespeople who have not sold high tech equipment are being brought back to the home office for retraining, and those in the field must increase their efforts.

Over the past three months June has been consistently late in filing her regional sales reports. She is also quite concerned over the fact that she needs to be trained in high tech selling because she has always been on the consumer goods side. June's energy level has been slipping, and she has been taking sleeping pills, something she has never done before, in order to overcome a recent case of insomnia.

Despite all the changes she is encountering, June intends to maintain her current pace. As she explained to a friend, "Our basic product composition is being changed, and we are going through adjustment pains. But everything will work out. We just have to hang in there."

1. Is June underloaded or overloaded? Explain.
2. What stressors are causing problems for June?
3. What are some of the effects of stress on June?
4. Is June a Type A or Type B personality?
5. What can June do to deal with her stress? What can the organization do to help?

Write down your answers to these questions and put them aside. We will return to them later.

THE NATURE OF STRESS

Stress refers to feelings of pressure, anxiety, and tension.

Stress can be defined in many different ways.[1] In general terms, **stress** refers to feelings of pressure, anxiety, and tension. Stress and work are organizational behavior considerations because *excessive* stress can result in work-related problems. Additionally, stress is found not only among managerial and professional personnel but among blue-collar workers as well.[2]

How Stress Works

Organizational stress consists of four factors.

Organizational stress consists of four factors: stressors, stress, outcomes, and consequences. **Stressors** are environmental factors that bring about stress. Common examples include the physical environment (light, noise, and temperature), individual-level stressors (role ambiguity, work overload, and responsibility for other people), group-level stressors (lack of group cohesiveness, intragroup conflict, and intergroup conflict), organizational-level stressors (organizational culture and structure), and extra-organizational-level stressors (family relations, financial problems, and relocation problems).

When one or more of these factors is present, job-related stress can result. The seriousness of the stress is often dictated by the individual. Some people can tolerate a lot of stress; others can tolerate very little. Some people thrive on hard work; others are severely burdened by it.[3] Some have excellent health and low blood pressure; others have poor health and high blood pressure.

Stress can lead to various outcomes. Physiologically, it can bring about a faster heart beat, higher blood pressure, sweaty palms, rapid breathing, and dilation of the pupils of the eyes. Behaviorally, it can affect absenteeism, turnover, productivity, job satisfaction, and career goals. In the case of excessive stress, the consequences can be many and varied. Typical examples include coronary heart disease, headaches, apathy, nervous exhaustion, and ulcers.

Stress and Behavior

Underloading can lead to boredom.

On the positive side, some degree of stress is good. Figure 13–1 illustrates this point. Notice that if stress is too low, it is possible for a person to be **underloaded**. When this occurs, the individual is often bored, irritable, and lethargic. It is also common to find the person expressing a negative attitude toward the job and frequently being absent. Productivity also tends to be low when a person is underloaded.

As stress is increased into the optimal stress level (again, see Figure 13–1) productivity goes up. Notice that under this condition, the worker tends to be more motivated and mentally alert and have a higher level of energy than the underloaded employee.

Overloading can be stressful.

There are a number of signs of overloading.

If the degree of stress increases further, however, the degree of productivity will decline. Once there is too much pressure on the person, the individual will begin showing signs of being **overloaded**. These signs include:

Working late, or more obsessively than usual, or harder than seems appropriate to the situation.

Difficulty making decisions, large and small, that the person would normally make easily.

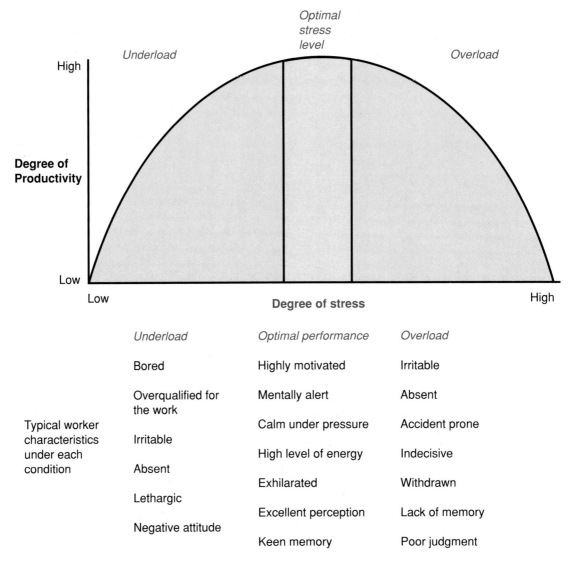

FIGURE 13-1
The Underload–Overload Continuum

Excessive daydreaming or fantasizing, always wishing he or she were elsewhere.
Sudden increase in drinking or smoking habits.
Use of antidepressants, tranquilizers, or mind-altering drugs.
Excessive worrying, especially over relative trivia (or extreme casualness and unconcern in the face of real problems).[4]

Another area that has become a focal point of attention among behaviorists studying stress is that of **workaholism**. Workaholics are people who never stop working.

They often place themselves under stress because they enjoy it, and managers some-times fail to realize the problems these people have because: (a) they have never seen these workers behave in any other way, thus their day-to-day habits look perfectly normal; and (b) workaholics are often willing to volunteer for just about any assign-ments, so changing their behavior could be detrimental to departmental output. Yet, workaholics merit consideration because of the potential they have for becoming over-loaded. Are you a potential workaholic? Take the workaholic quiz and judge for yourself.[5]

Are You a Workaholic?

A workaholic is a person who is compulsively overcommitted to work. The individual works all of the time, never seems to slow down, has a merciless schedule of things to do, and seems to greatly enjoy this pace of events. While it is difficult to say exactly where the dividing line is between a hard worker and a workaholic, the following ten questions provide some guidance. Answer each with a yes or a no.

	Yes	No
1. Do you get up early in the morning, no matter how late you went to bed the night before?	_____	_____
2. If you are eating alone, do you usually bring along something to read or work on while you dine?	_____	_____
3. Do you make a list of things to do each day?	_____	_____
4. Do you find it difficult to just do nothing?	_____	_____
5. Are you an energetic and competitive person?	_____	_____
6. Do you like to work on weekends and holidays?	_____	_____
7. Do you find that you can work anywhere, anytime, under just about any conditions?	_____	_____
8. Do you find it hard to take vacations of more than just a few days?	_____	_____
9. Do you think when you reach retirement age you will begin to dread having to give up work?	_____	_____
10. Do you really enjoy your work?	_____	_____

If you answered yes to eight or more of these questions, you are a potential workaholic.

STOP

Review your answer to Question 1 and make any changes you would like.

1. Is June underloaded or overloaded? Explain.

June is overloaded. Her long hours and increased responsibility are beginning to wear her down. Additionally, notice that she is beginning to be late with her reports and is beginning to feel the effects of stress. In Figure 13–1, June would be on the right-hand side.

SPECIFIC STRESSORS

Stressors can be divided into five categories: the physical environment, individual stressors, group stressors, organizational stressors, and extraorganizational stressors. The following subsections examine each.

Physical Environment

Physical environment stressors can be found everywhere. Common examples include light, noise, temperature, and vibration. Sometimes they are referred to as blue-collar stressors because they tend to be concentrated more in blue-collar occupations than in any others.

Improper lighting can make a task more difficult to perform. Noise can impair hearing, and deafness may result. Temperature is a stressor when the work environment is either too hot or too cold. Heat stress in the form of extreme heat can bring about increased blood flow and heart rate, higher oxygen demands, and fatigue. Extreme cold can affect work quality and bring about decreased levels of energy and motivation. Vibration, as caused by pneumatic drills or transportation vehicles, can blur one's vision, cause headaches, lead to muscle tension, and even affect physical balance.

Individual Stressors

There are many forms of individual stressors. Some of the most common include role ambiguity, role conflict, and work overload.

Role ambiguity occurs when individuals are unclear about their job role, objectives, or responsibilities. Ambiguity has been linked to depressed moods, lowered self-esteem, decreased life satisfaction (in addition to decreased job satisfaction), lower levels of work motivation, and expressed intention to leave the job. Research has also linked ambiguity to anxiety, depression, and feelings of resentment.[6]

Role conflict results when individuals are given two or more roles that are in conflict with one another. A supervisor who is told to keep the pressure on workers for increased output and also to try to employ a more democratic approach to leadership is likely to be caught in a quandary. It may seem to the individual that one cannot keep the pressure on and be democratic at the same time.

Work overload is both a quantitative and qualitative factor. Quantitatively it takes such forms as bringing work home at night, being responsible for a large number of projects, or simply having more work to do in a single day than is possible. Qualitatively it takes such forms as believing that work demands are unreasonable, perceiving assigned tasks as too complex, or feeling that one's training or experience are insufficient to properly discharge the duties of the job.

Group Stressors

Group stressors take numerous forms. Four of the most common are lack of group cohesiveness, inadequate group support, intragroup conflict, and intergroup conflict.

Group cohesiveness is the tendency of group members to stick together. Individuals who are not part of a close-knit team or whose work group has no status or prestige often suffer lack of cohesiveness. So do those individuals whose work groups are disorganized or place too much pressure on the individual.

Group conflict is stressful.

Inadequate group support is common among disorganized groups, those that lack direction, and those that offer no protection from unfair managerial work demands. Individuals need the support and understanding of their peers. When it is not forthcoming, stress often results.

Intragroup and intergroup conflict come about when there is misunderstanding or friction within or between groups. Intragroup conflict is related to low job satisfaction, high job stress, and high likelihood of employee termination.[7] This problem can affect both managers and subordinates. Intergroup conflict creates the biggest problem when two or more groups in conflict are required to coordinate their efforts in getting things done. This outcome is usually most stressful for managers.

Organizational Stressors

Organizational stressors are more encompassing than individual or group stressors. They are associated with the *overall* perspective of work. Some of the most common organizational stressors are organizational climate and organizational structure.

Organizational climate is the atmosphere or character of the organization.

Organizational climate is the atmosphere or character of the organization. This climate is often measured by asking questions such as: How much confidence and trust do you feel in the organization? Is this enterprise a good place in which to work? Do you feel that this company is concerned with your welfare? Organizations tend to have different types of climates, depending on their objectives and work patterns.

> An organization's climate may be conducive to a relaxed style of working, or it may generate a high-charged, crisis-oriented style. And the climate can affect people differently. One study has measured organizational climate through properties such as intimacy, production orientation, esprit, and aloofness. Nurses, hospital administrators, and diagnostic personnel were asked to record their perceptions of . . . climate properties and need satisfaction. The results indicated that nurses associated need satisfaction with a climate high in esprit, while administrators reported satisfaction in a climate high in consideration.[8]

Structural design can cause tension.

Organizational structures are of many different shapes and configurations. Some enterprises use narrow spans of control and are very bureaucratic in their approach; others employ wide spans of control and are heavily decentralized. These designs influence the way things are done, and this can prove stressful. For example, a high-achieving person who likes a lot of autonomy will feel a great deal of stress in a bureaucratic organization. Conversely, a low risk taker who enjoys rules and regulations will feel out of place in a heavily decentralized structure.

Extraorganizational Stressors

Extraorganizational stressors are actions, situations, or events outside of the organization that prove stressful to individuals. Three of the most important are family, financial problems, and relocation.

Many people find that family problems cannot be left at home. They continue to occupy the individual's time at work and can result in changes in job performance. For example, a person who learns that his daughter must have an operation to correct an eye problem may find that his thoughts continue to wander back to this problem, even while the boss is telling him about a new project that requires his assistance. The individual is worried about his child.

A second extraorganizational stressor is financial problems. When the economy turns down or when unexpected expenses occur, the average person's work performance tends to suffer. Many people believe that this stressor affects only those in the lower- and middle-income levels, but even high-paid executives find themselves worrying about financial problems. The family that sends its children to a private school, belongs to the country club, eats out often, and takes several yearly vacations to exclusive resort areas often has to exercise as much budgetary constraint as does a family that earns far less money. From a stress standpoint, many working people find financial concerns to be a constant problem.

A third extraorganizational stressor is relocation of the family. Moving to another part of the city or to another location across the country can be extremely stressful. New friends have to be made; new schools have to be located for the children; a new doctor, dentist, lawyer, accountant, and so on have to be found. All of this takes a physical and psychological toll.

Life Events

Life events cause degrees of stress.

When these stressors—individual, group, and extraorganizational—are evaluated, it becomes obvious that stress is a result of both job-related and home-related factors. Sometimes these are collectively referred to as **life events**: experiences that have occurred to the individual over the last six to twelve months. Some of these are minor or have only short-term impact; others are more serious.

In examining stressors from the standpoint of severity, Holmes and Rahe studied the impact of major life changes on over 5,000 patients who were suffering from stress-related illnesses. On the basis of their research, they developed a series of life events and assigned a numerical value to each. In research to validate this social readjustment rating scale, they found that 80 percent of those with high scores and 53 percent of those with medium-range scores suffered from some form of stress-related illness. On the other hand, less than a third of those with low scores suffered from stress-related illnesses.[9] Life-event scales have been constructed for specific groups. The chart on the right is designed to address stress among college students.

STOP

Review your answer to Question 2 and make any changes you would like.

2. What stressors are causing problems for June?

There are a number of stressors that are causing problems for June. One is work overload in terms of both quantity and quality. A second is responsibility for others. A third is that expected behaviors, actions, and values are being altered to reflect the focus on high tech. A fourth is the life events that are beginning to come into play. A brief review of the Holmes-Rahe Social Adjustment Scale illustrates this.

EFFECTS OF STRESS

Stress is an important organizational behavior topic because its effects can be work-related. Three of the most common results of excessive or prolonged stress are physical disorders, alcoholism, and burnout. The following subsections examine each.

Read each of the following life events and check those that have happened to you during the last twelve months. Then total all of the points associated with the events you checked off. A score of 150 puts you in the group that has a 50–50 chance of suffering an adverse health change.

Life Event	Points
1. Death of spouse	100
2. Unwed pregnancy	92
3. Death of parent	80
4. Father in unwed pregnancy	77
5. Divorce	73
6. Death of close relative	65
7. Death of close friend	65
8. Parents' divorce	63
9. Jail term	61
10. Major injury or illness	60
11. Flunking out	58
12. Marriage	55
13. Loss of job	50
14. Loss of financial aid	48
15. Failing important course	47
16. Sexual difficulties	45
17. Argument with partner	40
18. Academic probation	39
19. Change in major	37
20. New love interest	36
21. Increased workload	31
22. Outstanding achievement	29
23. First semester	28
24. Conflict with instructor	27
25. Lower grades than expected	25
26. College transfer	24
27. Change in social activities	22
28. Change in sleeping habits	21
29. Change in eating habits	19
30. Minor violations of law	15

Source: Reported in The New York Times, August 24, 1989, p. 20.

Physical Disorders

CHD can be stress-related.

Stress can bring about many types of physical disorders. For example, some executives have ulcers because of job tensions. Other common stress-related physical disorders include strokes, diabetes, and headaches. Yet the most commonly cited is coronary heart disease (CHD). The U.S. Public Health Service reports that of all deaths in the 25 to 34 age category, 10 percent are the result of heart disease. For those in the 35 to 44 age category, this percentage rises to 30 percent. Death due to heart disease increases to 38 percent for those in the 45 to 54 age group and 47 percent for those in the 55 to 64 age category.[10] Clearly, CHD is not a disease confined to the very old. Working people, those most likely to be under stress, also suffer greatly from its effects. In fact, "At current incident rates, one out of five American men will have a heart attack *before* he retires."[11]

Alcoholism

Alcoholics are often highly stressed.

Many people drink as a means of reducing stress. In moderation, alcohol can serve as a mild tranquilizer. Unfortunately, for some the stresses of the job are so great that alcohol becomes a crutch on which they depend every day. How closely linked are stress and alcoholism? Williams, Calhoun, and Ackoff conducted a study of alcoholics and nonalcoholics drawn from the same geographic region of the country and found the former to have far greater levels of tension and anxiety than the latter. Some of their findings include:

1. More alcoholics tended to respond anxiously to the failure to meet expectations by themselves or by others than did nonalcoholics.
2. The peak levels of anxiety provoked by unmet expectations generally lasted longer for alcoholics than for nonalcoholics.
3. Alcoholics differed most consistently from nonalcoholics on the basis of the reported "normal" levels of anxiety in response to unmet expectations. At work, the percentages reporting strong or very strong anxiety reactions were: all alcoholics, 66%, nonalcoholics, 21%.[12]

The cost of problem drinking has given rise to a growing number of company programs designed to curb alcoholism. The National Council of Alcoholism believes that such programs are the most promising means of treatment. Many businesses agree. In 1970, there were approximately 300 in-company alcohol problems throughout the United States. By 1975, this number was over 600. Today it is approaching 1,000. Realizing that many business people fall into the trap of alcoholism while carrying out job-related activities such as entertaining clients or trying to pass the time while cooped up in hotel rooms while on road trips, many firms have programs designed to help managers identify those who seem to have drinking problems and to encourage them to willingly submit to treatment.

Burnout

Burnout results in emotional or physical exhaustion.

Burnout is a response to chronic stress that results in emotional or physical exhaustion, or both.[13] Table 13–1 provides a contrast of stress and burnout. Notice that there is a very big difference between the two.

TABLE 13–1
Stress versus Burnout

Stress	Burnout
The person feels fatigued.	→ The individual encounters chronic exhaustion.
The person is anxious.	→ The individual is hypertensive.
The person is dissatisfied with his or her job.	→ The individual is bored and cynical about the work.
The person's job commitment has dropped off.	→ The individual's job commitment is virtually nil; he or she is mentally detached from the organization.
The person feels moody.	→ The individual feels impatient, irritable, and unwilling to talk to others.
The person feels guilty.	→ The individual encounters mental depression.
The person is having difficulty concentrating; he or she tends to forget things.	→ The individual does not seem to know where he or she is; forgetfulness is becoming more and more frequent.
The person undergoes physiological changes such as increased blood pressure and heart beat.	→ The individual begins to voice psychosomatic complaints.

Of course, not all people are equally vulnerable to burnout and not all jobs are high-stress ones. The National Institute for Occupational Safety and Health offers the following contrast:[14]

Examples of Some High-Stress Jobs	Examples of Some Low-Stress Jobs
Managers	Farm laborers
Secretaries	Maids
Clinical lab technicians	Craft workers
Waitresses and waiters	Stock handlers
Inspectors	Heavy equipment operators
Foremen on assembly lines	College professors

It is also important to realize that not all high-stress jobs create burnout. Executives who are able to deal with a high degree of stress have no burnout problems. Conversely, low-level employees who are unable to tolerate any degree of stress can burn out doing menial jobs. Another interesting fact is that stress does not appear to be greatest at the top. It tends to peak at the upper-middle to lower-upper management positions. Those at the top often surround themselves with individuals who are charged with filtering out information overload or reformatting it so that the top manager can deal with it quickly and easily. When this happens, the assistants to the executive and the members of the immediate line staff are often the ones under the greatest stress (see Figure 13–2). Finally, it should be noted that burnout, just like stress, is *self-*

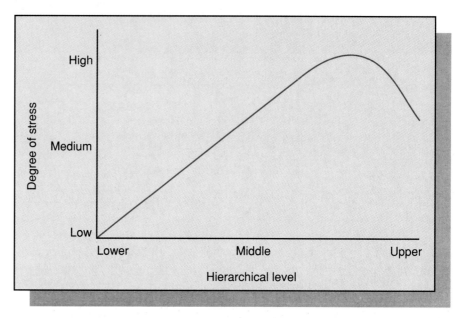

FIGURE 13–2
Stress and Hierarchical Level

generated. Thus, even the hierarchical level is not the best indicator of who will suffer burnout. Rather, it is the internal psychological makeup of the person that must be examined.

In looking at the topic of stress and work, it is necessary to consider these individual differences. The following section addresses this topic.

Review your answer to Question 3 and make any changes you would like.

3. What are some of the effects of stress on June?

There are a number of effects of stress on June. One is the physical exhaustion which is beginning to wear her down. A second is her use of medication to help her sleep. A third is her tardiness in submitting reports.

INDIVIDUAL DIFFERENCES

Why are some people more affected by stress than others? Some of the specific reasons can be traced to demographic differences and cognitive affective differences.

Demographic Differences

Demographics is the study of the characteristics of human populations including age and physical health. When extended to include behavior, it encompasses such factors as education and occupation. These characteristics or factors differ from person to person.

Age affects stress because most people go through life stages during which certain things are expected of them. When a child is three years old, little is expected of the person. At thirteen, the child is expected to do many things personally (get dressed, keep his or her room clean, have homework done on time). At twenty-three, many people are entering their first career stage in which they are expected to perform well and keep their noses to the grindstone. At thirty-three, many are already in middle management positions and hoping to move up even further. The pressure is now beginning to increase since there are fewer places in the top ranks than there are in the middle. At forty-three, some individuals are in upper middle management. As seen in Figure 13–2, the pressure is now even greater. If the person makes it into the top ranks, this stress may begin to abate. If the person is sidetracked along the way and can learn to live with it, the pressure slackens even earlier. Yet, regardless of one's career path, age does help create stress.

Another important individual stress factor is health. Some doctors claim that life longevity depends heavily on heredity. Coupled with heredity is the overall state of the individual's health. Some people are always in good physical health, while others always seem to feel poorly. Some are seldom sick, while others seem to have more than their share of illnesses. Research shows that healthy people tend to be better able to cope with stress than are their more sickly counterparts.[15]

Education impacts on stress in two ways. On the negative side, when an individual has not attained a certain educational level that has been attained by everyone else holding a similar job, the person may feel "unworthy" to be in that particular position. This can cause stress. On the positive side, however, education can help people moderate or control the negative effects of stressors.[16]

Another important factor is occupation. In every occupation, we find different types of stressors with which people working there must cope. Consider the field of accounting. What kinds of stress do accountants experience? Strawser, Kelly, and Hise studied a random sample of accountants, all of whom were members of the American Institute of CPAs, using a number of personal and job-related variables including age, educational level, annual income, sex, marital status, job experience, and management level. Table 13–2 reports their findings in terms of specific stressors. They also found that the older and the higher up the organization the individual was, the greater the amount of stress.[17]

Cognitive Affective Differences

Cognitive affective differences are psychological in nature. They deal with factors such as need satisfaction, locus of control, and type of personality.

Some people are driven very hard to attain certain types of need satisfaction. Consider the overachiever. This individual has a very strong need to excel, to surpass others, and to be the best (or one of the best) in a particular area. This need for self-actualization can be the basis for overwork and burnout.

TABLE 13–2
Factors That Cause Stress among Accountants

Factor	Ranking*
Feeling that you may not be liked and accepted by the people with whom you work	3.75
Feeling that you have to do things on the job that are against your better judgment	3.72
Not knowing just what the people you work with expect of you	3.67
Being unclear on just what the scope and responsibilities of your job are	3.59
Thinking that you will not be able to satisfy the conflicting demands of various people above you in the organization	3.57
The fact that you cannot get information needed to carry out your job	3.55
Feeling unable to influence your immediate superior's decisions and actions that affect you	3.53
Not knowing what your superior thinks of you, and how he or she evaluates your performance	3.49
Not knowing what opportunities for advancement or promotion exist for you	3.46
Feeling that you have too little authority to carry out the responsibilities assigned to you	3.42
Feeling that your job tends to interfere with your family life	3.40
Feeling that you have too heavy a work load, one that you cannot possibly finish during an ordinary work day	3.27
Having to decide things that affect the lives of individuals, people that you know	3.25
Thinking that the amount of work you have to do may interfere with how well it gets done	3.25
Feeling that you are not fully qualified to handle your job	1.76
Average for all 15 items	3.50

*Based on the following scoring key; 1 = never; 2 = rarely; 3 = sometimes; 4 = rather often; 5 = nearly all the time. Answers are an average of all respondent replies.

Source: Robert H. Strawser, J. Patrick Kelly, and Richard T. Hise, "What Causes Stress for Management Accountants?" Reprinted from Management Accounting, March 1982, p. 330. Copyright 1982 by National Association of Accountants, Montvale, NJ 07654.

Lack of control can affect stress.

Another cognitive affective difference is locus of control, a person's perception of the extent to which he or she is able to control the surrounding world. The greater an individual's perception of control or mastery over the environment, the less the amount of stress the person generally feels, and vice versa. Managers who give their people autonomy and allow them the personal freedom to make decisions and set their own pace often have subordinates with less stress.

Type A personalities are agressive and hard driving.

A third cognitive affective difference is personality type. In terms of stress, there are two basic types of people: Type A personality and Type B personality.[18] The Type A personality is of most interest to those studying the effects of stress. **Type A personalities** are continually involved in a chronic, incessant struggle to get more and more done in less and less time. They tend to be high achieving and have a high need for power.[19] In the process, they tend to produce a type of psychological and physical havoc that is not found in their Type B counterparts, who are more patient and easier-going. The latter may be just as interested in attaining goals, but they go about it in a different way.

Type A behavior can cause CHD.

A number of research studies have been conducted on Type A personalities. One of these, the Western Collaborative Group Study, evaluated over 3,000 male employees from eleven different companies. For eight to nine years, these individuals, ranging in age from thirty-nine to fifty-nine and free of coronary disease at the start of the study, were evaluated for Type A behavior.[20] By the end of the study, it was found that twice as many Type A men had coronary disease than did Type B men. Does this mean that executives with Type A personalities will become victims of heart attacks? The relationship between stress and coronary problems is not that clear because so many variables are involved. Moreover, some recent research has found that Type A people are much more likely to survive a heart attack than are their Type B counterparts. One major reason appears to be that Type A people are better at changing their diets and adhering more closely to their doctor's orders.[21] Thus, when it comes to heart disease, the proper lifestyle for one person may be disastrous for another.

STOP

Review your answer to Question 4 and make any changes you would like.

4. Is June a Type A or Type B personality?

June is a Type A personality. There are a number of facts in the case that support this conclusion. One is June's hard-driving nature. Notice from the information at the end of the case that she intends to hang in and keep working hard. A second is that she is a high achiever, and many Type A personalities are. A third is that she continually tries to get more and more done in the work day. She is time-driven, which is a typical characteristic of a Type A.

MANAGING STRESS

In recent years, a great deal of attention has been directed to ways of managing stress. The focus has been both on what an individual can do and what the organization can do to help the individual.[22] As seen in Table 13–3, there are many different strategies that can be used in coping with stress, from physical (diet, rest, and exercise) to psychological (psychoanalysis, development of a stress plan, and the use of meditation). Four of the major and *complementary* approaches that are quite popular today are diet,

TABLE 13–3
Strategies Designed to Cope with Stress

Physical maintenance strategies:
  Paying attention to diet and nutrition.
  Getting required amounts of sleep.
  Exercising.
  Participating in leisure and recreational activities.

Internal assistance strategies:
  Using relaxation response.
  Using biofeedback.
  Using autogenic training.
  Using meditation.

Personal organizational strategies:
  Developing a stress plan.
  Delegating responsibility.
  Choosing or altering the work environment.
  Engaging in creative problem solving and decision making.
  Setting goals.
  Managing time.
  Managing conflict.
  Restructuring jobs.
  Using self-assessment measures.

Outside assistance strategies:
  Using psychoanalysis.
  Using stress counseling.
  Participating in development programs.
  Using behavior-change techniques.

Stress-directed strategies:
  Engaging in systematic desensitization.
  Using dynamic psychotherapy.

Situational and support group strategies:
  Using assertiveness training and role playing.
  Developing supportive relationships.

Negative strategies:
  Avoiding substance abuse.

Source: Heather R. Sailer, John Schlacter, and Mark R. Edwards, "Stress: Causes, Consequences and Coping Strategies." Reprinted, by permission of publisher, from *Personnel,* July–August 1982, p. 48. © 1982 American Management Association, New York. All rights reserved.

physical fitness, mental relaxation, and organizational approaches. The following subsections examine each.

Diet

Diet is important.

Many experts in the area of stress believe that "you are what you eat." Food, nutrition, and general diet can help reduce stress and keep one in generally good health. The number of diets that have been popular in recent years, such as the Pritikin Diet, the Beverly Hills Diet, and so on, all bear witness to the fact that people are concerned with what they eat.

Most doctors agree that the average American eats too much salt, sugar, red meat, eggs, and butter. They recommend more consumption of fruit, vegetables, juices, water, dairy products made from skimmed milk, foul, fish, whole grain breads, and decaffeinated beverages. Does this really help? Pritikin claims that those who follow his diet, which is similar to the one noted above, do indeed have better health.

On the other hand, there are many who dispute the claim that the results are tied directly to diet. For example, noting that Pritikin patients are on a strict dietary regimen that includes daily exercise, lectures and seminars related to health, and continual medical exams, his critics ask how much these other factors contributed to the patient's improvement. Most experts believe that in addition to diet, physical fitness and psychological factors are also important.

Physical Fitness

Today there are hundreds of companies that offer their personnel some form of physical-fitness program. Examples include Xerox, Rockwell International, McDonald's, Pepsi Cola, and Kimberly Clark.

Exercise is important.

The initial impetus in establishing these programs typically comes from a high ranking corporate proponent of physical fitness. With this person behind the program, resources are allocated, programs are developed, and the staff are encouraged to participate.

How physically fit are most employees? Kreitner and his associates conducted a study whose results are undoubtedly typical for many firms. Over 600 participants in a multinational electronics subsidiary completed a questionnaire providing general health-related background information. They then took a physical exam. The results showed that while the average person saw himself or herself as physically fit and in good health, from the standpoint of objective coronary risk, the individual was in unsatisfactory shape.[23] One of the primary reasons was because most of them engaged in no regular physical exercise. Fortunately, many firms are now beginning to address this problem by offering personally designed exercise programs.[24]

Mental Relaxation

Mental relaxation consists of physical and psychological techniques that are used to help people slow down. They are particularly popular with business executives who find themselves continuously on the go. Those managers who can operate at a level of personal calm are often the most successful.

One of the most common mental relaxation techniques is abdominal breathing, which calls for the person to place his or her hands on the abdomen with fingertips touching and breathe deeply for five to ten minutes twice a day. This procedure helps one slow down and relax. Another technique is progressive relaxation, which requires the individual to lie down and slowly progress down (or up) the body by first stiffening

Organizational
Behavior
In Action

STRESS AND WOMEN AT WORK

The number of women in the workplace has been steadily increasing. By the turn of the century the work force will be almost 50 percent female. Many of these individuals will face stress that is unique to women. Chusmir and Durand, for example, have noted that three of these areas include: (a) socialization at work; (b) sex-role conflict and family pressures; and (c) job-sex typing and discrimination.

Some women find it hard to adapt to "male" values typified by assertiveness, competitiveness, and teamwork. Others discover that when they do accept these values, their male counterparts resent their behavior. As a result, women find themselves isolated, not taken seriously, and/or believe that managers accept behavior from men that they would not accept from women.

Many women also find that they are caught between two roles: homemaker and worker. One often precludes the other or makes it difficult to carry out properly. The multiple roles result in stress.

Job-sex typing can result in women ending up in typically "female" jobs. This often involves boring work, repetitive tasks, dead-end jobs, and underuse of talent.

What are organizations doing to reduce female stress? Some of the most important steps that are being implemented include:

1. Eliminating male-only practices such as old-boy networks and withdrawing any tacit or overt company support of these practices.
2. Encouraging workers to include women in all informal groups.
3. Encouraging other female employees to help newcomers.
4. Encouraging the formation of female support groups to help women overcome the feeling of being alone.
5. Finding male mentors for women with advancement potential.
6. Treating women as colleagues, in nonsexual terms.
7. Carefully examining expectations of women subordinates.
8. Reassuring women that their approach to work is okay—that both men and women have individual styles and that any approach is acceptable if it accomplishes the desired goal.
9. Equalizing promotion opportunity.
10. Reevaluating salary policies.

Source: Nick Nicyodym and Katie George, "Stress Busting on the Job," *Personnel,* July 1989, pp. 56–59; and Leonard H. Chusmir and Douglas E. Durand, "Stress and the Working Woman," *Personnel,* May 1987, pp. 38–43.

the muscles and then relaxing them. Slowly working one's way down the body, the person eventually tenses the toes and then relaxes them. By this time, the entire body is relaxed.

A third popular technique is **transcendental meditation (TM),** which requires the meditator to shut out all distractions and concentrate on a mantra, which is a single word or sound. For fifteen to thirty minutes, the individual works to attain a physical and mental relaxation peak. TM can have useful payoffs. For example, when Marcus investigated the effects of TM on thirty-six managers at a General Motors plant, he found that they now needed less sleep, fell asleep faster, used less coffee and aspirin, and were more self-confident and emotionally stable than before they started using TM.[25] Results such as these undoubtedly help account for TM's current popularity.[26]

Organizational Approaches

Organizational approaches take a number of different forms. Some, as we have seen, consist of physical fitness programs. Some consist of recreational efforts[27] and special programs.[28] Others are more behavioral in scope and include management training in how to clarify assigned tasks, give encouragement and support,[29] and provide subordinates feedback on their performance (also see "Organizational Behavior in Action: Stress and Women at Work"). This type of training is particularly helpful to those who are unsure of exactly what their job entails or how they are going to be evaluated. Included in this training are ways of opening up communication channels, getting a two-way dialogue established, and developing a style of management that is perceived as helpful rather than punitive to the subordinates.[30]

Another popular approach is teaching stress management principles to the organizational personnel. By making the employees realize that much stress is personally generated and can be controlled if the person knows how, the firm gets its people actively involved in the stress management program.[31]

How effective have such efforts been? To date, the results are encouraging. For example, after conducting stress programs for salaried personnel at the Mead Corporation's Packaging Division, Pelligrino reported that: (a) the number of salaried personnel in the counseling/referral program increased by almost 40 percent; (2) the seminars made the participants more aware of both the symptoms and the consequences of unmanaged stress; (3) some of the participants reported fewer incidents of insomnia, tension, headaches, and other stress-related problems; and (4) throughout the work force there was a renewed interest in physical fitness.[32]

Finally, it is important to realize that there are a number of reasons why organizations want to help their people manage personal stress. In addition to those described in this chapter, another is the legal liability that firms bear for job-related stress.[33] As court decisions continue to favor employees who suffer stress-related problems caused by the job, employers are going to increasingly make stress a target of concern.

STOP Review your answers to Question 5 and make any changes you would like.

5. What can June do to deal with her stress? What can the organization to do help?

There are a number of things that June can do. One is to watch her diet and to get a thorough physical exam. A second is to work on learning mental relaxation. A third is start forcing herself to limit work hours and not feel guilty about taking time off.

The organization can help by providing her high-tech training, hiring more people, and reducing her work load. As the firm begins doing this, it is likely that June will start feeling a reduction in tension, and everything will begin to straighten out for her.

SUMMARY

1. Stress is the feeling of pressure, anxiety, and tension. Organizational stress consists of four factors: stressors, stress, outcomes, and consequences. Stressors are environmental factors that bring about stress, and there are many different types of them. In the physical environment, they include light, noise, and temperature. At the individual level, they consist of role ambiguity, role conflict, and work overload. At the group level, common examples include lack of group cohesiveness, inadequate group support, and intragroup and intergroup conflict. At the organizational level, they include organizational climate and structure. Extraorganizationally, some primary examples are family, financial problems, and relocation.

2. Stress has a number of different negative effects. One of the most common is physical disorders such as coronary heart disease. A second is alcoholism. A third is burnout.

3. Some people are better able to withstand stress than are others. This can be accounted for by demographic differences and cognitive versus affective differences. Demographic differences include age, physical health, education, and occupation. Cognitive versus affective differences include need satisfaction, locus of control, and type of personality.

4. In recent years, a great deal of attention has been directed to ways of managing stress. Some of the most common include diet, physical fitness, mental relaxation, and organizational approaches such as stress management seminars. Organizations are now beginning to realize that effective stress management can improve the mental and physical health of personnel, reduce outlays for medical costs, and bring about increased productivity and improved organizational climate.

KEY TERMS

stress
stressors
underloaded
overloaded

workaholism
organizational climate
life events
burnout

Type A personalities
transcendental meditation (TM)

REVIEW AND STUDY QUESTIONS

1. In your own words, what is meant by the term *stress*?

2. How does stress work? In your answer, be sure to discuss stressors, stress, outcomes, and consequences.

3. Why is a person who is underloaded as likely to suffer the negative effects of stress as is a person who is overloaded?

4. What kinds of specific stressors can be found in each of the following categories: physical environment, individual stressors, group stressors, organizational stressors, and extraorganizational stressors? Describe a few in each category.

5. What are life events all about? What effect do they have on stress? Explain.

6. What are some of the effects of stress? In your answer, be sure to address the areas of physical disorders, alcoholism, and burnout.

7. How do demographic differences help explain why some people are more affected by stress than are others? Explain.

8. How do cognitive affective differences help explain why some people are more affected by stress than are others? Explain.

9. How does a Type A person behave? Why are Type A personalities more likely to have heart attacks than Type B personalities? Explain.

10. How can diet help manage stress? How can physical fitness help? How can mental relaxation help? Explain.

11. What are some of the organizational approaches that are being used currently to help manage stress? Identify and discuss two.

CASES

She Loves the Work

Roberta Rodriguez had been in health care for fifteen years before she was finally promoted into the upper ranks of management. That was eight months ago. As head of one of the major departments in her hospital, Roberta finds the challenges extremely interesting and the psychological rewards highly stimulating. Those who work with her are aware of her feelings and attitude and are delighted that she has been promoted to head of the department. Since Roberta came on board, the number of departmental personnel who are absent or tardy has decreased by 21 percent. Everyone enjoys showing up for work because Roberta makes the day interesting. She delegates tasks and follows up to see if there are any problems. She reads and personally responds to all memos and other correspondence within twenty-four hours. She attends all meetings fully prepared to discuss the agenda items. There does not seem to be anything that she does not get done quickly and accurately.

At least, that is the way it has been in the past. During the last month, however, both the hospital administrator and her personnel have noticed some marked changes in Roberta's behavior. Last week, she missed a major meeting of the top staff, and earlier this week she was unprepared to present a report to the administrator on an issue he had asked her to research and have ready for the weekly meeting. Even her twenty-four hour turnaround time on memos has dropped to three days, and the responses are sometimes incomplete or vague.

The administrator was the first one to see this change in her behavior, and he has been monitoring it for the last three weeks. Earlier today, he talked to one of the in-house psychiatrists, explaining Roberta's changing work behavior patterns and increased forgetfulness. The doctor has promised to talk to Roberta about it and see if she is indeed overworking herself. For his part, the administrator has promised to keep tabs on Roberta to see if she continues to have these problems. "Perhaps," he told the psychiatrist, "it's something at home that is bothering her. However, whatever it is, I want to know about it and help her before she suffers a total collapse." The psychiatrist smiled. "I know what you mean. We spend our time trying to help other people deal with their physical and mental problems and then find our own staff are suffering the same ones. Maybe this is what the sage meant by 'physician heal thyself'."

1. What are some of the symptoms of overload? Does Roberta seem to have any of them? Explain.

2. Why is Roberta suffering this problem? After all, she has been in the health-care business for a long time. Should she not be aware of the problem and know how to deal with it?

3. Can anything be done to help Roberta? Offer your suggestions.

A Matter of Burnout

When Sean Flaherty started working at the State Bank, he was determined to succeed. That was ten years ago, and since then he has been promoted six times. Compared to all of the other individuals who started at the bank at the same time he did, Sean's progress has been the fastest. Currently, his job requires him to work ten hours a day, including Saturdays. He is also on the road approximately two days a week.

Sean is well liked at State. There are some who wish they had been promoted as fast as he, but all admit that Sean earns everything he gets. One of his friends recently commented, "If you are willing to put in the time and effort to get ahead at this bank, you can achieve your goals. The big question is whether the race is worth the prize. Sean works like a madman. I don't know how long he's going to be able to keep up this pace. However, if that's the way he wants to spend his life, that's his decision. The bank is willing to promote a person with drive and ambition, and Sean has enough of both to make it all the way to the top."

The top is apparently where Sean wants to go. Last week, he applied for the opening as head of the midtown branch. This job is one of the most important in the bank, and if he gets it Sean will most certainly be in line for the senior vice-president's job when the latter retires in two years. There are a number of individuals in the bank who have applied for the midtown branch position, but the president of the bank has decided that Sean can have it if he wants it. He told him so last week at a closed-door conference.

Early this morning, there was a development that may throw a monkey wrench into the works. Every year the bank requires its top personnel to have a complete physical. Even though Sean is only thirty-five years old, he too must submit to one. The results, by agreement of the personnel, can be made available to the individual's superior if the ex-

amining physician feels the patient's health is being jeopardized by the job. Today the president received a copy of Sean's physical examination results, along with a note from the physician. The note explained that Sean was seriously overworked and recommended that he be given an immediate four-week vacation. The physician also recommended that Sean's work activity be reduced and that the president encourage Sean to take up an active sport such as jogging or tennis. The report concluded by noting, "Sean is physically burning himself out. Unless he slows down dramatically, I predict that he will suffer a heart attack or some other major physical calamity within six months."

After reading the doctor's note, the president sat back in his chair. Three things were running through his mind. First, how would Sean take the news? Second, how many other people around the bank were also suffering these same symptoms? Third, since the environment helps to create the problem, what could the bank do to help alleviate it? "Maybe," thought the president, "we ought to get more actively involved in some type of stress-management program for our personnel. Also, creating a physical fitness area might help." With these things in mind, he asked his secretary to set up a meeting with the doctor and some key staff members as soon as possible. "Perhaps between us," he thought, "we can figure out how to handle this problem before it gets any worse."

1. What is meant by burnout? What are its symptoms? What are its effects? Explain.

2. Given what you know about the bank, what type of climate exists there? How is this causing stress for Sean?

3. If you were giving advice to the president on this matter, what would you recommend? Be complete and realistic in your answer.

SELF-FEEDBACK EXERCISE

Identifying Type A and Type B Personalities

This self-feedback experiential exercise is designed to help you determine whether you exhibit Type A or Type B behaviors. For each item, there are two alternatives: A and B. Indicate which of the two is most descriptive of you by using the following scale:

If statement A is totally descriptive of you and B is not descriptive at all, give yourself 5 points.

If statement A is mostly descriptive of you and B is only somewhat descriptive, give yourself 4 points.

If statement A is slightly more descriptive of you than is statement B, give yourself 3 points.

If statement B is slightly more descriptive of you than is A, give yourself 2 points.

If statement B is mostly descriptive of you and A is only somewhat descriptive, give yourself 1 point.

If statement B is totally descriptive of you and A is not descriptive at all, give yourself 0 points.

1. _____ A. Looking back on my average day, I usually work at a hectic pace.

   B. Looking back on my average day, I usually work at a relaxed pace.

2. _____ A. I really hate days off. It means I don't get to do any job-related work.

   B. I enjoy days off. Getting away from the job is really relaxing.

3. _____ A. I like fighting a deadline. It's one way I'm assured of getting the work done.

   B. I seldom have to fight deadlines. I pace myself so everything gets done on time.

4. _____ A. My primary satisfaction comes from my work.

   B. My work is personally rewarding, but I also enjoy sports, social gatherings, time with family and friends, and so on.

5. _____ A. I talk fast. Few people can say more in a minute or two than I can.

   B. I talk at a moderate rate. This is more than adequate to convey what I have to say.

6. _____ A. I set very high standards for myself, and if I don't get things done according to my plan, I become quite upset.

   B. I establish a reasonable amount of work, and if I get it done, I am happy. I want to accomplish things, but I do not allow myself to get upset if I fall short.

7. _____ A. When I play games, I play to win. It doesn't matter against whom I'm playing—young kids, novices, people less alert than I am to the rules and shortcuts—I want to emerge on top.

   B. I enjoy playing games, but I don't always have to win. In fact, I try to find games in which I can obtain enjoyment just from the participation.

8. _____ A. When I listen to people who speak slowly or who make their point in a roundabout fashion, I find myself wanting to complete the conversation for them or just walk away. They bore me.

   B. When I listen to people who are slow or rambling in their conversation, I try to get enjoyment out of what they are saying rather than the way they are saying it.

9. _____ A. When I have to eat, I eat very fast. I know it may not be very good for my health, but by eating fast I can more quickly get back to other activities such as working.

   B. When I eat I like to take my time and enjoy the meal. This is one activity I really like to perform at a leisurely pace.

10. _____ A. When I stop to think about it, I am always in a hurry even when I don't have to be.

    B. I seldom rush anywhere. I try to plan my daily calendar so that I know where I am supposed to be going and can arrange things so that I can proceed at a reasonable pace.

11. _____ A. I often try to do two things at the same time. Sure it takes some getting used to, but I find that if I do things this way, I increase my output by almost 100 percent.

    B. I concentrate on doing one thing at a time. This way I know that I'm doing it right and won't have to repeat it later.

12. _____ A. Even though I don't usually show it, I find that I'm often angry and upset at the way people behave and things get done. I know there is no sense getting angry, but underneath, I feel that way.

B. I seldom get angry about things. People make lots of mistakes and sometimes things don't go my way. However, life is too short to spend it getting angry.

13. _____ A. Waiting makes me nervous. When I do wait, I find myself biting my nails, tapping my feet, scribbling on a pad, or doing something to pass the time.

B. I do not enjoy waiting, but when it is necessary, I try to take the time to relax. If I do have a lot of work, I make it a point to bring some of it along with me so I can read or fill out papers at a leisurely pace.

14. _____ A. I measure progress in terms of time and performance. For example, when I am given an assignment, I write down what I am to do and break it into time periods. Then I monitor progress closely. If I fall behind in something I am doing, I make it a point not to go home or go to sleep until I have completed the assignment for that day.

B. I try to get things done in an agreed upon time. However, I do not worry about progress on an hourly or daily basis. Rather I realize that sometimes I will work faster than others. So I try to keep up a good pace that ensures progress while not proving to be excessively demanding.

15. _____ A. When I go to bed, I cannot wait until morning so that I can get going again.

B. When I go to bed, I try to get a good night's sleep without thinking about what I'll be doing first thing the next day.

16. _____ A. I want people to respect me for what I do. Praise for my accomplishments is important.

B. I want people to respect me for who I am. Even if I'm only an average worker, I'm entitled to respect.

17. _____ A. I often find myself scheduling more and more work in less and less time.

B. I set goals for myself, and when they are accomplished I sit back and relax.

18. _____ A. When I speak I tend to overemphasize key words and speed up the delivery of the last few words in a sentence.

B. When I speak I tend to talk at an evenly paced, moderate speed throughout.

19. _____ A. When I engage in conversation, I find myself changing the topic to subjects that interest me. If I have to wait for a chance to talk, I pretend to listen while thinking of what I am going to say when the chance comes.

B. When I engage in conversation, I try to listen to what the other person has to say and draw some enjoyment out of what I am hearing.

20. _____ A. I wear myself out by doing too much. Yet I enjoy it. When I fall into bed totally exhausted, this is a sign of a good day's work.

B. I seldom wear myself out. If something does not get done today, I'll do it tomorrow. No job warrants wearing myself to a frazzle every day.

Review all your answers. Make sure that on each of the twenty, you have placed a score between 0 and 5. Now place your scores below and add them.

1. _____	11. _____
2. _____	12. _____
3. _____	13. _____
4. _____	14. _____
5. _____	15. _____
6. _____	16. _____
7. _____	17. _____
8. _____	18. _____
9. _____	19. _____
10. _____	20. _____

_____ + _____ = TOTAL _____

Interpretation: Compare your total to the key at the top of page 359. Most people are a mixture of Type A and Type B personalities. If you are a strong Type A personality, you might want to talk to some of your friends or classmates to see if they agree with you. If they do, the material in the last part of the chapter should be reread carefully to see if you can begin taking steps to "loosen up" a little.

0–19 You have a strong Type B personality.
20–39 You have a moderate Type B personality.
40–59 You have a mixture of Type A and Type B personalities; you do not exhibit any clear pattern.

60–79 You have a moderate Type A personality.
80–100 You have a strong Type A personality.

NOTES

1. John M. Ivancevich and Michael T. Matteson, *Stress and Work: A Managerial Perspective* (Glenview, IL: Scott, Foresman & Co., 1980), pp. 5–9; and Terry A. Beehr and Rabi S. Bhagat, *Human Stress and Cognition in Organizations: An Integrated Perspective* (New York: John Wiley & Sons, 1985), pp. 6–7.

2. Cary L. Cooper and Michael J. Smith (eds.), *Job Stress and Blue Collar Work* (New York: John Wiley & Sons, 1985).

3. Kent L. Streat and Nellie Sabin, "Is the Assignment Doable?," *Management Solutions,* July 1988, pp. 4–8.

4. Philip Goldberg, *Executive Health* (New York: McGraw-Hill Book Co., 1978), p. 41.

5. Also see Geraldine Spruell, "Work Fever," *Training and Development Journal,* January 1987, p. 44.

6. Ivancevich and Matteson, *Stress and Work,* p. 112.

7. Thomas F. Lyons, "Role Clarity, Need for Clarity, Satisfaction, Tension and Withdrawal," *Organizational Behavior and Human Performance,* January 1971, pp. 99–110.

8. Ivancevich and Matteson, *Stress and Work,* p. 130.

9. T. H. Holmes and R. H. Rahe, "The Social Readjustment Rating Scale," *Journal of Psychosomatic Medicine,* Vol. 11, 1967, pp. 213–218.

10. Michael T. Matteson and John M. Ivancevich, "Organizational Stressors and Heart Disease: A Research Model," *Academy of Management Review,* July 1979, p. 347.

11. Ivancevich and Matteson, *Stress and Work,* p. 91.

12. Trevor A. Williams, George Calhoun, and Russell L. Ackoff, "Stress, Alcoholism, and Personality," *Human Relations,* June 1982, pp. 494–497.

13. Baron Perlman and E. Alan Hartman, "Burnout: Summary and Future Research," *Human Relations,* April 1982, pp. 284–291.

14. National Institute for Occupational Safety and Health, Department of Health, Education and Welfare. Reported in *U.S. News & World Report,* March 13, 1978, pp. 80–81.

15. Hans Selye, *The Stress of Life* (New York: McGraw-Hill Book Co., 1976).

16. Ivancevich and Matteson, *Stress and Work,* p. 170.

17. Robert H. Strawser, J. Patrick Kelly, and Richard T. Hise, "What Causes Stress for Management Accountants?," *Management Accounting,* March 1982, pp. 32–35.

18. Meyer Friedman and Ray H. Rosenman, *Type A Behavior and Your Heart* (New York: Alfred A. Knopf, 1974).

19. Leonard H. Chusmir and Jacqueline A. Hood, "Relationships Between Type A Behavior Pattern and Motivational Needs," *Psychological Reports,* Vol. 58, 1986, pp. 783–794.

20. R. Rosenmann, R. Brand, C. Jenkins, M. Friedman, R. Straus, and M. Wrum, "Coronary Heart Disease in the Western Collaborative Group Study: Final Follow-Up Experience of 8 1/2 Years," *Journal of the American Medical Association,* no. 233, 1975, pp. 872–877.

21. Edward R. Ragland and Richard J. Brand, "Type A Behavior and Mortality from Coronary Heart Disease," *New England Journal of Medicine,* January 14, 1988, pp. 65–69.

22. Orlando Behling and F. Douglas Holcome, "Dealing with Employee Stress," *MSU Business Topics,* Spring 1981, pp. 53–61.

23. Robert Kreitner, Steven D. Wood, and Glenn M. Friedman, "Just How Fit Are Your Employees?" *Business Horizons,* August 1979, pp. 39–45.

24. For additional insights see Len Kravitz, "The Executive Workout," *Working Woman,* February 1990, pp. 115–120.

25. Jay B. Marcus, *TM and Business* (New York: McGraw-Hill Book Co., 1978).

26. Also see James C. Quick, Lawrence Schkade, and Mark E. Eakin, "Thinking Styles and Job Stress," *Personnel,* May 1987, pp. 44–48.

27. M. Michael Markowich, "Using Task Forces to Increase Efficiency and Reduce Stress," *Personnel,* August 1987, pp. 34–38.

28. Fairlee E. Winfield, "Workplace Solutions for Women Under Eldercare Pressure," *Personnel,* July 1987, pp. 31–39.

29. Sandra L. Kirmeyer and Thomas W. Dougherty, "Work Load, Tension, and Coping: Moderating Effects of Supervision Support," *Personnel Psychology,* Spring 1988, pp. 125–139.

30. See also David Hingsburger, "Learning How to Face That Stressful Situation," *Management Solutions,* February 1988, pp. 41–45.

31. John Pelligrino, "Teaching Stress Management: Meeting Individual and Organizational Needs," *S.A.M. Advanced Management Journal,* Spring 1981, p. 36.

32. *Ibid.,* p. 38.

33. John M. Ivancevich, Michael T. Matteson, and Edward P. Richards III, "Who's Liable for Stress on the Job?" *Harvard Business Review,* March–April 1985, pp. 60–72.

PART V
ORGANIZATIONAL PROCESSES

Conceptual Model for this Book

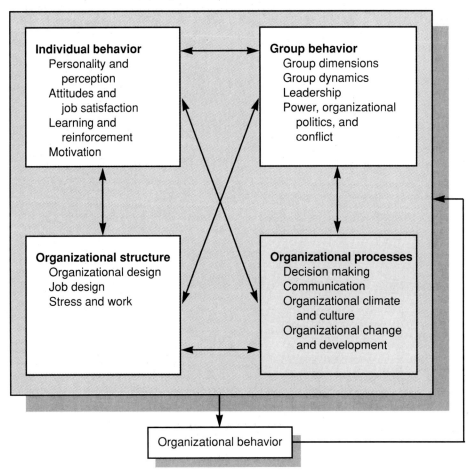

Now that we have examined individuals, groups, and the organizational structure, we are ready to look at these interactions or *interfaces* that occur between these three. These interfaces occur in the form of *organizational processes,* and there are three in all: decision making, communication, and monitoring culture and change.

In Chapter 14 we will examine the decision-making process. This is the process of choosing from among alternatives. We will see that there are two basic ways of studying this process. The first is to take a very logical, rational, efficiency-oriented approach. The second is to examine the process as one in which the decision maker actually accepts less than ideal solutions in many cases, just as long as the results are "good enough." We will study both approaches and point out the roles played by simplification, subjective nationality, and rationalization in the decision-making process.

In Chapter 15, the focus of our attention will be on the communication process. After defining this process, we will explain the roles and functioning of formal communication channels and relate how the grapevine can be of value to the manager. We will also discuss the most typical forms of communication media used in organizations, identify and describe common barriers to communication, and present some of the most useful techniques for overcoming these barriers.

In Chapter 16, organizational climate and culture will be examined. Particular attention will be focused on factors influencing this climate. Then the topic of culture and its ramifications for the organization will be studied. Both identifying and managing culture will be considered.

In Chapter 17, the topic is change. Strategies will be reviewed and we will note how resistance to change can be overcome and new equilibriums reestablished. Organizational-development (OD) interventions used in accomplishing planned change are also considered. Some of the most popular personal, group, intergroup, and overall organizational interventions will be studied. Particular attention will be given to the latter interventions, especially grid organizational development.

The overriding goal of this section is to study the organizational processes in which individuals, groups, and organizational structures interface. These processes are not confined to any one of these three, nor are they limited to any particular level of the hierarchy. In pursuing its objectives, however, management must carry out these processes, and sooner or later they affect everyone. ◆

CHAPTER 14
The Decision-Making Process

GOALS OF THE CHAPTER

Decision making in organizations is both an objective and a subjective process. On the one hand, it involves identifying goals and formulating an orderly, efficient process for attaining them. On the other hand, the decision maker's human characteristics may encourage expediency, shortcuts, and accepting less-than-ideal alternatives. Meanwhile, in the actual process of making decisions managers use different styles or approaches. The goal of this chapter is to examine models and styles of decision-making behavior to determine how both organizational and personal decisions are made. When you are finished reading this chapter, you should be able to:

1. distinguish between prescriptive and descriptive decision theory;
2. define the term *rationality* as it applies to decision making;
3. describe the decision-making steps in an econologic model and identify the shortcomings of this model;
4. describe the decision-making steps in a bounded rationality model and discuss the accuracy of the model;
5. relate the roles played by simplification, subjective rationality, and rationalization in the decision-making process;
6. describe typical decision-making styles and relate the role of right-brain and left-brain hemisphere functions.

OPENING CASE: MARTIN'S CHOICE

As head of the marketing department, Martin Schenkler's job is to make the final decisions on new product offerings. For the last two weeks Martin has been examining the benefits of two new consumer goods. Due to limited budget, only one of these will be chosen. The first is a revolutionary microwave oven which will sell for under $300 and would be more efficient than anything currently on the market. The other is a high-resolution, color portable television which will sell for $250.

Marketing research indicates that the microwave should provide the company with a return on investment of 22 percent annually for the first five years and 16 percent annually for the next five years. The portable television will provide a 20 percent return for the first five years and a 15 percent return for the next five years. The minimum annual return that the company will accept from a new product is 13 percent.

Martin believes that the television is a better choice because it lends itself to more creative selling. "Microwaves are boring products," he told his marketing research team. "I want something that allows us to use our talents in moving the product through the marketing channel." One of the members of the research team reminded Martin that the return on investment figures indicated that the television is not the best choice. Martin became very angry when he heard this. "I'm paid to make the decisions around here, so let me make them," he told the man. "I have a hunch that this TV is going to do a lot better than any of you believe."

1. Did Martin make any use of econologic decision making in arriving at his decision? Explain.
2. Did Martin make any use of the bounded rationality decision model in arriving at his decision? Explain.
3. In what way did Martin use simplification and rationalization in his decision?
4. What type of information-gathering orientation did Martin use? Explain. Is he a left-brain or right-brain thinker? Give an example.

BASIC DECISION-MAKING TERMINOLOGY

Decision making is the process of choosing from among alternatives. This activity is important to understanding organizational behavior[1] because choice processes play a vital role in communication, motivation, leadership, and other aspects of individual, group, and organizational interfaces.[2] Before we examine decision making in an organizational behavior context, however, it is important to have a clear understanding of some basic decision-making terminology, including the differences between prescriptive and descriptive theory and what is meant by the term *rationality*.

Decision making is the process of choosing from among alternatives.

Prescriptive and Descriptive Theories

When people talk about decision theory, they often intermix prescriptive theory and descriptive theory. **Prescriptive decision theory** attempts to explain how decision making *ought* to be carried out. It is a normative approach that outlines steps to be followed and critical questions that should be considered. Illustrations of the latter include: Is this an optimal decision, and if not, how can it be improved? How should a rational decision maker go about formulating alternatives and making a final choice? In an overall organizational setting, how should decisions be made?

Prescriptive theory relates how decisions ought to be made.

Descriptive decision theory is concerned with describing how decisions are *actually* made. Many times decision making is influenced by subjective factors, such as the individual's personality or the pressure of the situation. Descriptive theory is concerned with answering such questions as: What factors influence the behavior of the decision maker? What decisions are actually being made in the organization? How did these decisions turn out? In this chapter, we will be initially concerned with prescriptive theory and then turn our attention to descriptive theory. Before doing so, however, a discussion of rationality in decision making is in order.

Descriptive theory relates how decisions are actually made.

Rationality in Decision Making

Anytime we discuss decision making there is the implied presence of *rationality*. Yet there is a great deal of disagreement regarding exactly what this term means.[3] One way to define rationality is to use *economic* terms and consider a rational decision as one which *objectively maximizes* one's advantage. For example, if an organization has $50,000 in extra cash that it does not intend to invest in capital resources for the next year, there are a number of short-run decision alternatives. By merely computing the rate of return from each of these alternatives, the manager can determine the one that will provide the greatest payoff.

Rationality can be defined in various ways.

A second way of viewing rationality is by choosing a course of action that is "personally acceptable," *regardless* of whether it can be objectively measured. For example, a salesperson may choose to put 5 percent of his or her gross income into a retirement annuity in order to guarantee a fixed income in later years. The individual may not maximize his or her income, but for personal purposes the individual certainly has made a logical or rational decision.

A third way of viewing rationality is simply to examine the decision process itself and determine if it is *orderly* and *logical*. Does it follow a systematic, sequential flow that moves the decision maker from the problem identification to resolution? If it does, it is rational.

The first of these definitions is often used by people who feel the decision maker should be an **economic man** who always maximizes outcomes. The second is more subjective and implies that the decision maker is often an **administrative man** who chooses alternatives that are satisfactory or "good enough." Our third definition can be used by both the economic and the administrative person. The model that best represents the economic perspective is the econological model, while the administrative perspective is best explained by the bounded rationality model.

THE ECONOLOGIC DECISION-MAKING MODEL

The econologic model assumes economic rationality.

The **econologic decision-making model** proceeds from the assumption that people are economically rational and attempt to maximize outputs in an orderly and sequential process. These steps have been outlined in various ways by different authors.[4] All, however, seem to agree that decision making involves: (a) identifying the problem to be solved or goal to be reached; (b) listing the various alternatives that can be employed in accomplishing this mission; (c) determining the expected results from each alternative; and (d) comparing and evaluating the results to choose the best one. Most econologic model authors also contend that not only is each step in the process indispensable, but one must proceed in the specified order, since each step receives inputs from the prior one and provides outputs for use in the next succeeding step.

Econologic Decision-Making Process

Depending upon how detailed one would like to be, the econologic decision-making process can contain as few as four or as many as ten specific steps. For our purposes we shall use seven:

There are seven steps in the econologic decision-making process.

1. Uncover the symptoms of the problem or difficulty.
2. Identify the specific problem to be solved or goal to be realized.
3. Develop a decision criterion for evaluation.
4. Develop and list all alternative solutions.
5. Determine the outcomes of all these alternative solutions.
6. Select the one best course of action.
7. Implement this decision.

These steps, illustrated in Figure 14–1, provide a representation of econologic models in general.

Symptoms are uncovered.

Uncover the Symptoms. The first step in the decision-making process is to uncover the symptoms. Every problem has accompanying symptoms. The business manager who finds his employees reporting late for work is seeing only the symptom of some underlying problem, such as his failure to go to bat for them with top management on some matter relevant to working conditions. The hospital administrator who is being faced with the loss of three of her department

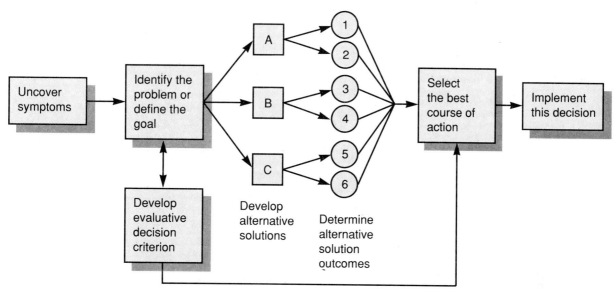

FIGURE 14–1
An Econologic Model

administrators may be witnessing a symptom caused by her failure to approve competitive salary increases for these personnel. In each case, the problem eventually manifests itself through symptoms.

Problems or goals are determined.

Identify the Problem or Define the Goal. Having identified the symptoms, the manager must identify the problem to be solved or the goal to be realized. In short, what needs to be done? The answer to this question will establish the overall direction of the decision-making process.

A decision criterion is established.

Develop Decision Criterion for Evaluation. The decision maker must now develop a criterion for evaluating the alternative courses of action. This criterion, whenever possible, is stated in objective terms so that the decision maker can arrive at a definite decision. However, when objective criteria cannot be developed, it is common to find econologic models using basic economic concepts, such as preference or indifference curves, in an attempt to quantify qualitative criteria. Such approaches, of course, are used only as last resorts.

Alternative solutions are developed.

Develop All Alternative Solutions. In this stage, the decision maker lists the possible solutions. Some, of course, may be highly unrealistic because they are long shots (a million to one likelihood) or would result in ridiculous results (an alternative with an expected value of minus $1 million). Nevertheless, they are placed on the list of possible outcomes. Meanwhile, if the problem or objective requires creativity, such as formulating an advertising campaign for a new product, techniques such as brainstorming may even be employed. But keep in mind that economic rationality is going to govern this process, so as little time as possible will be squandered on formulating overly creative or exaggerated alternatives.

Alternative solution out-
comes are determined.

Determine All Alternative Solution Outcomes. Once all the alternatives have been identified, it is necessary to measure their payoffs objectively. This is done under one of three conditions: **certainty, risk** or **uncertainty,** thereby plunging the manager into the area of quantitative decision making. While an in-depth quantitative analysis of alternative solutions is beyond our present concern, an examination of this selection process is worth a cursory view because such an objective approach is highly regarded by managers who are economic men.

For purposes of illustration, assume that Company A has formulated three plans—Plan 1, Plan 2, and Plan 3—in an effort to achieve a goal of profit maximization. Furthermore, by gathering all of the data possible through external surveillance, Company A has determined that its major competitor has formulated three major strategies (which we shall simply label Strategies 1, 2, and 3, respectively). Comparing its three plans against those of the competition, Company A has constructed the matrix shown in Table 14–1. The matrix reveals that if the competition adopts Strategy 1 and Company A opts for Plan 1, the latter will gain $20,000. If the competition chooses Strategy 2, the company will gain $4,000 with Plan 1; and if the competition goes with Strategy 3, Plan 1 will return $15,000 to the firm. This same reasoning applies in interpreting the remainder of Table 14–1.

If Company A's information allows it to know *exactly* what the competition will do, the firm is operating under conditions of *certainty*. In this case, the decision is quite simple. If the competition chooses Strategy 1, the firm should go with Plan 1. If the opposition elects Strategy 2, then Plan 2 is the proper countermove, and if Strategy 3 is going to be employed, then the company should choose Plan 3. A close look at Table 14–1 will illustrate that, given the competition's available strategy, each of our respective choices would maximize profit.

Of course, organizations seldom operate under certainty. Usually we have some idea of what the competition is likely to do, but we cannot say for sure. In this case, the organization is operating under *risk* conditions, in which there is a calculable probability of gain or loss. For example, what is the probability that the competition will opt for Strategy 1? Let us assume that on the basis of its information, Company A assigns a probability of 20 percent. Meanwhile, for Strategies 2 and 3, it assigns likelihoods of 60 percent and 20 percent, respectively.

Given this data, for which of the three alternative plans should the company opt? To answer this, we must compute the *expected value* of each plan, which is determined by multiplying the profit payoff from each plan and competitive strategy by the proba-

TABLE 14–1
Profit Payoff Matrix (In Thousands of Dollars)

		COMPETITION		
		Strategy 1	Strategy 2	Strategy 3
	Plan 1	20	4	15
Company A	Plan 2	10	25	9
	Plan 3	6	11	30

bility associated with each of these payoffs, and then totaling the results for each of the three plans. Doing so results in the following:

$$\text{Expected Value Plan 1} = 20(0.2) + 4(0.6) + 15(0.2) = 9.4$$
$$\text{Expected Value Plan 2} = 10(0.2) + 25(0.6) + 9(0.2) = 18.8$$
$$\text{Expected Value Plan 3} = 6(0.2) + 11(0.6) + 30(0.3) = 16.8$$

Given the above information, Company A should opt for Plan 2.

In some situations, the organization will be at an impasse in assignment probabilities of gains or losses. In such cases, the decision maker is operating under *uncertainty* and needs to turn to criteria that have been developed for handling such situations. The most popular of these is the *maximin criterion,* in which the individual chooses the plan with the highest minimum payoff, regardless of the competition's strategy. Applying this logic to Table 14–1, we can see that the lowest company payoff for Plan 1 is $4,000, for Plan 2 it is $9,000, and for Plan 3 it is $6,000. Following the maximin criterion of choosing the highest minimum, the decision maker should select Plan 2.[5]

The best alternative is selected.

Select the Best Alternative.   Once the alternative solution outcomes have been determined, selecting the best one is simply a matter of comparing the net results against the decision criteria. In the case of return on investment (ROI), the manager need only answer the question, which alternative promises the highest ROI? Keep in mind, of course, that while this step is basically simple, it depends upon the mathematical techniques and probabilities assigned to the various alternatives in the previous step. An error in probability assignment can give one alternative a higher expected value than another, resulting in the selection of the wrong alternative.

The decision is implemented.

Implement the Decision.   The final step in the decision-making process is to carry out the decision. This poses two possible pitfalls. One is that the personnel will make a mistake in bringing the process to fruition because of a misunderstanding about exactly how the action should be implemented. This is often a communication problem. The second is that the decision or strategy, despite all objective, rational analysis, will simply prove unworkable.

Econological Shortcomings

The econologic model has numerous shortcomings.

The econologic model we have just examined provides a very orderly, logical method for processing data and making decisions. Unfortunately, from an organizational behavior standpoint it contains two major shortcomings.

First, for *strict* econologic model theorists there is the problem of obtaining *complete* information on all available alternatives and outcomes. Seldom can the decision maker identify all of the alternative actions for solving a particular problem, and even then knowledge of the consequences of each is always fragmentary.

Second, even in those econologic models that do not require full knowledge of all alternatives and outcomes, there is the problem of processing capability.[6] For example, if a complex problem has six alternative solutions, the amount of data associated with each will probably be mind boggling. In order to make an economically rational decision, the manager will have to be capable of:

1. mentally storing the information in some stable form;
2. manipulating it via a series of complex calculations designed to provide expected values;
3. ranking all of the consequences in some consistent manner for the purposes of deriving one preferred alternative.

Research reveals that the human mind is actually unable to meet these rigorous requirements. None of the main features of the econologic model are supported by available information.[7] Thus, while the model provides useful insights into how people *should* make decisions, it fails to describe how they *actually* make them. A more realistic view is provided by the bounded rationality model.

STOP

Review your answers to Question 1 and make any changes you would like before continuing.

1. Did Martin make any use of econologic decision making in arriving at his decision? Explain.

He certainly did. The specific goal was clearly stated—identify a new consumer product for the firm to sell. Additionally, the marketing research team conducted analysis on the profit potential of both products, and the financial outcomes for both had been quantitatively computed.

THE BOUNDED RATIONALITY DECISION MAKING-MODEL

The bounded rationality model sees the decision maker as an administrative person.

The **bounded rationality decision-making model** presents the decision maker as an *administrative man* with limited information-processing ability. As a result, the person's view of the alternatives and outcomes is restricted or bounded to varying degrees. Simon has explained the concept in this way:

> When the limits to rationality are viewed from the individual's standpoint, they fall into three categories: he is limited by his unconscious skills, habits and reflexes; he is limited by his values and conceptions of purpose, which may diverge from the organizational goals; he is limited by the extent of his knowledge and information. The individual can be rational in terms of the organization's goals only to the extent that he is *able* to pursue a particular course of action, he has a correct conception of the *goal* of the action, and he is correctly *informed* about the conditions surrounding his action. Within the boundaries laid down by these factors, his choices are rational—goal-oriented.[8]

Thus, while the individual would like to make the best decision, the final choice is usually something less than the ideal. This occurs for two reasons: (a) there is a lack of opportunistic surveillance; and (b) the decision maker usually employs satisficing behavior.

Lack of Opportunistic Surveillance

There is often a lack of opportunistic surveillance.

Ideally, the decision maker continually performs **opportunistic surveillance,** scanning the environment in a never-ending search to improve conditions. Is there a new product line the customer would like? How can we improve service to our clients? Are there some cost-cutting programs we can introduce that will improve overall efficiency?

Questions such as these are futuristic and designed to deal with problems and take advantage of opportunities before the need to do so becomes mandatory. In reality, however, decision makers seldom perform opportunistic surveillance. Most decision making is designed to deal with problems that demand immediate attention, since when things are going well decision makers are not inclined to perform opportunistic surveillance.

Furthermore, individuals often begin problem solving by choosing the most obvious alternatives, only taking others into consideration if these initial choices prove inadequate. Thus, the totality of available alternatives is seldom examined, resulting in a decision-making process that is not only simpleminded but often downright biased. According to the bounded rationality model, the decision maker is a human being who wishes to make a good decision but who is a far cry from the economic man in the econologic model.

Use of Satisficing Behavior

The decision maker commonly employs satisficing behavior.

The second major characteristic of decision making under bounded rationality is the use of **satisficing behavior**. By this we mean that the final alternative may not maximize outcomes, as would occur in an optimal solution, but it is *good enough* to meet minimum standards of acceptability. This is the usual approach taken by decision makers.[9] March and Simon put it this way:

> Most human decision-making, whether individual or organizational, is concerned with the discovery and selection of satisfactory alternatives; only in exceptional cases is it concerned with the discovery and selection of optimal alternatives.[10]

Once the decision maker finds a satisfactory alternative, it is implemented. So for all practical purposes, the major question for the individual is which alternative is most acceptable.[11] The satisficing solution will provide a greater outcome for some people than for others because the latter are more selective and demand higher levels of acceptability. Research shows that if the individual has an easy time in discovering alternatives, the optimal decision will have higher standards (if not immediately, then in similar future problems) than if the person has a difficult time in finding satisfactory solutions.[12] Applying this idea to our earlier illustration of the manager who was seeking to invest $50,000, the man might find government notes providing the greatest return, but if there were a lot of paper work involved in making the investment, he might have the check mailed to a local bank for deposit in a savings account.

Bounded Rationality Model Process

The steps involved in the econologic and bounded rationality models are really quite different because of the underlying assumptions that accompany each. We have already examined those involved in the econologic model. The steps contained in the bounded rationality model, which is illustrated in Figure 14–2, are:

There are eight steps in the bounded rationality process.

1. Identify the problem to be solved or goal to be defined.
2. Determine the minimum level or standard that all acceptable alternatives will have to meet.
3. Choose one feasible alternative that will resolve the issue.
4. Appraise the acceptability that will resolve the issue.
5. Determine if it meets the minimum levels that have been established.
6. If the alternative is not acceptable, identify another and put it through the evaluation process.
7. If the alternative is acceptable, implement it.
8. After implementation, determine how easy (or difficult) it was to discover feasible alternatives and use this information to raise or lower the minimum level of acceptability on future problems of a similar nature.[13]

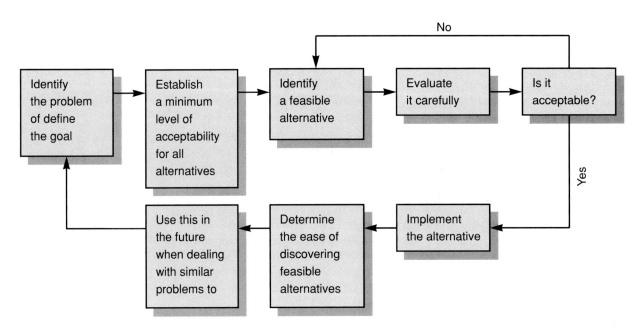

FIGURE 14–2
A Bounded Rationality Model

Most of the steps in this process are readily understandable. One comment, however, is in order. No consideration has been given to uncovering symptoms, since action is taken only after a problem arises; no initial preventive measures are enacted.

Accuracy of the Bounded Rationality Model

When the econologic and bounded rationality models are compared, it does seem that the latter represents a more realistic view of decision making. Yet how accurate is the model when subjected to empirical testing? The answer appears to be "very accurate," although much of the evidence supporting the model has been obtained from computerized simulations of the decision-making process, as seen through the work conducted by Cyert and March and by Clarkson.[14]

Empirical Testing

Empirical testing supports the accuracy of the bounded rationality model.

Cyert and March attempted to test the theory of bounded rationality by developing a computerized behavioral model to simulate price and output decisions in a large retail department store. The department they chose to investigate was primarily concerned with meeting specific sales objectives and obtaining a specified average markup on goods sold. By studying the department's decision-making process, Cyert and March formulated rules that they felt governed both sales and markups. They then built a model for predicting decision-making behavior within the department. In particular, they were interested in seeing if they could predict advance (initial) orders, markups, sale pricing, and markdowns. Their model proved to be a very accurate simulation of actual decision making in the department.

In order to test the model's ability to predict markup decisions on new merchandise, 197 invoices were randomly drawn and the data fed into the computer model. Using this information as a basis for analyzing past price decisions, the model then proceeded to forecast how the new merchandise would be priced.

> The definition of a correct prediction was made as stringent as possible. Unless the predicted price matched the actual price to the exact penny, the prediction was classified as incorrect. The results of the test were encouraging; of the 197 predicted prices, 188 were correct and 9 were incorrect. Thus, 95 percent of the predictions were correct. An investigation of the correct predictions showed that with minor modifications the model could be made to handle the deviant cases.[15]

Successful results were also obtained in the case of sales prices. Of the fifty-eight predictions made by the model, fifty-six (98 percent) were perfect. This same high result factor was obtained when markdowns were computed. Of the 159 price predictions that were made, 140 (88 percent) were totally accurate. Having built their model around the assumptions of bounded rationality, Cyert and March illustrated that decision makers are undoubtedly closer to being administrative men than economic men.

Another computer simulation model, constructed by Clarkson,[16] attempted to duplicate the investment decisions of a bank trust investment officer. After interviewing departmental officers at several bank trust departments, he focused his attention on one investment officer who was primarily responsible for making all of the portfolio choices within his respective bank.

Clarkson examined the histories of several accounts and constructed naive behavioral models to uncover those decision processes that seemed to remain the same among accounts. He also asked the trust officer questions about how portfolio decisions were made, and a transcript of the responses was studied. In addition, Clarkson asked the man to read certain articles and financial reports and comment upon them. On the basis of this research, he then constructed a model of the trust investment process used by this officer. The model relied heavily upon satisficing criteria in the form of rules of thumb and standard operating procedures.

In order to test the accuracy of the model, Clarkson then attempted to produce the portfolios for four accounts that had not been used in developing his program but were under the jurisdiction of the trust officer. A comparison of the portfolios selected by the trust officer and the program model revealed that Clarkson's simulated decision-making process produced results almost identical to those of the bank official. And to further test the model's ability to reproduce the actual behavior of the trust officer, the computer program's portfolios were compared with those generated by random models. The results showed that Clarkson's model was more accurate than any of these random models.

STOP | Review your answers to Question 2 and make any changes you would like before continuing.

2. Did Martin make any use of the bounded rationality decision model in arriving at his decision? Explain.

Yes he did. First, Martin knows the minimum return on investment that is acceptable to the company. Second, he has chosen an alternative that meets this level (satisficing behavior) even though it is not as profitable as the other choice.

OTHER EMPIRICAL RESEARCH FINDINGS

Thus far, we have illustrated two decision-making models and showed that the bounded rationality one is superior to the econologic model in terms of describing the decision maker's behavior. However, there is far more to the area of behavior and the decision-making process than these two models, and an examination of some other related empirical research is in order.[17]

Simplification Is Important

Most decision makers use a simplified model of reality.

Considerable evidence indicates that most decision makers employ a *simplified model of reality*. When confronted with a situation they have faced in the past, they often use the same general strategy as they did before if it was previously successful. They opt for a new approach only if the previous strategy did not work out well. For example, many people make decisions based on their recollection of the facts as opposed to laboriously checking their notes or other data sources.[18] Only if they feel their information is incomplete or they recently made an important mistake by relying on recollection will they change to a more sophisticated data retrieval strategy.

Additionally, people often dislike getting new information that distorts their prior beliefs. Individuals will attempt to reduce their dissonance by either ignoring, rationalizing, or refuting (in their own minds) the validity of the new information. For example, people who smoke often either ignore cancer warnings or say, "It won't happen to me." In either case, we can reiterate our decision-making proposition: simplified models of reality are used by most decision makers.

Subjective Rationality Is Ever-Present

Decision makers also respond to subjective criteria.

Many individuals believe they are highly scientific and logical when making decisions. Actually, research shows that most tend to respond to subjective criteria as well. For example, regardless of their initial goals, people often become more conservative as the complexity of a situation increases. At the same time, most will stop seeking additional information (which could be obtained cheaply and prove to be highly beneficial) and start relying more heavily on personal judgment. Laboratory experiments confirm that the probabilities assigned to outcomes by subjects are often quite different from those objectively determined.

What accounts for such behavior? Numerous personality traits can be cited, including aggression, autonomy, intelligence, and even fear of failure. All of these traits tend to affect decision making. The effect of fear of failure is particularly noticeable when people are asked to wager their own money. When betting small amounts such as $1, people are often high risk takers, accepting an even money payoff on an event whose likelihood is 4 to 1. On the other hand, when the stakes are very high, such as $5,000, they will turn down a payoff of 3 to 1 on an event with the likelihood of 50 percent. Their fear of failure (subjective rationality) outweighs the favorable odds (objective rationality).[19]

Finally, people tend to develop general decision-making rules that seem logical but are actually fallacious. For example, it is common to find individuals predicting the occurrence of a particular event because it has not occurred recently. If a fair coin has come up heads three times in a row, they bet on a tail for the next flip. People also tend to overestimate the probability of favorable events and underestimate unfavorable ones. Additionally, individuals often overestimate the likelihood of events with low probabilities and underestimate those with high probabilities.[20] It is even common to find individuals who have formally studied quantitative methods using subjective rationality when an objective approach would provide the best answer.[21] "Organizational Behavior in Action: The Subjective MBAs" provides an example.

Rationalization Often Transcends Rationality

Additionally, decision makers rationalize their decisions.

Empirical evidence reveals that decision makers not only are satisficers, but also are often *rationalizers*. As we noted earlier, search behavior is often concerned with the discovery of satisfactory alternatives. However, when is an alternative "good enough"?

Organizational Behavior In Action

THE SUBJECTIVE MBAS

How well do people analyze alternatives and make the best decisions from the available facts? Research shows that individuals often use a subjective process even when they have all of the necessary information and could give an objective response. For example, a group of forty-five MBA students recently were given a decision problem and asked if they would select the first option, the second option, or be indifferent regarding the two choices. The decision problem was framed in both positive and negative terms and the students were randomly assigned one of these sets of statements. The two sets were these:

Positive Statements
The National Cancer Institute has two possible treatments for cancer which could become standard treatments across the country.
　　If treatment 1 is adopted, of every 1,000 people who get cancer 400 will be saved.
　　If treatment 2 is adopted, there is a two-fifths chance that 1,000 of every 1,000 will be saved and a three-fifths chance that no people of every 1,000 will be saved.
Negative Statements
The National Cancer Institute has two possible treatments for cancer which could become standard treatments across the country.
　　If treatment 1 is adopted, of every 1,000 people who get cancer 600 will die.
　　If treatment 2 is adopted, there is a two-fifths chance that no people of every 1,000 will die and a three-fifths chance that 1,000 of every 1,000 will die.
　　There are adequate resources to implement only one treatment program. Which of the two programs would you favor for national implementation?

Since the statements in both groupings say the same thing, an econologic manager would be indifferent between them. The major difference between each pair is that the first statement is risk aversive while the second is risk seeking. Fifty-two percent of those who read the positive statements and 40 percent of those who read the negative statements opted for the first choice. On average, only 32 percent of the respondents were indifferent.

Then, after taking a ten-week course in statistical decision theory, the students were again given the decision problem. This time, on average, 57 percent chose the first statement and 26 percent were indifferent. Quite obviously, the MBAs were not using their statistical decision theory information. They were being influenced by their desire to avoid risk. Simply put, subjective rationality often outweighs objective rationality.

Source: N. S. Fagley and Paul M. Miller, "The Effects of Decision Framing on Choice of Risky vs. Certain Options," *Organizational Behavior and Human Decision Processes,* April 1987, pp. 264–277.

If a person is in a hurry, the first feasible choice may be implemented under the reasoning, "I had to make a fast decision so I chose the first likely alternative." Even if objective evidence shows that there was time for consideration of another alternative, the individual will often claim there was not. In short, the choice is rationalized.

Furthermore, individuals with sufficient time to consider many alternatives will often make a final choice *before* they have actually finished examining all the alternatives. They then rationalize their decision by finding some problem or shortcoming with each of the remaining choices. Their ultimate choice, known as the *implicit favorite,* is, of course, found to be superior to all the others.

While some people feel that this process is more a matter of rationalization than decision making, the two are actually intertwined. Except in the most objective cases, the final outcome is a matter of decision-maker preference, and when choosing from among similar outcomes, people are innately motivated to justify the final choice to themselves.

In a study conducted among business graduate students who were graduating from the Massachusetts Institute of Technology, Soelberg discovered that many of them actually made their final employment decision prior to the time they ended their job interviews. Using questionnaires and interviews, Soelberg also found that after the implicit favorite was chosen, individuals searched through the other alternatives and selected the most attractive one as the confirmation candidate. Then decision rules were developed and modified in such a way that the implicit favorite was shown to be superior to the confirmation candidate. During this process, the student continually reported a great deal of uncertainty regarding the final choice. Eventually, of course, a decision was made and the implicit favorite won out.[22]

Soelberg uncovered this rationalization process by gathering job-decision data from thirty-two of the degree candidates via a biweekly questionnaire. After analyzing the information and identifying the implicit favorite and confirmation candidate, he made predictions regarding job choices. In 87 percent of the cases, the researchers were able to identify accurately the final choice two to eight weeks before the student admitted having made it!

Unfortunately, the **implicit favorite decision-making model** is not definitive in its description of the decision-making process. First, it relies upon the individual knowing all of the available alternatives. Second, it really does not explain how the implicit favorite is justified. Third, it fails to address nonprogrammed decision making—decision making in which the alternative courses of action are poorly defined. An example of this last shortcoming is provided in the case of creative decision making in which alternatives have to be invented or dreamed up by the individuals. Finally, it does seem that the implicit favorite model is more applicable to individual than organizational decision making. On the positive side, however, the model provides some very valuable insights into the role of rationality in individual decision making.

STOP   Review your answers to Question 3 and make any changes you would like before continuing.

3. In what way did Martin use simplification and rationalization in his decision?

Martin simplified the process by choosing the product line that he liked best and ignoring the information that was contrary to this decision. He rationalized his choice by: (a) noting that the portable television line would allow the firm to use its creative marketing skills; (b) conveying his hunch that the TVs will do a lot better than expected; and (c) realizing the fact that this product line will meet return on investment minimums. Martin probably had chosen the TV line before the marketing research people had even presented their data, so his approach was more rationalizing than rational in nature.

ORGANIZATIONAL DECISION MAKING

Up until now, we have been analyzing decision making from the standpoint of the individual. Yet many of the models and concepts we have presented apply to organizational decision making as well. After all, to a large degree, group decision making is a function of the individuals who are participating in the process, and each uses at least some of the concepts we have examined in this chapter.

The econologic model is most descriptive of upper-level decision making.

On the other hand, organizational decision making is often more rational in terms of rigorously evaluating alternatives and choosing the one with the best cost-benefit ratio. In fact, many organizations formulate specific goals, strategies, policies, procedures, and rules to provide enterprise direction while ensuring the formal coordination of resources (workforce, money, machines, and materials). At the same time, performance standards and check points are established to ensure that goal and targets are met within the assigned time and cost parameters; when they are not, corrective action is taken. These planning, organizing, and controlling functions are carefully thought out and implemented. Thus, when we talk about organizational decision making, we are more likely to find the econologic model gaining in descriptive accuracy.

Alternatively, it is misleading to believe that organizational decisions are not influenced by individuals. As long-range objectives are formulated at the top and passed down the line, the idealism of the econologic model gives way to the realism of the bounded rationality and implicit favorite models. Subjectivity and expediency replace much of the previous objectivity; those charged with the final implementation of directives use techniques that employ both satisficing and rationalization. As a result, decision making tends to be a combination of objective and subjective processes; while top management would like it to follow the steps of the econologic model, in the individual-group organization interface decision making is highly influenced by behavioral input.

DECISION-MAKING STYLES

Whether managers are making decisions that fall within the purview of the econologic or the bounded rationality model, each person brings to the process a particular style of decision making.[23] This can be more clearly seen if we consider the two major activities of decision making: information gathering and data evaluation. Each of these activities is quite different from the other and has its own set of orientations.

Information Gathering and Evaluation Orientations

Information gathering involves two psychological functions: sensation and intuition. People who are **sensation types** like to solve problems in standard ways. These individuals do well in routine work, and at the lower levels of the hierarchy they are quite effective. Working with standard, familiar problems, they are typically assertive and fast-paced, employing a "let's get it done now" approach. However, if sensation types have to learn new skills or deal with complicated details, they often become impatient or frustrated.

Intuitive types like to solve new problems. In fact, doing the same thing over and over again bores them, and they are likely to become impatient and make snap decisions in handling such problems. Intuitive decision makers rely on hunches, non-verbalized cues, spontaneity, and an openness in redefining and reworking problems until they are solved. These individuals also keep the total picture in mind and modify or alter their approaches in an effort to continually focus on the major problem. Intuitive types are found among the ranks of entrepreneurs, scientists, and politicians—individuals who rely heavily on reading each situation in deciding how to proceed.

As seen in Figure 14–3, if an individual is high on sensation, he or she will be low on intuition. These two psychological functions represent extreme orientations used by individuals in gathering information.

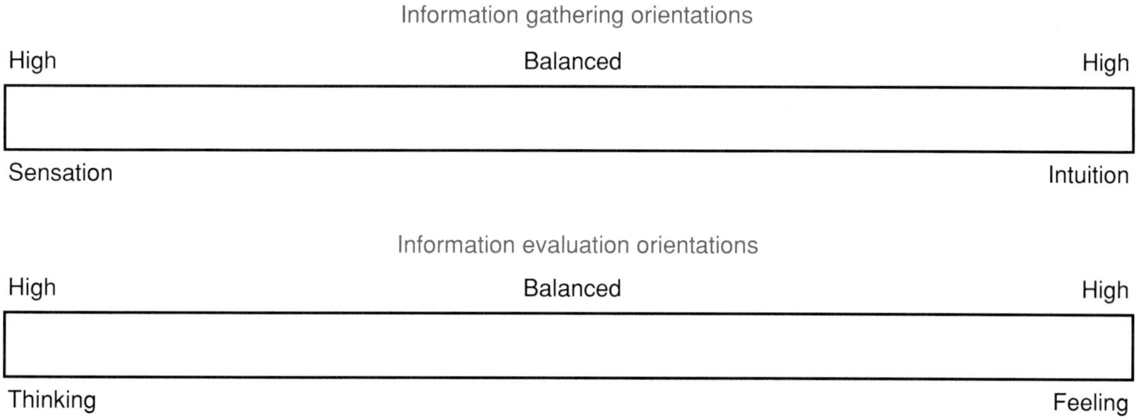

Sensation types like standard problems.

Intuitive types like new problems.

Information gathering orientations

High	Balanced	High

Sensation   Intuition

Information evaluation orientations

High	Balanced	High

Thinking   Feeling

FIGURE 14–3
Information Gathering and Evaluation Orientations

Thinking types are unemotional.

Feeling types relate well to others.

There are four basic decision styles.

The other two psychological functions that affect problem-solving styles and relate to evaluation are thinking and feeling. These are opposite extremes used in evaluating information. (Again, see Figure 14–3.)

Thinking types tend to be unemotional and uninterested in the feelings of others. Their decisions are controlled by intellectual processes based on external information and generally accepted ideas and values. These people usually organize information well and seldom reach a conclusion before carefully considering all options. Thinking types make excellent detectives or managers who function in situations in which personal feeling has to be secondary to making the right decision.

Feeling types like harmony and pleasant environments. They tend to be sympathetic and relate well to others. They also enjoy pleasing people and believe that much of the inefficiency and ineffectiveness in the organization is a result of interpersonal difficulties. Feeling types often do well as counselors, personnel training and development managers, and leaders of highly motivated, knowledgeable subordinates.

According to the famous psychologist Carl Jung, an individual tends to be dominant in only one of the four functions (sensation, intuition, thinking, or feeling) backed up by only one of the functions from the other set of paired opposites.[24] For example, a person could be high on sensation followed by thinking. Or the individual could be high on intuition followed by feeling. The four basic decision style combinations are: sensation-thinking (ST), sensation-feeling (SF), intuition-thinking (NT), and intuition-feeling (NF). These are referred to as basic decision styles.

The four basic decision styles can be classified as in Figure 14–4. Commenting on them, Taggart and Robey have noted:

> The ST processing style relies on sensing of the environment for perception and rational thinking for judgment. ST processors attend to facts and handle them with impersonal analysis. They tend to be practical and matter of fact and develop abilities more easily in technical work with facts and objects. In contrast, NF types rely on intuition perceptions and nonrational feeling for judgment. Such people attend to possibilities and handle them with personal warmth. They tend to be enthusiastic and insightful, and their abilities are more easily expressed in understanding and communicating.
>
> NT people attend to possibilities, as do NF's, but they approach them with impersonal analysis, like ST's. NT's are logical and ingenious, and express their abilities easily in theoretical and technical developments. SF people attend to facts, as do ST's but they handle them with personal warmth, like NF's. SF's tend to be sympathetic and friendly, and find their abilities best developed in practical help and services for people. Occupationally, the NT is typified by a planner; the ST, a technician; the SF, a teacher; and the NF, an artist.[25]

A number of different tests have been developed for helping individuals determine their own basic decision styles. Most of these are self-description inventories such as the Myers-Briggs Type I indicator (MBTI) in which the individual is given a series of questions that help identify the person's perception of his or her decision-making style. The MBTI has produced some interesting management research findings. For example, when Mitroff and Kilmann used the instrument and asked managers to relate stories

	Left hemisphere			Right hemisphere
	←	Decision style		→
	ST Sensation/Thinking	NT Intuition/Thinking	SF Sensation/Feeling	NF Intuition/Feeling
Focus of attention	Facts	Possibilities	Facts	Possibilities
Method of handling things	Impersonal analysis	Impersonal analysis	Personal warmth	Personal warmth
Tendency to become	Practical and matter-of-fact	Logical and ingenious	Sympathetic and friendly	Enthusiastic and insightful
Expression of abilities	Technical skills with facts and objects	Theoretical and technical developments	Practical help and services for people	Understanding and communicating with people
Representative occupation	Technician	Planner	Teacher	Artist
	←	Manager		→

FIGURE 14–4
The Range of Decision Styles in Human Information Processing (Reprinted with permission of the authors and publisher from: William Taggart and Daniel Robey, "Minds and Managers: On the Dual Nature of Human Information Processing and Management," *Academy of Management Review,* April 1981, p. 190.)

about their ideal organization, the authors reported a "remarkable and very strong similarity between the stories of those individuals who have the same personality type (e.g., ST) and . . . a remarkable and very strong difference between the stories of the four personality types."[26] ST's described their ideal organization as emphasizing factual details, the physical features of the work, certainty, specificity, and impersonal organizational control. NT's had stories that emphasized broad global issues and offered theories of organization that were impersonally idealistic. NF's also told stories with global theory emphases but they focused on general, personal, and humanistic values; they also described the organization as one that exists to serve humankind. SF's focused on facts and precision but did so in terms of human relationships within a specific organization.[27]

In another research investigation using the MBTI to study management decisions, Henderson and Nutt examined risk taking and the adoption of hypothetical capital expenditure proposals. They found that ST types were more reluctant to adopt the proposals and saw the greatest amount of risk in making decisions. SFs tolerated greater risk and were more likely to adopt the same projects. The NT and NF decision makers fell between these two groups in their likelihood to adopt proposals.[28]

Left-Brain, Right-Brain Hemispheres

Another current interest of behavioral scientists who are concerned with decision-making styles is the topic of left-brain, right-brain hemispheres. Table 14–2 provides an abbreviated summary of some of the specialized hemisphere functions. Notice from the table that individuals who are **left-brain dominant** tend to recognize and remember names; **right-brain dominant** people tend to recognize and remember faces. Left-brain people tend to respond best to verbal instructions; their right-brain counterparts respond best to visual instructions. There are also different approaches used in carrying out the decision-making process. For example, left-brain (when compared to right-brain) people tend to be more conforming (as opposed to nonconforming), prefer structure (as opposed to open-ended assignments), discover things systematically (as opposed to through exploration), recall verbal matter better than spatial imagery, look for specific facts (as opposed to main ideas), work best with sequential ideas (as opposed to those that show a relationship), and like to solve problems logically (as opposed to intuitively).[29]

Researchers such as Robey and Taggart believe that there is a link between decision styles and left-hemisphere and right-hemisphere domination. Referring to Figure 14–4, they point out that:

> At the top of [the figure], we suggest a link between left hemisphere domination and the ST type, and one between right hemisphere domination and the NF type. The two intermediate types, NT and SF, can be considered less indicative of hemispheric domination. The placement of NT to the left of SF suggests that thinking (T) judgment is more characteristic of left hemisphere processes than in intuitive (N) perception. The feeling (F) type, in contrast, is dominated by the right hemisphere, which "pulls" the SF person to the right of the NT. This implies that the second-named element (judgment) takes precedence over the first (perception); in other words, characterization of style depends more on how information is *processed* (judgment) than on how it is *gathered* (perception).[30]

TABLE 14–2
Twelve of the Specialized Brain-Hemisphere Functions

Left Brain	Right Brain
Recognize and remember names	Recognize and remember faces
Respond to verbal instructions	Respond to visual instructions
Dislike improvising	Like to improvise
Solve problems systematically	Solve problems playfully
Logical problem solvers	Intuitive problem solvers
Responsive to logic appeals	Responsive to emotional appeals
Deal with one problem at a time	Deal with several problems at a time
Not psychic	Highly psychic
Produce logical ideas	Produce humorous ideas
Seldom use metaphors	Often use metaphors
Give information verbally	Give information with movement
Depend on words for meanings	Interpret body language

The second, and perhaps more important, idea conveyed by Figure 14−4 is that managers have to be flexible in their processing style. Since they face a wide variety of technical and human-oriented questions, they will be more effective if they can change their style to fit their problems; that is, a manager sometimes has to be a technician, other times a planner, still other times a teacher, and in some cases an artist. This can be illustrated by looking at how each of the four managers listed at the bottom of Figure 14−4 might respond to a situation that calls for the individual to deal with a subordinate whose performance has been marginal. Consider how each of the four might act:

Manager	Response	Characteristics of the Response[31]
ST	Improve your performance or you're fired!	Factual, impersonal, practical
NT	If your performance does not improve, you will be transferred to another position.	Possibilities, impersonal, ingenious
SF	You need to change; what can we do to help you?	Factual, personal, sympathetic
NF	You can improve your performance; let me suggest an approach.	Possibilities, personal, insightful

Researchers interested in decision styles and left-brain, right-brain dominance are currently studying how and why left-brain dominant people process information differently from right-brain dominant people. They are also interested in integrated and mixed problem-solving strategies. An integrated problem-solver uses the left *and* right hemisphere simultaneously without a clear preference for either. If pressured to express a preference, individuals do tend to favor one over the other. However, the strong connection between the two hemispheres indicates that the real preference is for using both together. A *mixed* problem solving strategy is used by individuals who employ *either* a left- or a right-dominant strategy, depending on the situation. So there are actually four categories of problem-solving strategies: right brain, left brain, integrated, and mixed.

At the present time, human information processing researchers are interested in three specific areas of inquiry. One is how managers can be provided with learning experiences to improve right-hemisphere imaginative decision skills while continuing to educate them for success as left-hemisphere (logical) managers. For business schools and training and development departments, this means balancing the curriculum to encompass the complete range of processing styles and strategies that are offered in Figure 14−4.

The second area of inquiry is that of developing more systematic measurement instruments for identifying individual processing styles. These styles can be inferred from observed behavior and self-description inventories. However, "more work must be done to study correlations between the various approaches, their reliability, and validity and their links to existing and emerging theory."[32]

A third area of interest is the value of human information-processing data in assigning decision-making tasks. A practical example was provided by the Hawaii Telephone Company (HTC), which administered diagnostic tests to identify left-brain and right-brain managers. It then assigned each to a group with similar thinking styles. The left-brain managers were charged with dealing with decisions that required a creative approach, while the right-brain managers were charged with addressing decisions that required a logical and analytical approach. This "dual" approach to dealing with decision making has proven very effective for HTC.[33] Other firms are providing training to their people in becoming more "other" brained. For example, left-brain thinkers are encouraged to develop their right brain by engaging in unstructured activities such as creative daydreaming, observing colors, listening to sounds in the immediate environment, and joking with others. Right-brain thinkers are encouraged to develop their left brain by outlining things, solving mathematical problems, and engaging in analytical thinking.[34]

STOP

Review your answers to Question 4 and make any changes you would like before continuing.

4. What type of information-gathering orientation did Martin use? Explain. Is he a left-brain or right-brain thinker? Give an example.

Martin is an intuitive type of information gatherer. He uses intuition, hunch, and spontaneity in making decisions. He is a right-brain thinker as reflected by the fact that he likes to employ a creative approach in getting things done. Notice how he believes that a creative marketing effort will result in greater sales than the marketing research people are predicting.

SUMMARY

1. Decision making is the process of choosing from among alternatives, and there are two ways of examining this process: prescriptively and descriptively. The former attempts to describe how decisions ought to be made, and the latter describes how decisions are actually made. Whichever approach is taken, of course, there is the implied presence of rationality.

2. The econologic model proceeds from the basic assumption that people are economically rational and attempt to maximize outputs in an orderly and sequential fashion. These steps involve: (a) identifying the problem to be solved or goal to be achieved; (b) listing the various alternatives that could be used to accomplish this mission; (c) determining the results from each alternative; and (d) making a comparative evaluation of them to choose the best one.

The econologic model has several shortcomings. First, there is the problem of obtaining complete information on all alternatives and outcomes. Second, there is the difficulty of processing all of this information.

3. The bounded rationality model portrays the decision maker as an administrative person with limited information-processing capability. As a result, the individual's final choice is usually something less than ideal. This occurs for two reasons: (a) decision makers seldom employ opportunistic surveillance; and (b) many people employ satisficing behavior in which they choose an alternative that is "good enough" rather than expending time and effort to identify the one best possible alternative. The steps in the bounded rationality process are: (a) identifying the problem to be solved or goal to be attained; (b) determining the

minimum level of acceptability for all alternatives; (c) choosing one feasible solution; (d) determining if it meets the minimum levels of acceptability; (e) if the alternative does, implementing it; if not, going back and choosing another; and (f) after implementation, determining how easy or difficult it was to identify feasible alternatives and using this information to raise or lower the minimum level of acceptability on future problems of a similar nature. Empirical research tends to support the superiority of the bounded rationality model over the econologic model in terms of describing how personal decision making is carried out.

4. Other data-based research has shed further light on the decision-making process. For example, there is considerable evidence that decision makers use a simplified model of reality. Furthermore, people tend to use subjective rationality as the situation becomes more complex, even though objective rationality would provide higher payoffs. Additionally, rationalization often transcends rationality.

5. At the organizational level, the econologic model gains in descriptive accuracy. However, as top management decisions are delegated down the hierarchy, those implementing them often employ a process similar to that presented by the bounded rationality model.

6. Decision makers have different styles. Using the psychological functions of sensation, intuition, thinking, and feeling, four different style combinations can be derived. These combinations were illustrated in Figure 14–4. Each of the four styles results in a different type of decision-making approach. In addition to studying these four styles, behavioral scientists have also been investigating left-brain, right-brain hemisphere functions. As pointed out in Table 14–3, left-brain dominant people tend to approach decision making in a different way than do right-brain people. What is the connection between decision styles and brain dominance? Some researchers have offered tentative findings, but for the moment the area remains one of substantive inquiry.

KEY TERMS

decision making	uncertainty	intuitive types
prescriptive decision theory	maximin criterion	thinking types
descriptive decision theory	bounded rationality decision-	feeling types
economic man	making model	left-brain dominant
administrative man	opportunistic surveillance	right-brain dominant
econologic decision-making	satisficing behavior	
model	implicit favorite decision-making	
certainty	model	
risk	sensation types	

REVIEW AND STUDY QUESTIONS

1. How does prescriptive decision theory differ from descriptive decision theory?

2. How can you tell if a decision is rational or not? Explain, including in your answer a definition of the word *rational.*

3. Many people use the econologic model rather than the bounded rationality model in describing the decision-making process. Why is this so?

4. What are the major shortcomings of the econologic model? Describe them.

5. What are the basic decision-making steps in the bounded rationality model? Identify them.

6. Why do most decision makers fail to carry out opportunistic surveillance? Explain.

7. How does satisficing behavior influence the average decision maker's behavior? Give an example in your answer.

8. In what way have Cyert, March, and Clarkson helped validate the accuracy of the bounded rationality model? Explain.

9. How do people tend to deal with cognitive dissonance? Give an illustration.

10. Why is it true that, regardless of their initial goals, people often become more conservative as the complexity of a situation increases?

11. In what way is subjective rationality always present in the decision-making process? Cite an example in your answer.

12. In a rationalization model of decision-making behavior, what role is played by the confirmation candidate? Where does the implicit favorite enter the process? Explain.

13. "When we talk about organizational decision making, we are likely to find the econologic model gaining over the bounded rationality model in terms of descriptive accuracy." What is meant by this statement?

14. How do sensation types go about gathering information? How do intuition types do so?

15. How do thinking types go about evaluating data? How do feeling types go about evaluating data?

16. Using the four types of functions described in the above two answers, what basic decision-style combinations are there?

17. How do decision makers who are left-brain dominant differ from those who are right-brain dominant? Compare and contrast the two.

18. Is there any link between decision styles and left-hemisphere and right-hemisphere domination? Explain your answer.

CASES

A Down-Home Decision

Chet Andrews and his family have lived in southern California for the last fifteen years. Recently, Chet was called in by the president of his company and offered a promotion to vice-president and the opportunity to head up the firm's east coast operations. The company feels that by expanding to the other coast it can increase sales by 30 percent annually. No final decision had been made regarding where the east coast headquarters would be established, but a committee that had been studying the matter felt the two most promising locations were Buffalo, New York, and Orlando, Florida. The president promised Chet that if he accepted the job, he could make the final site choice himself. After conducting a preliminary review of the committee's data, Chet concluded that Buffalo would be the best choice.

Upon returning home that evening, Chet shared the news about the promotion with his wife. She was delighted to learn that he was finally going to be rewarded for all of the hard work he had done for the firm. However, she was not very pleased with the site location news. "I don't want to move to Buffalo," she told him. "It's cold there, and the children have never really had to spend a winter in that type of climate. Also, our parents are in their mid-sixties, and you know how much they like to come here to visit the kids. If we live in the north, the chance of their coming as often is going to be a lot less. Besides, I thought that a promotion is supposed to be a reward for doing a good job. It doesn't seem to me that this is much of a reward."

Chet listened quietly. When his wife was done, he asked her, "What do you want me to do? How would you like to handle this situation?" His wife measured her words carefully. "If I were you, I'd opt for the Orlando site. After all, the president is going to follow your recommendation. How much better is Buffalo going to be for the company than Orlando? Orlando is growing by leaps and bounds. So the company will be able to get its foot into a dynamic market, and at the same time it will be able to do you a favor." Chet said that he would think about it.

The next day, Chet told the president he would take the promotion. He also told him that after careful consideration of the committee's report, coupled with his own appraisal of the situation, he had decided that Orlando would be the best site location. The president gave his approval and told Chet to begin making plans to implement the expansion. When he called home to tell his wife the news, she was overjoyed. "Great, the children are going to be so happy. And Mom and Dad will be too. I can hardly wait to tell them."

1. Was Chet's decision rational?

2. Is the decision best described by an econologic or a bounded rationality model?

3. How did the concept of satisficing behavior enter into the decision? Explain.

It Was in the Bag

Last month, Mary Berdley, an accounting major, was graduated from a large midwestern university. During her last semester, Mary had interviews with seven large certified public accounting firms and nine intermediate and small ones. Her accounting grade point average of 3.75 and her overall GPA of 3.88 helped attract her to these firms, and some of them were very competitive in their hiring efforts. One company flew her to the home office 700 miles away and gave her a full-day tour of the facilities. They then proceeded to throw a small dinner party for her, and at the height of the dinner the president of the firm offered her a job. Mary was in a state of shock, but quickly recovered her composure and mumbled something about "wanting to think about it." Another firm interviewed her on campus. When they learned that Mary was thinking of getting married during the next year, they told her that the company would guarantee her fiancé a job as well.

During the semester Mary continually talked to her faculty advisor regarding the offers she was receiving. The advisor offered her general advice but tried not to influence the final decision in any way. During one of their last communications, the advisor said, "There are three weeks until graduation. You need to start concentrating on your studies. When the exam period is over, you can then sit back and make a decision. Besides, with sixteen offers in hand, it doesn't sound like you have an easy choice ahead of you." Mary just smiled.

A week before graduation, Mary dropped by to talk to the advisor. She informed the woman that she had accepted a job with one of the best-known national accounting firms. When the woman asked her why she had opted for this one, Mary said that several factors had influenced her decision. First, the money was better than that offered by any of the other firms. Second, there was a chance that she might someday become a partner. Third, if she decided to quit, it would be a lot easier to find another good job because the reputation of her employer was so high that competitors were quick to snap up those who were leaving.

This, however, was not the story the advisor received from other students. They told her that Mary had taken the job with the national accounting firm because her uncle was a partner there and had helped her out. "Her family wanted her to take that job and she was happy to comply," said one of the students. "There was never any doubt in any of our minds that she'd get an offer from that accounting firm and she'd accept it. It was in the bag all along."

1. Are any of Mary's comments to the advisor accurate? Explain.

2. Describe Mary's decision-making process, bringing the concepts of implicit favorite and confirmation candidate into your discussion.

3. Assuming Mary intended all along to take the job with the large national firm, why did she still go ahead and have interviews with the other companies?

SELF-FEEDBACK EXERCISE

Are You a Left-brain or a Right-brain Hemisphere Person?

As noted in the chapter, some people tend to be left-brain dominant, while others are right-brain dominant. The following questions are designed to help you determine which you are. Before answering the twenty-five questions, however, please keep in mind that this assignment is designed only to provide you with some preliminary information regarding your perception of the type of decision maker you are. Also remember that many people are not totally left- or right-brain dominant, but rather use an integrated or mixed decision-making process. The following does not measure the latter two strategies. It provides feedback only on your preference for left or right brain thinking.

Answer each of the following as accurately as you can. It is a forced-choice test, so circle the letter of the option you like best (or dislike least), but remember to answer each one!

1. When you solve problems, your basic approach is:
    a. logical, rational
    b. intuitive

2. If you were able to write books, which type would you prefer to write?
    a. fiction
    b. nonfiction

3. When you read, you read for:
   a. main ideas
   b. specific facts and details
4. Which of these types of stories do you most like to read?
   a. realistic
   b. fantasy
5. When you study or read:
   a. you listen to music on the radio
   b. you must have silence
6. How do you prefer to learn?
   a. through ordering and planning
   b. through free exploration
7. How do you like to organize things?
   a. sequentially
   b. in terms of relationships
8. Which of these statements best describes you:
   a. almost no mood changes
   b. frequent mood changes
9. Do you enjoy clowning around?
   a. yes
   b. no
10. How would you describe yourself?
    a. generally conforming
    b. generally nonconforming
11. Are you absentminded?
    a. frequently
    b. virtually never
12. What types of assignments do you like best?
    a. well structured
    b. open-ended
13. Which is most preferable to you?
    a. producing ideas
    b. drawing conclusions
14. Which is the most fun for you?
    a. dreaming
    b. planning realistically
15. Which of these would be most exciting for you?
    a. inventing something new
    b. improving on something already in existence

16. What type of stories do you prefer?
    a. action
    b. mystery
17. Which do you like best?
    a. cats
    b. dogs
18. What do you like best?
    a. creating stories
    b. analyzing stories
19. Do you think better:
    a. sitting up straight
    b. lying down
20. If you could be either, which would you prefer to be?
    a. a music composer
    b. a music critic
21. Could you be hypnotized?
    a. yes, quite easily
    b. no, I don't think so
22. Which would you prefer to do?
    a. ballet dancing
    b. interpretive impromptu dancing
23. Which are you best at?
    a. recalling names and dates
    b. recalling where things were in a room or picture
24. When it comes to getting instructions, which do you prefer?
    a. verbal instructions
    b. demonstrations
25. When getting verbal instructions, how do you generally feel?
    a. restless
    b. attentive

Now take each of your answers and compare them to the key below. *Circle* your response to each, and then add up the total of circled responses in each column.

	I	II
1.	b	a
2.	a	b
3.	a	b
4.	b	a

5.	a	b
6.	b	a
7.	b	a
8.	b	a
9.	a	b
10.	b	a
11.	a	b
12.	b	a
13.	a	b
14.	a	b
15.	a	b
16.	b	a
17.	a	b
18.	a	b

19.	b	a
20.	b	a
21.	a	b
22.	b	a
23.	b	a
24.	b	a
25.	a	b
TOTAL _____		_____

Column I measures your perceived preference for using right-brain functions while Column II measures your perceived preference for using left-brain functions. If you want more information on the way you perceive yourself as a decision maker, go back and reread Table 14–2.

NOTES

1. Henry Mintzberg, Dura Raisinghani, and Andre Theoret, "The Structure of 'Unstructured' Decision Processes," *Administrative Science Quarterly,* June 1976, pp. 246–275.

2. This is true for both national and international firms as explained in Richard M. Hodgetts and Fred Luthans, *International Management* (New York: McGraw Hill Book Co., 1991), pp. 178–183.

3. Herbert A. Simon, *Administrative Behavior,* 3rd ed. (New York: The Free Press, 1976), pp. 76–77.

4. See for example Richard M. Hodgetts, *Management: Theory, Process, and Practice,* 5th ed. (San Diego, CA: Harcourt Brace Jovanovich, 1990), p. 268.

5. Other decision criteria often used under uncertainty include the maximax (in which the decision maker opts for the greatest payoff of all) and the LaPlace criterion (in which equal probabilities are assigned to all of the competition's strategies). For a more detailed description of decision making under uncertainty see Hodgetts, *Management,* pp. 277–278.

6. O. I. Larichev and H. M. Moshkovich, "Limits to Decision-Making Ability in Direct Multiattribute Alternative Evaluation," *Organizational Behavior and Human Decision Processes,* Spring 1988, pp. 217–233.

7. For additional insights see Alexander Pollatsek, Arnold D. Well, Clifford Konold, Pamela Hardiman, and George Cobb, "Understanding Conditional Probabilities," *Organizational Behavior and Human Decision Processes,* October 1987, pp. 255–269; and Phipps Arabie and Carman Maschmeyer, "Some Current Models for the Perception and Judgment of Risk," *Organizational Behavior and Human Decision Processes,* June 1988, pp. 300–329.

8. Simon, *Administrative Behavior,* p. 241.

9. See for example Robert S. Billings and Lisa L. Scherer, "The Effects of Response Mode and Importance on Decision-Making Strategies: Judgment versus Choice," *Organizational Behavior and Human Decision Processes,* February 1988, pp. 1–19.

10. James G. March and Herbert A. Simon, *Organizations* (New York: John Wiley & Sons, 1958), pp. 140–141.

11. See for example Jan J. J. Christensen-Szalanski, "A Further Examination of the Selection of Problem-Solving Strategies: The Effects of Deadlines and Analytical Aptitudes," *Organizational Behavior and Human Performance,* February 1980, pp. 107–120.

12. Herbert A. Simon, *Models of Man* (New York: John Wiley & Sons, 1977), p. 253.

13. Jerome R. Busemeyer, "Choice of Behavior in a Sequential Decision Making Task," *Organizational Behavior and Human Performance,* April 1982, pp. 175–207.

14. Richard M. Cyert and James G. March (eds.), *A Behavioral Theory of the Firm* (Englewood Cliffs, NJ: Prentice-Hall, 1963); and G. P. E. Clarkson, "A Model of Trust Investment Behavior," in Richard M. Cyert and James G. March (eds.), *A Behavioral Theory of the Firm* (Englewood Cliffs, NJ: Prentice-Hall, 1963), pp. 253–267.

15. Cyert and March, *A Behavioral Theory*, p. 147.

16. Clarkson, "Trust Investment Behavior," pp. 253–267.

17. Also see Herbert A. Simon, "Making Management Decisions: The Role of Intuition and Emotion," *Academy of Management Executive*, February 1987, pp. 57–64.

18. Charles R. Schwenk, "The Use of Participant Recollection in the Modeling of Organizational Decision Processes," *Academy of Management Review*, July 1985, pp. 496–503.

19. Paul H. Schurr, "The Effects of Gain and Loss Decision Frames on Risky Purchase Negotiations," *Journal of Applied Psychology*, August 1987, pp. 351–359; Michele Cohen, Jean-Yves Jaffray, and Tanios Said, "Experimental Comparison of Individual Behavior Under Risk and Uncertainty for Gains and for Losses," *Organizational Behavior and Human Decision Processes*, February 1987, pp. 1–22; and Don N. Kleinmuntz and James B. Thomas, "The Value of Action and Inference in Dynamic Decision Making," *Organizational Behavior and Human Decision Processes*, June 1987, pp. 341–364.

20. For more on subjective rationality see Henry Montgomery and Thomas Adelbratt, "Gambling Decisions and Information about Expected Value," *Organizational Behavior and Human Performance*, February 1982, pp. 39–57; and Roger Johansson and Berndt Brehner, "Inferences from Incomplete Information—A Note," *Organizational Behavior and Human Performance*, August 1979, pp. 141–145.

21. N. S. Fagley and Paul M. Miller, "The Effects of Decision Framing on Choice of Risky vs. Certain Options," *Organizational Behavior and Human Decision Processes*, April 1987, pp. 264–277.

22. Peter O. Soelberg, "Unprogrammed Decision Making," *Industrial Management Review*, Spring 1967, pp.

19–29. For more on this see Daniel J. Power and Ramon L. Aldag, "Soelberg's Job Search and Choice Model: A Clarification, Review, and Critique," *Academy of Management Review*, January 1985, pp. 48–58.

23. See for example Jeanette R. Scollard, "How to Tell a Smart Risk From a Dumb One," *Working Woman*, February 1990, pp. 78–79.

24. C. G. Jung, *Psychological Types* (London: Routledge & Kegan Paul, 1923).

25. William Taggart and Daniel Robey, "Minds and Managers: On the Dual Nature of Human Information Processing and Management," *Academy of Management Review*, April 1981, p. 190.

26. I. I. Mitroff and R. H. Kilmann, "On Organization Stories: An Approach to the Design and Analysis of Organization through Myths and Stories," in R. H. Kilmann, L. R. Pondy, and D. P. Slevin (eds.), *The Management of Organization Design*, vol. 1 (New York: Elsevier North-Holland, 1976), p. 193.

27. *Ibid.*, pp. 193–195.

28. John C. Henderson and Paul C. Nutt, "The Influence of Decision Style on Decision-Making Behavior," *Management Science*, April 1980, pp. 371–386.

29. For more on this see Dudley Lynch, "Is the Brain Stuff Still the Right (or Left) Stuff?," *Training and Development Journal*, February 1986, pp. 23–26.

30. Taggart and Robey, "Minds and Managers," p. 191.

31. *Ibid.*

32. Daniel Robey and William Taggart, "Measuring Managers' Minds: The Assessment of Style in Human Information Processing," *Academy of Management Review*, July 1981, p. 382. See also Terence Hines, "Left Brain/Right Brain Mythology and Implications for Management and Training," *Academy of Management Review*, October 1987, pp. 600–606.

33. Richard M. Hodgetts, *Modern Human Relations at Work*, 4th ed. (Hinsdale, IL: Dryden Press, 1990), pp. 130–131.

34. *Ibid.*, p. 131.

CHAPTER 15
The Communication Process

GOALS OF THE CHAPTER

As we noted in the introduction to this section, some basic processes link the individual, the group, and the organization. One of these is the communication process. The goals of this chapter are to examine this process, to study some of the common barriers to effective communication, and to review techniques useful in surmounting these obstacles. When you are finished reading this chapter you should be able to:

1. describe the communication process;
2. explain the role and functioning of formal communication channels;
3. relate how the grapevine can be of value to the manager;
4. discuss the most typical forms of communication media used in organizations;
5. identify and describe common barriers to communication;
6. present some of the most useful techniques for overcoming these barriers.

OPENING CASE: THERE'S NOTHING TO WORRY ABOUT

All correspondence for the senior vice-president is opened by Anne Putnam, executive secretary, and placed on the manager's desk. Two weeks ago Anne put a one-page memo on her boss's desk. As she did so, she read the message. It said that the firm's major aerospace contracts would be reduced by 20 percent, effective next year. The memo contained an error. The word "contracts" should have been singular.

Anne immediately placed a call to her two best friends, Phil Carter and George Robaina. Within three days Phil had submitted a request asking to be transferred to the consumer products division. George passed the information to his best friend and counselor, Terri Mattson, and to his boss, William Sallers, for whom he has great respect.

William found the news hard to believe and immediately passed the information to his boss. At the same time William told George that the information was incorrect. However, George did not believe this because Anne's information had always been accurate in the past.

The message eventually was communicated through four hierarchical levels and resulted in William receiving a brief memo from the company president. "May I please see you regarding the rumor that all of our business is scheduled to be cut back by 20 percent," it read.

William and the president met for ten minutes. Part of the conversation was as follows:

President: I think you should know that the information you heard about business being cut by 20 percent is nothing but rumor.

William: I know. In fact, I wanted to ask your support in refuting the rumor. Can I explain why?

President: Oh, that's not necessary. You and I both know it's untrue, and that's all that counts. We're not going to cut any personnel.

William: That's great news but . . .

President: So there's no need to worry about anything. Well, it's been good to see you.

William: But don't you think . . .

President: Well, have a nice day.

1. What type of informal communication network was used in conveying Anne's message? Explain.
2. In what way did perception help influence George's refusal to believe William's message? What communication barrier accounted for the message being changed as it went through five hierarchical levels?
3. What type of a listener is the president? What type of listener would William have found to be most effective? Explain.

Write down your answers to these questions and put them aside. We will return to them later.

THE NATURE OF COMMUNICATION

Communication is the process of transmitting meanings from sender to receiver.[1] True communication requires an understanding of the message: the receiver must comprehend the meaning.[2] The process by which this is done comprises seven key elements (see Figure 15–1), and the process is universally applicable.[3]

There are seven key elements in the communication process.

First, there must be an idea or thought to be conveyed. Second, the idea must be encoded or put into some form for transmission; the sender must organize his or her ideas in some coherent fashion. Third, the means for transmission have to be determined. Fourth, noise or message interference must be overcome. Fifth, the message must be received by the other party. Sixth, the transmission must be correctly decoded to reconstruct the intended meaning.[4] Seventh, action must follow so that the person knows the message was correctly received.

COMMUNICATION IN ORGANIZATIONS

Communication channels hold the organization together because they provide the means for transmitting information vital to organizational activity and goal attainment.[5] Much of this information is carried along formal lines, while the remainder is transmitted informally.

FIGURE 15–1
The Communication Process

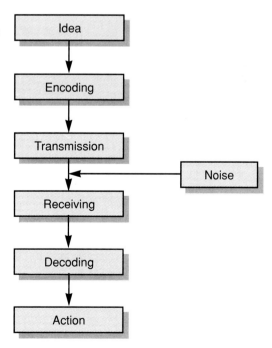

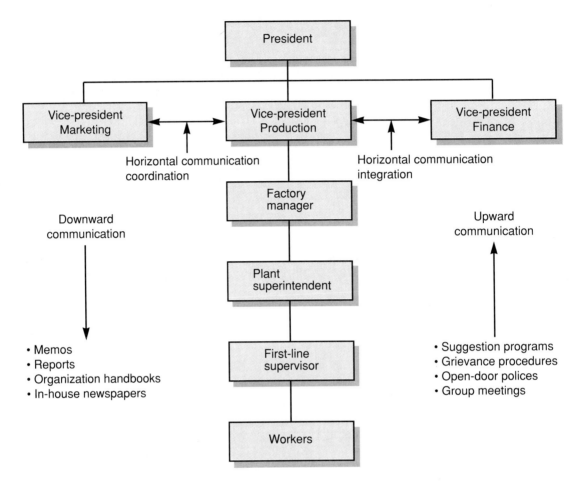

FIGURE 15−2
Formal Communication Channels

Formal Communication Channels

Formal communication channels are established by the organization's structure. Figure 15−2 provides a simple illustration of the three most common types of channels (downward, upward, and horizontal) in a manufacturing firm.

Downward channels convey directives from superior to subordinate.

Downward Communication. **Downward communication** is used to convey directives from superior to subordinate. One of the most common purposes of these communiques is to provide specific job instructions regarding what is to be done, by whom, and when. Such information can help clarify operational goals, provide a sense of direction, assist in indoctrinating workers as to the organization's mission and philosophy, and provide subordinates with data related to their performance. A downward orientation also helps link the levels of the hierarchy by providing a basis for coordinative activity.

Upward channels provide feedback from subordinates.

Upward Communication.

Upward communication provides management with feedback from the subordinates. The major benefit of upward communication is that it creates a channel from which management can gauge organizational climate and deal with problem areas, such as grievances or low productivity, before they become major issues. Unfortunately, this type of communication is often given minimum consideration in many organizations.

Horizontal Communication.

Horizontal communication takes place between people at the same level of the hierarchy. Support for this particular form of communication is often traced back to Henri Fayol, the father of modern management theory. In his famous *gangplank principle,* Fayol recommended that individuals at the same level of the hierarchy be allowed to communicate directly, provided they have permission from their supervisors to do so and they tell their respective chiefs afterward what they have agreed to do. In this way, while the integrity of the hierarchy is never threatened, it is possible to avoid following the formal chain of command by having to send messages up one part of the organization and down the other. In Figure 15–3, for example, to get a message from D to I it is necessary, if the person is to follow the scalar chain, to go up the hierarchy to A and then down to I. Following the gangplank principle, much of this red tape is avoided via a direct horizontal channel.

Horizontal channels are used for integration and coordination.

Most horizontal communications have integrative and coordinative purposes. At the upper levels of a manufacturing firm, for example, the vice-presidents of marketing, production, and finance will coordinate their efforts in order to arrive at an integrated master plan. The same is true in a major hospital in which the associate administrators for nursing, medical services, and support services will work together in constructing a long-range plan. In a university setting it is common to find departments coordinating their activities in order to ensure that all segments of the college are working toward the same general goals.

Informal Communication

The informal organizational communication network is known as the **grapevine**. Davis has called it "the network of social relations that arises spontaneously as people associate with one another. It is an expression of people's natural motivation to

FIGURE 15–3
Fayol's Gangplank Principle

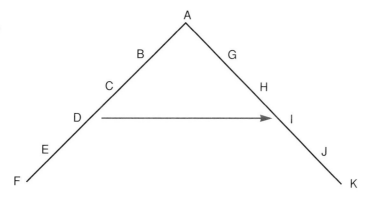

communicate."[6] Personnel use the grapevine to supplement formal channels. Some of the most likely causes for grapevine activity are the following:

1. When there is a lack of information about the situation, people try to fill in the gaps as best they can via informal channels.

2. When there is insecurity in the situation, people tend to increase their informal communication in an effort to create cohesiveness and protect each other against the unknown.

3. When individuals have a personal or emotional interest in a situation, such as when a friend has had a conflict with a supervisor, they will talk about it informally.

4. When people dislike others, they will often try to gain an advantage by passing undesirable rumors about these individuals through the grapevine.

5. When people have just received new information and want to spread the word as quickly as possible, they will often use informal channels.[7]

In most cases the grapevine relies on word of mouth. As a result it is common to find members of this informal organization coming into contact with each other during their daily work routine. For example, in one company the chief informal link between two offices was a manager's secretary who stopped by the other office right after lunch to pick up reports. During these visits information on topics of mutual interest was exchanged. In another office, the link between two offices was an accounting clerk who telephoned 300 yards across company property to secure some cost data. The conversations typically involved information in addition to that required by the organization. In a similar manner, employees having nearby desks are more likely to communicate via the grapevine than two employees in separate buildings. Opportunity is a prime requirement for being involved in a grapevine communication network.[8]

Informal Network and the Manager.   The grapevine carries rumor, gossip, and other informal communiques. Many times this information is either erroneous or incomplete. Sometimes, however, it is accurate. In any case, information transmission tends to follow a logical pattern. There are some people to whom messages are deliberately passed, and there are others who are deliberately bypassed. This selective form of communication is most prevalent in informal networks and is known as the **cluster chain**. To a large degree the informal organization relies on this chain for its survival. If individuals who are not supposed to receive certain types of information do receive them, the results may be detrimental to members of the informal group; and those responsible for passing the information to the "wrong" person(s) may well be excluded from future transmissions.

However, the cluster chain is not the only type of chain used in informal communications. There are three others. One is the **single-strand chain**. As seen in Figure 15–4, when information is conveyed by means of this channel, it moves from one person to the next. Everyone receives information from one (and only one) person and passes it on to one (and only one) person.

A second informal communication network is the **gossip chain**. When this channel is used, information is passed from one person to all of the others. In Figure 15–4

The cluster chain is most prevalent in informal networks.

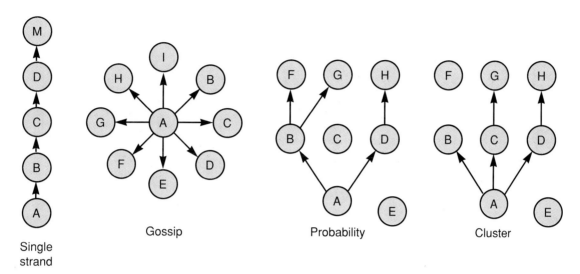

Single strand

Gossip

Probability

Cluster

FIGURE 15–4
Informal Communication Networks

the gossip network diagram looks like a wheel, with the person who is passing the information serving as the hub. This individual, quite obviously, is the most important person in the chain, since without him or her no information would be passed along.

A third informal communication network is the **probability chain,** in which information is passed along on a random basis. For example, an individual who learns that there are salary raises of 11 percent, in contrast to the expected 7 percent, may tell everyone he or she meets in the course of a walk down the hall. In this case, the information is passed on the basis of "who is in the nearby area." If the chain continues to exist, each individual who receives the information will also randomly pass it on to others in the network. Notice in Figure 15–4 that some people are not told the news. These are the individuals who do not happen to bump into one of the people with the latest salary data.

Many managers believe the grapevine to be a source of erroneous information that helps foster dissatisfaction, anxiety, and other dysfunctional attitudes. From a positive standpoint, however, this information channel has some very favorable features.

First, the grapevine can help build morale by carrying the positive comments people make about the organization. Second, the grapevine can provide satisfaction and stability to work groups by giving them a sense of belonging and security. Third, the grapevine provides employees with a safety valve for their emotions. For example, when someone gets extremely angry at the boss, he or she might risk being fired by entering into a confrontation with the individual, but by sharing this anger with other grapevine members the worker can find a harmless release for the frustration. Fourth, the grapevine encourages managers to plan and act more carefully than they would otherwise because it provides a check and balance on poorly conceived plans, emotional decisions, and the rise of favoritism. Fifth, the grapevine is a source of feedback to

The grapevine has numerous benefits.

managers; they can use it to find out what is going on around the organization and in this way learn the types of problems their employees are facing.[9]

Communication Media

Communication in organizations can take a variety of forms, including words, pictures, or actions. Words are the most common form, as seen by the wide use made of written and oral communication in organizations. Pictures are useful as visual aids and are employed in charts, blueprints, and posters to help convey the message. Actions take many different forms, especially in nonverbal cues. Receivers employ them as supplements to the main message. (What is this person really saying?) Senders use them in gauging how well the message is being received and the types of clarification or discussion, if any, that are needed. (Does this person understand what I am saying, and will the individual take the action I want taken?) Nonverbal channels are those of which people are least aware in themselves and most aware in others. The following subsections examine all three of these communications forms: written, oral, and nonverbal, with particular attention given to the latter.

Written Communication. Some of the more common forms of written communications are memos, reports, and organizational handbooks. Many managers like written communications because they provide a record of what was transmitted and can be reread and studied if they are initially unclear. Additionally, written messages carry a degree of formality not present in their verbal counterparts.

On the other hand, written communications present a number of major problems. First, many managers have difficulty expressing themselves in writing, so they deemphasize this medium. Second, superiors often refuse to read written reports of any substantial length, preferring to be briefed verbally on their content. Third, some written communications, such as job descriptions and policy manuals, are continually in need of updating, a task that is very time consuming.

Oral Communication. Most managers prefer oral communication to written because it is faster and allows for immediate feedback. Some of the most common forms include face-to-face verbal orders, telephone discussions, speeches, and discussions at meetings. Of these, face-to-face communication is considered most effective since it allows each party to respond directly to the other. Through this give-and-take problems and barriers can often be cleared up and a more complete transmission of meanings obtained.

Of course, face-to-face communication is not always possible. In dealing with large groups the manager is often forced to choose a more appropriate form of communication, such as a speech. Even with a small group, an informal talk with limited discussion afterward may be the best the manager can do. Each step away from one-on-one communication reduces the degree of interaction and, therefore, the extent of information exchanged.

Nonverbal Communication. Nonverbal communication can take many different forms. For purposes of analysis, the area has three major components: kinesics, proxemics, and paralanguage.[10]

Kinesics is another name for body language, and it includes such things as facial expressions, gestures, and posture.[11] Of all body expressions, the eyes seem to hold

---

Written communications provide a record of what was transmitted.

Most managers prefer oral communication.

There are three major forms of nonverbal communication: kinesics, proxemics, and paralanguage.

the most significance. For example, research reveals that speakers tend to perceive those who look at them as being more instrumental to their goals than those who do not.[12] The most important thing to remember about body language is that it is often just as important as verbal activity.

Proxemics deals with the way people use physical space and what it says about them. An excellent example is provided by the way managers arrange things in their office. Figure 15–5 offers an example.[13] Notice that layouts A and B are traditional and formal. The desk is placed between the manager and the visitor and serves to create a degree of formality. Layouts C and D are more client-related or participative in nature and help create a more favorable environment for open communication.

Keep in mind, however, that the manager may *not* want such a relaxed environment. When this is true, the study of proxemics takes status (the manager is showing how important he or she is) into account. The next time you visit a high-ranking executive, notice that the individual has an office that: (a) is larger than those of the subordinates; (b) has a window; (c) contains better quality furniture and more trappings than anyone else; and (d) is often in the corner of the building. Managers use physical space to send messages to others.

Paralanguage, closely associated with verbal communication, deals with *how* things are said. A person's rate of speech, voice tension, pacing, and loudness all

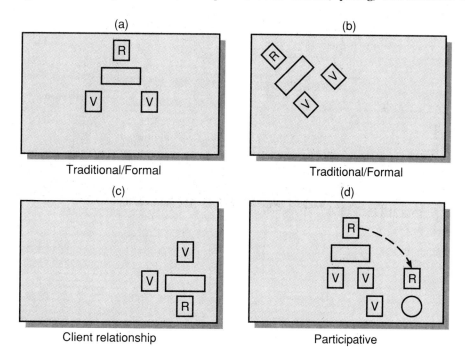

(a)

Traditional/Formal

(b)

Traditional/Formal

(c)

Client relationship

(d)

Participative

R = resident office holder

V = visitor

FIGURE 15–5
Different Forms of Office Layout

influence what is being said. Sometimes paralinguistic communication is unintentional; in other cases, it is entirely premeditated. Consider the case of the State Department spokesperson who was known to communicate different messages by varying voice quality. This individual had three different ways of saying, "I would not speculate." *Newsweek* explained them this way:

> Spoken without accent, it means the department doesn't know for sure; emphasis on the "I" means "I wouldn't but you may—and with some assurance"; accent on "speculate" indicates that the questioner's premise is probably wrong.[14]

Before continuing, review your answer to Question 1 and make any changes you would like.

1. What type of informal communication network was used in conveying Anne's message?

Anne's message was conveyed via the cluster chain. The message was selectively passed. (This becomes particularly clear when Figure 15–4 is examined.) Notice that the information in this case was conveyed based on friendship and on respect.

BARRIERS TO COMMUNICATION

Not all attempts at communication are successful. Sometimes a breakdown in transmission is brought about by a communication barrier. In overall terms there are four major barriers to effective communication.

First, some people do not communicate well because they have emotional blocks. This often happens to managers who are overly concerned with such things as whether the subordinates like them or whether the staff considers them qualified. Anger, fear, defensiveness, and uncertainty are all causes of emotional blocks.

Second, some people have trouble communicating because of different frames of reference. The manager who tells his subordinates that "this new work program is going to be good for you" may have trouble making the subordinates believe it, especially if they are union members. Conversely, when the subordinates tell the manager that management is not offering a fair contract, the boss is likely to label their communication "union rhetoric." Each sees things from a different point of view, each so inflexible that it cannot accommodate the other.

Third, some people cannot communicate well because they are incapable of expressing themselves properly in either written or oral terms. They lack the capacity to use words, and since words are the medium through which thoughts, ideas, and feelings are conveyed, they are poor communicators.

Finally, some people are poor communicators because they cannot use their personalities effectively. Communication depends not only on what individuals say, but also on how they say it. In verbal communication a person's outward appearance, as manifested by gestures, smiles, voice quality, and vitality, is all important in helping to transfer meanings. When managers or subordinates fail to use their personalities to complement the basic communication process, they are often ineffective. The following subsections examine these communication barriers in more specific terms. [15]

Perception

Perception is a person's view of reality.

As noted in Chapter 3, perception is a person's view of reality. This view, determined by values, beliefs, and past experiences, influences the way people see things. [16] Research shows that in order to overcome serious perception problems, all parties to a communication must have some common ground or frame of reference. For example, in recent years Eastern Airlines and its union have had major problems. The primary reason is that neither felt there was much common ground for negotiation. As a result, negotiations broke down, and the firm became enmeshed in a prolonged strike. This contrasts with firms like Chrysler and Ford which have been able to find common ground with their unions and negotiate contracts that were beneficial to both sides. (Also see "Organizational Behavior in Action: The Audience Analysis Grid.")

Most managers perceive themselves as effective communicators.

Interestingly, research shows that most managers perceive themselves as effective communicators. In one study, for example, Mann found that top staff personnel said they always (70 percent) or nearly always (30 percent) told their subordinates in advance about change. Only 63 percent of the foremen, however, agreed with this statement. Additionally, while 92 percent of the foremen said that they always (40 percent) or nearly always (52 percent) told their subordinates in advance about change, only 47 percent of the men agreed. [17] As seen in Table 15–1 on page 406, this same basic pattern has been reported when personnel were asked if superiors make use of the ideas and opinions of their subordinates in the solution of job problems.

Many managers express surprise when informed of results such as those listed in Table 15–1. They see their actions as being misinterpreted by the subordinates. Actually the results occur because there are two types of reality—sensory and normative. **Sensory reality** is physical reality, such as a car, a machine, and a desk. When people communicate about physical things there are few communication problems because everyone knows what a car, a machine, and desk are. Meanings become unclear, however, when people discuss normative, or interpretive, reality. What one person says and what another person hears may be two different things. Table 15–2 (p. 407) provides an illustration.

Normative reality comes into play when people communicate about issues that are open to interpretation or are matters of opinion. The manager who tells a subordinate that he or she will have to spend at least a year in the field in order to gain the experience needed for promotion may believe that a career path is being spelled out for that subordinate. The latter, however, may feel that the boss has to stick someone with this rotten assignment, and has chosen him or her. What the manager sees as a clear-cut statement of fact is interpreted in negative terms. Although the boss believed he was operating within the realm of sensory reality, he had actually entered the area of normative reality, and—given the subordinate's interpretation—the situation seems headed toward a communication breakdown.

Organizational Behavior In Action

THE AUDIENCE ANALYSIS GRID

One of the most effective ways of dealing with perception problems is to analyze the receiver of the message and find out where this person is "coming from." An excellent way of doing this is to make an analysis of the audience. The audience analysis grid presented on the right is one way of accomplishing this.

The grid places considerations on two variables: audience knowledge and audience friendliness. Audience knowledge is measured by the amount of information that the listeners understand about the material to be presented. Audience friendliness is the degree to which the listeners are friendly, neutral, disinterested, or hostile.

The grid is designed to help the presenter formulate a plan of action. For example, if the audience is knowledgeable but hostile, the speaker should consider Strategy D: Find and emphasize important benefits for the audience. If the audience has little knowledge about the subject and is also viewed as disinterested, the speaker should consider Strategy K: Give them the facts but do not waste time trying to be friends.

These strategies are not definitive; they need to be adjusted to the situation. However, they are useful in helping the speaker analyze the audience and formulate an initial plan of action.

© Richard M. Hodgetts and Jane W. Gibson, 1990.

Language and Semantics

Many managers have trouble expressing themselves in writing.

Even though the manager and subordinates all speak English, language can be a communication barrier.[18] This is particularly true because many organizational communiques should be in written form, whereas a significant percentage of managers have difficulty expressing themselves in writing. Recent research reveals that many schools are dropping or deemphasizing standard English. Poor grammar and improper sentence construction often go uncorrected.[19] This trend not only gives rise to a new brand of English, but also inadequately prepares managers for dealing with the challenge of written communication.

Then there is the problem associated with words themselves. We call this area **semantics,** which has been popularly defined by the cliche, "Different words mean different things to different people." One of the most common semantic problems is caused by the use of technical jargon or terms that are understood by only a select few. New employees, for example, often misunderstand messages containing technical

| | THE AUDIENCE ANALYSIS GRID | | | |
| | The Friendliness Continuum | | | |
	1. Friendly	2. Neutral	3. Disinterested	4. Hostile
4. Resistant to Learning	(A) Show them personal profit from presentation	(B) Need a dramatic start to grab interest	(C) Stress benefit of this presentation given the fact they're there anyway	(D) Find and emphasize important benefit for them
3. Neutral to Learning	(E) Get them involved in the presentation	(F) Use ice-breakers or humor to get their attention	(G) Get their interest fast	(H) Concentrate on benefits of learning
2. Little Knowledge; Eager to Learn	(I) Pedagogy important for best results	(J) Quickly give them the facts they want	(K) Give them the facts; don't waste time trying to be friends	(L) Emphasis on education
1. Knowledge-able	(M) Straight-forward presentation	(N) Warm them up by referring to their expertise	(O) Find a point to grab their interest	(P) Identify source of hostility and try to diffuse it

words. Consider, for instance, the case of the manager in an engineering firm who gave her secretary a set of blueprints and told her to burn them. Imagine the manager's surprise when she saw her put the drawings in a trash can and throw a lighted match on top of them. The manager had failed to tell the secretary that in this firm the word *burn* meant photocopy. Incidents such as this are not uncommon, as explained by a training and development specialist.

Different people are reared in different environments, developing different attitudes and social values. Their educations are different and their levels of understanding of the same word can also be quite different. This was illustrated in a class I conducted for a company not long ago. A supervisor said to one of the employees, "Go out back and pull the stacks of buckets apart." It was at most a 20-minute job. Two hours later, the supervisor found the employee literally tearing the buckets apart. Obviously, for the supervisor "pull apart" meant one thing and to the employee something quite different. They both had a meaning for "pull apart," but they didn't have the same meaning.[20]

TABLE 15–1

Do Superiors Use Subordinates' Ideas and Opinions in the Solution of Job Problems?

	Top Staff's View of Their Own Behavior	Supervisors' View of Top Staff's Behavior	Supervisors' View of Their Own Behavior	Workers' View of Supervisors' Behavior
Always or nearly always get subordinates' ideas and opinions	70%	52%	73%	16%
Often get subordinates' ideas and opinions	25%	17%	23%	23%
Sometimes or seldom get these ideas and opinions	5%	31%	4%	61%

Source: Adapted from Rensis Likert, *New Patterns of Management* (New York: McGraw-Hill Book Co., 1961), p. 53, with permission of McGraw-Hill, Inc.

Some words, while similar in meaning, convey entirely different messages. For example, consider the following two lists:

List A	List B
Firm	Unyielding
Aggressive	Ruthless
Compassionate	Weak
Concerned with detail	Nit-picking
Certain	Cocky
Easygoing	Unconcerned
Selective	Arbitrary
Respects lines of authority	Bureaucratic
An independent thinker	A nonconformist
Blunt and direct	Tactless

Most people tend to view the terms in List A more favorably than those in List B. When describing their friends, therefore, they will opt for words from the first list. Conversely, when describing those they dislike, most people will choose words from the second list. However, if someone means to convey a positive image of an individual but chooses a word from our second list, the receiver may well conjure up a negative image of this person. Communication theorists like to sum up this problem by noting that "meanings are not in words, they are in people. When people do not have the same meaning for a word, communication breakdown usually occurs."[21]

TABLE 15–2
Communication Breakdown

What the Manager Said	What the Manager Meant	What the Subordinate Heard
I'll look into hiring another person for your department as soon as I complete my budget review.	We'll start interviewing for that job in about three weeks.	I'm tied up with more important things. Let's forget about the hiring for the indefinite future.
Your performance was below par last quarter. I really expected more out of you.	You're going to have to try harder, but I know you can do it.	If you screw up one more time, you're out.
I'd like that report as soon as you can get to it.	I need that report within the week.	Drop that rush order you're working on and fill out that report today.
I talked to the boss but at present, because of budget problems, we'll be unable to match your competitive salary offer.	We can give you 95 percent of that offer, and I know we'll be able to do even more for you next year.	If I were you, I'd take that competitive offer. We're certainly not going to pay that kind of salary to a person with your credentials.
We have a job opening in Los Angeles that we think would be just your cup of tea. We'd like you to go out there and look it over.	If you'd like that job, it's yours. If not, of course, you can stay here in Denver. You be the judge.	You don't have to go out to L.A. if you don't want to. However, if you don't you can say good-bye to your career with this firm.
Your people seem to be having some problems getting their work out on time. I want you to look into this situation and straighten it out.	Talk to your people and find out what the problem is. Then get together with them and jointly solve it.	I don't care how many heads you bust, just get me that output. I've got enough problems around here without you screwing things up too.

Number of Links

The greater the number of links, the greater the potential for communication problems.

In the case of verbal transmissions, the number of links, or people through whom the message must be passed, constitutes a major communication barrier. Each individual will often rephrase or reinterpret the message to give it greater clarity. In the process, however, they often end up changing the basic content. This is readily seen by the parlor game in which one person gives another some message. The message is then passed to someone else, until it goes all the way around the room to the last person. In most cases the message that emerges at the end is completely different from the one that went in at the beginning.

The same pattern holds for organizational communiques that are passed down the line. At each level of the hierarchy information is often lost. After studying communication efficiency in 100 business and industrial firms, Nichols has reported the following loss of information between six levels in the hierarchy:[22]

Level	Percentage of Information Received
Board	100
Vice-president	63
General supervisors	56
Plant managers	44
General foremen	30
Workers	20

Such findings illustrate why communication problems in large organizations with many hierarchical levels can be so much greater than those in small ones with only a few levels. In all cases, however, the information loss between levels is dramatic. For example, in the study just mentioned there was a 37 percent loss between the board and the vice-presidents. Meanwhile, between the general foremen and the workers, it was 50 percent!

Inference-Observation

Inference is a problem in both written and oral communication.

In communication terms, an **inference** is an assumption made by the receiver of a message. Vague or incomplete transmissions require the receiver to fill in the hidden meanings by observing the situation and drawing assumptions about it. If the assumptions the individual makes are wrong, communication breakdown may result.

Inference is a major stumbling block in both written and oral communication. As an illustration, consider the case of the shipping clerk who received a memo from management saying that in the future all orders were to be either mailed or shipped by truck. The following week the clerk received a call from the vice-president of marketing telling him to send a rush order of parts to a firm located 1,500 miles away. The fastest way to fill the order was to send it by air, but remembering the memo's instructions, the clerk sent out a special truck. Not only was this mode more costly than air shipment, but the order also took two days to arrive. Since the company needed the parts within twenty-four hours, it filled the order locally and refused the truck shipment.

In retrospect it turned out that the clerk believed the memo said that goods could never be shipped by air. The management, however, meant that no more regular orders were to go by air, but special rush shipments could be sent this way.

In this story the company had two opportunities to clear up the communication barrier before it became a major problem. First, the written memo could have spelled out exceptions to the rule by noting that air shipments were acceptable in the case of rush orders. Second, the marketing manager could have asked the clerk how the parts were going to be shipped and cleared up the problem at that point. Since neither of these two things occurred, the clerk used inference-observation, and the company suffered high transportation costs and an order cancellation.

Message Competition and Selective Listening

There are four steps in message transmission.

There are four basic steps in transmitting messages from sender to receiver. First, the sender must get the receiver's attention. Second, the receiver must understand the essentials of the communique. Third, the receiver must be ready and willing to comply with the missive. Fourth, the action required by the message must be carried out.

The most difficult part of this four-step process is getting the individual's attention. One of the primary barriers is message competition. Many things can distract a listener, and the sender must be able to surmount these obstacles. In the case of the manager, for example, there may be reports sitting on her desk, telephone messages that have to be answered, and subordinates outside the door waiting to discuss some work-related matter. Each of these is competing for her time. If she chooses to talk with the subordinate first, there is still the problem of putting the reports and telephone messages out of her mind for a while. However, if the discussion starts to break down or slow up, it is likely that her mind will wander back to the other chores competing for her attention.

In the case of subordinates, meanwhile, there may be a basic message they wish to convey. If they feel the manager is beginning to stray from this central theme, the subordinates may ignore what she has to say, feeling it is irrelevant to their main point. In this case they are employing selective listening, blocking out all new ideas and information that either conflicts with or fails to address those things most important to them. Many subordinates hear only what they want to hear. Message competition and selective listening are interrelated. Each stems from a different source, but both require the same solution—getting and holding the listener's attention.

Status

Status refers to the attributes that rank and relate individuals in an organization. The formal organization provides a variety of status symbols to its people, including private offices, carpets, secretaries, position titles, keys to the executive washroom, and membership in the country club. As a result, not everyone in the organization is equal in status, which is often a result of personal ambition or drive.

Status affects the way people communicate.

Status affects the way organizational personnel communicate with each other. In particular, people tend to avoid sending bad news up the line for fear that it will anger their boss. As a result, a great deal of filtering takes place, in which the personnel either remove or cover up negative information. Perhaps the major reason for filtering is that management makes merit evaluations, gives salary increases, and promotes individuals based on what it receives from these people. A manager who gets only good news from his or her people is more likely to treat subordinates better than is one who receives a great deal of bad news from his or her people.

Before continuing, review your answer to Question 2 and make any changes you would like.

2. In what way did perception help influence George's refusal to believe William's message? What communication barrier accounted for the message being changed as it went through five hierarchical levels?

Perception influenced George's refusal because he had always found Anne's information to be accurate. George's view of reality was that Anne's information was correct, thus William's message was wrong.

As William's message went up the hierarchy, it was changed as a result of the number of links in the chain. Notice that the original message said that the firm's major aerospace contracts would be reduced by 20 percent. The message that emerged at the top was that overall business would be reduced by 20 percent.

ACHIEVING EFFECTIVE COMMUNICATION IN ORGANIZATIONS

In order to improve their communication ability, managers must overcome the barriers described in the previous section.[23] While there are many ways to do this, all require feedback from subordinates.[24] One of these ways, which we have already discussed, is the use of the grapevine. Others include face-to-face communication, simplicity and repetition, empathy, the understanding of nonverbal behavior, and effective listening.

Using Face-to-Face Communication

When possible, face-to-face communication should be used.

When possible, the manager should use face-to-face communication. This approach allows the individual both to see the other people and to note how they are reacting to the message. As James and Jongeward have pointed out, "Gestures, facial expressions, body posture, tone of voice, and so forth, all contribute to the meaning in every transaction. If a verbal message is to be completely understood, the receiver must take into consideration the nonverbal aspects as well as the spoken words."[25]

One of the primary benefits of face-to-face communication is that it allows for immediate feedback. If the transmission begins to break down or the manager believes that a particular point needs clarification, this can be done at once. Additionally, this communication form permits both parties to review and summarize their positions before terminating the conversation. As a result, it is often much easier for each side to get the other's attention, achieve understanding, obtain acceptance, and get the necessary action follow-up (Table 15–3). Many firms encourage their managers to use this approach, especially in the initial stages of handling employee rights and grievances. At the Bank of America, for example, a "let's talk it over approach" is employed *before* any written communication is used. The bank's president has described the process this way:

> Employees who have problems, questions, or complaints are urged to talk first to their operations officers and supervisors and next (if necessary) to their

TABLE 15–3
Some Important Dos and Don'ts of Face-to-Face Communication

The Dos

1. Learn how to express yourself properly.
2. Use your personality in winning over the other party.
3. Employ a confident, cordial, and quiet voice.
4. State your point of view clearly and then be done, without repeating parts of the message.
5. Accept the fact that not everyone is going to agree with what you say.
6. Give the other party the freedom to express, honestly and reasonably, any differences he or she may have about what you've said.
7. Accept these differences of opinion without getting upset or angry or developing a negative attitude toward the other party.
8. After hearing the other party out, think over what has been said, make the best possible decision you can, and stick to it.
9. Whether they are good or bad, learn to live with your decisions and go on from there.

The Don'ts

1. Do not be bossy with the other party.
2. Avoid the use of sarcasm in your dialogue.
3. Never use your power to threaten the listener(s).
4. Refrain from getting angry.
5. Do not swear.
6. Never take anything that is said as a personal attack.
7. Try not to lose your poise or act frightened.
8. Refrain from taking a position from which you are unable to deviate.
9. Never lose your patience.

managers, department heads, or district administrators. If the problem is still not resolved, or if the employee feels uncomfortable talking to these people, he or she can contact an employee assistance officer. All of these contacts are kept confidential. If the employee gives permission, the employee assistance officer will go to the supervisor and attempt to resolve the problem equitably. Thus employee assistance officers often fulfill the role of an ombudsperson.[26]

Simplicity and Repetition

Messages should contain simple, understandable language.

Regardless of the communication medium, messages should contain simple, understandable language. Words such as *esoteric, biennial,* and *peripheral* may be recognized by many, but their proper meaning is often misunderstood. Or consider the case of the manager who sent his people a memo saying that as of October 1 there would be biweekly meetings. What does the word biweekly mean? Obviously it means either twice a week or once every two weeks, but which is it? Simple words are always preferable to complex ones.[27]

Message repetition is also useful.

Additionally, message repetition is necessary in all but the simplest transmissions. The more information being conveyed, the more likely it is that the listener will suffer communication overload. People can absorb only a limited amount of information at one time. As more and more data, facts, and figures are transmitted, the receiver becomes deluged and either stops listening or tries to integrate all the material into some general pattern or framework. If this proves impossible, the overall communication will break down. Such an outcome can be avoided, however, if the sender communicates in small bits, rephrasing and reviewing what has been said as he or she goes along. This technique is especially helpful when technical or sophisticated data are being conveyed.

Empathy

Empathy involves putting yourself in another's shoes.

Empathy is the process of figuratively putting oneself in another's shoes. It requires communicators to sensitize themselves as much as they can by assuming the viewpoints and emotions of the receiver.[28] This skill can greatly reduce communication barriers. Unfortunately, many managers do not really empathize with their people. Consider the example of the plant manager who announced to his foremen that new work flow operations would be installed within the next sixty days and "all of your people will be taken care of." At this point some of the subordinate managers began to raise questions. They were particularly concerned about the fact that the grapevine was forecasting manpower layoffs if the new system were implemented. The plant manager quickly brushed these aside, saying, "Oh, c'mon, you know there's nothing to worry about. Now let's get on to other business." What he failed to realize was that although there was nothing for him to worry about, his subordinates were still very concerned with what might happen to some of their people. Empathy can help overcome problems such as these.[29]

Understanding Nonverbal Behavior

Managers who understand nonverbal behavior are able to complement what is being said with how the person is acting. Do the two fit together, or is the individual saying one thing but acting a different way? In order to answer this question, the manager has to know something about body language, and this is often much more than intuitive feeling. For example, is it true that an honest person will look the listener in the eye whereas a dishonest individual will not? The answer is no. Many people who are lying do so while staring directly into the listener's eyes. Cliches regarding how to tell when someone is lying are often wrong. Generally it helps if the manager looks at the person's *entire* posture and gestures. Some nonverbal behavior findings that have been empirically proven are the following:

Some nonverbal behavior findings have been empirically proven.

1. A high degree of relaxation generally indicates a lack of respect or a dislike of the other person, while a lesser degree of relaxation indicates a liking for the person.

2. An absence of relaxation indicates that the person feels threatened or is being threatening to someone else.

3. Higher status people are generally more relaxed than their lower status counterparts if the status difference is recognized and accepted.

4. When one person stands up and the other remains sitting it is commonly a sign that the former is attempting to dominate, control, or influence the latter.

5. The way an individual organizes his or her office, walks down the hallway, and greets people are all signs of this person's self-esteem as well as the way he or she wants to be treated.

6. The distance that remains between people when they talk helps explain the way they regard each other, i.e., a respectful subordinate will generally remain farther away from the boss than will one of the latter's fellow managers because distance often equates with respect, friendship and/or trust.[30]

The foregoing are only guidelines and are not meant to be accepted as hard and fast rules. However, they do indicate the value of trying to read the other person. If only because of its value in supplementing other forms of communication feedback, an understanding of nonverbal behavior is important to the manager.

Effective Listening

Approximately 70 percent of the manager's day is spent communicating.

Communication experts estimate that approximately 70 percent of the manager's day is spent communicating. Of this, 45 percent involves listening to others.[31] Yet most managers are ineffective in this process. For them listening is simply a matter of "doing what comes naturally." In reality, listening is hard work and demands a great deal of concentration and effort.[32]

One of the most common bad listening habits is faking attentiveness. A second is tuning out difficult or technical presentations. A third is letting emotional words disrupt the listening process. A fourth is wasting thought power.

Most people speak at the rate of 125 words per minute. However, the brain is capable of handling almost five times that number. If the speaker goes on for more than a few minutes, it presents a temptation to the listener to wander mentally, returning only periodically to check in and see where the speaker is.[33] Habits such as these help explain why research reveals that when people listen to a ten-minute talk, they operate at only 25 percent efficiency.[34] Some ways of overcoming these habits and improving listening skills are presented in Table 15–4.[35]

Another way of improving listening effectiveness is by developing an active listening style. This style employs empathetic, supportive behaviors that tell the speaker, "I understand. Please go on." Many managers believe they already are active listeners. Actually, they are best described by one of the other four possible listening modes. All five listening styles are summarized here:

There are five listening modes.

1. **Directing listener**: This person directs the speaker by establishing the limits and direction of the counteraction. For example, an employee who tells his supervisor that he is unable to get along with Jim, a co-worker, could expect the directing supervisor to say something like, "If I were you, I'd just ignore him." The manager seeks to direct the worker's behavior.

2. **Judgmental listener**: This individual introduces personal value judgements into the conversation, often in the form of advice or prescribed right and wrong behavior. In response to the problem we are considering, the judgmental listener might respond by saying, "Everybody regards that guy as a jerk." This manager seeks to influence the listener by telling the latter, "Be like the rest of us; regard Jim as a fool."

3. **Probing listener**: This listener asks questions in an attempt to get to the heart of the matter. In the process, he or she tends to lead the conversation and satisfy personal needs rather than those of the speaker. A probing listener might respond

TABLE 15–4
Twenty Steps for Improving Reception Ability

1. Be aware that listening is hard work.
2. Be prepared to listen by becoming familiar with the subject under discussion and by getting into the correct mental attitude.
3. Know your own biases so that you are better able to control them and prevent them from interfering with the message reception.
4. Choose a position in the room from which you can hear (and if necessary, see) all of the information being presented.
5. Bring along a pencil and paper and take notes on important, difficult, or unfamiliar material.
6. Concentrate on the message and fight any tendency to daydream.
7. Avoid becoming distracted by the presenter's voice, appearance, vocabulary, or style of presentation.
8. Keep an open mind by not feeling threatened, insulted, or resistant to messages that contradict your values, attitudes, beliefs, and ideas.
9. Remain interested and attentive by looking for ways in which the message can be relevant to you and your job.
10. Empathize with the speaker by putting yourself in that person's shoes.
11. Refrain from composing mental arguments over points made by the speaker; instead, concentrate on the rest of the message.
12. Delay judging the speaker until you have heard the entire message.
13. Listen critically to the talk so that when it is over you can pass judgment on it in an enlightened fashion.
14. Don't just listen to the words; look for nonverbal clues that provide you further information.
15. Stay alert for the main points of the message.
16. Give the speaker reinforcement by nodding your head slightly or, if verbal feedback is appropriate, saying, "I see" or "Right."
17. Do not interrupt the speaker to ask questions; make certain that the individual has finished before taking over the reins.
18. If something is unclear and you are sure you will not disrupt the source, use a reflecting phrase such as "What do you mean?" or "How is that so?" to obtain elaboration on a point.
19. When the person is finished, if you still need additional information, ask for it.
20. During the question and discussion period, limit your own input and let the source do most of the talking.

to the employee from item 1 by asking "How long has this situation existed?" or "Why are you unable to get along with him?"

4. **Smoothing listener**: This person tries to pat the speaker on the head and make light of the problem. The individual believes that conflict is bad and should be avoided at all costs. A smoothing listener might tell the employee in our example, "Hey, the

two of you have had a bad day. Relax. By tomorrow everything will have blown over."

5. **Active listener**: This listener works to develop an atmosphere in which the speaker can express his or her problem and, if possible, also solve it. In so doing, active listeners feed back neutral summaries of what they hear, thereby ensuring that understanding has occurred and allowing the individual to continue talking. An active listener might say to the employee, "It seems that you're troubled by the fact that you and Jim can't get along."

Active listening has four behavioral components: empathy, acceptance, congruence, and completeness. Empathy is the quality of trying to understand the speaker from his or her own viewpoint rather than from that of the listener's past experience or personal preference. Acceptance is the quality of concern for the other individual's welfare. Congruence is the quality of openness, frankness, and genuineness on the part of the listener. Concreteness is the quality of focusing on specifics and avoiding vagueness by helping the speaker concentrate on real problems and avoid generalities regarding the issue. Among the important benefits that active listening offers to managers are that it:

1. encourages the individual to speak his or her mind fully;
2. provides the speaker with a sounding board in solving problems;
3. offers a motivational benefit to the speaker, who feels important in the eyes of the listener;
4. encourages the speaker to think through his or her problem and not be quickly diverted;
5. encourages the speaker to become more open and less defensive in communication, thus fostering emotional maturity;
6. makes the speaker feel his or her ideas are worthwhile and can be helpful in stimulating creative thinking;
7. makes the speaker listen to his or her own ideas more carefully;
8. provides the listener with a wealth of information on facts, attitudes, and emotions that were previously unexpressed;
9. provides a growth experience for both the speaker and the listener.[36]

The major problem for many managers is using the active style and deemphasizing their reliance on the other four. Notice from Table 15–5 that each of the other four styles have serious shortcomings that prevent managers from becoming truly effective listeners. Yet these four are often personally satisfying because they help listeners pursue their own goals. Unfortunately, this is often done at the expense of the speaker.

TABLE 15–5
Listening Response Pattern Identification

Pattern	Listener's Focus	Response Mode	Responds to	Listener's Attitude and Posture	Speaker's Reaction
Directing	Listener's own ideas	Limited to the listener's way of looking at the problem	Speaker's content	Superior attitude	Speaker's focus is lost as the listener pursues his or her own track
Judgmental	Listener's own ideas	Gives the verdict of what to do or not do	Speaker's content	Superior attitude	Speaker may feel defensive, resentful, or misunderstood
Probing	Speaker's ideas or listener's ideas	Directing or leading by asking questions	Speaker's content	Impatient; wants to get to the point	Speaker must focus on listener's questions even if they go away from the central problem
Smoothing	Speaker's feelings	Ignores the problem; feels it is not important	Speaker's content and emotion	Healing and encouraging	Speaker feels frustrated at listener's attempts to smooth things over and ignore the central issue
Active	Speaker's ideas and feelings	Encouraging and accepting behavior	Speaker's emotion	Attentive, forward leaning, good eye contact	Speaker must look more closely at own problem; is free to continue talking

STOP

Before continuing, review your answer to Question 3 and make any changes you would like.

3. What type of a listener is the president? What type of listener would William have found to be most effective? Explain.

The president is a directing listener. He directed the conversation by establishing the limits and direction of the counteraction. William made a few suggestions, but the president was not listening. He apparently did not have time. He was simply interested in getting across his point of view and ending the conversation. William would have preferred that the president be an active listener. William wanted the opportunity to gain the president's support in refuting the rumor. William had had no success in convincing George, and perhaps a statement from the top manager would help. An active listening style would have provided William with the information he needed to set forth his position.

SUMMARY

1. Communication is the process of transmitting meanings from sender to receiver. This process comprises seven key elements: an idea; an encoding of the message; the means for transmission; noise or message interference; message reception; recoding of the message; and action.

2. In organizational communication there are both formal and informal channels. The formal channels consist of downward, upward, and horizontal communication. Some informal channels, popularly known as the grapevine, are a network of social relations that arise spontaneously as people associate with one another. Although the grapevine carries rumor, gossip, and other informal communiques, some of its transmissions are accurate. In any case, these transmissions tend to follow a logical pattern represented most accurately by the cluster chain, although there are other informal chains, including the single strand, gossip, and random.

3. Communication in organizations can take a variety of forms, including words, pictures, and actions. Written communication is widely used when a record is needed of

what was transmitted. Oral communication is used when time is of the essence and/or immediate feedback is desired. Nonverbal communication can take many different forms, as can be seen by an analysis of its three components: kinesics, proxemics, and body language.

4. Regardless of the communication form used, however, not all attempts at communications are successful. Sometimes a breakdown in transmission is brought about by such barriers as perception, language, semantics, the number of links in the chain, inference-observation, message competition, selective listening, and status. Some of the most common approaches useful for overcoming these barriers include face-to-face communication, simple and understandable language, message repetition, empathy, and effective listening habits, especially developing an active listening style. All are important in organizational communication because they promote feedback from receiver to sender, thereby turning communication into a closed-loop process.

KEY TERMS

communication	horizontal communication	single-strand chain
downward communication	grapevine	gossip chain
upward communication	cluster chain	probability chain

kinesics	**semantics**	**judgmental listener**
proxemics	**inference**	**probing listener**
paralanguage	**status**	**smoothing listener**
sensory reality	**empathy**	**active listener**
normative reality	**directing listener**	

REVIEW AND STUDY QUESTIONS

1. How does the communication process work? Put it in your own words.

2. Many communication theorists believe that of the three types of formal communication channels—downward, upward, and horizontal—upward receives the least emphasis from management. Do you think this is an accurate statement? Explain.

3. What are some of the most likely causes for grapevine activity?

4. In what way can the grapevine be of value to the manager?

5. What role do kinesics, proxemics, and paralanguage play in nonverbal communication? In your answer, be sure to define each term.

6. Why do most managers prefer oral communication to written communication?

7. In what way is perception a barrier to communication?

8. What is meant by the term semantics, and how is it a communication barrier?

9. Why might large organizations with many hierarchical levels have more communication problems than small ones with only a few levels?

10. Is there any way to avoid inference-observation problems in communication? Explain.

11. What are some of the dos and don'ts of face-to-face communication?

12. Some people believe that effective communication is simply a case of empathizing with the other person. What is the logic behind this statement? Do you agree or disagree with this statement?

13. Why is an understanding of nonverbal communication so important to managers? Explain.

14. Why are many managers ineffective listeners? Explain.

15. How do the following listening styles work: directing, judgmental, probing, smoothing, active? Compare and contrast each.

CASES

Grapevine Activity

Pat Wilson has been head of the Administration Department in his company for three months. Last month, Pat received word from the president of the firm that a meeting of all department heads would be held in the board room later that day. The president began his presentation by saying, "We have been having a great many problems with internal inefficiency. As a result, I have decided that we are going to have to reorganize ourselves. The reason that I have called all of you together is to discuss how this reorganization should take place. All of you have been the heads of your respective departments for at least ninety days, so you know basically how your end of the operation works. What I would like to see you do is work as a team in deciding how your departments can be reorganized to achieve greater

internal efficiency. I think that there are many things that can be done to improve coordination between your groups. I also think that some of you know ways that we can be more efficient but because you have never been asked, you haven't shared these ideas with the rest of us. I'd like all of you to work as a reorganization team and restructure our internal operations. What do you say?"

The response was extremely positive. A number of the department heads stood up and told the chief executive that he could rely on them to pitch in and give it their best effort.

Pat joined in, remarking, "I know that I'm new on the management team, but I have a few ideas about how we can be more efficient, and I welcome any ideas any of you have for my department." The meeting closed on a very positive note.

The committee met for two hours on each following day. In the beginning the managers talked about general ideas they had for improving efficiency. By the end of the fifth meeting, however, it was obvious that they were ready to turn their ideas into action. Over the next week they generated hundreds of suggestions that could be useful in reorganizing parts of the structure. The third week was spent translating these ideas into action plans for each department.

Throughout this entire period, the heads of the departments told no one what they were doing. The logic was simple. If the employees found out that management was reorganizing operations, there might be a general panic. The managers felt that once they had their plan all worked out, they would then tell the people in their respective departments what they had decided to do. Everyone on the committee agreed with this line of action.

Before doing anything, however, the committee requested a meeting with the president and discussed its ideas with him. The chief executive had a few questions and a couple of important suggestions, but in the main he agreed with their plan of action. The only major recommendation he had was that the reorganization take place in one department first to "work out any bugs." Then the other departments could all be reorganized according to plan. The department the president chose for the first reorganization was Pat's.

Early the next morning, Pat sent a memo to his department managers telling them that a reorganization of the unit would be taking place over the next couple of weeks. He stressed that there would be no change in the number of personnel and that if anyone's job was eliminated, the individual would be given work elsewhere in the department. Pat had two weeks to complete his reorganization and de-

termine if there were any problems. If there were none, then the other departments would begin their own reorganizations. Unfortunately, things did not go according to plan.

The grapevine learned about the reorganization and started passing the word that orders from the president called for Pat to cut departmental personnel by 10 percent. Some of the people in Pat's department called the rumors to his attention, but Pat assured them that there was no truth in the stories. Meanwhile, Pat was reluctant to send out a second memo directly refuting the grapevine story because he felt such action might give credence to the rumor. He believed that if he just left things alone, the rumors would die by themselves.

Unfortunately, yesterday he received a visit from one of the other department heads. The individual told him that things seemed to be getting out of hand. Some of her departmental personnel are requesting transfers to offices in branches where no reorganization is scheduled. Apparently just about everyone in the firm knows about the proposed changes, and although they do not know exactly what new changes will be introduced, they are quite concerned about them. Pat is now confused regarding what he should do. On the one hand, he feels he should continue to implement the reorganizational changes and just be as open and honest as he can with his people. On the other hand, he believes it might now be necessary for him to take some positive action related to dispelling the rumors.

1. How do rumors such as the one described in this case get started? Explain.

2. Do you think that these rumors will die by themselves, or would you suggest that Pat take some action? Explain your reasoning.

3. If Pat does decide to take some action, what should he do? Be complete in your answer.

A Difference of Opinion

Metropolitan Hospital is a large public institution located on the west side of a major city. Since it is tax-supported, the hospital finds that its salaries often do not compete with those offered by private hospitals in the nearby area. This has undoubtedly helped account for the tardiness and absenteeism rate at Metropolitan. Six months ago the administrator of the hospital resigned, and Margaret Shane was brought in to take over the reins. Margaret was an associate administrator at another large local hospital and has been in the health care field for twenty-three years.

Realizing that her institution cannot compete directly on a salary and fringe benefit basis, Margaret has decided to try to make the hospital the best health care institution in the area by approaching the tardiness and absenteeism issue from the standpoint of quality of work life. In order to do this, she first needs to find out something about the organizational climate. One of her assistants has designed a detailed questionnaire survey to provide feedback on what the personnel like and dislike about work at Metropolitan.

One part of the questionnaire, designed specifically for the workers, asked them to give their impression of their managers' behavior. Another part of the questionnaire, designed specifically for the managers, asked the latter to give their opinion of the same items, thus rating their own behavior. When the responses from the two groups were compared, the following resulted:

	Workers Said of Their Managers	Managers Said of Themselves
Keeps you informed about what is going on	25%	91%
Takes the time to explain difficult jobs to you	65%	100%
Listens to what you have to say when you have a grievance or complaint	33%	95%
Praises you when you do a good job	30%	96%
Makes you feel at ease when talking to him or her	35%	90%
You can discuss business-related matters on a confidential basis with him or her	45%	95%
You can discuss personal matters on a confidential basis with him or her	20%	85%
Is as concerned about you as a person as he or she is about you getting the work done	40%	98%
Uses your ideas and opinions in making decisions	20%	80%
Goes to bat for you	15%	100%

When the workers heard the results, they expressed little surprise. Many of the managers, however, questioned the findings. One of them said that the workers had exaggerated the situation. "It isn't half as bad as that," this manager asserted.

1. What barriers to communication exist in this firm? Describe them.

2. Exactly what did the manager mean about the workers exaggerating the situation? Do you agree or disagree with this statement? Explain.

3. How can the situation now be straightened out? Give your recommendations.

SELF-FEEDBACK EXERCISE

Identifying Your Own Listening Style

Read each of the following fifteen comments and choose your preference for *each* reply. Put a 1 on the line to the left of the reply you like best and a 5 on the line to the left of the one you like least. Continue until you have completed comment 15.

1. "I'm sorry I'm late. The bus came by early today, and I missed it and had to wait half an hour for another."

   _____ a. You better start getting here on time.

   _____ b. You should have gotten to the bus stop earlier.

   _____ c. Does the bus often arrive early?

   _____ d. Everyone is late from time to time.

   _____ e. You seem upset over your tardiness.

2. "I don't know when I'm going to get to that special report for the boss. I'm already swamped with work."

   _____ a. You ought to tell the boss to give you some assistance.

   _____ b. You sound concerned about your work load.

   _____ c. Don't sweat it. Get to it as you go along.

_____ d. How long have you been swamped with work?

_____ e. All of us know that feeling, believe me.

3. "Salary recommendations are to be forwarded up the line by next week. I wonder if I should talk to the boss again to be sure she remembers all the good things I did this year."

_____ a. Does she often change her mind when talked to?

_____ b. Don't worry; a good person like you will be well treated.

_____ c. You're right. If you don't stand up for yourself, no one else will.

_____ d. You appear concerned about your salary recommendation.

_____ e. See if you can schedule a meeting with her for later today.

4. "I'm beat. I don't think I can get anything else done today."

_____ a. It happens to all of us. You can do that stuff tomorrow.

_____ b. Sit down and rest. You'll feel better later on.

_____ c. You sound exhausted.

_____ d. You better learn how to keep your stamina up.

_____ e. What have you been doing that's got you so tired?

5. "The president asked me to make a special report to the board, but I don't think there's enough time to work up a detailed presentation."

_____ a. You sound nervous about the assignment.

_____ b. Haven't you done these presentations before?

_____ c. Once you get into it, it will prove much easier than you think.

_____ d. You should start working up your presentation right now.

_____ e. You should have told him no.

6. "I hear that top management is going to cut our work force by 20 percent. I hope I won't be laid off."

_____ a. Don't worry about it. It's probably just a rumor.

_____ b. Maybe you ought to consider sending out some resumes.

_____ c. Do you think you'll be included?

_____ d. Not you. They're only cutting the deadwood.

_____ e. You sound concerned that you might be laid off.

7. "Nuts! I've just been scheduled to go to Chicago on Friday. This is the third weekend in a row that I'll be away from my family."

_____ a. You ought to learn to say no to the boss.

_____ b. Is going on the road a burden to you and your family?

_____ c. Why don't you talk to the boss about it?

_____ d. Does everybody have to eventually go out on field trips?

_____ e. I'm sure this is the last trip you'll have to take for a while.

8. "I'm delighted over my promotion. However, I'm concerned about whether I have the ability to do the job well."

_____ a. What do you want me to do about it?

_____ b. I'm sure you wouldn't have been promoted if you didn't have the ability.

_____ c. Don't worry; most people feel that way.

_____ d. What makes you think you don't have the ability?

_____ e. Don't worry; you'll learn the job as you go along.

9. "Performance evaluation time is always a difficult one for me. I'd like to give everyone a good rating, but I know it's not possible."

_____ a. Don't worry. We all feel that way.

_____ b. Just do the best you can.

_____ c. Performance evaluations seem to upset you.

_____ d. You're going to have to learn to live with this problem; everyone does.

_____ e. What makes you feel this way?

10. "I've talked to Anne three times about getting her monthly cost control report in on time. This week she was late again."

_____ a. Does her tardiness upset you?

_____ b. When did all of this start?

_____ c. I'm sure there's a good reason for her being late.

_____ d. If I were you, I'd ignore the situation.

_____ e. You better do something about it quickly.

11. "George is my best worker, but he's been late for the fifth day in a row and that calls for a formal reprimand. Gosh, I hate to do this!"

    _____ a. Listen, just follow the rules and let the chips fall where they may.

    _____ b. If you can't take the heat, you have to stay out of the kitchen.

    _____ c. Does reprimanding him make you feel bad?

    _____ d. I know what you mean. I empathize.

    _____ e. It seems that this situation has you upset.

12. "I'd sure like to hire that woman I interviewed today, but she wants 10 percent more than my budget allows. And you know how the boss is about staying within the budget."

    _____ a. So what? If she doesn't know what a great organization we have here, that's her loss.

    _____ b. Does this upset you?

    _____ c. If I were you, I'd just try to forget it.

    _____ d. What are you going to do about it?

    _____ e. I understand. I've also lost some people I wanted.

13. "If I take this promotion, I'll have to move to Buffalo. If I turn it down, I may not get another for five years."

    _____ a. What's wrong with going to Buffalo?

    _____ b. I'm sure whatever decision you make will be the right one.

    _____ c. You should be glad you have a potential promotion.

    _____ d. You sound nervous about the situation.

    _____ e. Look at your decision in terms of the long run.

14. "Ted is griping again about work assignments. It seems to me that the only time he drops by my office is to lodge another complaint."

    _____ a. I'm sure he only comes by because he feels you really care about what happens in the department.

    _____ b. Ignore him and he'll quit coming by.

    _____ c. Do his actions upset you?

    _____ d. If I were you I'd set him straight right now.

    _____ e. Why does he keep bothering you?

15. "That stock clerk I fired last week is threatening to sue us for job discrimination. The company attorney wants to see me in his office after lunch. I wonder how serious this situation is."

    _____ a. You sound anxious about the meeting.

    _____ b. Do you think there might be a problem?

    _____ c. It's only natural to be nervous, but the attorney will handle everything.

    _____ d. Let the attorney handle things. He's the expert.

    _____ e. You did things by the book, so don't sweat it.

Enter your answers to each comment on the score sheet below. Make sure that in each row you have a 1, 2, 3, 4, and 5. Then add all five columns.

	I	II	III	IV	V
1.	__ a.	__ b.	__ c.	__ d.	__ e.
2.	__ c.	__ a.	__ d.	__ e.	__ b.
3.	__ e.	__ c.	__ a.	__ b.	__ d.
4.	__ b.	__ d.	__ e.	__ a.	__ c.
5.	__ d.	__ e.	__ b.	__ c.	__ a.
6.	__ a.	__ b.	__ c.	__ d.	__ e.
7.	__ c.	__ a.	__ d.	__ e.	__ b.
8.	__ e.	__ c.	__ a.	__ b.	__ d.
9.	__ b.	__ d.	__ e.	__ a.	__ c.
10.	__ d.	__ e.	__ b.	__ c.	__ a.
11.	__ a.	__ b.	__ c.	__ d.	__ e.
12.	__ c.	__ a.	__ d.	__ e.	__ b.
13.	__ e.	__ c.	__ a.	__ b.	__ d.
14.	__ b.	__ d.	__ e.	__ a.	__ c.
15.	__ d.	__ e.	__ b.	__ c.	__ a.
Totals	__	__	__	__	__

Your totals show your preference for each of the five listening styles discussed in this chapter. The lowest totaled column is your favorite style; the highest totaled column is the style you like least. The styles identified by each column are as follows:

Column I	Directing
Column II	Judgmental
Column III	Probing
Column IV	Smoothing
Column V	Active (or emphathetic)

For further clarification, go back and reread the section of the chapter related to listening styles. Also, look at the choices in each of the 15 situations and notice that you were offered all five styles *each* time. If your overall favorite style was not active, a close analysis of the scoring key can help you pick out why it was not, and a review of the choices can help you understand how you can become a more effective listener.

NOTES

1. Jane W. Gibson and Richard M. Hodgetts, *Organizational Communication: A Managerial Perspective,* 2nd ed. (New York: Harper Collins, 1991), p. 5.

2. Anne Donnellon, Barbara Gray, and Michael Bougon, "Communication, Meaning, and Organized Action," *Administrative Science Quarterly,* March 1986, pp. 43–55.

3. Richard M. Hodgetts and Fred Luthans, *International Management* (New York: McGraw-Hill Book Co., 1991), pp. 335–340.

4. John S. Fieldon, "Meaning Is Shaped by Audience and Situation," *Personnel Journal,* May 1988, pp. 107–110.

5. Robert E. Lefton, "The Eight Barriers to Teamwork," *Personnel Journal,* January 1988, pp. 18–20.

6. Keith Davis, "Understanding the Organizational Grapevine and Its Benefits," *Business and Public Affairs,* Spring 1976, p. 5.

7. *Ibid.,* pp. 7–9.

8. *Ibid.,* p. 8.

9. Alan Zaremba, "Working with the Organizational Grapevine," *Personnel Journal,* July 1988, pp. 38–42.

10. Jane W. Gibson and Richard M. Hodgetts, *Business Communication: Skills and Strategies* (New York: Harper & Row, 1990), pp. 454–467.

11. Julius Fast, *Body Language* (New York: Pocket Books, 1971).

12. Jane Gibson and Richard M. Hodgetts, *Organizational Communication* (New York: Harper Collins, 1990), pp. 121–122.

13. Also see Regina Barabas, "Get Organized," *Working Woman,* January 1990, pp. 116–119.

14. "Crisis Spokesman," *Newsweek,* October 5, 1970, p. 106.

15. For more on this see Jerie McArthur and D. W. McArthur, "The Pitfalls (and Pratfalls) of Corporate Communications," *Management Solutions,* December 1987, pp. 15–21.

16. Hazel J. Rozema and John W. Gray, "How Wide is Your Communication Gender Gap?" *Personnel Journal,* July 1987, pp. 98–105.

17. Reported in Rensis Likert, *New Patterns of Management* (New York: McGraw-Hill Book Co., 1961), p. 52.

18. Larry Blake, "Communicate with Clarity: Manage Meaning," *Personnel Journal,* May 1967, pp. 43–50.

19. See Merrill Sheils, "Why Johnny Can't Write," *Newsweek,* December 8, 1975, pp. 58–62.

20. J. Thomas Miller III, "Communication. . .Or Getting Ideas Across," *S.A.M. Advanced Management Journal,* Summer 1980, p. 34.

21. For more on language see Bruce H. Drake and Dennis J. Moberg, "Communicating Influence Attempts in Dyads: Linguistic Sedatives and Palliatives," *Academy of Management Review,* September 1986, pp. 567–584.

22. Ralph G. Nichols, "Listening Is Good Business," *Management of Personnel Quarterly,* Winter 1962, p. 4.

23. Harold P. Zelko, "Rate Your Communication Skills," *Personnel Journal,* November 1987, p. 133.

24. Roger L. Kirkham, "Communicating to Influence Others More Effectively," *Personnel Journal,* December 1987, pp. 52–55.

25. Muriel James and Dorothy Jongeward, *Born to Win: Transactional Analysis with Gestalt Experiments* (Reading, MA: Addison-Wesley Publishing Co., 1971), p. 24.

26. A. W. Clausen, "Listening and Responding to Employees' Concerns," *Harvard Business Review,* January–February 1980, p. 104.

27. Eric M. Eisenberg and Marsha G. Witten, "Reconsidering Openness in Organizational Communication," *Academy of Management Review,* July 1987, pp. 418–426.

28. William C. Himstreet and Wayne Murlin Baty, *Business Communications,* 9th ed. (Boston: PWS/Kent Publishing, 1990), p. 152.

29. Robert A. Giacalone and Stephen B. Knouse, "Reducing the Need for Defensive Communication," *Management Solutions,* September 1987, pp. 20–24.

30. Gibson and Hodgetts, *Organizational Communication,* p. 122.

31. Ralph G. Nichols, "Listening, What Price Inefficiency?" *Office Executive,* April 1959, pp. 15–22.

32. Cynthia Hamilton, "Steps to Better Listening," *Personnel Journal,* February 1987, pp. 20–21.

33. Richard M. Hodgetts, *Management: Theory, Process, and Practice,* 5th ed. (San Diego, CA: Harcourt Brace Jovanovich, 1990), p. 444.

34. Nichols, "Listening," pp. 15–22.

35. For more on this topic see Richard M. Hodgetts, *Modern Human Relations at Work,* 4th ed. (Hinsdale, IL: Dryden Press, 1990), pp. 440–442.

36. Gibson and Hodgetts, *Organizational Communications,* pp. 72–73.

CHAPTER 16
Organizational Climate and Culture

GOALS OF THE CHAPTER

Organizations are in a constant state of flux. For example, the work climate is often changing. A slightly autocratic manager may be moved to another unit and replaced by a more participative individual. Some individuals will like the first manager better than the second and vice versa, so for each the perceived climate is different. This climate is affected, among other things, by the enterprise's values and beliefs. These properties, often referred to as organizational culture, have been the focus of attention in recent years because the wave of mergers and acquisitions and increased competition all directly affect every enterprise's culture.

The first goal of this chapter is to examine what is meant by the term *organizational climate,* review some of the key climate factors, and illustrate how this climate can be measured. The second goal is to examine the nature of organizational culture and the ways in which cultural profiles can be determined. The third goal is to look at the ways in which culture is developed and managed. When you are finished reading this chapter, you should be able to:

1. define the term *organizational climate;*
2. discuss some key climate factors and how they can be measured;
3. define the term *organizational culture* and describe the four common types of culture;
4. explain how organizational culture is developed and the benefits of culture to an enterprise;
5. describe some of the steps that organizations take in managing their culture.

Until six months ago the Grattling Company had specialized in research and development (R&D) work. The firm consisted of 749 people, most of whom were in either the R&D laboratory or associated with research-related activities. A small number of the personnel were in managerial positions and were responsible for negotiating contracts with outside clients. These contracts took two forms. The most common was "research for hire" contracts whereby Grattling agreed to conduct R&D for the client. Because of its high tech facilities and the reputation of Grattling's research staff, many firms that did not want to fund their own in-house R&D would turn to Grattling under a "cost plus" contract. The second most common R&D activity was research directed at developing new processes and products that would then be sold to a client who, in turn, would bring them to market.

The above arrangement had proven very profitable for Grattling, but the company also began to feel that it was passing up too much profit by developing new products for other firms. "We should be doing our own product development and marketing," the president told the board of directors, and they agreed. Beginning nine months ago, the firm started rapidly increasing its work force. There currently are seventy-five people in the marketing department, and within a month the fifty-two of them in sales will begin calling on clients around the country in an effort to persuade them to carry Grattling's two new consumer products. One is a lightweight, portable cellular phone that will compete directly with Motorola and other leading competitors. The other is a pocket-size color TV that can operate for 1,000 hours off a battery charge. The firm believes that both products will be big winners. As the president put it, "For years we've been developing outstanding consumer products for other firms. Now we're going to sell directly into the marketing channel and end up with a lot more of the profits. My only real concern is the effect that this new direction will have on our R&D people. They used to be the only important people around here, but now they're going to have to share the spotlight with the marketing people. I know this is going to cause some friction, but I think we can keep everything under control."

1. How can the company measure its organizational climate to find out the current state of affairs?
2. What did the firm's organizational cultural profile look like when it was doing strictly R&D work? What changes are likely to occur in this profile over the next year?
3. What value would a strong corporate culture provide to Grattling? Explain.
4. What steps can management take to manage this new culture? Identify and describe two.

Write down your answers to these questions and put them aside. We will return to them later.

ORGANIZATIONAL CLIMATE

Organizational climate has been defined in many different ways.[1] On an individual basis, it is a person's perception of the kind of organization in which he or she is working. On a macro basis, it is a set of attributes which can be perceived about a particular organization or its subsystems, based on the way that the organization or subsystems deal with the personnel. The term is a difficult one to define because there are often a *number* of organizational climates, depending upon one's place in the hierarchy. We know, for example, that the climate at the top sets the stage for that in the middle, which in turn affects the climate at the bottom. As a result, the situation is similar to the one depicted in Figure 16–1. Organizational structure and policy influence leadership behavior, and both of these factors affect the work process. In turn, the work process influences performance, satisfaction, and organizational climate, with the climate at the top setting the stage for that at the intermediate and lower levels.

Organizational climate consists of the work environment properties that serve as a major force in influencing job behavior.

In specific terms, organizational climate refers to a set of properties of the work environment that are perceived by individuals who work there and serve as a major force in influencing their job behavior. Illustrations include structure, job descriptions, performance standards, rewards, leadership style, challenge, supportiveness, and work

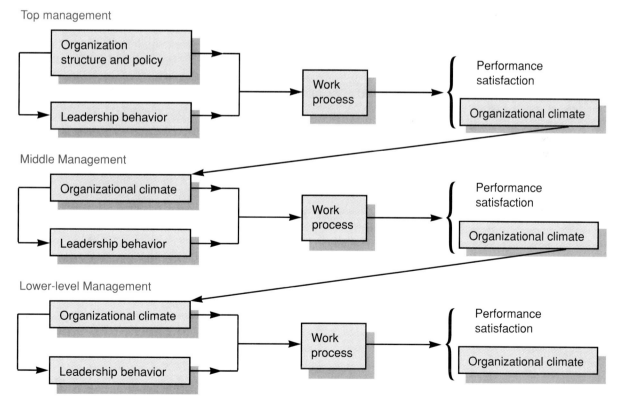

FIGURE 16–1
The Cumulative Effect of Organizational Climate

values. These interacting **climate factors** influence such key variables as satisfaction, production, and efficiency.

Climate Factors

Various classifications of climate factors have been proposed. In a public school organization that they studied, Halpin and Crofts identified eight factors: (a) the consideration management had for the personnel as people; (b) the emphasis that was placed on getting work done; (c) the emotional distance that existed between manager and subordinate; (d) the perception people had that their social needs were being satisfied; (e) the enjoyment they received from social relationships in the organization; (f) the desire management showed, through task-oriented behavior, to motivate the work force; (g) the perception people had regarding whether they were simply going through motions to complete a task; and (h) the feeling they had of being burdened with busy work.[2]

Another classification has been offered by Field and Abelson. After making a thorough review of the literature, they have synthesized current research in the form of a climate model, presented in Figure 16–2. Notice that the model takes into account a series of climate factors. It also incorporates much of the material that has been presented in this text, including individual behavior, group behavior, and organizational processes.[3]

A third categorization has been offered by the Likerts. Simpler to understand than Field and Abelson's model, the six variables that they set forth help establish the foundation of Figure 16–2. An analysis of each can actually provide important insights regarding how well things are going in the organization. The six, along with the questions that can be used in examining each, are as follows:

1. Communication flow. How well do subordinates know what is going on? How receptive are superiors to communiques? Are subordinates given sufficient information to do their jobs well?

2. Decision-making practices. Are subordinates involved in the decision-making process? Is the know-how of all the personnel at every level being utilized?

3. Concern for people. Does the organization organize work activities sensibly, try to improve working conditions, and show an interest in the individual's welfare?

4. Influence on the department. Do lower-level supervisors and employees who have no subordinates have an influence on the department?

5. Technological adequacy. Are equipment and resources well managed and improved methods quickly adopted?

6. Motivation. Do people in the organization work hard for both extrinsic and intrinsic rewards, and are they encouraged to do so by the organization?[4]

There are both overt and covert aspects of organizational climate.

Note that in all three of the above descriptions organizational climate consists of two major categories. The first contains those things that can be seen or measured. Illustrations include the hierarchy, the goals of the organization, performance standards, and efficiency measurements. The factors in the second category are not visible, but they also play key roles in helping to shape the organizational climate. Illustrations include attitudes, feelings, supportiveness, and satisfaction. The former are **overt**

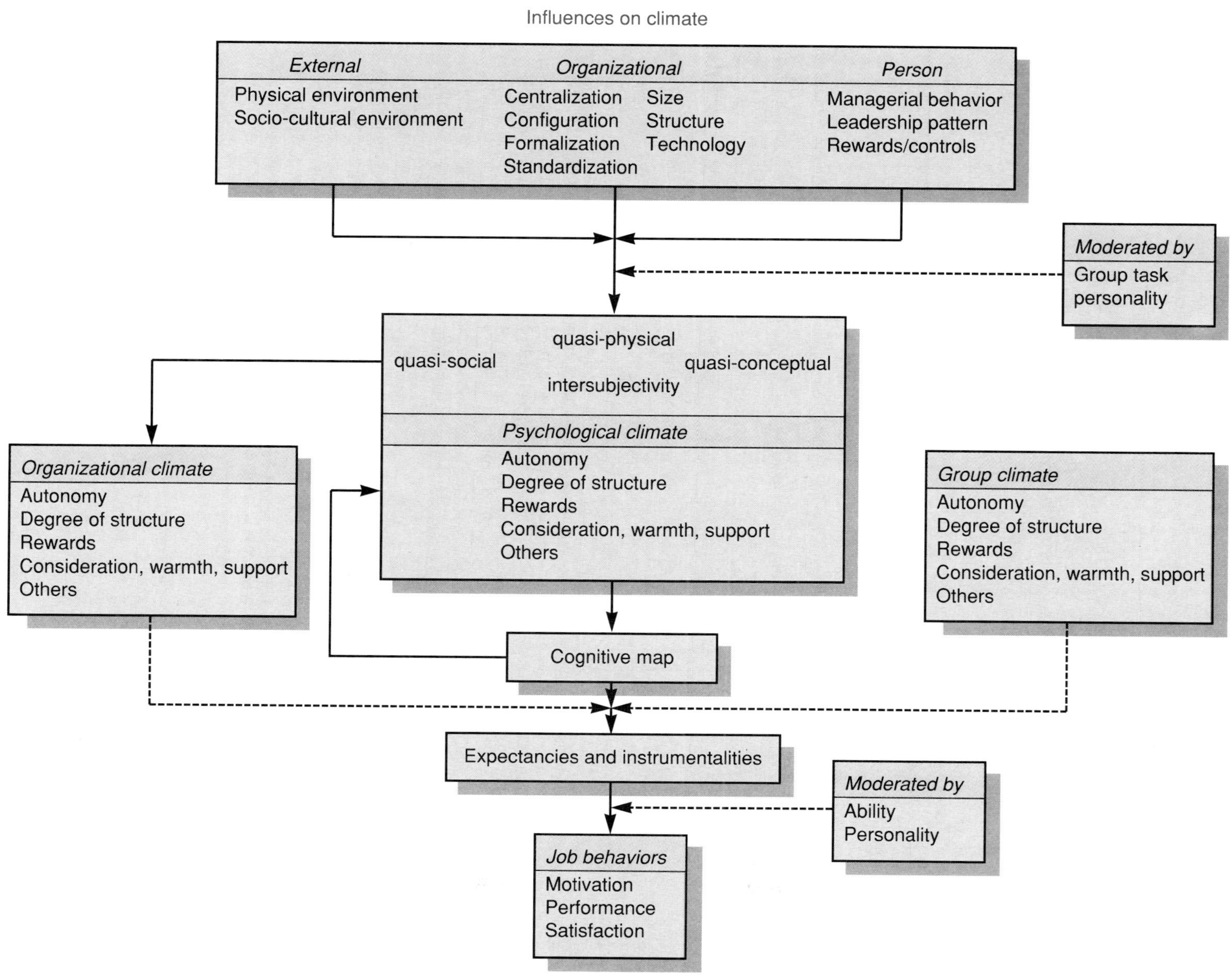

Influences on climate

FIGURE 16–2

A Climate Model (Source: R. H. George Field and Michael A. Abelson, "Climate: A Reconceptualization and Proposed Model," *Human Relations*, March 1982, pp. 194–195.)

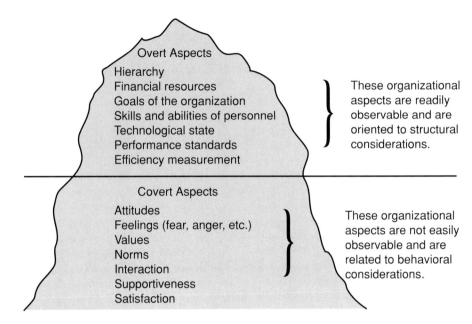

Overt Aspects

Hierarchy
Financial resources
Goals of the organization
Skills and abilities of personnel
Technological state
Performance standards
Efficiency measurement

} These organizational aspects are readily observable and are oriented to structural considerations.

Covert Aspects

Attitudes
Feelings (fear, anger, etc.)
Values
Norms
Interaction
Supportiveness
Satisfaction

} These organizational aspects are not easily observable and are related to behavioral considerations.

FIGURE 16–3
The Organizational Iceberg

aspects of the organization, while the latter are **covert aspects**. When we examine an organization's climate, it is akin to studying an iceberg (see Figure 16–3). Everything we see is important, but there is a great deal under the surface, not readily visible, that also merits close attention. In recent years, behavioral scientists have attempted to identify and measure these causal inputs that affect organizational climate.

Measuring Organizational Climate

There are a number of ways of measuring organizational climate.

There are a number of ways to measure the status of an organization's climate, whether it be for a department, a division, or the entire organization. One way is by using structured survey instruments in which the personnel are asked to evaluate key organizational variables such as leadership, motivation, communication, decision making, goals, and control. Figure 16–4 presents an illustration of the organizational characteristic profile popularized by Likert and his associates at the Institute for Social Research.[5] Each variable has four dimensions, and each dimension contains five degrees. By giving such a questionnaire to departmental members and then averaging the scores, an overall general profile can be obtained. Note that none of the continua in Figure 16–4 are presented in an either/or fashion. Furthermore, the climate in one area, such as leadership, may be different from that in another, such as motivation.

Using the Likert profile, an organization has a starting point for determining: (a) the climate that currently exists in each category; (b) what it should be; and (c) the types of changes that must be undertaken to attain the desired profile. Of particular importance is the fact that the survey instrument attempts to measure causal

Organizational Variables	Exploitive Autocratic	Benevolent Autocratic	Consultative Democratic	Participative Democratic
Leadership How much confidence and trust is shown in the subordinates?	Almost none	Some	A substantial amount	A great deal
Motivation Is predominant use made of (1) fear, (2) threats, (3) punishment, (4) rewards, (5) involvement?	1, 2, 3, and occasionally 4	4 and sometimes 3	4 and sometimes 3 and 5	5 and 4 predominantly
Communication What is the usual flow of information?	Down	Mostly down	Down and up	Down, up and sideways
Decision making At what levels are decisions made?	Mostly at the top	Policy is set at the top; some delegation occurs	Broad policy is set at the top; more delegation occurs	Decisions are made throughout the entire organization
Goal setting How are goals determined?	Orders are issued from the top	Orders are issued; some comments are invited	After discussion, orders are issued	Except in crisis situations, there is group action
Control How concentrated are review and control functions?	Very highly at the top	Quite highly at the top	Moderately; delegation to the lower level	Widely shared

FIGURE 16–4

A Profile of Organizational Characteristics (Adapted from Rensis Likert and Jane Gibson Likert, *New Ways of Managing Conflict* (New York: McGraw-Hill Book Co., 1976), p. 75, with permission of McGraw-Hill, Inc.)

inputs—inputs that help determine the organizational climate and, in the final analysis, bring about effectiveness in the form of high productivity and satisfaction and low absenteeism and turnover. Sometimes this climate must be changed in order to maintain the organization's viability. For example, many companies are now finding that a consultative or democratic climate is more conducive to productivity than an autocratic climate. This climate is often created through the emergence of a new organizational culture.

STOP — Review your answers to Question 1 and make any changes you would like before continuing.

1. How can the company measure its organizational climate to find out the current state of affairs?

There are a number of ways that this climate can be measured. One of the simplest and most direct is to use a form of the Likert profile and find out the system of management currently being used. Of particular value is the baseline profile that this information provides. Once the company gathers this information, it can measure its organizational climate in the future and compare it to this earlier profile. This will allow management to identify those changes that have occurred and to determine whether this new climate is acceptable or if efforts should be made to modify it.

ORGANIZATIONAL CULTURE

Organizational culture consists of expected behaviors, actions, and values.

Organizational culture consists of the expected behaviors, actions, and values that people in an enterprise are expected to follow.[6] Some individuals have simplified this term and defined it as "the way we do things around here."[7] In any event, organizational culture is important because many organizations are finding that their cultures must undergo change if the enterprise is to remain viable.[8] In the process, the climate is also changed, but this is a price the organization must pay if it hopes to survive. In recent years such major firms as General Motors, IBM, 3M, Johnson & Johnson, and AT&T have undergone culture change.[9] One of the most popular approaches during the 1980s was the adoption of Japanese management practices, which put a strong emphasis on group cooperation and long-term commitment to the firm.[10] Many American firms have found that the acceptance of certain Japanese practices has resulted in a combination American-Japanese approach to operations.

In a number of cases, acceptance of these ideas has brought about greater efficiency. For example, in 1982 General Motors closed its Fremont, California, assembly plant. The unit had an 18 percent daily absenteeism rate and a long history of labor relations problems. The plant was reopened the next year in a joint venture between Toyota and GM, and 85 percent of the original workers were rehired. The new culture, with its Japanese-style emphasis on having assembly line workers maintain their machines and focus on work quality and improvement of the production process, resulted in record high productivity. Quite obviously, the new culture has had a dramatic, positive effect on the operation.

The GM example provides some important insights into the value of understanding corporate culture. In particular, it points out that many times the current culture needs to be changed because it is not resulting in productive behaviors. Sometimes, however, a joint venture or merger can produce the opposite effect. When personnel are accustomed to doing their jobs in a particular way and the organization suddenly makes a major strategic change, the impact of the new culture on the personnel may bring about negative results. For example, when General Motors bought Electronic Data Systems from Ross Perot, the giant auto maker found that it was unable to achieve the desired synergy between the two companies. The cultures were so different that the personnel were unable to work in harmonious fashion. So although a change in culture can bring about positive results, other times it creates problems.[11]

Cultural Profiles

Cultural profiles are characteristics that distinguish the expected behaviors and values of people in a particular organization.

No two organizations have identical cultures. There are always some differences between the two. One way of comparing and contrasting cultures is through the use of *cultural profiles,* characteristics that distinguish the expected behaviors and values of people in a particular enterprise. One of the most comprehensive views of these profiles has been offered by Deal and Kennedy. They have found that there are four types of cultural profiles: tough-guy macho, work hard/play hard, bet your company, and process. (See Table 16–1.)

There are two criteria that can be used in identifying and describing cultures: risk and feedback. In some organizations risk is high while in others it is low; in some organizations feedback is fast while in others it is slow. Deal and Kennedy have used these four criteria combinations to create the culture profiles in Table 16–1. Notice that when comparing the tough-guy macho culture with the process culture that there are dramatic differences in the way things are done. In a **tough-guy macho culture** the emphasis is on high risk taking and fast feedback. Owner-managed firms that are run by entrepreneurial types are often personified by this culture. Conversely, in the **process culture** risk taking is low and feedback is slow. Governmental agencies with their typical bureaucratic approach to doing things are an excellent example of this culture.

The other two cultures, work hard/play hard and bet your company, are much more common. Sales organizations, in particular, often develop a **work hard/play hard culture;** they rely heavily on teamwork and short-term goal accomplishment. Research and development laboratories and airplane design and manufacturing firms are good examples of a **bet your company culture;** the risks are high and the personnel do not find out how well they have done for an extended period of time.

Cultural profiles are useful in understanding the impact of culture on organizational behavior.

These four profiles are useful in understanding the impact of culture on organizational behavior. For example, before the court-ordered breakup of the telephone industry, AT&T used to place its greatest focus on research and development. The company was technology driven. It worked to develop cheaper long distance dialing equipment so that more and more people would be enticed to use this service. And it continued to turn out new products such as touch-dial phones (as opposed to rotary dial) and portable phones, so that phone calling would be easier and more available. After the breakup, however, the firm found that it had to compete with a host of other companies for both the long distance market as well as telephone products. Over the last five years AT&T's culture profile has become much more work hard/play hard. The firm is now very heavily customer-driven.

Cultural profiles can also be used to examine behavior within specific departments. For example, entrepreneurs tend to be tough-guy macho types. Production and sales people are often work hard/play hard types. Strategic planning people tend to be

TABLE 16–1
Organizational Culture Profiles

Name of the culture	Tough-Guy, Macho	Work Hard/Play Hard
Type of risks that are assumed	High	Low
Type of feedback from decisions	Fast	Fast
Typical kinds of organizations that use this culture	Construction, cosmetics, television, radio, venture capitalism, management consulting	Real estate, computer firms, auto distributors, door-to-door sales operations, retail stores, mass consumer sales
The ways survivors and/or heroes in this culture behave	They have a tough attitude. They are individualistic. They can tolerate all-or-nothing risks. They are superstitious.	They are super salespeople. They often are friendly, hail-fellow-well-met types. They use a team approach to problem solving. They are nonsuperstitious.
Strengths of the personnel/culture	They can get things done in short order.	They are able to quickly produce a high volume of work.
Weaknesses of the personnel/culture	They do not learn from past mistakes. Everything tends to be short-term in orientation. The virtues of cooperation are ignored.	They look for quick-fix solutions. They have a short-term time perspective. They are more committed to action than to problem solving.
Habits of the survivors and/or heroes	They dress in fashion. They live in "in" places. They like one-on-one sports such as tennis. They enjoy scoring points off one another in verbal interaction.	They avoid extremes in dress. They live in tract houses. They prefer team sports such as touch football. They like to drink together.

Source: Adapted from Terrence E. Deal and Allan A. Kennedy, *Corporate Cultures: The Rites and Rituals of Corporate Life* (Reading, MA: Addison-Wesley Publishing Co., 1982), Chapter 6.

bet your company types. Personnel in the accounting department often operate in a process culture. Despite these differences, however, there will be one overall cultural focus that tends to drive the company. For example, while IBM is technology focused, it is market driven. The company is more represented by the work hard/play hard culture than by the bet your company culture. So there is an overall cultural profile and unit or departmental profiles that exist simultaneously. These cultures help the orga-

Bet Your Company	Process
High	Low
Slow	Slow
Oil, aerospace, capital goods manufacturers, architectural firms, investment banks, mining and smelting firms, military	Banks, insurance companies, utilities, pharmaceuticals, financial-service organizations, many agencies of the government
They can endure long-term ambiguity. They always double check their decisions. They are technically competent. They have a strong respect for authority.	They are very cautious and protective of their own flank. They are orderly and punctual. They are good at attending to detail. They always follow established procedures.
They can generate high quality inventions and major scientific breakthroughs.	They bring order and system to the workplace.
They are extremely slow in getting things done. Their organizations are vulnerable to short-term economic fluctuations. Their organizations often face cash-flow problems.	There is lots of red tape. Initiative is downplayed. They face long hours and boring work.
They dress according to their organizational rank. Their housing matches their hierarchical position. They like sports such as golf, in which the outcome is unclear until the end of the game. The older members serve as mentors for the younger ones.	They dress according to hierarchical rank. They live in apartments or no-frills homes. They enjoy process sports like jogging and swimming. They like discussing memos.

nization function by the way in which they establish priorities and direct ongoing activities on both a macro and micro basis.

Cultural profiles also help illustrate changes that can occur in corporate climate when moving from one culture to another.

A third benefit of cultural profiles is for illustrating the changes that can occur in corporate climate when an enterprise or department moves from one profile to another. Using Table 16–1 as a point of reference, personnel in a department that once operated in a process culture and now have to function in a work hard/play hard culture would find themselves undergoing a great deal of stress. Many would be unable to cope. The pace of work and the degree of responsibility would weigh heavily on most of the people. Conversely, individuals who are accustomed to a work hard/play hard culture would have great difficulty functioning effectively in a process culture. The red tape and bureaucratic procedures would lead to high stress for many of them.

Review your answers to Question 2 and make any changes you would like before continuing.

2. What did the firm's organizational cultural profile look like when it was doing strictly R&D work? What changes are likely to occur in this profile over the next year?

When it was doing strictly R&D work, the firm had a bet your company cultural profile. This profile is characterized by high risk taking and slow feedback. Now that it is adding a marketing focus, the firm's basic profile will be complemented by a work hard/play hard culture characterized by low risk taking and fast feedback. The two cultures will exist side-by-side. However, one will be dominant. At the present time, it is the bet your company culture because the firm is technology-driven. First it creates new products, then it sells them. If the focus were to change and the company began selling low tech goods or served as a marketing arm for other R&D firms, it is possible that the primary culture would become work hard/play hard.

The Development of Culture

Organizational culture can be developed in a number of ways. Typically these steps or mechanisms involve developing norms and behaviors that are reinforced by top management. For example, at the Wal-Mart Corporation, Sam Walton, founder and president, spends three days a week on the road where he visits his stores and talks to customers and employees. This hands-on approach helps reinforce Sam's belief in the principle of "management by walking around." Aware of his practices, store managers emulate Sam and find that they, too, are able to get feedback on what is going on in the store and what changes need to be made to ensure that the unit is responding to customer needs. Typically, four mechanisms are used in developing culture: participation, symbolic action, information from others, and comprehensive reward systems.[12] Sometimes all four are used, but many organizations find they can create and sustain the necessary culture by relying on just a couple of these mechanisms.

Participation is important in reinforcing desired activities.

Participation.   Participation is used to encourage people to get involved in desired activities and to let them know that their contributions are desired. A wide number of methods are typically used, including quality circles, suggestion systems, and advisory boards. Such participation is voluntary because this is the most effective way of getting people to "buy into" the system. Then, as the personnel get involved and realize that they are responsible for their actions, they develop a commitment to the enterprise and its way of doing things. Thus participation helps build and reinforce this culture.

Symbolic actions indicate what is important to management.

Symbolic Action.   Symbolic action typically takes the form of management behavior that is used to indicate what is important in the organization. Sam Walton's frequent store visits reinforce the importance of management by walking around. At IBM the attention to customer service lets everyone know that this is one of the important values of the culture. At the 3M Company the focus on creativity is continually stressed by management, and those who are creative are given the authority to follow through on their projects and bring them to fruition. In the process, management lets everyone know the importance of creativity.

Storytelling is a common form of symbolic action.

Another common form of symbolic action is storytelling. Many organizations have seasoned managers talk to new recruits and tell the latter how it was "in the old days." These stories almost always involve some action that the manager took as a young employee to solve a problem or land a sale, such as personally working through the night with a store manager to install a computerized inventory system. After the story is told, the moral is presented: Don't work a 9 to 5 schedule; work until the job is done. If you do that, you'll succeed in this company. These stories are used to reinforce beliefs and attitudes that are critical to the success of the enterprise and, in the process, they help build and sustain the corporate culture.

Another form of symbolic action is using ceremonies to reinforce culture. At Mary Kay Cosmetics the annual sales awards have become legendary. People are honored for their contributions and the rewards, which range from cash to jewels and furs, are used to encourage everyone to continue working even harder.

Coworkers are important in reinforcing cultural values.

Information from Others.   Cultural values are also reinforced by coworkers. When individuals enter the organization, they often are unsure of how to act or to handle certain situations. In strong cultures, seasoned employees know what to do, and they guide and direct their new counterparts. In the process, a consistency of understanding ensures that everyone is doing things in a uniform way. For example, if the company's philosophy is one of customer service, the new employees learn that anyone who wants to return merchandise to the store can do so. There should be no hesitation about accepting the goods. When this message is communicated by the older employees and the new workers see it carried out in practice, they quickly adopt the same approach. This uniformity of action eliminates the contradictory interpretations common in enterprises with weak cultures where what is communicated and what is done are often not the same thing.

Sometimes this culture affects off-the-job behavior as well. For example, work teams in the Japanese-GM assembly plant in Fremont are each given a semiannual budget that must be spent only on team-sponsored activities where the entire team participates. The result is a stronger bond of teamwork than if the workers interacted only in the work place.

Reward systems support desired behavior.

Comprehensive Reward Systems.   Reward systems include both monetary and nonmonetary rewards. Most organizations make wide use of recognition and approval of proper behavior. Primary attention is given to developing a sense of satisfaction and accomplishment within the personnel for a job well done. One of the primary principles that is often employed is "catching people doing things right."

At the same time, the organization will work to reduce and eliminate negative rewards that can undermine the culture. For example, 3M emphasizes creativity. However, not everyone will be successful in their creative efforts. It is therefore important not to punish those who fail because this will have a dampening effect on the rest of the personnel and will eventually result in a very risk aversive work group. In turn, creative efforts will diminish and eventually cease.

The Importance of Culture

A well-developed organizational culture can provide a number of important benefits to an enterprise. Some of the primary ones include effective control, normative order, the promotion of innovation, the effective positioning of strategy, and strong commitment from the personnel.

Culture helps control behavior.

Effective Control. Organizational culture serves as a control mechanism in directing behavior. As the culture is diffused throughout the organization, people understand what they are supposed to do (for example, work hard, be ethical, focus on quality) and what they should not do (for example, fail to cooperate with others, be rude to customers, not keep machinery well maintained). When individuals are not in accordance with the beliefs and values of the culture, managers and coworkers will step in and insist on corrective action. A strong culture is characterized by shared beliefs and expectations to which all must adhere.[13] In fact, sometimes situations arise that are not governed by formal rules and procedures, and culture serves as the determinant in helping decide what to do. For example, in a high risk-taking culture a person with an idea for a new good or service will be encouraged to proceed with the idea even though no formal mechanism gives the go ahead.

Strong cultures have both consensus and intensity regarding norms.

Normative Order. Closely linked to effective control is the use of norms to guide behaviors. These expectations regarding appropriate and inappropriate behaviors are greatly influenced by culture, and strong cultures have both consensus and intensity regarding these norms. Everyone understands the culturally based norms (consensus), and there is strong support (intensity) for them. In weak cultures, consensus may be present but intensity is not. This comparison helps explain why some organizations are very successful at what they do. It also helps explain why organizations with strong cultures often have great difficulty changing their strategies and behaviors. The norms that dictate these actions have been reinforced so strongly that the personnel are reluctant to abandon them in favor of other behaviors. A good example is provided in the case of AT&T. (See "Organizational Behavior in Action: AT&T's New Aggressive Culture.")

Cultures can also promote innovation.

Innovation Promotion. Organizational cultures can also promote innovation. In firms like Cray Research, Hewlett-Packard, Intel, Johnson & Johnson, and 3M, the culture encourages creative thinking. This is done through promoting norms that support such activity. O'Reilly investigated these norms across a wide diversity of industries, including consumer products, computers, manufacturing, pharmaceuticals, and semiconductors.[14] The norms supporting innovation are reported in Table 16–2. Several things are notable about this list. First, regardless of the industry or technology, managers identified virtually the same list of norms as important. Second, these norms were all found to be useful in supporting and facilitating the

Organizational Behavior In Action

AT&T'S NEW AGGRESSIVE CULTURE

For almost ten years now AT&T has been trying to develop a more competitive posture. It has not been easy to shed its old culture and develop one that is more market-driven. The firm still has a top-heavy bureaucracy and performance has been lackluster. However, under its new chairman, Robert E. Allen, a new culture is being developed, and things seem to be falling into place. For example, revenues from the sale of equipment and long-distance services are now up and operating margins have started to increase. Yet there is still a long way to go. In particular, AT&T is finding that its old culture, developed during the days when it held a virtual monopoly in the telephone business, is difficult to change and every time the firm makes a new strategic move, it is countered by the competition.

The firm's bread and butter business is the long distance market. However, MCI has been taking away 30,000 to 40,000 customers a week because AT&T has not been aggressive in its competitive moves. The firm's computer business has long been a loser in a market dominated by well-entrenched competitors, and its Consumer Products Division has had annual losses in excess of $10 million. On the other hand, there is good news.

Under Allen the company is beginning to reduce excessive layers of management and flatten out the structure. It is also beginning to win back market share from MCI, and computer losses have been dramatically cut. Some industry experts believe that the company will turn a profit in computers during the early 1990s. At the same time Allen is changing the corporate culture by carving the company into nineteen different business units and pushing decision making down to the presidents of these units. These executives now have the authority to make pricing and new product decisions. This is creating a new form of aggressiveness that, hopefully, will make the firm more profitable. Even at the company's venerable Bell Laboratories a new approach is in place. Each business unit has a manager and a crew of engineers, and the managers' annual compensation is being tied to the unit's sales performance. The objective is to force the Labs into creating more marketable designs and reducing the time needed to get products to market.

In an effort to show that he is serious, Allen has slashed 75,000 jobs, pushed manufacturing work offshore where costs are significantly lower, and put in place a strategy for gaining market share. The firm has three major goals for the 1990s: increase shareholder value, be a technology leader, and improve service. At the same time, authority is being delegated down the line, and managers are being held accountable for performance.

Will Allen's plan work out? It is still too early to tell. In an operation as large as AT&T, changes often take place in fits and starts. However, Allen is determined to make the company more aggressive and to stay the course. If nothing else, old timers are finding that the company culture they came to know and love is fast disappearing.

Source: John J. Keller and Mark Maremont, "Bob Allen is Turning AT&T Into a Live Wire," *Business Week,* November 6, 1989, pp. 140–152.

TABLE 16–2
Norms That Promote Innovation

A. Norms to Promote Creativity

1. **Risk Taking**
   - freedom to try things and fail
   - acceptance of mistakes
   - allow discussion of "dumb" ideas
   - no punishments for failure
   - challenge the status quo
   - forget the past
   - willingness *not* to focus on the short term
   - expectation that innovation is part of your job
   - positive attitudes about change
   - drive to improve

2. **Rewards for Change**
   - ideas are valued
   - respect for beginning ideas
   - build into the structure:
     - budgets
     - opportunities
     - resources
     - tools
     - time
     - promotions
   - top management attention and support
   - celebration of accomplishments
   - suggestions are implemented
   - encouragement

3. **Openness**
   - open communication and share information
   - listen better
   - open access
   - bright people, strong egos
   - scanning, broad thinking
   - force exposure outside the company
   - move people around
   - encourage lateral thinking
   - adopt the customer's perspective
   - accept criticism
   - don't be too sensitive
   - continuous training
   - intellectual honesty
   - expect and accept conflict
   - willingness to consult others

B. Norms to Promote Implementation

1. **Common Goals**
   - sense of pride in the organization
   - teamwork
   - willingness to share the credit
   - flexibility in jobs, budgets, functional areas
   - sense of ownership
   - eliminate mixed messages
   - manage interdependencies
   - shared visions and a common direction
   - build consensus
   - mutal respect and trust
   - concern for the whole organization

2. **Autonomy**
   - decision making responsibility at lower levels
   - decentralized procedures
   - freedom to act
   - expectation of action
   - belief that *you* can have an impact
   - delegation
   - quick, flexible decision making
   - minimize the bureaucracy

3. **Belief in Action**
   - don't be obsessed with precision
   - emphasis on results
   - meet your commitments
   - anxiety about timeliness
   - value getting things done
   - hard work is expected and appreciated
   - empower people
   - emphasis on quality
   - eagerness to get things done
   - cut through the bureaucracy

Source: Charles O'Reilly, "Corporations, Culture, and Commitment: Motivation and Social Control in Organizations." © 1989 by the Regents of The Univ. of California. Reprinted from the *California Management Review*, vol. 31, no. 4 (Summer 1989, p. 15). By permission of The Regents.

innovation process. In addition to encouraging creative thinking, the norms helped the personnel deal with the conflicts that often arise when new ideas are proposed and implemented. The result is "creative conflict" rather than destructive conflict.

Organizational cultures help enterprises both formulate and implement their strategies.

Strategy Formulation and Implementation.

Organizational culture also helps an organization position itself vis-a-vis the competition. For example, in the case of Allen at AT&T the company is reducing its personnel and streamlining operations to become more competitive. At the same time the culture is promoting a new-found aggressiveness to both increase and retain market share. As this culture begins to take hold, it supports and encourages the desired strategy. Similar examples can be cited for many other firms. For example, Wal-Mart's culture is built around customer service. This has resulted in a highly responsive strategy and structure that continue to change to accommodate customer needs. The 3M Company emphasizes innovation and gives people time to work on special projects and develop ideas that eventually result in new product development. These products, in turn, are manufactured and marketed within a strategy that has been formulated to handle this new input. Thus the system feeds off itself. The culture creates innovative ideas and the strategy brings them to fruition.

Personnel in strong cultures identify with their firm.

Personnel Commitment.

The interactive reinforcement of culture and people often results in a highly committed work force. As the personnel learn their jobs and ways to interact effectively, morale increases and commitment to the enterprise is strengthened. This commitment often goes through three phases: compliance, identification, and internalization. In the **compliance phase,** individuals allow themselves to be influenced and swayed by other members of the group in order to obtain external rewards such as pay and promotions. In the **identification phase,** individuals accept influence in order to maintain a satisfying relationship; they feel pride in belonging to the organization. In the **internalization phase,** individuals find the values of the organization to be intrinsically rewarding and in harmony with their own values. The personnel in strong cultures are in the internalization phase: they identify with their firm.

STOP

Review your answers to Question 3 and make any changes you would like before continuing.

3. What value would a strong corporate culture provide to Grattling? Explain.

A strong corporate culture would provide a number of benefits to Grattling. The culture would help control organizational behavior. It would also promote innovation, help the company formulate and implement strategy, and serve as a catalyst in creating high commitment from the personnel. In addition, it is important to remember that the firm currently is developing two cultures, and it must be careful that there is no clash between them. If the R&D people do not respect the marketing people and vice versa, the company will have a great deal of difficulty operating profitably.

Managing Culture

Once a culture is in place, an organization will maintain it by reinforcing these beliefs and ensuring that the values are supported and sustained. Figure 16–5 illustrates how this process works. Beliefs and values are communicated to the personnel, commitment to the culture is attained, and the people are rewarded for this commitment.

Effective enterprises seek to manage their cultures.

    A good example of culture management is found in the case of Motorola, which has built its culture around three basic foundations: strong research and development, high quality, and zealous customer service.[15] This culture has reinforced the company's strategy and helped it develop such new products as the sleek, lightweight MicroTac cellular phone and the wristwatch pager, which have proven to be major technological breakthroughs. These products were the result of a strong commitment by Motorola to invest heavily in R&D and then "stay the course." In the process, the company's quality reached new heights; between 1983 and 1989 defects dropped from 3,000 per million products to under 200.[16] In the process, operating profits climbed from under $100 million in the early 1980s to over $500 million by the end of the decade. At the same time, the firm has been able to compete effectively with both domestic and foreign firms. In fact, Motorola quality is so high that it currently sells over $750 million annually in the Japanese market.

STOP   Review your answers to Question 4 and make any changes you would like before continuing.

4. What steps can management take to manage this new culture? Identify and describe two.

One thing that management can do is to convey its cultural values to the personnel through both words and deeds. The management has to let the personnel know what the company stands for and what its basic direction is to be. Second, the company must reward those who support its culture. This can be done through salary increases, promotions, and, most common of all, approval in the form of verbal reinforcement. These steps are critical to the company in managing this new culture.

FIGURE 16–5

How Culture Is Managed (Charles O'Reilly, "Corporations, Culture, and Commitment: Motivation and Social Control in Organizations." © 1989 by the Regents of the Univ. of California. Reprinted from the *California Management Review*, vol. 31, no. 4. (Summer 1989, p. 23.) By permission of The Regents.)

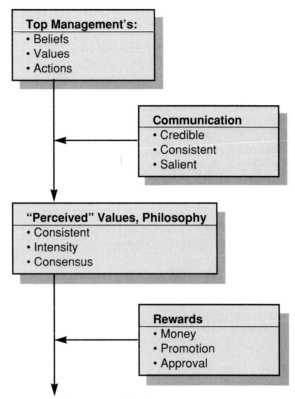

Top Management's:
• Beliefs
• Values
• Actions

Communication
• Credible
• Consistent
• Salient

"Perceived" Values, Philosophy
• Consistent
• Intensity
• Consensus

Rewards
• Money
• Promotion
• Approval

Employee's beliefs, attitudes, and behaviors expressed as norms

SUMMARY

1. An organization's climate is influenced by a number of key factors, including structure, job descriptions, performance standards, leadership style, and work values. These interacting forces affect such major variables as satisfaction, production, and efficiency. Some of these factors are readily observable and are oriented toward structural considerations; others are not as easily observable and are related to behavioral considerations. In measuring them, organizations have relied on a number of methods, including structured survey instruments such as the profile popularized by Likert and his associates at the Institute for Social Research.

2. Organizational climate consists of the behaviors, actions, and values that people in an enterprise are expected to follow. There are two criteria that can be used in identifying and describing cultures: risk and feedback. In some organizations risk is high while in others it is low; in some organizations feedback is fast while in others it is slow. These two criteria are the basis for four different cultures: tough-guy macho, work hard/play hard, bet your company, and process. Each was described in the chapter.

3. Organizational culture can be developed in a number of ways. These steps or mechanisms typically involve participation, the use of symbolic actions, information from others, and comprehensive reward systems. Of particular importance are symbolic actions such as storytelling, which is used to identify and reinforce organizational values and norms.

4. A number of important benefits can be derived from creating a strong culture. These include effective control, using norms to guide behavior, promoting innovation, formulating and implementing strategy, and creating personnel commitment. For example, organizations with strong cultures typically have personnel who identify closely with their firm.

5. Managing culture ensures that the norms and values of the enterprise are reinforced and maintained. This process includes communicating the culture to the personnel, ensuring that it is accepted, and rewarding the people for this commitment.

KEY TERMS

organizational climate	**organizational culture**	**bet your company culture**
climate factors	**tough-guy macho culture**	**compliance phase**
overt aspects	**process culture**	**identification phase**
covert aspects	**work hard/play hard culture**	**internalization phase**

REVIEW AND STUDY QUESTIONS

1. What is meant by the term *organizational climate*? Identify and describe some of the key climate factors.

2. How can organizational climate be measured? Explain.

3. What is meant by the term *organizational culture*?

4. What is a cultural profile? What importance do risk taking and feedback have in understanding cultural profiles?

5. How does the tough-guy macho culture differ from the work hard/play hard culture? Explain.

6. How does the bet your company culture differ from the process culture? Explain.

7. If an individual working in a process culture were trans-

ferred to a tough-guy macho culture, would this present the individual with any problems? Defend your answer.

8. What are some of the benefits of understanding cultural profiles? How can this information be of practical use?

9. How are organizational cultures developed? What steps or mechanisms are involved? Explain.

10. Of what value is an organizational culture? What benefits does it offer to the enterprise? Identify and describe three.

11. How do organizations manage their cultures? What steps or procedures do they use? Explain.

CASES

It's Not Business as Usual Any More

When the Urban Bank (UB) was founded 50 years ago, its primary customer focus was small businesses that needed financial assistance. In many cases these businesses proved successful and outgrew their need for UB's services. However, there were so many small businesses coming to UB every year that the bank management was not concerned about losing these growing firms. "We really couldn't deal with their needs," the chairman of the board explained recently. "We were set up for handling fledgling enterprises that needed $20,000 or less and were willing to pay an interest rate a half-percent above that being charged by other banks. The two main reasons they came to us were that most other banks did not want their business, and we were known for our expertise in helping small, growing firms."

Three years ago UB's board of directors made a major strategy decision. The bank would begin seeking medium and large business accounts. In order to meet the capital needs of these businesses, UB established banking relationships with some of the largest banks in the country. "We put the deal together," the president explained, "and if we need help from our banking partners, we get it from them in exchange for a piece of the profit. Of course, we won't have to rely on them forever. If we keep growing as we have over the last couple of years, we'll be able to handle all of our deals with in-house funds."

The bank has also been making a concerted effort to attract professional business people. UB's research shows that these individuals often keep large deposits and are very profitable accounts. However, there is strong competition for this market niche, and the bank realizes that it will take at least five more years before it will have over 5 percent of the local market. On the other hand, UB is determined to continue its efforts in this direction because it believes that this market will be critical to its growth plans for the upcoming decade.

At a recent board meeting, the chairman explained the bank's emerging strategy. "We used to be a sleepy bank that was interested only in small business accounts. Over the last thirty-six months, however, we have been expanding our business and becoming much more competitive in attracting larger accounts. And this is only the beginning. By the turn of the century we intend to be one of the five largest banks in the region. Those who have been with us for five or more years understand what I mean when I say, 'It's not going to be business as usual any more.'"

1. What type of organizational culture did the bank have five years ago? Describe it.

2. What type of corporate culture is the bank now trying to develop? Put it in your own words.

3. What are some steps that the bank will have to take to ensure that this new culture continues to gain strength? Describe two.

It's a Whole New World

When Karla Cooper took early retirement from the Social Security Administration (SSA), her friends liked to kid her. "You retired from the Social Security Administration so you can draw social security? Is this your way of telling us that the government is running out of money and you wanted to get yours before it's all gone?" Karla just smiled. She had no intention of remaining retired. In fact, last month she took a full-time job with a large consumer goods firm. The company is trying to develop and market foods to people fifty years of age and older. The firm believes that these people are more interested in good health than is any other segment of the population, and the company's new product lines emphasize high nutrition, low fat, and low cholesterol.

Karla is now working with a sales group in Florida that will be doing direct marketing to retail stores. "These foods are new to the market," she explained to her husband, "and they require personalized selling. It will be my job to show the retailer the benefits offered to the customer and why the store owner or manager should give us shelf space."

Karla likes her new job but finds it very demanding. "It's not like it was at Social Security," she recently told a friend. "The work pace is a lot faster and the company expects bottom-line performance. I'm expected to make a sale at one of every three retail stores I call on. This is no easy chore because a lot of retailers are skeptical or feel that they don't need our product line. This market is highly competitive, and there are plenty of substitute products so I have to show them why our products are superior to what they are already carrying. You know, it's a lot different from working at the SSA where we used to have rules and procedures for handling everything. Now I find myself improvising a lot and using my initiative to get things done. It's a whole new world out here. I don't think many people from the SSA could make this transition. However, even more interesting, I doubt whether many people in my sales group would survive very long at the SSA."

1. What was the organizational culture profile at the SSA? Put it in your own words.

2. What is the organizational culture profile at Karla's current firm like? What are some of the major ways in which it differs from the SSA?

3. Why would it be difficult for people to make the transition from one of these cultures to the other? Explain.

SELF-FEEDBACK EXERCISE

Evaluate Your Own Organizational Climate

The following twelve statements are designed to measure the behavioral climate in your organization. Read each statement carefully and place an *X* at the appropriate place on the accompanying continuum. If you do not have a job now, think of one for which you could currently qualify and fill in the continua based on that job.

	A	B	C	D
1. In your department/unit, how are most decisions made?	Decided by the boss and told to me.	Decided by the boss, and I am urged to go along with them.	Decided by the boss after talking to me.	Decided by the boss and me after discussion.
	1 | 2 | 3 | 4 | 5	6 | 7 | 8 | 9 | 10	11 | 12 | 13 | 14 | 15	16 | 17 | 18 | 19 | 20
2. How much confidence and trust does your boss have in you?	None	Very little	Some	A substantial amount
	1 | 2 | 3 | 4 | 5	6 | 7 | 8 | 9 | 10	11 | 12 | 13 | 14 | 15	16 | 17 | 18 | 19 | 20
3. How much notice are you given regarding change in your department/unit?	None	Very little	Some	A substantial amount
	1 | 2 | 3 | 4 | 5	6 | 7 | 8 | 9 | 10	11 | 12 | 13 | 14 | 15	16 | 17 | 18 | 19 | 20
4. How much control does your boss exercise over how you do your job?	A substantial amount	A good deal	A fair amount	A minimum amount
	1 | 2 | 3 | 4 | 5	6 | 7 | 8 | 9 | 10	11 | 12 | 13 | 14 | 15	16 | 17 | 18 | 19 | 20
5. In terms of Maslow's need hierarchy, what needs can you fulfill on the job?	Physiological and safety	Physiological, safety, and social	Physiological, safety, social, and esteem	Physiological, safety, social, esteem, and self-actualization
	1 | 2 | 3 | 4 | 5	6 | 7 | 8 | 9 | 10	11 | 12 | 13 | 14 | 15	16 | 17 | 18 | 19 | 20
6. How much is teamwork encouraged and developed in your department/unit?	None	Very little	Some	A great deal
	1 | 2 | 3 | 4 | 5	6 | 7 | 8 | 9 | 10	11 | 12 | 13 | 14 | 15	16 | 17 | 18 | 19 | 20

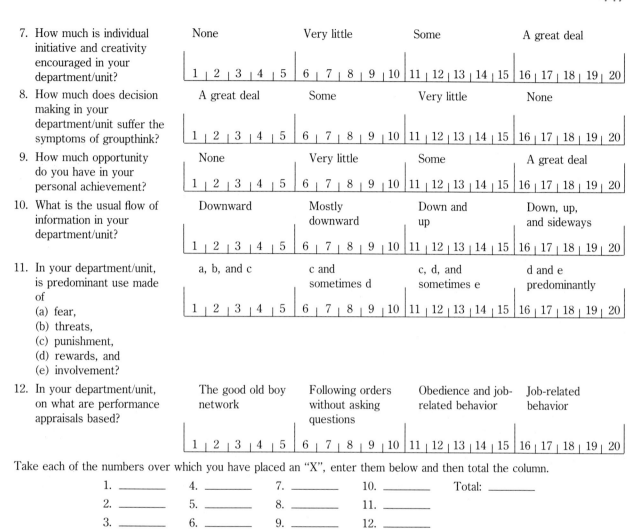

7. How much is individual initiative and creativity encouraged in your department/unit?

None | Very little | Some | A great deal

1 | 2 | 3 | 4 | 5 | 6 | 7 | 8 | 9 | 10 | 11 | 12 | 13 | 14 | 15 | 16 | 17 | 18 | 19 | 20

8. How much does decision making in your department/unit suffer the symptoms of groupthink?

A great deal | Some | Very little | None

1 | 2 | 3 | 4 | 5 | 6 | 7 | 8 | 9 | 10 | 11 | 12 | 13 | 14 | 15 | 16 | 17 | 18 | 19 | 20

9. How much opportunity do you have in your personal achievement?

None | Very little | Some | A great deal

1 | 2 | 3 | 4 | 5 | 6 | 7 | 8 | 9 | 10 | 11 | 12 | 13 | 14 | 15 | 16 | 17 | 18 | 19 | 20

10. What is the usual flow of information in your department/unit?

Downward | Mostly downward | Down and up | Down, up, and sideways

1 | 2 | 3 | 4 | 5 | 6 | 7 | 8 | 9 | 10 | 11 | 12 | 13 | 14 | 15 | 16 | 17 | 18 | 19 | 20

11. In your department/unit, is predominant use made of
(a) fear,
(b) threats,
(c) punishment,
(d) rewards, and
(e) involvement?

a, b, and c | c and sometimes d | c, d, and sometimes e | d and e predominantly

1 | 2 | 3 | 4 | 5 | 6 | 7 | 8 | 9 | 10 | 11 | 12 | 13 | 14 | 15 | 16 | 17 | 18 | 19 | 20

12. In your department/unit, on what are performance appraisals based?

The good old boy network | Following orders without asking questions | Obedience and job-related behavior | Job-related behavior

1 | 2 | 3 | 4 | 5 | 6 | 7 | 8 | 9 | 10 | 11 | 12 | 13 | 14 | 15 | 16 | 17 | 18 | 19 | 20

Take each of the numbers over which you have placed an "X", enter them below and then total the column.

1. _____   4. _____   7. _____   10. _____   Total: _____

2. _____   5. _____   8. _____   11. _____

3. _____   6. _____   9. _____   12. _____

Now compare your total to the following description to see your overall interpretation of your departmental/unit climate:

A. 12–60   Exploitive Autocratic Climate. This climate is characterized by a management that has little confidence in the subordinates. The latter are seldom involved in decision making, and management tends to use threats or punishment and coercion to get things done. Superiors and subordinates deal with each other in an environment of distrust.

B. 61–120   Benevolent Autocratic Climate. This climate is characterized by a management that acts in a condescending manner toward the subordinates. While there is some involvement by the subordinates in decision making, this usually occurs within a prescribed framework. Rewards and punishments are used to motivate the personnel toward staying in line. The basic philosophy of the management is one of conning the subordinates into doing things the organization's way by using phrases such as, "this is going to be good for your career," or "go along with me on this one and I'll take care of you later on," and so on.

C. 121–180   Consultative Democratic Climate. This climate is characterized by a management that has quite a bit of confidence and trust in the subordinates. While important decisions are made at the top of the structure, subordinates make specific decisions at the lower levels. There is some confidence and trust in the subordinates, and two-way communication is in evidence. Managers tend to consult with their people even though they, themselves, make most of the important decisions.

D. 181–240   Participative Democratic Climate. This climate is characterized by a management that has complete confidence and trust in the subordinates. Decision making is highly decentralized, and communication flows not only down and up the line but among peers, as well. Interaction between superiors and subordinates occurs in a friendly environment and is characterized by mutual trust and confidence.

NOTES

1. William F. Joyce and John W. Slocum, Jr., "Collective Climate: Agreement as a Basis for Defining Aggregate Climates in Organizations," *Academy of Management Journal,* December 1984, pp. 721–742.

2. A. W. Halpin and D. B. Crofts, *The Organizational Climate of Schools* (Chicago: Univ. of Chicago, Midwest Administration Center, 1963).

3. R. H. George Field and Michael A. Abelson, "Climate: A Reconceptualization and Proposed Model," *Human Relations,* March 1982, pp. 194–195.

4. Rensis Likert and Jane Gibson Likert, *New Ways of Managing Conflict* (New York: McGraw-Hill Book Co., 1976), p. 73.

5. For further elaboration of this profile see Rensis Likert, *New Patterns of Management* (New York: McGraw-Hill Book Co., 1961), Chapter 14; Rensis Likert, *The Human Organization* (New York: McGraw-Hill Book Co., 1967), Chapters 1–3; and Rensis Likert and Jane Gibson Likert, *New Ways of Managing Conflict* (New York: McGraw-Hill Book Co., 1976), Chapter 5.

6. Andrew M. Pettigrew, "On Studying Organizational Cultures," *Administrative Science Quarterly,* December 1979, pp. 570–581.

7. Terrence E. Deal and Allan A. Kennedy, *Corporate Cultures: The Rites and Rituals of Corporate Life* (Reading, MA: Addison-Wesley Publishing Co., 1982), p. 4.

8. Stephen R. Barley, Gordon W. Meyer, and Debra C. Gash, "Cultures of Culture: Academics, Practitioners and the Pragmatics of Normative Control," *Administrative Science Quarterly,* March 1988, pp. 24–60.

9. For more on this see Tom Peters, *Managing In Chaos* (New York: Alfred A. Knopf, 1987).

10. William G. Ouchi, *Theory Z: How American Business Can Meet the Japanese Challenge* (Reading, MA: Addison-Wesley Publishing Co., 1981).

11. For more on this topic see A. Wilkins and W. G. Ouchi, "Efficient Cultures: Exploring the Relationship Between Culture and Organizational Performance," *Administrative Science Quarterly,* September 1983, pp. 468–481.

12. Charles O'Reilly, "Corporations, Culture, and Commitment: Motivation and Social Control in Organizations," *California Management Review,* Summer 1989, pp. 19–22.

13. For an interesting view of how cultures are changing see Alma S. Baron, "What Men are Saying About Women in Business: A Decade Later," *Business Horizons,* July–August 1989, pp. 51–53.

14. *Ibid.,* p. 14.

15. Louis Thierren, "The Rival Japan Respects," *Business Week,* November 13, 1989, pp. 108–120.

16. *Ibid.,* p. 114.

CHAPTER 17
Organizational Change and Development

GOALS OF THE CHAPTER

As we saw in the last chapter, organizational climate and culture are important in achieving enterprise effectiveness. So are the proper management of change and organizational development, topics that will be examined in this chapter.

The first goal of the chapter is to examine the nature of organizational change and some of the important steps in implementing this process. The second goal is to examine how the organizational development (OD) process works. The third goal is to study how selected OD interventions work. The fourth goal is to review the overall effectiveness of OD.

When you have finished reading all of the material in this chapter, you should be able to:

1. identify some of the common reasons that individuals and organizations resist change;
2. describe the steps involved in implementing the change process;
3. define the term *organizational development;*
4. identify the basic components and characteristics of organizational development;
5. describe some of the common personal, group-intergroup, and overall organizational interventions;
6. discuss the difficulties associated with evaluating some of these interventions.

OPENING CASE: IMPROVING ORGANIZATIONAL EFFECTIVENESS

The southeast branch office of Hamilton Insurance had been the most troublesome office for almost two years. During this time the branch lost an average of $10,000 per month, turnover was high, and an attitude survey conducted by an outside consulting firm revealed that attitudes were poor and the personnel were not supportive of company efforts designed to increase productivity and efficiency. Based on the consulting company's report, the firm changed branch managers and promoted Pete Josephson to the position.

Within a week of the time he took over, Pete called a meeting of the personnel and began discussing the overall problems that existed. He then followed up and visited with each individual on a one-to-one or small-group basis. From these meetings Pete concluded that there were two major problems: salaries were noncompetitive vis-a-vis competition, and the home office had not taken sufficient interest in what was going on at the branch.

Pete then set about determining competitive salary levels and discussed these with the other managers to ensure that he was on the right track. He then visited the home office and told the president that it would be necessary to spend an additional $200,000 to bring salaries into line with the competition. At first the president resisted. "If I give you this much money, our return on investment will be lowered by at least a half-percentage point. This money would have to come from our profits." Nevertheless, Pete persisted, and the president relented. Pete also persuaded his boss to personally visit the branch within the next two weeks and announce these salary changes at that time.

Pete would also like to create better understanding and cooperation between his branch and the home office. The president has suggested that Pete look into using the services of an organizational development (OD) specialist. "Look into this," he told Pete. "These guys can often be very helpful, and my people will be happy to cooperate."

1. Why did the president initially resist Pete's recommendation about increasing salaries?
2. In what way did Pete work to strengthen the forces for change? Explain.
3. What form of OD intervention would be most helpful in improving cooperation between the branch and the home office? Explain.

Write down your answers to these questions and put them aside. We will return to them later.

ORGANIZATIONAL CHANGE

As noted in the previous chapter, organizational culture is often in a state of flux as enterprises seek to adapt to change. Moreover, change is becoming more commonplace. For example, deregulation and increasing competition have brought about major changes in such companies as Honeywell,[1] Bank of America,[2] and Southwestern Bell,[3] to name but three well-known enterprises. In Honeywell's case, the firm has been striving to integrate marketing and manufacturing processes. Bank of America has been trying to develop a product/market matrix structure that coordinates branches selling the same products and services. Southwestern Bell has been working to separate its nontelephone business from its telephone business.[4] In many organizations, these types of changes will result in individual resistance that must be carefully managed.[5]

Individual Resistance to Change

Some of the most common reasons for individual resistance to change include: (a) selective perception; (b) habit; and (c) a desire for security.

Selective Perception. People see reality within a particular construct that is created and influenced by their own attitudes, experiences, and beliefs.[6] This personally biased interpretation of reality is known as **selective perception**. In the case of unionized workers, for example, management is stereotyped as untrustworthy. As a result, union members typically oppose any management-initiated changes, no matter how helpful they might be to the rank and file.

> Selective perception is a biased view of reality.

Managers also use selective perception in resisting change. For example, many of those who attend training programs will categorize the speaker's ideas into two groups. The first group contains the ideas that they are already using, so there is no need to worry about these. The second group contains the remainder of the speaker's ideas, which are labeled "too theoretical to be of practical value to me" and discarded. As a result, the manager brings nothing away from the session. With selective perception, the individual manages to sidestep the need for any change in leadership style.

> Habits are programmed decision-making methods.

Habit. Individuals handle many of their personal and organization-related activities in an established manner. These habits not only provide a programmed method for decision making but also serve as a source of personal satisfaction. As a result, any proposed change that will affect a habit tends to be resisted.

> Individuals find security in established procedures.

Desire for Security. Individuals tend to find security in the past. Doing things the old way is given priority over trying new methods. In bureaucracies a great deal of faith is placed in established procedures, and people cling to the security of these practices. Furthermore, the people who fill positions in bureaucracies are often those who find security very important.[7] Change scares them. As a result, it is common to find a lot of activity going on without any tangible results taking place.

Organizational Resistance

> Individuals often fight changes.

While organizations have to adapt to their environment, they tend to resist change. Some of the most common reasons include: (a) stability; (b) prior investments; and (c) past contracts.

Stability is important to organizations, especially large ones.

Stability Is Important.   Most organizations (especially large ones) pay a great deal of attention to maintaining stability. Narrow job descriptions, limited lines of authority, and small spans of control are employed to ensure both predictability and productivity. Additionally, while the organization must respond to external forces, it tries to minimize their impact on the overall structure by assigning specific groups or departments the task of dealing with them. In this way each division or unit needs to confront only a minimum number of these forces. The rest of the time can be devoted to organizational efforts.

Prior investments cause resistance to change.

Prior Investments.   Many organizations resist change because they have invested their resources in a given project or location and are locked into a particular strategy. The big manufacturing firms that pollute air and water may be unable to afford an increased investment in antipollution equipment. They therefore fight ecological restrictions because this is their only profitable recourse. Meanwhile, in the case of technology, the organization may simply be unable to buy the latest equipment or machinery because it has not obtained an adequate return from its current equipment. In this case the company will resist the advance of science by simply turning out a higher-cost product and seeking to compete on a nonprice (advertising, personal service, or so on) basis.

Past contracts cause resistance to change.

Past Contracts.   Every organization enters into contracts with others. Agreements with unions, suppliers, competitors, and customers are all illustrations. In the case of the union, the organization may have agreed to certain work rules and hiring policies that preclude the introduction of newer, faster machinery during the life of the contract. Or if the machinery can be introduced, the workers may be guaranteed employment elsewhere in the organization, making it unprofitable for the firm to implement this strategy. In cases such as these, the organization may find itself unable to change the current situation until the contract expires.

Review your answers to Question 1 and make any changes you would like before continuing.

1. Why did the president initially resist Pete's recommendation about increasing salaries?

The president initially resisted Pete's recommendation because of its effect on return on investment. The two main underlying reasons were probably prior investments and past contracts. The company had already committed its resources to other projects and did not have the available funds for increased salaries unless they were taken out of profits.

INTRODUCING CHANGE EFFECTIVELY

Organizational Behavior In Action

Many companies are undergoing change, but few have been as successful in managing this process as Southwestern Bell. The firm relies heavily on training to help its employees understand what they want from their work and how they can go about getting it. The process is win-win in nature for both management and the personnel.

The company's training requires the participants to work through a series of exercises to clarify their job satisfaction criteria. In the process, the workers determine their own skills, strengths, and weaknesses and identify those parts of their job that they like best and least. They then indicate what they might do to make their work more satisfying.

The entire exercise is designed to prepare the employee to initiate a job-developmental discussion with his or her supervisor. Unlike most such discussions, which are initiated by the boss and center on job-performance, the employees like these talks because. . .there is something specific to talk about and the talk centers on skills, not job performance. Another plus: The employee calls for and directs the session, which is held in a neutral setting away from the job to preclude interruptions.

By helping the workers focus on their self-interests, the company is finding that it is easier to get them to accept and to deal with change. During a time when corporate downsizing is very common and organizations are reducing their personnel ranks, people are concerned that the next change will result in their being thrown out of work. This fear can result in a decline in productivity and morale. Southwestern Bell is working to overcome these problems by meeting them head-on. By identifying the needs and goals of the individual and effectively tying them into the corporation's culture and goals, the firm believes that it can sidestep many of the problems associated with change. In particular, this approach helps people focus on their careers and the changes that they would like to see occur. The result is that change is no longer viewed as negative by many of the people. Instead, they see the process as inevitable, and they believe that their input can help mold the result so that it is in the best interests of both themselves and the organization. In this way, it becomes a win-win process.

Source: Stanley J. Modic, "If You Win, I Win," *Industry Week,* April 3, 1989, p. 11.

Strategies for Change

Change can be participative or coerced.

Given that people tend to resist new developments, management needs a well-designed strategy for initiating change.[8] This strategy can be participative or coerced. In a participative change, the individual or group selects the new goals and methods for obtaining them. By informing the people about the need for change and getting them to adopt a positive attitude toward it, management can often end up gaining personal acceptance. (See "Organizational Behavior in Action: Introducing Change Effectively.")

With immature people who like directive leadership, however, a forced-type change is often the only recourse. In this case the manager uses position power to get the group to comply. Rather than working up from the individual to the group, as in the case of participative change, the manager imposes the change on the group and lets it filter down to the individual.[9] In most cases, management will attempt to use a participative change strategy. This approach employs a three-step process.[10]

Change Process

In getting people to change their attitudes or work habits, a three step **change process** is necessary: (a) unfreezing the old way; (b) introducing new behaviors; and (c) refreezing the new equilibrium.

In order to unfreeze the situation, the manager must first analyze the reasons for resistance to change. These can be pictured as forces supporting the status quo. Pushing in the other direction are the forces for change.

The first step is to unfreeze the old ways.

When two force groups exist, it may be a standoff with neither one being any stronger than the other. This is illustrated in Figure 17–1. The forces against change (labeled A) have strengths equal to those forces pushing for change (labeled F).

An example of four forces pushing in each direction is seen in the case of the organization that has announced the introduction of a new monthly cost report. After careful analysis, a top manager may find various reasons given by subordinates for

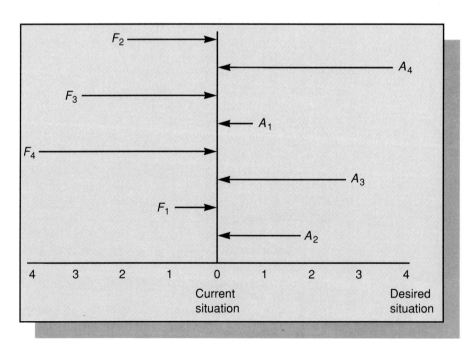

FIGURE 17–1
Equal Forces for Change

resisting change, on the one hand, or for promoting change, on the other hand. Among the reasons given for resisting change might be:

1. The old report is easy to fill out because the data are readily available.
2. The old report takes very little think time.
3. Top management has never used this report in the past for control purposes.
4. The new report will be very comprehensive and require more time to fill out.

Among the pressures for advocating change might be:

1. An organizational streamlining of reporting forms is necessary.
2. Organizational control is getting out of hand.
3. If a report is going to have to be filled out, why not make it a meaningful one?
4. This new report is going to be analyzed by staff personnel, and useful recommendations will be forwarded to each manager who has filled one out.

The second step involves the introduction of the change and the third step involves refreezing the new behaviors.

In dealing with this situation, the top manager must unfreeze the current equilibrium. In doing so, three courses of action are available: (a) increase the strength of those pressures pushing for change; (b) decrease the strength of those forces resisting change; or (c) change a resisting force into one supporting the change. In our illustration, the top manager might well *unfreeze* the situation by changing the subordinates' perceptions of the value of the new reporting system by showing them how the system could help them. Then the manager could move into the *change* phase by getting the reports filled out, showing the people who have problems with it what to put in and what to leave out, and creating a series of new behavioral patterns. As the subordinates complete the reports, the process becomes part of their monthly routine. The manager can then work on *refreezing* the situation by reinforcing these new behaviors with some pre-determined schedule. Such reinforcement schedules were discussed earlier in Chapter 4 when the area of learning was examined.[11]

During this three-phase change strategy the manager may confront some disheartening effects. In particular, during the time when attitudes and beliefs are in a state of transition those forces resisting change may be stronger than those supporting change. Here is where the manager's leadership style comes into play, as the individual seeks to bolster those forces supporting the transition and to weaken or eliminate those favoring the old status quo. As this is done, the change will begin to be accepted, and a new equilibrium will be established. Prior to this, however, there is a high likelihood that the change will result in a decrease in efficiency.

This is particularly evident when a quantitative illustration is used. For example, suppose that a manufacturing firm has just announced new work procedures designed to increase production output. At first, the personnel object to the change because they believe it will mean more work for the same pay. However, as the manager takes the people through the unfreezing and change stages, pointing out how the new procedures will simply make things easier for everyone, initially negative attitudes are supplanted by positive ones. Note in Figure 17–2, though, that this change process is not without

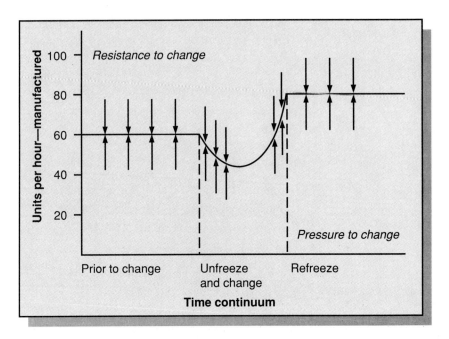

FIGURE 17-2
The Change Process and Productivity

negative effects. The management must be willing to accept some short-run decline in output in order to introduce and freeze these new behaviors. After the change is accepted, output rises to a higher level.

STOP

Review your answers to Question 2 and make any changes you would like before continuing.

2. In what way did Pete work to strengthen the forces for change? Explain.

Pete worked to strengthen the forces for change by altering employee attitudes. By convincing the personnel to cooperate and support the company, he did two things: (a) reduced the forces opposed to cooperating with the firm and increasing productivity; and (b) increased the forces supporting cooperation and increased productivity. In some cases, the personnel may have stopped opposing but not cooperated, but that is all right because in the process Pete managed to weaken the force against change. In most cases, he undoubtedly got the personnel to switch from pushing against cooperation to pushing for it.

THE NATURE OF ORGANIZATIONAL DEVELOPMENT

Effective organizational change is a result of a carefully designed strategy. In recent years, the term **organizational development (OD)** has been used in referring to the wide range of behaviorally oriented strategies used for this purpose. Although there is some disagreement regarding the specific boundaries of OD, French and Bell have offered the following comprehensive definition:

> Organization[al] development is a long-range effort to improve an organization's problem-solving and renewal processes, particularly through a more effective and collaborative management of organization culture—with special emphasis on the culture of formal work teams—with the assistance of a change agent, or catalyst, and the use of the theory and technology of applied behavioral science, including action research. [12]

OD strives to develop individual and organizational harmony.

At the heart of OD is a concern for vitalizing, activating, and renewing the organization's human resources. This renewal process helps establish conditions encouraging individual motivation and development. At the same time, the overall purpose and direction of the organization is blended with a problem solving and action orientation. Thus OD is not merely a process of change for the sake of change or a series of behavioral interventions designed to motivate individuals throughout the structure. Rather it is an action program in which the needs of both the organization *and* the personnel are examined, and steps are developed for getting both to work in harmony toward the goals they feel are in their best *collective* interests.

It is important to realize that any effective OD program relies on management support. Unless the top people in the firm want to see the necessary changes occur, nothing substantive will happen. On the other hand, if they do, the chances of OD paying off become much greater, and there have been many instances of success. [13]

However, the percentage of managers with a working knowledge of OD is very small. Digman has estimated that in organizations with less than ten managers, virtually no one knows what OD is all about; in enterprises with ten to 500 managers, only about 3 percent understand the nature of OD; and in organizations with over 500 managers, this number is but 5 percent. [14] Additionally, many managers, even when they do understand what OD is all about, are reluctant to use it. Why? Some of the most common reasons include: (a) they are uncomfortable with the techniques; (b) they have a mistrust of consultants; (c) they are unsure of what OD can really do for them; and (d) they are wary of what they consider to be touchy-feely approaches to management. [15] On the other hand, like it or not, managers are finding that they must learn about OD.

OD Components and Characteristics

There are many forms of OD interventions. All, however, have three basic components: (a) diagnosis; (b) action; and (c) process maintenance. In addition, there are a series of characteristics or underpinnings (see Figure 17–3).

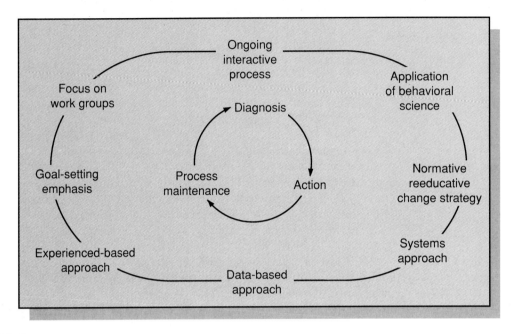

FIGURE 17–3
The Nature of Organizational Development

First, a diagnosis is made.

The Diagnostic Component.   The first step in an OD process is to diagnose the situation by gathering information on the state of things. Sometimes this diagnosis is conducted over the entire organization or in major subunits. Other times the diagnosis will focus on groups or individuals within units or departments. In this initial step, the OD practitioner will examine the organizational processes that are taking place. "These include decision-making processes, communication patterns and styles, relationships between interfacing groups, the management of conflict, the setting of goals, and planning methods."[16]

Then an OD intervention is used.

The Action Component.   The action component is characterized by **OD interventions,** a catchall term used to describe the structured activity in which the targeted individuals, groups, or units engage in accomplishing task goals related to organizational improvement. This emphasis on action planning and action taking is a distinguishing feature of OD because, in contrast to many traditional education and training activities through which people learn something in the classroom and then take it back to the job, both the learning and the doing usually take place in the same setting. Additionally, OD problem-solving interventions usually focus on real organizational problems central to the needs of the organization rather than on hypothetical, abstract problems that may be peripheral to the members' needs.

Finally, there is feedback and follow up.

Process-Maintenance Component.   As the action stage is initiated, the OD practitioner must monitor the feedback and ensure that everything is going according to plan. Are the interventions proving to be timely and relevant? Is there continued involvement, commitment, and investment in the program by the members? Effective management of this OD process often spells the difference between success and failure for the entire effort.

Characteristics. The OD process contains a series of distinguishing characteristics. First, the process is an ongoing, interactive one. Its objective is to teach people new skills while getting them to forget old ones.

The OD process is ongoing and interactive.

Second, heavy emphasis is placed on applied behavioral science principles from areas such as social psychology, social anthropology, sociology, and psychiatry. Diagnosis by OD practitioners is based on scientific knowledge derived primarily from organizational theory, group dynamics, and personality theory.

The OD process is based on applied behavioral science principles.

Third, OD is a normative-reeducative strategy that assumes that norms form the basis for behavior and change comes about through a reeducative process in which old norms are replaced by new ones. In accomplishing this reeducation, the client (the organizational personnel) tells the OD practitioner the changes and improvements the organization would like to make. The practitioner then works with the organization in a cooperative way to define the problems, identify the solutions, overcome any roadblocks, and then implement the necessary action steps.

OD uses a normative-reeducative strategy.

Fourth, the OD process views the organization from a systems approach. The practitioner realizes that one part of the organization cannot be changed without influencing other parts as well.

OD also uses a systems approach.

Fifth, OD employs a data-based approach to change. Information is collected from the particular organization, so that a *specific* analysis can be made and solutions can be tailored to its own needs.

OD is a data-based approach to change.

Sixth, the OD process is experience based. OD interventions focus on real organizational problems. When lab training is used, it takes place in the form of experimental learning in which the group members are assigned specific tasks from which they can derive information related to problems they face.

OD is also experience-based.

Seventh, the process is oriented toward goal setting. There are targeted objectives to which the intervention is directed.

OD is oriented toward goal setting.

Eighth, and finally, OD activities focus on intact work groups. Many of an organization's activities are carried on by work teams.

OD focuses on intact work groups.

The OD process can be diagrammed in the form of an action research model (Figure 17–4). This model contains the basic components and characteristics of organizational development. Note that in the figure there is a continuous process of data gathering, analyses, feedback, and determination of a plan of action, followed by a reassessment of the situation through data gathering, thereby restarting the cycle.[17]

OD Interventions

OD interventions cover a wide range of planned activities in which both change agents and clients engage. The purpose of these activities is to improve the organization's efficiency by helping the members better manage their personnel and jobs. In making a final decision on what intervention(s) to use, the OD expert will try to blend consideration of the needed change mechanism with the different types of interventions that can be effectively used with the particular target group.

The intervention is specifically designed to deal with the problem.

The following examines some of the most popular types of interventions.

FIGURE 17–4
OD Action Research Model (Adapted from Wendell L. French and Cecil H. Bell, Jr., *Organization Development*, 2nd ed. (Englewood Cliffs, NJ: Prentice-Hall, 1978), p. 86.)

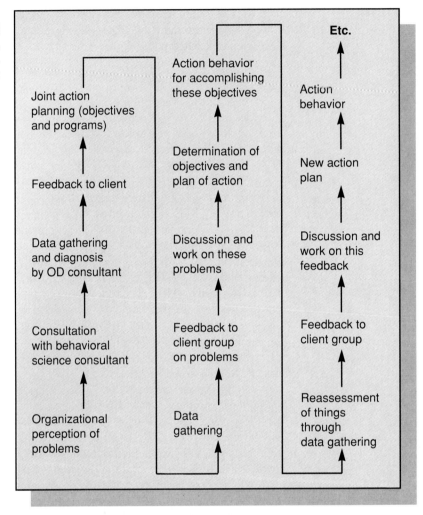

Sensitivity Training Laboratories. **Sensitivity training laboratories,** or **T-groups** (T for training), were a cornerstone of early organizational development efforts. While they have been partly supplanted by other OD techniques, they are still very effective today when used for personal growth and individual development.

T-groups generally consist of ten to fifteen members and a professional trainer who serves as the catalyst and group facilitator. This individual will typically begin the first T-group session by pointing out that: (a) there will be no agenda, agreed-upon procedures, or structure for the group; (b) the focus will be on the "here and now"; and (c) the overall purpose of the lab is to help each person increase his or her understanding of individual behavior and group performance.

In this ambiguous setting, then, the members may try to organize, select a leader, determine topics for discussion, and get things going. Regardless of their activity, however, the here-and-now focus requires them to start discussing such things as how

T-groups function in ambiguous settings.

they feel (not think) and what their reaction is to others in the group. As this disclosure process begins, the individuals are given feedback on how they are perceived by the other members. This mutual interaction allows each to obtain insights into his or her own behavior.

Research shows that T-groups can have various effects, both positive and negative, on individuals. On the positive side, the opportunity exists to obtain insights into personal blind spots, become aware of group norms, experience a sense of group belonging, and achieve role flexibility. On the negative side, however, some people report a feeling of manipulation, experience a decline in self-confidence, feel pressured to abide by group norms, and resent giving up their autonomy in order to lose themselves in the group. [18]

Of all of the OD interventions, T-groups are probably the most controversial because of the possible harm they can have on individual participants. If handled properly, however, they can be very helpful.

While controversial, T-groups can be helpful.

Life and Career Planning Interventions.

Life and career planning interventions focus on the goals of the individual members, providing them a basis for controlling their own destinies. These interventions can concentrate on the past, present, or future. Most tend to follow a basic pattern in which individuals put together **life inventories** in which they note their peak experiences, the things they do well and poorly, the things they would like to learn to do well, and the peak experiences they would still like to have. A life inventory presents the individual's past and provides insights into desired future direction. It is common to have each individual discuss the inventory with other members of a small group. Then each sets down a series of action steps for achieving the goals he or she has identified as desirable.

A life inventory is constructed.

Sometimes these life and career planning exercises take only a day; other times an entire week is spent generating data about oneself, analyzing the results individually and in groups, and then formulating goals and action plans. However, the intervention can be very helpful to individual personnel. In particular, OD change agents have found that these kinds of exercises are highly beneficial for organizational members who are contemplating a career change, feel they are in a rut, or have seldom systematically examined their own life style and career pattern.

RAT Intervention.

One reason why some individuals do not perform well is that they are unclear about what they should be doing and the types of support help they can expect from other organizational personnel. **Role analysis technique (RAT)** intervention is designed to clarify both role expectations and obligations of team members.

Role expectations and obligations are clarified.

The first step in the process is to choose one of the jobs, which is called the *focal role,* and then list the duties and behaviors expected of the individual filling this role. The role, the rationale for its existence, and its place in the organization are all examined. Both the individual and the group discuss these issues, and between them they arrive at a defined role that is satisfactory to all.

In the next two steps the individual and the group identify and discuss what each expects from the other. After these expectations are agreed upon the focal role person puts together a summary of the job. This *role profile* contains a description of the job's activities, the obligations to the group associated with the role's enactment, and the expectations the other group members have concerning this role. This procedure is used with every job in the group so everyone knows what is expected of him or her and what can be expected from the other members.

Many OD consultants have had success with the RAT interventions because, if handled properly, they constitute nonthreatening activities. In particular, team members like this intervention because it helps them understand what the other people in the group are doing. In addition, role analysis serves not only to clarify work roles but also to ensure commitment to them.

Process Consultation.   **Process consultation,** P-C for short, is an intervention method that is used in an ongoing system. There are many variations of P-C, but the goal is always the same: To help the organization to solve its own problems by making it aware of the organizational processes, the consequences of these processes, and the mechanisms by which they can be changed.[19]

The process consultant typically functions in a work-group setting, helping the team develop the skills necessary to diagnose and solve its problems. Typical examples of the latter include communication breakdowns, problems with authority and leadership, and difficulty in achieving intergroup cooperation. The consultant typically employs the following approach: (a) the client contacts the consultant about the problem; (b) the two parties enter into a formal agreement, spelling out the services, times, and fees that will be involved, as well as the hoped-for results; (c) an understanding is reached regarding where and how the consultant will do the job; (d) the consultant gathers data about the problem and makes a preliminary diagnosis; and (e) the consultant conducts an actual intervention in the form of feeding back information to the group, coaching or counseling the members, and providing them with guidance regarding how to achieve more harmonious interpersonal relations.

There are a number of advantages of P-C. One major advantage is that the intervention is aimed at helping people help themselves. A second is that the consultation addresses the types of interpersonal and intergroup problems that are commonly found in today's organizations. A third is that the consultant's role is much more passive than it is in other interventions. Rather than telling people what they ought to do, the individual listens to their problems, feeds back what they say, and encourages them to come up with solutions to their own problems. The consultant helps the group members observe their own behavior and learn how to become more effective through their own efforts. The change agent's role is greatest in diagnosing what is going on and helping the members understand it. To the extent that the group members want the intervention to succeed, it will. The ultimate responsibility rests with the client group.

Intergroup Team Building.   Organizational groups often compete with one another. One way of increasing cooperation and communication between them is with **intergroup team building interventions**. While the steps involved in the process may differ slightly, depending upon the OD consultant,[20] the following steps represent the general pattern:

Step 1. The leaders (or total membership) of the groups meet with the consultant and are asked if the relations between them can be improved. If the groups give an affirmative reply, the intergroup team building process can start.

Step 2. The intergroup intervention begins with the two groups meeting in separate rooms and building two lists. The first list consists of the group's perceptions, attitudes, and feelings about the other group. The list contains answers to such questions as, What do they do that we like? What do they do that upsets us?

The second list consists of the group's predictions concerning what the other group is saying about them on their particular list. In constructing this second list, the group asks questions such as, What does the other like about us? What do they dislike? Exactly how do they see us?

Step 3. The two groups then come together to share the information on their respective lists. The first group reads its list of how it sees the second. Then the second group reads its list of how it sees the first. During this period the OD consultant imposes the rule that there will be no discussion of the items. The only questions permitted are those related to clarification of meanings on specific items. When Group 2 is finished reading its first list, Group 1 then reads its list regarding what it expected Group 2 to say about it. Then Group 2 reads its list of what it expected Group 1 to say.

Step 4. The two groups then return to their individual meeting places to discuss what they learned about themselves and the other group. Many of the areas of disagreement or friction between the two groups are found to rest on erroneous perceptions and communication breakdowns. Once this is realized, the problems between them are seen to be far fewer than imagined. Each group is now given the task of constructing a list of priority issues that still need to be resolved between the two groups.

Step 5. The two groups meet again and share their lists. After the lists are compared, they work together in constructing one overall list of the issues and problems that still need to be resolved. Each item on the list is given a priority, and action steps are formulated for handling each. These steps outline who will do what and when. In this way the groups ensure that all the priority items will be addressed. At this point, the intervention is concluded.

Step 6. In some team building activities a follow-up determines whether the action steps have indeed been implemented. The purpose of this follow-up is to ensure that the intergroup intervention momentum has not been lost.

This team building intervention is often used with groups in the same department or groups in different departments who must coordinate their efforts for maximum organizational efficiency. Additionally, it has also been employed with large groups drawn from two very large populations.[21]

Grid OD is both thorough and systematic.

Grid Organizational Development. Perhaps the most thorough and systematic OD intervention is that designed by Blake and Mouton. Commonly referred to as **grid organizational development,** the program has six phases that take from three to five years to implement. At the heart of the program is the concept of the managerial grid, also developed by Blake and Mouton. This grid is a two-dimensional scheme for examining and improving the practices of individual managers. One dimension of the grid measures "concern for production," while the other measures "concern for people." Additionally, each dimension contains nine degrees ranging from low concern to high concern; in all there are five basic styles (see Figure 17–5). The program is designed to help managers identify their current and "ideal"

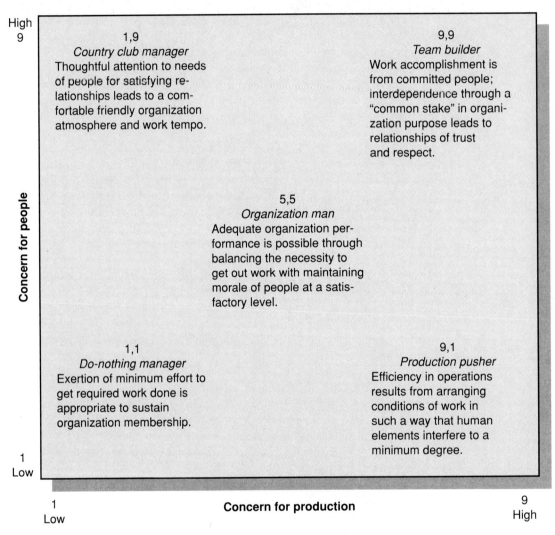

High
9

1,9
Country club manager
Thoughtful attention to needs
of people for satisfying relationships leads to a comfortable friendly organization
atmosphere and work tempo.

9,9
Team builder
Work accomplishment is
from committed people;
interdependence through a
"common stake" in organi-
zation purpose leads to
relationships of trust
and respect.

5,5
Organization man
Adequate organization performance is possible through
balancing the necessity to
get out work with maintaining
morale of people at a satisfactory level.

1,1
Do-nothing manager
Exertion of minimum effort to
get required work done is
appropriate to sustain
organization membership.

9,1
Production pusher
Efficiency in operations
results from arranging
conditions of work in
such a way that human
elements interfere to a
minimum degree.

Concern for people

1
Low

1   **Concern for production**   9
Low   High

FIGURE 17–5
The Managerial Grid

leadership style and then start moving from the former to the latter. The overall
program consists of six basic phases.[22]

The first phase is basically a seminar for the organization's managers during which
they diagnose their leadership styles, study reading material, learn problem-solving and
critiquing skills, work at improved communication, and develop team action skills. This
seminar is usually conducted away from the organization and lasts about a week.

The focus of phase two is on perfecting teamwork. This is done by having the
manager and his or her subordinates apply what they have learned in the first phase to
their specific situation. During this process the group is encouraged to identify and
diagnose those barriers that are impeding work-group effectiveness, determine how the

members want to operate, establish a timetable and objectives for improving team performance, and create a climate for examining and critiquing the work of each individual.

During the third phase, the emphasis moves from intragroup to intergroup to develop closer integration between work groups. Each group individually analyzes what an ideal relationship would be, and these ideas are then shared with the other groups. Representatives from units that are in direct contact are asked to develop these ideal relationships by discussing the problems associated with attaining them and then formulating a plan of action for moving toward them.

The fourth phase, which may take up to one year, focuses on developing an ideal strategic plan for the overall organization. The top management group is charged with designing an ideal strategic planning model. These plans, structures, policies, and ideas are then tested, evaluated, and critiqued, thereby providing top management with a clear picture of the changes that will be necessary to achieve excellence. Once this ideal strategic model is built, attention is directed toward implementation.

The fifth phase requires the greatest amount of time, often two to three years. During this period the organization attempts to close the gap between "where it is" and "where it wants to be." To achieve this transition, the organization may set up planning teams to conduct conversion studies and to determine exactly what needs to be done. At the same time, top management is charged with handling those tasks that do not fall within the bailiwick of the planning teams, as well as reviewing the progress of these teams.

Grid OD has six basic phases.

The sixth phase consists of a systematic critique of the five phases. Progress is evaluated, barriers are identified, and further action steps are determined. The new methods that have been developed during these five phases are consistently reinforced so that they become standard practices. The organization tries very hard to prevent any pressure toward "slipping back."

Blake and Mouton report that organizations that have adopted grid OD programs have had significant organizational improvements, particularly in terms of lower costs and greater profits. Practicing managers have also reported increased organizational efficiency resulting from this OD intervention.

STOP

Review your answers to Question 3 and make any changes you would like before continuing.

3. What form of OD intervention would be most helpful in improving cooperation between the branch and the home office? Explain.

Pete needs an OD intervention that is group-oriented. He can use one of two methods described in this part of the chapter: process consultation and intergroup team building. Process consultation offers the greatest benefit. The focus should be on improving communication, dealing with problems of authority and leadership, and achieving intergroup cooperation, and the process consultation intervention provides this.

Evaluation of OD

OD effectiveness must be evaluated.

The OD interventions we have examined can be helpful in increasing an organization's effectiveness.[23] However, some of them have been criticized by opponents who claim that there is simply no basis for determining their overall value. Commenting on training labs, for example, Campbell and his associates have concluded that "no basis exists for judging the potential worth of T-group training from an institutional or organizational point of view. Instead, its success or failure must be judged by each individual trainee in terms of his own personal goals."[24]

Other researchers have found that some interventions have produced no measurable results. For example, Woodman and Sherwood conducted a team development intervention using both test and control groups and found that the groups experiencing team development performed no better than the control groups. Also, no statistically significant differences were found between the two groups in terms of perceived learning or expressed satisfaction with the group.[25] Eden conducted a three-day team development workshop with nine logistics units in the Israel Defense Forces and compared the outcomes with those groups that had not received team development. The intervention did not improve unit efficiency.[26] In another study Buller and Bell examined the effects of team building and goal setting on hard-rock miners' productivity. Although there were slight improvements in performance, it was not clear that these improvements were results of the interventions.[27]

Another recent concern about OD interventions is their application in the international arena. Most interventions are based on openness, honesty, and willingness to communicate. However, many foreign cultures do not promote these values. As a result, in choosing those interventions to use, the OD change agent is often limited to a small number of alternatives.[28]

In overall terms, some OD interventions have proven more successful than others. The future is going to see better matching of interventions with situations, so that the right choice is made. More effective evaluation of OD results will allow the outcome of the intervention to be clearly determined.[29] Another emerging concern will be ways of dealing with ethical issues in OD such as protecting people's privacy and not manipulating or coercing participants during the intervention. Some critics claim that not enough has been done along these lines.[30]

SUMMARY

1. In dealing with change, management needs a well-designed strategy. This strategy can be either participative or coerced. Whenever possible, the former is preferred. It entails a three-phase change process: (a) unfreezing the old ways; (b) introducing new behaviors; and (c) refreezing this new equilibrium. Unfreezing requires the manager to increase the strength of those pressures pushing for change, decrease those resisting change, and change resisting force(s) into one(s) supporting the change. During the second phase the manager needs to introduce the change and

help the personnel accommodate it. The refreezing stage requires reinforcing these new behaviors.

2. There are many ways of increasing an organization's effectiveness. In recent years, the term *OD* has been used to refer to the wide range of behaviorally oriented strategies used for this purpose. The heart of OD is a concern for vitalizing, activating, and renewing the organization's technical and human resources. In OD interventions, the needs of the organization and the personnel are exam-

ined, and steps are developed for getting both to work in harmony toward goals they feel are in their best collective interest.

3. OD interventions have three basic components. The diagnostic component consists of analyzing the situation and gathering information on its current state. The action component consists of the intervention itself, in which the targeted individuals, groups, or units accomplish tasks related to organizational improvement. The process-maintenance component monitors the feedback to ensure that everything is going according to plan. In addition to these components, the OD process contains a series of distinguishing characteristics. The process is seen as an ongoing, interactive one; heavy emphasis is placed on ap-

plied behavioral science; a normative-reeducative strategy is employed; the process views the organization from a systems approach; it employs a data-based approach to change; experience-based exercises are used; the process is oriented toward goal setting; and the activities focus on intact work groups.

4. There are many OD change strategies or interventions that can be employed, including T-groups, life and career planning, role analysis technique, process consultation, intergroup team building, and grid development. These interventions can be extremely useful, but care must be taken in choosing them and evaluating the results to ensure that the desired effects were achieved.

KEY TERMS

selective perception
change process
organizational development (OD)
OD interventions
sensitivity training laboratories
   (T-groups)

life and career planning
   interventions
life inventories
role analysis technique (RAT)
process consultation

intergroup team building
   interventions
grid organizational development

REVIEW AND STUDY QUESTIONS

1. Why do individuals resist change? How do they resist it?

2. Why do organizations resist change? How do they resist it?

3. When is a participative change most likely to succeed? When is a coerced change the best course of action?

4. What are the three steps involved in the change process? Explain each.

5. "During this three-phase change strategy, the manager may confront some disheartening effects." What is meant by this statement?

6. What is meant by the term *organizational development*?

7. An OD intervention consists of three basic components: (a) diagnosis; (b) action; and (c) process maintenance. What kinds of activities take place in each?

8. In what way is the OD process an ongoing, interactive one? A normative-reeducative strategy? A data-based approach to change?

9. How does an OD intervention work? Put it in your own words.

10. How does a sensitivity training laboratory work? What are its advantages and limitations?

11. How can life and career planning intervention be of value to organizational members?

12. What are the steps involved in a RAT intervention? Why is this intervention so well liked by group members?

13. How does process consultation work? Explain.

14. How is an intergroup team-building intervention conducted? Identify the steps involved.

15. Why is grid organizational development, as developed by Blake and Mouton, considered to be the most thorough and systematic OD intervention?

16. What are the major steps involved in grid organizational development?

17. How can the effectiveness of an OD intervention be judged? In addition, which of the OD components and characteristics are most important in ensuring that maximum value is obtained from the intervention?

CASES

A Matter of Change

For the last three years a small private hospital in the East has been reporting financial losses. At first the annual loss was less than $10,000. However, last year it swelled to over $100,000, and the board of directors became very concerned. After holding a special meeting, the board voted to bring in a management consulting firm to look over the situation. Everyone on the board, with the exception of the hospital administrator, voted in favor of this action.

The consulting group arrived three weeks ago. The team broke up into a number of different groups to gather as much information as possible about the hospital's performance. The group took five days to get all the information it needed. At the end of this time, it prepared a one-hour talk for the board of trustees. In essence, the consultants concluded that the hospital could not last more than six more months in its current condition. The first priority was to get it out of the red as soon as possible. In this regard, the consultants felt that two major steps would have to be taken. First, an accountant would have to be brought in to help identify profit centers and pinpoint those services that were costing the hospital the greatest amount of money. By pruning the big losers and concentrating on the big winners, the consultants felt that the hospital could reverse its negative financial posture in the shortest time possible.

They recommended that at the same time the administrator and his staff, working closely with the board of trustees, formulate overall long-range goals for the organization. These goals would then be broken down to the departmental level and finally to the unit level. The aim of the consultants was to have each group in the organization pinpoint exactly what it was going to be doing over the next year and do the same for each individual in its respective group. In this way, the consultants believed, standards of efficiency and effectiveness could be determined and maintained for the organization at large.

At first, the hospital administrator opposed any such plan of action. However, after a long session with the consultants he began to believe that their ideas might have a great deal of merit. Yet he was still concerned that he would have problems getting the other members of his staff to accept the idea and to give him their full effort in implementing the plan throughout the organization. In an effort to put his mind at ease, the consultants spent a whole day explaining the importance of change and how an overall change strategy could be implemented. The administrator was particularly impressed with the unfreeze, change, and refreeze cycle suggested by the consultants.

Before they left his office yesterday, he told them he was going to adopt their ideas and begin to implement them immediately. "When I took this job I never realized how much time would have to be spent dealing with organizational behavior. Right now, I see my biggest challenge as that of introducing a major change, and I wonder if my staff is going to buy the idea. I think it has merit, but selling it to them may be a different story."

1. Why might the administrator's staff be opposed to this new idea of a master plan with carefully defined objectives?

2. What will the administrator have to do at each step of the changing process: unfreeze, change, and refreeze? Be explicit in your answer.

3. With which of these three steps do you think the administrator will have the greatest difficulty? Why?

The Consultant's Report

A large southern insurance company had a team of management consultants analyze its operation last month. When the consultants were finished, they presented a short report to the board of directors. In the report they noted those areas in which they felt the firm was having problems. Among their findings were the following:

1. Approximately 25 percent of all middle and top management personnel openly admit that they do not know what the future holds for them. They have no career plans and believe that over the next five years their career direction will be determined strictly on the basis of openings that occur in the upper ranks due to retirement or resignation. Another 7 percent of the managers candidly admit that they are looking for jobs with other organizations because they feel that if the organization had any long-range career plans for them, they would have been informed about these plans by now. Lacking such knowledge they can only surmise that they are not going to be promoted in the near future. A review of the performance appraisal files of these latter 7 percent show that

most of them are regarded as superior performers and, if they stay with the firm, will eventually be promoted.

2. Approximately 11 percent of all the personnel in every department are either confused about their jobs or lack an understanding of how to accomplish them. One-third of this group admit that they have never been formally trained in their job. Twenty-five percent say that they have never seen a job description related to their work, and they doubt whether one has ever been written.

3. Approximately 22 percent of overall productivity is being lost because of infighting within groups and departments. This problem is most noticeable in areas in which output is directly measurable. However, the problem even exists in areas like human resources and public relations. A one-page attitude questionnaire distributed to all personnel clearly revealed this. Additionally, when questioned about the matter, most managers openly admit that the amount of infighting and intragroup conflict seems to have increased dramatically over the last six months.

4. Almost all of the personnel except for the top managers say that they are confused regarding the objectives of their own particular department. They also say that, as far as they can tell, the organization has not really given much attention to formulating specific overall goals.

The consultants believe that these problems can be resolved with the use of tailor-made OD interventions.

They see the entire program taking approximately one year, although certain parts of it will take much less time. For example, solving the first problem described above should take much less time than solving the last problem.

The board of directors believe that the consultants are on the right track. They basically agree that the four problem areas described above are, indeed, in need of attention. They also believe that there are a number of other significant problems that will surface once work begins on solving these initial four problems. On the other hand, the board members would like to get more information about how the consultants are going to address the problems. Most of the members are totally unfamiliar with OD and how interventions work. They would like to know what an intervention involves, how long one lasts, and the relationship between an intervention and the way a problem is solved.

1. What type of intervention do you think the consultants would use in dealing with the first problem listed above? The second? The third? The fourth?

2. How can OD interventions of the type you have identified in the answer above be of value in solving the problems the consultants have identified?

3. In handling the fourth area described above, what specific steps would you expect the consultant to take? Outline them and be as complete as possible in your answer.

SELF-FEEDBACK EXERCISE

What Is Your Management Style?

The following exercise contains statements related to eight areas in which managers make decisions. In each case, there are five statements describing the type of behavior that might be exercised in that particular area. Read each of the five statements carefully and choose the one that is most typical of you. Place a 1 next to this statement. Continue this ranking process with the remaining statements, placing a 2 next to the statement that is the next most typical of you on down to a 5 next to the statement that is least typical of you. (Remember that in each group of five statements you must assign a 1, 2, 3, 4, and 5.) When you have finished, record all of your answers on the scoring sheet at the end of the exercise.

1. Planning the Work

    a. _____ Along with my people, I look at the whole picture, try to get reactions, comments, and commitments from them, and see that goals, schedules, and control points are developed.

    b. _____ I sit down with each of my people, discuss goals, targets and schedules with them, plan out the work and make individual assignments, and then let each person know that if further assistance is needed, he or she is to check back with me.

    c. _____ In the arrangement of their activities, I make suggestions to my people and offer my assistance to them.

    d. _____ I let my people have the planning responsibilities for their own parts of the job.

    e. _____ I set up the work assignments, quotas, and check points for my people and make it a point to know how well they are doing.

2. Handling Subordinate Mistakes

a. _____ After making an examination of the facts, I then determine what corrective action to take.

b. _____ I tend to overlook mistakes except when doing so is going to get me in trouble.

c. _____ I help my people try again by working in every way I can to encourage them and keep up their morale.

d. _____ I discuss mistakes with my subordinates in order to find out their causes; this also serves to prevent their recurrence.

e. _____ When my people make repeated mistakes, I take corrective action; however, I try to use these problems as an opportunity to teach them how to prevent their recurrence rather than to punish them.

3. Dealing with New Ideas from My People

a. _____ I tend to evaluate the idea, and if it is sound, I will implement it; if it is not sound, I will reject it.

b. _____ I will take the idea and either table it or pass it up the line; I neither accept nor reject new ideas.

c. _____ I will compliment the individual for the idea and encourage the person to develop it further.

d. _____ I will review the idea to make sure that it has not been presented before. If the idea then looks usable, I will recommend that the person develop it further.

e. _____ I try to stimulate new ideas by analyzing their usefulness with those who present them. In this way, if the idea is employed the individual will get credit for his or her contribution, and if the idea is not employed the person will understand why it was not used.

4. Handling Information Requested by Subordinates

a. _____ I obtain whatever information is needed by my people, and I keep them fully informed about what is going on.

b. _____ I decide if this information is really important, and if it is, I see that they get whatever they need.

c. _____ The minute I find out what they need, I pass the request right on up to my boss.

d. _____ I get them whatever information is needed and, in so doing, really get a personal kick out of being helpful to them.

e. _____ I get whatever information is needed but make sure that I edit the material so that what they receive is for the overall good of the entire group and not just for the good of the individual.

5. Handling Decisions Affecting Subordinates

a. _____ I am the type of person who makes decisions and, this having been done, stays with them.

b. _____ I make decisions that follow the thinking of my superior.

c. _____ I tend to discuss the matter with those who will be affected by the decision, getting their input and sharing mine with them and evaluating alternative approaches to the situation before reaching a decision based on mutual understanding.

d. _____ I like to meet with each person who will be affected by the decision to get this individual's input, and then I make the decision and tell those who are affected the reasons behind my choice.

e. _____ I work to get a picture of what my subordinates want and use this as the basis for making decisions that will affect them.

6. My Personal Pace

a. _____ I try to maintain a good, steady work pace.

b. _____ I drive myself and my subordinates as well.

c. _____ I seldom lead, but I do extend quite a bit of help.

d. _____ I put out enough effort to get by but not much more than this.

e. _____ I exert a lot of vigorous effort, and my people tend to join in.

7. Time Management

a. _____ My work schedule is flexible so if my boss or my subordinates need some help from me, I can give it to them.

b. _____ I set up an orderly routine for getting things done; in this way, I can reach a satisfactory level of performance without having to push too hard.

c. _____ I schedule my work activities within a time framework that incorporates long-term objectives. In this way, if an emergency arises I can take care of it without facing a crisis.

d. _____ I have no need to schedule my work activities; day-to-day demands keep me busy enough.

e. _____ I have a plan of activities worked out in advance so that I get a maximum use of my time; I do not allow too much to upset this schedule.

8. Self-Development

a. _____ I really do not need to review my performance; if some changes are needed, my boss will tell me about them.

b. _____ I try to analyze myself to maintain a pleasing personality that helps me secure acceptance by others.

c. _____ My chances for success in the organization are increased through the process of self-appraisal, because in this way I am able to tell when I am doing things well and when I am not.

d. _____ My contribution to the organization is increased as I improve my skills in analyzing the causes of my successes and my failures.

e. _____ I analyze my record to make sure that I am staying ahead. Performance appraisals are helpful in pinpointing failures, but a more diligent personal effort is what really gets results.

Scoring

Take each of your answers above and transfer them to the scoring key below. Be careful to match your numbers with the letters associated with each number. For example, the number that you gave to alternative b in number one should be placed in row 1, column A; your answer to alternative c in number two should be placed in row 2, column E, and so on.

	A	B	C	D	E
1.	__ b	__ d	__ e	__ a	__ c
2.	__ e	__ d	__ b	__ a	__ c
3.	__ d	__ b	__ a	__ e	__ c
4.	__ e	__ c	__ b	__ a	__ d
5.	__ d	__ b	__ a	__ c	__ e

6.	__ a	__ d	__ b	__ e	__ c
7.	__ b	__ d	__ e	__ c	__ a
8.	__ c	__ a	__ e	__ d	__ b
Total	__ +	__ +	__ +	__ +	__ = 120

Your totals for each column provide self-feedback regarding your favorite leadership style, your secondary style, on down to your least favorite style. In interpreting your answers, you will have to refer back to Figure 17–4. Column A indicates your preference for the 5,5 style; column B indicates your preference for the 1,1 style; column C reveals your preference for the 9,1 style; column D shows your preference for the 9,9 style; and column E indicates your preference for the 1,9 style.

Which is your favorite style? It is the column with the *lowest* total. Remember, you put a 1 next to the description that was *most* representative of you and a 5 next to the one that was *least* representative of you. So lower-total columns indicate a higher preference for the respective leadership style. The closer your totals are to each other, the more indifferent you are between these styles. For example, if your total for columns A and E are within a few points of each other, this means that you really have little preference between the two. On the other hand, if the difference is ten or more points, it means that you greatly prefer one style over the other.

Is your favorite style the 9,9? For most people it is. And the 1,1 is their least favorite choice. How about you? Regardless of your answer, the important thing is not how you perceive your leadership style but rather that you become aware that in OD the measurement of your approach to managing others and yourself is an object of consideration. An OD consultant, in conducting an overall intervention, will often use a self-appraisal instrument similar to the one we have employed here. By determining how people see themselves, the individual is in a position to compare their perceived behavior with their actual behavior. Information on the latter can be obtained by simply having your subordinates and your superior fill out the same instrument describing you. In this way the OD consultant can compare your perceptions with those of people around you. Also, the consultant would have asked you to describe the managerial style that would be best for you without telling you that you were about to take a test related to the managerial grid. When you were finished, the consultant could then compare your perceived style with the one you reported would be best for you. If there were a difference between your perceived and your desired styles, attention would then be focused on how this could be corrected.

NOTES

1. James J. Remer, "Turnaround of Information Systems at Honeywell," *Academy of Management Executive,* February 1987, pp. 47–50.

2. Robert N. Beck, "Visions, Values, and Strategies: Changing Attitudes and Culture," *Academy of Management Executive,* February 1987, pp. 33–41.

3. Zane E. Barnes, "Change in the Bell System," *Academy of Management Executive,* February 1987, pp. 43–46.

4. Michael Beer, "Revitalizing Organizations: Change Process and Emergent Model," *Academy of Management Executive,* February 1987, pp. 51–55.

5. Stanley J. Modic, "If You Win, I Win," *Industry Week,* April 3, 1989, p. 11.

6. Marcia Kleiman, "Ease the Stress of Change," *Personnel Journal,* September 1989, pp. 106–112.

7. Richard M. Hodgetts, *Modern Human Relations at Work,* 4th ed. (Hinsdale, IL: Dryden Press, 1990), p. 474.

8. Murray M. Dalziel and Stephen C. Schoonover, *Changing Ways* (New York: American Management Association, 1988).

9. Amir Levy and Uri Merry, *Organizational Transformation: Approaches, Strategies, Theories* (New York: Praeger Pubs., 1986), pp. 3–6.

10. John D. Adams and Sabina A. Spencer, "People in Transition," *Training and Development Journal,* October 1988, pp. 61–63.

11. For more on this see Clay Carr, "Follow Through on Change," *Training,* January 1989, pp. 39–44.

12. Wendell L. French and Cecil H. Bell, Jr., *Organization Development,* 2nd ed. (Englewood Cliffs, NJ: Prentice-Hall, 1978), p. 14.

13. Douglas M. Soat, "An OD Strategy at Parker Pen," *Personnel,* March–April 1979, pp. 39–43.

14. Lester A. Digman, "Let's Keep the OD People Honest," *Personnel,* January–February 1989, p. 25.

15. *Ibid.,* pp. 25–28.

16. Richard Beckhard, *Organization Development: Strategies and Models* (Reading, MA: Addison-Wesley Publishing Co., 1969), p. 26.

17. For more on this subject see D. D. Warrick, (ed.), *Contemporary Organization Development: Current Thinking and Applications* (Glenview, IL: Scott, Foresman & Co., 1985).

18. M. Likin, *Experiential Groups: The Use of Interpersonal Encounter, Psychotherapy Groups and Sensitivity Training* (Morristown, NJ: General Learning Press, 1972), p. 11.

19. E. H. Schein, *Process Consultation: Its Role in Organizational Development* (Reading, MA: Addison-Wesley Publishing Co., 1969), p. 135.

20. Thomas H. Patten, Jr., "Team Building Part 1. Designing the Intervention," *Personnel,* January–February 1979, pp. 11–21; Thomas H. Patten, Jr., "Team Building Part 2. Conducting the Intervention," *Personnel,* March–April 1979, pp. 62–68; and S. Jay Liebowitz and Kenneth P. DeMeuse, "The Application of Team Building," *Human Relations,* Vol. 35, no. 1, pp. 1–18.

21. For more on this topic of team building see S. Jay Liebowitz and Kenneth P. DeMeuse, "The Application of Team Building," *Human Relations,* January 1982, pp. 1–18.

22. Robert R. Blake and Jane S. Mouton, *Building a Dynamic Corporation through Grid Organization Development* (Reading, MA: Addison-Wesley Publishing Co., 1969), pp. 76–109.

23. See for example Robert M. Frame and Warren R. Nielsen, "Excellence According to Plan," *Training and Development Journal,* October 1988, pp. 37–40; Robert T. Golembiewski, Richard Hilles, and Rick Daly, "Some Effects of Multiple OD Interventions on Burnout and Work Site Features," *Journal of Applied Behavioral Science,* vol. 23, no. 3, 1987, pp. 295–313; and Jane Moosbrucker and Emanuel Berger, "Know Your Customer," *Training and Development Journal,* March 1988, pp. 30–34.

24. John R. Campbell, Marvin D. Dunnette, Edward E. Lawler III, and Karl E. Weich, Jr., *Managerial Behavior: Performance and Effectiveness* (New York: McGraw-Hill Book Co., 1970), p. 323.

25. Richard W. Woodman and John J. Sherwood, "Effects of Team Development Intervention: A Field Experiment," *Journal of Applied Behavioral Science,* vol. 16, no. 2, 1980, pp. 211–226.

26. Dov Eden, "Team Development: A True Field Experiment at Three Levels of Rigor," *Journal of Applied Psychology,* February 1985, pp. 94–100.

27. Paul F. Buller and Cecil H. Bell, Jr., "Effects of Team Building and Goal Setting on Productivity: A Field Experiment," *Academy of Management Journal,* June 1986, pp. 305–328.

28. Alfred M. Jaeger, "Organization Development and National Culture: Where's the Fit?," *Academy of Management Review,* January 1986, pp. 178–190.

29. Richard W. Woodman and Sandy J. Wayne, "An Investigation of Positive-Findings Bias in Evaluation of Organization Development Interventions," *Academy of Management Journal,* December 1985, pp. 899–913.

30. Gordon A. Walter, "Organizational Development and Individual Rights," *Journal of Applied Behavioral Science,* vol. 20, no. 4, 1984, pp. 423–439; and Louis P. White and Kevin C. Wooten, "Ethical Dilemmas in Various Stages of Organizational Development," *Academy of Management Review,* December 1983, pp. 690–697.

PART VI
HORIZONS

Now that we have examined the nature and processes of organizational behavior, we want to take a look at behavioral challenges and issues. The two that are given attention in this part of the book are international organizational behavior and career planning and development. These are not new topics, but they are critical to an understanding of the field, and they are continuing to emerge as important areas of consideration.

More and more businesses are going international. This means that American firms are going to need a basic understanding of the cultures and behaviors of foreign business people. This will be necessary in dealing with businesses in overseas environments as well as with foreign firms operating here in the United States. Chapter 18 considers the four cultural dimensions that distinguish countries from each other. Attention is also focused on common communication problems faced by managers in overseas environments and why leadership styles in other countries are often different from those in the United States. The value of cultural assimilators in training managers for overseas assignments will also be addressed.

In Chapter 19 career planning and development are discussed. This chapter helps explain why individuals and organizations alike are concerned with career development and the way in which people make career choices. Consideration is also given to the four career stages through which most individuals progress and the benefits that can accrue from career planning. The last part of the chapter describes some of the most common career developments programs, including career pathing, mentoring, universal programs, and preretirement programs.

The objective of this part of the book is to examine two critical areas of organizational behavior that will be increasing in importance during the 1990s. While these areas have been of interest during the 1980s, their significance will be greater than most other topics that have been covered in this book. For this reason they are addressed at this point. ◆

CHAPTER 18
International Organizational Behavior

GOALS OF THE CHAPTER

No study of organizational behavior would be complete without considering the international aspects of the subject. The growing trend of internationalism makes this topic critical for the 1990s. The goals of this chapter are to examine the cultural dimensions that account for behavioral differences between cultures and to look at the ways in which these differences are reflected in the communication, motivation, and leadership processes. The use of cultural assimilators in helping prepare people for overseas work assignments is also considered. When you have finished reading this chapter, you will:

1. know the four cultural dimensions that distinguish countries from each other and be able to describe each of these dimensions;
2. be aware of some common communication problems faced by managers in overseas environments;
3. understand some of the value changes that are occurring in the international work environment;
4. be aware of the importance of work centrality in motivating people;
5. know why leadership styles in other countries are often different from those in the United States;
6. understand how cultural assimilators are being used to train managers for overseas assignments.

OPENING CASE: THEY ARE CONVINCED THEY CAN'T LOSE

Franden Inc., a medium-size manufacturing firm, has found that it is more efficient to farm out some of its work than to do everything in house. Some small manufacturers specialize in producing certain types of parts, and they can provide them to Franden at 15 to 20 percent below the company's own cost. For the last six years Franden has increasingly relied on outsourcing.

A few months ago the company was approached by a manufacturing firm in Singapore that offered to manufacture and deliver parts to Franden at 30 percent less than it is currently paying its outside suppliers. The company turned down the firm because it felt that if something went wrong in Singapore, the company might end up losing some of its biggest accounts. On the other hand, the firm is interested in setting up operations in Singapore if it could cut 30 percent off its current outsourcing costs.

Last month two Franden executives met with a local businessman in Singapore. This individual came highly recommended by Franden's bank, which does quite a bit of business there. The essence of the conversation was that this man will help Franden set up operations in Singapore. The company will send three managers to run the operation, and the local businessman will help hire a 120-person work force and purchase the necessary machinery. The overseas factory should be up and running within four months.

The board of directors of Franden is quite pleased. After looking over the financial projections associated with the venture, the president called the decision to go international one of the best the company ever made. "I'm convinced," he said, "that we can't lose."

1. Is Singapore likely to be a high power distance or low power distance country? Explain.
2. Is management likely to find the employees to have high individualism or high collectivism?

3. Of the clusters in Figure 18–1, in which is Singapore located? Explain your answer.
4. Are communications in this country likely to be more explicit or implicit than they are in the United States?
5. Would you expect to find high or low work centrality in Singapore? Explain.
6. Would a cultural assimilator be of any value in training managers for this overseas assignment? Why or why not?

Write down your answers to these questions and put them aside. We will return to them later.

INTERNATIONAL DEVELOPMENTS

A number of important developments are making international organizational behavior an area of interest. One of the primary developments is the growth of international operations.[1]

Greater Internationalism

International organizational behavior is becoming important.

More and more countries are buying goods from abroad as well as setting up operations overseas.[2] In order to carry out these activities successfully, it is important to understand how the parties to these transactions think and act. What are some of the most common communication barriers in dealing with people from other countries? What motivates these individuals? What leadership style is most effective when trying to influence them?

These types of questions are becoming more important because the United States is the world's leading international country in terms of both foreign investment here and American investment overseas. At the present time, foreigners have direct investment of over $300 billion in the United States with the British and Dutch accounting for 46 percent of this total and the Japanese making up another 16 percent.[3] On the other side of the coin, American firms have invested hundreds of billions of dollars abroad, and as the European Common Market moves toward its goal of total elimination of trade barriers by 1992, U. S. firms are hurrying to gain a bigger foothold in this market.[4] At the same time, as the Communist bloc takes steps toward allowing free market operations within their sphere of control, American companies are looking to do business behind the Iron Curtain.[5] The same is true in the Pacific Rim countries such as China, Japan, South Korea, Taiwan, Hong Kong, and Singapore.[6]

The Need to Think Internationally

The above developments are resulting in organizational managers beginning to "think internationally."[7] This is occurring in a number of different ways. One is through training programs that teach managers about other cultures and familiarize them with the "right" way to behave. A second is through direct contact with overseas customers and clients. The outcome is a manager who is able to understand the cultural barriers that exist between countries and knows how to overcome them.

There are important differences between those who can think internationally and those who cannot.

A number of significant differences exist between those managers who are able to think internationally and those who are not. Table 18–1 presents some of these contrasts. These profiles were drawn from those of young executives studying at two of Europe's leading business schools for international management: The London Business School and INSEAD in Fountainbleau, France. The researchers found that the most effective international managers were those who relied on intuition, watched and listened carefully, tried to tune in to the social situation around them, and were able to follow the flow of people and events. Their less successful counterparts tended to analyze things rationally, looked for patterns of behavior that could be used to formulate overall explanations, and tended to be socially withdrawn.[8]

TABLE 18–1
A Comparison of Managers Best Able to Think Internationally with Those Who Are Not

Characteristic	Best Able	Not as Able
Objective	Be able to adapt to individual people	Be able to adapt to society
Perceived requirements for successful interaction with others	No special skills are needed; effective adaptation depends on the demands of the situation	Special skills are needed such as patience, empathy, honesty, broadmindedness, and flexibility
Question to ask in adapting to a new culture	What is happening? Search for descriptions, interpretations, and meanings	Why is this happening? Search for explanations and reasons
Relevant data	Feelings and impressions are most important	Facts and information are most important
Process of analyzing culturally-related information	Try to qualitatively describe cultures in an attempt to differentiate between them	Try to quantitatively compare and evaluate cultures
Results: internal	Modify stereotypes and clarify impressions and interpretations	Confirmation of stereotypes and impressions
Results: behavioral	Socially flexible and open	Socially judgmental and withdrawn

Source: Reprinted from Indrei Ratiu, "Thinking Internationally," *International Studies of Management and Organization,* Spring–Summer 1983, p. 146, by permission of M. E. Sharpe, Inc., New York 10504.

Other researchers have found that to be successful in the international arena it is important to develop the right "mind set" and to view the organization as multinational in nature. Some of the specific behavioral steps that are taken in implementing this strategy include: (a) creating organization designs that can handle unique international problems and challenges; (b) developing a communication system that keeps the company informed about political changes that can have an impact on operations; (c) forming management teams that are international in nature and are able to respond to the various demands of the respective world markets; (d) creating a board of directors that is truly international in composition; and (e) developing a cadre of top managers that feel comfortable operating in the world arena.[9]

THE CULTURAL CHALLENGE

One of the primary challenges faced by many people working in the international arena is that the culture of the country is so different from their own. These differences can be explained in terms of cultural dimensions.[10]

Cultural Dimensions

Cultural dimensions are behavioral and attitudinal differences that distinguish groups from each other. Hofstede has found four cultural dimensions that are useful in examining and comparing countries: power distance, uncertainty avoidance, individualism/collectivism, and masculinity/femininity.

Power distance relates to accepting the fact that power is distributed unequally.

Power Distance. **Power distance** is the extent to which less powerful members of institutions and organizations accept that power is distributed unequally.[11] When people blindly obey orders, there is high power distance. When people often question orders or are reluctant to obey regardless of the formal authority possessed by the other person, there is low power distance. In some countries such as those in Latin America (Panama, Venezuela, and Equador, for example) and the Orient (Hong Kong, Korea, and Singapore, for example) there is high power distance. Conversely, in many European countries such as Great Britain, the Netherlands, and Denmark, in North American nations such as Canada and the United States, and in Anglo cultures in the South Pacific such as New Zealand and Australia, power distance is very small.

There are many ways of comparing high power and low power countries. Some of these include the following:[12]

High Power Countries	Low Power Countries
There is a high value on conformity	There is a low value on conformity
Managers make autocratic and paternalistic decisions	Managers consult with their people before making important decisions
The work ethic is weak	The work ethic is strong
Managers see themselves as benevolent decision makers	Managers see themselves as practical and systematic, and they admit a need for support from their people

Companies in high power distance countries tend to have centralized and tall organization structures and use autocratic leadership styles. Companies in low power distance countries tend to have decentralized and flat organization structures and use participative approaches in managing their personnel.

Review your answers to Question 1 and make any changes you would like before continuing.

1. Is Singapore likely to be a high power distance or low power distance country? Explain.

Singapore will be a high power distance country. As noted in the text, the country places a high value on conformity, and managers will tend to be autocratic or paternalistic in their decision making.

Uncertainty avoidance re-
sults in a high need for security.

Uncertainty Avoidance.   **Uncertainty avoidance** is "the extent to which people feel threatened by ambiguous situations, and have created beliefs and institutions that try to avoid these."[13] Countries with high uncertainty avoidance tend to have strict laws and severely punish those who break them. These nations are also characterized by a high need for security and a strong belief in experts and their knowledge. Organizations in these countries tend to have low risk-taking managers, low labor turnover, and less ambitious employees. Managers feel that they must know the answer to all subordinate questions and must personally be knowledgeable about details related to company operations. Conversely, cultures with low uncertainty avoidance have fewer or less strict laws, and citizens have strong feelings of personal competence. Organizations in these countries tend to have higher risk-taking managers, higher labor turnover, and more ambitious employees. Managers have a more generalist point of view and do not try to develop a detailed knowledge of all facets of the enterprise's operations.

Individualism/Collectivism.   **Individualism** is the tendency of people to look after themselves and their immediate family only. **Collectivism** is the tendency of people to belong to groups or collectives and to look after each other.[14] Individualism is high in the United States, Canada, Great Britain, and other Anglo nations. Collectivism tends to be high in Latin and Oriental countries such as Costa Rica, Mexico, South Korea, and Japan.

High individualism results in
high personal initiative.

Countries with high individualism encourage people to take care of themselves and not rely on others. Emotional independence is promoted, and achievement, individual initiative, autonomy, financial security, and the belief in individual decision making is nurtured. Countries with low individualism encourage people to look after each other in exchange for loyalty. Emphasis is on belonging, developing expertise, assuming a sense of duty, and believing strongly in the importance of group decisions.

STOP   Review your answers to Question 2 and make any changes you would like before continuing.

2. Is management likely to find the employees to have high individualism or high collectivism?

Management is likely to find employees with high collectivism. This pattern of behavior is common in Far Eastern countries. The company will find some of the individualistic approaches it uses in the United States will not work in this country.

Highly masculine societies
prize earnings, advance-
ment, and challenge.

Masculinity/Femininity.   **Masculinity** is "a situation in which the dominant values of society are success, money, and things."[15] This is in contrast to **femininity** which is "a situation in which the dominant values in society are caring for others and the quality of life."[16] Countries with high masculinity place great importance on earnings, recognition, advancement, and challenge. People are encouraged to be independent decision makers, and achievement is defined in terms of recognition and wealth. This thinking tends to favor high work drive and high stress. Countries with high masculinity include Japan, Austria, Germany, and Great Britain. The United States is characterized by moderately high masculinity.

Countries with low masculinity (high femininity) place great importance on cooperation, a friendly atmosphere, and employment security. Individuals are encouraged to be group decision makers, and achievement is defined in terms of human contacts and the living environment. In the workplace there is low stress, and managers tend to give their people greater authority and autonomy. Nordic countries such as Finland, Norway, and Sweden have a low masculinity index.

Attitudinal Dimensions of Culture

Hofstede's work on cultural dimensions has proven useful in explaining the reasons for behavioral similarities and differences between countries. His research has also allowed him to form **cultural clusters,** which are groupings of similar cultures. This approach has been extended through the work of a number of other researchers, the best-known being Ronen and Shenkar who formulated the cluster synthesis in Figure 18–1.[17]

Researchers have uncovered eight basic cultural clusters.

Their research found that most countries can be placed into eight basic cultural clusters. As seen in Figure 18–1, each country has been placed in a cluster that is culturally similar to the others located there. This clustering concept is particularly important in the study of international organizational behavior because of the benefits it provides in understanding other cultures. The concept also has advantages for those doing business overseas.

> As multinational companies increase their direct investment overseas, especially in less developed and consequently less studied areas, they will require more information concerning their local employees in order to implement effective types of interactions between the organization and the host country. The knowledge acquired thus far can help one to understand better the work values and attitudes of employees throughout the world. American theories work very well for Western nations. Are they equally applicable in non-Western countries? Clearly, more cluster research is called for, including research in countries from all parts of the globe.[18]

 STOP Review your answers to Question 3 and make any changes you would like before continuing.

3. Of the clusters in Figure 18–1, in which is Singapore located? Explain your answer.

Singapore is located in the Far Eastern cluster. It has a culture similar to that of Hong Kong, Malaysia, and the Philippines, among others, and is quite different from that of the United States.

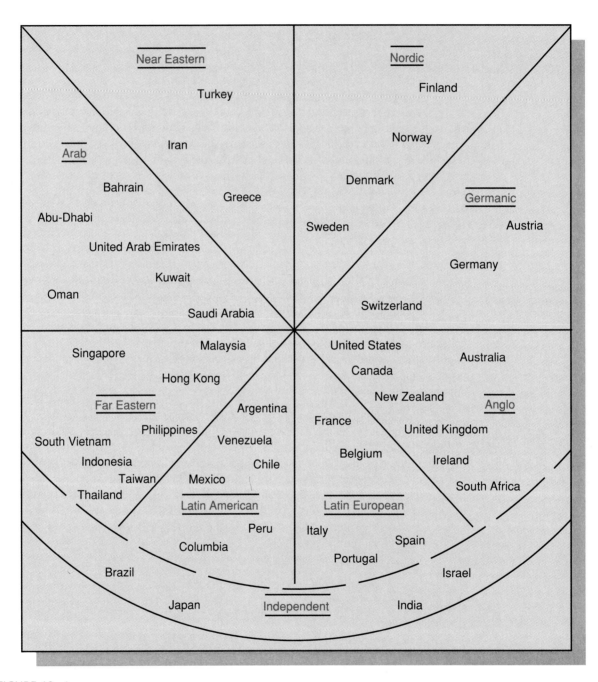

FIGURE 18–1

A Synthesis of Country Clusters (Source: Simcha Ronen and Oded Shenkar, "Clustering Countries on Attitudinal Dimensions: A Review and Synthesis," *Academy of Management Journal*, September 1985, p. 449.)

COMMUNICATION IN INTERNATIONAL ENVIRONMENTS

Communication in an international setting can be a major stumbling block for a number of reasons. One is perception, because some words have different meanings in different languages while other words do not translate directly. For example, in the United States when a Broadway play does poorly it is said to have "bombed." In England the word means just the opposite and is used to indicate a highly successful production. Similarly, in the United States the term "Mickey Mouse" is often employed to mean something that is trite, simplistic, or easy, i.e., I did not sign up for that course because it is too Mickey Mouse. This term does not translate into most other languages. While the receiver is likely to know who Mickey Mouse is, the person is unlikely to understand the meaning of the sentence because he or she has never heard the term used this way. Some of the other common problems relate to the use of one-way, two-way communication flows, explicit vs. implicit communication, and language difficulties.

One-Way, Two-Way Communication

Two-way communication is more popular in the United States.

Managers in most countries do not put as strong an emphasis on feedback (two-way communication) as do American managers. Table 18–2, for example, shows that on average, American managers prefer two-way communication more than managers from other countries.

Additionally, in some countries downward flows are used to pass on more than just business-related information. Inzerilli and Laurent found that French managers were much more likely than their American counterparts to use their authority to try to influence subordinates in nonwork-related matters, including the type of person they should marry, how many children they should have, and whether or not their spouse should work.[19]

Explicit and Implicit Communications

Implicit communication is widely used in other countries.

Another major difference in the international communication process is that in some countries communications are more explicit than they are in the United States and in others they are more implicit. Figure 18–2 provides an illustration of these differences.

In the United States, people are taught to say exactly what they mean. In many foreign countries such as those in the Orient, Middle East, and Latin America there is a great deal of implied meaning. Ouchi, a well-known expert on Japanese management, offers the following explanation of why many Americans feel frustrated in their attempts to do business in a country where implied communication is widely used.

> Americans expect others to behave just as we do. Many are the unhappy and frustrated American businessmen or lawyers returning from Japan with the complaint that, "If only they would tell me who is really in charge, we could make some progress." The complaint displays a lack of understanding that, in Japan, no one individual carries responsibility for a particular turf. Rather, a group or team of employees assume joint responsibility for a set of tasks. While we wonder at their comfortableness in not knowing who is responsible for what, they know quite clearly that each of them is completely responsible

TABLE 18–2
Preferences Regarding One-Way and Two-Way Communication

	Belgium	Denmark	India	Italy	Norway	United Kingdom	United States	Total
Number of managers	47	30	34	47	88	36	31	313
Number of groups	5	5	6	7	18	4	6	51
Percent preferring as sender*								
1-way communication	6.4	10.0	20.6	6.4	3.4	13.9	6.5	8.3
2-way communication	87.2	83.3	79.4	91.5	95.5	86.1	93.5	89.5
Percent preferring as receiver**								
1-way communication	2.1	10.0	11.8	0.0	1.1	8.3	0.0	3.8
2-way communication	95.7	90.0	88.2	95.7	97.7	91.7	100.0	94.9

*Percentages may not total 100; the remainders represent those expressing no difference in their attitude.
**Found significant at the 0.05 level, chi-square analysis.

Source: Adapted from G. V. Barrett and R. H. Frank, Communication Preference and Performance: A Cross Cultural Comparison, MRC Technical Report No. 29, August 1969 and reported in Simcha Ronen, Comparative and Multinational Management (New York: John Wiley & Sons, 1986), p. 105.

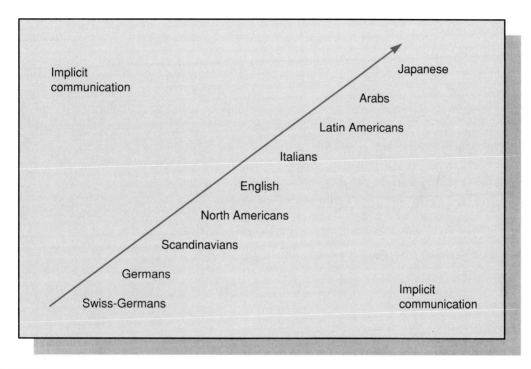

FIGURE 18–2
Explicit/Implicit Communication: an International Comparison (Source: Adapted from "Signif-
icance of Message" from Martin Rösch, K. G. Segler "Communication with Japanese," in
Management International Review, vol. 27, no. 4, p. 60.)

for all tasks, and they share that responsibility jointly. Obviously, this approach
sometimes lets things "fall through the cracks" because everyone may think
that someone else has a task under control. When working well, however, this
approach leads to a naturally participative decision making and problem solving
process.[20]

Language Difficulties

**Language continues to be a
stumbling block.**

A third international communication problem is language difficulties, which are caused
when the manager does not understand the language of the other country. Hildebrandt
found that among the American subsidiaries he studied in Germany language was the
major problem when sending written communications to the home office. The process
involved a series of elaborate procedures for translating and reworking reports before
finally communicating them. A typical set of steps was the following: (a) a staff conference would be held to determine what to include in the written message; (b) an initial
draft of the material would be written in German; (c) the draft would be rewritten in
German; (d) the message would then be translated into English; (e) bilingual staff

members would examine the translation; and (f) the message would be rewritten until it was judged acceptable for transmission. Summing up the problem, Hildebrandt noted:

> The general manager or vice president cannot be asked to be an editor. Yet they often send statements along, knowingly, which are poorly written, grammatically imperfect, or generally unclear. The time pressures do not permit otherwise. Predictably, questions issue from the States to the subsidiary and the complicated bilingual process now goes in reverse, ultimately reaching the original. . .staff member, who receives the English questions retranslated.[21]

The problems associated with translating information from one language to another have been made even clearer by Schermerhorn, who found that when Hong Kong Chinese who were fluent in English were queried in Chinese they gave different answers than when they were queried in English.[22] Quite obviously language plays a key role in conveying information between cultures.

STOP

Review your answers to Question 4 and make any changes you would like before continuing.

4. Are communications in this country likely to be more explicit or implicit than they are in the United States?

The communications are likely to be more implicit than they are in the United States. A close look at Figure 18–2 shows that the Japanese are very implicit. The same is true for other countries in the Far Eastern cluster.

MOTIVATION IN DIFFERENT CULTURES

Many things motivate people in an organizational environment. Sometimes it is the work itself; other times it is the money people are paid for doing the work; still other times it is the status and prestige that accompany the job. Table 18–3 provides an example. Notice that the Japanese are highly motivated by money; the Israelis and the Dutch prize work that is interesting and satisfying; the Belgians, British and Americans like work that allows for social interaction; and the British and Americans like work that gives them status and prestige. It is erroneous to say that all people are motivated by identical things. Additionally, recent research shows that some values are changing, so what motivates people today may not do so in the future.

Values in Transition

Stateside Japanese have different values than their counterparts at home.

Research shows that personal value systems are relatively stable and do not change rapidly.[23] However, changes are taking place in managerial values as a result of both culture and technology. The Japanese are a good example. Reichel and Flynn examined the effects of the American environment on the cultural values of Japanese managers

TABLE 18–3
Average Number of Points Assigned to Working Functions by Country Samples

Country	Working Provides You with an Income That Is Needed	Working Is Basically Interesting and Satisfying to You	Working Permits You to Have Interesting Contacts with Other People	Working Gives You Status and Prestige
Japan	45.4	13.4	14.7	5.6
Germany	40.5	16.7	13.1	10.1
Belgium	35.5	21.3	17.3	6.9
United Kingdom	34.4	17.9	15.3	10.9
Yugoslavia	34.1	19.8	9.8	9.3
United States	33.1	16.8	15.3	11.9
Israel	31.1	26.2	11.1	8.5
Netherlands	26.2	23.5	17.9	4.9
All countries combined	35.0*	19.5	14.3	8.5

*The combined totals weigh each equally, regardless of sample size.

Source: Adapted from MOW International Research Team, The Meaning of Work: An International Perspective, (New York: Academic Press, 1985) and reported in Simcha Ronen, Comparative and Multinational Management (New York: John Wiley & Sons, 1986), p. 144.

working for Japanese firms in the United States. In particular, they focused attention on such key organizational values as lifetime employment, formal authority, group orientation, seniority, and paternalism.[24] Some of their findings included: (a) while lifetime employment is widely accepted in Japanese culture, Japanese managers located stateside do not believe that unconditional tenure with one firm is of major importance; (b) obedience and conformity to hierarchical positions are important in Japan, but stateside managers did not perceive them to be very important; (c) group orientation and compromise are important in Japan, but stateside managers believe that these factors must be balanced with a consideration for individual orientation; (d) in Japan rewards are often given on the basis of seniority, but the longer the managers were located in the United States, the greater their preference for rewards based on merit; and (e) while paternalism is very strong in Japan, the longer the managers remained stateside, the greater the likelihood that they disagreed with this policy.[25]

Other researchers have found supporting evidence that managerial values are changing in Japan. Schwind and Peterson examined value systems among three groups of Japanese managers: (a) a group that had graduated from the Japanese Institute for International Studies and Training during the previous ten years; (b) a group of management trainees that were currently enrolled in the institute; and (c) a group of American MBA students who were taking MBA courses at the institute.[26]

Their data showed that Japanese managers, for the most part, are greatly concerned with job security and group success, while the MBAs value achievement and personal success. In the main, the two groups have contrasting values. The Japanese students, on the other hand, fall between these two extremes. This has led Schwind and Peterson to conclude, "The data seem to indicate a significant difference in values between Japanese respondents who have already attained responsible managerial positions in their organization and the Japanese management trainees who have held lower positions and been employed less long with their present company or government agency."[27]

The Importance of Work

Another key area of motivation is the importance assigned to work. In some countries work is a way of life; in others, leisure is a desirable activity, and people work only as much as they feel is necessary. Similarly, in some countries working conditions are not given major priority, while in others the quality of working life ranks very high.

Work is very important to the Japanese.

In one of the most recent studies related to the importance of work, England and Misumi examined **work centrality,** the degree of general importance that working has in the life of an individual at any given point in time.[28] A total of 4,228 workers and managers in the United States and Japan responded to a questionnaire designed to determine how important work, leisure, family, community, and religion were to them. As seen in Figure 18–3, the researchers found that work was more important to the Japanese than to the Americans, and this was true regardless of occupational area. They also found that while the Americans and Japanese under the age of twenty had similar work centrality profiles, after this age the point gap jumped dramatically and the Japanese reported average differences of 12 to 15 points higher than Americans of the same age. After the age of sixty, the importance of work declined for both groups but the large point spread remained.[29]

Other research studies echo the importance of work in the Orient. For example, Putti and his associates examined work values in Thailand, Singapore, the Philippines, Malaysia, and Indonesia.[30] They found that pride in work and job involvement ranked at the top of the list; earnings, for most respondents, were at the bottom. Nor did these findings change when the data were examined on the basis of religion. Christians, Buddhists, Islamites, and Hindus, on average, all ranked pride in work and job involvement at the top of their list; earnings were at or near the bottom. The researchers also found that individuals with no religion ranked earnings lowest of all.

Motivating foreign personnel is likely to be different from motivating American workers.

These data show that ways to motivate foreign personnel are likely to be different from those of American workers.[31] On the other hand, it is erroneous to believe that these differences are extremely large and new motivation systems must be developed. There is a great deal of similarity between all workers, and as Third World countries become more economically advanced, they are likely to adapt motivation systems similar to those in the United States. This is even true in the case of Japan. Recent research shows that the Japanese approach of rewarding people based on seniority is beginning to give way to a system based on merit.[32] Mroczkowski and Hanaoka report that between 1978 and 1987 among surveyed Japanese firms, the relative contribution of seniority declined from 58 percent to 46 percent and merit rose from 42 percent to 54 percent.

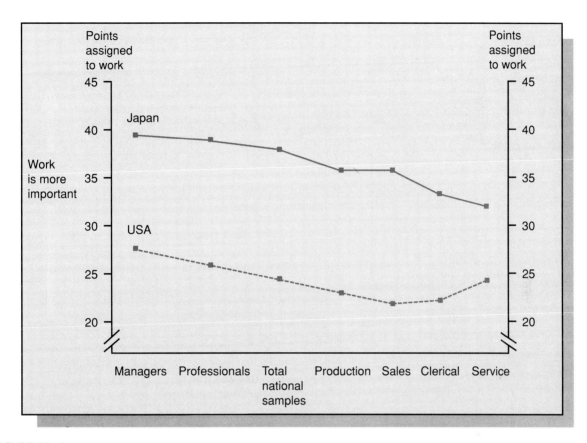

FIGURE 18–3
Work Importance Scores for Occupational Groups in Japan and the United States (Source: George W. England and Jyuji Misumi, "Work Centrality in Japan and the United States," *Journal of Cross-Cultural Psychology,* December 1986, p. 410.)

 STOP   Review your answers to Question 5 and make any changes you would like before continuing.

5. Would you expect to find high or low work centrality in Singapore? Explain.

High work centrality is likely in Singapore. The personnel would have great dedication to work, and work would be a central part of their lives. They would have the same basic values as the Japanese for whom work is a critical dimension of their life.

	PREPARING PEOPLE FOR OVERSEAS ASSIGNMENTS
Organizational Behavior In Action	As more firms do business overseas, preparing people for these assignments will become a major area of consideration. There are a number of reasons for this. One is that many people return home early because they are unable to adjust to their new assignments. A second is that foreign competitors such as the Europeans and Japanese do not have the high failure rate that the Americans do in other countries because they better prepare their people before sending them abroad. This has led internationally known firms such as IBM, Xerox, Colgate-Palmolive, and Dow Chemical, among others, to develop tailor-made international management programs.

IBM, with operations in 132 countries, conducts internal executive development programs at its management development centers in the United States, Australia, Singapore, Japan, and Belgium. Bringing in managers from all over the world, the firm offers a six-week course related to a wide variety of international topics designed to help personnel function more effectively in overseas environments. Additionally, every year all IBM managers receive forty-two hours of training on topics such as managing multinational groups.

Xerox has developed its own program for international managers and sends all top managers through the training. This approach is important given the fact that the company used to develop products for the United States and then market the goods overseas, but it has changed its strategy so that some products are now marketed directly in foreign countries.

Sources: Richard M. Hodgetts and Fred Luthans, *International Management* (New York: McGraw-Hill Book Co., 1991), Chapters 7 and 8; Richard M. Hodgetts and Fred Luthans, "Japanese HR Management Practices: Separating Fact From Fiction," *Personnel,* April 1989, pp. 42–45; Madelyn R. Callahan, "Preparing the New Global Manager," *Training and Development Journal,* March 1989, pp. 29–32; Mark E. Mendenhall and Gary Oddou, "The Overseas Assignment: A Practical Look," *Business Horizons,* September–October 1988, pp. 78–84; Paul L. Blocklyn, "Developing the International Executive," *Personnel,* March 1989, pp. 44–47; and Rosalie L. Tung, "Expatriate Assignments: Enhancing Success and Minimizing Failure," *Academy of Management Executive,* May 1987, pp. 117–125.

LEADERSHIP IN OTHER CULTURES

The leadership process is also influenced by cultural variables, so the most effective style with a group of American workers may prove highly ineffective with a group workers in another country. Two of the most important reasons for this are the differences in managerial backgrounds and the decision making preferences of the managers. In dealing with these and similar leadership-related challenges, many firms are now turning to the use of cultural assimilator programs.

Managerial Backgrounds

Many foreign managers come from a particular economic stratum.

American managers come from every economic strata: lower, middle, and upper. However, many foreign managers are from a particular economic stratum. For example, in

Colgate-Palmolive uses a two-year orientation program that prepares people for overseas assignments. Additionally, each manager sent overseas develops a relationship with a senior manager at the vice-presidential level, and the latter serves as a mentor.

Dow's training starts with an orientation program and then provides relocating executives with language training and a briefing packet with information on the host country. Each person going overseas is then assigned a high-level manager who keeps track of the individual's career through continuous communication with the person.

These firms, as well as other international companies, are also finding that a series of procedures can be helpful in preparing their people for overseas assignments. These procedures include: (a) selecting people whose educational backgrounds and experiences are appropriate for overseas assignments; (b) choosing people whose personalities and family situations can withstand the cultural changes that will be encountered in their new environments; (c) briefing candidates fully and clearly on all relocation policies; (d) giving the relocating personnel comprehensive training in the new country's culture and language; (e) providing the executives with a mentor to monitor their overseas careers; and (f) establishing a repatriation program that will help returning personnel to readjust to their professional and personal lives in their home country.

Turkey top managers often come from the upper class, but in Poland most business leaders are from the lower middle class. In Argentina and Peru, business leaders are often middle class, and in Chile the landed aristocracy are the managerial leaders.

In some countries top managers have attended the best schools and have been singled out for leadership positions. In Japan, Tokyo University is a "must" school for the potentially successful manager. In France it is the *grand ecoles*. In Russia it is the University of Moscow. In Korea, surprisingly perhaps, American universities are most highly regarded because the Koreans believe that their ability to build strong ties with the United States, their number one business market, will be critical to their future.[33]

Other key background factors that influence leadership include family upbringing and the relationship between old and young people. In India, for example, it is common to accept the authority of elders, so there is often little delegation of authority. Everyone does whatever the head of the enterprise wants done. One senior Indian executive with a Ph.D. from a prestigious American university explained it this way:

What is most important for me and my department is not what I do or achieve for the company, but whether the [owner's] favor is bestowed on me. . . . This I have achieved by saying "yes" to everything [the owner] says or does. . . . To contradict him is to look for another job. . . . I left my free-dom of thought in Boston.[34]

Decision-Making Preferences

The way people make decisions in other countries is often different from that in the United States. For example, American managers are taught to be risk takers, and this activity is encouraged and rewarded. However, many other cultures discourage risk taking. Cummings and his associates have found that American managers are greater risk takers than most European managers.[35]

Similarly, in some countries managers do not put much emphasis on the need for data analysis and careful decision making because they believe things will eventually work themselves out. This strong belief in fate is in sharp contrast to the American belief in self-determination and the need to take control of one's own situation.

A third major decision-making difference is individual versus group action. In the United States managers are encouraged to make individual decisions; in the Far East decisions are often the result of collective action. In Japan decisions are discussed by groups of workers, and the final course of action is a result of everyone's input. This process helps explain why the Japanese prefer group incentive plans rather than indi-vidual incentive plans.

Cultural Assimilators

One of the most effective approaches to improving leadership in an international setting is to provide training through the use of a cultural assimilator. (Also see "Organizational Behavior in Action: Preparing People for Overseas Assignments.") A **cultural assim-ilator** is a programmed learning approach designed to expose members of one culture to some of the basic concepts, attitudes, role perceptions, customs, and values of another culture.[36] These assimilators typically are developed for each culture. For example, if a company is going to send three American managers from New York to Bejing, a cultural assimilator would be developed to familiarize the three Americans with Chinese customs and culture.

In most cases these assimilators require the trainee to read a short episode of an intercultural encounter and to choose an interpretation of what has happened and why. If the individual's choice is correct, the person goes on to the next episode. If the response is incorrect, the individual is asked to reread the episode and choose another response. Table 18–4 provides an example.

The incidents in the cultural assimilator are typically developed through interviews with managers who have spent time in that country and who can help pinpoint things that should be known and can describe situations that the newly-appointed manager is likely to confront. These incidents can be pleasant, unpleasant, or simply nonunder-standable occurrences.

The cultural assimilator approach to training can be quite expensive. A typical 75- to 100-incident program often requires approximately 800 hours to develop. Assuming that a training specialist is costing the company $50 an hour including benefits, the cost is around $40,000 per assimilator. On the other hand, this cost can be spread over many

TABLE 18–4
An Example of a Cultural Assimilator Situation

Sharon Hatfield, a school teacher in Athens, was amazed at the questions that were asked of her by Greeks whom she considered to be only casual acquaintances. When she entered or left her apartment, people would ask her where she was going or where she had been. If she stopped to talk she was asked questions like, "How much do you make a month?" or "Where did you get that dress you are wearing?" She thought the Greeks were very rude.

Page X-2

Why did the Greeks ask Sharon such "personal" questions?
1. The casual acquaintances were acting like friends do in Greece, although Sharon did not realize it.

Go to page X-3

2. The Greeks asked Sharon the questions in order to determine whether she belonged to the Greek Orthodox Church.

Go to page X-4

3. The Greeks were unhappy about the way in which she lived and they were trying to get Sharon to change her habits.

Go to page X-5

4. In Greece such questions are perfectly proper when asked of women, but improper when asked of men.

Go to page X-6

Page X-3

You selected 1: The casual acquaintances were acting like friends do in Greece, although Sharon did not realize it.
Correct. It is not improper for in-group members to ask these questions of one another. Furthermore, these questions reflect the fact that friendships (even "casual" ones) tend to be more intimate in Greece than in America. As a result, friends are generally free to ask questions which would seem too personal in America.

Go to page X-1

Page X-4

You selected 2: The Greeks asked Sharon the questions in order to determine whether she belonged to the Greek Orthodox Church.
No. This is not why the Greeks asked Sharon such questions. Remember, whether or not some information is "personal" depends upon the culture. In this case, the Greeks did not consider these questions too "personal." Why? Try again.

Go to page X-1

Page X-5

You selected 3: The Greeks were unhappy about the way in which she lived and they were trying to get Sharon to change her habits.
No. There was no information given to lead you to believe that the Greeks were unhappy with Sharon's way of living. The episode states that the Greeks were acquaintances of Sharon.

Go to page X-1

TABLE 18–4
continued

Page X-6

You selected 4: In Greece such questions are perfectly proper when asked of women, but improper when asked of men.

No. Such questions are indeed proper under certain situations. However, sex has nothing to do with it. When are these questions proper? Try to apply what you have learned about proper behavior between friends in Greece. Was Sharon regarded as a friend by these Greeks?

Go to page X-1

Source: Fred E. Fiedler, Terence Mitchell, and Harry C. Triandis, ''The Culture Assimilator: An Approach to Cross-Cultural Training,'' *Journal of Applied Psychology*, April 1971, pp. 97–98. © 1971 by the American Psychological Association. Reprinted by permission.

trainees, and the program may not need to be changed for five or more years. A firm that sends forty people a year from the United States to a foreign country for which an assimilator has been constructed is paying only $200 per person for this programmed training. In the long-run the costs are often more than justified. Additionally, the concept can be applied to virtually all cultures. Many different types of assimilators have been constructed, including Arab, Thai, Honduran, and Greek, to name but four. Most importantly, research shows that these assimilators improve the effectiveness and satisfaction of those being trained as compared with other training methods.[37] During the 1990s this approach will undoubtedly increase in use.[38]

Before ending our discussion of this topic, however, one additional point merits consideration. Increasing evidence indicates that leadership styles throughout the world are not as markedly different from that in the United States as many people believe, and there currently appears to be a movement *toward* more American-type leadership patterns. After conducting a thorough review of the literature on leadership, Hodgetts and Luthans found that there is much more similarity in international leadership styles than has been previously believed, leading the researchers to conclude:

> As countries become more economically advanced, participative styles may well gain in importance. Of course, this does not mean that MNCs [multinational corporations] can use the same leadership styles in their various locations around the world. There must still be careful contingency application of leadership styles (different styles for different situations). However, many of the more enlightened participative styles used in the U.S. and other economically advanced countries. . .may also have value in managing international operations. . .in developing countries.[39]

STOP

Review your answers to Question 6 and make any changes you would like before continuing.

6. Would a cultural assimilator be of any value in training managers for this overseas assignment? Why or why not?

A cultural assimilator certainly would be of value because it would help familiarize the managers with the values, attitudes, beliefs, and customs of the people with whom they would be doing business. The assimilator is an excellent way of teaching managers about various cultures before the individuals actually go to that geographic region.

SUMMARY

1. A dramatic increase in international business is occurring. As a result, international organizational behavior is becoming a major area of consideration in the study of organizational behavior. Primary areas of interest include communication, motivation, and leadership.

2. Why do managers in one country use different communication patterns than those in other countries? How does motivation vary between cultures? How do leadership patterns vary between cultures? These questions are becoming focal points for organizational behavior research. In developing an overall profile on the behavioral and attitudinal differences between countries, researchers have examined cultural dimensions.

3. There are four cultural dimensions: power distance, uncertainty avoidance, individualism/collectivism, and masculinity/femininity. Based on these differences, it has been possible to develop cultural clusters such as those in Figure 18–1.

4. Communication in an international setting can be a major stumbling block for a number of reasons. These include one-way, two-way communication, explicit and implicit communication, and language difficulties. Motivation differences are often a result of changing values and of work centrality. Leadership differences are often accounted for by factors such as managerial backgrounds and decision-making preferences.

5. In an effort to help train their personnel for overseas assignments, organizations are now turning to the use of cultural assimilators. This programmed learning approach is proving to be very effective.

KEY TERMS

cultural dimensions	collectivism	cultural clusters
power distance	masculinity	work centrality
uncertainty avoidance	femininity	cultural assimilator
individualism		

REVIEW AND STUDY QUESTIONS

1. How do effective organizational managers "think internationally"? How do their less-effective counterparts think? Explain.

2. What is a cultural dimension? Give an example.

3. If a country has high power distance, how would this affect organizational behavior? Give an example.

4. If a country has low uncertainty avoidance, what conclusions can be drawn about managers who operate in that culture? Give two examples.

5. Does the United States have high or low individualism? Does Japan have high or low individualism? What do your answers relate about managing personnel in both countries?

6. If a country has high masculinity, how will its managerial leadership styles be different from a country that has low masculinity? Explain.

7. What is the value of cultural clusters to the study of international organizational behavior? Be complete in your answer.

8. In what ways do explicit and implicit communication affect organizational behavior? Why might these types of communication prove to be communication barriers?

9. Why is language an international organizational behavior problem? Why can interpreters not totally resolve the problem?

10. Are international managerial values changing? Defend your answer.

11. Why is work centrality an important issue in the study of international organizational behavior? Explain.

12. How can managerial background influence leadership behavior? How can family upbringing influence this behavior? How can decision-making preferences influence this behavior?

13. What is a cultural assimilator? Of what value are assimilators in preparing people for overseas assignments?

CASES

Giving It His Best Shot

For the last five years Jack Philby's company has had a plant just outside of Mexico City. The operation was not very profitable, but because Mexican law required that majority ownership be held by Mexicans, Jack's firm did not try to assume a strong leadership role. The government recently changed its regulations, and Americans can now hold a controlling interest in Mexican-based companies. Upon hearing the news, the firm offered to put $4 million into the plant to update the facilities and to expand operations, in return for an increase of 15 percent of the ownership. Their Mexican partners agreed, and next month Jack will be going to Mexico to take charge of the operation.

Between now and then the firm has decided to help Jack prepare for his new position by giving him some basic language training and acquainting him with many of the values and customs of Mexico. In particular, they want Jack to take control of the reins and quickly establish himself as the president. "You're going to be our main person down there," the vice-president of foreign operations told him. "We want you to go in there and let them know that you are running the operation. Of course, we don't want you to start running all over people, but we don't want to find that you

are president in name only. Most of the managers are locals who are accustomed to working for a Mexican president, but they'll respond to you if you handle things correctly."

Jack is not sure exactly what the vice-president is talking about, but he does realize what the individual wants done. As a result, Jack is spending ten hours a day preparing himself for the assignment. In particular, he is working hard to master the language and to learn how employees think and act. "I'd like to communicate, motivate, and lead them in a way that they're accustomed to without changing my own style a lot in the process," he told his wife. "However, I'm wondering if this is going to be possible. In any event, I'm going to give it my best shot."

1. Will Jack find any differences between the cultural dimensions in the United States and those in Mexico? Explain.

2. How important will language training be for him? Defend your answer.

3. Will the leadership style he is accustomed to using in the states be of value to him, or will he have to make major adjustments? Why?

Picking the Best

Joint ventures are one of the most common ways of going international. Last month Madrick & Matson (MM), a sys-

tems engineering firm, entered into a major deal with a large Swedish electronics firm. Under the terms of the arrangement, MM and its new partner will both invest $50 million in the design and production of state-of-the-art office electronics equipment. The partnership hopes to become a major competitor in this field by the mid-1990s.

The first product to be manufactured was already on MM's drawing board, and the Swedish firm is going to complete tooling up for it within four months. It is believed that the product will be on retailers' shelves within nine months.

In an effort to ensure that the product is built correctly and that MM is allowed to play a role in the process, the Swedish manufacturer has insisted that MM send four managers to Sweden to work alongside its own people. These managers will help directly supervise the project and will be able to give MM's top management a first-hand report on what is going on.

MM has not decided who to send because the company is not sure how different working conditions in Sweden are from those in the United States. The management wants to send people who will fit in well and is concerned that if this first team over does not work out well, this could jeopardize the entire venture. "We've got to give this our best shot," the president told the selection committee. "Pick the four best people we've got and give them whatever training is necessary before they leave. I want glowing reports on them from our Swedish partners."

1. How is the cultural dimension of masculinity likely to effect the way operations are run in Sweden vis-a-vis the United States?

2. What type of leadership approach would you expect the Swedes to use with their people? Would it be similar to that used in the United States?

3. Would a cultural assimilator be of any value in training these managers? Why or why not?

SELF-FEEDBACK EXERCISE

What Do You Kow About International Organizational Behavior?

There are twenty true-false questions below. Using your best judgment, decide whether each is true or false and circle your choice. Answers and a scoring key are provided at the end of the exercise.

T F 1. Managers from India are very concerned about bureaucratic rules.

T F 2. French managers are not as cooperative with others as are many other managers.

T F 3. Portuguese managers try to be very aware of the feelings of others.

T F 4. In contrast to many other managers, American managers tend to rely much more on facts than on intuition.

T F 5. Most countries of the world see Americans as very energetic or industrious.

T F 6. Work that is intrinsically satisfying is more important to the Dutch than to the Germans.

T F 7. The ability to socialize on the job is not that important to the Dutch.

T F 8. Swedish managers believe it is very important to have on hand precise answers to most subordinate questions.

T F 9. Money is a bigger motivator among Israeli workers than among Japanese workers.

T F 10. British managers are more likely to bypass the hierarchical chain than are French managers.

T F 11. Indian managers have higher power distance than Austrian managers.

T F 12. Japanese managers tend to rely very heavily on intuition.

T F 13. The ability to socialize on the job is important to the Belgians.

T F 14. Spanish managers try to be very aware of other's feelings.

T F 15. Indonesian managers believe that a formal hierarchical structure is very important.

T F 16. British managers have higher uncertainty avoidance than do German managers.

T F 17. Italian managers are more likely to bypass the hierarchical chain than are German managers.

T F 18. Dutch managers tend to be very uncooperative.

T F 19. Japanese managers believe it is very important to have at hand precise answers to most subordinate questions.

T F 20. Mexican managers have a higher masculinity index than do American managers.

Answers

Most respondents get twelve right. If you had fourteen or more correct, your score is above average and if you had sixteen or more correct you are in the top 10 percent of all people who have taken this quiz.

1. T	6. T	11. T	16. F
2. F	7. F	12. F	17. F
3. T	8. F	13. T	18. F
4. T	9. F	14. T	19. T
5. T	10. T	15. T	20. T

NOTES

1. Rae Sedel, "Europe 1992: HR Implications of the European Unification," *Personnel,* October 1989, pp. 19–24.

2. See for example Oded Shenkar and Yoram Zeira, "International Joint Ventures: A Tough Test for HR," *Personnel,* January 1990, pp. 26–31.

3. Jonathan P. Hicks, "The Takeover of American Industry," *New York Times,* May 28, 1989, Section 3, p. 1.

4. Shawn Tully, "Europe Gets Ready for 1992," *Fortune,* February 1, 1988, p. 81.

5. Peter Gulaszka and Rose Brady, "The Chill is Gone, and U.S. Companies are Moscow-Bound," *Business Week,* June 5, 1989, p. 64.

6. John Naisbitt and Patricia Aburdene, *Megatrends 2000: New Directions for the 1990's* (New York: William Morrow & Co., 1990), 178–215.

7. See Richard M. Hodgetts and Fred Luthans, "Japanese HR Management Practices: Separating Fact from Fiction," *Personnel,* April 1989, pp. 42–45; and Sedel, "Europe 1992" pp. 19–24.

8. Indrei Ratiu, "Thinking Internationally," *International Studies in Management and Organization,* Spring–Summer 1983, pp. 139–150.

9. Some of this information can be found in James F. Bolt, "Global Competitors: Some Criteria for Success," *Business Horizons,* January–February 1988, pp. 34–41.

10. Arthur M. Whitehill, "American Executives Through Foreign Eyes," *Business Horizons,* May–June 1989, pp. 43–48.

11. Geert Hofstede and Michael Bond, "The Need for Synergy Among Cross-Cultural Studies," *Journal of Cross-Cultural Psychology,* December 1984, p. 419.

12. Geert Hofstede, *Culture's Consequences: International Differences in Work-Related Values* (Beverly Hills: Sage Publications, 1980), p. 180.

13. *Ibid.*

14. *Ibid.*

15. *Ibid.,* pp. 419–420.

16. *Ibid.,* p. 420.

17. Simcha Ronen and Oded Shenkar, "Clustering Countries on Attitudinal Dimensions: A Review and Synthesis," *Academy of Management Journal,* September 1985, pp. 435–454.

18. *Ibid.,* p. 452.

19. G. Inzerelli and A. Laurent, "The Legitimacy of Managerial Authority—A Comparative Study," paper presented at the annual meeting of the Academy of International Business, 1979.

20. William G. Ouchi, *Theory Z* (New York: Avon Books, 1981), p. 39.

21. H. W. Hildebrandt, "Communication Barriers Between German Subsidiaries and Parent American Companies," *Michigan Business Review,* July 1973, p. 9.

22. John R. Schermerhorn, Jr., "Language Effects in Cross-Cultural Management Research: An Empirical Study and a Word of Caution," *National Academy of Management Proceedings,* 1987, p. 103.

23. George W. England, "Managers and Their Value Systems: A Five-Country Comparative," *Columbia Journal of World Business,* Summer 1978, p. 39.

24. A. Reichel and D. M. Flynn, "Values in Transition: An Empirical Study of Japanese Managers in the U.S.," *Management International Review,* vol. 23, no. 4, 1984, pp. 63–72.

25. *Ibid.,* pp. 69–70.

26. Hermann F. Schwind and Richard B. Peterson, "Shifting Personal Values in the Japanese Management System," *International Studies of Management & Organization,* Summer 1985, pp. 60–74.

27. *Ibid.,* p. 72.

28. George W. England and Jyuji Misumi, "Work Centrality in Japan and the United States," *Journal of Cross-Cultural Psychology,* December 1986, pp. 399–416.

29. *Ibid.*, p. 412.

30. Joseph M. Putti, H. Jack Shapiro, and Loo Boon Kang, "Intrinsic and Extrinsic Work Values in the Asian Subsidiaries of a Japanese Company," *National Academy of Management Proceedings,* 1984, pp. 105–109.

31. See Rabindra N. Kanungo and Richard W. Wright, "A Cross-Cultural Comparison Study of Managerial Job Attitudes," *Journal of International Business Studies,* Fall 1983, pp. 115–129; Theodore A. Chandler, Deborah D. Shama, and Fredric M. Wolf, "Gender Differences in Achievement and Affiliation Attributions: A Five Nation Study," *Journal of Cross-Cultural Psychology,* June 1983, pp. 241–256; and Peter D. Machungwa and Neal Schmitt, "Work Motivation in a Development Country," *Journal of Applied Psychology,* June 1983, pp. 31–42.

32. Tomasz Mroczkowski and Masao Hanaoka, "Continuity and Change in Japanese Management," *California Management Review,* Winter 1989, pp. 39–53.

33. A. R. Negandhi and S. B. Prasad, *Comparative Management* (New York: Appleton-Century-Crofts, 1971), p. 128.

34. L. L. Cummings, D. L. Hartnett, and O. J. Stevens, "Risk, Fate, Conciliation and Trust: An International Study of Attitudinal Differences Among Executives," *Academy of Management Journal,* September 1971, p. 293.

35. Laxmi Nakarmi and William J. Holstein, "Korea's New Corporate Bosses: Made in America," *Business Week,* February 23, 1987, pp. 58–59.

36. Fred E. Fiedler, Terence Mitchell, and Harry C. Triandis, "The Culture Assimilator: An Approach to Cross-Cultural Training," *Journal of Applied Psychology,* April 1971, p. 95.

37. *Ibid.*, p. 102.

38. For more on this topic see Robert C. Maddox and Douglas Short, "The Cultural Integrator," *Business Horizons,* November–December 1988, pp. 57–59.

39. Richard M. Hodgetts and Fred Luthans, *International Management* (New York: McGraw-Hill Book Co., 1991), pp. 419–420.

CHAPTER 19
Career Planning and Development

GOALS OF THE CHAPTER

Career planning and development is one of the latest steps that organizations have undertaken to improve organizational behavior and performance. This trend is important for two reasons. First, a growing shortage of managerial talent is making it critical for organizations to maintain and develop their human resources. Second, by allowing personnel to plan and heavily control their career progress, enterprises are able to motivate their people to remain with the firm. The goals of this chapter are to introduce the concept of career planning and to present some of the programs that firms are developing to assist with career development. When you have finished reading this chapter, you should have a solid understanding of the current status of this area. You should also:

1. understand the reasons why both individuals and organizations are concerned with career development;

2. be aware of how individuals make career choices;

3. know the four career stages through which most individuals progress;

4. know the benefits that can accrue from career planning;

5. be able to describe some of the most common career development programs, including career pathing, mentoring, universal programs, and preretirement programs.

OPENING CASE: GETTING READY

Although he has worked twenty hours a week during his college career, Mark Segrine has been able to carry a full-time course load and will receive his accounting degree in June. In the interim, Mark is planning on signing up for a host of interviews at the university placement service. He would like to interview with a number of large accounting firms. Mark also wants to talk to a couple of smaller accounting firms that will be visiting the campus because these companies often offer the opportunity for people to enter their consulting business. "I think an accountant can be a good consultant as well," he recently told one of his friends. "After all, a lot of strategy is based on financial projections and analyses, and an accountant knows a lot about this."

However, Mark has not decided on a career course. He is just thinking out loud. Most accounting firms, he knows, require their people to per-form well if they hope to remain with the company past the first five years. This is why many of them hire large numbers of new graduates. Both business growth and employee turn-over create a large number of vacancies industry-wide. So it is highly likely that Mark will have to dig in, work hard, and prove himself if he hopes to succeed at any of the accounting firms.

As a result, he has decided to do a little research of his own and find out the type of career path that he is likely to encounter, regardless of the firm for which he works. "I know that career progress will be heavily influenced by the type of organization I choose," he told his father. "However, there must be general career patterns during which specific things happen, such as promotions come quickly or they slow up and are tough to get. So if I know what to expect, I think this puts me in a better position to start off fast and get a jump on the other new people who are coming in at the same time I am. This career stage investigation is going to be part of my preparation for interviews, and I think it's really going to pay off."

1. After completing his interviews, what does Mark need to do to decide which offer to take? Explain.
2. During the first couple of years on the job, what career stage will Mark be in? What does he need to know about this career stage?
3. If Mark were to make a career self-assessment at the end of his second year with a firm, how would he go about doing it? Explain.
4. What type of career development programs would be of most value to Mark during his early career? Identify and briefly describe two.

Write down your answers to these questions and put them aside. We will return to them later.

THE CAREER CONCEPT

A **career** is a series of work-related positions that a person holds during his or her lifetime. Since most people work for a living, career planning and development is important to them, although this importance will vary and is typically a function of both individual and organizational concerns.[1]

Individual Concern

Career concern is an important issue for many individuals, especially those who are upwardly mobile and hope to attain high managerial positions. Two major issues for these people are: How can they improve their chances of promotability? What should they do if they find themselves sidetracked?

Over the last five years many successful managers have found themselves pushed out of jobs because their organizations have been cutting back middle and upper-middle management positions. People making $60,000 to $120,000 have been finding themselves unemployed, and the demand for their services is quite limited.[2] Others have found that their technical jobs (research and development, design, etc.) have left them sidetracked while others who hold line jobs (sales, production) have been promoted into the upper ranks.[3] These developments help explain why many individuals are becoming increasingly interested in career development.[4] Figure 19–1 provides an example of a generic career management approach that is used by individuals in planning their career.

Organizational Concern

Organizations are becoming concerned with career planning management for two reasons. First, there is a growing labor shortage in the United States, and it is going to get worse by the turn of the century. Unless organizations are able to develop and maintain highly skilled pools of talent, they are going to pay dearly for new talent in the open market. Career planning and development can help them sidestep this problem.

Second, as the needs of the enterprise change, the focus of the personnel will also have to change. The abilities and talents needed to do today's jobs are unlikely to be the same that will be required in the year 2000. So career planning must include training and development, and this overall plan must be understood and agreed to by the personnel. In this way enterprises can ensure that there is a match between their needs and the employees' abilities.[5] This will be no small challenge during the decade of the 1990s, especially when successful managers and other skilled workers find their services in demand by competitors. This overall career planning process actually begins with individual career choices.

CAREER CHOICES

Researchers have long been interested in the way an individual chooses one career option over another. While a number of conclusions have been forthcoming, there have been three common findings. First, career decision making does not start in college; the process takes place much earlier in life and often extends over several years. Second,

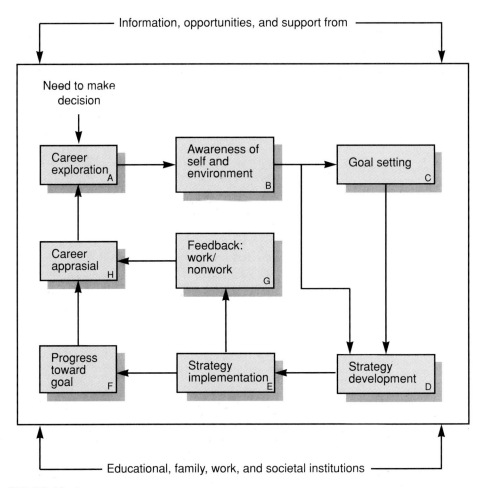

FIGURE 19–1

A Model for Career Management (Source: "A Model for Career Management" from *Career Management* by Jeffrey Greenhaus, copyright © 1987 by The Dryden Press, a division of Holt, Rinehart and Winston, Inc., reprinted by permission of the publisher.

people look for a "fit" between their needs and abilities and the opportunities and demands of different careers. Third, as individuals get older and come closer to making an occupational choice, they also become increasingly aware of the specific challenges and hurdles associated with a career and begin weighing both the likelihood of gaining entry into an occupation and the chance of achieving success in that type of work.[6]

Occupational Choice

There are three stages of career choice.

There are three stages of career choice. Before the age of eleven many people day-dream about a variety of different jobs such as police officer, airplane pilot, and teacher. The primary focus of attention is on what it is like to be an adult. Between the ages of eleven and sixteen people engage in realistic tentative career planning. They think about their interests, their talents, and their personal values and how they can mesh all of these in a work-related setting. The third career stage begins around the age of seventeen as individuals begin to more sharply focus their preferences. This eventually results in a final choice or set of choices from which a decision is made.

Perhaps the best-known research on career choice is that by Holland, who has identified six personality types.[7] Research on Holland's model (see Table 19–1) suggests that people in each personality type do indeed gravitate to a small set of jobs.[8] They do so because they seek work that is consistent with their likes and dislikes. Follow-up research on Holland's model also reveals that when people choose a career consistent with their personality they are more likely to be satisfied with their choice and not change professions.[9]

Organizational Choices

Once an individual has made a career choice, the next step is finding a job. Who is hiring people for these positions? What specific demands will the enterprise put on these new hires?

TABLE 19–1
Holland's Model of Vocational Choice

Personality Types	Occupational Environment
1. *Realistic:* Involves use of tools and machines, physical activity requiring skill, strength, and coordination	Forestry, farming, architecture, police work, carpentry
2. *Investigative:* Involves observing, organizing, and understanding data. Dislikes social and persuasive activities.	Biology, mathematics, oceanography, engineering, geology, dentistry
3. *Social:* Involves interpersonal rather than intellectual or physical activities. Enjoys informing, training, and enlightening others.	Clinical psychology, clergy, education, foreign service, social work
4. *Conventional:* Involves structured, rule-regulated activities and subordination of personal needs to an organization or person of power and status. Enjoys ordered, systematic activities.	Accounting, finance, bookkeeping, secretarial and clerical work, military
5. *Enterprising:* Involves verbal activities to influence others, to attain power and status. Enjoys activity rather than observation.	Management, law, publishing, labor relations, sales
6. *Artistic:* Involves self-expression, artistic creation, expression of emotions, and individual activities. Dislikes repetitive, ordered activities.	Art, music, drama, advertising, interior design

Reprinted from John L. Holland, *Making Vocational Choices: A Theory of Careers* (Englewood Cliffs, N.J.: Prentice-Hall, 1973), pp. 112–117.

Information on job opportunities must be obtained.

The first step in this process is gaining information on job opportunities. This often is resolved by using the services of the college placement office, private employment firms, or employment service organizations. Additional sources include family, friends, acquaintances, former and current employees, and the help-wanted section of newspapers. Without such sources of information, individuals would be unaware of available opportunities.

Organization demands must be in harmony with individual needs.

The second step is ensuring that the organization's demands are in harmony with individual needs. For example, some jobs require people to relocate to other sections of the country, and this is not always acceptable either to new job applicants or to veteran employees.[10] Factors such as salary, advancement opportunity, and life style will all influence the final decision. This is true both for those seeking their first job as well as for experienced employees who are considering job changes.

Before continuing, review your answers to Question 1 and make any changes you would like before continuing.

1. After completing his interviews, what does Mark need to do to decide which offer to take? Explain.

Mark needs to ensure that his personal desires and ambitions match those of the organization. What will the company want him to do? What types of opportunities and challenges will he face? Are these in line with his own values and aspirations? By comparing job opportunities and personal ambitions, Mark can ensure that the "match" will be a good one.

CAREER STAGES

Individuals who work for a living typically find that their career has a number of stages. A **career stage** is a time period in an individual's work life during which the person faces predictable career tasks and psychological issues. For example, in what is often

In the pre-career stage the individual seeks the appropriate education.

called a **pre-career stage** it is typical to find individuals looking for a career and seeking the education that is appropriate for this work. The psychological issues the person confronts during this time period often include: (a) discovering their own needs and interests; and (b) developing a realistic self-assessment of their abilities.[11] This process helps them make an initial career choice, but if things do not work out the process may be repeated later in their career as they seek to change jobs or careers.

There is no universal agreement regarding the number of career stages. Some people opt for as few as three,[12] while others suggest that there are twice this number.[13] The following discusses four of the most commonly accepted: entry, advancement, maintenance, and withdrawal.

Entry

The entry stage is the beginning of the career path.

The **entry stage** is characterized by an individual securing an initial full-time job and beginning progress on a career path. A person faces a number of tasks at this stage, including learning the work routines and adjusting to the demands of the enterprise. Individuals who successfully move through this stage of their career are characterized by high output and the ability to work well with others.[14] As a result, they often are identified as competent and are tabbed for promotion.

Those who are not identified as promotable typically find their careers bogging down and soon find themselves unable to catch up with their faster-moving peers. However, this does not mean that rapid promotion is always good for one's career, especially if the person starts out as a supervisor or other type of manager. McEnrue has found a strong, positive relationship between the length of job experience among early-career managers and their performance. Those who stayed in their initial position for a longer time were more effective[15] because they gained valuable early managerial experience and were not moved up before they were prepared to assume the responsibilities of the next position. Such a strategy also prevented them from making errors and having their upward progress sidetracked due to poor performance.

During this time period, it is often likely that the employee will find a mentor. A **mentor** is an individual who provides advice and assistance to a younger, junior member of the organization and who acts as a counselor and sponsor for the person.[16] In some organizations mentors are formally assigned; in others, individuals voluntarily assume these roles.

> A mentor provides advice and assistance.

Advancement

The **advancement stage** is typically characterized by promotions, transfers, and the opportunity to use one's abilities in assuming responsibility and getting things done. Performance feedback is critical during this stage and typically determines whether the person will continue being promoted or eventually will be sidetracked.

> Most people begin to specialize during this stage.

Most people begin to specialize during this stage and become identified with one particular functional area. For example, a young person with a liberal arts degree might start out as a management trainee but eventually end up in the sales department. During the advancement stage, this person will become a sales supervisor or regional manager and begin making his or her way up the line in sales. Specialization is particularly important because it helps management identify the person's expertise, and it often dictates how quickly the person will be promoted. For example, in some companies individuals with sales experience are promoted fastest because the company is sales-driven and top managers come from the sales group. Apple Computer where John Sculley, a marketing person, heads the firm, is a good example. In other firms individuals in finance or accounting have the best opportunities for top-level management because the company has found that these people provide the best overall leadership. Most major banks follow this pattern of promotion.

> This stage is also characterized by job hopping.

The advancement career stage is also characterized by job hopping. Outstanding performers often find themselves being contacted by other firms or by executive recruiters who want to hire them away. Those who stay typically are promoted and may end up moving to other geographic locales as the firm attempts to balance its needs for personnel with the demands of its various offices and departments.

At the same time many people find themselves being tied more closely to the organization and unable to leave. This is particularly true for those making large salaries or having lucrative benefit packages (company car, country club membership, stock options, deferred compensation plan) that they cannot get elsewhere. These people will remain with the company indefinitely. This is often viewed positively at this stage of their career because they are doing so much better than their counterparts in other companies. On the other hand, if their career progress eventually levels off they may find themselves unable to go anywhere else or unable to find a similar compensation package if the company lets them go. Some of the benefits of advancement can become drawbacks later on if the person's career begins to plateau.

Relationships with peers also become important during this career stage. Mentors start playing less of a role because the person is on the way up. Peers become the reference group and provide support, guidance, and encouragement to the individual.[17] Work and personal life also become intertwined during this time period. Longer hours, more travel, and the likelihood of relocation all influence family life. For many, however, this is simply regarded as part of the price that must be paid for success.

Maintenance

The **maintenance stage** is characterized by a reassessment of one's progress followed by adjustments to changing demands. This stage often takes place during one's late 30s or early 40s and can result either in further advancement or a leveling off of career progress. This will depend on whether the individual is deemed to be a star, solid citizen, or deadwood.

A **star** is a person who has been identified as top management timber and is given greater promotions and responsibility. Typical examples include special assignments designed to provide the person experience in areas that will be important to his or her career growth. Sometimes these assignments are within the firm; other times they require the individual to work with clients and customers or to interface with governmental agencies.

Solid citizens are individuals who are hard working and reliable, but who have little chance for further promotion. There are a number of reasons for this,[18] including: (a) the individuals have inappropriate skills and abilities; (b) they lack motivation; (c) they have suffered excessive stress or burnout; (d) they feel that the rewards associated with higher positions are not commensurate with the responsibilities; (e) they are happy in their current position and do not want any further promotions; and (f) the company has encountered slow growth and their promotional opportunities have been affected. Regardless of the reason, these individuals have reached a **career plateau,** which is a point at which the likelihood of further hierarchical promotion is very low and, for many, represents the final career step.[19]

The career plateau has been the focus of much interest in recent years because of the effects that it can have on personnel morale and behavior.[20] For example, Stout and his associates have found that employees who become organizationally plateaued view themselves as less marketable and have lower commitment to their organization.[21] Many of them believe that their best hope lies in moving to another firm. Moreover, the plateau is not always a result of individual performance; sometimes it is caused by industry conditions. For example, Slocum and his associates have found that firms in mature industries with established product lines and little growth potential have a higher

A star is regarded as top management timber.

A solid citizen is hard working and reliable, but has little chance for promotion.

incidence of plateaued employees than those firms that are able to add new products in high growth segments of the market.[22]

Organizations can take a number of steps in dealing with plateauing.

What can be done to prevent plateauing? If it does occur, how should it be managed? These two questions have been of great interest to researchers. Felmand and Weltz have proposed a series of different managerial interventions that can be used, including training, use of rewards, job enrichment, and reassignment of personnel (see Figure 19–2). Others have offered additional suggestions including:

1. Letting the employees know the facts about plateauing.
2. Trying to eliminate plateauing by moving people to other jobs in the organization (lateral promotions).
3. Using nonmonetary rewards for plateaued people, including recognition programs for those who do their jobs well.
4. Giving honest performance appraisal feedback so people know if their careers are plateauing.
5. Not placing nonplateaued employees in jobs where there is little likelihood for advancement or promotion.[23]
6. Creating a climate in which it is all right to seek help with personal problems.
7. Giving plateaued individuals the opportunity to do independent and challenging work.
8. Encouraging plateaued people to create new initiatives at work and rely on themselves, not the organization, to improve their lives.[24]

Individuals who have been identified as having little potential for advancement and whose performance has fallen to an unsatisfactory level are known as **deadwood**.[25] These people are often in less important jobs, are no longer given challenging assignments, and are accorded minimal salary raises. Some are simply hanging on until retirement, although many will leave the organization and find jobs elsewhere long before this time.

Deadwood have little potential for advancement.

Veiga has found that those who fit into this deadwood category are often identifiable fairly early in their careers, and they are passed over for promotion. Many of them see what is happening and change companies.[26] As a result, sometimes it is difficult to know if someone is a star or deadwood based solely on their willingness to change firms since both groups are mobile, albeit for different reasons. It also is important to remember that a person who is deadwood in one organization may be a star in another where new work opportunities and organizational climate are more conducive to the individual's personality and performance. Similarly, early promotions do not always signal a successful career. Some people initially succeed and then plateau or become deadwood.[27]

Withdrawal

The **withdrawal stage** is a career stage in which the individual faces retirement or other end-of-career options. This often happens when people are in their late 50s or

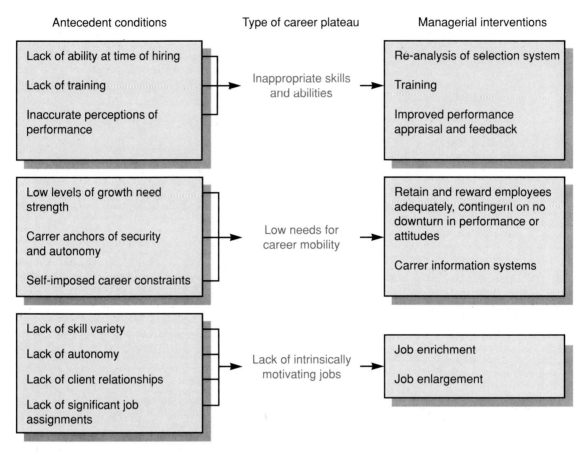

FIGURE 19–2
Career Plateaus in Organizations (From *Managing Careers in Organizations* by Daniel C. Feld-man, pp. 138–139. Copyright © 1988 by Scott, Foresman and Co. Reprinted by permission of HarperCollins, Publishers.)

In the withdrawal stage the individual faces retirement or other end-of-career options.

early 60s. This stage can be a positive, rewarding one for individuals because it allows them to play a more active mentoring role, offer assistance and guidance to their replacement and other managers, and mentally prepare themselves for retirement. Moreover, in some cases individuals do not retire but go on to other jobs that allow them to continue using their abilities and talents. However, for some this stage is difficult to accept, and they suffer severe loss of self-esteem. In an effort to deal with these problems and other career-related issues, many organizations are now focusing attention on career planning that covers the gamut, from the entry stage to the with-drawal stage.

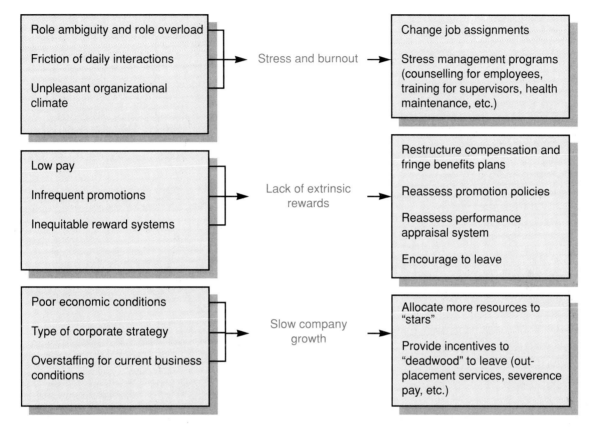

FIGURE 19–2
continued

 STOP

Before continuing, review your answers to Question 2 and make any changes you would like before continuing.

2. During the first couple of years on the job, what career stage will Mark be in? What does he need to know about this career stage?

Mark will be in the entry stage. During this time he will be learning the work routines and adjusting to the demands of the enterprise. He needs to quickly learn his job and to gain as much experience as possible. He should also try to be an outstanding performer because this will help tab him as a potential star. Finally, he should consider getting a mentor who can help him improve his chances for advancement.

CAREER PLANNING

Career planning is the process of identifying personal interests, abilities, and work goals and then making decisions regarding a career path. This process has become extremely important in recent years as organizations seek to develop integrated human resource systems that ensure they will have the necessary personnel for operating their enterprise today and in the future.[28] Figure 19–3 provides one illustration of how this process works. Notice from the bottom of the figure that career planning is critical to

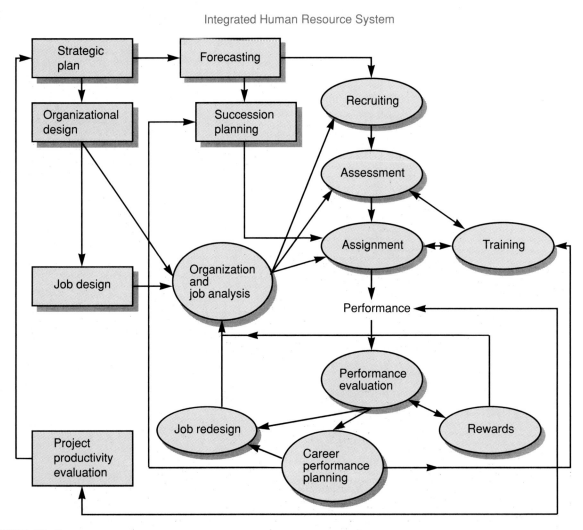

Integrated Human Resource System

FIGURE 19–3

Integrated Human Resource System (Source: Mary Ann von Glinow, Michael J. Driver, Kenneth Brousseau, and J. Bryce Prince, "The Design of a Career Oriented Human Resource System," *Academy of Management Review,* January 1983, p. 26.)

the entire operation because it generates information useful for both training and succession planning.

Benefits

A number of benefits can accrue from career planning.

A number of benefits can accrue from career planning. These include: (a) helping improve the quality of working life by providing employees with information regarding job options and strategies; (b) helping attract talented personnel who see the organization as interested in helping them attain their career aspirations; (c) helping people anticipate work-related changes and identify new skills that will have to be developed in order to succeed in the future; (d) creating job satisfaction and reducing absenteeism and turnover;[29] (e) helping organizations meet the need to provide increased opportunities for women and minorities; (f) improving the overall abilities and talents of personnel by assisting those in dead-end or no-growth jobs to move into areas more in line with their talents and ambitions; (g) increasing the chances of attracting topnotch personnel;[30] and (h) improving profits and productivity.[31] While organizations use a number of approaches to help their personnel with career planning, many of these begin with self-appraisal.

Self-Appraisal

Self-appraisal is a systematic process of generating data about oneself and analyzing the information to determine career and life decisions. This information provides a basis for making career decisions such as: (a) jobs and positions to seek or to avoid; (b) strategies to use in getting a particular job; (c) selecting a job from among a series of job offers; (d) making decisions related to assignments, transfers, and location changes; and (e) determining a sequence of job moves in attaining a desired position.[32] There typically are seven steps in this process.

There are seven steps in career self-assessment.

1. Generate personal information without evaluating it.
2. Generate information from multiple methods and sources regardless of redundancy; i.e., quantity is more important than quality.
3. Examine all the data and determine what it means in relation to career planning.
4. Organize the information into identity statements or comments such as: Freedom to do the job my own way is important to me. I have a high need to achieve. I like challenges.
5. Assess the accuracy and importance of the identity statements.
6. Cluster identity statements by putting them into groups based on common characteristics such as: desire for control, need for security, importance of social interaction, and desire to accomplish things.
7. Draw implications for career decision making.[33]

These steps are typically carried out as part of a formal organizational career development program. No matter what career direction the individual chooses, self-appraisal is a critical foundation because it provides a basis for goal setting,[34] and it focuses the ultimate responsibility for career success on the employee.[35]

Before continuing, review your answers to Question 3 and make any changes you would like before continuing.

3. If Mark were to make a career self-assessment at the end of his second year with a firm, how would he go about doing it? Explain.

Mark would have to generate data about himself and then analyze the information for the purpose of determining career and life decisions. This information could be grouped into identity statements and then used as a basis for decisions in a host of specific areas, including the desire to accomplish things, the need for social interaction, the desire for control, etc.

ORGANIZATIONAL CAREER DEVELOPMENT PROGRAMS

There are many different types of career development programs,[36] and most are continually undergoing change in order to remain viable.[37] Examples include career pathing, mentoring, universal programs, career planning for high-potential managers, dual track programs, and preretirement programs. ("Organizational Behavior in Action: Some Formal Programs" provides examples of what Coca-Cola and IBM are doing along these lines.)

Career Pathing

Career pathing is the process of identifying job assignment sequences by which a person can get from one position to another. These paths have often existed in organizations if only on an informal basis.[38] Today, however, the process is becoming formal and is used to help individuals develop a detailed plan of action.[39] Some organizations have even developed career path-based forecasts that allow them to link their human resource demand needs with their internal work force and thus determine who will be promoted or transferred in the future as vacancies become available.[40]

There are three basic steps in career pathing. First, the subordinate is given feedback on his or her major strengths and weaknesses. This serves as a basis for discussing a career path.

Second, the individual is given feedback on the level of performance that will be rewarded and what the rewards are likely to be. This helps the person evaluate the abilities and drive that will be required for a particular career path and the rewards that are available for doing a good job.

Third, the subordinate is apprised of the types of training and development needed to meet the different job demands along the career path. Primary attention is focused on the next step along the path. At Sears Roebuck, for example, a formal job progression plan has been developed. As a person examines possible job moves, the requirements for the position are spelled out. Changes in technical, managerial, and

There are three basic steps in career pathing.

SOME FORMAL PROGRAMS

In recent years a number of organizations have begun creating formal career management programs. Coca-Cola and IBM are examples.

Coca-Cola's objective is to help people attain their career goals through a carefully designed program. Every employee is given the opportunity to complete a career interest form on an annual basis. This form is then used by the individual and his or her manager to discuss an overall plan of action and to make the organization aware of the employee's career goals. Among others, the form is sent to the human resource department so that the latter know who is interested in what types of jobs. The ultimate responsibility for career planning is left with the employee, but the company tries to keep the individual apprised of new job openings and career opportunities. This is done in a number of different ways including: (a) *Newsmakers,* a monthly publication that lists the number and kinds of internal career moves taking place within the company; (b) job posting of lower and mid-level management openings; and (c) career opportunity booklets that provide a broad overview of each department as well as the specific qualifications for typical positions.

IBM's approach is even more detailed. The company offers a career workshop that helps employees develop a plan that they can review with their boss and can then use as a guide in directing their own careers. During the workshop the personnel carry out a self-assessment, make career decisions regarding what they would like to do, and develop a plan of action for reaching these goals.

IBM reports that after attending this workshop, 80 percent of the participants say that they feel they have control over their own career development, and 81 percent felt that their opportunity to move into a better job in the company has improved. Clearly the program is accomplishing its objectives.

Sources: Lynn Slavenski, "Career Development: A Systems Approach," *Training and Development Journal,* February 1987, pp. 56–60; and Carolyn A. Bardsley, "Improving Employee Awareness of Opportunity at IBM," *Personnel,* April 1987, pp. 58–63.

human relations skills are identified and serve as the basis for the necessary training and development. Other firms have similar approaches.

Mentoring

Mentoring can be very important in helping develop organizational talent. Research shows that many individuals find that a mentor is extremely important in helping them get ahead. For example, one study of twenty-five successful female managers found that almost all of them had used men as role models, and they often credited their male mentors with the encouragement and training they needed to rise to upper management.[41] Another study of 520 executives found that the mentor relationship increased the self-confidence of protégés as they advanced to more responsible positions.[42] This undoubtedly helps explain why organizations such as Bell Laboratories, Johnson & Johnson, Merrill Lynch, and NCR[43] are requiring their managers to also be career coaches.[44]

Mentors can perform many important functions for those they are helping.[45] Some of the primary ones include:

Mentors perform many important functions.

- Teaching—mentors provide instruction in specific skills and knowledge necessary for successful job performance.

- Guiding—mentors help those they are advising to understand the unwritten rules of the organization and how to avoid saying or doing the wrong things.

- Advising—mentors answer important questions and provide insights that the average manager is unable to offer.

- Counseling—mentors provide emotional support during stressful times by listening to concerns and communicating an empathetic understanding of these concerns.

- Role modeling—mentors serve as role models.

- Validating—mentors evaluate, sometimes modify, and endorse the goals and aspirations of those whom they are mentoring.

- Motivating—mentors help those they are advising believe in their own goals, and they provide the encouragement and impetus to these people to act toward achieving these goals.

- Protecting—mentors serve as a buffer for those whom they are advising so that the latter can make mistakes without losing self-confidence.

- Communicating—mentors establish open lines of communication through which the concerns of those they are helping can be discussed clearly and effectively.[46]

Over the last decade, mentoring has become so useful in developing personnel talent that more and more organizations are now making it a formal part of their operations.[47]

Universal Programs

There are many different types of universal programs.

Universal programs are designed to provide participants with insights to themselves, a knowledge of opportunities available to them, and an understanding of the actions they now can take in availing themselves of these opportunities. There are many types of universal programs sponsored by a wide variety of firms including AT&T, Corning Glass, Exxon, the 3M Company, and RCA, to name but five. The following programs are sponsored by still others.

Polaroid's Career Development Series. The objective of Polaroid's career development series is to address organizational and career planning concerns. The program consists of four workshops. The first focuses on self-assessment, the next two deal with building skills, and the last concentrates on gathering information about Polaroid job opportunities and how to best use the company's job posting and education systems. The career development series often results in additional training and development for the participants and also helps establish more systematic staffing decisions via the firm's posting system.

General Electric's Career Dimensions Program. General Electric (GE) has a career development program called "Career Dimensions." The program relies on four workbooks. The first two are self-directed and are designed for use by employees. The third is a how-to-do-it guide for managers to use in coaching employees regarding their careers and for dealing with difficult career questions raised by subordinates. The fourth handbook is for professionals in human resource management to use in implementing career planning programs. W. D. Storey reports that the results of the GE program have been very good. "Experienced benefits for the business have included improved fitting of jobs to people, higher quality of data for manpower reviews, development of a framework for affirmative action, and allocation of scarce dollars for employee education."[48]

Bell Of Pennsylvania's Program. This four-unit program is designed for managers in low and middle management positions. The participants' supervisors are offered a one-day workshop to help them participate in discussions with their subordinates. The first unit is a self-assessment workbook containing exercises designed to help the individual identify personal values, evaluate training and development experiences, and relate these to general skills. Other exercises in the workbook require the individual to assess his or her managerial potential, identify career goals, and set up a reasonable schedule for attaining these objectives.

The second unit focuses on career exploration and requires the participant to clarify career goals and, using company-provided information, potential opportunities. The third unit is devoted to a personal development plan that helps the individuals prepare for a career development discussion with their supervisors. During this unit the participants prepare a preliminary work action plan, summarize their talents, and list plans for developmental experiences such as the types of job assignments they would like to have. The last unit calls for the formulation of a five-year personal development plan and a corresponding work preference document. This information is put into the company's personnel data base for use in job matching when vacancies occur.

Typical Programs. The preceding represent typical universal programs.[49] Table 19–2 draws together their major elements. Notice that there are seven basic phases, although these can be reduced to three primary ones: initial self-assessment and goal setting, planning of a course of action, and followup and monitoring of the plan.[50] All universal programs incorporate these three.

Career Planning for High-Potential Managers

Some firms offer career planning programs for high-potential managers.

Some firms also offer career planning programs for those designated as having high managerial potential. The initial approach used in selecting and developing these employees typically consists of: (a) an initial evaluation by recruiters of job applicants; and (b) a performance evaluation by supervisors of their subordinates. During this phase, management seeks to identify new employees who are management timber as well as current personnel who can be promoted into the management ranks. These people are

TABLE 19-2
Overall Design for a Universal Career Planning Program

Phase	Activities	Time Frame
I	Self-assessment testing, feedback from friends and peers regarding participant's skills values, strong points, weak points, etc.	One week before the program begins plus one full workshop day.
II	Carrying out skill assessment exercises and setting career goals.	One (maybe two) workshop days.
III	Integration of all information gathered thus far into an initial career and life planning exercise.	One workshop day.
IV	Skill building in areas such as interviewing, resume writing, exploring career opportunities.	One (maybe two) workshop days.
V	Development of a career plan of action along with work preferences.	One workshop day.
VI	Sharing relevant information with supervisors, peers, and family and an identification of career actions.	Immediately following the workshop and from time to time thereafter.
VII	Follow-up and review of career progress with an eye toward identifying necessary changes and modifications.	Once every 2-3 months.

then placed into an initial high-potential manager program. In this program, which usually lasts one to two years, they receive orientation, training, and special assignments designed to develop their management talent. Their performance is then evaluated and, on the basis of the evaluation, the best performers are designated for an accelerated program. Those who are not designated enter regular career paths.

The accelerated program is more challenging than the previous one, although the basic process is similar. After meeting with the superior to jointly set targets and goals, the individual is given critical job assignments followed by periodic evaluations. The latter are used to screen out those who do not do well. The remainder are designated as promotable and put on a list of those to be considered for the next available opening. In some cases the individual is designated for one particular job, but in most cases the person is assigned based on his or her place on the list and when an opening becomes available it goes to the individual.

Dual-Track Plans

Some firms have developed dual career tracks.

Some organizations have developed **dual career tracks** that allow a person to remain in his or her present track or switch to another one. This dual approach is more common in enterprises with salaried professionals who want to advance in their company but not by becoming managers. Employees in research and development (R&D) laboratories, new product engineering departments, and legal departments often benefit from the dual-ladder approach. This helps explain their popularity in the chemical, electronics, insurance, pharmaceutical, and petroleum industries. Firms such as Aetna Life and Casualty, IBM, Mobil Oil, Texas Instruments, Union Carbide, and Westinghouse have all successfully introduced dual ladders for their scientific and engineering professionals.

The two-track career plan gives the employee an opportunity to decide whether he or she wants to remain in a professional capacity or become a manager. This decision is generally made after the person has received two or three promotions and is well along the career path. Figure 19–4 provides an example of a dual career track. Once the individual has reached the rank of senior engineer, the individual decides whether he or she wants to become a department head or an engineering associate.

Whatever the person's choice, the salary and benefits at that level of the structure are similar because the organization wants to encourage both professional and managerial development, and to pay one more than the other would result in the lower-paid track being less attractive. In truth, this is where many organizations run into problems.

FIGURE 19–4
A Dual Career Ladder in the Engineering Department (One Example)

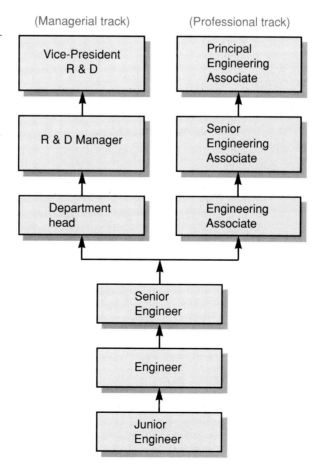

They find that the vice-president of R&D can command a higher salary in the market-place than the principal engineering associate. See Figure 19–4 as an illustration. As a result, they pay the R&D manager more money. An additional problem with dual career tracks is that hard feelings often develop between the two groups. Those who leave the professional track to become managers are seen as only marginally qualified. On the other hand, those who move onto a managerial track often regard the professionals as prima donnas who lack the ability to work well with people and make difficult, strategic decisions.

At the present time, only limited use is being made of dual career tracks. However, as the number of professionals in organizations grows, there will be greater attention given to the benefit of this career development approach. Additionally, while the petty jealousies between the two groups will have to be overcome, many organizations feel this is a small price to pay for providing career opportunities to two important groups in the hierarchy.[51]

Preretirement Programs

In recent years an increasing number of firms have developed preretirement programs. The objective of these programs is to help employees close out their careers with a future-oriented plan of action.[52] Siegel found that in 1977 only 29 percent of *Fortune* 500 firms had preretirement programs. By 1984 this had risen to 51 percent, and, based on survey responses, he predicted that over 75 percent would have them by the early 1990s.[53]

Some firms set minimum age eligibility for employee participation. This usually ranges between fifty-five and sixty years of age, although some companies allow eligibility as early as fifty. In recent years, because of the elimination of mandatory retirement at sixty-five, many firms have raised the eligibility age for participation in preretirement programs.[54] However, anyone taking early retirement is automatically eligible for the program.

There are a number of different types of program content. The most emphasized element is financial planning.[55] This includes consideration of topics such as social security, pension planning, life insurance conversion, medical/hospital benefits, and the effect of tax regulations. More recently, other areas of concern have been added to these programs, including the mental aspects of retiring, work after retirement, and leisure-time planning. There also is a trend toward supplementing HRD in-house efforts with the use of outside, professionally trained counselors.

If retirement does not work out, some companies offer their retirees a chance to return to work. For example, the Travelers Insurance Company has an Unretired Program. Under this arrangement, retired employees who have tried retirement for six months "can come back and—if they qualify—fill job openings on a part-time basis."[56] At the Walt Disney Company retired employees can return to the company on an as-needed basis.[57]

The format of preretirement programs runs the gamut from lectures to computer disks. Some firms have also developed workbooks to support the program. The Walt Disney Company, for example, uses lectures. Grumman employs a combination workbook and cassette tape package. Others have computerized interactive diskettes that help the participant identify and deal with preretirement issues. However they go about structuring and delivering the preretirement program, companies are beginning to realize that career planning involves all time phases of the employee's career. As Watts has noted:

> Opportunities for older workers continue to broaden. They no longer face a gold watch after 40 years of service directly followed by endless domino games on the front porch. But the new opportunities hinge on looking ahead as realistically as possible. Preretirement planning can show employees what options are available and educate them to make wise choices early to help make their final years a reward, not a burden. [58]

STOP Before continuing, review your answers to Question 4 and make any changes you would like before continuing.

4. What type of career development programs would be of most value to Mark during his early career? Identify and briefly describe two.

Since Mark is in the early stages of his career, he would benefit most from programs designed to help him get his career off the ground. Career pathing would be useful. With this program, he and his boss would determine the next couple of positions Mark could hold as he makes his way up the ladder. Mentoring would be useful because it would provide him an advisor and counselor who could help him make important career choices and understand some of the things to do and to avoid doing. A third is a universal program that could help Mark put together an overall plan of action.

SUMMARY

1. A career is a series of work-related positions that a person holds during his or her lifetime. In recent years career concern has been evidenced by both individuals and organizations. Both want more systematic career planning.

2. In choosing a career, most individuals go through three stages, culminating in a sharp focus of preferences. For example, Holland's research shows that people with a particular personality tend to gravitate toward certain types of jobs. Having made a career choice, people then tend to gain information on job opportunities and seek to ensure that there will be a match between their needs and the organization's demands.

3. A career stage is a time during which an individual faces predictable career tasks and psychological issues.

Most people go through four career stages: entry, advancement, maintenance, and withdrawal. During the entry stage the individual masters the job and sometimes finds a mentor. During the advancement stage the person is promoted, transferred, and given the opportunity to use his or her abilities. During the maintenance stage the person may continue rising in the organization, level out, or be phased out. This will depend on whether the individual is a star, a solid citizen, or deadwood. At this stage many people find their career plateauing. The withdrawal stage is a phase during which the individual faces retirement or other end-of-career options.

4. Today many organizations have formal career planning programs. These programs often begin with a self-

appraisal followed by a structured approach which ultimately results in the individual developing a career plan. Some of the most common programs include career pathing, men-toring, universal programs, dual-track programs, and pre-retirement programs. Each of these was described in the chapter.

KEY TERMS

career	maintenance stage	career planning
career stage	star	self-appraisal
pre-career stage	solid citizens	career pathing
entry stage	career plateau	universal programs
mentor	deadwood	dual career tracks
advancement stage	withdrawal stage	

REVIEW AND STUDY QUESTIONS

1. What is meant by the term *career*? Why are individuals concerned with career choice? Why are organizations?

2. There are three stages of career choice for most individuals. What are these three stages? Identify and briefly describe each.

3. "Research suggests that people choose jobs that fit their personality." What does this statement mean? Include a discussion of Table 19–1 in your answer.

4. What are the two steps that individuals take after they have made a career choice? Identify and describe each.

5. In what types of activities does an individual engage during the pre-career stage? Explain.

6. What takes place during a person's entry career stage? What can the individual expect to happen?

7. What happens during a person's advancement career stage? Explain.

8. Who is most likely to continue getting promoted during the maintenance career stage? Who is least likely? Explain.

9. How can organizations help their people deal with the career plateau? Offer five suggestions.

10. When does the withdrawal career stage occur? What happens during this stage?

11. Why is self-appraisal so important to the career planning process?

12. How does career pathing work? Give an example.

13. How useful are mentors for young, career-minded people? Explain.

14. How do universal programs work? Give an example.

15. How do career planning programs for high potential managers work? Give an example.

16. What is a dual career track? Who would be interested in this type of program? Explain.

17. How do preretirement programs work? In what way are they beneficial to organizational personnel?

CASES

Moving Up

For the past two years Natalie Forsyth has been a supervisor at the Concordia Company, a bank holding company. Natalie supervises six employees in the check-clearing department and has continually received excellent ratings from her boss. The general pattern of promotion in the company is that supervisors are promoted every three years, on av-erage, if they are considered stars. Those who are considered solid citizens usually end up staying where they are. Deadwood are let go as soon as possible.

Natalie is certain that she will be promoted within the next twelve months, and she would like to discuss this possibility with her boss. She would also like to get an idea of the path she might take in reaching a middle management position over the next five years. She knows that most people are promoted to group head, and then on to senior supervisor before getting a department head job. She also knows that after reaching the middle ranks, most people's careers slow down. The average department head has been in this position for eight years. This is why the turnover rate at this level is so high. Each year many department heads are passed over for promotion, and they leave the firm. These vacancies are filled through both in-house promotions and outside hiring. Those who are promoted from within usually have a sponsor or mentor who goes to bat for them and helps get their name past the promotion committee. The rest of the vacancies are filled with new college recruits from master's programs.

The promotion pattern at Concordia, in Natalie's view, is somewhat unpredictable, and she believes that it will be very difficult to get a middle management job if she does not formulate a career plan. Later this week Natalie will be meeting with her boss for the purpose of working out a plan of action. In particular, she would like to talk to him about potential promotions she can expect over the next five years and about some of the in-house promotion and career development programs that she might attend. These programs are offered monthly by the personnel department.

1. Would it be helpful for Natalie to talk to her boss about career pathing? What should the conversation deal with? Explain.

2. If Natalie does not have a mentor, should she get one? Why or why not?

3. What type of career development program would you recommend for Natalie? Defend your answer.

Sheldon's Plans

Sheldon Manning began working for Gifford Products, a large electronics firms, more than thirty-five years ago. He started out as a repairman while he finished his undergraduate degree by attending night school at a nearby university. He was then promoted into the management ranks and eventually ended up as head of their largest production department.

About three years ago Sheldon accepted a special position of advisor to the president of the firm. In this job, Sheldon serves as a member of the board of trustees and helps the firm develop its long-range plans for the next decade. The work is very rewarding, but is quite different from that of line management where he was making operating decisions on a daily basis.

Sheldon is sixty-five years old and has decided that he will retire in five years. In the interim, he would like to, in his words, "make a meaningful contribution to the firm before I leave." In doing so, Sheldon has become a formal mentor for Paul Prentiss, one of the bright up-and-coming middle managers. He enjoys meeting with the young man and offering guidance and assistance. The two have lunch every Tuesday and Friday, in addition to talking on the phone daily. Sheldon believes that this mentor relationship will be very fruitful for Paul and, in the final analysis, will also benefit Gifford.

Sheldon is also interested in making some post-career plans of his own. He has learned the company has hired an outside consulting group to offer a program entitled "Getting Ready for Retirement." The program will be offered every three months, and Sheldon wants to be in the first group. "I've been so busy working, I haven't had time to plan for retirement," he told his wife. "I better start figuring out what I'm going to do with myself five years from now." His wife agreed that this would be a very good idea.

1. What types of assistance is Sheldon offering to Paul? Be complete in your answer.

2. In addition to mentoring, what other steps might Sheldon take to help Paul or other up-and-coming middle managers? Identify and describe two of these steps.

3. What will Sheldon learn in the retirement program that will be offered by the consultants? Why are programs like this proving so beneficial to those in the preretirement stages of their careers? Explain.

SELF-FEEDBACK EXERCISE _____

Early Career Analysis

In deciding the type of career you would like and the kind of job you would enjoy, it is important to make a self-analysis. This analysis can include a number of different avenues of consideration. The following is designed to help you better understand what you would like in a job and how to proceed with a career plan of action.

First, begin your evaluation by identifying the type of job you would like. Then list the types of education, training, and experience that are necessary to get the job.

Job _____

Education and/or training _____

_____

_____

Experience _____

_____

Now identify the basic skills and characteristics that you possess that would be of value in getting this first job. The following should be useful as an initial list, but skip over any that do not apply and add any at the end of the list that you feel are important. Also note any skills and characteristics that you do not possess and should, since this will help you identify areas you need to work on or which can prevent you from getting that desired job. In each case, rank yourself from 1 (excellent) to 5 (poor).

	1	2	3	4	5
1. job knowledge	—	—	—	—	—
2. honesty	—	—	—	—	—
3. confidence	—	—	—	—	—
4. communication skills	—	—	—	—	—
5. trustworthiness	—	—	—	—	—
6. ability to interact well with others	—	—	—	—	—
7. enthusiasm	—	—	—	—	—
8. flexibility	—	—	—	—	—
9. willingness to work hard	—	—	—	—	—
10. ability to solve problems	—	—	—	—	—
11. organizational ability	—	—	—	—	—
12. willingness to follow orders	—	—	—	—	—
13. ability to learn quickly	—	—	—	—	—
14. willingness to study further	—	—	—	—	—
15. high initiative	—	—	—	—	—
16. good listener	—	—	—	—	—
17. empathetic	—	—	—	—	—
18. well-groomed	—	—	—	—	—

19. mature	—	—	—	—	—
20. good judgment	—	—	—	—	—
21.	—	—	—	—	—
22.	—	—	—	—	—
23.	—	—	—	—	—
24.	—	—	—	—	—
25.	—	—	—	—	—

Now identify those factors or characteristics that you are looking for in a job. There are many possibilities, but the list provided below should help you get started. Add any others in the space provided at the bottom. Note those that are of most importance to you and then place them on a pie chart by dividing up the chart appropriately; i.e., if challenging work is more important than anything else, give it a large section of the pie. Use just the number of each in the chart (rather than the full description), so that there is enough room to put in all the important factors. Then note the three factors that are most important to you, since these will be the ones that will have to be provided by the organization and undoubtedly will be the major focal point of any discussions you have with potential employers.

1. money
2. working conditions
3. benefits
4. recognition
5. independence
6. job variety
7. opportunity for advancement
8. challenging work
9. the opportunity to succeed
10. the chance to help others
11. the opportunity for social interaction
12. prestige and/or status

The adjacent pie chart should be very useful to you in deciding what you are looking for in a company. It can be used as a basis for comparing one organization to another in making the employment decision.

NOTES

1. See for example Leah Rosch, "Switching Careers and Getting a Good Reception," *Working Woman,* February 1990, pp. 92ff.

2. Peter Nulty, "Pushed Out at 45—Now What?" *Fortune,* March 2, 1987, pp. 26–34.

3. Aaron Bernstein, Richard W. Anderson, and Wendy Zellner, "Help Wanted," *Business Week,* August 10, 1987, pp. 48–53.

4. Barbara A. Williamson and Fred L. Otte, "Assessing the Need for Career Development," *Training and Development Journal,* March 1986, pp. 59–61; and Zandy B. Leibowitz, Beverly Kaye, and Caela Farren, "Overcoming Management Resistance to Career Development Programs," *Training and Development Journal,* October 1986, pp. 77–81.

5. Cherlyn Skromme Granrose and James D. Protwood, "Matching Individual Career Plans and Organizational Career Management," *Academy of Management Journal,* December 1987, pp. 699–720.

6. Daniel C. Feldman, *Managing Careers in Organizations* (Glenview, IL: Scott, Foresman & Co., 1988), p. 31.

7. John Holland, *Making Vocational Choices: A Theory of Careers* (Englewood Cliffs, NJ: Prentice-Hall, 1973).

8. See David L. Reutefors, Lawrence J. Schneider, and Tom D. Overton, "Academic Achievement: An Examination of Holland's Congruency, Consistency, and Differentiation Predictions," *Journal of Vocational Behavior*, April 1979, pp. 181–189; and J. C. Latack, "Person-Role Conflict: Holland's Model Extended to Role-Stress Research, Stress Management, and Career Development," *Academy of Management Review*, January 1981, pp. 89–103.

9. D. C. Feldman and H. J. Arnold, "Personality Types and Career Patterns: Some Empirical Evidence on Holland's Model," *Canadian Journal of Administrative Sciences*, June 1985, pp. 192–210.

10. Sam Gould and Larry E. Penley, "A Study of the Correlates of the Willingness to Relocate," *Academy of Management Journal*, June 1985, pp. 472–478.

11. Feldman, *Managing Careers in Organizations*, p. 14.

12. Michael K. Mount, "Managerial Career Stage and Facets of Job Satisfaction," *Journal of Vocational Behavior*, June 1984, pp. 340–354; and John Slocum, Jr. and William L. Cron, "Job Attitudes and Performance During Three Career Stages," *Journal of Vocational Behavior*, April 1985, pp. 126–145.

13. Feldman, *Managing Careers in Organizations*, pp. 14–15.

14. Kenneth Oldfield, "Survival of the Newest," *Personnel Journal*, March 1989, pp. 53–59.

15. Mary Pat McEnrue, "Length of Experience and the Performance of Managers in the Establishment Phase of Their Careers," *Academy of Management Journal*, March 1988, p. 181.

16. See Kathy E. Kram, "Mentoring in the Workplace," in Douglas T. Hall and Associates (eds.), *Career Development in Organizations* (San Francisco: Jossey-Bass Publishers, 1987), pp. 161–164.

17. For more on this see Kathy Kram and Lynn A. Isabella, "Mentoring Alternatives: The Role of Peer Relationships in Career Development," *Academy of Management Journal*, March 1985, pp. 110–132.

18. Thomas P. Ference, James A. F. Stoner, and E. Kirby Warren, "Managing the Career Plateau," *Academy of Management Review*, October 1977, pp. 602–612.

19. John W. Slocum, Jr., William L. Cron, Richard W. Hansen, and Sallie Rawlings, "Business Strategy and the Management of Plateaued Employees," *Academy of Management Journal*, March 1985, p. 133.

20. Beverly Kaye, "Are Plateaued Performers Productive?," *Personnel Journal*, August 1989, pp. 57–65.

21. Suzanne K. Stout, John W. Slocum, Jr., and William L. Cron, "Dynamics of the Career Plateauing Process," *Journal of Vocational Behavior*, February 1988, pp. 75–91.

22. Slocum, Cron, Hansen, and Rawlings, "Business Strategy," pp. 133–154.

23. John W. Slocum, William L. Cron, and Linda C. Yows, "Whose Career Is Likely to Plateau?" *Business Horizons*, March–April 1987, pp. 31–38.

24. Judith M. Bardwich, "The Plateauing Trap, Part 2: Setting Employees Free," *Personnel*, November 1986, pp. 35–40.

25. Ference, Stoner, and Warren, "Managing the Career Plateau," p. 604.

26. John F. Veiga, "Plateaued Versus Nonplateaued Managers: Career Patterns, Attitudes, and Path Potential," *Academy of Management Journal*, September 1981, pp. 566–578.

27. J. Benjamin Forbes, "Early Intraorganizational Mobility: Patterns and Influences," *Academy of Management Journal*, March 1987, pp. 110–125.

28. Cheryl Getty, "Tapping the Power for Career Development," *Training and Development Journal*, February 1986, pp. 36–37.

29. Dennis C. Sweeney, Dean Haller, and Frederick Sale, Jr., "Individuality Controlled Career Counseling," *Training and Development Journal*, August 1987, pp. 58–61; and Neal A. Chalofsky and Carlene Reinhart, *Effective Human Resource Development* (San Francisco: Jossey-Bass Publishers, 1988).

30. Michael A. Sheppeck and Craig Taylor, "Up the Career Path," *Training and Development Journal*, August 1986, pp. 46–48.

31. Tom Jackson and Alan Vitbert, "Career Development, Part 2: Challenges for the Organization," *Personnel*, March 1987, pp. 68–72.

32. Manuel London and Stephen A. Stumpf, *Managing Careers* (Reading, MA: Addison-Wesley Publishing Co., 1982), p. 33.

33. For more on this see Frank W. Archer, "Charting a Career Course," *Personnel Journal*, April 1984, pp. 60–64; and Karen N. Gaertner, "Managers' Careers and Organizational Change," *Academy of Management Executive*, November 1988, pp. 311–318.

34. Lewis Newman, "Career Management: Start with Goals," *Personnel Journal,* April 1989, pp. 91–92.

35. Lorraine M. Carulli, Cheryl L. Noroian, and Cindy Levine, "Employee-Driven Career Development," *Personnel Administrator,* March 1989, pp. 67–70; Barbara Moses, "Giving Employees a Future," *Training and Development Journal,* December 1987, pp. 25–28; and Dennis C. Sweeney, Dean Haller, and Frederick Sale, Jr., "Individually Controlled Career Counseling," *Training and Development Journal,* August 1987, pp. 58–61.

36. See for example W. Bruce Walsh and Samuel H. Osipon, (eds.), *Career Decision Making* (Hillsdale, NJ: Lawrence Erlbaum Associates, Publishers, 1988).

37. Richard J. Mirabile, "New Directions for Career Development," *Training and Development Journal,* December 1987, pp. 30–33.

38. Kenneth B. McRae, "Career-Management Planning: A Boon to Managers and Employees," *Personnel,* May 1985, p. 56.

39. Robert E. Hastings, "Career Development: Maximizing Options," *Personnel Administrator,* May 1978, pp. 58–61.

40. John D. Gridley, "Who Will Be Where, When?" *Personnel Journal,* May 1986, pp. 51–58.

41. Harry L. Wellbank, Douglas T. Hall, Marilyn A. Morgan, and W. Clay Hamner, "Planning Job Progression for Effective Career Development and Human Resources Management," *Personnel,* March–April 1978, pp. 54–64.

42. Patricia Berry, "Mentors for Women Managers: Fast-track to Corporate Success," *Supervisory Management,* August 1983, p. 37. For more on this topic see Murray J. Reich, "The Mentor Connection," *Personnel,* February 1985, pp. 50–56.

43. Michael G. Zey, "A Mentor for All," *Personnel Journal,* January 1988, p. 46.

44. Pamela R. Jones, Beverly Kaye, and Hugh R. Taylor, "You Want Me to do What?" *Training and Development Journal,* July 1981, pp. 56–62.

45. For additional discussion of this topic see Kram, "Mentoring in the Workplace," p. 162.

46. Daniel Lea and Zandy B. Liebowitz, "A Mentor: Would You Know One If You Saw One?" *Supervisory Management,* April 1983, pp. 33–35.

47. Linda Phillips-Jones, "Establishing a Formalized Mentoring Program," *Training and Development Journal,* February 1983, pp. 38–42; George S. Odiorne, "Mentoring—An American Management Innovation," *Personnel Administrator,* May 1985, pp. 63–70; Michael G. Zey, "Mentor Programs: Making the Right Moves," *Personnel Journal,* February 1985, pp. 53–57; Donald D. Bowen, "Were Men Meant to Mentor Women?" *Training and Development Journal,* February 1985, pp. 30–35; Kathy E. Kram, "Improving the Mentoring Process," *Training and Development Journal,* April 1985, pp. 40, 42–43; and James G. Clawson, "Is Mentoring Necessary?" *Training and Development Journal,* April 1985, pp. 36–39.

48. W. D. Storey, "Self-Directed Career Planning at the General Electric Company." Paper presented at the National Academy of Management Meeting, Kansas City, MO, August 1976.

49. For additional information on other programs such as Jones Laughlin, AT&T, and Kodak see Tom Jackson and Alan Vitberg, "Career Development, Part 3: Challenges for the Individual," *Personnel,* April 1987, pp. 54–57.

50. Les Cross, "Career Management Development: A System That Gets Results," *Training and Development Journal,* February 1983, pp. 54–63.

51. James A. Raelin, "Two-Track Plans for One-Track Careers," *Personnel Journal,* January 1987, pp. 96–101.

52. James Wynbrandt and Jack J. Feldy, "Managing Corporate Retirement Policy," *Management Review,* May 1987, pp. 47–50.

53. Sidney R. Siegel, "Preretirement Programs in the '80s," *Personnel Administrator,* February 1986, pp. 77–78.

54. *Ibid.,* p. 80.

55. Patrick J. Montana, "Preretirement Planning: How Corporations Help," *Personnel Administrator,* June 1986, p. 128; and Malcolm H. Morrison and Kathryn Jedrziewski, "Retirement Planning: Everybody Benefits," *Personnel Administrator,* January 1988, p. 79.

56. Patti Watts, "Preretirement Planning: Making the Golden Years Rosy," *Personnel,* March 1987, p. 34.

57. *Ibid.*

58. *Ibid.,* p. 39.

GLOSSARY

The following definitions of many of the concepts and terms used in this book for the most part correspond to those given in the text and represent ones that the reader is most likely to encounter in modern organizations.

Active listener A listener who works to develop an atmosphere in which the speaker can express his or her problems and, if possible, also solve them.

Action tendencies The "inclinations" people have to approach or avoid certain things.

Ad hoc committee A committee formed for a specific purpose and disbanded upon completion of the job.

Administrative man A term used to describe a decision maker who chooses alternatives that are satisfactory or good enough in contrast to an individual who attempts to maximize the outcome every time. (See also *economic man.*)

Advancement stage Period in a person's work life characterized by promotions, transfers, and the opportunity to use one's abilities in assuming responsibility and getting things done.

Affective component The emotional feeling attached to an attitude.

Affiliation motive The need to be part of a group, associated with social motives and for group dynamics.

Affluence power Power based on an organization needing an employee more than he or she needs the organization.

Ambiguity Uncertainty of meaning, alternatives, or instructions, which is a major factor accounting for conformity.

Anthropology The science of man.

Attitudes An individual's feelings about people, objects, events, or activities.

Attribution theory A behavioral theory that provides explanations of how individuals observe behavior and then attribute causes to it.

Authoritarian leaders Leaders who delegate very little authority and prefer to make most decisions themselves.

Authoritarian personalities Personality that rigidly adheres to conventional values, obeys recognized authority, and is concerned with such things as power and toughness.

Behavior modeling A behavioral program in which a person is asked to emulate the behavior of a successful role model.

Behavior modification A system of motivation that tries to change an individual's responses by rewarding the individual for proper responses and failing to reinforce him or her for improper ones.

Behavioristic model A model of individuals that presents people as being controlled by their environments; theorists who subscribe to this model are interested in observable behavior.

Bet your company culture An organizational culture in which the risks are high and the personnel do not find out how well they have done for an extended period of time.

Bounded rationality decision-making model A model of the decision-making process in which "ideal" decision models are modified to reflect the way decisions are often made. This includes a lack of opportunistic surveillance and the use of satisficing behavior. (See also *econologic decision-making model.*)

Bureaucracy An idcally mechanistic structure characterized by a clear-cut division of labor, a formal chain of command, rules and standards, impersonality in the evaluation of performance, and employment based on technical qualifications.

Burnout A response to chronic stress that results in emotional and/or physical exhaustion.

Career A series of work-related positions that a person holds during his or her lifetime.

Career pathing The process of identifying job assignment sequences by which a person can get from one position to another.

Career planning The process of identifying personal interests, abilities, and work goals and then making decisions regarding a career path.

Career plateau A point in a person's career at which the likelihood of further hierarchical promotion is very low and, for many, represents the final career step.

Career stage A time period in an individual's work life during which the person faces predictable career tasks and psychological issues.

Certainty A decision-making situation in which all the outcomes are known with a probability of 1.0.

Change process A three-part process by which change is brought about; it includes: (a) unfreezing the current situation; (b) introducing the new changes; and (c) refreezing the situation by reinforcing these new behaviors.

Charismatic leaders Individuals who lead by virtue of their ability to inspire devotion and extraordinary effort from their followers.

Classical conditioning A term that refers to unlearned behaviors in which, for example, an unconditioned stimulus brings about an unconditioned response. In Pavlov's experiment, the dog was not trained to salivate when it was first presented the meat; it did so automatically. Thus it was an unlearned or unconditioned response to an unconditioned stimulus.

Classical management theory Early management thought that developed from the work and writings of the scientific managers, administrative management theorists, and bureaucracy advocates.

Climate factors Factors that influence such key variables as satisfaction, production, and efficiency. Illustrations include structure, job descriptions, performance standards, rewards, leadership style, challenge, supportiveness, and work values.

Cluster chain An informal communication chain in which transmissions follow a logical and selective pattern, with some people being deliberately included in the chain and others deliberately excluded.

Coalescing The formation of a joint venture between one group and another, usually for the purpose of attaining mutually desirable objectives.

Coercive power Power based on fear.

Cognitive component The beliefs a person has about an object or event.

Cognitive dissonance A mental state in which there is a lack of consistency between what an individual believes and the information the person is receiving from the surrounding environment. For example, Ralph does not have a college degree and believes such a degree is not necessary for promotion to the vice-presidential level. While no one lacking such a degree has ever been promoted to vice-president, Ralph continues to believe he will receive such a promotion.

Cognitive theories Theories of human motivation that view behavior largely as a function of what will happen in the future. Supporters of these theories believe that a major determinant of human behavior is the beliefs, expectations, and anticipations that individuals have regarding future events.

Cohesiveness A term used to describe the closeness or interpersonal attractions that exist between members of a group.

Collectivism The tendency of people to belong to groups or collectives and to look after each other.

Communication The process of transmitting meanings from sender to receiver.

Communication network The way in which members of a group or organization go about communicating with each other.

Compliance phase The first phase of personal commitment to the organization in which individuals allow themselves to be influenced and swayed by other members of the group in order to obtain external rewards such as pay and promotions.

Consensus The extent to which others in the same situation behave in the same way.

Consideration factor One of the dimensions of leadership uncovered by the Ohio State researchers, it refers to leadership behaviors indicative of friendship, respect, mutual trust, and warmth.

Consistency The extent to which the same person behaves in the same way at different times.

Consistency theory A set of ideas about how attitudes change; based on the notion that people strive to see the world as orderly and consistent and that they adjust their attitudes to maintain this consistency.

Content theories of motivation Motivation theories that attempt to explain the specific things in the individual or environment that motivate people.

Contingency theory of leadership effectiveness Fiedler's theory of leadership, based on the relationship between organizational performance and leader attitudes.

Continuous reinforcement schedule A reinforcement schedule under which the individual receives a reward every time he or she performs a desired behavior.

Contracting The negotiation of an agreement between two or more groups for the purpose of controlled exchange or guaranteed interaction.

Contrived reinforcers External reinforcers such as coffee breaks, free lunches, country club privileges, and money.

Co-opting The process of absorbing new groups into the leadership or policymaking structure of an organization in order to avert threats to stability or survival.

Core job dimensions Characteristics that job enrichment experts attempt to design into the work to increase worker motivation. Some of the most important are skill variety, task identity, task significance, autonomy, and feedback.

Covert aspects One of two major categories of organizational climate, consisting of attitudes, feelings, supportiveness, and satisfaction.

Cultural anthropology That branch of anthropology that studies the impact of culture on behavior.

Cultural assimilator A programmed learning approach designed to expose members of one culture to some of the basic concepts, attitudes, role perceptions, customs, and values of another culture.

Cultural cluster Groupings of cultures on the basis of similarities.

Cultural dimensions Behavioral and attitudinal differences that distinguish groups from each other.

Culture Beliefs, values, and techniques used by individuals in dealing with their environment. These are shared among contemporaries and transmitted from one generation to the next.

Customer departmentalization The organization of an enterprise along customer lines. Retail stores and banks are typical illustrations.

Deadwood Individuals who have been identified as having little potential for advancement and whose performance has fallen to an unsatisfactory level.

Decentralization A system of management in which a great deal of decision-making authority rests at the lower levels of the hierarchy.

Decision making The process of choosing from among alternatives.

Delegation of authority The process a manager employs in distributing work to the subordinates.

Delphi group A group put together to generate ideas and pool judgments. The individuals' ideas are often gathered via structured questionnaires and fed back to the participants, who are then asked to make additional decisions based on the information.

Democratic leaders Leaders who delegate a great deal of authority to their subordinates.

Departmentalization The process of combining identified and defined tasks into groups.

Descriptive decision theory A description of how decision making is actually carried out. (See also *prescriptive decision theory.*)

Deterministic systems Systems that provide predictable outcomes, as in the case of an adding machine that, when functioning properly, will total 10 and 25 and provide an answer of 35.

Differentiation A concept that refers to the process by which subunits in an organization develop responses to the demands imposed by their particular subenvironments.

Directing listener A listener who directs the speaker by establishing the limits and direction of the counteraction.

Distinctiveness The extent to which the person behaves in the same way in different situations.

Dogmatism The rigidity of one's belief system.

Downward communication Communication used to convey directives from superior to subordinate.

Drive The intensity of behavior.

Drive and reinforcement theories Theories of human motivation that hold that decisions about present behavior are based largely on the consequences or rewards of past behaviors.

Dual career tracks Career planning programs that allow an individual to remain in his or her present track or switch to another one.

Econologic decision-making model A model of the decision-making process in which: (a) the steps are carried out in an orderly sequential order; (b) all attempts are made to identify and analyze all alternative courses of action; and (c) the best one is then chosen. The model is considered more idealistic than realistic. (See also *bounded rationality decision-making model*.)

Economic man A term used to describe an individual who always seeks to maximize the outcome of the decision by obtaining, for example, the greatest profit, output, or return on investment. (See also *administrative man*.)

Economic model A model of individual behavior that describes individual differences in terms of economic orientation.

Emotional model A model of individuals that presents people as heavily controlled by their emotions, many of which are unconscious in nature.

Empathy The process of figuratively putting oneself in another's place.

Enacted role The way an individual in a group actually behaves.

Entry stage The period in a person's work life during which the individual secures an initial full-time job and begins progress on a career path.

Equity theory A motivation theory that holds that in order to be motivated, individuals must believe the rewards they are receiving are fair. This results in people determining whether their salary is commensurate with the work they are doing and is fair when compared to the salaries others are receiving for the work they are doing.

Esteem needs These motives include the need to feel important and to receive recognition from others who support such feelings. They are satisfied through feelings of self-confidence and prestige.

Existence needs Needs at the lowest level of hierarchy; these include physiological and certain safety needs.

Expectancy A term used in expectancy/valence theory; it refers to the perceived probability of attaining a first-level outcome.

Expectancy-valence theory A theory of motivation; it postulates that individuals are thinking, reasoning beings who have beliefs and anticipations about future events in their lives and in deciding what to do they evaluate rewards, the relationship between performance and these rewards, and the likelihood of attaining the desired performance level.

Expected role The way an individual in a group is expected to behave.

Expert power Power based on competence.

Expressed behavior Behavior people initiate or show to others.

Extinction A learning intervention strategy that reduces undesirable behavior by simply failing to reinforce such behavior. Extinction works along the lines that if one fails to reinforce a particular behavior, such behavior will cease.

Extinction-positive reinforcement strategy A learning intervention strategy that attempts to eliminate a given behavior by using extinction while positively reinforcing the person every time he or she performs desirable behavior.

Extraneous power Sources of power outside the leader's direct work environment, such as organizational policies and procedures.

Feeling types An information-gathering style characterized by people who like harmony and pleasant environments.

Femininity A situation in which the dominant values in society are caring for others and the quality of life.

Field experiment A common research design; it applies the laboratory method to a real-life situation.

Field study A common research design; its basic purpose is to gather information from the respondents, as opposed to trying to change or influence them in any way. Interviews and/or questionnaires are often used to gather this information.

FIRO (fundamental interpersonal relations orientation) A way of studying interpersonal relations by examining an individual's need for such things as inclusion, control, and affection.

Fixed-interval schedule A reinforcement schedule based on a fixed passage of time rather than on a specific response.

Fixed-ratio schedule A reinforcement schedule given after a specific number of responses. While this can be 1:1 (continuous reinforcement), it is more common to find organizations shifting the ratio to 3:1, 5:1, 10:1, and so on as learning progresses.

Flat organizational structure An organizational structure with few hierarchical levels and, usually, a wide span of control.

Friendship groups Groups formed on the basis of common beliefs, concerns, or activities.

Frustration An unavoidable part of organizational life due to situations when one person succeeds at the expense of others.

Functional departmentalization The organization of an enterprise around those basic or organic activities that the enterprise must perform. In a manufacturing firm these are production, marketing, and finance.

Functional group A group composed of individuals all performing the same basic tasks.

Goal setting An expectancy theory of motivation; its basic premise is that an individual's conscious objective will influence his or her work behavior.

Gossip chain An informal communication channel in which one person conveys the message to all of the others.

Grapevine The name given to the informal communication network that exists in most organizations.

Grid organizational development A total organizational development intervention based on the concepts of the managerial grid; it consists of six phases designed to examine and improve organizational performance at all levels of the hierarchy.

Group A collection of two or more interdependent and interactive individuals who are seeking to attain common objectives.

Groupthink Social conformity to group ideas by members of the group.

Growth needs Needs related to the upper levels of Maslow's hierarchy: esteem and self-actualization.

Habit The strength of the relationship between past stimulus and response.

Hawthorne studies Behavioral research studies that provided early insights into group norms and behavior.

Hedonism A psychological theory which holds that individuals will tend to seek pleasure.

Heterogeneous group A group in which the individuals have varied needs, motives, and personalities. This type of group is often very effective in handling complex tasks.

High achievers Individuals with a strong need to succeed; they tend to: (a) like situations in which they take personal responsibility for finding solutions to problems; (b) take moderate, rather than high or low, risks; and (c) want concrete feedback on their performance.

Homogeneous group A group in which the individuals have similar needs, motives, and personalities. This type of group is often effective in handling simple, routine tasks.

Horizontal communication Communication that takes place between people at the same level of the hierarchy.

Human relations theory A management theory that holds that employees should be treated as human resources who welcome the opportunity to satisfy upper-level needs and contribute to the overall success of the organization.

Human resources theory A theory of modern behavioralists that extends the view of human relationists, viewing the employee as a highly capable entity with untapped resources. In this theory, the manager's role is not to control subordinates but to facilitate employee performance.

Humanistic model A model of individual behavior that views people as capable of surmounting irrational behavior through conscious reasoning.

Hygiene Identified by Herzberg in his two-factor theory of motivation. Hygiene factors will not motivate people by their presence but will cause dissatisfaction by their absence; examples include money, security, and working conditions.

Hypothesis A statement about the relationship between two or more variables.

Identification phase The second phase of personal commitment to the organization in which individuals accept influence in order to maintain a satisfying relationship and feel pride in themselves in belonging to the organization.

Implicit favorite decision-making model A model that describes individual decision making by pointing out that people often make choices based on bias and subjective rationality.

Incentive The anticipatory reaction to future goals.

Individualism The tendency of people to look after themselves and their immediate family only.

Inference An assumption made by the receiver of a message.

Initiating-structure factor One of the dimensions of leadership uncovered by the Ohio State researchers; it refers to leadership behaviors related to organizing and defining the relationship between the leader and the subordinates.

Instinct theory A psychological theory that holds that people have instincts which cause them to behave in a given way.

Institutionalized conflict A situation that arises in the hierarchical structure when each division is more concerned with its own needs than with those of other departments.

Instrumentality A term used in expectancy/valence theory; it refers to the perceived relationship between a first-level and second-level outcome.

Integration A concept that refers to the process of attaining unity of effort among the organization's various subsystems.

Inter-role conflict Conflict that occurs when an individual has a number of roles to play and they conflict with each other.

Interacting groups Groups that come into contact with each other.

Interest groups A group formed on the basis of common beliefs, concerns, or activities.

Intergroup behavior Behavioral interactions between two or more groups.

Intergroup team building interventions OD interventions in which the change agent gets both groups to identify their real and imaginary problems, develop steps for intergroup harmony, and then implement these steps.

Intermittent reinforcement schedule A reinforcement schedule under which desired behavior is reinforced on a variable or random basis. (See also *fixed-ratio schedule, fixed-interval schedule, variable-ratio schedule,* and *variable-interval schedule.*)

Internalization phase The third phase of personal commitment to the organization in which individuals find the values of the organization to be intrinsically rewarding and in harmony with their own values.

Intragroup behavior Behavior within groups; it involves communication and decision making by the members.

Intragroup relationships Relations between members of a group.

Intrarole conflict Conflict that results when someone receives different and conflicting messages and is unable to carry out one without ignoring or violating the other.

Intrasender conflict Role conflict that results when an individual is unable to obey an order without violating some company policy or directive.

Intuitive types An information-gathering style characterized by people who like to solve new problems.

Job characteristics model A work motivation model that shows the relationships between core job dimensions, critical psychological states, and personal and work outcomes.

Job definition Descriptions of the authority and responsibility contained in a particular job.

Job depth The amount of power an individual has to alter or influence the job or the surrounding environment.

Job design Job content, the methods to be used on the job, and the manner in which the particular job will relate to others in the organization.

Job enlargement Increasing the range of a job by giving the individual more to do.

Job enrichment Building psychological motivators into a job, such as increased responsibility and a feeling of accomplishment, by giving the person increased authority to: (a) plan the work by organizing and scheduling the tasks; and (b) control the job by taking care of follow-up functions, such as inspecting, testing, and repairing.

Job enrichment principles Principles that can be effective in creating core job dimensions.

Job range The number of operations or tasks an individual performs.

Job rotation Moving an individual from one job to another to reduce boredom.

Job satisfaction An emotional response to a job situation, typically influenced by how well outcomes meet or exceed personal expectations.

Judgmental listener A listener who introduces personal value judgments into the conversation, often in the form of advice or prescribed right and wrong behavior.

Kinesics Another name for body language, it includes such things as facial expressions, gestures, and posture.

Laboratory experiment A common research design; its basic purpose is to observe the effects of an independent variable(s) on a dependent variable(s).

Leader Behavior Description Questionnaire (LBDQ) A questionnaire developed by the Ohio State researchers and used to identify the two dimensions of leadership: consideration and initiating structure.

Leader-member exchange theory A theory that explains leadership in terms of the interaction between superior and subordinate; it is also known as vertical-dyad theory.

Leader-member relations dimension The quality of the relationship between the leader and the group.

Leader participation theory Theory proposed by Vroom and Yetton, and expanded by Vroom and Jago, which relates leadership and decision making. It prescribes a leadership style appropriate to a given situation.

Leadership The process of influencing people to direct their efforts toward the achievement of some particular goal(s).

Leadership-behavior theory A theory of leadership that seeks to explain leadership in terms of what leaders do.

Leadership-trait theory Early leadership theory that sought to identify those traits or characteristics that distinguish successful leaders from unsuccessful leaders.

Learning A relatively permanent change in behavior.

Least preferred co-worker scale (LPC) A series of adjective comparisons used to describe the individual with whom the leader can work least well.

Left-brain dominant People who are logical problem solvers, deal with one problem at the time, give information verbally, and depend on words for meanings.

Legitimate power Power vested in the manager's position or role in the hierarchy.

Life and career planning interventions OD interventions that focus on individual goals, providing participants in the intervention the opportunity to assess where they currently are in their career, where they want to be, and how they might bridge the gap.

Life events Stress-causing experiences (either home-related or job-related) that have occurred to a person over the last twelve-month period.

Life inventories An OD intervention in which people note their peak experiences, the things they do well and poorly, the things they would like to learn to do well, and the peak experiences they would still like to have.

Locus of control The extent to which individuals believe that events that occur to them are (or are not) basically under their control.

Maintenance Stage Period in a person's work life characterized by reassessing one's progress and adjustments to changing demands.

Masculinity A situation in which the dominant values of society are success, money, and things.

Matrix departmentalization A hybrid combination of both project and functional structures; project managers operating within this form of departmentalization are forced to rely on the functional managers for support and assistance, since the former have no line authority.

Maximin criterion A criterion in which the individual chooses the plan with the highest minimum payoff, regardless of the competition's strategy.

Mechanistic organization An organizational structure that is often effective in a stable environment in which external factors have little impact on organizational performance.

Mentor Individual providing advice and assistance to a junior member of the organization; a counselor and sponsor.

Motivators Identified by Herzberg in his two-factor theory of motivation, motivators are those factors that will build high levels of motivation and job satisfaction; examples include recognition, advancement, and achievement.

Natural reinforcers Heavily social reinforcers such as verbal praise, friendly greetings, and solicitations of advice.

Need achievement theory Popularized by David McClelland, the theory attempts to describe and explain people's desire to achieve and the means they use in doing so.

Need hierarchy A widely accepted framework of motivation; developed by Abraham H. Maslow, it holds that everyone has five levels of needs, unsatisfied needs influence behavior, and once needs are satisfied the individual moves on up the hierarchy to the next level.

Negative reinforcement A learning intervention strategy that increases the frequency of a behavioral event while bringing about termination or withdrawal of some condition.

Nominal group A group whose members have structured face-to-face meetings, make a proactive search for problem solutions, and in which there is equality of participation.

Normative reality Interpretive reality in which meanings are sometimes unclear. People deal in normative reality any time they communicate about issues that are open to interpretation or are matters of opinion.

Norms Behavioral rules of conduct that have been established by the group members.

OD interventions A catchall term used to describe the structured activity in which targeted individuals, groups, or units engage in accomplishing task goals related to organizational development.

Operant conditioning A term that refers to learned behaviors that occur because of some reinforcement schedule. In operant conditioning the desired response may not be present in the subject, but the person is taught to respond in the desired manner via a reinforcement schedule. (See *fixed-interval, variable-interval, fixed-ratio,* and *variable-ratio schedules.*)

Opportunistic surveillance Scanning the environment in a never-ending search to improve conditions.

Organic organization A highly unstructured, flexible form of organization that is particularly effective in helping organizations function in a dynamic, changing environment.

Organic organizational design An organizational structure that is often effective in a dynamic environment in which external factors have a significant impact on organization performance.

Organizational behavior An academic discipline that is concerned with describing, understanding, predicting, and controlling human behavior in an organizational environment.

Organizational climate A set of properties of the work environment perceived by individuals who work there and which serve as a major force in influencing their job behavior.

Organizational culture Expected behaviors, actions, and values that people in the enterprise are expected to follow.

Organizational development (OD) A long-range effort to improve an organization's problem-solving and renewal processes; it relies on the assistance of a change agent and the use of applied behavioral science, including action research.

Organizational politics Acts designed to protect and/or enhance the self-interest of individuals or groups.

Overloaded A condition that exists when an individual is subjected to too much stress.

Overt aspects One of two major categories of organizational climate, consisting of things that can be measured; e.g., the hierarchy, the goals of the organization, performance standards, and efficiency measures.

Paralanguage The study of how things are said, such as rate of speech, voice tension, pacing, and loudness.

Path-goal theory of leadership A leadership theory that holds the manager's job is to: (a) clarify the tasks to be performed by subordinates; (b) clear away any roadblocks to goal attainment; and (c) increase the opportunity for subordinates to obtain personal satisfaction.

Perceived role Those activities or behaviors an individual believes are required to fulfill his or her place in the group.

Perception A person's view of reality.

Perceptual defense The screening out of information that is disturbing or that the individual does not care to acknowledge.

Person-role conflict A conflict that arises when the expected behavior is incompatible with the person's own values.

Personal factors Reasons why individuals belong to certain groups, such as age, sex, intelligence, and authoritarianism.

Personality An individual's characteristics and behaviors, organized in such a way as to reflect the unique adjustment the person makes to his or her environment.

Personalized power Power characterized by personal aggrandizement.

Physiological needs Basic physical needs, such as food, clothing, and shelter.

Pooled interdependence One of the common forms of interdependence; it occurs whenever groups are relatively independent of each other, although each has some effect on the overall organization.

Position power The formal authority that comes with a particular job.

Positive reinforcement A learning intervention strategy in which a reward is given for the performance of some act; it leads to a repetition of the act in the future.

Power The ability to influence someone to do something that he or she would not otherwise do.

Power distance The extent to which less powerful members of institutions and organizations accept that power is distributed unequally.

Power motive The need to manipulate others or be superior to them; the need to feel in charge.

Pre-career stage The period in a person's work life during which he or she is looking for a career and seeking the education appropriate for this work.

Prescriptive decision theory Description of how decision making ought to be carried out. (See also *descriptive decision theory*.)

Primary groups Groups that are characterized by intimate face-to-face association and cooperation.

Probability chain An informal communication channel in which people communicate on a random basis.

Probabalistic systems Systems that do not provide uniquely determined outcomes, as seen in the case of organizational systems.

Probing listener A listener who asks a lot of questions in an attempt to get to the heart of the matter and in the process tends to lead the conversation.

Process consultation An OD intervention used in an ongoing system; it consists of making the organization aware of its process and problems and how these problems can be solved.

Process culture An organizational culture emphasizing low risk taking and slow feedback.

Process theories of motivation Motivation theories that attempt to explain how behavior is initiated, directed, sustained, and halted.

Product departmentalization The organization of an enterprise around its major product lines. Illustrations include Ford Motor, DuPont, and Columbia Pictures.

Project group A group formed to accomplish a particular objective and, once this is accomplished, disbanded.

Projection A defense mechanism; it involves attributing one's own unworthy impulses or motives to other people.

Proxemics The study of the way people use physical space and what it says about them.

Psychology The study of human behavior.

Punishment A learning intervention strategy used for reducing undesirable behavior.

Punishment-negative reinforcement strategy A learning intervention strategy in which undesirable behavior is punished; punishment is not terminated until the undesirable response is replaced by a desirable one.

Punishment-positive reinforcement strategy A learning intervention strategy in which undesirable responses are punished, while desirable responses are reinforced.

Quality circles (QC) A group of well-trained employees and a team leader that study job-related problems and make recommendations for improvement.

Rational model A model of individuals that presents people as highly rational persons who possess computer-like characteristics.

Reciprocal interdependence One of the common forms of interdependence; it occurs when the outputs of each group become inputs for the other groups.

Referent power Power based on the follower's identification with the leader.

Relatedness needs Needs related to the middle of Maslow's hierarchy: safety needs, social needs, and some esteem needs.

Research design A plan, structure, and strategy of investigation used for obtaining answers to the researcher's questions.

Research design plan The overall scheme or program of the research, including everything the investigator is going to do from writing the hypothesis, to collecting and analyzing the data, to submitting the final report.

Research design strategy The methods to be employed in gathering and analyzing the data, as well as deciding how the research objectives will be met and how problems encountered along the way will be resolved.

Research design structure The construct of the research design; it contains the variables to be measured and the relationships that exist between these variables.

Reward power Power based on the ability to offer rewards in exchange for compliance.

Right-brain dominant People who are intuitive problem solvers, deal with several problems at a time, give information with movement, and interpret body language.

Risk A decision-making situation in which there is some information regarding the outcomes associated with alternatives. Since the decision maker does not have complete information, probability assignments are used.

Risky-shift phenomenon The tendency of individuals to be greater risk takers when acting as members of a group than when acting alone. One reason is that a decision maker in a group allows for diffusion of responsibilities in the event of a wrong decision.

Role An expected behavior.

Role ambiguity A role-related condition that occurs when job duties are unclear and the person is unsure of what to do.

Role analysis technique (RAT) An OD intervention designed to clarify both role expectations and the obligations of team members.

Role conflict A situation that arises when a person tries to undertake two or more mutually exclusive roles, such as teeing off at the golf course at 9:00 A.M. and taking the children to a swimming meet at 9:30 A.M.

Role overload conflict A problem that results when a person is given so much work to do that it is impossible to fulfill the expected role.

Role sendings The messages an individual receives from others that let him or her know the manner in which to behave consistent with a role assignment.

Safety needs Needs for security, stability, and the absence of pain; these are often satisfied in organizational settings by such things as medical insurance, a retirement program, and fringe benefits.

Satisficing behavior Decision-making behavior in which the final alternative may not maximize outcomes, as in an optimal solution, but is good enough to meet minimum standards.

Scientific management A system of management that was heavily work-oriented; its adherents placed major emphasis on ways of increasing productivity by making the work easier to perform and developing methods of motivating the workers to take advantage of these labor-saving tools and techniques.

Selective perception A person's personally biased interpretation of reality which is created and influenced by one's own attitudes, experiences, and beliefs.

Self-actualization needs The desire to become more and more what one is, to become everything one is capable of becoming. Individuals try to fulfill this need through self-development and creativity.

Self-actualizing model A model of individual behavior that describes people as motivated by the opportunity to grow, mature, and become all that they are capable of becoming.

Self-appraisal A systematic process of generating data about oneself and analyzing the information for the purpose of determining career and life decisions.

Self-concept The way a person feels about and perceives himself or herself.

Semantics A term popularly defined by the cliche, "Different words mean different things to different people."

Sensation types An information-gathering style characterized by people who like to solve problems in standard ways.

Sensitivity training laboratories (T-groups) Training designed to make individuals more aware of both their own feelings and those of others.

Sensory reality Physical reality, such as a car, machine, or a desk.

Sequential interdependence One of the common forms of interdependence; it occurs when the outputs of one group become inputs for other groups.

Single-strand chain An informal communication chain in which messages are passed from one person to another, with each being the sole link to the next position.

Situational factors Variables such as group size, unanimity of the majority, and structure of a group.

Skill variety The degree to which the job allows the worker to use a number of different abilities or talents in carrying out tasks.

Smoothing listener A listener who tries to pat the speaker on the head and make light of the problem.

Social needs Needs for affiliation and interaction in which people give and receive friendship and affection; these needs are often satisfied on the job by joining informal groups.

Social learning theory A belief that learning can take place via modeling and self-control processes.

Social power Power characterized by, among other things, a concern for others.

Socialization The acquisition of behavior patterns that help people interact with others.

Sociology The study of social behavior, particularly among societies, institutions, and groups.

Solid citizens Individuals who are hard working and reliable, but who have little chance for further promotion.

Span of control The number of people who report to a superior.

Standing committee A committee that exists for an indefinite period of time.

Star A person who has been identified as top management timber and is given greater promotions and responsibility.

Status The relative ranking of an individual in an organization or group.

Status discrepancy A status problem that occurs when people do things that do not fit with their status ranking in the group.

Status incongruency A form of emergent people or things on the basis of perceived similarities.

Stereotyping The processing of categorizing people or things on the basis of perceived similarities.

Stress A condition characterized by emotional strain and/or physical discomfort which, if it continues unabated, can impair one's ability to cope with the environment.

Stressors Environmental factors that bring about stress.

Subculture A narrow range of society consisting of people whose ways of behaving are peculiar to their particular group within the larger society.

System An organized unit that consists of two or more interdependent parts, or subsystems, and that can be distinguished from the environment in which it exists by some identifiable boundary.

Tall organizational structure An organizational structure with many hierarchical levels and usually a narrow span of control.

Task concept The single most prominent element in scientific management; it consisted of planning out the work of every workman at least one day in advance and relating in detail what the individual was to accomplish, as well as the means to be used in doing the work.

Task groups Groups formed to accomplish a particular objective and, once this is accomplished, disbanded.

Task structure dimension The degree to which the task is programmed or spelled out via established procedures.

Territorial departmentalization The organization of an enterprise along geographic lines. Many large multistore retail chains use this form of departmentalization.

Theory X A set of managerial assumptions that hold that people: (a) dislike work; (b) have little ambition; (c) want security above all else; and (d) must be coerced, controlled, and threatened with punishment in order for them to attain organizational objectives.

Theory Y A set of managerial assumptions that hold that: (a) if conditions are favorable, people not only will accept responsibility but also will seek it; (b) if people are committed to organizational objectives, they will exercise self-direction and self-control; and (c) commitment is a function of rewards associated with goal attainment.

Theory Z A management approach that blends Japanese and American management practices in arriving at a modified American approach that employs consensual decision making, lifetime employment, slower evaluation and promotion, informal control, a moderately specialized career path, and holistic concern for the employee.

Thinking types An information evaluation style characterized by people who tend to be unemotional and uninterested in the feelings of others.

Tough-guy macho culture An organizational culture emphasizing high risk taking and fast feedback.

Transcendental meditation (TM) A popular technique used to shut out distractions and attain a physical and mental relaxation peak.

Two-factor theory of motivation A motivation theory developed by Frederick Herzberg; it holds that motivation derives from two sets of factors: motivators and hygiene factors. The former, consisting of factors such as achievement, recognition, and the work itself, are motivational in content, while the latter, consisting of factors such as money, security, and working conditions, will not motivate by their presence but will cause dissatisfaction by their absence.

Type A personalities Personalities characterized by aggressive involvement in a chronic, incessant struggle to achieve more and more in less and less time.

Uncertainty A decision-making situation in which there is no information available regarding the outcomes associated with the alternatives, or the information is so limited that the individual feels unable to make probability assignments. In such cases there are specific quantitative techniques to which the person can turn in resolving the dilemma.

Uncertainty avoidance The extent to which people feel threatened by ambiguous situations and have created beliefs and institutions that try to avoid these.

Underloaded A condition that exists when an individual is not subjected to sufficient stress.

Universal design theory Design theory developed by the classical theorists; it held that there was one best way to design an organization.

Universal programs An organizational career development program designed to provide participants with insights to themselves, a knowledge of opportunities available to them, and an understanding of the actions they now can take in availing themselves of these opportunities.

Upward communication Communication that provides management with feedback from the subordinates.

Valence A term used in expectancy/valence theory; it refers to a person's preference for a particular outcome.

Variable-interval schedule A reinforcement schedule where reinforcement is given on a random basis, and the reward is given at the end of randomly determined intervals of time.

Variable-ratio schedule A reinforcement schedule which varies randomly based on the number of right responses.

Vertical loading A job enrichment principle that involves closing the gap between the "doing" and the "controlling" aspects of the job.

Wanted behavior The way people want others to act toward them.

Withdrawal stage A career stage in which the individual faces retirement or other end-of-career options.

Workaholism Compulsive overcommitment to work.

Work hard/play hard culture An organizational culture which relies heavily on teamwork and short-term goal accomplishment.

Work centrality The degree of general importance that working has in the life of an individual at any given point in time.

NAME INDEX

SUBJECT INDEX